Leopold of Austria

A Compilation

on the

Science

of the Stars

Translated & Edited by
Benjamin N. Dykes, PhD

The Cazimi Press
Minneapolis, Minnesota
2015

Published and printed in the United States of America

by The Cazimi Press
515 5th Street SE #11, Minneapolis, MN 55414

© 2015 by Benjamin N. Dykes, Ph.D.

All rights reserved. No part of this publication may be reproduced, stored in or introduced into a retrieval system, or transmitted, in any form or by any means (electronic, mechanical, photocopying, recording or otherwise), without the prior written permission of both the copyright owner and the above publisher of this book.

The scanning, uploading, and distribution of this book via the Internet or via any other means without the permission of the publisher is illegal and punishable by law. Please purchase only authorized editions and do not participate in or encourage electronic piracy of copyrighted materials. Your support of the author's rights is appreciated.

ISBN-13: 978-1-934586-43-3

Acknowledgements

I would like to thank the following friends and colleagues, in alphabetical order: Wade Caves, Richard Mohr, and Robert Switzer.

Also available at www.bendykes.com:

Designed for curious modern astrology students, *Traditional Astrology for Today* explains basic ideas in history, philosophy and counseling, dignities, chart interpretation, and predictive techniques. Non-technical and friendly for modern beginners.

This excellent and popular introduction to predictive techniques by contemporary Turkish astrologer Öner Döşer blends traditional and modern methods, with numerous chart examples.

The first two volumes of this medieval mundane series, *Astrology of the World*, describe numerous techniques in weather prediction, prices and commodities, eclipses and comets, chorography, ingresses, Saturn-Jupiter conjunctions, and more, translated from Arabic and Latin sources.

Two classic introductions to astrology, by Abū Ma'shar and al-Qabīsī, are translated with commentary in this volume. *Introductions to Traditional Astrology* is an essential reference work for traditional students.

The classic medieval text by Guido Bonatti, the *Book of Astronomy* is now available in paperback reprints. This famous work is a complete guide to basic principles, horary, elections, mundane, and natal astrology.

This first English translation of Hephaistion of Thebes's *Apotelesmatics* Book III contains much fascinating material from the original Dorotheus poem and numerous other electional texts, including rules on thought-interpretation.

The largest compilation of traditional electional material, *Choices & Inceptions: Traditional Electional Astrology* contains works by Sahl, al-Rijāl, al-'Imrānī, and others, beginning with an extensive discussion of elections and questions by Benjamin Dykes.

The famous medieval horary compilation *The Book of the Nine Judges* is now available in translation for the first time! It is the largest traditional horary work available, and the third in the horary series.

The Search of the Heart is the first in the horary series, and focuses on the use of victors (special significators or *almutens*) and the practice of thought-interpretation: divining thoughts and predicting outcomes before the client speaks.

The Forty Chapters is a famous and influential horary work by al-Kindī, and is the second volume of the horary series. Beginning with a general introduction to astrology, al-Kindī covers topics such as war, wealth, travel, pregnancy, marriage, and more.

The first volume of the *Persian Nativities* series on natal astrology contains *The Book of Aristotle*, an advanced work on nativities and prediction by Māshā'allāh, and a beginner-level work by his student Abū 'Alī al-Khayyāt, *On the Judgments of Nativities*.

The second volume of *Persian Nativities* features a The second volume of *Persian Nativities* features a shorter, beginner-level work on nativities and prediction by 'Umar al-Tabarī, and a much longer book on nativities by his younger follower, Abū Bakr.

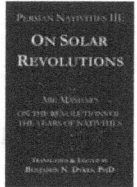
The third volume of *Persian Nativities* is a translation of Abū Ma'shar 's work on solar revolutions, devoted solely to the Persian annual predictive system. Learn about profections, distributions, *firdārīyyāt*, transits, and more!

This compilation of sixteen works by Sahl b. Bishr and Māshā'allāh covers all areas of traditional astrology, from basic concepts to horary, elections, natal interpretation, and mundane astrology. It is also available in paperback.

Expand your knowledge of traditional astrology, philosophy, and esoteric thought with the *Logos & Light* audio series: downloadable, college-level lectures on MP3 at a fraction of the university cost!

Enjoy these new additions in our magic/esoteric series:

Astrological Magic: Basic Rituals & Meditations is a basic introduction to ritual magic for astrologers. It introduces a magical cosmology and electional rules, and shows how to perform ritual correctly, integrating Tarot and visualizations with rituals for all Elements, Planets, and Signs.

Available as an MP3 download, *Music of the Elements* was composed especially for *Astrological Magic* by MjDawn, an experienced electronic artist and ritualists. Hear free clips at bendykes.com/music.php!

Nights is a special, 2-disc remastering by MjDawn of the album GAMMA, and is a deep and powerful set of 2 full-disc MP3 soundtracks suitable for meditation or ritual work, especially those in *Astrological Magic*. Hear free clips at bendykes.com/music.php!

Aeonian Glow is a new version of the original ambient work mixed by Steve Roach, redesigned by MjDawn and Vir Unis from the original, pre-mixed files. This MP3 album is entrancing and enchanting: hear free clips at bendykes.com/music.php!

TABLE OF CONTENTS

Table of Figures iv
Book Abbreviations viii
Translator's Introduction 1
   §1: The text and content of the *Compilation* 1
   §2: Important Vocabulary 18
Treatise I: On the Spheres, & their Circles & Motions 21
   Chapter I.1: The cosmic orbs 21
   Chapter I.2: The great circles of the local horizon 24
   Chapter I.3: Stars, signs, mansions 29
   Chapter I.4: The faces 38
   Chapter I.5: Stars co-rising with the zodiacal constellations 39
   Chapter I.6: Physical dimensions of the universe 40
   Chapter I.7: The seven climes 43
   Chapter I.8: Miscellaneous astronomical comments 43
Treatise II: On the Spheres of the Planets, their Circles & Motions ... 46
   Chapter II.1: Introduction 46
   Chapter II.2: Solar theory 47
   Chapter II.3: Lunar theory 55
   Chapter II.4: Theory of the superiors and Venus 64
   Chapter II.5: Theory of Mercury 77
   Chapter II.6: Latitudes, stations, and tables 80
Treatise III: On the Proof of the Science of the Stars 83
Treatise IV: On the Introductory Matters of Judgments 88
   Introduction 88
   Chapter IV.1: The signs and houses 88
   Chapter IV.2: Introduction to the natures of the planets 104
   Chapter IV.3: Introduction to the planets in themselves and in co-operation 117
   Chapter IV.4: On the introductory matters of judgments 137
   Chapter IV.5: On Lots 143
Treatise V: On the Revolutions of Years 179
   Chapter V.1: Introduction 179
   Chapter V.2: General evaluation of an ingress 180
   Chapter V.3: "Al-Qabīsī" on planetary conjunctions in the signs 186
   Chapter V.4: Prices 189
   Chapter V.5: General conjunctional theory 190
   Chapter V.6: Comets 192
   Chapter V.7: Planets' rulerships over places and regions 197
Treatise VI: On the Changing of the Atmosphere 198
   Introduction 198
   Chapter VI.1: The signs and fixed stars 198
   Chapter VI.2: Planets and their combinations in the signs 201

 Chapter VI.3: Rules about winds 212
Treatise VII: On Nativities **217**
 Introduction 217
 Chapter VII.1: Early deaths 217
 Chapter VII.2: Monsters 218
 Chapter VII.3: On completed births, conception, and character 221
 Chapter VII.4: Longevity and natal predictions 227
 Chapter VII.5: Prosperity and wealth 241
 Chapter VII.6: Siblings 248
 Chapter VII.7: Parents 249
 Chapter VII.8: Marriage 252
 Chapter VII.9: Children 254
 Chapter VII.10: Infirmities 256
 Chapter VII.11: Qualities of the soul 264
 Chapter VII.12: Travel and faith 267
 Chapter VII.13: Rulership and mastery 270
 Chapter VII.14: Friendship 274
 Chapter VII.15: Enmity 275
 Chapter VII.16: Death 277
 Chapter VII.17: Planets in their own and others' houses 279
 Chapter VII.18: Planets in the twelve places 282
Treatise VIII: On Interrogations **288**
 Chapter VIII.1: Introduction 288
 Chapter VIII.2: Questions of the 1st house 291
 Chapter VIII.3: Questions of the 2nd house 297
 Chapter VIII.4: Questions of the 3rd house 304
 Chapter VIII.5: Questions of the 4th house 304
 Chapter VIII.6: Questions of the 5th house 318
 Chapter VIII.7: Questions of the 6th house 324
 Chapter VIII.8: Questions of the 7th house 341
 Chapter VIII.9: Questions of the 8th house 356
 Chapter VIII.10: Questions of the 9th house 359
 Chapter VIII.11: Questions of the 10th house 365
 Chapter VIII.12: Questions of the 11th house 373
 Chapter VIII.13: Questions of the 12th house 375
Treatise IX: On Elections & Images **377**
 Chapter IX.1: Principles of elections 377
 Chapter IX.2: A few specific elections 383
 Chapter IX.3: Making magical images 389
 Chapter IX.4: Individual elections 393
 Chapter IX.5: Elections of the first house 399
 Chapter IX.6: Elections of the second house 403
 Chapter IX.7: Elections of the third house 403
 Chapter IX.8: Elections of the fourth house 403

Chapter IX.8: Elections of the fifth house 404
Chapter IX.9: Elections of the sixth house 405
Chapter IX.10: Elections of the seventh through tenth houses 406
Chapter IX.11: Elections of the eleventh house 406
Chapter IX.12: Elections of the twelfth house 408
Chapter IX.13: Sahl on elections 408
Chapter IX.14: Miscellaneous lore, and monitoring daily activities 411
Treatise X: On Intentions 416
Appendix: Al-Khayyāt's Interpretation Template 422
Glossary 424
Bibliography 447

TABLE OF FIGURES

Figure 1: Late medieval, 10-sphere universe (Dykes, after Leopold) 21
Figure 2: Three great circles, viewed from middle of Earth at 0° latitude (Dykes) 25
Figure 3: Celestial equator and ecliptic (Dykes) 26
Figure 4: Star at altitude 50° from local horizon (Dykes) 27
Figure 5: Star at *azimuth* 50° (Dykes) 27
Figure 6: Signs of the zodiac (Leopold) 29
Figure 7: Table of lunar mansions (Leopold, Dykes) 31
Figure 8: Three-orb system of Mars (Dykes, after Leopold) 47
Figure 9: Solar apogee and eccentricity, 2000 AD (Dykes) 48
Figure 10: Mean and true Suns, solar equation of center (Dykes) 50
Figure 11: Simplified Ptolemaic theory of the Moon (Dykes) 56
Figure 12: Theory of superiors and Venus (Dykes) 65
Figure 13: Effect of retrogradation on true position (Dykes) 66
Figure 14: Mean longitude of Mars (Dykes) 66
Figure 15: Apogee of the epicycle (Dykes) 67
Figure 16: True longitude of Mars (Dykes) 68
Figure 17: Equation of the center of Mars (Dykes) 69
Figure 18: Equation of the epicycle (Dykes) 70
Figure 19: Approximate apsidal points, 2000 AD (Dykes) 71
Figure 20: Theory of Mercury (Dykes) 79
Figure 21: Retrogradation of Saturn (Dykes) 81
Figure 22: Signs of the triplicities (Dykes) 88
Figure 23: Signs with same ascensions (Dykes) 92
Figure 24: Seven advantageous places, in gray (Dykes) 95
Figure 25: Table of major dignities and corruptions/debilities (Dykes) ... 96
Figure 26: Table of Egyptian bounds (Dykes) 97
Figure 27: Dorothean triplicity lords (Dykes) 97
Figure 28: Chaldean faces or decans (Dykes) 98
Figure 29: Points for weighted victors (Dykes) 99
Figure 30: Masculine and feminine degrees (Leopold) 99
Figure 31: Degrees in the signs (Leopold) 100
Figure 32: The welled degrees (Leopold) 101
Figure 33: Degrees increasing fortune (Leopold) 101
Figure 34: Degrees of chronic illness (Leopold) 102
Figure 35: Degrees of bodily chronic illness (Leopold) 102
Figure 36: Degrees of bodily chronic illness (Leopold) 103
Figure 37: Fixed star degrees of chronic illness (from *BA*) 103
Figure 38: Sol 104
Figure 39: Table of planetary years (Dykes) 105
Figure 40: Luna 106
Figure 41: Saturnus 108

Figure 42: Jupiter..109
Figure 43: Mars...110
Figure 44: Venus 112
Figure 45: Mercurius...113
Figure 46: Planetary hours from sunrise (Dykes).................................115
Figure 47: Planetary hours from sunset (Dykes)..................................116
Figure 48: Mars increasing and decreasing in number and light (Dykes) 118
Figure 49: Nodes of the Moon (Dykes)..119
Figure 50: Planets in their domains in a diurnal chart (Dykes)...........120
Figure 51: House strengths according to ibn Ezra (Dykes, from *Search* Appendix F)...121
Figure 52: Mercury, Jupiter, Saturn in the facing of the Sun, Mars in the facing of the Moon (Dykes)..122
Figure 53: Synodic cycle of superiors (Dykes, adapted from Abū Ma'shar) 124
Figure 54: Four types of direct configuration (Dykes)........................125
Figure 55: An example of transfer (Sahl, via Leopold).......................128
Figure 56: An example of collection (Leopold)....................................129
Figure 57: An example of reflection type #1 (Dykes, *ITA* III.13)...........130
Figure 58: Two examples of blocking (Sahl, via Leopold)..................131
Figure 59: Examples of returning virtue (Leopold) 132
Figure 60: Table of ninth-parts (Dykes)...139
Figure 61: Table of twelfth-parts (Dykes) 140
Figure 62: Medieval way of projecting Lots (Dykes)...........................145
Figure 63: Abū Ma'shar's example chart (Dykes)..................................174
Figure 64: Centers of the Moon (Dykes, from 'Umar and al-Kindī) 209
Figure 65: Examples of miscarriage and early death (Leopold)...........219
Figure 66: Trutine of Hermes (Dykes) 222
Figure 67: Distribution of the Ascendant to age 50 (Dykes) 229
Figure 68: Ptolemy's releaser by primary direction and *horimaia* (Dykes) 233
Figure 69: Table of planetary periods for longevity (Leopold) 235
Figure 70: A nativity showing copious riches (Leopold)........................241
Figure 71: A nativity showing prosperity and good fortune (Leopold)...242
Figure 72: Angular triads for ages of life (Dykes) 246
Figure 73: A nativity showing many good siblings (Leopold)...............248
Figure 74: A nativity showing the good condition of the father (Leopold) 250
Figure 75: A nativity showing the good condition of the mother (Leopold) 251
Figure 76: A nativity showing a good and useful marriage union (Leopold) 252
Figure 77: A nativity showing many good children (Leopold)..............255
Figure 78: A nativity showing many long infirmities (Leopold) 257
Figure 79: A nativity showing prosperous travels, firm faith (Leopold) .268

Figure 80: A nativity showing loftiness, mastery, and good work (Leopold) 270
Figure 81: A nativity showing many good and noble friends (Leopold) .275
Figure 82: A nativity showing many harmful enemies (Leopold) 276
Figure 83: A nativity showing a natural death in the fatherland (Leopold) 277
Figure 84: A figure showing that the querent will obtain it easily (Leopold) 292
Figure 85: A figure showing that the querent will obtain it with difficulty (Leopold, after Sahl) 293
Figure 86: A figure showing that the querent will obtain assets (Leopold) 299
Figure 87: A figure showing the good status of fourth-house matters (Leopold) 305
Figure 88: Al-Kindī's example of finding treasure 311
Figure 89: Finding a hidden object (Dykes, from Jirjis) 313
Figure 90: A figure showing the effecting of an uncertain matter (Leopold) 317
Figure 91: A figure showing that a messenger will arrive safely (Leopold) 321
Figure 92: A figure showing that a sick person will be cured (Leopold) .325
Figure 93: Lunar mansions applied to the body (Leopold) 328
Figure 94: Humoral virtues, planets, & functions (Dykes, after Saunders 1677) 335
Figure 95: A figure showing that a sick person is spitting up blood (Leopold) 337
Figure 96: A figure showing that a marriage-union will be perfected (Leopold) 341
Figure 97: A figure showing that a lost object will be recovered (Leopold) 348
Figure 98: Sahl's angular significations for partnerships (Dykes) 351
Figure 99: A figure showing that someone inquired about is dead (Leopold) 357
Figure 100: A figure showing that a messenger is returning immediately (Leopold) 361
Figure 101: A figure showing that the querent will attain a dignity (Leopold) 366
Figure 102: A figure showing that the querent will attain the thing hoped for (Leopold) 373
Figure 103: Advancing/upright and remote/falling Midheavens (Dykes) 382
Figure 104: A figure showing that something cannot be well hidden (Leopold) 383

Figure 105: A figure showing the changing of a lodging-place (Leopold) 394
Figure 106: A figure showing that something sought from the king will be obtained (Leopold)..396
Figure 107: A figure showing the good nursing of a boy (Leopold)........399
Figure 108: A figure showing the good incision of a vein or limb (Leopold)..401
Figure 109: A figure showing praise and reputation (Leopold) 407
Figure 110: A figure showing someone will have an honor (Leopold) ...412
Figure 111: Table of twelfth-parts (Dykes) 417
Figure 112: Hermes's thought of sick mother (Leopold) 420

BOOK ABBREVIATIONS

AW (1-2)	Dykes, *Astrology of the World* Vols. I-II
BRD	Abū Ma'shar, *On Historical Astrology: The Book of Religions and Dynasties*
Choices	Dykes, *Choices & Inceptions: Traditional Electional Astrology*
ITA	Dykes, *Introductions to Traditional Astrology*
JN	Al-Khayyāt, *The Judgments of Nativities*
Judges	Dykes, *The Book of the Nine Judges*
PN (1-3)	Dykes, *Persian Nativities* Vols. I-III
RYW	Māshā'allāh, *On the Revolutions of the Years of the World*
Search	Hermann of Carinthia, *The Search of the Heart*
Skilled	Al-Rijāl, *De Iudiciis Astrorum* [*The Book of the Skilled in the Judgments of the Stars*]
Tet.	Ptolemy, Claudius, *Tetrabiblos*
WSM	Dykes, Benjamin trans. and ed., *Works of Sahl & Māshā'allāh*

TRANSLATOR'S INTRODUCTION

§1: The text and content of the *Compilation*

This is the first modern translation of a well-known medieval compilation of all branches of astrology, written by a "Leopold of Austria," living close to the last few decades of Guido Bonatti (late 13th Century), during the striking 13th Century explosion in sophisticated European astrology, philosophy, the medieval university system, and so on. In recent years, this work has sometimes been known in the astrological community as a "shorter Bonatti," which in a sense is accurate but in fact there seems to be no relation between the two men's books: for example, while Bonatti often uses the easy-to-read translations of John of Spain (11th Cent.), Leopold draws on the same Arabic authors but from other translators, notably Hugo of Santalla (11th Cent.). It is absolutely clear that when explaining horary questions, Bonatti quotes John's translations of Sahl and shows no knowledge of the same material in Hugo's *The Book of the Nine Judges*; but just the reverse is true for Leopold.[1] So, shorter though the *Compilation* is, it is not exactly a shorter *Bonatti*.

In fact, Leopold's identity is unclear. According to a handwritten note in the opening pages of the Wolfenbüttel edition, the author was Leopold, Duke of Austria, either living or reigning from 1292-1326 AD; but he is also described in two other sources[2] as being Leopold II, the son of Leopold I. Moreover, the title of the work and his own introduction describes him either as the "son of the Duchy of Austria," or "son of a/the Duke of Austria" (*ducatus Austriae filius*), an important distinction. Carmody[3] believes it was written about 1271 AD, since Ch. IV.4, **35** calculates the mundane *firdaria* for that year. Indeed, some of the charts in the book can be tentatively dated to around that time. But chart dates in themselves are not definitive because one can always search one's ephemeris for days when planets are in the position one wants; but there would be no particular reason for calculating the mundane *firdaria* for a specific day unless one was living at that time. So, I am

---

[1] My own translation of John's version of Sahl is in my *Works of Sahl & Māshā'allāh* (2008), with an expanded edition from Arabic forthcoming in 2016. My translation of *Nine Judges* was published in 2011.
[2] See McKay 1899, p. 504, and Thomas 1887/2009, vol. III, p. 1408.
[3] Carmody 1960, p. 172.

inclined to agree with Carmody that the book was written circa 1271, whatever the regnal or lifespan dates of these other Leopolds are. The book itself was printed in 1489, and its printer, the famous Erhard Ratdolt (from Augsburg) dedicated it to an Ulrich von Frundsberg (*Ularicus de Fronsperg*), Bishop of Trent from 1486-1493. (I have omitted the dedication, as it is comprised only of Ratdolt's praises and beggings, offering nothing useful about the work itself.)[4]

Concept and style

As I mentioned, most of the texts in the *Compilation* have already been translated by me from their earlier Latin versions (such as *Nine Judges*), so what is the purpose of this volume, both according to Leopold and relative to my other translations? Leopold's intention was clearly to provide a handy, one-volume treatment of all branches of astrology—so that perhaps one might not need other books or help in studying and practicing. Unfortunately, I cannot say that he succeeded, since the text is not written in a way such that a student can start from scratch without extra help. Leopold's choice of text and organization is sometimes puzzling, the typesetting includes many misspellings, and worst of all he often uses awkward and abridged ways of expressing himself in Latin. Moreover, he almost never states what authors he is drawing on, so without a great deal of acquaintance with his source texts, some passages can hardly be deciphered and understood. It is sometimes hard to tell where to place the blame: with Leopold or later editors.

However, since I have indeed translated virtually all of the source texts already, it became easy (albeit tedious) to correct and comment on the *Compilation*: clarifying sentences, providing commentary, and so on. The result is a compilation that now accurately reflects his sources and is understandable by the modern student. My own concept of the *Compilation* then, is that of a single succinct volume that will help students otherwise leery of buying many other translations. It is not really a course in astrology, but one could think of it as something of a manageable bridge between my *Traditional Astrology for Today* and both more extensive traditional texts, and the astrology course I am currently writing. And unlike my *Introductions to*

---

[4] I have also omitted Leopold's short but tortured introduction; the only interesting bit of information in it is that Leopold praises a Raymond de Laudun, one of several possible minor French rulers in the 13th-14th Century.

Traditional Astrology, which is more of a resource guide to basic principles, Leopold teaches the applied interpretations which he finds in his source texts and authors: Sahl b. Bishr, Māshā'allāh, Abū Ma'shar, al-Qabīsī, Ptolemy, al-Imrānī, 'Umar al-Tabarī, al-Khayyāt, magical texts, and others.

In the rest of this Introduction, I will briefly describe the contents and sources of each of his ten Treatises, and then move to some important issues of vocabulary. All important terms are already in the Glossary, but because of Leopold's Latin and my more recent word choices in Latin and Arabic, the reader needs to be reminded of certain terms up front so as not to be confused.

Also, the reader should know that in the past few years I have begun to add boldface sentence numbers in my translations, to better help the reader find citations. So in this book, if I refer to Chapter IV.2, **25**, this means "Treatise IV, Chapter 2, sentence 25."

Treatise I: Geocentric Astronomy Part A

Primary texts:
- An unknown Latin book of astronomical theories and tables, or *zīj*.[5]
- Ptolemy: *Almagest, Tetrabiblos, The Planetary Hypotheses.*
- Abū Ma'shar: *The Great Introduction.*
- John of Spain/Seville: *Treatise on Rains and the Changing of the Atmosphere* (see *AW1*).

Unlike many treatments of astrology, Leopold begins with basic geocentric astronomy. His treatment is brief and accurate for its time, but for most moderns it will be impenetrable, because few of us are taught classical astronomy.[6]

Treatise I describes the universe in the broadest terms, discussing its three outer "orbs": the first movable or *primum mobile*, the zodiacal sphere or orb of the signs, and the orb of the fixed stars. As I point out in my *Comment* to Ch. I.1, this ten-orb scheme was formed by inserting the orb of the signs just

---

[5] However, in Ch. II.3, **62** Leopold does indicate familiarity with the *zīj* of al-Zarqālī (11th Cent. AD); this indicates that Leopold might have used the *Alphonsine Tables*.
[6] In the future I will produce a short paperback on classical astronomy for contemporary astrologers.

under the first movable, as a way of explaining precession through the theory of "trepidation."

The first two orbs are dealt with very briefly (Ch. I.1). Then Leopold discusses several of the types of great circles and other concepts which are essential for many things in astronomy and astrology, from determining terrestrial latitude to house division (Ch. 1.2). From here, Leopold gets a bit more concrete by variously grouping and attributing qualities to the signs, fixed stars, lunar mansions, and faces/decans (Chs. I.3-I.5). He ends with some not-well-expressed material on the physical dimensions of the universe and other things, largely drawn from Ptolemy (Chs. 1.6-1.8). Apart from my *Comment* to Ch. I.1, little of this needs much explanation beyond my footnotes – with the exception of some passages that are impenetrable or confused.

Treatise II: Geocentric Astronomy Part B

Primary text:

- An unknown Latin book of astronomical theories and tables, or *zij*, which draws heavily on Ptolemy's *Almagest*.[7]

In Treatise II, Leopold turns to the last seven orbs of his medieval scheme: namely, all of the Ptolemaic planetary theories. Most of this Treatise simply describes the geometry or mechanism of the theories, but in Ch. II.1 he makes reference to the medieval "three-orb" system, in which each planet's set of circles is contained within three shell-like orbs with a specific outer limit, so that the concentric planetary systems do not crash into one another.

I have added lengthy *Comments* to all of the planetary models discussed, which should be read along with the models in the following order: the Sun (II.2), the superiors and Venus (II.4), Mercury (II.5), and the Moon (II.3). Here I would simply like to summarize Ptolemy's approach, and highlight three special terms which will help readers understand this and especially certain mundane texts: *mean*, *true*, and *equation*.

Ptolemy's planetary models are excellent examples of high scientific achievement. Given a few known planetary motions and periods, Ptolemy

---

[7] Carmody (1960, p. 172) claims that there are elements of Indian astronomy in Tr. II as well.

strove to create geometrical models that would explain and predict planetary motion with as few objects as possible: namely, just a few circles turning at certain rates and arranged in simple ways. If the orbits of the planets were centered on earth and moved at a uniform rate, with no retrograde motion, then planetary models would be easy: we would always know where the planet was, is, and will be. But there were two types of "anomalies" that Ptolemy had to account for in most of the planetary models. The first is the "zodiacal" anomaly, which means that planets move at different rates in different parts of the zodiac: for example, the Sun's motion is a little bit slower in Cancer than in Capricorn. So while we know how long it takes for the Sun to return to any position (namely, exactly one tropical year), he will not always be where he is "expected" to be, because he sometimes moves slower, sometimes faster. Ptolemy's answer was to give the planets a large circle set off-center ("eccentric") from the earth, so that when they are in the farthest parts of the circle, they will appear to move more slowly, and when in the nearer parts they appear to move more quickly. The farthest point is called the "apogee," and the nearest point is called the "perigee." This large eccentric circle is sometimes called the "deferent." The eccentric or deferent rotates exactly once for each planet's tropical period. This accounts for the first anomaly.

The second kind of anomaly or odd behavior is retrograde motion. Again, once we know how long each planet's retrogradation period is, and how far back and forth they move during it, we can put the planet on a smaller circle of the correct size, the "epicycle," and make it rotate exactly once per retrogradation period. This epicycle is carried along on the eccentric, so that the retrogradation behavior moves throughout the zodiac as the planet works its way through its tropical period. Apart from some other basic geometry needed to make everything the right size and coordinate the planets with each other, this is the basic model of Ptolemy (at least, for the superiors, Venus, and the Sun, who does not have an epicycle).

However, Ptolemy made one other important innovation which made calculation easier, and which will lead us to the three special terms above. It turns out that if we stick with this basic model, and assume that the planets (or rather their epicycles) move along their deferents at a constant speed, the positions do not quite work out. This is evident in the retrograde loops, which will either be the wrong size or spaced incorrectly. To correct this, Ptolemy discovered a point out in space, from which, if one measures the planets from it, they will appear to move at a constant rate: the "equant" point. In other words, Ptolemy identified three points to account for three astronomical functions: planets are *measured* from the equant, *revolve* around the center of their eccentric, and are *observed from* the earth. A diagram of the system for Mars is in Ch. II.4. This leads us to our three terms.

Ptolemy's method for calculation is simple and requires only addition and subtraction (and some interpolation) using special tables. First, we find out where the planet *ought* to be, if we assume constant, uniform motion: this is its "mean" motion or the "mean" position, as calculated from the equant point. Whenever you see the word "mean," you should assume that it refers to the expected position of a planet based on constant uniform motion, which is always measured from the equant. So if a planet moves around the zodiac once in exactly 10 years, then from the equant's perspective it will have moved exactly halfway around after 5 years, three-quarters of the way around in 7.5 years, and so on. This will not be so from the earth's perspective, because of the zodiacal anomaly. But it is true for someone in space at the equant point.

However, as astronomers and astrologers, we want to cast charts that show where the planet is, not for the equant point, but for an observer on earth: this is its "true" position, and its motion as observed from earth is its "true" motion. Again, whenever you see "true," you should assume it means "as observed from earth." So the trick is to somehow convert the mean position into the true position: from the measurement out in space, to the observation on earth. Since we know how far off-center the various circles are, it takes just a bit of geometry to figure out how to add or subtract the correction we need: this correction is called an "equation." Sometimes the mean position is farther ahead than the true, so we need to subtract the equation to get the true position; sometimes it is a bit behind, so we need to add the equation. There are equations for both the eccentric (to account for the zodiacal anomaly) and the epicycle (to account for the retrogradation anomaly). Ptolemy grouped all of this into just a couple of tables for each planet. So long as our planetary parameters (lengths of cycles, etc.) are correct, Ptolemy's tables are highly accurate for many centuries. For now, the student should read Leopold's text along with my *Comments*, and try to get the main gist of each model without worrying about its details.

Treatise III: Defense of Astrology

Primary text:
- Abū Ma'shar's *Great Introduction* I.3 - I.6 (no English translation available at this time)

Further reading:
- Guido Bonatti's *Book of Astronomy*, Tr. 1 (in *Bonatti on Basic Astrology*).

Treatise III is mainly a select and condensed review of Abū Ma'shar's arguments in favor of astrology, and his responses to critics. Many of these arguments and responses are interesting, and I have made some comments in the footnotes to this Treatise. Here I will summarize some of the points of view, which Abū Ma'shar divides into ten "sects" or attitudes.

The first sect does not understand in general how the stars could "signify" changes in the world, the coming-to-be of things and their passing away or corruption. "Signify" might be the central concern here, since astrological literature tends to oscillate between a view of planets as signifying things, and *causing* them. Since Abū Ma'shar is a naturalist about astrology (at least, for the most part), he provides a naturalistic response: the elemental makeup and natural motions of things contributes to their change, their coming-to-be and passing away. But, he adds, the planets themselves have similar operations (such as heating, drying, etc.), and their circular movements communicate these changes to our world of the elements. Therefore, planets signify these changes because they actually cause many of them. In Leopold's version, the objector does not see how the planets can cause things to be *destroyed* or pass away or change into something else; but Abū Ma'shar's treatment shows he is interested in both sides of the equation.

The second sect admits that the planets cause change, but that they only cause change in general and basic categories of things, such as the elements or classes of beings like "human," or "horse." But, they say, the planets do not have power over individual and particular things which are produced by them (such as a particular human, or a particular horse). Leopold combines Abū Ma'shar's two responses, to the effect that generic beings like "the human" do not exist, only individuals do: but since individual humans are composed of, and change in accordance with, their elemental qualities, the planets must have power over the changes in individuals. Moreover, Leopold says that planetary influences target specific ways in which the individual operates: the power of speech, emotions, the blood, and so on.

The third sect uses some categories of modal logic to say that phenomena fall into three categories: the necessary (such that fire is hot), the impossible (such that fire is cold), and the possible (such that a human may write or not write). Now, this whole topic is too difficult to go much into here (and Abū Ma'shar goes on for several pages), but the objection is this: that when a particular person does write or does not write, that action becomes either necessary or impossible. That is, when he does write, it is necessary that he writes because he has done what it takes to write, so that *not* writing has become impossible (and *vice versa*). Therefore, there is not really such a category as the possible—and since astrologers concern themselves with possible actions, giving advice, and so on, they are deluding themselves about the logical character of what they do. Abū Ma'shar responds that the category of the possible extends to things we have choices over, and even then there are gradations in the possible. Moreover, people only deliberate and choose when it comes to things that are really possible—otherwise, the whole process of thinking and deciding would be illusory. But it is not illusory: therefore the possible exists, and that is the realm that astrology deals with.

The fourth sect argues that the planets only have power over large-scale changes like seasons, but not daily effects in individuals and their lives. Abū Ma'shar observes that seasonal changes are elemental too, and effect changes in individuals like us, who are made up of the elements. So of course even seasonal changes have effects: the objector, he says, is admitting the causes of change (seasonal shifts), but is not bothering to pay attention to how these causes generate change all the way down to individuals.

The fifth sect targets the principle of replication in science. Since similar causes should have similar effects, then when planets recur in the same places or configurations, we should expect effects similar to their previous occurrence. But not only do some of these recurrences happen over long stretches of time (so that reports of them are unreliable), but they do not occur in isolation: there is always some other configuration or feature of a chart which could mitigate the effect we are expecting to happen each time. Abū Ma'shar responds that the ancient sages *did* observe the planets over long periods of time (he mentions Ptolemy, but might also be thinking of the Babylonians here), and moreover we already know that many general changes *are* repeated and replicable: such as the Sun's process of heating, or the Moon's role in relation to moisture.

The sixth sect attacks the differences between planetary tables: for example, Ptolemy's *Almagest* has planetary parameters that differ from the tables of the Indians, or the *Zīj al-Shāh*, and so on: these differences mean that the astrologer never knows *precisely* where the planet is, and so cannot properly judge the effects. Abū Ma'shar's response is that judgment is difficult, and does not rely simply on the zodiacal position of the planet: it relies on angularity, rulerships, and so on. These factors sometimes have an overriding factor that makes the exact position of the planet less important.

The seventh sect is something of an odd one, but refers to people who deny astrology out of envy, but because of their laziness they never bother to study it. I suppose we could include some professional astronomers here, or people who attack astrology out of cultural prejudice. To these, Abū Ma'shar responds that since their laziness and prejudice is not an argument, these people can be dismissed. Of course, they cannot be dismissed *culturally*, but here Abū Ma'shar is concerned with actual arguments against astrology.

The eighth sect refers to medical doctors who want to treat their science as independent of astrology. But as Abū Ma'shar points out, all sorts of environmental changes *do* lead to changes in our bodies and health; and besides, experience and authority shows that when people are sick it is important to draw up decumbiture charts, monitor the Moon, and so on. Therefore, doctors really ought to pay attention to astrology.

The ninth sect involves everyday people who believe that it is enough to have practical success in life: for example, if one has earned a lot of money, knowing astrology would not change that, so what is the point of astrology? Abū Ma'shar's response has to do with the dignity of humans and knowledge. What sets us apart from the animals is knowledge and reason (which the Latin edition also summarizes as "wisdom"): therefore, to the extent that someone does care about the knowledge of future things, he is strengthening his humanity. Concentrating only on animal needs like the means of subsistence (or, money) does not ennoble us, and indeed treats us as only being animals. The implication here is also that things like money and fame are not certain and are changeable, whereas having knowledge and wisdom is something we can possess in our own right, so that we are more in control of our happiness and humanity when we focus on that.

Finally, the tenth sect points to the prevalence of errors among astrologers. Abū Ma'shar's response is simply that the astrologer has to know all sorts of things, including areas of the natural world—people make mistakes (or at least, big mistakes) when they do not know all of these things but call themselves astrologers anyway. Therefore, it is important for astrologers to be well trained in all sorts of subjects, in addition to the complicated realm of astrology.

In a future work (most likely the translation of Abū Ma'shar's *Great Introduction* from Arabic), I hope to address these sects in detail, based on his fuller discussion of them. But in conclusion, Leopold raises one more issue: the moral effect of astrology on the human being. Apparently alluding to *Gr. Intr.* I.6, Leopold finally raises the question as to whether predictive knowledge would be too depressing: for just as we may see something good happening in the future, we will also see that it comes to an end. So why should we depress ourselves with the knowledge of things that will come to an end, or get involved with them when they will not last? Abū Ma'shar's response is that *everything* comes to an end: if this argument were good, it would mean that we should not eat, because eating will end; not love, because loving will end. If we followed this advice, then we would not do anything at all: it has little to do with astrology.

Treatise IV: Introductory Principles and Lots

Primary texts:
- Al-Qabīsī's *Introduction to Astrology*.
- Sahl b. Bishr's *Fifty Judgments* or *Fifty Aphorisms* (in *WSM*, and forthcoming in my translation from Arabic).
- Abū Ma'shar, *Great Introduction*.

Further reading:
- Dykes, *Introductions to Traditional Astrology*.
- Dykes, *Works of Sahl & Māshā'allāh*.
- Dykes, MP3 audio workshop on Lots (see www.bendykes.com).

Treatise IV is a long and varied treatise, which covers basic astrological vocabulary, planetary configurations and planetary natures, and Lots. Much of this is taken from the sources mentioned above, and because it largely consists of simple definitions and lists of significations, there is not much to say about its content and organization here. However, it is important for the beginning student to understand the role these lists and definitions play in traditional texts.

In most modern astrology, there is very little interpretive distance between certain basic concepts and their application in a chart. For example, we might learn that Venus naturally signifies things like love and passion, and Aries signifies energy patterns that are dramatic or forceful; in virtually the next sentence we then learn that Venus in Aries means something like "forceful passion." One reason for this simple pairing of key words is because in most modern astrology (a) the conceptual vocabulary is rather small, and (b) the chart is taken to be a picture of your mind. So we are already dealing with a narrow context of psychological needs and expression, and a limited vocabulary of signs, aspects, and such.

But traditional astrology has a much greater vocabulary, and this vocabulary is virtually context-free: Venus in Aries might mean one thing in a horary chart about getting a job, another thing in the natal sixth house, another thing in a mundane chart, and so on. Indeed, there is hardly anything that *can* be said about "Venus in Aries" all by itself, except that Venus is in detriment (or that she is in a movable sign, etc.): being in detriment does mean something, but unless we know the context of the chart, it does not help us much. Traditional texts are more like geometry books: we begin with definitions of lines and angles and such, but unless we are faced with a specific diagram or problem, the definitions do not bring us very far all by themselves. So when we learn that a planet on the Midheaven is strong, but in the eleventh it is not as strong, this can seem trivial until we know the context. Suppose we have a question chart about two litigants in a court case, and we want to know which party is more likely to win: in this case, it is very valuable to know that the lord of the Ascendant is on the Midheaven, while the lord of the seventh is in the eleventh. In short, we could look at the situation like this: Treatise IV provides the definitions, but later Treatises on questions, nativities, mundane ingresses, elections, and so on, explain and explore the *applications*.

After his chapters on definitions and planetary significations, Leopold turns to Lots or so-called "Arabic Parts" (Ch. IV.5), most of which is taken from Abū Ma'shar's *Gr. Intr.* VIII. Recently I recorded an MP3 workshop on six useful Lots, exploring their meaning and interpretation,[8] and here I would just like to give a short summary—especially since some Lots (like Lots for commodities) ought to be treated somewhat differently than others.

All Lots are based on a ratio: we measure the distance between two points that naturally signify something (such as Saturn and the Sun for fathers), and then project that same distance from a third point (normally the Ascendant). Where the counting stops, that degree (or more usually that sign) is the location of the Lot. By projecting from some personal point like the Ascendant, we personalize the position and meaning of the Lot for a particular native, or nation, or whatever.

Although there is still a lot of work to do in this exciting area, in general Lots describe people and situations which are not really under our control: people or events which are external to us, or which involve complex patterns of behavior and phenomena. In a natal chart, they often seem to deal with our own subjective experience of these people and things. For example, the Lot of the father should objectively describe something about the father and his life, but especially the *native's experience* of having that father, and the role that father plays in the native's life. (It is not always easy to distinguish the meaning of the Lot from the meaning of a house; this is part of the ongoing research.)

Interpreting most Lots should be based on the same simple procedures we follow in interpreting house topics. First, the house of the Lot (and perhaps its sign, quadruplicity, etc.) should be interpreted, and benign or difficult effects upon it based on aspects from planets to its sign. So if the Lot of the father is in the sixth house, then the experience of the father and who he was should be related to sixth-house people and events. Second, the lord of the Lot: its nature and location. If the lord of the Lot is Venus, and she is in the ninth, then the father's activity and the experience of him should be somehow Venusian, and linked to ninth-house affairs: perhaps the father was a musician, and loved to travel. Third, the planet which most closely aspects or influences the lord, should be interpreted as giving extra qualities and behaviors. For example, if Jupiter is the most closely-aspecting planet to this Venus, then perhaps the father was very interested in justice, or religion, or philosophical concerns. Some Lots have special planets associated with them, such that transits to the Lot allow for predictive statements; one must consult each Lot in order to see what Abū Ma'shar has to say about them.

---

[8] See www.bendykes.com.

Treatise V: Mundane Astrology

Primary texts:
- Māshā'allāh, *On the Revolutions of the Years of the World* (see *AW2*).
- Abū Ma'shar, *The Book of Religions and Dynasties (On the Great Conjunctions)*.
- "Al-Qabīsī," a short work on planetary conjunctions (see *AW2*).
- Jirjis, excerpts from *The Book of the Nine Judges*.

Further reading:
- Dykes, *Astrology of the World* Vols. I-II (*AW1* and *AW2*, see Bibliography).
- Dykes, MP3 audio lectures on traditional mundane astrology (www.bendykes.com),

Treatise V is a somewhat disorganized but overall good introduction to the style of thinking in traditional mundane astrology, with many aphoristic descriptions of what to expect from various planets and various charts. But it would be difficult to practice any of the techniques on the basis of Leopold's summary. Instead, I recommend my *Astrology of the World* (*AW*) series, which contains lengthy *Comments* and Introductions that explain the rationale and procedures behind all of these techniques. My best advice to the reader is to follow along and get the main gist of what the various authors say, and then look to my full translations and explanations in *AW1* and *AW2*.

Treatise VI: Weather Prediction

Primary texts:
- Ptolemy, *Tetrabiblos*.
- John of Spain, *Treatise on Rains* (see *AW1*).
- Hermann of Carinthia, *Book of Heavy Rains* (see *AW1*).
- Al-Kindī, *Letter on Air & Rains* (see *AW1*).

Further reading:
- Dykes, *Astrology of the World* Vol. I (*AW1*).

Leopold's treatment of weather prediction is brisk and moves quickly from an account of decans or faces from Ptolemy, lunar mansions, the "opening of the doors," planetary combinations, and a host of other rules whose sources are not known. Some of the descriptions, such as winds and thunder (Ch. VI.3) are of uncertain application or relevance, certainly when it comes to different geographical regions. For more on this topic, including a lengthy introductory essay on all these techniques, see my *AW1*.

Treatise VII: Nativities

Primary texts:
- 'Umar al-Tabarī, *Three Books on Nativities* (see *PN2*).
- Ptolemy, *Tetrabiblos*.
- Al-Qabīsī, *Introduction to Astrology*.
- Abū 'Alī al-Khayyāt, *On the Judgment of Nativities* (see *PN1*).
- Māshā'allāh/Jirjis, *What the Planets Signify in the Twelve Domiciles of the Circle* (see *WSM*).

Further reading:
- Dykes, *Persian Nativities* Vols. I-III (*PN1-3*).
- Dykes, *Introductions to Traditional Astrology* (*ITA*).
- Dykes, *Works of Sahl & Māshā'allāh* (*WSM*).

Treatise VII is a pretty comprehensive treatment of nativities, at least from the few sources used. Chapters VII.1-4 cover the basics of physical life and temperament, which could be grouped into the first house: gestation, birth and birth defects, body type and character, and longevity. These are taken mainly from Ptolemy and 'Umar, with some additions from al-Qabīsī on primary directions. Following this, Chs. VII.5-16 (based on 'Umar and Abū 'Alī) cover house topics such as assets, profession, and so on—with the exception of VII.11, which does more with Ptolemy's views on character and personality. Readers should be aware that Leopold's version of Ptolemy on illness (VII.10, **25ff**) is pretty much as intelligible as Ptolemy's own version, which is to say it is frustrating and sometimes so specific as to planetary configuration that its practical use is uncertain. I have had to add much clarifying material in brackets to make it readable.

Finally, Chs. VII.17-18 are cookbook-style renditions of Abū ʿAlī's and Māshā'allāh's/Jirjis's lists of planets in the houses and signs. These should be read closely, and while the student should try to memorize many of them, they should not be taken as precise interpretations. The purpose of these lists is to get the student to understand how planetary placements work, *by means of* the interpretations. For example, the Moon is the principal symbol of change in the chart, and her closeness to the earth makes her signify well the daily, concrete activities and people we spend our life with. So, Abū ʿAlī says that the Moon in a sign of Mars makes the native associate with bad people and robbers: this leads us to the conclusion that the lord of a sign has a lot to say about the concrete application of a planet's signification, in this case the types of people (Moon) that the native associates with. It is more important to understand why a signification exists, and how to generate it from principles, than to *merely* memorize it.

Treatise VIII: Questions (Horary)

Primary texts:
- Various, *The Book of the Nine Judges.*

Further reading:
- Dykes (trans. and ed.), *The Book of the Nine Judges.*
- Sahl's *On Questions* (in *WSM*, and in a forthcoming translation from Arabic).
- Bonatti, Guido (Dykes trans. and ed.), *The Book of Astronomy* Tr. 6 (also published as *Bonatti on Horary*).

Treatise VIII is a standard treatment of questions (horary), almost completely comprised of passages from *The Book of the Nine Judges*, a medieval Latin compilation of question texts translated from Arabic by Hugo of Santalla (11th Cent.). Of the various "judges" or Arabic authors Hugo collects, Leopold concentrates on passages from Sahl, ʿUmar al-Tabarī, and al-Kindī. This makes sense, due to their popularity in the medieval period (although ʿUmar was mainly known through his natal work)—but surprisingly, Leopold also employs many passages from "Aristotle" and Jirjis, minor authors whose identity is unknown.

In this Treatise especially, readers need to be aware of a major style change in Leopold's language—that is, Leopold begins to mimic or quote Hugo's Latin style, which differs greatly from the easier style of translators such as John of Spain (11th Cent.). Some of this comes down to simple vocabulary: for example, "Ascendant" is usually expressed in Latin as *ascendens* (lit., "the rising"); but Hugo prefers *oriens*, which also means "the rising" but also more specifically "the east." In fact, Hugo often has very good reasons for his choice of terms, and *oriens* translates the Arabic just as validly as *ascendens* does. But for people used to a certain style of expression in astrology, some of Hugo's/Leopold's style in this Treatise can seem odd. For the most part, the trick is simply to slow down. For instance, we are normally used to if-then statements, such as "If a benefic is in the Ascendant, or if the lord of the Ascendant is in the Ascendant…it will hasten [the effect]." But in Ch. VIII.6, **8** Leopold follows Hugo by saying "And a fortune in the east, or with the lord of the east being in the east…hastens [the effect]." The information is the same, but expressed in a way that may take a little more time to digest.

Treatise IX: Elections & Talismans

Primary texts:
- Sahl b. Bishr, *On Elections* (in *WSM* and in Dykes ed., *Choices & Inceptions*).
- Al-Imrānī, *On Elections* (in Dykes ed., *Choices & Inceptions*).

Further reading:
- Carmody, *The Astronomical Works of Thābit b. Qurra*.

The word "election" means "choice," and Treatise IX is devoted to choosing opportune times for many types of actions, from getting a haircut (!) to conceiving children. The Treatise is not well organized, in my opinion. Chapters IX.9-12 do indeed move through their topics according to the order of the houses. But many basic principles are sprinkled throughout, from the importance of planetary signification (IX.1) to the quadruplicities of the signs (IX.13). Ch. IX.14 is an interesting account of how to track the success of daily events.

The most striking addition to the usual description of elections is IX.3, which gives advice on "images," namely talismans: normally, magical material is omitted from normal books on chart-reading. According to Carmody,[9] the development of Leopold's material stands somewhere between what is found in Thābit b. Qurra and the medieval grimoire *Picatrix*. Some of the details for the precise design of talismans are missing (including if any magical operation ought to take place), but the instructions amount to inscribing astrological names at the proper elected time (and in some cases making more than one talisman), and burying or carrying the talisman in the appropriate way.

Treatise X: Thought-Interpretation

Further reading:
- Hermann of Carinthia, *The Search of the Heart*.

This short Treatise is on a little-known practice called "thought-interpretation" or "investigating" or "drawing out" the "heart." For some centuries thought-interpretation was used as a prelude to, or in conjunction with, question charts (and perhaps election charts). When a client approaches an astrologer, the astrologer casts a chart and interprets it in order to figure out the hidden thoughts, intentions, and wishes of the client—as a kind of independent check on what is going on with the client. In some cases, thought-interpretation was used as a basis of discussion, which would then lead to a particular question or election; in other cases, it was used to identify *and answer* a question or issue on the clients mind (as Leopold shows here, with the chart of the sick mother). For much more on thought-interpretation, see my *The Search of the Heart* and my MP3 audio lecture on it (with examples), at www.bendykes.com.

---

[9] Carmody, p. 172.

§2: Important Vocabulary

There are a number of terms used in this book which are important to note, partly because of the Latin works Leopold is drawing on, and partly because of my own changes in Latin translation over the past few years. None of these is difficult, but I thought it would be better to list a few of the more notable ones here. The reader is also directed to the extensive Glossary at the back of the book.

- **Aversion**. This is the counterpoint to aspecting or **looking**: a planet is in aversion to something when its sign and the other thing's sign do not aspect each other by any classical aspect. For example, since Cancer and Virgo are configured by a sextile aspect, anything in Cancer can see Virgo and anything in it by a sextile (these are considered sign-to-sign aspects). But Cancer and Leo are not configured by any aspect, so anything in Cancer is in aversion to Leo and anything in it. Since aspects involve a relationship, knowledge, and some kind of control, things that are in aversion are characterized by a lack of relationship, lack of communication, lack of control.
- **Falling**. Not to be confused with a planet's fall (such as Cancer being the fall of Mars), "falling" usually refers to being cadent, whether in a cadent sign or a cadent house. (*Cadens* means "falling" in Latin.) A related term is "falling away from," which means the same as **aversion**.
- **Foreign**. Equivalent to "peregrine" (*peregrinus* means "foreigner" or "pilgrim" in Latin).
- **Fortune, infortune**. Equivalent to "benefic" and "malefic." Similar terms are "benevolent" and "malevolent," and "good one" and "bad one."
- **Good one / bad one**. Equivalent to "benefic" and "malefic."
- **Leader**. This is used by Hugo of Santalla to translate the Arabic word referring to a "significator" or "indicator," as the Arabic verb (*dalla*) also means to point out or lead someone's attention to something.
- **Look at**. Equivalent to "aspect."

- **Pivot**. Equivalent to "angle," but with the usual ambiguity as to whether this refers to a house or an axial degree itself.
- **Possessing**. This is a more colorful word used by Hugo of Santalla to mean that a planet is "in" a certain sign or house.
- **Regard**. Equivalent to "aspect," or **look at**.
- **Rendering/gathering counsel**. These phrases are used by Hugo of Santalla to mean that a planet is pushing or accepting management to or from another planet. For example, if Mars is a significator and is applying to Jupiter, he renders or pushes his management responsibility to Jupiter, who gathers or accepts it.

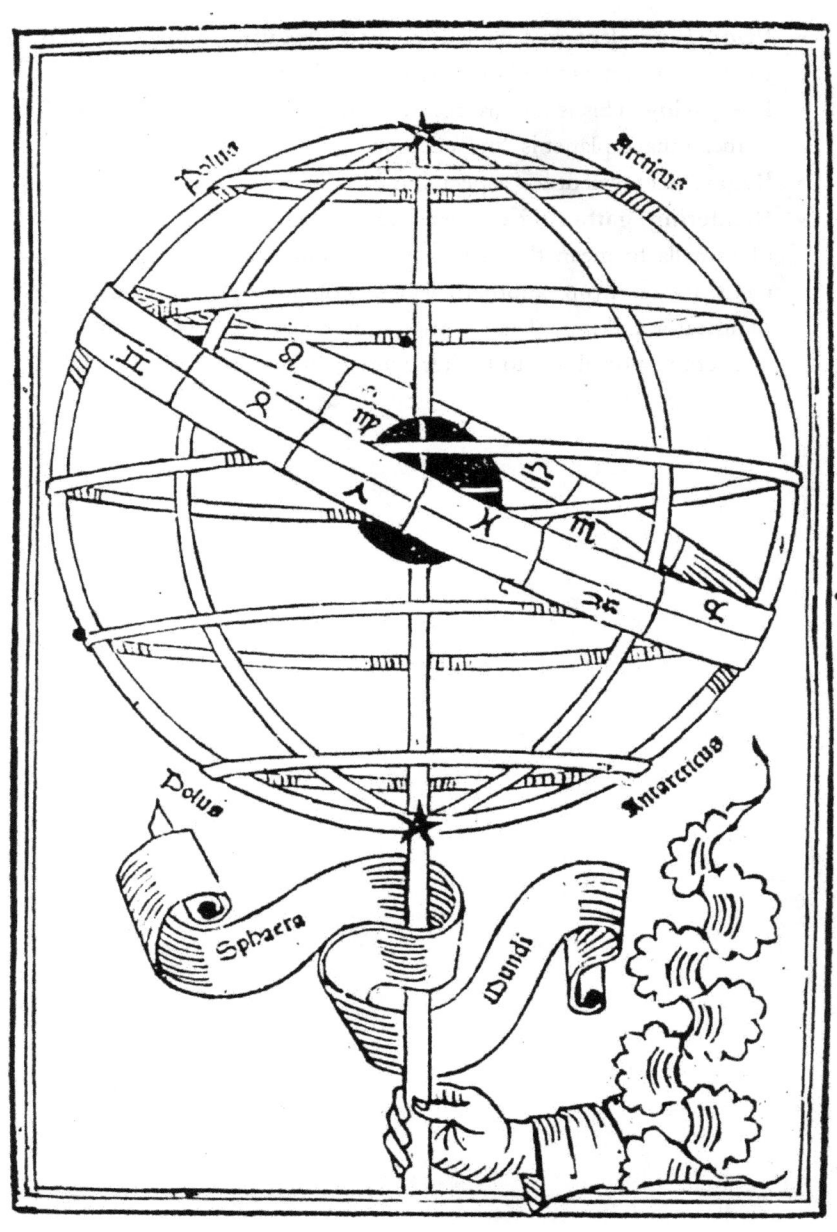

TREATISE I: ON THE SPHERES, & THEIR CIRCLES & MOTIONS

[Chapter I.1: The cosmic orbs]

1 A sphere is a solid body contained by exactly one surface. **2** There are ten heavenly spheres: the first is the firmament or circumference; the second, the orb of the signs; the third, the starry orb; the fourth, that of Saturn; the fifth, that of Jupiter; the sixth, that of Mars; the seventh, that of the Sun; the eighth, that of Venus; the ninth, that of Mercury; the tenth, that of the Moon.

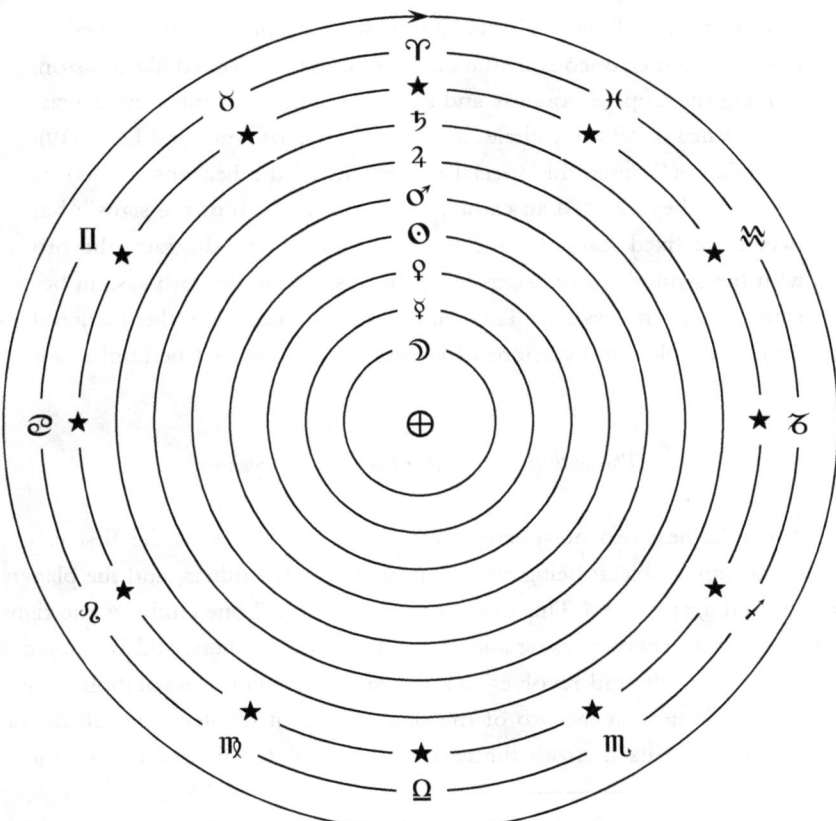

Figure 1: Late medieval, 10-sphere universe (Dykes, after Leopold)

Comment by Dykes. Leopold's universe was of a late medieval type (inherited from Arabic astronomy) which inserted an extra sphere into the older, nine-orb universe.[1] At the center of the universe is the earth, with the four elements. Around it are the seven planetary orbs, and just beyond them the sphere of visible fixed stars (called by Leopold the "starry orb"). Now, in the traditional Aristotelian universe the final sphere was the sphere of diurnal rotation (or "first movable," the *primum mobile*), depicted here with an arrow pointing to the right and called by Leopold the "firmament or circumference." And in Leopold's universe, this sphere is indeed the outermost. But medieval Arab astronomers believed that precession did not proceed at a uniform rate, being confused by some incorrect measurements by Ptolemy. To explain this assumed periodic change in the rate of precession, astronomers such as Thābit b. Qurra (fl. 9th Cent. AD) developed an ingenious but erroneous mathematical device that worked like a piston, moving the tropical equinox and starry orb back and forth on the circumference of two tiny circles at the beginning of Aries and Libra (**19**): "trepidation." Since this special movement of the heavens needed its own orb, they inserted an extra orb (Leopold's "orb of the signs") between the fixed stars and the first movable (in the diagram, the orb with the symbols of the signs in it). In this way, a nine-orb system became a ten-orb system. Trepidation was worked into the medieval books of tables, and versions of it were assumed to be true until about 1550 AD!

[The tenth sphere: the firmament or circumference]

3 The highest orb or sphere is moved by the virtue of the first cause, which is immovable: it being moved, it moves all the others, and the planets are moved against it.[2] **4** This orb is called the "great" one, and it is the right [sphere], more encompassing and faster than all the others, and it embraces them within itself, and revolves in a day and night with a revolution of 360 portions,[3] along with the orb of the signs. **5** And it revolves the orb of the fixed stars with itself, from the east to the west. **6** And the orb of those

---

[1] See for example Evans, pp. 276-77, 280.
[2] That is, while the outermost orb sweeps everything around the heavens daily by diurnal motion, the planets move in a contrary direction, in the order of signs.
[3] That is, "degrees."

[stars] revolves by itself[4] toward the east, 1° in 100 years (according to Ptolemy).[5] **7** Then, the other orbs [revolve] according to the amount of their limit and size.

8 And on account of [the firmament] there is day and night, and diverse seasons of spring and summer, autumn and winter, and it alters the seven planets.[6] **9** And the earth is fixed in the middle of it: which if it did not exist, day and night would never be balanced. **10** And it is not starry, and some say that it is spiritual.

[The ninth sphere, the orb of the signs]

11 The orb of the signs[7] is that to which a star (in whatever sign) is said to be aligned, and its northern pole is distant from the pole of the orb of the signs by approximately 24°[8] (and likewise the southern pole). **12** It is not even starred, on account of the fact that the forms of the signs are not able to be put in it—but they are *referred to* the 12 parts of the orb of the signs. **13** For already *Cor Leonis*[9] and other fixed stars are in more degrees of the orb of the signs than they were at the time of the Flood, and we see the stars only if they are the fixed ones—which are not called "fixed" because they are in no way moved, but because periods of time do not change their *shapes*. **14** And they divide off from the orb of the signs according to the quantity of the course in their own orb.[10] **15** And the 12 parts in the orb of the signs are named according to the shape which the stars placed in those parts, form. **16** Therefore, there are forms of signs and images in the starred heaven, but those signs themselves are in a non-starred one, inasmuch as individual forms are put under individual signs. **17** And the signification of the images and things is from the proper quality of the signs.

---

[4] *De ipso.*
[5] A modern value for precession is 1° every 71.59 years, or 1° 23' 45" in 100 years.
[6] *Permutat.* I am not exactly sure what Leopold means here, except that perhaps the planets' significations in various areas (such as in weather prediction) are changed based on the season, signs, and night and day.
[7] Again, this is the invisible orb which accounts for precession, and in which the tropical signs are measured.
[8] Lit., "24 parts" (*partes*). That is, the obliquity of the ecliptic, which in 2000 AD was about 23° 26'.
[9] That is, Regulus.
[10] Namely, via precession.

18 The step of the fixed stars[11] is the recession of the eighth sphere or the ninth, by 1° every 100 years.[12]

[The eighth sphere, the fixed stars]

19 The mean motion of the eighth sphere is the motion of the small circle from the beginning of Aries or Libra.[13] **20** Its equation[14] is the arc of the zodiac which is from the beginning of starred Aries up to the intersection of that same zodiac and the equator.

[Chapter I.2: The great circles of the local horizon]

1 For an understanding of the circles, let a man be placed standing directly under the equator at the true center of the earth. **2** Then understand, through the regard of the one standing [there], one point in the east (in the sphere of heaven), another in the west, a third in the north in the sphere of heaven, a fourth in the south, a fifth directly above the head of the one standing [there] (which is called the zenith), a sixth opposite it in the angle of the earth, a seventh in the place where he stands.

3 Once this is done, understand a circle going out from the point of the east, which proceeds through the zenith of the one standing, and through the point of the west, and the angle of the earth, and let it return to the one from which it went out: and this is the equator, the poles of which are the northern and southern point which it is revolved around. **4** And along with itself it leads the whole machine of heaven from east to west, and the elevation of its pole is always equal to the latitude of the region [one is in].

---

[11] Or, the "precession of the equinoxes."

[12] See above for a better, modern rate.

[13] These are the tiny circles of about 4° 30" which later trepidation theory put in the eighth sphere at the intersection of the equator and the "fixed" equinoctial point: see the description of trepidation above.

[14] That is, the difference between 0° sidereal Aries, and 0° tropical Aries or the equinox. In traditional astronomy, an "equation" (Lat. *equatio, aequatio*) is a correction: an amount that must be added to a value from a table, in order to get a more accurate value. This passage suggests that Leopold or his source was working with Ptolemaic positions for fixed stars, which then had a correction applied so as to get their tropical position for the year a chart was cast. Unfortunately, most medievals did not have the correct rate of precession so the "equation" would have been wrong in any case.

5 Let a second circle go out from the northern point and cross through the zenith, that is, through the point of the south and the angle of the earth, and let it return whence it went out, and this is the meridian. **6** But the meridian circles of the regions are those which, going out from the poles, cross the vertex of the regions.

7 Let a third circle go out from the east, through the point of the north and west and south, and let it return whence it went out, and this is the horizon, which divides the part of heaven which is above the earth from that which is under the earth.

8 The center of all is what is between the feet of the one standing [there]. **9** Therefore, of the three aforesaid circles there are three chords, and six poles which are the extremities of their chords.[15]

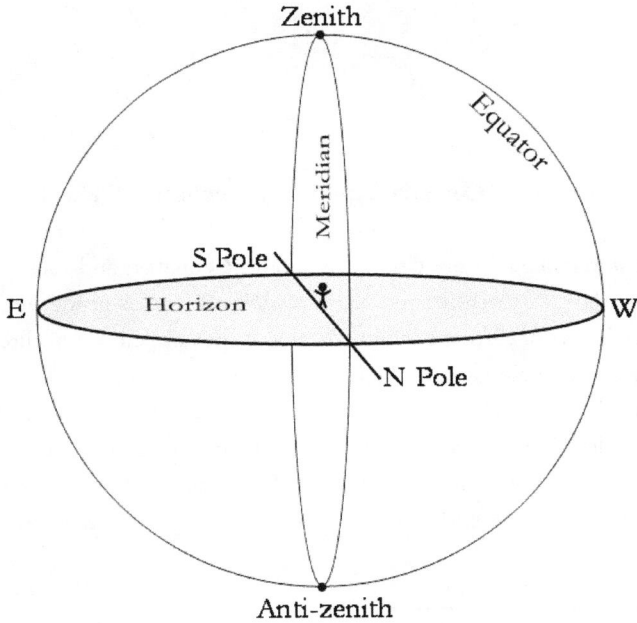

Figure 2: Three great circles, viewed from middle of Earth at 0° latitude (Dykes)

---

[15] I have not shown all of the poles, so as to keep the diagram simple.

10 Moreover, let a circle go out to the side of the equator on both sides, about 24° askew,[16] and let it be drawn around so that it returns to the same [place] in the sphere whence it went out, and this is the zodiac.

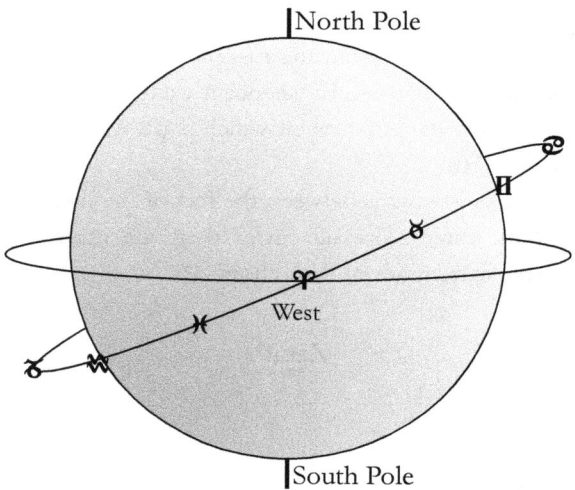

Figure 3: Celestial equator and ecliptic (Dykes)

11 The *almucantarath*[17] are circles dividing the equator, and these are circles of elevation [above the horizon]. **12** *Azimuth*[18] are circles going out from the pole of the horizon, through the horizon: and they are circles of direction.

13 The arctic circle is that which circles the northern pole at a distance of approximately 24°.[19] **14** The antarctic pole is that which likewise circles the southern pole. **15** The circle of elevation or altitude is that which, crossing through the zenith over one's head, [being] elevated over anything, falls upon the horizon.[20] **16** The zenith is the point directly above the head of any thing.

---

[16] Lit. "in width" or "in latitude."

[17] *Almicanthorat*. These are parallel circles of elevation above the local horizon, up to the zenith (from Ar. *al-muqanṭarāt*, which refers to arches and vaulting). Since astronomers have used this transliteration for many centuries, I retain it here.

[18] *Azimuth*, from Ar. *al-sumūt*, "the ways/roads." Azimuth is the angular distance of some point when viewed from a particular location: it is measured from due north around to the east, south, and west.

[19] The difference between the arctic circle (66° N) and the north pole (90°) is 24°.

[20] I am not sure what Leopold means here; it sounds like an awkward combination of both *almucantarath* and *azimuth*.

17 The arc of elevation is that portion from the circle of elevation (which is even called the circle of altitude) elevated from a thing toward the horizon.[21]

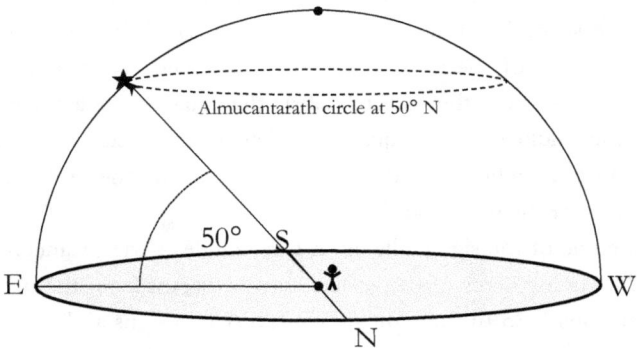

Figure 4: Star at altitude 50° from local horizon (Dykes)

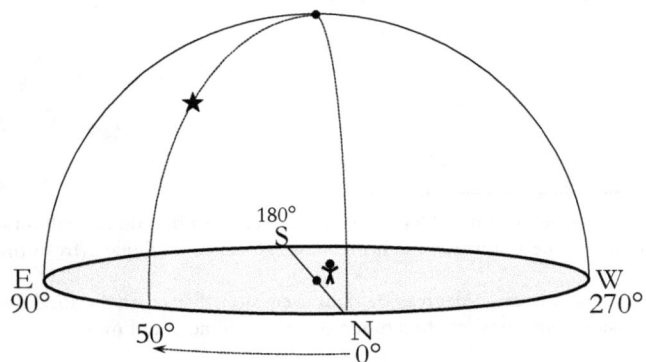

Figure 5: Star at *azimuth* 50° (Dykes)

18 The ascensions of the right sphere[22] are ascensions of the equator above the head of one whom we said before was standing, or [ascensions] which it makes there with the signs.[23] **19** The ascensions of the oblique

---

[21] See the diagram above of the star at altitude 50°: the arc from the star down to the horizon is equivalent to the 50° angle as observed from the center of the horizon.
[22] That is, "right ascension" or RA. These are the equivalent of terrestrial longitude, but projected onto the celestial equator.
[23] See the diagram above, described in **1-9**. This simply means that degrees on the celestial equator are measured in degrees called "right ascension," and that degrees of the zodiac or in the ecliptic correspond to and can be converted to them.

sphere or clime,[24] are ascensions of the equator according to the diversity of the climes.[25] **20** Whence, if you hear "ascensions of the signs," understand "ascensions of the circle of the equator"—or, in the first way in the right circle, or the second way in the oblique circle, which it makes there along with the elevation of the signs.[26] **21** But understand "equal degrees" to be "degrees of the signs in the zodiac." **22** At the equator, the ascensions of the signs and the Midheaven are equal, and likewise the ascensions of the Midheaven and of the whole world: and for that reason, one table of the right circle suffices for the whole world.[27]

23 The circle of the signs falls upon three circles: Aries, Cancer, and Capricorn.[28] **24** Any two arcs of the zodiac equally distant from the tropics, have equal ascensions.[29] **25** In the right sphere, every two signs and their opposites have equal ascensions.[30] **26** In the right sphere, in the equinoctial quarters more of the zodiac arises than that of the equator;[31] in the solstitial quarters, more of the equator [arises] than of the zodiac.

---

[24] That is, "oblique ascensions." Degrees of right ascension that do not fall on the meridian circle but somewhere towards the horizon are all called "oblique" (from the Latin for "slanted").

[25] This means that the exact degrees of right ascension that cross the local horizon (i.e., oblique ascensions) are sensitive to latitude or one's "clime" (and must be measured trigonometrically).

[26] This confusing sentence refers to ascensional times. Each zodiacal sign is rather slanted when it crosses the local horizon, and the exact degree of the slant is sensitive to latitude. In order to measure how long each sign takes to cross the horizon at a particular latitude, Babylonian astronomers calculated how many degrees of RA crossed the meridian, as all 30° of a sign rose in the east. The number of degrees were called "ascensions" or "times" or "ascensional times." Because ascensional times are a function of local latitude, they are related to the practice of mapmaking. They are also used for timing mechanisms in astrology, and were an early way of calculating primary directions.

[27] That is, the relationship of the zodiac itself to the celestial equator is the same for everyone; but how this translates into ascensional times and the angles of the signs at a particular location (e.g., how an astrological chart will look), must be calculated in special tables or trigonometry for a specific place and time.

[28] Namely, Aries (and Libra) at the equator, the Tropic of Cancer, and the Tropic of Capricorn.

[29] So, for any latitude, Aries-Pisces have identical ascensional times, as do Taurus-Aquarius, Gemini-Capricorn, and so on.

[30] See the figure at Ch. IV.1, **55** below.

[31] Reading *equatore* for *equinoctiali*.

[Chapter I.3: Stars, signs, mansions]

46 The stars taken up into knowledge are 1,022,[32] among which are the seven planets, 5 nebulous, [and] 9 dark. **47** And one is called the king of all the stars, and it is *Cor Leonis*,[33] because of which the science of astronomy was discovered.

48 There are 12 signs of the zodiac, and they are the following shapes:

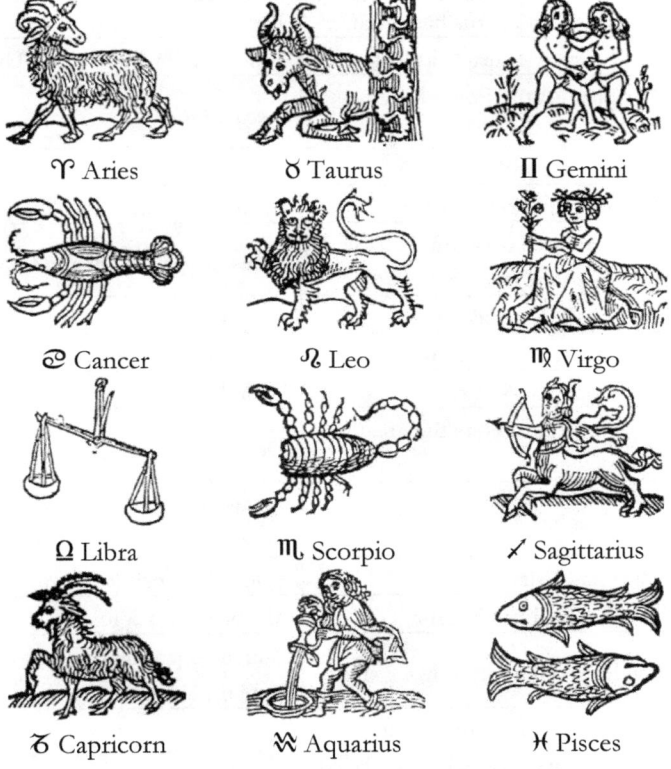

Figure 6: Signs of the zodiac (Leopold)

---

[32] Reading with Ptolemy VIII.1, for *1029*.
[33] I.e., Regulus.

[Mansions of the Moon][34]

49 There are 28 mansions of the Moon in the aforesaid twelve signs, to each one of which they grant 12° 51' and about 26". **50** And they are these:

	Mansion	Likely Stars
1	The horns of Aries has 2 stars.	Sheratan (β Aries), Mesarthim (γ)
2	The belly of Aries has 3 stars.	Botein (δ), ε, ϱ Aries
3	The Head of Taurus has 6 stars.	Pleiades
4	The heart of Taurus has 9 stars.	Aldebaran (α Taurus), or Hyades
5	The head of the Powerful Dog has 5 stars.	λ and φ Orion?
6	A small star with a great light.	Alhena (γ Gemini), ξ?
7	The arm of Leo has 3 stars.	Castor (α Gemini), Pollux (β)
8	There are two nebulous stars with a cloud in the middle.	Praesepe (nebula near ε Cancer)
9	The eye of Leo has 3 stars.	ϰ Cancer, Alterf (λ Leo)
10	The forehead of Leo has 4 stars.	Around ζ, γ, η, α Leo; ε Gemini
11	The mane has 4 stars.	Zosma (δ), θ Leo
12	[In] the tail of Leo is the greatest star.	Denebola (β Leo)
13	The Dog has 4 stars.	Zavijava (β Virgo), Zania (η), Porrima (γ), δ, Vindemiatrix (ε)
14	Spica has 1 star.	Spica/Azimech (α Virgo)
15	The Covered has 3 stars.	Maybe ι and ϰ Virgo
16	The horns of Scorpio has 2 stars.	Zuben Elgenubi (α Libra) & Zuben Eschemali (β)
17	[In] the crown are three stars above the head of Scorpio, placed in a line.	Maybe Acrab/Graffias (β Scorpio), Dschubba (δ)
18	The heart of Scorpio is a great red star put between two [others].	Antares (α Scorpio)

---

[34] In the following table, Leopold has clearly drawn on John of Spain's *Treatise on Rains & the Changing of the Atmosphere*, which I partially translated for *AW1* (Section I.16). Leopold provides the verbal descriptions in the "Mansion column," while have numbered them and added the "Likely Stars" column based on my table in *AW1*.

19	The tail of Scorpio has 2 great stars, and 9 others in the same line.	Shaula (λ Scorpio), Lesath (υ); Acumen & Aculeus (in sting of Scorpio)
20	The Beam has 8: 4 in the belt[35] and 4 outside.	Near Ascella (ζ Sagittarius)
21	The Desert is a place without stars.	Maybe π Sagittarius
22	The Shepherd has 2 small stars, and in front one which is called "the Ram."	Algedi (α Capricorn), Dabih (β)
23	The Gulping has 3 stars.	Albali (ε Aquarius), μ, ν
24	The Star of Fortune [has] two, and one shines more.	Sadalsuud (β Aquarius), ξ; *46 Capricorn?*
25	The Butterfly has 2 stars behind, and 4 stars in front.	Sadachbia (γ Aquarius), π, ζ, η
26	The First Pourer has 2 stars.	Maybe Markab (α Pegasus) & Scheat (β)
27	The Second Pourer has 2 bright ones.	Maybe Algenib (γ Pegasus), Alpheratz (α Andromeda or β Pegasus)[36]
28	The Fish [has] 15.	β Andromeda[37]

Figure 7: Table of lunar mansions (Leopold, Dykes)[38]

[Planetary qualities of the fixed stars: Ptolemy][39]

51 The stars at the summit[40] of Aries are of the nature of Saturn and Mars, and mixed temperately in heat, exceeding in dryness; those which are in the mouth are of the nature of Mercury, those in the tail of Venus.

---

[35] That is, 4 on or very near the ecliptic.
[36] According to Kunitzsch and Smart (pp. 15, 47), there was some confusion between the names and stars for α-γ Pegasus and α Andromeda.
[37] According to Kunitzsch and Smart (p. 50), this mansion originally involved a faint curve of stars meant to be like a rope, connecting to the Square of Pegasus.
[38] The list of mansions is from Leopold, but the likely stars are from *AW1* and its sources.
[39] See *Tet.* I.9. Not every sentence in here comes from Ptolemy (or accurately reports the *Tetrabiblos*), and Leopold's texts omits some stars. Some words are clearly transliterations of Arabic.
[40] That is, its head.

52 In Taurus, [those on the line cutting it off are][41] of the nature of Venus and little of Saturn. **53** *Al-Thurayyā* or the Pleiades, of Mars and the Moon. **54** *Aldabarān* or the eye of Taurus, of the nature of Mars. **55** Others, the same [as] Saturn and a little bit Mercury; those in the horns of Taurus are of Mars.

56 Those in the feet of Gemini are of Mercury and a little bit of Venus. **57** The bright ones in the hips of Gemini, Saturn. **58** Two large stars are contained in their two heads: the first is of Mercury,[42] and is called *acurta*,[43] about which Haly says that when the releaser[44] reaches it, it sometimes blinds; the other one is of Mars,[45] and is called "the hand."

59 Those which are placed in the foot of Cancer are of the nature of Mercury and somewhat of Mars. **60** Those which are in its claws, of Saturn and Mercury. **61** A certain oblong one in the arrangement[46] of Cancer (those in its chest), nebulous; those in other places are said to make redness, and the one called Praesepe, of Mars and the Moon. **62** Two stars which are on each side of Praesepe (and they are the "Asses"), of Mars and the Sun,[47] whose complexion cuts and destroys.

63 Those in the head of Leo, of Saturn and a little bit Mars; likewise those which are in the neck. **64** The heart of Leo, which is called "royal," is of the nature of Jupiter and Mars. **65** Those which are on [its] back, and clear in the tail, of Venus and Saturn, and a little of Mercury. **66** And two which are in the hips, of Venus and Mercury.

67 Those which are at the summit[48] of Virgo and at the extremity of the southern wing, have the effect of Mercury and a little bit of Mars. **68** And the two bright stars in its northern wing, and which are on the back, are like Mercury and somewhat Mars.[49] **69** The bright star in its northern wing, Vindemiatrix,[50] of Saturn and Mercury. **70** The star Spica,[51] that is *altum alaizel*,[52] that is, "the departure,"[53] of Venus and a little bit of Mercury. **71** At

---

[41] Adding with Ptolemy.
[42] *Castor.*
[43] Transliteration unknown at this time.
[44] *Ylech.* See "releaser" in the Glossary. This is probably from al-Rijāl, *Skilled* IV.
[45] *Pollux.*
[46] *Constitutione.*
[47] Omitting *aequantur*, which seems to serve no purpose in the sentence.
[48] Again, the head.
[49] Ptolemy has: Venus.
[50] *Altaf*, which may be a transliteration for *al-Kitāf* (Allen, p. 471).
[51] *Adymet*, perhaps a transliteration related to *hazimet* (Allen, p. 467).
[52] *Altum* is unknown, but *alaizel* is clearly one of the many transliterations of al-A'zal, "the Defenseless" (Allen, p. 467).

the end of its feet where they drag the borders [of the robe], of Mars and Mercury.

72 Those which are in Libra at the end of the two claws (in other respects, Scorpio),[54] of Saturn[55] and Mercury; and those which are in the middle, of Saturn and a little bit of Mars.

73 In Scorpio, bright ones on the brow [are] of Mars, and somewhat of Saturn; that one of the three which [is] in the mouth, is middling white,[56] the brighter one on the back, with redness (called *Cor Scorpionis*)[57] is of Mars and a little of Jupiter. **74** Those which are in the tail of the knot,[58] of Venus and Saturn; and those in the sting, of Mars and Mercury. **75** Those in the cluster which is called "filthiness"[59] [are] cloudy, of Mars and the Moon.

76 The star in Sagittarius which is at the tip of the arrow, of Mars and Venus.[60] **77** Those which display the shape of the bow and are in the right hand, of Jupiter and Mars. **78** Those in the cluster, which is a feature[61] like clouds, of the Sun and Mars. **79** Those which are in the place where the stars encircle the bow,[62] of Jupiter and a little bit Mercury. **80** Those which are in the legs are of Jupiter and Saturn, those in its tail of Venus and Saturn.

81 The stars in the horns of Capricorn are of Venus and a little bit of Mars; those in the mouth, of Saturn and a little bit Venus and Mars;[63] those in the tail, of Jupiter and Saturn.

82 In the spout[64] of Aquarius and in the left hand, of Saturn and Mercury; those in the hips [are] more of Mercury, a little of Saturn. **83** The stars in the flow of water are of Saturn and a little bit of Jupiter.

84 In the southern summit[65] of Pisces, of Mercury and a little bit Saturn; those in the mouth, of Jupiter and Mercury; those above the tail and upon the southern line, of Saturn and a little bit Mercury. **85** In the body of the

---

[53] *Exitus*, which does not seem to translate any of the ancient names for Spica.
[54] The two pans of Libra comprise the two claws of Scorpio.
[55] Ptolemy has: Jupiter.
[56] Reading *alba* for *alibi*. Ptolemy reads much more simply, that of the three in the body, "the middle one...is reddish brown and fairly bright."
[57] *Antares*.
[58] Ptolemy: "upon the joints."
[59] *Inquinatio* (?).
[60] Ptolemy: Moon.
[61] *Linimentum*, read as *lineamentum*.
[62] Ptolemy: the shoulder-blades.
[63] Ptolemy associates Mars with the feet and belly.
[64] *Hauritorio*.
[65] Again, "head."

northern fish (namely, in the spine), of Jupiter and a little bit Venus. **86** In the northern thread, of Saturn and Jupiter. **87** The bright star in the ligature (that is, in the mouth of the fish, since it is tied there), of Mars and a little bit Mercury.

[Stars north of the zodiac]

88 Around the zodiac, the stars (namely the northern ones) in Ursa Minor are of Saturn and a little bit Venus.

89 In Ursa Major, Mars.

90 Those like the lesser cluster under the tail of Ursa Major,[66] of Venus and the Moon.

91 The bright stars making the square,[67] of Saturn and Mars.

92 Those which are in the assassins, that is, in the shape of an inflamed man,[68] of Jupiter and Saturn.

93 Those in the spine of the back,[69] of Mercury and Saturn, Jupiter and Mars; sometimes they allot [it] the nature of *azimoth*[70] (that is, "high"); the bright [star] *al-Rāmih*[71] (that is, the Lance-bearer), of Jupiter and Mars.

94 Those in Alphecca,[72] that is, in the [Northern] Crown,[73] of Venus and Mars.

95 Those in Hercules, [or] *al-Rakhīs*,[74] [or] "upon the knees," of Mercury.

96 Those in the Cymbal,[75] which is called the Falling Vulture, of Venus and Mercury.

97 Those which are like a chicken,[76] of Venus and Mercury.

---

[66] That is, *Coma Berenices*.
[67] The constellation Draco.
[68] The constellation Cepheus (see Allen p. 157).
[69] The constellation Bootes (see Allen pp. 92ff). Leopold or his source has messed this passage up terribly. For Ptolemy, most of these stars are of the nature of Mercury and Saturn, *except* for Arcturus (see below), which has the nature of Mars and Jupiter.
[70] A Latin transliteration of *al-Simāk*, the first half of the full Arabic title (*al-Simāk al-Rāmih*), referring to Arcturus. But Leopold has mistaken this for the astronomical notion of *azimuth*, which refers to how elevated something is from the local horizon. He was probably encouraged in this by the fact that Bootes does extend far northward.
[71] *Alrameth*, again Arcturus, and the last half of the full title mentioned in the previous footnote.
[72] *Alpheta*.
[73] The constellation Corona Borealis.
[74] *Alernix* (see Allen p. 242).
[75] *Asange*, a transliteration for *al-Sanj*. That is, the constellation Lyra.
[76] The constellation Cygnus.

98 Those which have the shape of one having a seat,[77] of Saturn and Venus.

99 Those of Perseus bearing the head of Algol, of Saturn and Venus.[78]
100 And the ones like a cluster which are contained in the handle of the little knife, of Mars and Mercury.

101 The bright stars in the figure one of one holding reins,[79] of Mars and Mercury.

102 The stars in the figure of a man holding a serpent,[80] Saturn and a little bit Venus. **103** The stars in [his] Serpent, of Saturn and Mars.

104 Those placed in the Arrow,[81] of Mars and a little bit Venus.

105 Those in the Flying Vulture,[82] of Mars and Jupiter.

106 Those in the Dolphin[83] work as Saturn and Mars.

107 The clear stars in the Horse,[84] of Mars and Jupiter.[85]

108 The stars of Andromeda, of Venus.

109 The stars of the Triangle,[86] of Mercury.

[Stars south of the zodiac]

110 Beyond the zodiac, the bright star in the mouth of the Southern Fish[87] which is in Capricorn, [is] of Venus and Mercury.

111 Those which are in the body of the Fish[88] are of Saturn.

112 Those which are in Orion (that is, of the most strong one), in each shoulder of his, of Mars and Mercury. **113** All the other bright ones there [are] of Jupiter and Saturn.

114 The last one in the brightest Stream,[89] of Jupiter; the others, Saturn.

115 Those which are in the Hare,[90] of Mercury and Saturn.

---

[77] The constellation Cassiopeia.
[78] Ptolemy: Jupiter.
[79] The constellation Auriga.
[80] The constellation Ophiuchus.
[81] The constellation Sagitta.
[82] The constellation Aquila.
[83] The constellation Delphinus.
[84] The constellation Pegasus.
[85] Ptolemy: Mercury.
[86] The constellation Triangulum.
[87] The constellation Piscis Australis.
[88] The constellation Cetus.
[89] The constellation Eridanus.
[90] The constellation Lepus.

116 Except for the one which is in the mouth, [the stars of Canis Major are][91] of Venus; and the bright one in the mouth, which is called *al-Shi'rā al-Yamaniyyah* ("from such a place"),[92] is of Jupiter.

117 The bright stars in the Preceding Dog[93] are of Mercury and a little bit Mars.

118 Those which have the form of a great-souled man (that is, Hydra), of Saturn and Venus.

119 Those which are in Crater, of Venus and somewhat of Mercury.

120 The stars in Corvus, of Saturn and Mars.

121 The stars in the Ship[94] are likened to Saturn and Jupiter.

122 In the Centaur,[95] the stars having the human form are of Venus and Mars;[96] the clear stars in the horse-like shape, of Jupiter and Venus.

123 The bright ones in the form of a Wolf,[97] of Saturn and somewhat of Mars.

124 Those which are in the Censer or Hearth[98] are of Venus, and have a little bit of the powers of Mercury.

125 The bright stars in the Southern Crown,[99] which is called the Southern Alphecca, imitate Saturn and Mars.

126 Of these, however, the greater stars are stronger than the smaller ones, and the ones which are above the heads of these [are stronger than] those which decline [away from them]; and those which are in the orb of the signs [are stronger than] the northern ones, and the northern ones [more so] than the southern ones.

127 And the aspects of all of them amongst each other, and with the planets, ought to be considered in the nativity. **128** And if they are eastern from the Sun up to the square, they are moist, from thence to the opposition hot, to the next square dry, in the last quarter up to the Sun (up to the same minute) they are cold.

---

[91] Adding based on Ptolemy; Leopold mixed this sentence up with the previous constellation.

[92] That is, the star Sirius. The Arabic here was transliterated as *azehere gemema*; the name refers to it being more southerly, in the direction of Yemen (apparently the source of Leopold's "from such a place").

[93] The constellation Canis Minor (sometimes called Procyon).

[94] The constellation Argo.

[95] The constellation Centaurus.

[96] Ptolemy has: Mercury.

[97] The constellation Lupus.

[98] The constellation Ara.

[99] The constellation Corona Australis.

[*Number of stars in each region: Ptolemy*][100]

129 There are 360[101] stars on this side of the zodiac, in the direction of the north: 3 in the first magnitude, 18 in the second, 81[102] in the third, 177 in the fourth, 58 in the fifth, 13 in the sixth, 9 of the cloudy ones (that is, of the hidden ones).[103]

130 In the zodiac are 346: 5 in the first magnitude, 9 in the second, 64[104] in the third, 133 in the fourth, 105[105] in the fifth, 27 in the sixth, 3 of the cloudy ones, and two small ones not entering into the counting.[106]

131 There are 316 stars beyond the zodiac in the direction of the south: 7[107] of which are in the first magnitude, 18 in the second, 63[108] in the third, 164[109] in the fourth, 54 in the fifth, 9 in the sixth, 1 cloudy one.

132 In Aries are 13 stars, around Aries[110] 5. **133** In Taurus 32, around [it] 11. **134** In Gemini 18, around [it] 7.[111] **135** In Cancer 9,[112] around [it] 4. **136** In Leo 27, around [it] 5.[113] **137** In Virgo 26, around [it] 6. **138** In the six northern signs, and around [them], there are 523.[114]

139 In Libra 8, around [it] 9. **140** In Scorpio 21, around [it] 3. **141** In Sagittarius 31, around [it] 0. **142** In Capricorn 28, around [it] 0. **143** In Aquarius 42, around [it] 3. **144** In Pisces 34, around [it] 4.

---

[100] Leopold or his source has read the following material directly off the summaries in Ptolemy's tables in the *Almagest* VII.5-VIII.1, but many of the numbers have been mistyped or read wrong by scribes.
[101] Reading for 340.
[102] Reading for 131.
[103] This should be 9 faint stars, and 1 nebulous one.
[104] Reading for 44.
[105] Reading for 120.
[106] That is, Coma Berenice.
[107] Reading for 8.
[108] Reading for 83.
[109] Reading for 64.
[110] That is, around it but not in the constellation itself.
[111] Reading for 4.
[112] Reading for 11.
[113] Reading for 8.
[114] The stars in the northern constellations are 360, and in the northern zodiacal signs 346, which makes 706; I am not sure where Leopold gets 523.

[Chapter I.4: The faces][115]

1 In the first face of Aries ascends the form of a black man wrapped in a white garment.[116] **2** In the second face, the form of a woman on whom [are] red cloths. **3** In the third face, the form of a man of pale color, with red hair on the head.

4 In the first face of Taurus ascends a male executioner,[117] and a nude man.[118] **5** In the second face, a nude man in whose hand [is] a key. **6** In the third face, a man in whose hand [is] a serpent and an arrow.

7 In the first face of Gemini ascends a man in whose hand [is] a switch, and serving another.[119] **8** In the second face, a man in whose hand [is] a flute,[120] and another one bent over. **9** In the third face, a man seeking weapons.

10 In the first face of Cancer ascends the form of a virgin girl. **11** In the second face, a man on whom are decorative cloths.[121] **12** In the third face, a girl on whose head [is] a crown.

13 In the first face of Leo ascends the form of a lion and a man on whom are raised clothes.[122] **14** In the second face, an image with elevated hands and a man on whose head [is] a crown. **15** In the third face, a young man in whose hand [is] a whip and an intense[123] man of sorrow and a foul face.

16 In the first face of Virgo ascends the face of a good girl. **17** In the second face, a black man on [whom are] vestments of leather, and a man having a mane. **18** In the third face, a white, deaf woman.

19 In the first face of Libra ascends the form of an angry man in whose hand is a flute. **20** In the second face, two angry and serving men. **21** In the third, an intense man in whose hand is a bow, and a nude man.

---

[115] The faces listed below are versions of the faces described by Abū Ma'shar in *Gr. Intr.* VI.1: many are the "Indian" faces, but Leopold has also mixed these up with those which Abū Ma'shar attributes collectively to the Persians, Babylonians, and Egyptians. In some cases, I cannot tell where he is getting the descriptions and we could assume some creative reimagining is going on. For a recent book on the faces from many different traditions, see Coppock 2014.

[116] Reading *veste* for *vase*.

[117] *Vir spiculator*.

[118] I am not sure if these are two different figures or the same one.

[119] I do not know where Leopold is getting the bit about serving another.

[120] Or specifically, a pan flute or shepherd's flute (*fistula*).

[121] *Decoratio panni*.

[122] *Elevati*. I am not sure what this means or where Leopold is getting it.

[123] *Vehemens*, which also has connotations of violence and power.

22 In the first face of Scorpio ascends a woman of good face and body. **23** In the second face, a nude man and nude woman. **24** In the third face, a man bent over his own knees.

25 In the first face of Sagittarius ascends the form of a dirty man. **26** In the second face, a woman on whom are rags. **27** In the third face, a man like the color gold.

28 In the first face of Capricorn ascends the form of a woman, and a black man. **29** In the second face, two women. **30** In the third face, a woman wise in body[124] and in deed.

31 In the first face of Aquarius ascends the form of a man. **32** In the second face that of another man with a long beard. **33** In the third face, an angry black man.

34 In the first face of Pisces ascends a man on whom are good clothes. **35** In the second face, a woman with a good face. **36** In the third, a nude man.

[Chapter I.5: Stars co-rising with the zodiacal constellations][125]

1 Nothing on this side[126] of the zodiac arises with Cancer, but beyond [it] all of Orion [and] the tongue of Canis Minor (a bright star), [and] practically all of Eridanus.

2 With Leo, nothing on this side; but beyond [it] the first part of Canis Minor, the head of Hydra, Lepus, [and] the other[127] [part of] Procyon.

3 Nothing on this side [arises] with Virgo, [but] beyond it the whole of Canis Minor, Hydra up to Crater, the stern of Argo.

4 With Libra, on this side one-half of the man,[128] the right foot of Bootes, beyond [that] the rest of Hydra except for the end of the tail,[129] the horse part of the Centaur.

---

[124] *Corpore.* Perhaps this could be read *colore* ("color"), which is a word used in the Latin description.
[125] The source of this section is unknown at this time.
[126] "On this side" means "northern constellations," while "beyond" means "southern constellations."
[127] Tentatively reading *alter.*
[128] This is probably Hercules.
[129] Reading *caudae* for *caudam*, which would mean "last tail."

40   A COMPILATION ON THE SCIENCE OF THE STARS

5 With Scorpio, on this side the whole *nixus*,[130] the Crown of Ariadne,[131] the head of Ophiuchus,[132] beyond the tail of Hydra, the whole Centaur except for the front feet of the Centaur.

6 With Sagittarius, on this side the whole of Ophiuchus,[133] Lyra, the head and shoulders of Cepheus, beyond [that] the first feet of the Centaur.

7 With Capricorn, on this side Cygnus, Aquila, Sagitta; beyond [that], the Altar.

8 With Aquarius, on this side Pegasus, beyond [it] nothing.

9 With Pisces, on this side the right part of Andromeda; beyond [it], Piscis Australis.[134]

10 With Aries, on this side the left part of Andromeda, Delphinus, Perseus up to *alium*;[135] beyond [it], nothing.

11 With Taurus, nothing on this side; beyond [it], the first part of Cetus and the left foot of Orion.

12 With Gemini, nothing on this side; beyond [it], the whole of Cetus [and] the beginning of Eridanus.

[Chapter I.6: Physical dimensions of the universe][136]

[Volumes of the planets and stars?][137]

1 There are fourteen magnitudes of the bodies of the world.[138] **2** The Sun has 166 and ¼ of 1/8 [times] the quantity of the earth, the greater stars [of first magnitude] 115, Jupiter 95, Saturn 91, the fixed stars of second magnitude 90, those of the third 70, those of the fourth 50, those of the fifth 36,

---

[130] This is probably Hercules, drawing on the Arabic name (see Ch. I.3, **95** above).
[131] The constellation Corona Borealis.
[132] *Osuilti*.
[133] *Osuiltus*.
[134] *Piscis Austrinus*.
[135] Perhaps Auriga?
[136] In this chapter, Leopold uses what are clearly Ptolemaic values for the dimensions of the universe, largely based on Ptolemy's *Planetary Hypotheses* (Goldstein 1967).
[137] While sentences **1-4** *seem* to describe the relative volumes of the planets and stars, and indeed Leopold lists them in this order (Goldstein p. 9), the values do not all make sense to me. For example, Ptolemy does make the volume of Mars 1.5 times that of earth; but Leopold seems to miss the numerator in some cases (reading 39 for the Moon when it should be 1/39 or 1/40), and in other cases gives numbers I simply cannot explain.
[138] Only 12 are listed here, but perhaps Leopold means to include the earth as an unstated value of 1.

those of the sixth 18, Mars 1 ½ and half of an eighth of one time, Venus with respect to the earth a thirty-seventh portion, the Moon 39 and a little more,[139] Mercury 1/7 of 22, or of the 22,000 parts of the earth.[140]

[Distance from earth to other spheres, in earth radii][141]

3 There are eight distances of the heavenly bodies from the earth.[142] **4** The diameter of the earth has 6,500 *miliaria*, the circumference of the earth 20,420 *miliaria*, 1,714 cubits, and there remain two undivided cubits.[143]

5 From the earth to the neighboring or closer place of the Moon, are 33 halves of the diameter of the earth. **6** To [the closest distance of] Mercury, 64; to [the closest distance of] Venus, 166; to the [closest distance of the] Sun 1,079[144] (elsewhere, 1,979); to [the closest distance of] Mars, 1,260; to [the closest distance of] Jupiter, 8,820; to [the closest distance of] Saturn 10,187 (otherwise 14,187);[145] to the fixed stars 17,360.[146] **7** Abū Ma'shar posits 128,094 *miliaria* from the earth to the nearer place of the Moon (he says a *miliarium* has 3,000 cubits).

---

[139] This should read 1/39, as he seems to intend with Venus.

[140] The fraction 7/22 (or 3.14286) was a common whole-number ratio for π (3.14159).

[141] See Goldstein, p. 7.

[142] That is, to each of the seven planets and to the fixed stars, for a total of 8.

[143] This sentence raises two points of interest. (1) I am not sure where the two undivided cubits come from, but if we ignore them, Leopold has a value of π that is accurately rounded to the 4th decimal place. Below (**7**), Leopold says there are 3,000 cubits to a *miliarium*, which makes his circumference 20,420.57133 *miliaria*. Since $c = d\pi$, dividing the circumference by his diameter 6,500 yields 3.1416 for π (a more accurate value is 3.14159). (2) If we assume that a cubit is about 18 inches (from elbow to fingertip) or 1.5 feet, then a *miliarium* is 4,500 feet and Leopold's diameter of the earth (6,500 *miliaria*) is 5,539.7 modern miles. The modern value for the diameter of the earth is 7,918 miles, so Leopold's earth is only 70% the size of the true earth.

[144] Ptolemy also gives another value for the Sun, 1,160: "there is a discrepancy between the two distances which we cannot account for" (Goldstein, p. 7).

[145] Leopold's text makes a confusing mistake here, saying "otherwise *4*," in connection with Jupiter. But Jupiter's value is faithful to Ptolemy. It is Leopold's value for Saturn which is wrong (10,187), and the comment about the *4* can be explained by substituting it for the *0* in Leopold's value. So, I have moved Leopold's reference here, and made it part of Ptolemy's own value (14,187).

[146] Since Saturn's farthest distance according to Ptolemy is 19,865 radii, the stars cannot be so close; I do not know the origin of this value for the stars.

8 The arc of the day is the arc of the circle equidistant to the equator, through which the Sun is moved on that day.[147] **9** The arc of the night is what remains of that circle [that is] not crossed over in that day.

10 An equal hour is the time in which 15° of the equator are elevated.[148] **11** A temporal hour[149] is that in which there is more or less [than that], and it is 1/12 of the day.

12 The inhabitable [portion of the earth] between the east and west does not have 4 hours.[150]

13 The earth does not have a sensible quantity as compared to the heavens.[151]

14 All horizons divide the equator in half; however, they divide the remaining ones equidistant from the equator, differently.[152]

15 The natural day is variable under the equator on account of the obliquity[153] of the zodiac, and on account of the obliquity of the horizon.[154]

16 Those living under the equator have two summers and two winters, and four shadows.[155] **17** The inseparable poles of the horizon are from the horizon under the equator.[156]

---

[147] That is, since the heavens always turn parallel to the equator, the Sun's position over the course of a day will also be parallel to the equator (if we ignore his tiny daily movement in the zodiac).

[148] The heavens turn along the equator by 360° in one day; therefore in each hour the equator will turn 15° (360°/24 = 15°).

[149] Otherwise known as planetary or seasonal hours: see Ch. IV.2, **87**.

[150] I do not understand this sentence.

[151] That is, for geometric purposes the earth is a point: this was Ptolemy's working assumption in the *Almagest*.

[152] That is, the local horizon will divide the celestial equator so that an equal amount of it is above and below; but other circles of latitude will be cut at different points, so that more or less of them is above the earth.

[153] Lit., "slantedness" (*obliquitatem*).

[154] This simply means that the length of the day is sensitive to one's geographical latitude.

[155] I do not understand this sentence.

[156] This seems to refer to the north-south and east-west lines that can be drawn on any local horizon. See Ch. I.2, **1-3**.

[Chapter I.7: The seven climes][157]

1 The latitude[158] of the first clime has 440 *miliaria*, 13 hours [and] 15 minutes of an hour; the altitude of the pole is 20°.[159]
2 The latitude of the second clime has 400 *miliaria*, 13 hours [and] 45 minutes of an hour; the altitude of the pole is 27°.
3 The latitude of the third clime has 350 *miliaria*, 14 hours [and] 15 minutes of an hour; the altitude of the pole is 30°.
4 The latitude of the fourth clime has 300 *miliaria*, 14 hours [and] 45 minutes of an hour; the altitude of the pole is 39°.
5 The latitude of the fifth clime has 250 *miliaria*, 15 hours [and] 15 minutes of an hour; the altitude of the pole is 41° 43'.
6 The latitude of the sixth clime has 200 *miliaria*, 15 hours [and] 45 minutes of an hour; the altitude of the pole is 45°.
7 The latitude of the seventh clime has 185 *miliaria*, 16 hours [and] 15 minutes of an hour; the altitude of the pole is 48°.
8 And always, the remainder of the altitude up to 90° is the southern altitude of the Sun at the equinox.
9 And the latitude of a clime is its distance from the equator. **10** The longitude of climes is the distance between their meridians, *etc.*

[Chapter I.8: Miscellaneous astronomical comments][160]

1 The difference in the viewing of the stars is threefold: first,[161] because they are greater or smaller, the greater ones appear more quickly, the smaller ones more slowly.

---

[157] I omit a complicated diagram from Leopold here. Climes are lines of geographical latitude, or bands of latitudes, which share similar ascensional times and days of longest daylight. For example, in **1**, Leopold has the first clime being at 20° N latitude (the "altitude of the pole"), with the hours of daylight at the summer solstice (the longest day of the year) being 13h 15m, and it is of a certain thickness (440 *miliaria*, an old standard of measurement). For more on climes, see my *AW1*.
[158] Lit., "width" (*latitudo*).
[159] The latitude of the pole is the same as the geographical latitude of the clime.
[160] I find some of this section (especially **2-6**) impenetrable.
[161] Lit. "either" (*aut*), beginning a list of ways (likewise, **2** lists the second option, with an "or").

2 Second, since they otherwise divide the heaven in half,[162] for those which are in the northern half of the orb of the signs from Capricorn to Cancer,[163] they divide the heavens in half first,[164] and the southern ones afterwards. **3** For the northern pole of the orb of the signs inclines towards the west, and the southern one towards the east. **4** But from Cancer to Capricorn, those which are southern from the orb of the signs, they divide the heavens in half first,[165] and the northern ones afterwards. **5** For the northern pole of the orb of the signs inclines towards the east, the southern one towards the west. **6** And the greater diversity in this is at the beginning of Aries and Libra, and [there is] none at the beginning of Cancer and Capricorn, because there the pole of the world and the pole of the orb of the signs are in that same surface, [and] proportionately so in the places in the middle.

7 Third,[166] because they otherwise arise above the horizon. **8** For in all parts of the world in which the northern pole of the world does not set, the northern stars arise first, and set afterwards: whence, they make a greater arc above the earth. **9** Whence, where that same pole sets, the northern ones arise more slowly and set more quickly: and therefore they make smaller arcs under the earth.

10 The diversity of the appearance of the Moon in longitude is null at the Midheaven, and is greatest in the east above the horizon.[167]

11 The cosmic arising above the horizon is threefold: "heliacal," at [a star's] exit from the rays of the Sun; "cronical," when first at night the stars begin to appear in the direction of the east.[168]

12 The amplitude of the horizon is the portion of the horizon which is between the equator and the arising of a thing. **13** The degree of advancement[169] is that degree which an arc encounters [when] going out from the pole of the world through the place of a star. **14** The degree of longitude is that which an arc encounters [when] going out from the pole of the signs through the place of a star.

---

[162] *Mediant.*
[163] Capricorn through Pisces are not signs of northern declination, but Leopold might mean "the signs which go *from* the south *northwards*," which would include Capricorn through Cancer.
[164] Omitting *quam/quae sui gradus.*
[165] Again, omitting *quam/quae sui gradus.*
[166] Again, "or."
[167] This seems to refer to refraction.
[168] Note that there are only two types listed here.
[169] *Profectionis.*

15 Concerning comets (or "haired" or "tailed" stars), I defer [discussion of them] until the treatise on revolutions, because then a prognostication is had as to whether in that year they ought to come about[170]—I will put the occurrence of them and [their] proper significations there.

---

[170] Leopold is referring to Ch. V.6, but he does not discuss timing there. For that, see *AW1* Section III.1.

Treatise II: On the Spheres of the Planets, & their Circles & Motions

[Chapter II.1: Introduction]

1 The orbs of the planets are seven, as was said. **2** The orbs of the planets and the planets themselves are of the fifth essence, and therefore they are not corrupted, nor are they converted into one another.[1] **3** The first cause has given to the planets their natural motions, which are always constant, but diversity comes to be on account of their motion in the epicycles, and that of the epicycles in the eccentrics, and that of each [eccentric] in the orb of the signs. **4** And it has given them their own proper significations, which they wield in subject materials according to [the latter's] proper quality and possibility.[2]

5 All spheres from the eighth downwards have the motion of advancement and recession, which is said to be the motion of the eighth sphere.[3]

6 All spheres are eccentric from the world, and indeed are thick so that they contain the eccentricity, and the semi-diameter of the epicycle, and the semi-diameter of the planet.[4]

7 All circles, both big and small, are divided into 360 parts and into 12 signs.[5]

---

[1] That is, unlike a corruptible material thing on earth (whose matter undergoes shifts and elemental transformations), the planets remain what they are.
[2] That is, a planet like Jupiter cannot affect something that lacks the ability to be *affected by* him.
[3] This is the sphere of the fixed stars, which (according to the theory of trepidation) moved back and forth over long periods of time. See my *Comment* in Ch. I.1, and Leopold in Ch. I.1, **1** and **19-20**.
[4] The figure below illustrates the medieval "three –orb" system for many of the planets. In this model, we can define three orbs or "shells," which mark out the limits of the spatial motion of a planet. The center of the whole model is the earth. The circles or orbs are: (1) the eccentric or deferent circle of the planet itself, depicted here as a white band centered on the "Mars center." We can see that the tiny epicycle of Mars, with him on it, fits exactly into the white band of (1). The second orb is (2) the white circle formed with the earth as center and extending to the nearest point of (1) ("limit of Earth's sphere"): this happens to correspond to Mars's perigee. The third circle is (3) the big, black circle which encloses everything else (the "limit of Mars's sphere"), centered on the earth. We must imagine that each of the planets has its own version of this model, nested one inside the other: so, the model for the Sun should fit precisely into (2). In this way, none of the planets will crash into the other by treading into another's sphere.

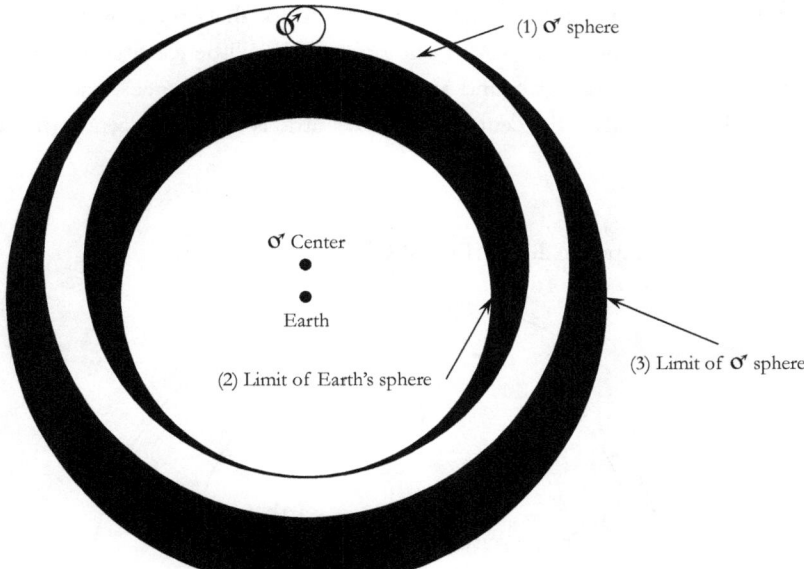

Figure 8: Three-orb system of Mars (Dykes, after Leopold)

[Chapter II.2: Solar theory]

1 The Sun has two orbs.[6] **2** The (1) great orb [is] the one which leads him away from the east and down towards the west: which, if he did not have it, the Sun would remain above the earth for one-half the year, and under the earth for the other half.[7] **3** He also has (2) an eccentric, which is so discovered because he stays more in one-half of his orb than in the other, and more in one quarter than in another, and more in one sign than in the other. **4** From this it was known that his circle or sphere in which he stays, inclines

---

[5] This convention is a convenience that allows one to picture where in any circle a planet happens to be, relative to its apogee.

[6] The Sun has no epicycle in Ptolemaic theory. He *could* have been given one, with exactly the same results (as Ptolemy and Apollonius of Perga knew, see Evans p. 212); but it is not strictly necessary to do so.

[7] This is diurnal rotation. Leopold means that if the Sun did not have 24-hour diurnal motion but only motion through the signs, it would take him one-half of the year to pass across the upper hemisphere in any location, and he would spend the other half under the earth—essentially making perpetual day for six months, and perpetual night for the other six months.

more to one side than another, and so the center of that sphere will be outside the center of the earth. **5** And one point of it will be elevated the most above the center of the earth, and we call this point the "apogee": and it is at 17° 50' Gemini.[8] **6** And the center of this eccentric is above the center of the world by 1° 59' 10".[9]

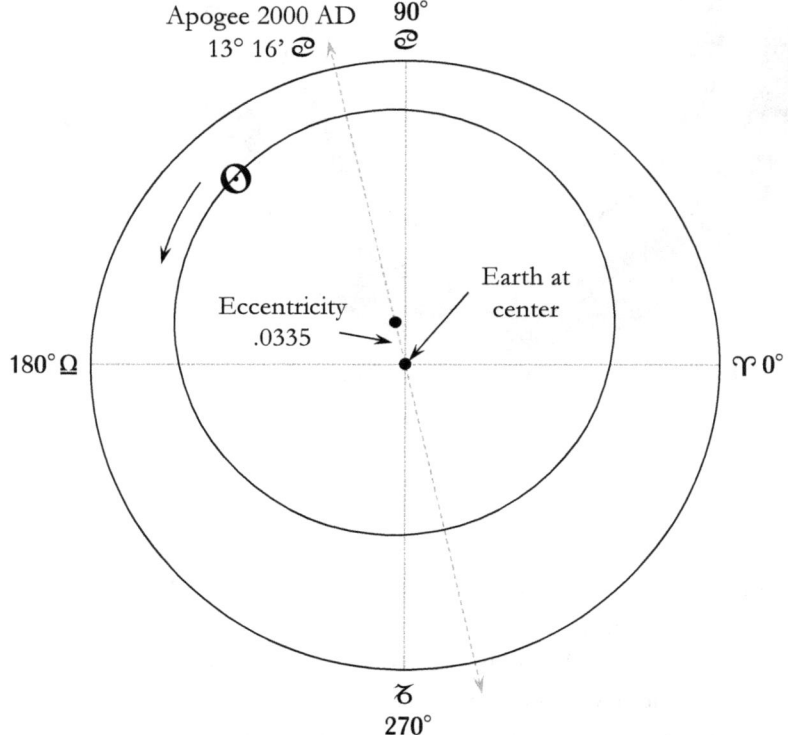

Figure 9: Solar apogee and eccentricity, 2000 AD (Dykes)

7 Since therefore it was necessary for the astronomer (who would scrutinize the effects of things which are put high up)[10] to know the true motions

---

[8] A good value for the solar apogee in 2000 AD, is 13° 16' Cancer (see diagram and my *Comment* below)

[9] This is known as the "maximum equation" (see diagram and my *Comment* below); its value in 2000 AD was 1° 55' 09". It is the arcsin of the eccentricity, which was .033490546 in 2000 AD. Leopold's statement means that his eccentricity was .034657236.

[10] Reading *sublime* or perhaps *sublimium* for *sublimia*.

and situation of the heavenly bodies with respect to the earth, it was therefore necessary for him to understand them insofar as they are arranged toward the center of the earth.[11]

8 The Sun for instance, completes equal parts in equal times in [his] eccentric, so that in a natural day [he completes] approximately 59' 08" 15'": and this is the "mean" or even motion of the Sun.[12] **9** However, the Sun's motion about the center of the earth is diverse and not uniform: and this is the "true" motion of the Sun which the astronomer seeks, so that from the true motion he may understand true effects on the earth. **10** This true motion is designated by a line going out from the center of the earth, through the center of the Sun, to the firmament: and this arc of the firmament which is between the beginning of Aries and the end of this line, is the true motion of the Sun—whence, to find the true motion of the Sun is to find this arc (and vice-versa). **11** But the mean motion of the Sun is the one which he has about the center of the eccentric, and is designated by a line going out from the center of the eccentric, through the center of the Sun towards the firmament, and the arc from the eccentric is the mean motion of the Sun—whence, to find the mean motion of the Sun is to find this arc (and vice-versa), and it is the distance from the beginning of Aries *within* the eccentric.[13]

12 The portion of the arc which falls between the boundaries of the two stated lines is the "equation" of the Sun: which is nothing when the Sun is in the apogee of the eccentric or in the opposite of the apogee (because these two lines have the same surface there). **13** But in the other places there is a difference in the contact of these two lines, and so the equation arises: by it being added or subtracted from the mean motion, the "true" [motion] emerges; and this begins from the apogee of the eccentric and is taken [in the tables of equations] with the "argument."

---

[11] That is, not within their own circles, but as observed *by us*—this is the difference between "mean" motion and "true" motion (see my *Comment* below).

[12] An accurate modern value would be: 59' 08" 19.8'". From Leopold's statement we can gather that his year was 365.2504756 days long (perhaps rounded to 365.25): for, 360°/59' 08" 15'" = 365.2504756.

[13] Leopold does not have this quite right, but I will explain it in my *Comment* below.

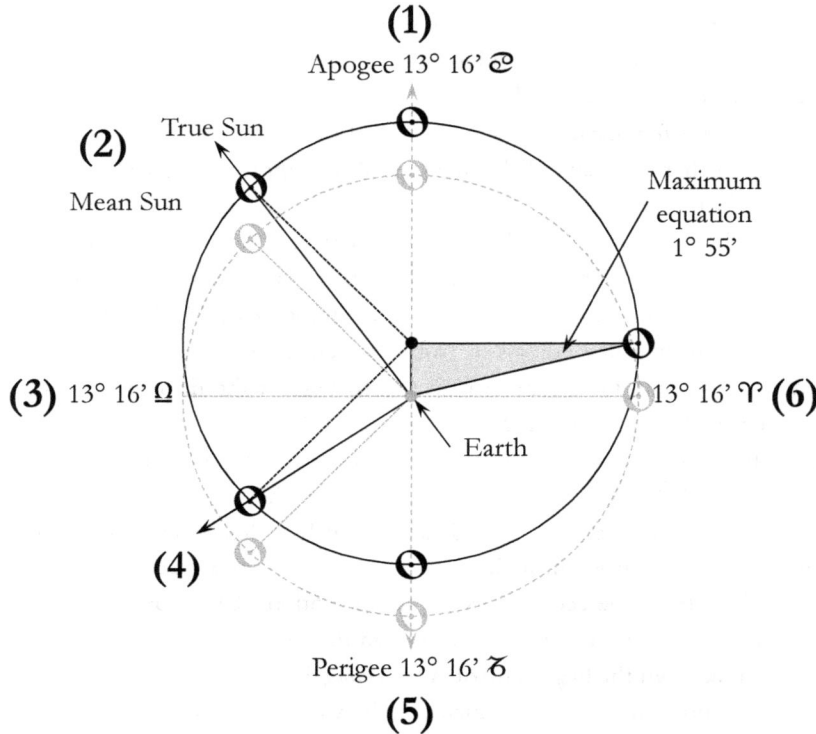

Figure 10: Mean and true Suns, solar equation of center (Dykes)

14 Now, the argument is the distance of the center of the Sun from the apogee of the eccentric.[14] **15** But where the mean motion comes to be greater or lesser than the true motion, is known thusly. **16** Let a line be drawn out from the center of the earth, parallel to the line which is drawn out from the center of the eccentric, through the center of the Sun, to the firmament. **17** You will see that from the apogee up to the opposite of the apogee, this line precedes the other, and thus you know that the mean motion is greater than the true. **18** Whence, the *Canon* well instructs that if the argument was less than 6 signs, subtract the equation from the mean motion.[15] **19** And since

---

[14] Actually this is called the "anomaly," the angular distance of the mean Sun from his apogee; in the diagram above at (2), I have made him be 45° away from his apogee, so he has an anomaly of 45°. An anomaly becomes an *argument* when it is looked up in a table: so, we would go down the column of "arguments" in Ptolemaic solar tables until we found the value of the anomaly: 45°.

[15] In other words, between 0° and 180° away from the apogee, the mean Sun is always ahead of the true Sun and so appears later in the zodiac; therefore we must subtract our

this line parallel to the opposite of the apogee up to the end of 12 signs follows the aforesaid, other[16] line, the true [motion] is greater than the mean, whence there it justly teaches that the equation should be added, so that the true motion may be had—which in the end, is what was sought. **20** And this equation increases from the apogee up to 3 signs, and decreases up to 6, whence just as at the highest point and lowest point there is no [equation], so in the middle it is the greatest—and proportionately by advancing toward the apogee or receding from the apogee.[17] **21** And because the equation of the Sun begins from the apogee, for that reason the tables of the Sun have, in equal distance, equal (or rather those very same) equations, as you see. **22** For the same equation is ascribed to 1° from the apogee of the eccentric, and to 11 signs and 29°—and thus with the others.[18] **23** The equations are found in increments of 5°:[19] and the lesser is subtracted from the greater, and the remainder is divided by 5, and what comes out is added to the equation of the first degree, and there is had the equation of the following, and thus one proceeds through the whole.[20]

24 The declination of the Sun[21] is his receding from the equator: he has the greatest [declination] at 23° 33' 30".

∞ ∞ ∞

---

correction (the "equation") in order to bring the position back to the correct, true Sun. But between 180° and 360°, the mean Sun will appear behind the true Sun or earlier in the zodiac, so the correction must be added.

[16] Reading the accusative *aliam* for *alia*.

[17] This simply means that because a circle is curved, the distortion created by the difference between the mean and true Suns will be greater in some portions of the circle than others: from 0° to 90° from the apogee, the difference or equation will become rather great, until it reaches "maximum equation," the maximum distortion; then it becomes smaller from 90° to 180°. Likewise, from 180° to 270° it starts to increase until it again reaches maximum equation, then decreases from 270° to 360°.

[18] Again, this simply means that because circles are symmetrical, there is a symmetry between the corrections on either side of the apogee. So if the mean Sun is 5° greater than the apogee, the amount of correction we *subtract* will be the same amount we would *add* if he were at 5° *less than* the apogee.

[19] Lit., "from five degrees to five."

[20] Leopold is describing interpolation: his tables of the solar equation would have been listed in 5° increments, so obviously one would interpolate between values in the table.

[21] Normally this is known as the "obliquity of the ecliptic." But Leopold is right to call this the declination of the Sun, since at 0° Cancer and 0° Capricorn the Sun is at his greatest declination, which is precisely the greatest obliquity of the ecliptic. The values of the obliquity on January 1, 2000, was 23° 26' 16".

Comment by Dykes. Ptolemy's solar theory is the easiest of his planetary theories, and is a good way to be introduced to Ptolemy's style of thinking as well as some vocabulary. Leopold first introduces two circles: the diurnal circle, or the fact that the heavens rotate once daily around the earth (**2**): this creates night and day. The Sun himself moves around his own circle once a year, which creates the seasons as he enters successive signs (**3**). Leopold points out that if there were no diurnal circle, than any place on earth would experience constant daylight for about half the year, because it would take that long for the Sun to move out of sight (**2**).

But the key to the solar theory is the fact that the seasons are of unequal length (**3**), meaning that the Sun moves more slowly in the zodiac in some seasons, and faster in others—in fact, knowledge of the lengths of the seasons provides all the data we need to create the solar theory, with the help of a little basic geometry.

Since things appear to move more slowly when they are farther away, we may tentatively conclude that the Sun's circle is not centered on the earth: it is off-center, or "eccentric"; and since summer is the longest season in the northern hemisphere (or winter in the southern), his eccentric circle must be off-center in the direction of the summer signs (Cancer through Virgo). That way, he will appear to move more slowly in the summer, and so by definition summer is longer. His farthest point from the earth is called the "apogee" (**5**), and his closest point is opposite it, the "perigee." It is clear that the apogee must fall on a line passing through the center of the earth and the center of the Sun's circle, since it defines the point at which he moves most slowly from our earthly perspective. Figure 9 shows this "apsidal" line pointing from us through the center of his circle, towards a point in the zodiac, the apogee.

But where exactly is the apogee? (In fact, it moves slightly forward over time.) With a little geometry, it is easy to prove that in 2000 AD, it was at 13° 16' Cancer (see Figure 9). Leopold says his apogee (ca. 1300 AD) was at 17° 50' Gemini (**5**), which would make spring his longest season (as it was in antiquity). But his apogee was actually closer to 0° Cancer, suggesting he was using older tables and did not know how fast the apogee advanced.

The seasonal lengths also tell us exactly how off-center from the earth the Sun's circle must be, which is called his "eccentricity" ("off-centeredness"). The longer the season and the slower his apparent motion, the farther away from earth the center must be. Now, the eccentricity is always expressed as a fraction of the radius of his circle (which is treated as being 1 unit in length). In 2000 AD it could be measured as being about .0335, so however many miles or kilometers wide the radius of his circle actually is, it is off-center from the earth by .0335 of that.

Part of Ptolemy's genius was in creating a simple, two-step process for determining the position of a planet which is off-center. First, he created a table of "mean" motion, which assumes a constant and unvarying, or "mean," motion about some point, and then—based on the eccentricity and where in the circle the mean position is—he created a table that showed how to add or subtract a little correction to get the "true" position, or the position as seen by us on earth. This correction is called an "equation" (see below). Modern ephemerides do all of this for us, and list only the true motions. But how does this really work? Leopold gives a somewhat long explanation of this in **6** and **8ff**. Let us look at Figure 10 to understand this.

In the figure, I have turned the Sun's circle so that the apogee is at the top. I have also put the Sun in six different positions around the zodiac. The black Sun is the actual body of the Sun, and the line from the center of the earth to him gives his "true" position (i.e., as seen by us). But there is also a gray Sun, called the "mean Sun." The mean Sun is a fictitious position that would show his true position *if* the Sun's circle was centered on the earth. The idea is this. Let us suppose that the Sun is at his apogee, at (1): both the mean Sun and true Sun are at 13° 16' Cancer. Now let each Sun move at a constant rate around its respective circle for exactly one year, until they return there. We can see that between his apogee and perigee (2) – (5), the mean Sun is always a little bit ahead of where we see the true Sun (**17**). This angular difference between the mean and true Suns is called the "equation of the center" (**14**): it starts from 0° at the apogee, gets larger around the middle, and then gets smaller until it is 0° again at the perigee. After that, the mean Sun always follows a little bit behind the true Sun, with the equation getting larger around the middle, then smaller again until it returns to the apogee (**19**).

What this means is the following. *If* the Sun's circle were centered on the earth, then he would always appear to move at a constant rate and be where the mean Sun is; but it is not, so his true position is sometimes behind, sometimes equal to, and sometimes ahead of, this mean position. The largest value for the equation is the "maximum equation" (**6**), which is always the arcsin of the eccentricity: Leopold says it is 1° 59' 10" (**6**), while a better modern value for 2000 AD is 1° 55' 09". In order to determine where the true Sun is on any day, we simply need to know where the mean Sun is on that day, and *add or subtract a correction*, based on *how large the equation is at that position*.[22] Ptolemy's table of solar equations tells us the exact amount of the correction, once we enter the mean position as an "argument" into the table (**13**). If the mean Sun is at the apogee or perigee, then no correction is needed (**20**). But if it is between the apogee and perigee, we need to subtract the correction to find the true Sun (**18**); if it is between the perigee and apogee, we need to add it (**19**). Since we are dealing with perfect circles, the correction we need to add for some distance on one side of the circle, will be the same correction we need to subtract at the same distance on the other (**21-22**). Since the maximum equation is around the middle, the correction needed will be greatest there (**20**), and by definition the correction will never be more than the maximum equation itself. Ptolemy's table of equations gives corrections in increments of 6° or less, so in most cases we will have to interpolate a bit (**23**).

This vocabulary of apogees, eccentricity, equations, and mean positions are also used for the other planets, but with some extra complications due to retrograde motion and certain factors pertaining to the Moon. In later chapters I will give a thumbnail sketch of how these work.

---

[22] To put it differently, the equation *is* the correction itself, because it defines how far away the true Sun is from the mean Sun. But we do not know the size of the equation until we know the position of the mean Sun and then look it up in the table of equations. The equation can also be calculated directly using a formula (which would have been used to create the table in the first place).

[Chapter II.3: Lunar theory]

1 The Moon has five circles. **2** The first is the great orb, which leads her every day from the east to the west and draws [her] down—which if it did not exist, the Moon would remain above the earth for one-half of a [lunar] month, and under the earth for one-half.

3 The second is the one which is said to be like the orb of the signs, in relation to which the Moon is said to enter or exit the signs, and it is concentric with the earth and equal to the eccentric of the Moon in magnitude.[23]

4 The third is the eccentric, in which the Moon is at one time more remote from the earth and at another closer [to it]: and the center of this is elevated above the center of the earth by about 11°.

5 The fourth is the epicycle, whose center is moved in the said eccentric, and it has 6 1/3 parts of the 60 parts which the middle of the eccentric has.[24]

6 The fifth, the circle of latitude, in which the Moon goes out from the zodiac, sometimes towards the north (and the point of her cutting it is called the "Head of the Dragon"), sometimes towards the south (and it is called the "Tail of the Dragon"); and it is gotten through the argument of the latitude of the Moon.[25]

7 The Moon also has a mean and true motion.[26] **8** Her mean motion is the one which, with respect to the second orb, the center of the epicycle makes, in the heaven of the Moon against the firmament, 13° 10' 53" in individual days, and it is designated by the boundary of the line which goes out from the center of the earth, through the center of the epicycle, toward the zodiac of the Moon (or the one like the zodiac). **9** Whence, just as the Sun is moved constantly about the center of his own eccentric, so the center of the Moon's epicycle [is moved] about the center of the world.

---

[23] That is, for the purposes of his model Ptolemy's Moon has its own zodiac, mirroring the greater zodiac.
[24] In determining the proportions of his model, Ptolemy assigned 60 fictional units (here, "parts") to certain lines, expressing the size of the others in terms of that. It was only later, in his *Hypotheses of the Planets*, that he tried to determine the actual spatial dimensions.
[25] The entire lunar model lies on a plane which is inclined away from the ecliptic, and intersects it at the Nodes. I have not depicted the latitude of the model here.
[26] Or rather, her mean *longitude*.

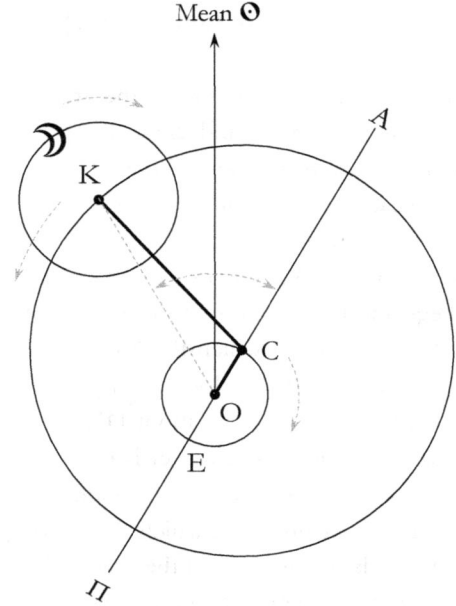
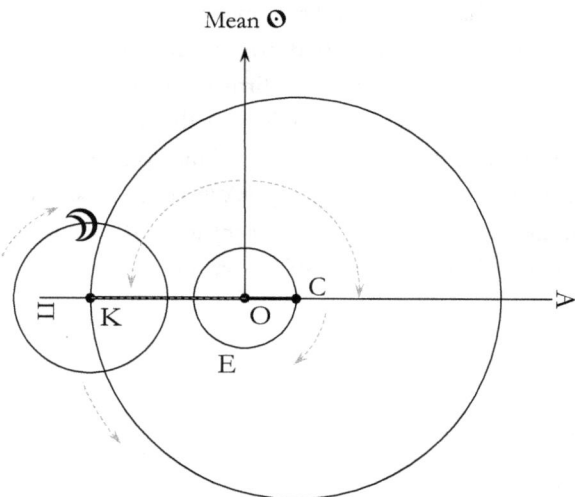

Figure 11: Simplified Ptolemaic theory of the Moon (Dykes)

10 The true motion is the arc of the already-stated orb, towards the boundary of the line of true motion. **11** The line of true motion is the one which goes out from the center of the earth, through the center of the body of the Moon, towards that same orb.

12 And the body of the Moon is moved in the upper half of the epicycle with the firmament, [but] in the lower [half] against the firmament, by 13° 03' 54" every day.[27] **13** Whence, the lower [half] is quick and the upper one slow—but she does not become retrograde on account of this, because the center of the epicycle is always moved more quickly than the Moon herself. **14** (But the other five planets become retrograde since they are moved contrarily: for they are moved against the firmament in the upper half: whence, aided by the motion of the epicycle, they are yet quicker.[28] **15** [But] the lower [half] is moved with the firmament toward the west, whence then they are subtractive from their course in the circle of signs. **16** And when it happens that what they subtract is more than the motion of the epicycle, then they are retrograde; and if it is less, they are direct; and if it is equal, then they are stationary.)

17 And the arc from the orb which is between the two boundaries of the stated lines designating the mean and true motion of the Moon, is the equation of the argument of the Moon. **18** And this is nothing when the center of the epicycle is at the apogee of the eccentric or in [its] opposite, so that then the Moon is in the farther or nearer longitude of her epicycle; and it is greatest when the center of the epicycle is in the middle longitudes of the eccentric. **19** And when the Moon is in the half which regards the west, her mean motion is greater than the true [motion]: therefore then the equation of the argument is subtracted and becomes the true [motion]. **20** In the other half it happens contrariwise, and then it is subtracted if the argument is less than 6 signs, because then the mean [motion] is less than the true [motion], and it becomes true beyond 6 signs (and *vice versa*).

21 The argument of the Moon is twofold: the mean [argument] is the small arc of the epicycle which is between the mean apogee and the center of the Moon: and this is according to the motion of the Moon in the epicycle, and from there begins the equation of the argument. **22** The true [argument]

---

[27] That is, the Moon moves in what we would call retrograde or clockwise motion, *within* her epicycle.
[28] *Diutius veloces*.

of the Moon begins from the true apogee in the epicycle, and is an arc between the true apogee and the center of the Moon.

23 There are two apogees in the epicycle of the Moon. **24** One [is] the mean [apogee],[29] which is an arc which the body of the Moon passes through after she was in the point which is called the mean apogee, which is designated by the boundary of the line which goes out from the point which is opposed to the center of the eccentric (which however is distant from the center of the earth by how much the center of the eccentric is), through the center of the epicycle toward the firmament: that point which this line touches in the upper part of the epicycle is the mean apogee, and this line bears the epicycle in the eccentric. **25** But the true apogee is what is designated by[30] the line going out from the center of the earth, through the center of the epicycle, toward the firmament:[31] the point which this line touches in the upper part of the epicycle, is the true apogee. **26** And the difference between these two apogees is the "equation of the center," which is nothing at the conjunction and opposition of the Sun, because then the line of the mean apogee and the true one, is the same.[32]

27 The center of the eccentric of the Moon is above the center of the earth by 11°, and this center describes a small circle about the center of the earth, and leads along with it the apogee of the eccentric toward the west, by 11° 12' 19" per day. **28** And the center of the epicycle is moved towards the east by as much as was stated above, and the Sun toward the east by 1°.[33] **29** Whence, if the Sun and the center of the epicycle are together, as well as the apogee of the eccentric (which happens at the conjunction or at the opposition of the Sun and Moon), after one day the Sun is in the middle of them—between the center of the epicycle and the apogee of the eccentric by a distance of 12°, and the center of the epicycle is distant by double [that] from the apogee of the eccentric (that is, by 24°). **30** And at the square of the Moon with the Sun, the center of the epicycle is in the opposite of the apogee of the eccentric: whence the Sun is either with them (as in the

---

[29] In the first diagram above, this is a line (not pictured) passing from E through K, towards the zodiac.
[30] Reading in the passive, to make the sentence flow more smoothly.
[31] In the first figure above, this would be the line OK, and extending through to the zodiac.
[32] In the first figure above, this would be the angle OKE, which represents the difference in perspective between E and O.
[33] Or rather, the *mean* Sun, by 59' 08" per day: the model of the Moon is oriented towards the mean Sun.

conjunction of the Sun with the Moon) or is opposed to them (as at the opposition of the Sun and Moon), or is equally distant from them in other places. **31** And the center of the Moon is the distance of the center of the epicycle from the apogee of the eccentric, and is said to be a double longitude or double interstice: namely, that the center of the epicycle of the Moon passes through the eccentric of the Moon twice in a month, because at the conjunction it is at its apogee (and likewise at the opposition), and at the square it is at the closer longitude.

32 However, that the Moon has an eccentric, is known thusly: because in equal times she does not describe equal arcs, and because sometimes she is found to be farther from the earth, sometimes closer. **33** However, that the apogee of the eccentric is moved against the motion of the epicycle towards the west, was known thusly: because the longitude of the center of the epicycle from the earth is 1, and that same thing [is] at the conjunction and opposition: which cannot be unless the apogee of the eccentric was moved, and that eccentric [is moved] against the motion of the epicycle.[34]

34 The short circle of the Moon, or the difference of the diameter of the short circle, is the difference between the equations of the argument—which, with the center of the epicycle appearing at the apogee of the eccentric, are lesser, [but] greater at the opposite: whence, the higher ones are subtracted from the lower ones. **35** And the compilers of tables stated the differences of the short circle, or the diversity of the short circle, which they had in due measure for all degrees of the epicycle: they would subtract the maximum equation of the three upper signs of the epicycle which they have at the apogee, from the greatest one which they have in the opposite of the apogee. **36** They put the remainder as 60', [and] afterwards in the apogee from the equation 5° from the apogee, and they saw what proportion it bore to the first, and thus with the rest. **37** And they took these in proportional minutes, because they bore that thusly towards 60, just as they bear a difference among themselves.

---

[34] In other words, *if* the diameter of the eccentric is standardized as being a length of 1, then *since* it is that far away at conjunctions and oppositions but *not* in other places (**32**), the obvious solution is to make the eccentric rotate on a small circle such that its apogee moves in the opposite direction to the epicycle, pushing and pulling it closer and farther throughout the month. Leopold's way of stating this puts it the other way around, as though the model itself is something that needed explaining, when in fact the model explains the phenomenon.

38 The equations of the argument in the tables are thus, as if the center of the epicycle is always in the apogee of the eccentric. **39** But it is certain that with the center of the epicycle appearing in other places of the eccentric, the equations of the argument increase in accordance with how the center of the epicycle approaches the center of the earth; and these arguments are taken with the proportional minutes which were said to be 60 little portions of the line appearing between the center of the earth and the center of the eccentric, divided into 60 parts; and the line drawn from the center of the earth to the opposite of the apogee has none of these parts; drawn towards the apogee, it has all of them. **40** And drawn to other places they have these according to the approach and withdrawal from the apogee and the opposite of the apogee.

41 The Dragon of the Moon, or the section by which the eccentric of the Moon (and that of all the other planets)[35] declines from the path of the Sun, is evident because when the Sun appears in Cancer, all [of them] are seen to decline by 5° beyond [and] 5° nearer.[36] **42** And the Dragon of the Moon is moved [retrograde] against the signs, which is known by the eclipses—but the Dragons of the other [planets] are immovable in the order of signs.[37] **43** And because the Dragon of the Moon is moved against the signs, for that reason the writers of the tables subtract from the 12 signs what they extract from the tables of the Dragon, and thus they find its true place. **44** And the intersection by which the eccentric of the Moon declines from the path of the Sun towards the north, is called the Head, where [it declines] toward the south is called the Tail, and these intersections are moved every day with the firmament by about 3'. **45** And a certain circle concentric with the world leads these intersections [along]: it is in the heaven of the Moon, equal to the eccentric of the Moon in magnitude, and it is on the surface of the orb of the signs or path of the Sun, and this motion is contrary to the motion of the planets.

46 But the motions proper to the Moon herself are five: [first], that of the epicycle in the deferent eccentric, by 13° 10' 39" every day against the firmament. **47** That of the eccentric toward the west [is] as was posited above.

---

[35] Since all of the other planets have zodiacal latitude, they all have Nodes as well.

[36] Lit., "on this side" (*citra*). Adding the symbol for "degrees," in accordance with Ptolemy's theory.

[37] Actually, the other planets' Nodes do move, as Leopold points out in Ch. II.4, **42**. For example, the exact North Node of Mars was at about 8° 31' Taurus in 2015 (on April 12), but it will be at about 22° 10' Aries in 2017 (February 27).

48 That of the body of the Moon [is] with the firmament in the epicycle, in the upper half. **49** Her motion through the sections of the Head and Tail of the Dragon are with the motion of the first movable, from the east to the west (and *vice versa*), every day.[38] **50** She [also] has a sixth [motion] in common with all of the stars and planets against the firmament, in 100 years per degree.[39]

51 The eclipse of the Moon at the farther longitude of the epicycle happens within 10°, in the nearer one within 13°, and she is totally eclipsed at the farther longitude within 4°, at the nearer one within 5°. **52** The digits[40] of the diameter of the shadow of the earth at the farther latitude, are 20.5, at the nearer one 21.5, of which the diameter of the Moon has 12. **53** The digits of an eclipse are 12, of the diameter of the lunar body.

54 The minutes of the occurrence[41] are the minutes of heaven which the Moon transits from the beginning of the eclipse to the middle (if she is not totally obscured), or up to the beginning of total obscuration (if she is totally obscured). **55** For the Sun, the minutes of the occurrence are the minutes which the Moon transits from the beginning of an eclipse of the Sun, up to the middle. **56** The minutes of one-half the stay are the minutes which the Moon transits from the beginning of the obscuration up to the middle, and for that reason if these minutes are divided by the motion of the Moon in 5 hours, the time in which she transits them are had.

57 The "points of the remainder" are the parts of the diameter of the epicycle which are from the apogee up to the direction or direct [line] of the Moon. **58** The diameters which are posited in the lines of the tables of eclipses, are the increases of latitudes of equal power[42] among themselves, or "equipollent" latitudes.

---

[38] Perhaps we can state this differently: there is (1) her motion in the epicycle; (2) the epicycle's motion on the deferent; (3) the deferent's motion around the earth; (4) her diurnal rotation; (5) her motion through zodiacal latitudes.

[39] This is Ptolemy's false value for the precession of the equinoxes. A better value is 1°/71.59 years. .

[40] This is a unit of measurement, whereby the diameter of an eclipse or of the Moon's body was taken to be 12 digits (see **53**).

[41] *Minuta casus*. I take *casus* ("fall") here and in **55** to be a translation of the Arabic verb "to fall," which by analogy means "to occur." But it might also refer to the shadow "falling" upon the Moon.

[42] Or perhaps, equal length?

59 A month[43] of the Moon has 29 days, 31 minutes, 50 seconds: which, 12 being taken, make 354 days and 22 minutes of a day (which are one-sixth and one fifth of a day, because 12 are one-fifth and 10 are one-sixth):[44] and these make a lunar year. **60** And the said days of the month, and minutes and seconds, are 29 days, 12 hours, 45 minutes. **61** And the said 22 minutes of a day are 8 hours, 48 minutes of an hour. **62** But al-Zarqālī, in his tables, [has] 11 minutes (making a day have 30 minutes), of which 30 [minutes] 6 are one-fifth, 5 one-sixth.[45] **63** And he collects 11 in individual years: however often he has 30, he gets one day, and he reckons the motion of that number (which he has presupposed) in the tables of the planets.

ஓ ஓ ଔ

Comment by Dykes. Ptolemy's theory of the Moon is much more complicated than that of the superiors and Venus (Ch. II.4), but is very similar to the theory of Mercury (Ch. II.5). It is best if the reader looks at the superiors and Venus first, as well as Mercury, before trying to understand the Moon. In describing the lunar theory here, I will mention several terms but not fully explain them as I do in my *Comments* on the other chapters.

The Moon has a number of odd motions which Ptolemy tried to account for in the *Almagest*, first using a model based on Hipparchus, then an intermediate theory which accounts for anomalies at the lunar quarters, and finally a third theory to explain her positions at the octants, or cross-quarters. Leopold presents the third theory, and rather than explain all of the reasoning Ptolemy used to develop it, I will describe its major features here. By the way, what Ptolemy accomplished was rather brilliant, and although further

---

[43] In this confusing paragraph, Leopold is treating a lunar month and the lunar year in terms of degrees, which he then converts to time units. (He is probably treating the month in terms of the motion of certain lines in Ptolemy's model.) The problem is that he explicitly *treats* his units in terms of time, even when they are degrees. At any rate, Leopold's rounded synodic lunar month—when the Moon returns to conjoin with the Sun—is 29.53105 days (**60**), about a minute less than the modern value.

[44] Leopold is using a short-cut method to turn the 22 minutes into a portion of the day. Leopold is treating 1 day as equivalent to 1°: so, since 22 is the sum of 12 and 10, it can be understood as one-fifth of a day (since 60/5 = 12) plus one-sixth of a day (since 60/6 = 10).

[45] This is simply another conversion system. Above (**61**), when Leopold was treating one day as 1°, 22' could be converted into 8h 48m (or 8.8), since 22'/60' = .3666, and .3666 of a day is 8h 48m. Now (**62**), al-Zarqālī treats one day as 30'. But .3666 of 30' is 11', so for al-Zarqālī "11" converts to 8h 48m. Again, in such a system 6' is one-fifth of a day, and 5 is one-sixth.

anomalies were discovered in later centuries, it should be pointed out that *even today* there is no complete theory of the Moon as there is with the other planets.

It is easiest to think of Ptolemy's final lunar theory as being more similar to his second (since the third largely just uses a different position as the basis for its tables). Ptolemy is trying to deal with two general problems or inequalities in her motion. First of all, the Moon's motion is variable throughout the month (**32**), particularly in the fact that the time when she returns to the same daily speed (the anomalistic month) varies with respect to the length of her return to the same point in the zodiac (the tropical month). To solve this problem, Ptolemy does the following. He first puts the Moon in an epicycle that revolves (ultimately, eccentrically) around the earth: the center of her epicycle K revolves around the earth (O) through the zodiac at the rate of a tropical month (**8**), while her body revolves in her epicycle in the opposite direction (clockwise), at the rate of an anomalistic month (**12-13**). This accounts, in theory, for variable motion.

However, Ptolemy proved that at the lunar quarters, her position could be several degrees off from what the model predicts. In order to account for this, he needed her epicycle to be drawn in closer to the earth, so that her position on it could appear wider from our perspective (**32**). Accordingly, instead of having a fixed center for her deferent (C), he put C on a smaller circle that rotated clockwise (in the opposite direction to K): C and her equant point E now form opposite points on a small circle (**27**).

Ptolemy's final and third theory of the Moon is represented in a simplified form above, with some of the auxiliary lines indicating various points on the epicycle omitted (**17-26**). The whole lunar apparatus revolves around the earth at the center (O). First, the deferent circle has a center C which revolves clockwise from east to west, thereby dragging the whole system around in a wide circle. The line OC points at one end towards the apogee of the eccentric, while the other end points at the perigee (**27**). But on this concentric deferent, the Moon's epicycle moves counterclockwise or west to east, with its center at K (**8-9**). While the epicycle itself moves counterclockwise, the Moon herself moves *clockwise*, in the opposite direction (**12**). One might think that this would falsely make the Moon retrograde, but because of the periods Ptolemy is using for the rotations, it actually only makes her speed up and slow down (**13**).

The really interesting feature of the theory is the coordination between the rotation of C on the small circle, and K on the deferent. They move such that each is equally distant from the mean Sun, but in the opposite direction (**28-31**). This creates what has been called a "crank mechanism," because as C moves clockwise and K counter-clockwise, the dragging of the deferent along with C brings K closer to, and farther away from, the earth. But because they move at the same rate in relation to the mean Sun, they will coincide at the New and Full Moons, where the Moon appears farthest away (and in the model, she is). But at other points of the cycle, she will be drawn towards us, appear bigger, and move faster. In the first figure, the mean Sun is arbitrarily placed at the top. The Moon is approaching one of the cross quarters: on the right, the apsidal line OCA has rotated 30° westward (angle: mean Sun-O-A), while the line OK has rotated 30° eastward (angle: mean Sun-O-K). The thick line CK is the radius of the deferent, which is always the same size. (The Moon's position on the epicycle is not to scale and should be ignored.)

As one can imagine, as OC approaches 90° (the first lunar quarter), it will drag the Moon towards the right, so as to be closer at the quarter. The second figure shows just this. Now, OCA and OK form 90° angles with the line to the mean Sun: OC points to the right, and overlapping it is the radius of the epicycle, which lies on OK. As the Moon approaches the fullness, OC and CK will point away from the mean Sun, and at the full Moon she will be extended fully downwards, at her farthest point. After that, OC and OK will switch sides and draw the Moon closer again.

[Chapter II.4: Theory of the superiors and Venus]

1 Saturn, Jupiter, and Mars have an orb which draws them around, as was said for the Sun and Moon. **2** They have four circles: [1-2] two eccentrics, [3] an epicycle, and [4] a circle of latitude.[46] **3** The [1] deferent eccentric is the one on which the center of the epicycle of each of these is moved contrary to the firmament.[47] **4** The [3] epicycle is grasped[48] by means of direct motion

---

[46] Reading singular for the epicycle and circle of latitude, so that each clearly has four apiece.
[47] That is, forward in the zodiac in the opposite direction to the diurnal motion of the heavens.
[48] That is, "understood to exist" (*deprehensus*).

and retrogradation. **5** The [2] equant eccentric is the one[49] whose center describes the center of the epicycle, equal arcs in equal times. **6** The [4] circle of latitude is the one in which a planet leaves the path of the Sun towards the north or south. **7** And both of the two eccentrics for each planet are equal.[50]

8 And for these three planets *and* for Venus, the center of the equant is above the center of the deferent by how much the center of the deferent is above the center of the earth. **9** (For Mercury it is otherwise.) **10** And all of the eccentrics of these four are immovable, except the amount [there is] toward the motion of the eighth sphere,[51] the daily dragging from the east to the east, and conversely around the center of the world.

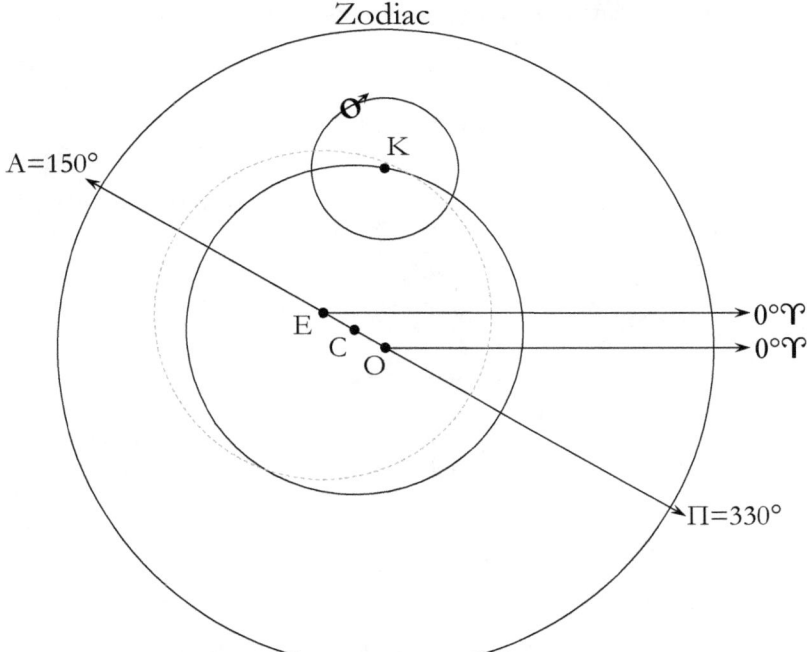

Figure 12: Theory of superiors and Venus (Dykes)

---

[49] Omitting *de quo ut super*, which does not make much sense; one possibility is that *super* goes with the following clause, which would then read, "around the center of which is described..."; but one would expect the passive *describitur* instead. In either case, the phrase does not actually contribute to the definition of the equant.
[50] That is, they are equal to each other in size.
[51] This may be a reference to the motion of their apogees.

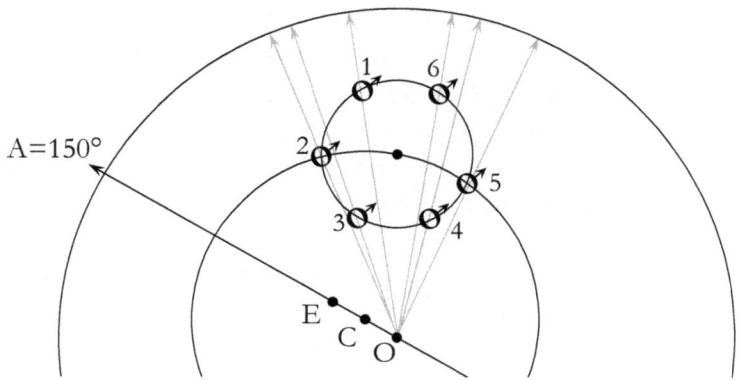

Figure 13: Effect of retrogradation on true position (Dykes)

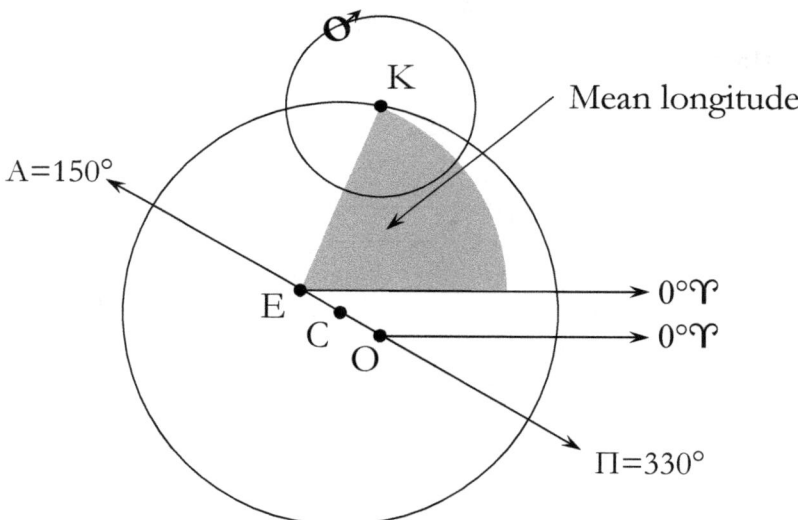

Figure 14: Mean longitude of Mars (Dykes)

11 Also, they have two motions: the mean and the true. **12** The mean is the one which is indicated by[52] the terminus of the line which goes out from the center of the equant, through the center of the epicycle, *in* the equant:

---

[52] Reading the passive for clarity.

whence the arc in[53] the equant from the beginning of its Aries to the terminus of the said line, is the mean or equal motion of the planet.[54]

13 The epicycle has two motions in the firmament. **14** The mean [motion] is the one signified by the terminus of the line of the mean motion, drawn forth towards the firmament.[55] **15** The true [motion] is the one signified by the line going out from the center of the earth, through the center of the epicycle, toward the firmament. **16** Where these two lines touch the epicycle, designates the two apogees in the epicycle: the line of the mean motion [indicates] the mean apogee, the line of true motion the true apogee.[56]

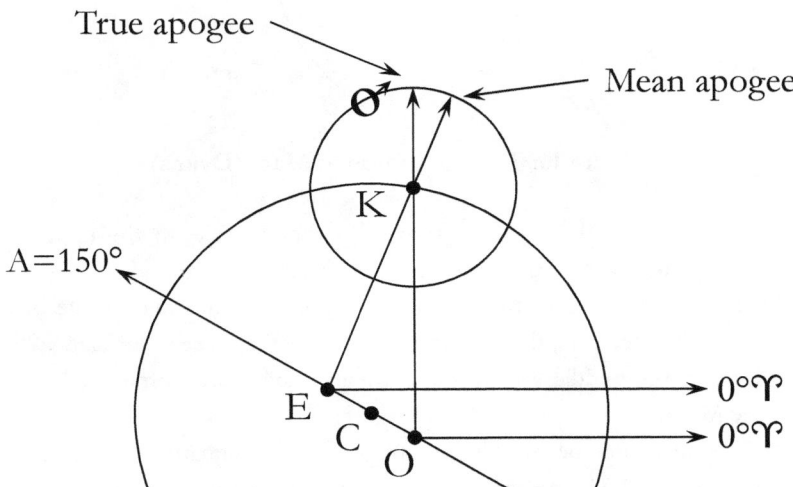

Figure 15: Apogee of the epicycle (Dykes)

17 The true motion[57] of a planet is designated by the line which goes out from the center of the earth, through the center of the planet, toward the firmament.

---

[53] Reading for "from" (*de*).
[54] This is the planet's "mean longitude."
[55] That is, pointing toward some degree of the zodiac.
[56] The difference between them is the equation of the center; in the solar theory, the equation of center had a similar meaning. The equation is nothing more than the difference between the assumed position based on mean motion, and the actual position as seen from earth. See **21** and my *Comment* below.
[57] Or rather, "position" or "longitude."

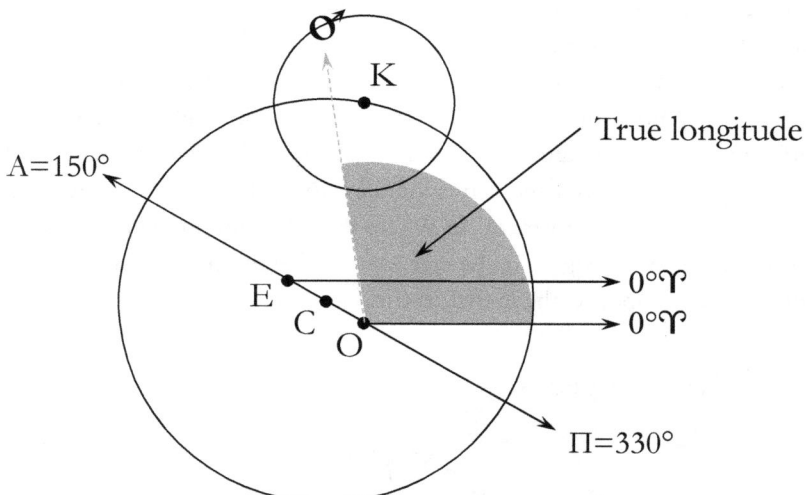

Figure 16: True longitude of Mars (Dykes)

18 The body of the planet is moved in the epicycle: in the upper half against the firmament; in the lower [half], with it.[58]

19 If the center of the epicycle is at the apogee (or in the opposite of the apogee) of the eccentric, the true apogee and mean apogee is the same. **20** In the places in the middle they differ, sometimes by more, sometimes less, as with the Moon.

21 The difference between these apogees is the "equation of the center" in the epicycle. **22** The equation of the center in the zodiac is the difference between true and mean motion in the firmament or epicycle. **23** The center is the distance of the center of the epicycle from the apogee of the eccentric of the equant.[59] **24** The apogee is the point most elevated in the eccentric from the beginning of Aries, in the equant.[60]

25 The center is two-fold: the mean [center is] what was stated before; the true [center] is the arc which is from the point of the firmament in the direct [line] of the apogee up to the terminus of the line designating the true motion of the epicycle. **26** And these two centers differ according to the equation of the center. **27** And this equation is taken along with the mean

---

[58] "Firmament" here refers to "diurnal motion."
[59] This is also called the "mean anomaly" (there is also a mean anomaly within the epicycle itself).
[60] As in the solar theory, the apogee is the point at which the planet (or rather, the center of its epicycle) is farthest from the earth.

center, because according to it the equation of the center varies, and this equation rectifies the center and the argument; and with the center it adds, [with] the argument it subtracts (and vice-versa), and each becomes the true.

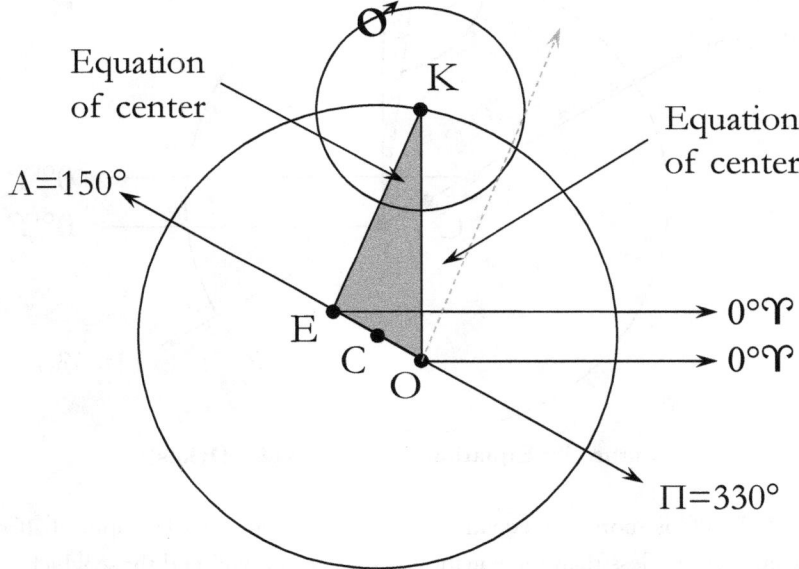

Figure 17: Equation of the center of Mars (Dykes)

28 The argument of the planet is the distance of the planet's body from the apogee of the epicycle.[61] **29** The equation of the argument is the difference between the true motion of the epicycle, and the true motion of the planet; and when the true argument is 0, that is [both] the true motion of the epicycle and the true [motion] of the planet. **30** But the true [motion] of the planet is greater than the mean when the argument is less than 6 signs: and therefore so that the mean might become true, the equation of the argument is added to the mean motion of the epicycle, and when [the argument] is greater than 6 signs it is subtracted for the contrary reason.

---

[61] Leopold might be referring to the mean epicyclic anomaly here.

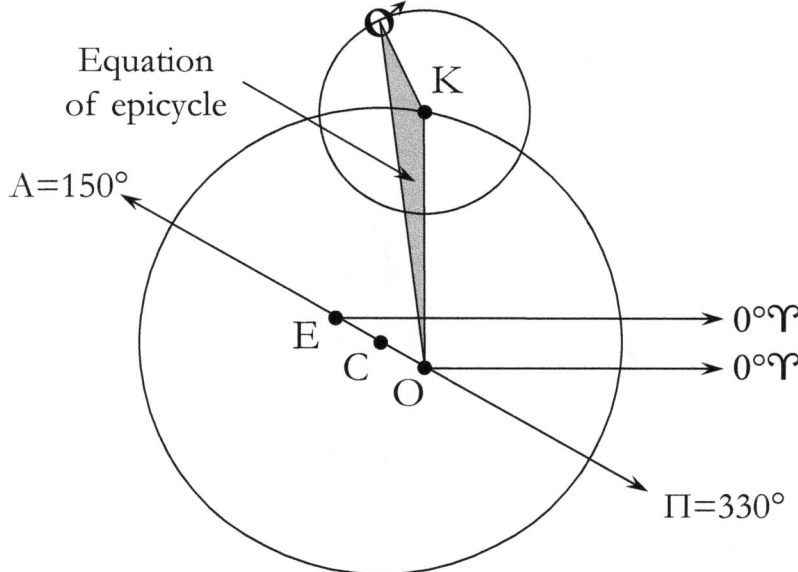

Figure 18: Equation of the epicycle (Dykes)

31 What[62] is more, the equations of the argument over the upper half of the epicycle are less than the equations in the lower half, and those which are in the middle are greater than those which are above the middle: whence, by comparing the lower ones to the middle ones, they say the longitude is closer, and by comparison and the excess of the middle ones with respect to the upper ones, they say the longitude is farther. **32** And the greatest difference among all of them they reputed to be 60'.

33 And[63] they have discovered [some] remaining differences: they took from the higher of the longitudes according to the proportion of the minutes (which they put as being up to 60), and they added the amount which they found by proportion [when the planet was] below [the center of the epicycle], and they subtracted the amount [if it was] above. **34** Because by how much more the center of the epicycle descends toward the opposite of the

---

[62] This refers to the fact that the corrections made to the epicyclic position are asymmetrical: the amount of the correction when closer to the epicyclic apogee differs from the corresponding positions closer to the perigee.

[63] This paragraph refers to the "interpolation coefficients," which are helpful numbers allowing one to interpolate between epicyclic corrections (see previous paragraph). When closer to the apogee, these coefficients help one subtract from the nearest number to get the right position, and when closer to the perigee they help one add to it.

apogee, the equation of the argument will be that much greater (and vice-versa); and because of this wherever the lesser is posited it becomes an addition, and where [it is] more than what is needed, it becomes a subtraction. **35** And because whenever the equation of the center is part of[64] the equation of the argument, now the lesser is subtracted from the greater, and the remainder is added to the mean motion; [but] sometimes it is not a part, and then one equation is added to the other, and they are added or subtracted together from the mean motion—as Tytulus[65] teaches.

36 And as the motion of the center of the epicycle of the three superiors, and the motion of their bodies in the epicycles every day are of equal value with the mean motion of the diurnal Sun in his eccentric,[66] because of this once their mean motion is subtracted from the mean motion of the Sun, their argument remains (that is, their motion in the epicycles from the mean apogee of the epicycle); and once their apogee is subtracted from their mean motion, the center remains, because the center is the distance of the center of the epicycle from the apogee of the equant—but the mean motion is from the beginning of Aries in the equant.

37 The apogee of Saturn is in 5° Sagittarius, Jupiter in 14° 30' Virgo, Mars in 5° 51' Leo.

	Apogee	Perigee
♄	3° ♐	3° ♋
♃	10° ♍	10° ♈
♂	0° ♍	0° ♓
☉	13° ♋	13° ♑
♀	11° ♋	11° ♑

Figure 19: Approximate apsidal points, 2000 AD (Dykes)[67]

38 And[68] the epicycle of Saturn has 6 ½ (of which the middle of his equant has 60), Jupiter has 11 ½, and Mars 3 ½.

---

[64] *Pars*, here and later in the sentence. I do not quite understand what Leopold means by it, but this is simply part of the instructions for interpolating between two numbers in Ptolemy's tables.
[65] This is probably an awkward transliteration of the Arabic for "Ptolemy."
[66] Leopold is probably referring to the fact that the radii of the superiors' epicycles run parallel to the mean Sun—as seen from earth.
[67] The apogees of the Moon and Mercury move constantly throughout their cycles (see below).

39 The latitude of the planets is their receding from the zodiac (which is the path of the Sun). **40** And these five have a double latitude: one from the epicycle, which is inclined from the eccentric, [and] the other from the eccentric, which is inclined from the path of the Sun.[69] **41** But the eccentric of the Moon is always distant in a uniform way from the path of the Sun, and the Moon's epicycle is always on the surface of the eccentric: and therefore the Moon has but one latitude.

42 And[70] the aforesaid five have the following: the place of the Head of the Dragon of Saturn is 3.13.12.57, its mean motion is 8.16.48.0. **43** The place of the Head of the Dragon of Jupiter is 2.23.11.0, its mean motion 9.7.59.0. **44** The place of the Head of the Dragon of Mars is 0.21.54.56, its mean motion 11.8.6.0. **45** The place of the Head of the Dragon of Venus is 1.29.17.18, its mean motion 0.0.0.39. **46** The place of the Head of the Dragon of Mercury is 0.21.10.0, its mean motion 11.8.5.0.

47 But the center of Venus's epicycle is only moved daily in the equant by how much the Sun is in his own eccentric, and likewise Mercury: because their centers are always with the Sun: and therefore their mean motion and the Sun's is the same.[71] **48** But the centers of their *bodies* are not always with the Sun, whence neither they…[72]

49 The epicycle of Venus has 43 1/6 (of which the middle of her equant has 60); [the epicycle] of Mercury [has] 22 ½.

50 Therefore, the motion of those four aforesaid [planets], namely Saturn, Jupiter, Mars, and Venus, are these:[73] the epicycles from the west to the east

---

[68] This sentence refers to the radius of the epicycle for the superiors (see Venus and Mercury below), which I will describe in a later work on geocentric astronomy.

[69] Leopold may be referring to the fact that notable changes in latitude occur not only in certain parts of the zodiac (which could be explained simply by the eccentric or deferent), but also around periods of retrogradation (which would have to be explained by an inclination of the epicycle, too).

[70] At present I am not sure exactly what the numbers here denote, though they are probably given in the Babylonian sexagesimal form: so, 8.16.48.0 indicates 8° 16' 48" 0'".

[71] In Ptolemy's theory of Venus and Mercury (both inferior planets), the line from their equant points to the center of their epicycles, runs parallel with the line from the earth to the mean Sun. So, the revolution of their epicycles around the deferent takes exactly as much time as the Sun's does on his eccentric: one tropical year.

[72] The sentence ends here at the bottom of Leopold's page, and resumes with the next sentence on the following page.

[73] The rest of this sentence is meant to describe two motions, to make five total (see below), but Leopold's language (and apparent reference to measuring from the equant circle) makes it hard to understand exactly how he conceives of them. The two motions are: (1) the rotation of the planet through the epicycle, and (2) the rotation of the epicycle itself around the eccentric or deferent circle.

in the deferent eccentric about the center of the earth, from the equant of the body in the epicycle. **51** Moreover, [they have] the motion of latitude outside of the path of the Sun, and in addition to this they have the motion of the eighth sphere. **52** Moreover, [they have] daily motion or dragging from the east to the west (and conversely [around]): and they are five [motions]. **53** Apart from this Mercury has the motion of the center of the epicycle from the east to the west, about which I will speak imminently [below].

54 The center of Saturn's epicycle every day completes about 2', his body in the epicycle 57'.[74] **55** The center of Jupiter's epicycle [completes] 5', his body in the epicycle 54'. **56** The center of the epicycle of Mars [completes] 31', [his] body 28'. **57** The centers of the epicycles of Venus and Mercury [complete] just as much as the Sun does every day: 59' 08".

58 And[75] when the Sun returns to the centers of the epicycles of the three superiors, then [the superior planet] completes its own epicycle, and the one whose center is in the mean [epicyclic] apogee. **59** And when he is opposed to them then it is in the opposite of its [epicyclic] apogee. **60** And in a square with the Sun they are at the middle of the epicycle.

℞   ℞   ℞

Comment by Dykes. In this comment I will discuss some of the main points of Ptolemaic planetary theory, which Leopold discusses in a straightforward but not always illuminating way. Some details of this chapter are too fine for the beginner, and I will discuss them at greater length in a later work on geocentric astronomy.

Ptolemaic planetary theory is designed to deal with two key astronomical problems, and his method for finding planetary positions involves a two-step process (or three, depending on how one counts). The two problems are the "inequalities" or irregularities in planetary motion. We saw the first inequality at work in the solar theory: the fact that planets move at different speeds in different parts of the zodiac. The Sun currently moves most slowly around

---

[74] This refers to his motion in mean longitude, and his mean motion in epicyclic anomaly, respectively.
[75] This sentence in particular is stated awkwardly, but Leopold is referring to the fact that for superior planets, their motion in epicyclic anomaly runs parallel to the mean Sun, so their retrogradation cycles are coordinated with it. For example, in the middle of their retrogradation they are opposed to (or rather parallel with) the mean Sun.

13° Cancer, and Ptolemy dealt with this by putting his circle off-center from the earth (i.e., an "eccentric" circle), in the direction of 13° Cancer. Thus, when the Sun appears to move more slowly it is because he is actually in the part of his circle which is furthest from the earth: his apogee. When he appears to move most quickly (around 13° Capricorn), he is in the part of his circle closest to earth. For the superior planets and Venus, Ptolemy does exactly the same thing to solve *their* zodiacal inequalities, giving them an eccen-eccentric in the direction of their apogees (**3, 37**).

The second inequality has to do with the cycles of direct motion, stationing, and retrogradation. Most people are aware that Ptolemy (following some predecessors) dealt with this by adding an epicycle: a circle whose center is on the eccentric, around which the planet revolves (**4, 18**, Figure 12). This epicycle in turn revolves around the eccentric. The eccentric is often called the "deferent," because the epicycle is "borne along" on it (from the Latin *defero*.)

The result is that we have (1) a planet which goes through cycles of retrogradation on (2) the epicycle, and which is also borne along through the zodiac on (3) the eccentric.[76] In this way, Ptolemy is theoretically able to solve the two inequalities and accurately predict the "true position" of the superiors and Venus. In geocentric astronomy, a true position is the actual position of a planetary body *as seen from earth*: it is the position given in the ephemeris, and is depicted geometrically in Figure 15.

In Figure 12, we can see the basic model for Mars. O is the earth, the center of the universe, with the zodiac around it. From the earth, an arrow points at 0° Aries, from which we measure zodiacal longitudes. C is the center of the smaller eccentric or deferent, which is off-center in the direction of Mars's apogee, currently at about 150° (0° Virgo). On the eccentric is a yet smaller epicycle, whose center K revolves counter-clockwise around the eccentric. The body of Mars revolves counter-clockwise around the epicycle. From our line of sight at O, the body of Mars will be at some degree of the zodiac (his true position), which will sometimes move forward or backwards, depending on where in his epicycle he is: Figure 13 shows six different perspectives on his true position, when he is in various positions on the epicycle.

Now, all of this is fine and good, except that when we actually track the motion of the planets—particularly through their retrogradation cycles—their true positions do not match what is predicted by the model. Specifically,

---

[76] In this little essay I omit Ptolemy's theory of latitudes (**6**).

as long as C is the center of the planet's uniform motion, then no matter where we put C, the retrogradations will either happen in the wrong location, or be of the wrong size. So, something else needs to be done.

Ptolemy's innovation[77] was to find a position in space, on the other side of C, which could act as the place from which to measure planets' uniform motions: the equant (E), which is the center of its own "equant circle." The equant circle is the same size as the deferent (**7**), and E, C, and O are spaced equally apart (**8**).[78] That is, the planets still move about C, but for an observer at C they no longer move at a constant rate. Instead, they only move at a constant rate for an observer *at E*. Put differently, Ptolemy has now given three separate functions to three separate points:

- Planets are *measured* from E.
- Planets *move about* C.
- Planets are *observed by us* from O.

The pre-Ptolemaic model used C both for the measurement of uniform motion *and* as the center of revolution, which did not yield accurate results.

I mentioned above that Ptolemy's method for finding true positions involved a two-step (or three-step) process. The steps are roughly these (1) find the *mean* positions of the planet on its deferent and in its epicycle as measured; (2) use certain corrections (called "equations") to convert these into *true* positions as observed from O. (We might consider this a three-step process because we need to add corrections to both the deferent and the epicycle.) Just as in the solar theory, a "mean" position or motion is where we would expect a planet to be *if it moved at a constant rate*. Since the planets do not revolve around the earth (but around C), nor do we observe mean motion from earth (but at E), we need to apply corrections so that the mean positions can be converted into true ones. This may seem awkward, but most of it is easy and allows planetary tables for thousands of years to be contained on a single piece of paper. Let us look briefly at each of these steps, beginning with Figure 14 and sentence **11**. For the sake of ease, I have removed the zodiac and the dotted equant circle so we can focus on the planet itself, centered on C.

---

[77] At least, we can find no other source for it.
[78] In the end, it happens that E is not *exactly* twice as far away from O as C is, but it was treated this way.

(1) *Mean positions*. As I stated, E is our point for measuring uniform motion. From E the motion of K is uniform, and at any moment K will be at some angular distance away from 0° Aries (**11-12**). The time it takes for K to revolve exactly once (as measured from E) is *exactly* the length of the planet's tropical period. Our example uses Mars: his period is 1.88 years, so for any position of K you like (measured from E, and on the equant circle), it will return there 1.88 years later. Likewise, from the perspective of E, Mars moves around his epicycle exactly once for each retrogradation period (779.9 days).

What this means is that we only need some fixed day (called the "epoch date"), on which we know where Mars's apogee is, where K is, and where Mars is on his epicycle. For any other day, we just need to know how much time has passed (forward or backward), and we can calculate where each of these is in the zodiac: these are the mean positions. For example, suppose our epoch date is January 1, 2000, at noon in Greenwich. Suppose also that we have a birth chart dated exactly 5 days later, on January 5, again at noon. Since Mars moves about 27' 41" per day in his epicycle, we know he has moved about 2° 18' 28" on it since the epoch date (5 x 27' 41" = 2° 18' 28"). We simply add this to the position on the epoch date, and we know where he was in the epicycle at the nativity as measured from E.

However, these are all positions as viewed from E. What we want for chart-casting are the true positions, which are seen from earth or O.

(2) *Equations and true positions*. The second (or second and third) step is simply to convert the mean positions into true ones, by applying certain corrections, called "equations." Since planetary circles are eccentric or off-center, we need to know how large their eccentricity is, so we know the difference in perspective between our measuring point (E) and the earth. An equation is precisely this difference: because of eccentricity, a viewer at E (or the Sun's C, in the solar theory) will usually see a planet as being in a slightly different place against the zodiac, as a viewer on earth will. Therefore, once we know the dimensions of the model, and we know the mean positions for some day, we can enter these into a special table and discover the "equation" or correction to add or subtract. One set of equations corrects, or "equates," the position of K; the other corrects the planet's position on the epicycle. In Ptolemaic jargon, we enter the mean positions as "arguments" or data into the first column of his table of equations; by reading across the table, we learn what corrections to make. In some cases, we must subtract something,

in other cases add something. The result is the true position as seen from earth, which is what we wanted.[79]

Ptolemy's general theories for the superiors and Venus were extremely accurate and can still be used today, albeit using some modern parameters, and moving their apogees at a certain rate; one must also tolerate certain small errors in longitude. Ptolemy's own errors—though they were still small, all things considered—had mainly to do with the motion of the apogees and some faulty parameters in the length of the year and the planetary cycles. In any given short period, this would not create a great problem. But over many centuries Ptolemy's parameters cause an accumulation of errors, especially in his theory of Mercury (see below). Nevertheless the final result was an astonishing achievement from a first-rate scientific mind.

[Chapter II.5: Theory of Mercury]

1 Mercury has as many circles as the four mentioned above.[80] **2** He has a different motion in this, because the center of his deferent is moved with the firmament to the west, just as much as the center of the epicycle [is moved] toward the east. **3** Whence, the center of the epicycle is with the point of the apogee of the deferent twice in the year, just as the center of the epicycle of the Moon is with the apogee of her own deferent twice in a month. **4** Whence a diversity of equations happens to Mercury, as well as longitude and approach to and from the earth (and because of this [there is] a difference in the proportional minutes), which nicely appears in the figure which is posited, in the theory of the planets.[81]

5 The center of the deferent is above the center of the world, double what the center of the equant is above the center of the earth, and the center of the deferent is above the center of the world by 9°, and above the center of the equant by 6°.[82] **6** And these are the reasons for the differences between

---

[79] Some further data helps us interpolate between values, along with some other minor corrections.
[80] *Memorati.* This is a bit misleading, as Mercury's "small circle" (invented for the Mercury theory) plays a different role here. See my *Comment* below.
[81] My own diagrams show this better than Leopold's: see below.
[82] This is contradictory, and may be a typesetter's mistake.

Mercury and the other four preceding [planets]. **7** And every day the body of Mercury describes virtually 3° of his epicycle.

☎   ☏   ☙

Comment by Dykes. Presented here are several diagrams showing the intriguing and more complicated Ptolemaic theory of Mercury. After understanding the theories of the superiors and Venus, as well as the Moon and her extra circle, Mercury is not difficult to understand. The basic difference involves the center of the deferent (C) moving around a fixed point (F) on the apsidal line, rather than C being on the apsidal line. In other words, *the entire combination of deferent and epicycle* now revolves around a small circle centered at F.

In the diagram, I have made the apsidal line point towards an apogee (A) and perigee (Π). It is important to think of this line as fixed in place, as is the center of the earth (O) on it, the equant point (E), and the center of a new, small circle (F). Note that the equant E and the deferent apparatus have switched places, so that E is closer to O. Between C and the epicyclic center K is an imaginary line of fixed length. This gives the model the appearance of being a "crank mechanism." Finally, for the sake of simplicity I have put Mercury on the epicycle but have not made him move on it, nor have I added the epicyclic apogees.

The motion of the model is as follows. (a) K moves counterclockwise or forward in the zodiac, as usual. And (b) as in the model for the superiors and Venus, the angle AEK (centered on the equant point E) shows the mean anomaly: how far away K is from the apogee A, measured in uniform motion. The innovation here is (c) that the center of the deferent C, and so the entire deferent circle itself, rotates around F *clockwise* or with diurnal motion, *at the same rate as K*. That is, angle AEK will always be equal to AFC, with K and C moving in opposite directions (**2**). Because the deferent circle is revolving around F, and C is connected to K by an imaginary line of fixed length, the entirety of the deferent-circle apparatus swings back and forth around the apsidal line. The effect is something of an ellipse shape.

TREATISE II: ON THE SPHERES OF THE PLANETS 79

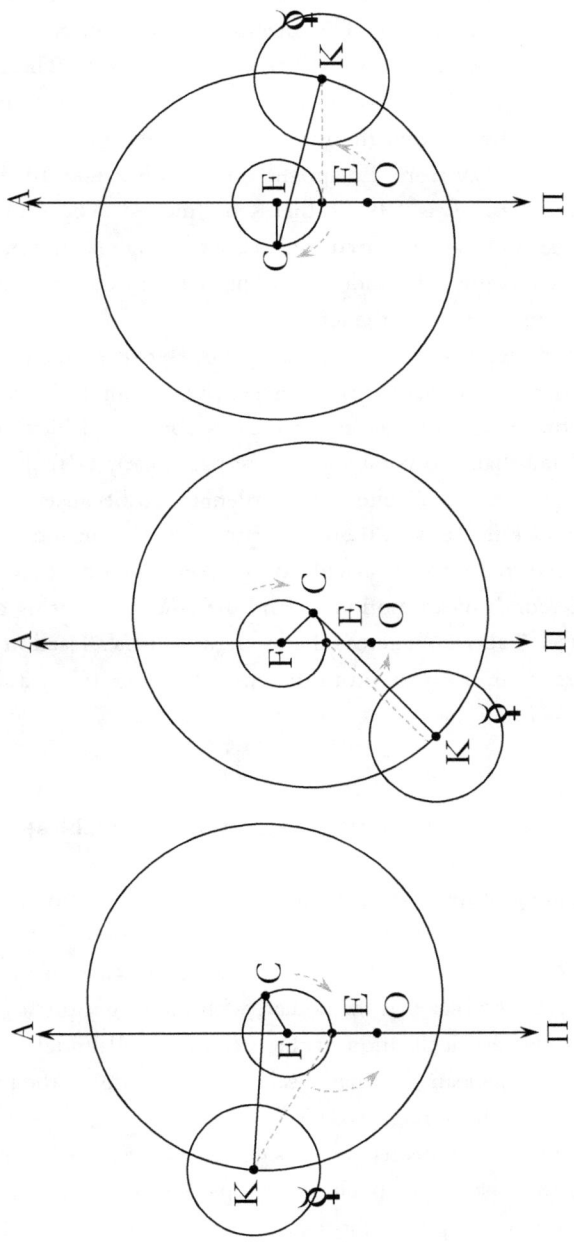

Figure 20: Theory of Mercury (Dykes)

In the first diagram, the mean anomaly is 60°. That is, AEK is 60°, so that K is 60° from the apsidal line. This means that deferent center C (or angle AFC) must be 60° from the apsidal line on the *other* side. The effect is that the deferent and epicycle are drawn towards the right. In the second diagram, K has moved further so that the mean anomaly (AEK) is 135°, so again C (or AFC) is 135° away from the apogee on the other side. In the third diagram, the mean anomaly is 270°, so that K has moved to be 270° or ¾ of the way around the circle, as measured from E; accordingly, C has moved so that AFC is 270° from the other side. Now the deferent-epicycle apparatus has revolved to be more towards the left.

It is worth noting that Ptolemy's own parameters eventually create a Mercury that runs about 5° behind on average, over about 1,000 years—but by the 12th Century the error was in some cases about 11°! Nevalainen (1996) showed in detail that two parameters were particularly at fault. First, Ptolemy's tropical year was not quite the right length, so because Mercury's (and Venus's) epicycles move with the mean Sun, any error in the length of year would be transferred into the calculation of their motions. Second, Ptolemy calculated Mercury's mean motion around the epicycle as being about 3° 06' 24" per day (see **7** above), whereas the modern value is a fraction of a second faster: this results in his position in the epicycle being off by a little over 1° over the course of a century.

[Chapter II.6: Latitudes, stations, and tables]

1 The declining of the planets [in latitude] is the distance of each degree of the epicycle from the plane of the zodiac, with the center of the epicycle put in the node. **2** The reflexion of the planets is the distance of each degree of the epicycle from the plane of the zodiac, with the center of the epicycle being put at the greatest declination of the eccentric [in latitude]. **3** Understand what is said here by means of what is said in the treatise on the theory of the planets, in the chapter on retrogradation.

4 The stations of the planets are designated by two lines going out from the center of the earth, and touching the epicycle on each side. **5** The first station is the contacted point closer to the apogee in the epicycle—closer, I say, according to the motion of the body of the planet in the epicycle—and the arc of the epicycle which is from the apogee up to that point, is the first station. **6** The second station is the other point, and the arc from the apogee to it is the second station. **7** What [there is] of the epicycle above, is direct motion, and what is below is retrograde. **8** And the said lines include more of the epicycle when the center of the epicycle is in the apogee of the eccentric, [but] less when it is in the opposite of the apogee: and because of this, the arc of the first station increases from the apogee up to the opposition of the apogee, and therefore the first station is found with the center because [the center] is the elongation of the center of the epicycle from the apogee of the eccentric.[83] **9** And the second [station] is had through the first, because it is the remainder of the epicycle which is from the second station to the first one. **10** Whence, when the first station is subtracted from the 12, the second [station] remains; and because the arc teaches the place of the planet in the epicycle, on account of this there justly comes to be a relationship[84] between the arc and the stations, so that it may be known whether the planet is direct or retrograde or stationary.

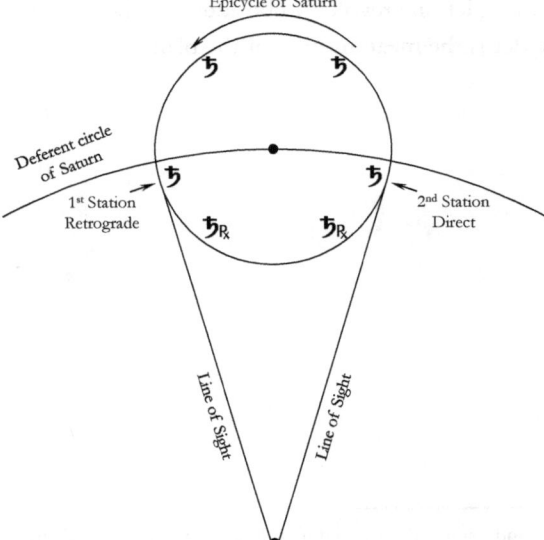

Figure 21: Retrogradation of Saturn (Dykes)

---

[83] That is to say, because retrogradation is based on a planet's true position (i.e., from our line of sight), the apparent length of the retrogradation (and the amount of the epicycle it takes up) will change based on where the epicycle actually is relative to us.
[84] *Collectio.*

11 He[85] who wishes the change the tables for another place than for the middle of the world (which is equally distant from the east and west, and from the northern and southern pole by 90°), should subtract the mean course of the planets if his place is closer to the east, or he should add if [closer to] the west, according to the hours of distance between his own place and that of the middle of the world: and you coordinate[86] this in his root. **12** And the city Arim[87] is held to be in the middle of the world.

13 You will find the distances between the places of the world thus: observe the Moon [at] the southern arc, and equate her by the tables of a known place, and by the difference of the equated place and the observed place of the Moon, is made clear the difference between the places: and thus it is not necessary for you to wait for an eclipse to know that.

14 For[88] a time which is not in the tables, you will find the mean motion thus: take the root of the sums,[89] and again in the expansions of the years among the mean ones which are between the first year of what is summed up and the year which you wanted to know. **15** And subtract[90] from the root if it can be done; if not, let one revolution be added to the root (namely 12 signs), and the remainder is the mean motion of the planet sought.

---

[85] I do not quite understand the procedures described here through the end of the chapter.

[86] Reading *collegis* for *collectis*; nevertheless Leopold's language here is unclear.

[87] Sometimes called "Arin," 'Ujjaīn is a city in India at 23° 10' N, 75° 46' E, and was a standard place from which to cast mundane charts because it was considered the neutral, geographical center of the world: see Pingree 1968, p. 45.

[88] This sentence is opaque to me, especially the use of *colligo / collectio / collectorum*, which must be an attempt to render a difficult Arabic word.

[89] *Collectorum.*

[90] *Extrahe.*

TREATISE III: ON THE PROOF OF THE SCIENCE OF THE STARS

1 Questions[1] are equal to the number of [things which][2] we [can] truly know, which are four: [1] whether it is, [2] what it is, [3] how it is, and [4] on account of what.

2 Certain people,[3] destroying the science of the stars, used to say that [the stars] did not effect anything in things: for if they made a thing come into being, they would not make it be destroyed—but the things in the world which are below the circle of the Moon, do come into being and are destroyed. **3** To whom let it be responded thusly: in this world, the generation of one thing is the destruction of another thing, and *vice versa*—as is clear with fire, whose burning, even though it is the corruption of the wood, is still the generation of charcoal.[4]

4 Other people[5] have said that the planets signify universal things (as are the four elements), and genera and species, but not individuals. **5** Which is to say nothing [at all], because species are preserved *in* individuals, and a man has, from the proper quality of the four elements, at diverse times,[6] the conversion of opposites, increase and diminution; [but] he has nothing of these from the species [itself]. **6** From the planets he has the agreement of the vital and rational soul with the body, and the Sun in particular signifies life, and therefore the brain and heart, along with the partnership of the planets. **7** Mercury [signifies] reasoning and speech, whence the tongue and mouth, with the partnership of the planets. **8** Saturn [signifies] the spleen, Jupiter the liver, Mars the blood, Venus the kidneys and flowing down of the sperm, the Moon the stomach.

9 A third sect[7] says that the stars do not have power over those things which [can tend] toward either [of two possible outcomes]—which is even

---

[1] See *Gr. Intr.* I.3, lines 723-28. In *Gr. Intr.* Abū Ma'shar himself proceeds to discuss each of these in relation to astrology; unfortunately, it contributes nothing to Leopold's chapter.
[2] Reading for the odd *his quicumque* [*quamcumque?*].
[3] This short Treatise concerns various types or "sects" of people who object to astrology; this is the first sect. See my Introduction, and *Gr. Intr.* I.5, lines 1157-1186.
[4] One might also call this the conservation of energy.
[5] This is the second sect. See broadly *Gr. Intr.* I.5, lines 1192-1251, but also I.4, lines 935-39.
[6] Reading in the plural, for "at a different time."
[7] See *Gr. Intr.* I.5, lines 1253-1268, and 1391ff.

an error. **10** Because even though there is necessity and impossibility in natural things, such as heat in fire and cold in snow [which are necessary], and that a man flies and fire is cold [which are impossible], still it is not that way in those things which are from the will and from choice—rather, they are the possible. **11** And the possible is threefold: one tends more towards being than not being, such as rain (when there is cloud cover); another is to the contrary, such as that an ignoble man should become king; a third [tends] equally to each, such as that a man should walk. **12** And the planets do signify the necessary, the impossible, and the possible: the astrologer does not look into necessary things (such as whether a fire becomes hot), nor into impossible things (such as whether fire becomes cold), but possible things.

13 The fourth sect[8] says that the stars have power over nothing except in the alterations of the seasons.[9] **14** But on the contrary let it be responded that the resolution of the elements follows the alteration of the seasons, and the generation and corruption of lower things [follows] this: if therefore the stars have power over the first, they also have power over the things which follow. **15** For knowledge is the fruit of this science, so that when the motion of the circles and planets is known, the proper quality and effect of the seasons in things which come to be in this world may be known. **16** And he who knew the motions and did not know the effects, is like one who has drugs and manufactured medicines, but does not know how to use them; and every such person denies that this science of the stars exists, lest he may be said to know the [the first and] incomplete path of knowledge, and be ignorant of the other.[10]

17 Those of the fifth [sect][11] have said that [the science of the stars] is not known, even if something is understood of the signification of the planets, because they do not return to the places in which they were at the time of [some] experience except after many years.[12] **18** To whom let it be responded that the early sages were experienced, and they left sufficiently tested things

---

[8] See *Gr. Intr.* I.5, lines 1519-1571.

[9] Reading *temporum* with the Latin here and in the next two sentences, for *corporum* ("bodies").

[10] In other words, these critics deny that horoscopic astrology exists, lest they be accused of being deficient because they do not know how to practice it.

[11] See *Gr. Intr.* I.5, lines 1573-1664. Abū Ma'shar is not speaking simply of (say) planetary cycles of so many years, but even the positions of the planets in direct and retrograde motion, etc.

[12] Therefore (Abū Ma'shar says), according to this sect we cannot properly make astrological claims and predictions.

to their posterity, and [the latter] have observed and found that when the planets have returned to the original places the same thing has followed, and [the tested things]¹³ were able to be applied to all differences.

19 The sixth sect¹⁴ speaks against [astrology] because according to different tables [of planetary positions], a different place of the planets is found [in each]: therefore judgment is uncertain. **20** To which let it be responded thusly: the astronomer takes the nature of the planets and their proper qualities, and the lord of the sign of each of them, and that of its exaltation, and the lords of their triplicity, and [their] places in the angles and the succeedents and [their] falling from the angle, and if it is in the house of assets or brothers, etc., [as well as] their significations over climes and the rest of their significations—and *afterwards* he judges.¹⁵

21 The seventh sect¹⁶ speaks against the science of the stars through envy alone, and on account of [their] laziness in investigation. **22** And because these people are nothing, let there be no response to them, because¹⁷ a denier should not speak unless by means of what curtails him and forces him to return to the inevitable truth.

23 The eighth sect,¹⁸ speaking against the science of judgments, is the laziness of medical doctors who have not read the books of the ancients, and say that the science of medicine does not have necessary knowledge of the stars, but in fact is certain and absolute in its own right. **24** But let it be said to them: doesn't the corruption of the weather bring about the corruption of bodies, and isn't the diversity of the atmosphere in bodies because of alteration? **25** But these do not happen except through the strength of the motion of the Sun and the planets. **26** But you reject this when you deny that the knowledge of the stars is necessary for you: therefore you are ignorant of the *causes* of the bodies (which you are seeking): therefore you do not know what is going to be by means of it. **27** And Hippocrates has already said generally how much the science of the stars is a cause of the knowledge of medicine;

---

¹³ Taking *illa* to refer to *experta* in the previous sentence.
¹⁴ See *Gr. Intr.* I.5, lines 1666-1706.
¹⁵ That is, while the exact position is sometimes necessary, astrological judgment covers much more than this.
¹⁶ See *Gr. Intr.* I.5, lines 1757-66.
¹⁷ Reading with the Arabic, as even John's Latin does not quite make sense. The point seems to be that envy drives people to a lack of self-control in their criticisms, because they are not actually focused on the truth, but rather their own feelings.
¹⁸ See *Gr. Intr.* I.5, lines 1768-1839.

and a medical doctor should never get involved in the curing of one about whose health one has lost hope according to the knowledge of the stars. **28** And it is certain that it is important to observe the critical days themselves (that is, the determinations of illness), so that they may know the strength and weakness, increase and diminishment of the disease, which they cannot know except through the course of the Moon and her mixture with the planets: whence, when such people disapprove of the science of the stars, they condemn themselves.

29 The ninth sect on the other hand spoke thusly: if a man had copious assets, not[19] knowing astronomy would not impede him; which, even if they were in their [financial position] deservedly, [they should be] despised. **30** However, let it be responded to them thusly: a man is more worthy than the rest of the animals through wisdom and thinking and the choice of the good and knowledge of what is true, and not through the possession of assets. **31** And the knowledge of a man about present things is great, but especially concerning future things: and by how much more a man recedes from wisdom, he will approach the brute animals by that much. **32** But the knowledge of future things is by means of the science of the stars: therefore the knowledge of future things is preferable to all other things, not assets.

33 The[20] tenth sect rejects the science of the stars on account of the frequent errors into which those judging, fall. **34** But this does not hinder the science, because those who go astray are ignorant of the science. **35** But they themselves count themselves[21] rashly among the number of the sages, so that they may get fame and profit for themselves, not knowing those things which are necessary for this science. **36** An astronomer ought to know this: what is the nature of the planets, their concord and diversity, the diversity of the climes and their condition, the diversity of the elements, the diversity of animals, seeds, metals, and their changing according to the diverse climes—which, if they knew all of the aforesaid, they would not err in judgments.

37 Therefore,[22] now that the aforesaid errors have been rejected, let the science be set down most truthfully. **38** Its usefulness is in escaping foreknown danger, if this is possible; and then either the whole or part of it, and perhaps after time it will cease. **39** And if it cannot be avoided, according to

---

[19] Omitting *quod* and adding *non*, as Leopold has otherwise not captured Abū Ma'shar's meaning here.
[20] See *Gr. Intr.* I.5, lines 1885-1931.
[21] *Se...applicant.*
[22] See *Gr. Intr.* I.6.

this [one may] foresee [it], and in these things even foreknowledge is useful, because the sudden weight of grief makes for a sudden death.[23] **40** Nor should foreknowledge be neglected on account of the terror of future danger, because every joy of this life has an end with grief.[24]

---

[23] Abū Ma'shar means that when we are hit with an unexpected tragedy, we can fall into greater problems due to a lack of proportion and caution, as well as succumb to death from grief (*Gr. Intr.* I.6, lines 2181-87).

[24] Leopold seems to be referring to *Gr. Intr.* I.6, lines 2259ff. The Latin reads: "And if a man declined to make use of every thing which induces grief in the end, it would be necessary for him to not listen to singing: because until the experienced singer is silent, grief will occupy him on account of the cutting-off of the joy and happiness [which was] at the hour of his listening to the song. And he should not be joined to beautiful women, nor eat food with a good flavor, nor drink more delightful things of the different kinds of drinks: because at the hour of the completion of all of these, in the end grief will follow from them on account of the absence of their happiness. And it would be necessary for him not to acquire many assets, because he would hasten to grieve and be sad about their preservation at first, [and] afterwards [that] he would acquire enemies for himself, and the envious, and he would be afraid of them." The point is that *everything* comes to an end, but we should not cease our activities, much less avoid foreknowledge of them, simply because we might be unhappy when they end. Only an unwise person would reject knowledge and *pretend* that pleasure could go on indefinitely.

TREATISE IV: ON THE INTRODUCTORY MATTERS OF JUDGMENTS

[Introduction]

1 This[1] fourth Treatise is divided into five parts:
  2 The first is on the signs and houses.
  3 The second, on the planets.
  4 The third, on the planets' bearings[2] in themselves and with respect to the signs.
  5 The fourth is on the [specialized] terms whose understanding is necessary in judgments.
  6 The fifth, on the Lots of the planets and houses, and certain other ones.

[Chapter IV.1: The signs and houses]

1 There[3] are twelve signs, as were posited above, whose triplicities are four. **2** For some are fiery: Aries, Leo, Sagittarius. **3** Others, earthy: Taurus, Virgo, Capricorn. **4** Others, airy: Gemini, Libra, Aquarius. **5** Others, watery: Cancer, Scorpio, Pisces.

Fiery	♈	♌	♐
Earthy	♉	♍	♑
Airy	♊	♎	♒
Watery	♋	♏	♓

Figure 22: Signs of the triplicities (Dykes)

---

[1] This division is based on al-Qabīsī, I.1.
[2] *Habitudine.* This refers to various conditions and configurations of the planets.
[3] See al-Qabīsī I.16.

6 And[4] the fiery and watery ones (which are opposites) are well placed at the extremes. **7** But the earthy ones are close to the fiery ones, because dryness is [akin to][5] heat, and thus to the airy ones remains the third place.

8 Those[6] which are from Aries up to Libra are northern, because they rise on this side[7] of the equator; from Libra to Aries [they are] southern, because they rise beyond the equator.

9 Aries[8] is masculine, Taurus feminine, and thus with all the rest of them.

10 There[9] are four movable signs: Aries, Cancer, Libra, Capricorn. **11** Four fixed ones: Taurus, Leo, Scorpio, and Aquarius. **12** Four common ones: Gemini, Virgo, Sagittarius, and Pisces. **13** And the movable ones signal quickness, the fixed ones stability, the common ones alteration.

14 There[10] are six rising straight: from [the beginning of] Cancer to [the beginning of] Capricorn; crookedly, from Capricorn to Cancer.

15 The obeying[11] [signs] are the crooked ones, [and they obey] the straight: like Cancer-Gemini, Taurus-Leo, and likewise with the others.[12]

16 The ones[13] agreeing [in the path] are equally distant from the beginning of Aries, and these have equal ascensions.[14]

17 The fiery[15] and airy ones are hot, diurnal, masculine. **18** The earthy and watery ones are cold, nocturnal, feminine.

19 Aries signifies domestic animals, Taurus wild human ones, Gemini men, Cancer watery [animals], Leo forest [animals], Virgo men, Libra men,

---

[4] See *Gr. Intr.* II.5, lines 338-45. This paragraph is about why the order of signs is fiery, earthy, airy, watery, as opposed to the descending natural order: fire, air, water, earth. In this theory, heat and cold are the two major, active qualities, and they predominate in fire and water; dryness and moisture are the minor, passive qualities, and they predominate in earth and air. Heat is the major principle allowing life and so comes first, while cold is the major principle destroying life, and so comes last (*Gr. Intr.* II.4, 300-315). But between the passive qualities, dryness (earth) is more like fire, and moisture (air) more like water, so these elements were placed closer to those active elements (*ibid.*, 346-48).
[5] Reading *affinis* with John's Latin, for *lima*.
[6] See al-Qabīsī, I.8.
[7] Leopold means "the northern" side, because he is in the northern hemisphere.
[8] See al-Qabīsī I.17, and Sahl's *Introduction* §1 (in *WSM*).
[9] See Sahl's *Introduction* §1 (in *WSM*).
[10] See al-Qabīsī, I.8. This is in the northern hemisphere; in the southern hemisphere these categories are reversed.
[11] See al-Qabīsī, I.8.
[12] So, in the northern hemisphere Gemini obeys Cancer, Taurus obeys Leo, and so on.
[13] See al-Qabīsī, I.9.
[14] So, Aries and Pisces agree in the path, also Taurus-Aquarius, and so on. See the figure after **55** below, showing signs with the same ascensions.
[15] See al-Qabīsī, I.16.

Scorpio savage [animals], the first half of Sagittarius, men, Capricorn forest animals, Aquarius men, Pisces fish.

20 The rational[16] (that is, human ones) are Gemini, Virgo, Libra, and Aquarius, and the first half of Sagittarius. **21** The domestic ones are Aries, Taurus, Capricorn. **22** The voluptuous ones are Aries, Taurus, Leo, Capricorn.

23 Those[17] of few children are Aries, Taurus, Libra, Sagittarius; those of many, Cancer, Scorpio, Pisces; the sterile ones, Gemini, Leo, Virgo, and the beginning of Taurus. **24** Those of twins are the common ones and the last half of Capricorn.

25 Gemini belongs to magnates, Aquarius to nobles, Capricorn, Libra, [and] Sagittarius the middle class, Aries and Gemini with their triplicities belong to nobles, Taurus and Cancer with their triplicities to ignoble people.

26 Leo in particular is difficult.[18] **27** Pisces signals arthritis of the foot.

28 Fixed[19] signs signify respectable women, movable ones signify unstable ones, common ones those in the middle.

29 Those[20] with limbs cut off are Aries, Leo, Scorpio.

30 Those[21] with loud voices are Gemini, Virgo, Libra; middle ones in this are Aries, Taurus, Leo, Sagittarius; weak ones, Capricorn, Aquarius; those lacking in voice, Cancer and its triplicity. **31** And if in a nativity the lord of the Ascendant or the Moon or the victor were there,[22] the native's tongue will be impeded, and perhaps he will be deaf and a stammerer.

32 The[23] Pleiades of Taurus signify pain of the eyes, as do the clouds of Cancer and the sting of Scorpio, and the arrow of Sagittarius, and the tail of Capricorn. **33** The falling of water in Aquarius signifies inflammation of the eyes, and Libra and Leo might impede the eyes.

34 The[24] signs of learning and cleverness are Leo, Sagittarius, Capricorn, and Aquarius. **35** Signs of grief are Leo, Scorpio, Capricorn. **36** And the signs of grief are the dark ones, and in Virgo and Libra the darkness is moderate.

---

[16] See al-Qabīsī, I.24.
[17] See *Gr. Intr.* VI.16.
[18] This must be a health-related reference, but I am not sure of its source.
[19] See *Gr. Intr.* VI.15.
[20] See *Gr. Intr.* VI.17.
[21] See *Gr. Intr.* VI.18.
[22] That is, in signs lacking a voice.
[23] See *Gr. Intr.* VI.20. See the table at the end of this chapter for identifying the modern location of these.
[24] See *Gr. Intr.* VI.21.

37 Gemini, Virgo, Sagittarius, Pisces, and the second face of Capricorn (because the Flying Vulture[25] is there, and the tail of the Hen)[26] signify birds. **38** Those of four-footed animals are Aries, Taurus, Leo, and the last half of Sagittarius, and the first one of Capricorn. **39** Those of serpents are Cancer, Scorpio, Sagittarius, and Capricorn, and [they are also] those of scorpions and creeping things and every land of unclean things.

40 Those[27] of tall trees are Gemini, Leo, Libra, and Aquarius; and other ones, Cancer, Scorpio, and the last half of Pisces. **41** Those of seeds are Taurus and its triplicity: Taurus of planting, Virgo of growth, Capricorn of har- harvesting.

42 The[28] half of the Sun is from Leo to Aquarius; the remaining one belongs to the Moon.

43 The[29] hot half is from Aries to Libra, beyond that the cold one.

44 The[30] descending half is from the Midheaven to the fourth house, the ascending one from the fourth to the tenth.

45 The quarter[31] from Aries to Cancer is hot and moist; to Libra, hot and dry; to Capricorn, cold and dry; to Aries, cold and moist.

46 The eastern[32] quarter is from the Midheaven to the first, and it is masculine. **47** The southern [is] from the seventh to the Midheaven, and it is feminine. **48** The western [is] from the fourth to the seventh, masculine. **49** The northern [is] from the first to the fourth, and it is feminine.

50 In[33] the eastern quarter, [planets] signify hours; in the southern one, months; in the western, years, in the northern, days—because the ascending half is quick, and the descending one is slow. **51** And the ascending half is from the fourth [to the Ascendant] to the tenth, the descending one from the tenth to [the Descendant to] the fourth.

---

[25] The constellation Aquila.
[26] The Hen is the constellation Cygnus.
[27] See *Gr. Intr.* VI.23.
[28] See al-Qabīsī I.10.
[29] See al-Qabīsī I.10.
[30] See al-Qabīsī I.56. I have reversed the attributions of this sentence as well as **51** below, which originally made the ascending half the region from the tenth down to the fourth (and vice versa).
[31] See al-Qabīsī I.11.
[32] See al-Qabīsī I.56.
[33] See Sahl's *On Times* §3 (in *WSM*).

52 And all the signs, everywhere they divide the heaven in half, as in the right circle.³⁴ **53** And under the equinoctial line likewise ascend Aries-Pisces [and] Libra-Virgo. **54** Moreover Taurus-Aquarius, [and] Leo-Scorpio; and likewise Gemini-Capricorn [and] Cancer-Sagittarius. **55** See the ascensions of the equator, with the signs whose degrees are said to be equal in the climes, in the tables of ascensions through the climes.

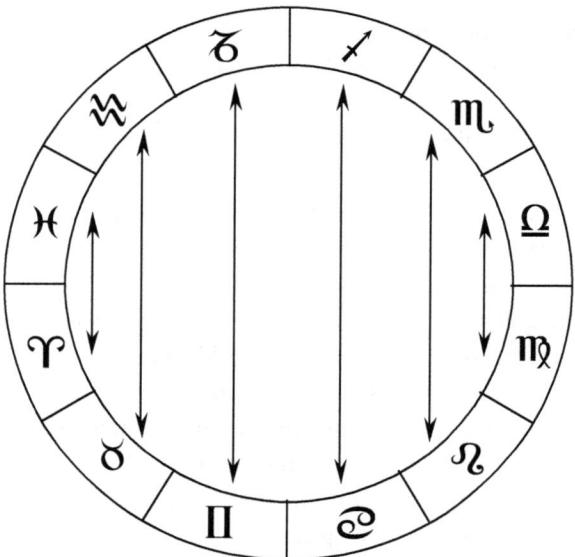

Figure 23: Signs with same ascensions (Dykes)

56 The³⁵ first quarter signifies soul, and in colors the white. **57** The second, neither body nor soul, and in colors the green. **58** The third quarter, body and soul, and black. **59** The fourth, only the body, and red.

60 And the four quarters respond to the four elements, and the four regions of the world, and the four winds, and the four ages (childhood, and youth, the manly age, and senility), and the quarters of the day and quarters of the night.

---

³⁴ That is, in ascensions of the celestial equator. In this paragraph, Leopold describes what signs have identical numbers of ascensional times: namely, those which are opposite each other across the equinoctial line (Pisces-Aries, etc.) For a table of ascensions arranged by latitude (**55**), see my site (www.bendykes.com).
³⁵ This paragraph is drawn from *Gr. Intr.* VI.27 and VI.29.

61 Some say that the hours of blood are from the tenth hour of night up to the fourth hour of the day; from thence six of choler, from thence six of black bile, from thence six of phlegm.

62 The world began from a Sunday,[36] and the Sun ascended in the first minute of Aries.[37]

63 Aries has the head and face, Germany and Britain. **64** Taurus, the neck, trees and plants, Asia Minor. **65** Gemini, the shoulders and arms, Greater Armenia, and Egypt. **66** Cancer, the chest and lungs, Africa, Babylon, and France. **67** Leo, the heart, sides, the stomach and back, Turkey and Damascus. **68** Virgo, the thighs and intestines of the belly, and Tela[38] and Greece. **69** Libra, tall trees, the loins, navel, pubic region, hips,[39] high places, and the land of the Romans and Greater Ethiopia. **70** Scorpio, the private parts and testicles, the bladder and anus, and hunts, Arabia and Khurāsān. **71** Sagittarius has the hips, mountains, and places of fire, Spain, Sicily, the Gardens,[40] and Palestine. **72** Capricorn, the knees and Macedonia. **73** Aquarius, the legs, shins, and the west, and Venetian rivers,[41] and Syria. **74** Pisces, the feet and northern parts, and Alexandria and the lands of the Angles. **75** Those of these which are fiery signify mountains, the earthy ones [have signification] over cultivated places, the airy ones over sandy places, the watery ones over moist and watery places.

[The houses][42]

76 There are twelve houses. **77** The first is the house whose beginning arises or ascends in the east at the hour of the interrogation or nativity or the inception of some work. **78** And this signifies life and the weakness of life, because it is the Ascendant of the life of someone, since it precedes his life while he goes out from the belly of his mother: for this sign ascends from the lower part of the earth to the upper one of it, and from darkness to the light of this world, and from the narrowness of the uterus to the breadth of the

---

[36] Reading *dominica* for *dnica*. In this case, the day of rest would be Saturday (as in the Jewish tradition).
[37] This is a Persian tradition.
[38] Unknown.
[39] Reading *anchas* for *authas*.
[40] *Viridaria*, I do not know if this refers to anywhere in particular.
[41] Reading tentatively for *flimina* [sic] *veneta*.
[42] For this section, see Sahl's *Introduction* §§3-4 (in *WSM*).

air. **79** And it shows one asking his question from the secret of his own heart, and it illuminates and uncovers what was previously hidden. **80** Therefore, it signifies bodies and life and every beginning and motion. **81** The[43] lord of this, and the Moon, if they were impeded by the conjunction, square aspect, or opposite aspect of the bad ones, if a fortune is joined from the square aspect it dissolves all the evil.

82 The second [house signifies] assets and the gathering and storing of them, and the cause of [one's] means of livelihood, and the situation of its giving and taking.

83 The third: brothers and their condition, sisters, older kin.

84 The fourth: fathers, prison, buildings, lands, hidden things, storehouses, death, and what follows burial and burning.

85 The fifth: children, delights, and legates.

86 The sixth: infirmity, slaves, and changing from place to place.

87 The seventh: contentions, women, and contrarieties.

88 The eighth: deaths, killings, [and] the instructions and assets of the dead. **89** In[44] this house a planet is said to be a murderer, and a fortune there does neither good nor bad; a bad one there magnifies evil.

90 The ninth: foreign travels, religions, dreams, divinations.

91 The tenth: loftiness, rulership, judges, the nobility, glory, boldness, mastery, works, and mothers.[45]

92 The eleventh: trust, the good fortune of friends, praise, and ministers.

93 The twelfth: limitation, enemies, labors in productive things, and animals.

94 And the first, tenth, seventh, fourth, are angular or pivots. **95** The second, fifth, eighth, and eleventh [are] the succeedents. **96** The twelfth, ninth, sixth, third, [are] falling or withdrawing. **97** And a planet after the angle within 5° is like one which is in the angles.

98 Sahl b. Bishr the Israelite said, the stronger one of all the places of the circle is the Ascendant, and this sign is more worthy than all the signs, and a planet which was in it is stronger than all the planets, especially if it was in its own house or exaltation or triplicity or bound or its own face. **99** Then follows in strength the angle of heaven, then the western angle (that is, the seventh from the Ascendant), after that the angle of the earth (that is, the

---

[43] This is from Sahl's *Fifty Judgments* (#36).
[44] Apart from the bit about being a murderer, this sentence is from Sahl's *Judgments* (#43).
[45] "Mothers" does not appear in the Arabic.

fourth from the Ascendant). **100** After this, there follows in strength the eleventh house, then the fifth, after that the ninth.

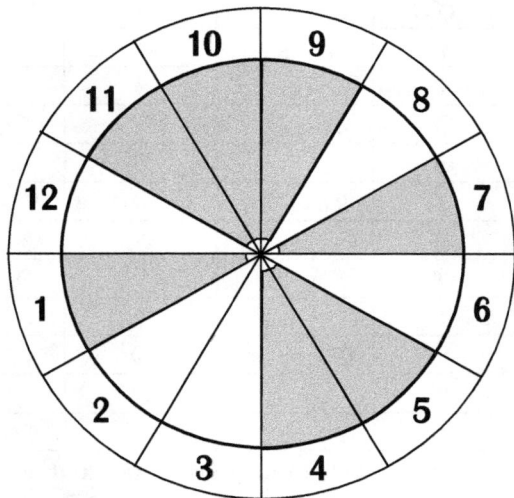

Figure 24: Seven advantageous places, in gray (Dykes)

101 These are the good places,[46] and strong, among which the first place is better than the second one, the second one [better] than the third one, and so on. And after this the third from the Ascendant is chosen because it is the place of the joy of the Moon, then the second place from the Ascendant because it ascends after the Ascendant. **102** However, in the eighth sign is misfortune, because it is the house of death. **103** But the sixth and the twelfth are the worst, and a planet in them does not benefit.

---

[46] Also known as busy or advantageous places (*ITA* III.3-4). These places are especially advantageous or good for the native (or whoever is represented by the Ascendant), because all of these signs are configured by some aspect to the Ascendant. There is also an eight-place system of good or advantageous houses, namely the angles and succeedents (as planets are particularly stimulated there): again, see *ITA*.

[Degrees and dignities in the signs]

	Domicile	Exaltation	Detriment	Fall
♈	♂	☉ (esp. 19°)	♀	♄ (esp. 21°)
♉	♀	☽ (esp. 3°)	♂	
♊	☿	☊ (esp. 3°)	♃	
♋	☽	♃ (esp. 15°)	♄	♂ (esp. 28°)
♌	☉		♄	
♍	☿	☿ (esp. 15°)	♃	♀ (esp. 27°)
♎	♀	♄ (esp. 21°)	♂	☉ (esp. 19°)
♏	♂		♀	☽ (esp. 3°)
♐	♃	☋ (esp. 3°)	☿	
♑	♄	♂ (esp. 28°)	☽	♃ (esp. 15°)
♒	♄		☉	
♓	♃	♀ (esp. 27°)	☿	☿ (esp. 15°)

Figure 25: Table of major dignities and counter-dignities (Dykes)[47]

104 The signs are distributed among the planets thus, so that to every one is given two (but one to the Sun, [and] one to the Moon): Aries and Scorpio to Mars, Taurus and Libra to Venus, Gemini and Virgo to Mercury, Sagittarius and Pisces to Jupiter, Capricorn and Aquarius to Saturn, Leo to the Sun, Cancer to the Moon. **105** And these are the houses of the planets.

106 The place[48] of the Sun's exaltation is Aries, 19°; the Moon's, 3° Taurus; the Head of the Dragon of the Moon, 3° Gemini;[49] Jupiter, 15° Cancer; Mercury, 15° Virgo; Saturn, 21° Libra;[50] Mars, 28° Capricorn; Venus, 27° Pisces.

107 The bounds[51] of the planets are these, and they are those of Hermes, and Abū Ma'shar judges through them:[52]

---

[47] In traditional texts there is widespread inconsistency between cardinal and ordinal numbers. For example, the exaltation of the Sun is variously given as "nineteen" degrees (19°), and the "nineteenth" degree (18°). My sense is that the authors probably meant "at the end of the nineteenth degree, namely at 19°."

[48] See al-Qabīsī I.15.

[49] The exaltation of the Nodes is a Persian concept (perhaps influenced by India), and not Hellenistic.

[50] Reading for *27*.

[51] See al-Qabīsī I.19.

♈	♃ 0°-5°59'	♀ 6°-11°59'	☿ 12°-19°59'	♂ 20°-24°59'	♄ 25°-29°59'
♉	♀ 0°-7°59'	☿ 8°-13°59'	♃ 14°-21°59'	♄ 22°-26°59'	♂ 27°-29°59'
♊	☿ 0°-5°59'	♃ 6°-11°59'	♀ 12°-16°59'	♂ 17°-23°59'	♄ 24°-29°59'
♋	♂ 0°-6°59'	♀ 7°-12°59'	☿ 13°-18°59'	♃ 19°-25°59'	♄ 26°-29°59'
♌	♃ 0°-5°59'	♀ 6°-10°59'	♄ 11°-17°59'	☿ 18°-23°59'	♂ 24°-29°59'
♍	☿ 0°-6°59'	♀ 7°-16°59'	♃ 17°-20°59'	♂ 21°-27°59'	♄ 28°-29°59'
♎	♄ 0°-5°59'	☿ 6°-13°59'	♃ 14°-20°59'	♀ 21°-27°59'	♂ 28°-29°59'
♏	♂ 0°-6°59'	♀ 7°-10°59'	☿ 11°-18°59'	♃ 19°-23°59'	♄ 24°-29°59'
♐	♃ 0°-11°59'	♀ 12°-16°59'	☿ 17°-20°59'	♄ 21°-25°59'	♂ 26°-29°59'
♑	☿ 0°-6°59'	♃ 7°-13°59'	♀ 14°-21°59'	♄ 22°-25°59'	♂ 26°-29°59'
♒	☿ 0°-6°59'	♀ 7°-12°59'	♃ 13°-19°59'	♂ 20°-24°59'	♄ 25°-29°59'
♓	♀ 0°-11°59'	♃ 12°-15°59'	☿ 16°-18°59'	♂ 19°-27°59'	♄ 28°-29°59'

Figure 26: Table of Egyptian bounds (Dykes)

108 The lords[53] of the fiery triplicity are the Sun [and] Jupiter in the day, and conversely in the night; the partner is Saturn. **109** The earthy one, Venus and the Moon in the day, conversely in the night, and the partner is Mars. **110** The airy one, Saturn and Mercury in the day, conversely in the night, and the partner is Jupiter. **111** The watery one, Venus and Mars in the day, conversely in the night, the partner is the Moon.

	Diurnal	Nocturnal	Partnering
Fire	☉	♃	♄
Air	♄	☿	♃
Water	♀	♂	☽
Earth	♀	☽	♂

Figure 27: Dorothean triplicity lords (Dykes)

112 Every[54] sign has three faces, which consist of 10°. **113** The lords of the faces of Aries are Mars, the Sun, Venus, of Taurus Mercury, the Moon, Saturn, etc., and extend [them] thus through all the faces of the signs. **114**

---

[52] I have put Leopold's table in a slightly different form, listing the actual degrees for each bound. For example, the bound of Mercury in Taurus comprised the six degrees from 8°-13° 59' (up to 14°), whereas Leopold only reads "6."
[53] See al-Qabīsī I.16.
[54] See al-Qabīsī I.20.

And when you are lacking [any more] planets, begin from the beginning of them.[55]

A	♂ 0°-9°59'	☉ 10°-19°59'	♀ 20°-29°59'
♉	☿ 0°-9°59'	☽ 10°-19°59'	♄ 20°-29°59'
♊	♃ 0°-9°59'	♂ 10°-19°59'	☉ 20°-29°59'
♋	♀ 0°-9°59'	☿ 10°-19°59'	☽ 20°-29°59'
♌	♄ 0°-9°59'	♃ 10°-19°59'	♂ 20°-29°59'
♍	☉ 0°-9°59'	♀ 10°-19°59'	☿ 20°-29°59'
♎	☽ 0°-9°59'	♄ 10°-19°59'	♃ 20°-29°59'
♏	♂ 0°-9°59'	☉ 10°-19°59'	♀ 20°-29°59'
♐	☿ 0°-9°59'	☽ 10°-19°59'	♄ 20°-29°59'
♑	♃ 0°-9°59'	♂ 10°-19°59'	☉ 20°-29°59'
♒	♀ 0°-9°59'	☿ 10°-19°59'	☽ 20°-29°59'
♓	♄ 0°-9°59'	♃ 10°-19°59'	♂ 20°-29°59'

Figure 28: Chaldean faces or decans (Dykes)

115 And when[56] a planet is in its own house, it is like a man in his own home. **116** In the exaltation, just like a king in [his] kingdom. **117** In the bounds, just like one among [his] relatives.[57] **118** In the triplicity, just like one among [his] supporters. **119** In the face, just like one in his own mastery and work.

120 And a planet[58] in its own house has 5 strengths, in the exaltation 4, and thus by descending down to one.

---

[55] Leopold simply means that when one reaches the Moon, start again from Saturn, Jupiter, Mars, etc. (as with Taurus, in **113**).
[56] See al-Qabīsī I.23.
[57] *Parentes.*
[58] See al-Qabīsī I.22. Leopold follows the later or "newer" Arabic authors (such as Abū Ma'shar) in assigning points to the dignities of a planet as shown in the right column below. But an older approach gives more points to the bounds than to the primary triplicity lord, as shown in the center column. For example, let the Ascendant be at 1° Pisces in a nocturnal chart. In the older system, the domicile lord of Pisces (Jupiter) gets 5, the exalted lord Venus 4, the bound lord Venus 3, the nocturnal triplicity lord Mars 2, and the face lord Saturn 1: Venus is the victor, with 7 points. But in the newer system the points for the bound and triplicity lords are switched: in this case Venus is still the victor, but now with 6 points.

	Older (Māshā'allāh)	Newer (Abū Ma'shar, Leopold)
House (Domicile)	5	5
Exaltation	4	4
Triplicity	2	3
Bound	3	2
Face	1	1

Figure 29: Points for weighted victors (Dykes)

121 Which degrees of the signs are masculine or feminine, follows:[59]

♈	M 8	F 1	M 6	F 7	M 8		
♉	F 5	M 6	F 6	M 4	F 3	M 6	
♊	F 5	M 11	F 6	M 4	F 4		
♋	M 2	F 6	M 2	F 2	M 10	F 4	M 4
♌	M 5	F 3	M 7	F 8	M 7		
♍	F 8	M 4	F 8	M 10			
♎	M 5	F 10	M 5	F 7	M 3		
♏	M 4	F 10	M 3	F 8	M 5		
♐	M 2	F 3	M 7	F 12	M 6		
♑	M 11	F 8	M 11				
♒	M 5	F 10	M 6	F 4	M 2	F 3	
♓	M 10	F 10	M 3	F 5	M 2		

Figure 30: Masculine and feminine degrees (Leopold)

122 If planets[60] were in the aforesaid masculine degrees, they signify the strength of things; but in the female ones, weakness.

123 Moreover, [the following table] denotes the bright (B), dark (D), and empty (E) [degrees]:[61]

---

[59] The following table sometimes differs greatly from the accounts of al-Qabīsī and Abū Ma'shar (who do not agree with each other): see *ITA* VII.8.
[60] See *Gr. Intr.* V.19. But Abū Ma'shar does not say that *any* planet in such degrees will be strengthened or weakened: he means that if a planet is in a degree whose gender matches that of the *native* or the *querent*, it will be stronger due to the gender match.

♈	D 3	B 5	D 8	B 4	E 4	B 5	E 1
♉	D 3	B 7	E 2	B 8	D 5	B 3	E 2[62]
♊	B 7	D 2	B 5	E 3	B 6	D 7	
♋	D 7	B 5	D 2	B 4	D 2	B 8	D 2
♌	B 7	D 3	D 6	E 5	B 9		
♍	D 5	B 4	E 2	B 6	D 4	B 7	E 2
♎	B 5	D 5	B 8	D 3	B 7	E 2	
♏	D 3	B 5	E 6	B 6	D 3	B 5	D 2
♐	B 9	D 3	B 7	D 4	B 7		
♑	D 7	B 3	D 5	B 4	D 2[63]	E 4	B 5
♒	D 4	B 5	D 4	B 8	E 4	B 5	
♓	D 6	B 6	D 6	B 4	E 3	B 3	D 2

Figure 31: Degrees in the signs (Leopold)

124 And planets[64] in the bright degrees signify good, beauty, profit, and good fortune; in the dark ones, harshness, slowness, and a horrible thing; in the empty ones, a little bit horrible.

125 The wells are [the following degrees]:[65]

♈	6th	11th	17th	24th	25th	
♉	5th	12th	14th	24th	25th	26th
♊	2nd	12th	17th	26th	30th	
♋	12th	18th	24th	26th	30th	
♌	7th	13th	15th	22nd	23rd	28th

---

[61] Leopold's table below (with minor corrections) differs greatly at points from al-Qabīsī, his putative source; note also that in Leo, Leopold follows dark degrees with other dark degrees. Moreover, Leopold has omitted an entire category of degrees, the "smoky," often simply calling them dark. But since few astrologers agree on these degrees, and since they are hardly ever used in practice, nor is their precise origin known, all of these discrepancies should probably not concern us.

[62] Reading for Leopold's "3," else the sign would have 31°.

[63] Reading for Leopold's "3," else the sign would have 31°.

[64] See *Gr. Intr.* V.20.

[65] The following table departs in so many ways from al-Qabīsī and Abū Ma'shar (*ITA* VII.9), that I have let it stand. In English-language Renaissance astrology, these are usually referred to as the "pitted" degrees; when planets or special degrees are in them, they are assumed to be weak, like someone who has fallen down a well. Their origin is unknown to me, but it likely has to do with fixed star positions. Please note that these are ordinal numbers: so, the "1st" degree of Libra is really 0°-59' Libra; likewise "30th" means 29°-29° 59'.

TREATISE IV: ON THE INTRODUCTORY MATTERS OF JUDGMENTS   101

♍	8th	13th	16th	21st	25th	
♎	1st	7th	20th	30th		
♏	8th	17th	22nd	27th		
♐	7th	12th	15th	24th	27th	30th
♑	2nd	7th	17th	23rd	24th	28th
♒	12th	17th	19th	24th	28th	
♓	4th	8th	24th	27th	28th	

Figure 32: The welled degrees (Leopold)

126 There are even degrees increasing good fortune in the signs:[66]

♈	19				
♉	3	15	17		
♊	11	5			
♋	1	2	7	15	
♌	2	5	7	19	
♍	3	13	20		
♎	3	5	13		
♏	5	18	20		
♐	12	20			
♑	12	13	24		
♒	4	16	17	20	
♓	13	15			

Figure 33: Degrees increasing fortune (Leopold)

---

[66] This list differs in so many ways from those by al-Qabīsī and Abū Ma'shar (*ITA* VII.9.3), that I have let it stand. Their origin is unknown to me, as well as whether Leopold means these to be ordinal degrees or cardinal: such as whether "1" Cancer means the "1st" degree (0°-59'), or 1°-1° 59'. Al-Qabīsī and Abū Ma'shar seem to mean the former.

127 For if⁶⁷ significators were in these degrees (such as the Moon or Lot of Fortune), or they were ascending, they make [matters] fortunate and lofty.

128 There are⁶⁸ even degrees which are called *azemene*,⁶⁹ that is, "weakness."

♈	6, 7, 8, 9, 10
♉	8, 9
♋	15
♌	15, 27, 28
♏	19, 29
♐	17, 18, 19
♑	27, 28, 29
♒	18, 20

Figure 34: Degrees of chronic illness (Leopold)

129 And in the signs are certain degrees which are called *azemene* for the body, such as is deafness, blindness, the loss of limbs—if the Moon or a planet was in them in the nativity of any child:⁷⁰

♉	7, 9, 10, 11
♋	7, 11, 12, 13, 14, 15, 16
♌	19, 28, 29
♏	10, 19, 20
♒	10, 19, 20

Figure 35: Degrees of bodily chronic illness (Leopold)

130 …this is according to Abraham ibn Ezra.⁷¹ **131** But elsewhere [they are listed as]:⁷²

---

⁶⁷ See *Gr. Intr.* V.22 and *ITA* VII.9.
⁶⁸ See al-Qabīsī I.52, and *ITA* VII.10.
⁶⁹ This comes from the Ar. *al-zamīn*, "chronic illness." Again, al-Qabīsī and Abū Ma'shar seem to take these as ordinal numbers (*ITA* VII.10).
⁷⁰ The next two tables list tropical degree positions in the signs, but they apparently derive from fixed stars or star clusters themselves: after the tables I provide a list of them (with modern positions) based on the so-called *Book of Aristotle* or *BA* (in *PN1*), which derive from Dorotheus and Rhetorius.
⁷¹ Source unknown at this time.
⁷² The following seems to be drawn (and partly misunderstood) from al-Qabīsī (*ITA* VII.10).

TREATISE IV: ON THE INTRODUCTORY MATTERS OF JUDGMENTS

Sign	Degrees
♉	6, 7, 8, 9, 10
♋	7, 9 to 15 inclusive
♌	18, 27, 28
♏	19, 29
♐	17, 18, 19
♑	26, 27, 28, 29
♒	18, 19

Figure 36: **Degrees of bodily chronic illness (Leopold)**

Constellation in *BA*	Name of stars/clusters	Modern zodiacal positions (2010)
Taurus	Pleiades	29° ♉ 26' (Alcyone)
Cancer	Praesepe (nebula in Cancer)	About 7° ♌
Leo	Coma Berenice	Around 8° ♎ (Diadem)
Scorpio	Face and sting of Scorpio	Face: around 2° ♐ (Graffias) Sting: around 25°-28° ♐ (Aculeus, Acumen)
Sagittarius	Point of Arrow in Sagittarius	About 0° 30' ♑ (al Nasl)
Capricorn	Spine (ε, κ) of Capricorn[73]	Around 13° ♒ (Dorsum, θ Cap.)
Aquarius	Pitcher of Aquarius	Around 6° ♓

Figure 37: **Fixed star degrees of chronic illness (from *BA*)**[74]

---

[73] That is, according to Burnett and Pingree.
[74] These positions derive from *Carmen* IV.1.108-11 and Rhetorius Ch. 61.

Chapter IV.2: Introduction to the natures of the planets

Figure 38: Sol

1 The Sun[75] is the authority of the day, a fortune, temperately hot and dry, he has authority in the soul and life and honor, and in the right side of the body, all [power] in the heart and brain, in the right eye in the day (in the left one in the night), he is good in the sextile and trine aspect, he is bad in the square and opposite. **2** Masculine, stronger than all the planets, his color is white,[76] his taste sweet, his glow 12° in front and behind,[77] the significator of the living and mundane soul, and the purgation of bodies inside and out, and of much gold.

3 Mixed with Saturn, he signifies the management of an estate, if Jupiter a principal place in faith and religion, if Mars the leadership of an army, if Venus rulership and women, if Mercury counselors and books, if the Moon legates.

4 In men the right eye, in women the left, and he has the heart, the marrow, and thighs, diseases in the mouth, the occurrence of water in the eye.[78]
5 According to the Indians, if he is in the Ascendant [the native] will have a

---

[75] This chapter is based on al-Qabīsī IV.18-24.
[76] The Ar. has "transparent."
[77] This should be 15°.
[78] That is, cataracts. Reading *descensum* (lit. "descent") as the typical Arabic "fall," which also means "to occur."

mark on his face. **6** And according to Dorotheus, the hair on the head [is] a little red, eyes a little saffron.

7 And he is a significator of praises, kings, authorities, and fathers.

8 The years of the authority of his *firdaria* are 10, the greatest years are 1461, the great ones 120, the middle ones 39 ½,[79] and the small ones 19.

	Lesser	Middle	Greater	Greatest
♄	30	43 ½	57	275[80]
♃	12	45 ½	79	427
♂	15	40 ½	66	284
☉	19	39 ½	120	1,461
♀	8	45	82	1,151
☿	20	48	76	480
☽	25	39 ½	108	520

Figure 39: Table of planetary years (Dykes)

---

[79] Adding ½ with al-Qabīsī. As Burnett and Yamamoto point out, the middle years for the Sun (reflected in numerous Arabic sources) is actually the average of his lesser years and *half* of his greater years: (19 + 60) / 2 = 39.5. But many Latin manuscripts use the average of the lesser and greater (69.5).

[80] Reading with al-Qabīsī for 265.

Figure 40: Luna

9 The Moon[81] [is] a fortune, female, nocturnal,[82] and signifies bodies and seeds.

10 And with a fortune she signifies respectability and rulership and allegiance. **11** With Mars the practice of whispering, with Saturn envy, with the Sun the management of royal things, with Mercury wisdom. **12** And in the night she has the right eye, in the day the left one, and planting.[83] **13** With Saturn, grief, with Jupiter reason, with Mars anger and hastiness, with Venus joy and fun, with Mercury learning. **14** Her color is whitish, in nature moderately cold and moist.

15 (I will put the quality of the atmosphere according to the quarters of the month, in the Treatise on the changing of the atmosphere.)[84]

16 She has mothers, sisters, and the wives of men, the stomach and lung, part of the brain, and the left side of a man by day,[85] the right eye in the night (and *vice versa*), powerful in infirmities, inceptions, interrogations, and thoughts. **17** [Of animals and minerals, she has a signification] in cows, cattle, and silver.

---

[81] This somewhat disorganized section is roughly based on al-Qabīsī II.36-40 (see *ITA* V.7), and Sahl's *Fifty Judgments* (in *WSM*).
[82] Adding with al-Qabīsī for Leopold's puzzling *legit*.
[83] This may be due to the practice of planting according to the phases of the Moon, but it does not appear in al-Qabīsī.
[84] See perhaps the centers of the Moon (Ch. VI.2).
[85] Reading *per diem* for *mediam*.

18 The Moon is impeded if she is eclipsed (and more seriously so if she is burned in the sign of the root),[86] or if found under the rays, [or] if conjoined to the bad ones, if in the twelfth house, if with the Head or Tail within 12°, if descending in the south,[87] if in the burnt path, if at the end of the signs in the bounds of the bad ones, if empty in course, if slower in course (that is, in less than [her] average course), if in the ninth house from the Ascendant. **19** Her rays in front and behind are 12°.

20 The years of [her] *firdaria* are 9, her greatest years are 520, the greater ones 108, the middle ones 39 ½,[88] and the lesser ones 25.

21 The Moon[89] is a significator of all things, and she hands over her own management to the one on whom she projects [her] rays, and she changes her being to the one to which she is conjoined. **22** And [the other planet] is the acceptor of the management, and she is the reporter [of it], and she pushes to them and she carries [it] away from certain ones to other ones.

23 The[90] Moon in an empty course impedes.[91]

24 The conjunction[92] of the Moon signifies what is going to be, according to the disposition of the one accepting [the application].

25 A planet[93] is not said to be impeded unless a bad one projects rays upon its light; and if it crossed over [it] by one complete degree, it does not impede the good (and it is likewise with respect to a good one).[94] **26** An impeding [planet that is] falling away from the Ascendant does not impede, likewise a good [planet] in a good [place].

27 When[95] the Moon is in one minute with a planet, it signifies what is going to be from the planet to which she is conjoined.

---

[86] That is, the nativity.
[87] This must be in ecliptical latitude.
[88] Adding ½ with al-Qabīsī.
[89] See Sahl's *Judgments* (#1).
[90] See Sahl's *Judgments* (#6).
[91] Omitting the puzzling *et ambulat* ("and she walks").
[92] Or rather, "application." See Sahl's *Judgments* (#7).
[93] See Sahl's *Judgments* (#4).
[94] That is, when a fortune passes beyond 1°, it will not be able to complete the matter.
[95] See Sahl's *Judgments* (#14).

Figure 41: Saturnus

28 Saturn[96] is masculine, diurnal, cold and dry. **29** He does not change [his] coldness, because it is an active quality; but dryness is a passive one.[97]

30 And his is the last age of a man, and black bile, and he has much eating, true esteem, deep counsel. **31** And he has the cultivation of lands, and the first clime, the right ear and the spleen, and he makes one ingenious and a seducer, and he has the color black and distresses. **32** And he has power in the father,[98] and stinking things, a sour taste, he is unfortunate and unclean, and anxious about long diseases from black bile, and makes melancholy and mania through passive phlegm, iron shackles, captivity in black places and pits, and uneasiness of the mind, a bad death in a river or the falling of heavy things, or stoning, or the bite of wild beasts. **33** He gives worthless[99] powers to a man, [and] he has iron, jackasses, and pigs, and slaves, and false people.

34 He is made malign in feminine signs, in the opposite of his own houses and his descension, and he is not particularly corrupted by the planets (and the Moon is so very much), and his works are hateful. **35** And he signifies death in a natal signification, whence Mars is below[100] him. **36** And if he is eastern from the Sun, above the earth, he is good in himself, and in his own

---

[96] This section is partly based on al-Qabīsī II.2-7 (see *ITA* V.1).
[97] Saturn has some signification over moist diseases and water-related topics, but he is never considered to be warming.
[98] Omitting the unknown *et illus imputredinis*, which has connotation with moldering and rotting.
[99] Or, "bad, vile" (*nequam*).
[100] *Deterior*.

place he signifies firm good fortune, and in the Ascendant in the body, in the second house in assets, [and] likewise in the other houses. **37** And he being with the Pleiades signifies expensiveness and famine, as does changing his sign, and the fiery signs.[101]

38 His light in front and behind is 9°, the years of his *firdaria* are 11, his greatest years 275,[102] great ones 57, middle ones 43 1/2,[103] small ones 30.

Figure 42: Jupiter

39 Jupiter[104] is a fortune, masculine, diurnal, hot and moist, a significator of the law and abundant assets, he signifies the soul, life, religion, patience, faith, and the good, and the fortune[105] of the future world [which] comes to be through faith.

40 He has a part in the heart and liver, the left ear is his. **41** His color is green, [and] tin, corn, and barley are his.

42 He is a star of truth and steadfastness. **43** If he is mixed with Saturn, he makes black magicians, enchanters, exorcists; if Mars, the knowledge of medicine; if the Sun, the knowledge of secrets and prudence in disputing; if

---

[101] Perhaps this should be read as changing *into* fiery signs.
[102] Reading with al-Qabīsī for *270*.
[103] Reading with al-Qabīsī for *33*.
[104] This section is partly based on al-Qabīsī II.8-12 (see *ITA* V.2).
[105] Reading the accusative for the nominative.

Venus, music; if Mercury, the knowledge of astronomy and arithmetic; if the Moon, the knowledge of disputation [and] the management of waters.

44 His light in front and behind is 9°. **45** The years of his *firdaria* are 12.

46 Jupiter[106] looking at a bad one turns its nature into good (Venus cannot do this unless she looks at Jupiter): Jupiter dissolves the malice of Saturn, and Venus [does so with] Mars.

47 His greatest years are 427,[107] the great ones 79, middle ones 45 1/2,[108] small ones 12, etc.

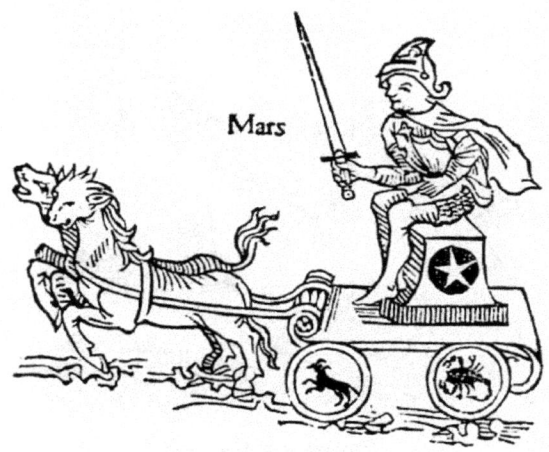

Figure 43: Mars

48 Mars[109] is masculine, nocturnal, bad, hot and dry, and he signifies brothers and the end of youth, the mastery of iron (and more so if Saturn is mixed with him), and bath-superintendents and blacksmiths and bakers. **49** If Jupiter is mixed with him, [it signifies] the working of copper, if the Sun a puncher of coins, if Venus the ornaments of women, if Mercury needles, if the Moon wool.[110]

50 The right ear is his, the liver, and dogs and poisonous animals, the occurrence of abuses through iron, arrogant men, perjurers, deriders, diseases

---

[106] See Sahl's *Judgments* (#34).
[107] Reading with al-Qabīsī for *429*.
[108] Adding ½ with al-Qabīsī.
[109] This section is based largely on al-Qabīsī II.13-17 (see also *ITA* V.3).
[110] Al-Qabīsī has scales and weights.

of the blood, burning, blisters, falling from a height, his taste bitter, the color red, the left nostril.

51 His light in front and behind is 8°. **52** The years of his *firdaria* are 7, the greatest years 284,[111] the great ones 66,[112] middle ones 40 ½,[113] and small ones 15.

[General comments on planetary behavior: Sahl][114]

53 The[115] bad planets signify evil on account of the excess of the cold of Saturn and heat of Mars. **54** A good [planet] received by a bad one in its house or exaltation, restrains its malice, and likewise if the good ones look at them by the trine aspect. **55** The fortunes are temperate, and therefore they always are responsible for good, and better if they receive: and wherever you saw a good one, say good (and the contrary).

56 Peregrine[116] bad ones increase evil, just as the good ones take away the good.

57 A planet[117] in its own descension signifies injustice, sorrow, prison, and distress. **58** A retrograde one [signifies] disobedience, contention, and discord.

59 And[118] a planet has 3° of its own strength: the one in which it is, another in front, the third one after [it].

60 A body[119] cuts off an aspect, and not the other way around; but an aspect [does not cut off] an aspect, but it *blocks* the effect.

61 A bad[120] planet eastern of the Sun in the morning, in its own house or exaltation, not conjoined to [the other] bad one, is better than an impeded good one.

---

[111] Reading with al-Qabīsī for *280*.
[112] Reading with al-Qabīsī for *55*.
[113] Reading with al-Qabīsī for *20*.
[114] Much of the following comes from Sahl's *50 Judgments* (in *WSM*).
[115] See Sahl's *Judgments* (##2-3).
[116] See Sahl's *Judgments* (#26 and #28).
[117] See Sahl's *Judgments* (#9 and #10).
[118] See Sahl's *Judgments* (#15).
[119] See Sahl's *Judgments* (#17).
[120] See Sahl's *Judgments* (#18).

Figure 44: Venus

62 Venus[121] is a fortune, nocturnal, [pertaining to] women, mothers, instruments of games, fornications, clothing, eating, drunkenness, music. **63** If Saturn is mixed with her, [it signifies] wailing over the dead and the singing of those building houses; if Jupiter, the chanting of the religious in the places of God Omnipotent; if Mars, the singing of battles and conflicts; if the Sun, the knowledge of singing before kings; if Mercury, the composition of verses; if the Moon, the singing of travelers.

64 She has diseases of the belly and genitals, the left ear, and the kidneys. **65** Her taste is sweet, the color white. **66** [She is] a star of beauty in the body, and in the face she is the left ear.

67 Her light in front and behind is 7°. **68** The fig and camels and vines and red copper are hers. **69** The years of [her] *firdaria* are 7, the greatest years 1,151,[122] the great ones 82,[123] the middle ones 45,[124] the small ones 8.

---

[121] This section is based largely on al-Qabīsī II.25-30 (see also *ITA* V.5).
[122] Reading with al-Qabīsī for *584*.
[123] Reading with al-Qabīsī for *45*.
[124] Reading with al-Qabīsī for *25*.

Figure 45: Mercurius

70 Mercury has a mixed nature, according to the one with whom he is mixed. **71** And [in himself] he signifies wisdom, [but] if [mixed] with Saturn he signifies numbers and measures [used in real estate and building]; if Jupiter, efforts in divine books; if Mars, counting[125] in the paying[126] of armies; if the Sun, the counting[127] of kings; if Venus, the counting[128] of [musical] chords and the pipes; if the Moon, counting [belonging to legations].[129]

72 He has the tongue, mouth, and bile, and men with long fingers. **73** His taste and color are diversified, and he is a star of children and all small animals. **74** He has power in the rational soul, in the sciences, in scribes, and in brief words. **75** The wisdom of Mercury is opposed to the games of Venus, and the sage has contempt for assets, because the lust for assets is contrary to the lust for wisdom.

76 His light in front and behind is 7°. **77** The years of his *firdaria* are 13, his greatest years 480,[130] the great ones 76,[131] the middle ones 48,[132] small ones 20.

---

[125] Reading *numerum* for *animum* ("the mind").
[126] *Solidis*, the coins traditionally paid as salary in the Roman army.
[127] Reading *numerum* for *munerum* ("of the services/gifts").
[128] Reading *numerum* for *munerum*.
[129] Adding with al-Qabīsī.
[130] Reading with al-Qabīsī for *115*.
[131] Reading with al-Qabīsī for *75*.
[132] Reading with al-Qabīsī for *28*.

[Good and bad qualities of the planets and Nodes]

78 The planets are good and bad not through their own nature, but through the peculiar quality of their own operations: and the Sun is the more fortunate of all the planets, then the Moon, from thence Jupiter, then Venus, Mercury is mixed, Saturn and Mars are bad.

79 The Head[133] of the Dragon is of the nature of Jupiter and Venus, it makes fortunate, and increases with the good and bad ones. **80** the Head increases life, money, honor—when it is with a fortune. **81** The Tail is contrariwise: the Tail of the Dragon is of the nature of Saturn and Mars, and always diminishes.

[Joys of the houses]

82 Mercury[134] rejoices in the Ascendant, the Moon in the third, Venus in the fifth, Mars in the sixth, the Sun in the ninth, Jupiter in the eleventh, Saturn in the twelfth (for he rejoices in lamentation and beating the breast and tribulation, which are signifies by the twelfth).

[Rulership of the planets during gestation]

83 When[135] a child is conceived, Saturn is in charge of the first month, and coagulates the seed; Jupiter [is in charge of] the second, and breathes in the spirit; Mars the third, and gives blood; the Sun the fourth, and gives life; Venus the fifth, and distinguishes the sex; Mercury the sixth, and makes the body and its orifices fit; the Moon the seventh, and the child is completed. **84** If it is born in the eighth month it is destroyed, because it is given over to Saturn; in the ninth it is complete because [it is given] to Jupiter.

---

[133] See al-Qabīsī II.45-48.
[134] See al-Qabīsī I.70.
[135] See al-Qabīsī II.44.

TREATISE IV: ON THE INTRODUCTORY MATTERS OF JUDGMENTS

[Ptolemy's Ages of Man]

85 If the native[136] was in the first four years, the Moon is in charge; from thence Mercury for 10, Venus for 8, the Sun for 20, Mars for 15, Jupiter for 12, [and] Saturn until the end. **86** But these two pertain more to nativities.[137]

[Planetary hours]

87 The hours[138] of the day and night are deputed to the planets, thus: begin from Sunday at the rising of the Sun, and give the first hour to the Sun, the second to Venus, and thus in order; and when no planets are left, begin from the top [with Saturn] and thus you will always find the first hour of that planet whose days it is.

	Sunday	Monday	Tuesday	Wednesday	Thursday	Friday	Saturday
1	☉	☽	♂	☿	♃	♀	♄
2	♀	♄	☉	☽	♂	☿	♃
3	☿	♃	♀	♄	☉	☽	♂
4	☽	♂	☿	♃	♀	♄	☉
5	♄	☉	☽	♂	☿	♃	♀
6	♃	♀	♄	☉	☽	♂	☿
7	♂	☿	♃	♀	♄	☉	☽
8	☉	☽	♂	☿	♃	♀	♄
9	♀	♄	☉	☽	♂	☿	♃
10	☿	♃	♀	♄	☉	☽	♂
11	☽	♂	☿	♃	♀	♄	☉
12	♄	☉	☽	♂	☿	♃	♀

Figure 46: Planetary hours from sunrise (Dykes)

---

[136] See al-Qabīsī II.44.
[137] This may be a truncated version of al-Qabīsī II.45, which goes on to discuss the Nodes and the years they have in natal *firdaria*.
[138] See al-Qabīsī II.49.

	Sunday	Monday	Tuesday	Wednesday	Thursday	Friday	Saturday
1	♃	♀	♄	☉	☽	♂	☿
2	♂	☿	♃	♀	♄	☉	☽
3	☉	☽	♂	☿	♃	♀	♄
4	♀	♄	☉	☽	♂	☿	♃
5	☿	♃	♀	♄	☉	☽	♂
6	☽	♂	☿	♃	♀	♄	☉
7	♄	☉	☽	♂	☿	♃	♀
8	♃	♀	♄	☉	☽	♂	☿
9	♂	☿	♃	♀	♄	☉	☽
10	☉	☽	♂	☿	♃	♀	♄
11	♀	♄	☉	☽	♂	☿	♃
12	☿	♃	♀	♄	☉	☽	♂

Figure 47: Planetary hours from sunset (Dykes)

[Friendships of the planets]

88 Jupiter[139] loves all planets, and all [love] him (except for Mars). **89** Venus loves all, and all her (except for Saturn). **90** Saturn loves Jupiter, the Sun, and Moon, and Mars and Venus hate him. **91** Venus loves Mars and the others hate him (and more so Jupiter and the Sun). **92** Jupiter and Venus [and Saturn][140] love the Sun, and Mercury and the Moon hate him. **93** Jupiter, Venus, and Saturn love Mercury, and the Sun, Moon, and Mars hate him. **94** Jupiter, Venus, and Saturn love the Moon, and Mars and Mercury hate her.[141] **95** Jupiter and Venus love the Head, and Saturn and Mars hate him; contrariwise the Tail.

96 The enmity[142] of the planets is even by the opposition [of their domiciles].[143]

[Climes of the planets]

97 The climes are deputed to the planets: the first to Saturn, and it is that of the Indians; the second to Jupiter, and it is of the Ethiopians; the third to Mars, and it is of the Egyptians; the fourth to the Sun, and it is of the Baby-

---

[139] See al-Qabīsī III.30.
[140] Adding with al-Qabīsī.
[141] Reading *eam* with al-Qabīsī for *eum* ("him").
[142] See al-Qabīsī III.30.
[143] That is, if the domiciles of two planets are opposed to each other, such as Saturn and the Sun due to the opposition of Aquarius and Leo.

Ionians; the fifth to Venus, and it is of the Romans; the sixth to Mercury, and it is Gog and Magog; the seventh to the Moon, and she is of the Persians.

Chapter IV.3: Introduction to the planets in themselves and in co-operation

1 The planets[144] are in the apogee when they are equated at the summit of their own apogee, or there is less than 90° from the right or left between any of them and its apogee: and then it is said to be diminished in light. **2** And if it was at the summit of the circle of its apogee, it will be at its least motion.

3 Now,[145] if there were 90° on either side between it and the summit of the circle of its apogee, it will be in the middle of the circle of its apogee and its equal motion. **4** And if it crossed over the summit of its apogee by 90° until it reached 270 equal degrees, it will be descending from the middle of the circle of its apogee, and then it will be increased in light, and especially if it was in the opposition of the apogee, most certainly (because then it is closer to the earth and so it appears greater), equal in the middle, less at the top—not that in its own being it grows or shrinks. **5** And if in addition to being at the summit of the apogee of the eccentric it is even at the summit of the short circle (or epicycle), it will be less.

6 And the[146] three higher than the Sun[147] are said to be "increased in calculation"[148] if the equation is added to their mean motions (and *vice versa*). **7** If indeed the place of the Sun is less than the mean course of Venus, or there remained 180 equal degrees, she will be with the Sun in the same minute, and she will have no equation.

---

[144] See al-Qabīsī III.2, and Tr. II on the planetary models.
[145] See al-Qabīsī III.2.
[146] See al-Qabīsī III.2. I omit any further description of this, as it would be too complicated for an introductory text.
[147] That is, the superior planets Saturn, Jupiter, Mars.
[148] Reading with al-Qabīsī for "number."

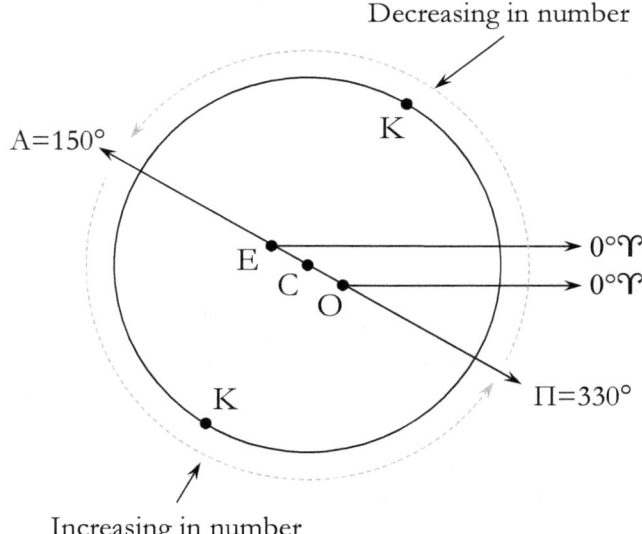

Figure 48: Mars increasing and decreasing in number and light (Dykes)[149]

---

[149] This diagram represents the deferent eccentric of Mars, as in Ch. II.4. His epicycle is not shown, but its center K is. See al-Qabīsī II.45-48.
[149] See al-Qabīsī I.70.
[149] See al-Qabīsī II.44.
[149] See al-Qabīsī II.44.
[149] This may be a truncated version of al-Qabīsī II.45, which goes on to discuss the Nodes and the years they have in natal *firdaria*.
[149] See al-Qabīsī II.49.
[149] See al-Qabīsī III.30.
[149] Adding with al-Qabīsī.
[149] Reading *eam* with al-Qabīsī for *eum* ("him").
[149] See al-Qabīsī III.30.
[149] That is, if the domiciles of two planets are opposed to each other, such as Saturn and the Sun due to the opposition of Aquarius and Leo.
[149] See al-Qabīsī III.2, and Tr. II on the planetary models.
[149] See al-Qabīsī III.2.
[149] This diagram represents the deferent eccentric of Mars, as in Ch. II.4. His epicycle is not shown, but its center K s seen to rotate clockwise around the deferent. As Leopold points out (**2**), as K moves from the apogee A (farthest from the earth O) towards the perigee Π (closest to the earth), the daily motion of K will be seen to speed up, or "increase in number." As K moves from the perigee towards the apogee, its daily motion will be seen to slow down or "decrease in number." Likewise, as it is closer to the apogee it will decrease in light, and increase in light when closer to the perigee (**1, 4-5**). Finally, Leopold points out that if Mars is also at the apogee of his epicycle, he will be seen to be even farther out than K is (**5**).

8 The planets are said to be eastern from the Sun if they appear sooner than the Sun above the upper[150] hemisphere, before the rising of the Sun.

9 A planet[151] is northern [in latitude] from the head of its own Dragon up to the Tail, southern from the Tail to the Head. **10** And from the Head by 90° it is more northern, and from the Tail by 90° it is more southern.

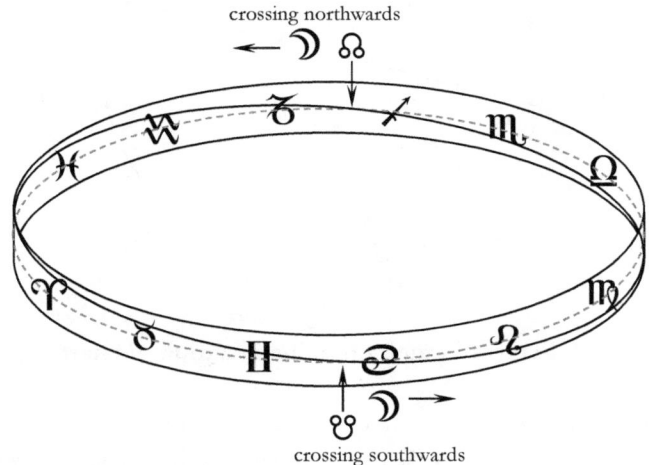

Figure 49: Nodes of the Moon (Dykes)

11 The "domain"[152] of a planet is that it is a masculine one in the day above the earth (in the night below the earth), in a masculine sign; [or], a feminine planet under the earth in the day (above the earth in the night), in a feminine sign. **12** [It is] to the contrary for Mercury.[153] **13** And the planets are stronger in their own work according to this.

---

[150] Reading *superiorem* for what seems to be *numerum* ("number").

[151] See al-Qabīsī III.3. Note that while we often speak of the Moon's Nodes, all of the planets have their own Nodes because they, too, pass between northern and southern ecliptical latitudes.

[152] See al-Qabīsī I.78, and my essay in *ITA* III.2. Really this should be a *diurnal* planet above or below the earth, and likewise a *nocturnal* one (see diagram).

[153] Typically, Mercury is considered to be a diurnal planet if he rises before the Sun; nocturnal if he rises after him. In the figure below, the planets are placed in their domains in a diurnal chart.

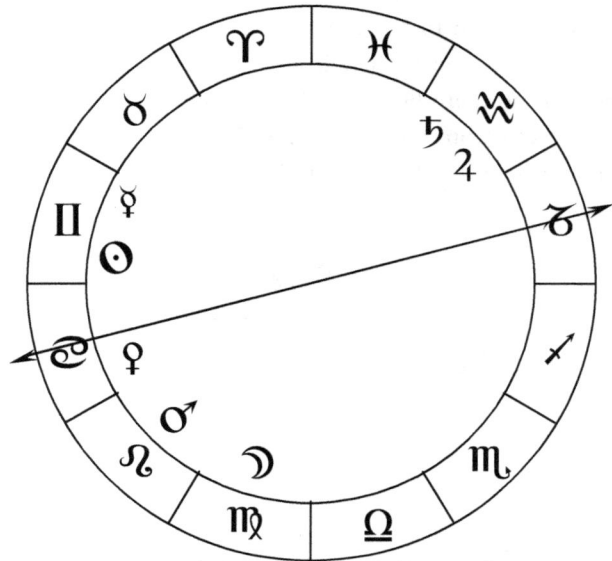

Figure 50: Planets in their domains in a diurnal chart (Dykes)

14 The planets[154] are *strong* in seven ways:[155] if they are [1] northern, [or] [2] when ascending in the circle of the apogee; [3] if they have recently gone out of the Sun's rays; [4] if in the second station; [5] if in an angular or succeedent house; [6] if the superiors are eastern of the Sun, in masculine signs and masculine quarters, [or] [7] if the inferiors are western of the Sun, in feminine signs and quarters. **15** Understand their weaknesses through their opposites.

16 The planets[156] are made *fortunate* in seven ways: if they [1] are with good ones; [2] if they are besieged by the good ones; [3] if the bad ones fall away from them; [4] if united to the Sun; [5] in a good aspect of the Moon; [6] [if swift in motion, increasing in light and number];[157] [7] if in any dignity of its own. **17** Understand their misfortune through the opposites.

18 The signification of the planets is varied in four ways: either from the circle of the apogee, or from their places in the signs, or from their places from the Sun, or from the quarters of the circle.

---

[154] See al-Qabīsī III.27.
[155] Reading for Leopold's "eight."
[156] See al-Qabīsī III.25-26.
[157] Adding with al-Qabīsī.

19 The regard of the planets is according to the houses.[158]

20 In the first house they have 12 powers, in the Midheaven 11, in the seventh 10, in the fourth 9; and less than that through the succeedents and the remote [places].

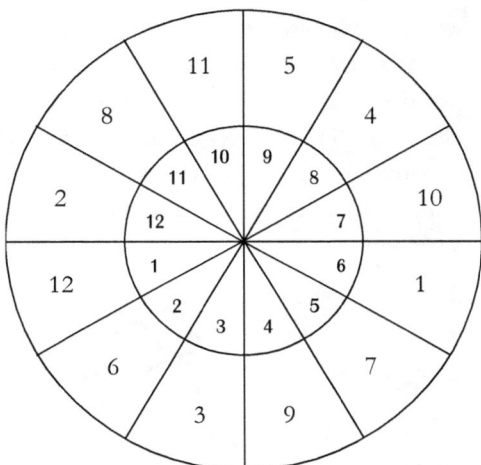

Figure 51: House strengths according to ibn Ezra (Dykes, from *Search* Appendix F)

21 The time[159] of the outcome of the planets' signification is known by: that which is between the significators,[160] and by that which is according to the figure when one goes to the place of the other (or of the matter sought),[161] by that which remains apart from addition or subtraction,[162] or by

---

[158] Leopold could be referring to the fact that aspects are based on configurations between signs that aspect or see each other, not through the abstract relationship of the planets alone. That is, if Mars in Aries squares Mercury in Cancer, it is first and foremost because Aries and Cancer are in such a position to square each other.

[159] This list is similar to many in traditional texts, and a particularly well-known one was from Sahl's *On Times* (see a discussion of the many methods in *Choices*, Introduction §7). Unfortunately, the Arabic of these lists was never well rendered into Latin, with many methods seeming redundant or confusing. I will try to decipher this list in the following footnotes.

[160] This is probably the degrees between them, converted into a unit of time (such as 5° being 5 days or months or years).

[161] This is probably the real-time transit, when one significator conjoins with the other by body.

[162] This may have to do with stationing and changing directions.

the renewal of the planet,[163] and when a planet goes to the place which is appropriate for it[164]—and these are seven.[165]

22 If a planet[166] is in the middle of the Ascendant, eastern and quick, and it applies to a quick [planet], the outcome of its signification will be within the hour (that is, one [hour]). **23** With one of the three conditions missing, [it is] within the day; with two [missing], within the month, etc.

24 The "facing"[167] of a planet is that it is western of the Sun, and between it and the Sun are as many signs as there are between the house of the Sun and the house of the planet (and between the Sun and Saturn are five full signs). **25** And [alternatively] it is eastern of the Moon, and between it and the Moon are as many signs as there are between the [house] of the planet and the house of the Moon.

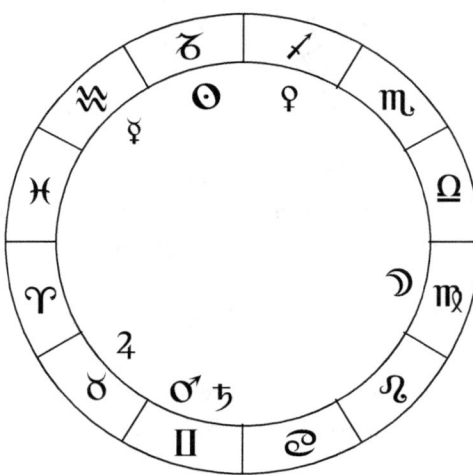

Figure 52: Mercury, Jupiter, Saturn in the facing of the Sun, Mars in the facing of the Moon (Dykes)

---

[163] This is probably a planet's going under the rays, and emerging from them again.
[164] This is probably when a planet enters its own domicile or exaltation, in a real-time transit.
[165] Many of the Latin lists of times also differed in how many there were; I do not count seven here. Again, see Sahl.
[166] This paragraph is probably based on Sahl's *On Times* (in *WSM*).
[167] See al-Qabīsī III.5, and *ITA* II.11. By "western," al-Qabīsī or Ptolemy means "later in the zodiac"; by "eastern," they mean "earlier in the zodiac." The idea is that it is archetypally significant if a planet is in a sign which bears the same relation to a luminary, as one of its own domiciles has to Leo or Cancer.

26 The condition[168] of the planets (namely, the superior ones) from the Sun is in many ways: for in the same minute with the Sun they are conjoined, but they are said to be united within 16', and united up to here because the magnitude of the Sun's lesser circle is 32':[169] and in this state a planet signifies good fortune. **27** From there, Saturn and Jupiter are burned up within 6°, and up to 18° under the rays (Mars is burned up to 10°, and up to 18° under the rays of the Sun): and then they are unable to give [their] greater years. **28** Beyond this they become strong, eastern: not that then they appear everywhere, but in some places yes, some places no. **29** With the Sun withdrawing [from them], they are elongated from him. **29** And they are stronger towards the sextile aspect. **30** From there they are to the right of the Sun and become weak: from thence they have the square aspect, from there they stand still, then they retrograde up to the opposition of the Sun. **31** After this they stand still again, they go direct, then they advance to 60° [from the Sun]. **32** Then the Sun crosses over them, and they become eastern, and again as before.

33 Venus and Mercury are burned up within 7°, [and are] under the rays of the Sun within 12°. **34** And Venus, with the Sun in 1', appears in the day if she is in 8° northern latitude.

35 The Moon is burned up within 6° of the Sun, under the rays within 12°. **36** But her appearance is different on account of the diversity of the setting of the signs which ascend then, according to which opposites ascend.[170] **37** And the burning of the Sun corrupts Venus and the Moon more so than the other planets.

38 The bearing of the planets is fourfold: [1] according to the circle (so that they are in a pivot, succeedent, or remote [place]); [2] according to the Sun (so that they are western or eastern or under the rays); [3] according to commixture, being conjoined, applied, or the converse; [4] according to themselves, like being direct, stationary, or retrograde.

---

[168] The following passages about relationships to the Sun seem to be based on *Gr. Intr.* VII.2.
[169] Or rather, the size of the Sun's body.
[170] This simply means that as straight or long signs ascend in the east, short signs set in the west (and vice-versa): the angles these signs make to the local horizon help determine when she is seen to exit the Sun's rays.

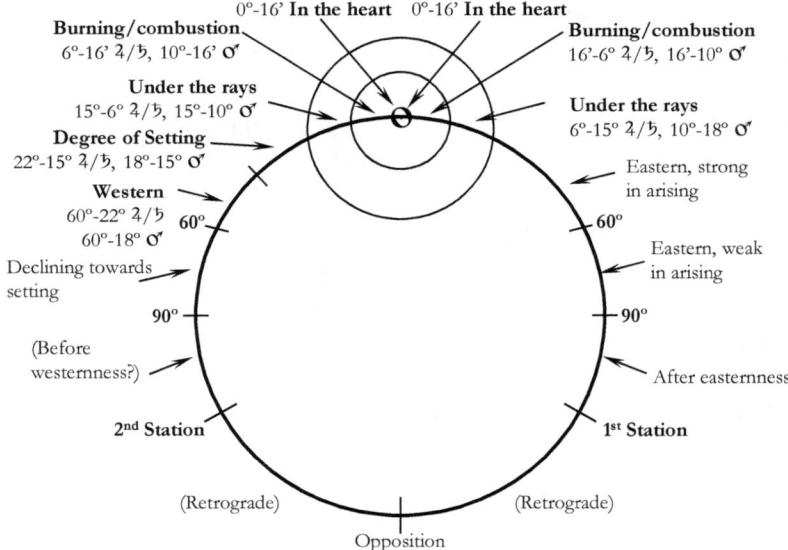

Figure 53: Synodic cycle of superiors
(Dykes, adapted from Abū Ma'shar)

[Planetary configurations]

39 A CONJUNCTION[171] is sometimes said in a general way, sometimes particular. **40** It is said in a general way whenever some lighter planet tends

---

[171] See al-Qabīsī III.11, and *ITA* III.5-7. In this paragraph, Leopold is speaking more specifically about different kinds of *connections* or *applications*, which can happen either in the same sign or signs which see (i.e., "aspect" or "regard") each other. The reason for these distinctions has in part to do with the fact that Arabic uses the same word for degree-based applications, whether in the same sign or aspecting signs. In his "general" sense (**40**), it is when a faster planet applies to a slower one, either in the same sign or involving signs which are configured to each other by aspect (such as between Leo and Sagittarius, which are configured by a trine). But if we want to get specific and distinguish same-sign connections from different-sign connections, then an application or connection within the same sign is a conjunction proper or "assembly" (**41-42, 44**), but from signs that are configured to or see or aspect each other it is an application or "regard" (**41**). What Leopold does not quite get right is that the Arabs also had a word for planets in the same sign, *even if* one did not apply to the other: this was more properly an assembly (*ITA* III.5). The diagram above shows a more accurate division of these into four categories: (1) planets which are merely assembled in the same sign, (2) merely see or aspect each other by sign, (3) apply or connect bodily in the same sign, and (4) apply or connect from aspecting signs. In (1), the Sun and Mars are in the same sign, but because the Sun is faster, he is not applying to Mars, so they are merely assembled. In (2), the Sun and Saturn are in signs which see or aspect or regard each other by square, but again the Sun is not applying

towards a heavier one, either in the same sign or in a regarding sign. **41** But it is said in a particular way whenever, in the *same* sign, a light planet tends towards a heavier one—from the other ones which regard, it is called a "regard."[172] **42** An application in a particular sense is not said to be the same as a conjunction in a general sense, but from one place it is called an application, from another a conjunction. **43** For it is called a *conjunction* on account of each planet, but an *application* on account of the lighter one tending towards the heavier one. **44** However, an "assembly" is said to be the same as a conjunction in the particular sense.

45 However, those planets are called "lighter" which have faster motion; "heavier" ones those with slower [motion]: whence, the Moon is judged the lightest, but Saturn the heaviest.

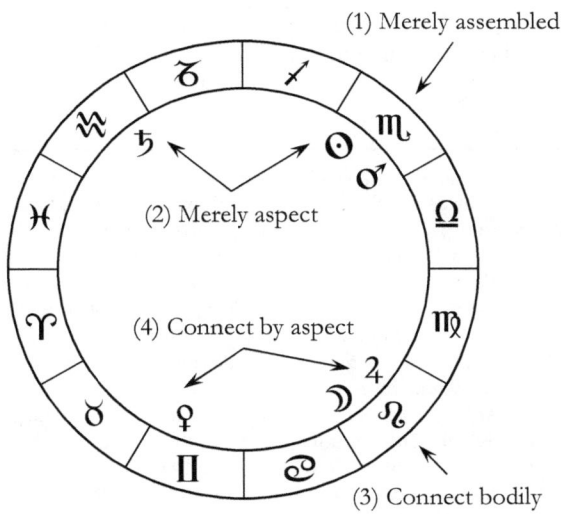

Figure 54: Four types of direct configuration (Dykes)

46 But a RAYING[173] is said to be the same as a regard, and there are four regards: the sextile, square, trine, opposite. **47** And one must know that there

---

to Saturn. In (3), the faster Moon is applying to slower Jupiter within the same sign. In (4), the faster Venus is applying to Jupiter within signs that sextile each other.
[172] Here Leopold is distinguishing between a connection by assembly (in the same sign) and by aspect (from another sign).
[173] This is the same as an aspect, but Leopold is pointing out that aspects can be taken in two ways. The first, proper way involves signs which aspect each other zodiacally, such as

is a "proper" and natural raying, and there is a less proper and accidental one. **48** A proper raying is from the signs regarding each other according to heaven; an accidental one is in the houses regarding each other according to the diversities of the figures. **49** In such figures it sometimes happens that one sign fills up two houses, and according to this a planet in the next sign is said to inspect another by a sextile aspect, and in the eighth by a trine aspect. **50** And even sometimes, a square aspect according to the heavens is a trine or sextile according to the figure.

51 There[174] are 120 conjunctions of the planets, among which one should especially note those which come to be in this world.[175] **52** For[176] there is conjunction of a planet with a star, and a planet with its own Dragon or that of another: and this is a conjunction of quality, not a mixture like that of water with wine, nor a commixture like flour with flour, nor a composition like wood with wood, in the knowledge of making [things].[177] **53** And the Moon is ruined[178] with Mars, the Sun with Saturn.

---

aspects between Leo and Sagittarius, which are configured by trine (**48**). This way is especially appropriate when using whole-sign houses. However, when using quadrant-based houses such as Alchabitius Semi-Arcs or Placidus, we can have intercepted signs or multiple cusps on the same sign (**48-49**). Older astrologers who used these systems tended to call the *cusps themselves* the houses, and so it was possible to aspect a house (or cusp) in a way that normally would not be allowed by whole signs. Leopold's first example of aspecting the adjacent sign seems to be an error (**49**), but his second example makes more sense. Suppose the Ascendant is in Aries, and the Placidean eighth-house cusp is in Sagittarius, the ninth sign. It would be possible for a planet in Aries to aspect the "eighth house" (namely, its cusp) by a trine, even though classically the first and eighth houses cannot see each other. Finally (**50**), Leopold points out that because of the obliquity of the ecliptic, planets aspecting each other from straight and crooked signs may suffer a mismatch between their *zodiacal* relationship (say, a square), and their distance considered along the celestial equator (say, a trine)—this is something only considered in specialized situations, and can safely be ignored by the beginner.

[174] This sentence is from pseudo-Ptolemy's *Centiloquy*, Aph. 50. This is based on the number of possible conjunctions among all of the planets: that is, the number of conjunctions between two planets, or three, or four, etc. However, it does not connect with the following sentences, which include conjunctions with the planetary Nodes.

[175] This is an awkward truncation by Leopold: the *Centiloquy* means that these conjunctions are the key to understanding the processes of generation and corruption in the world.

[176] The following statements about mixtures seem to be based on Gr. Intr. VII.4.

[177] *Pro scientia facienda*, which is not quite an accurate translation, but it pretty well mirror's Abū Ma'shar's statements about different ways of making medicine, constructing furniture, etc.

[178] *Defuncta*. Leopold might mean that Mars is destructive to the Moon's coolness and moisture, and Saturn is destructive to the heat of the Sun.

54 And[179] among the planets, the conjunction is the direct positioning of one under the other, and it is twofold: by body and by aspect. **55** By aspect is when one looks at another. **56** And if they are conjoined by the same latitude, then one obscures the other. **57** And a conjunction by longitude is when their degrees are equal, but a conjunction of latitude is that two planets would be joined either by longitude (so that their degrees are equal) or by opposition or according to any of the other aspects, so that if one is ascending in the north, the other is descending in the north, and if one is ascending in the south, the other is descending in the south.

58 And[180] the conjunction begins from the middle of the planet's orb, separation after the middle. **59** And the one which is closer to [its own] eccentric apogee is the stronger one.

60 And Saturn and Mars conjoined in the degree of the exaltation of a planet, destroys those things which belong to that planet.

61 Observe[181] the SEPARATION of a conjunction by 1°, because then come dreams and words and other things according to the nature of the planets, and according to the authority which they had in nativities.

62 The EMPTYING OF THE COURSE[182] is when a planet is being separated from another, and is not being joined to another.

63 A planet is WILD[183] when none at all is looking at it, and this happens more so to the Moon: and then she is said to be conjoined to the lord of the bounds in which she is.

64 TRANSFER[184] is when a light one is being separated from a heavy one, and it transfers the nature of the one from which it is being separated, to the one to which it is being conjoined—so that if the light one is being joined to a heavy one, and it to another, the light one crosses between them. **65** An example of which is [that] the Ascendant was Virgo, and an interrogation arose about a marriage-union, and the Moon was in 10° of the sign of Gemini, and Mercury in 8° of Leo, and Jupiter in 12° of Pisces. **66** And Mercury

---

[179] See al-Qabīsī III.11, and *ITA* III.7.2.
[180] See *Gr. Intr.* VII.4, and *ITA* II.6.
[181] See Sahl's *Fifty Judgments* #4-5. Leopold's strange mention of dreams and words is an elaboration of Sahl's, such that separating planets can indeed show fears and hopes, but without real effect.
[182] See al-Qabīsī III.12, and *ITA* III.9. It is important to note that in medieval Arabic astrology, a planet empty or void in course cannot complete an application *so long as it is in its current sign*.
[183] See al-Qabīsī III.13, and *ITA* III.10. That is, a wild planet even lacks aspects *by sign*.
[184] See Sahl's *Introduction* §5.5 (in *WSM*).

was the lord of the Ascendant, which was the significator of the one asking, and he was not looking at Jupiter (who is the lord of the marriage-union), who was in the eighth sign from him. **67** Therefore I looked at the Moon, whom I found in 10° of Gemini, separated (namely from Mercury) and applied to Jupiter: she was bearing away the light of each, and this signified the effecting of the matter [and its] attainment through the hands of legates running back and forth between each [party].[185]

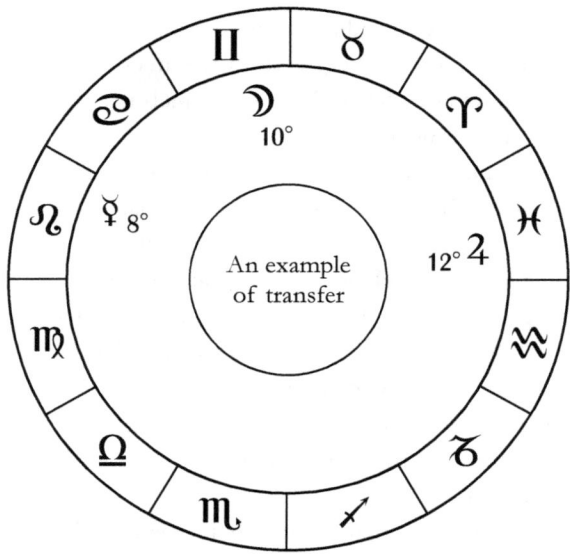

Figure 55: An example of transfer (Sahl, via Leopold)

68 COLLECTION[186] is that two or more are being joined to one planet: it will collect their lights, and accept their natures. **69** For example, a certain interrogation was made concerning a king, as to whether he would acquire a rulership or not: and the Ascendant was the sign of Libra, whose lord Venus (who was the significator of the one asking) was in 10° of the sign of Aries, and the Moon (the lord of the royal house, that is Cancer, which was the

---

[185] This is not a very helpful example, because it is actually an example of "reflection" (see **72** below). The key difference between transfer and reflection is that in transfer, the two key planets (here, Mercury and Jupiter) *do* aspect each other by sign, but are not applying to each other by degree. In reflection, the two key planets *do not* aspect each other even by sign, so are completely unconfigured.

[186] See *Gr. Intr.* VII.5, and *ITA* III.12. In this example, Venus is no longer applying to Mars, but they both apply to Jupiter, who collects their lights.

tenth house,[187] which signified the rulership) in 10° of the sign of Taurus, not looking at each other. **70** And Jupiter was in 15° Cancer, in the angle of heaven, in the royal house, and the Moon and Venus were applying to him. **71** Therefore, Jupiter was conjoining the light (that is the rays) of both, in the place of the matter asked about (that is, in the place of rulership), whence he signified the acquisition of the rulership through the hands of a judge or bishop or through the hands of some esteemed man, to which both planets willingly grant [their] assent.[188]

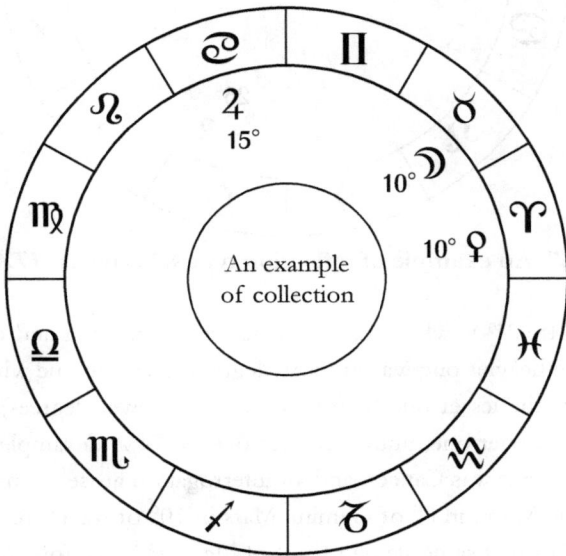

Figure 56: **An example of collection (Leopold)**

72 REFLECTION of light is when one planet or two are not being joined one to the other, nor do they look at each other, but they look at or are being joined to [a third planet], and it looks at or reflects the light to a certain place of the circle, and reflects their light to that place which it is looking at.

---

[187] Omitting a redundant *regie*.
[188] The example in **69-71** originally appeared under "reflection" and was titled as such in Leopold's book. However, Leopold's description is rather that of collection, so I have moved it up to this paragraph, and supplied my own example of reflection from *ITA* III.13 below.

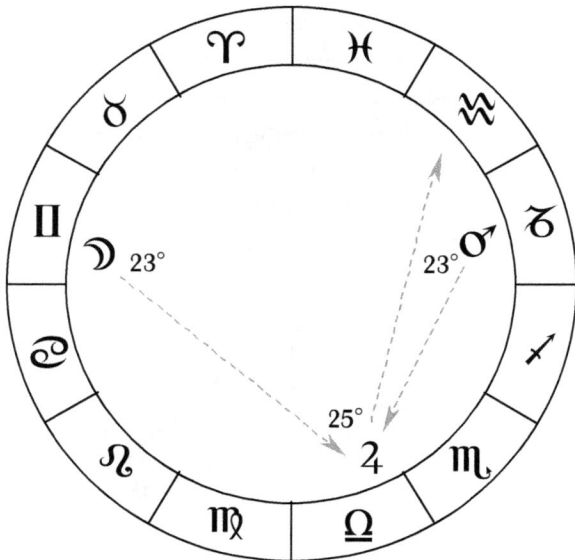

Figure 57: An example of reflection type #1 (Dykes, *ITA* III.13)

73 BLOCKING[189] is when three planets are in one sign and different degrees, and the heavier one was in more degrees: then the one which is in the middle blocks the lesser one (that is, which is in fewer degrees) from being joined to the heavier one, until it crosses over it. **74** An example of which is that the Ascendant was Cancer, and an interrogation arose about a marriage-union, and the Moon in 8° of Gemini, Mars in 10° of the aforesaid sign, but Saturn in 12° of that same sign, in front of Mars. **75** Therefore, Mars separated the Moon from Saturn, and took away their conjunction, and destroyed the matter.

76 Or, if two are in one sign, and the lighter one is conjoined to a heavier one by aspect, the one looking it blocked by the one which is in the same sign, and it destroys its conjunction, and the other one is being joined to the heavier one (if their degrees were equal), and even if the one looking was in fewer degrees than the lighter one. **77** But if the degrees of the one looking are closer to the conjunction, the one looking will come before the conjunction of the other.

---

[189] Often called "prohibition" (*prohibitio*). See Sahl's *Introduction* §5.7 (in *WSM*), al-Qabīsī III.16, and *ITA* III.14.

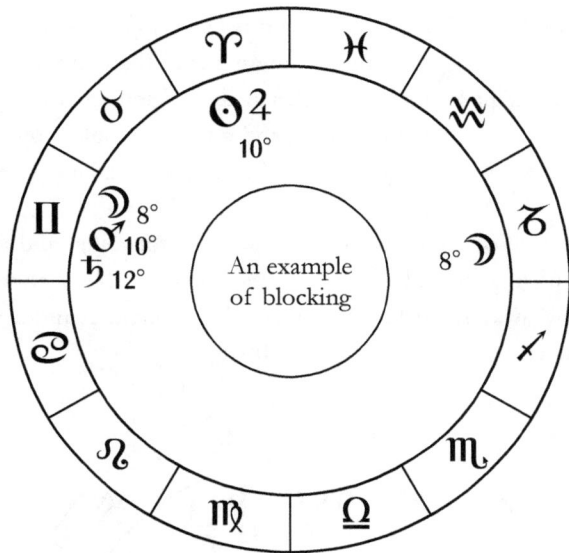

Figure 58: Two examples of blocking (Sahl, via Leopold)[190]

78 PUSHING [of nature][191] is when a planet is being joined to the lord of the sign in whose house it is (or only to the lord of the exaltation, or triplicity or face), and it is a pushing of the nature which was stated. **79** And[192] so that a diurnal one [is joined] to a diurnal one, and a nocturnal one to a nocturnal one, and in whatever way one is being joined to the other, it pushes its management, and it is a pushing of nature or handing over of management.

80 The RETURNING of virtue[193] is when a planet is being joined to another, burned planet (or one which is under the rays of the Sun), or a retrograde one: because then it cannot retain it, and it returns[194] it to the one which is being joined to it. **81** And if this happens in an angle or a succeedent, it will

---

[190] This chart contains two examples. The first is a question about marriage, and the Moon (the lord of the Ascendant) wants to connect with Saturn (the lord of the seventh) in Gemini; but Mars is between them, and so blocks their conjunction. In the second, the Moon is applying to the Sun from another sign, but Jupiter, who is in the same degree as the Sun, blocks her aspect. This second example is similar to a Hellenistic configuration called "intervention," in which the aspect from the *Moon* would block the conjunction of *Jupiter*, if he had been in an earlier degree (such as 7°).
[191] See al-Qabīsī III.17, and *ITA* III.15.
[192] This is Leopold's own addition.
[193] See al-Qabīsī III.20, and *ITA* III.19.
[194] Reading *reddit* for *addit* ("adds").

be with benefit. **82** And if the one which is being joined is falling,¹⁹⁵ and the one to which it is being conjoined is in an angle, the end will [not] be with benefit. **83** And if [it is] the reverse, then the beginning [will be good], because the applying one is the light one, and it is in an angle—but not the end, because the acceptor is falling. **84** And if both [were] falling, [it will be] with detriment.¹⁹⁶

85 An example of which is that Cancer was ascending, and the Moon in Sagittarius in 6° (namely, falling),¹⁹⁷ and she applies to Mars, appearing in 12° Gemini, falling away from the Ascendant: and then it signifies the destruction of the interrogation and end of this [matter].

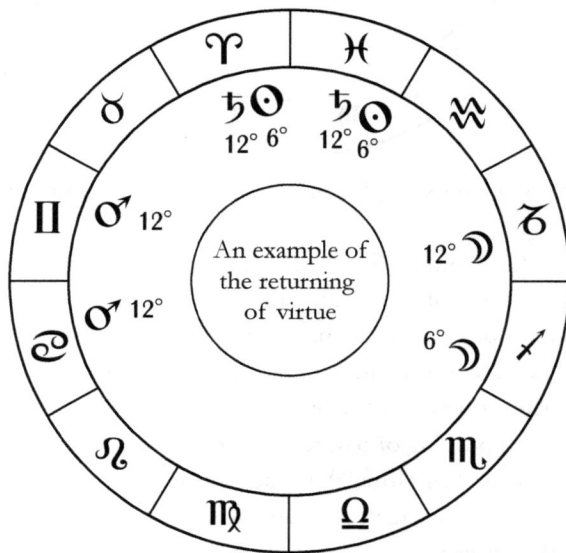

Figure 59: Examples of returning virtue (Leopold)¹⁹⁸

---

¹⁹⁵ Or, "cadent."
¹⁹⁶ The idea behind "returning" (see *ITA* III.19) is that the light and impetus of the matter is being applied or pushed by the first planet to the second, but the second is highly weakened and so unable to properly manage the matter: it therefore returns the matter back to the first planet. But it makes a big difference whether the first planet which takes it back, is in a strong place or not. See the example below and my footnote to the figure.
¹⁹⁷ The printed chart originally had "12" for the Moon, but I have changed it to match the text.
¹⁹⁸ This chart contains several examples. The first [1] is described by Leopold below: the Moon applies to Mars by opposition from Sagittarius, wanting to hand over the matter to him. But he is in a cadent or falling place (let's assume it is both by quadrant houses and whole signs to satisfy both interpretations), so he is too weak to maintain it. He returns it back to her. But since she is also falling or cadent, she cannot bring about the matter ei-

86 RESTRAINT[199] is when a planet wanting to be joined to another, first becomes retrograde: through this, its conjunction is destroyed.

87 CONTRARIETY of accident[200] happens when some light planet had many degrees (such as Mercury in 29° Virgo), and another heavier one [in fewer degrees][201] (such as Saturn in 28° of the same sign), and a third one lighter than the second one is less than that (such as Jupiter being in 24° of the same sign).[202] **88** And before Jupiter would be joined to Saturn, Mercury becomes retrograde and is joined to Saturn before[203] Jupiter is: whence the conjunction of Jupiter and Saturn is annulled.

89 FAILURE[204] is when a planet wants to be joined to another, and the first one goes out of the sign in which it is, and then another one (who is in few degrees [of its own sign]) looks at it: it makes it so that the conjunction of the first one fails.

90 The CUTTING of light[205] is when a planet wants to be joined to a heavier one, and [another] is in the following sign from the lighter ones, and before the lighter one comes to the conjunction of the heavier one, the one which is in the following sign goes retrograde, changes sign, and is joined to it, and cuts off its light from the planet with which it wanted to be joined. **91** Likewise, if a planet goes to the conjunction of another, and the one to which it wants to be joined seeks the conjunction of another, heavier one, and before the light one reaches the degree of the heavy one, the heavy one

---

ther, and so the matter falls apart. The next is probably [2] the Moon in Capricorn and the seventh applying to Saturn in the ninth: Saturn is burned and falling (i.e., cadent), so returns the virtue; but because the Moon is angular, she is able to maintain something of the matter and bring it forward. A third could be [3] the Moon in Sagittarius applying to Saturn in the ninth: he is burned and falling or cadent, but he receives her from his own domicile, which is a mitigating condition mentioned by Abū Ma'shar. A fourth is [4] the Moon in Capricorn applying to Saturn in Aries: not only does he receive her, but because they are both angular, he is able to give something of force to the matter even though he has to return the virtue to her. Mars in the first and Cancer, is angular and could be viewed as applying to either Saturn, as a further example of [2] and [4].

[199] Sometimes called "refrenation" in Renaissance/early Modern texts (*refrenatio*), but it is better understood with the Arabic as "revoking," as though revoking a promise to connect with the second planet. See al-Qabīsī III.21, and *ITA* III.20.

[200] This is better understood as "obstruction": see al-Qabīsī III.22, and *ITA* III.21.

[201] Adding with al-Qabīsī, for Leopold's puzzling *unus* ("one").

[202] In al-Qabīsī and Abū Ma'shar, the third planet is supposed to be lighter than the *first* planet (here, Mercury), not simply lighter than the second planet. But I suppose the example works either way.

[203] Reading *ante* for *inde*.

[204] Or rather, "escape," from the Arabic: see al-Qabīsī III.23, and *ITA* III.22.

[205] See al-Qabīsī III.24, and *ITA* III.23.

is joined to the other, heavier one: it cuts off the first[206] light from the lighter one, etc.

92 These conjunctions [of the planets] signify good, [but] cutting the reverse.

93 LARGESSE AND REPAYMENT[207] is that a planet which is in a well or in [its] descension,[208] would be joined to a planet friendly to it, having dignity in the sign of the pushing or receiving one: then the testimony leads him out of the well or descension.

94 RECEPTION[209] is when a planet is in another's house or exaltation or another dignity, [and is joined to it].[210] **95** And the one which is by house or exaltation is stronger, and that which is by a conjunction [in degrees], more so than that by [mere] aspect [by sign];[211] and you should know that reception cannot be annulled.

[Primary directions for significators between the angles][212]

96 The aspects of the planets are seven: two sextiles from 60°, two squares by 90°, two trines by 120°, and one is the opposite, by six signs. **97** For the direction of these aspects, take up [these] four rules:

98 If a planet is in the eastern quarter, take the right circle of the degrees of the Midheaven (that is, the ascensions which are in the straight line[213] of

---

[206] Reading *primum* for *primo*.
[207] See *Gr. Intr.* VII.5, and *ITA* III.24.
[208] Reading *in puteo aut in descensione sua* with John's Latin, for *in puncto vel in decursione*, here and at the end of the sentence.
[209] See *Gr. Intr.* VII.5, and *ITA* III.25.
[210] Adding with Abū Ma'shar.
[211] That is, Abū Ma'shar is suggesting that reception can happen by sign configuration alone, and not only by an application in degrees; but the latter is stronger.
[212] In this section, Leopold wants to explain how to use special tables to direct the aspects of planets (and not just their bodies), particularly when they fall in between two angles: these are the proportional semi-arcs which Ptolemy describes in *Tet.* III.10 (Robbins) or III.11 (Schmidt). But in trying to combine al-Qabīsī's general instructions (al-Qabīsī IV.11-12 and *ITA* VIII.2.2) with the topic of aspects, he starts to get lost, and never really finishes the instructions or relates them correctly. It is worth pointing out that when Leopold directs aspects, he does not use the right ascension or RA of the zodiacal position of the aspect, but first finds the RA of the planet, and adds the degrees of the aspect onto it, *in right ascensions*. That is, suppose we want to direct the sextile of the Sun, who is at 15° Gemini. His sextile is at 15° Leo. Finding the RA of 15° Leo is not the same as adding 60° to the RA of the Sun's own RA (which is what Leopold does): this will give different results. See Gansten 2009 and my audio lecture on "primary directions without tears" (www.bendykes.com) for more on traditional primary directions, as well as Appendix E of *ITA* (which is more technical).

TREATISE IV: ON THE INTRODUCTORY MATTERS OF JUDGMENTS   135

that same degree). **99** Likewise take the right circle of the degree of the planet, then subtract the right circle of the Midheaven from the right circle of the degree of the planet, and divide what remains by the parts of the hours [of the day belonging to] the degree of the planet: and what comes out will be the hours by which the planet is distant from the Midheaven.

100 And if the planet was between the Ascendant and the angle of the earth, take the right circle of the Midheaven, and the right circle of the degree of the planet, and subtract the right circle of the Midheaven from the right circle of the degree of the planet: preserve what remains. **101** After this,[214] take the parts of the hours [of the day] and multiply them by six, and subtract from what was preserved, and divide what remains by the parts of the hours of the degree opposite the planet, and what will have come out are the hours: and multiply by what the planet is distant from the Ascendant.

102 And if there were a planet between the angle of the earth and the seventh, take the right circle of the angle of the earth and the right circle of the degree of the planet, and subtract the right circle of the degree of the angle of the earth from the [right] circle of the degree of the planet, and divide what remains by the parts of the hours [of the day] of the degree opposite the planet, and what comes out is the distance of the planet from the angle of the earth, in terms of hours and parts of hours.

103 And if a planet was between the seventh and the Midheaven, take the right circle of the angle of the earth and the right circle of the degree of the planet, and subtract the circle of the angle of the earth from the right circle of the degree of the planet, and preserve what remains. **104** After [this], take the degree of the nadir and multiply by six, and subtract that from what was preserved, and divide what remains by the parts of the hours of [the day belonging to] the degree [of the planet], and what will have come out is the distance of the planet from the angle of the west.

105 Once you knew the distance of the planets from the four angles, and you wanted to know the projections of the rays of the left sextile or square or trine aspect, add on top of the right circle of the degree of the planet the left sextile aspect (60°), for the square 90°, for the trine 120°. **106** And enter the

---

[213] *Directo*. This word adds little, and simply means: "find the right ascension (RA) corresponding to the zodiacal degree where the planet is."
[214] Omitting a redundant *gradus planetae*. The rest of the instructions in this sentence are confused: see my footnote above on better sources for these instructions.

result[215] in the ascensions of the right circle and take what was in its direct line, of equal degrees from the sign in which it fell, and preserve it. **107** After this, take the ascensions of the region of the degree of the planet, and even add on top [of that] 60° for the left sextile aspect, 90° for the square, [and] 120° for the trine, and enter the result[216] in the table of ascensions for your city, and see in which direct line it falls, of the signs. **108** And if both ascensions fall in one degree and minute, the rays of the planet will be there. **109** And if [they are] in different places, take the difference between both places and divide by six, and multiply what comes out by the hours of the distance of the planet from the angle, and add the result on top of the place of the nearer planet by equal degrees: and if the ascensions were closer, add on top of those; and if the right circle was closer, add on top of that: and where it reached, there are the rays of the planet.

110 But for the right aspects (the sextile, square, and trine), subtract just as you added before, for each one: and add what came out on top of the farther place from the planet, by equal degrees, and where it reached, there are the rays of the planet. **111** However, the opposite aspect is always in the opposite degree and minute.

112 And if a planet was precisely on the Midheaven, operate only with the table of the right circle (and likewise for the angle of the earth). **113** And if it was in the Ascendant, [operate only] with the tables of the climes (if in the west, by the ascensions of the nadir of the climes). **114** And in this way direct the significators forwards and backwards from the houses, and from all of the planets, from the Lots backwards, and the significators which are from the fourth house to the tenth, as is said in the *Tetrabiblos* of Ptolemy, III.10.

[*False and true testimonies*]

115 All testimonies of the planets are false if they are burned up or retrograde; from the second station to the first, they are in the middle. **116** Saturn and Jupiter, when they are eastern within 6° [of the Sun] the testimonies are in the middle; when western they are false. **117** Mars eastern of the Sun by 10° has a middling testimony (less than that false). **118** Mercury under the rays of the Sun, eastern or western, has false testimony. **119** The Moon within 12° from the Sun has false testimony unless she is northern in latitude (then

---

[215] *Cum collecto.*
[216] *Cum collecto.*

it is in the middle). **120** Every star in an angle has full testimony; in a succeedent, the middle; in a remote [place], false. **121** The Moon within 12° from the Tail of her Dragon [is likewise]. **122** Firm signs have full testimonies, common ones middling, movable ones false. **123** Saturn and Mars in a bad [place], true; in a good one, false—Jupiter and Venus [are] to the contrary. **124** The Sun, Mercury, and the Moon are transformed.[217] **125** A testimony is the connection of the east or Sun [or] Moon with the significators, or of the others amongst themselves.

Chapter IV.4: On the introductory matters of judgments

1 The fourth part of the introductory matters begins, concerning names which astronomers (judging the effects of the significators) use:

2 First,[218] concerning conjunctions: [there are] six, of which the first is the conjunction of Saturn and Jupiter in 960 years, at the same point in which the preceding conjunction was made:[219] and this signals the greatest change in the world, in sects and in kingdoms. **3** The second is the conjunction of Saturn and Jupiter in 240 years, which even signifies a great alteration in the world. **4** The third is the conjunction of Saturn and Mars in Cancer[220] in 30 years, where it is the debility[221] of Saturn and the fall of Mars. **5** The fourth is the conjunction of Saturn and Jupiter in 20 years, which makes 12 in 240 years. **6** The fifth is the Sun's entrance into the sign of the vernal equinox every year. **7** And the sixth, the position of the heaven and places of the planets at a conjunction or prevention (and especially before the Sun's entrance into Aries, the one which more closely comes before it).

8 There[222] follows the "indicator,"[223] and this is the understanding of the degree of the Ascendant. **9** For this, take the figure of the [assumed] root, and see the place of the conjunction or prevention which more closely pre-

---

[217] Or perhaps, "reversed" (*permutantur*), meaning here uncertain.
[218] See al-Qabīsī IV.2, and *ITA* VIII.3.1, and *AW2* I.1. This largely concerns mundane techniques.
[219] That is, 960 years before, after a full circuit of triplicity shifts. Reading a little loosely for *in quo facta est coniunctio precedens*.
[220] Or rather, in the early parts of Cancer.
[221] Or, "detriment."
[222] See al-Qabīsī IV.3, and *ITA* VIII.1.2.
[223] Also called the *animodar* or *namudar*, after the Persian for "indicator." This is used in natal rectification. See Ch. VII.3, **22ff**.

ceded it, and the degree of the planet which is closer to the Ascendant or the Midheaven (or another angle).[224] **10** Take this [planet], and calculate the houses according to it, and you will have the figure of heaven at the [actual] root. **11** And for degree of the conjunction there is no difference [of opinion as to where it is], but [according to Ptolemy] the degree of the prevention is of that luminary which is above the earth at the prevention or the root.[225] **12** 'Alī explains[226] here concerning the planet which has many dignities at the conjunction or prevention, [that] he takes the degree of the Moon as the degree of the prevention.

13 But[227] the "releaser" is the lord of life in nativities and questions, and signifies the quality [of life], and is interpreted as the wife. **14** The "housemaster" is the giver of years and is interpreted as the husband. **15** And I will speak fully about these in [the Treatise on] nativities.[228]

16 The "victor"[229] is the one which is more powerful in a figure of heaven, in whatever root it was.

17 The "distributor"[230] is the one to whose bounds a direction reaches, from the root.

18 A direction[231] is the extension of degrees from the root (by the right circle or by ascensions of the clime, or by each proportionately), giving one year to every degree. **19** To 5' of one degree one grants a group of thirty (namely days), to 6 days 1'. **20** The art of [this] is completely had through the direction of the aspects, explained above.

21 "Profection"[232] is the extension of the houses from the root, by giving one year to every sign. **22** They grant 2° 30' to every month, 5' to one day, 12.5" to one hour. **23** And according to profection [using a year of 365.25

---

[224] Leopold has left out an important step, which is to find the planet which is the *victor over* the place of the conjunction or prevention—not just any planet which happens to be close.

[225] Or rather, at the prevention, *not* the root or nativity (but that would be an intriguing possibility).

[226] Source uncertain.

[227] See al-Qabīsī IV.4-5, and *ITA* VIII.1.3.

[228] See Ch. VII.4 below.

[229] Often spelled in its Latin transliteration, *almuten, almutem*, or *almubtez*. See al-Qabīsī IV.7, and *ITA* VIII.1.4, and Ch. IV.1, **120**.

[230] This refers to distributions through the bounds. See Ch. VII.4, **20ff**, al-Qabīsī IV.14, *ITA* VIII.2.2f, and my audio workshop on this topic at www.bendykes.com.

[231] See al-Qabīsī IV.11-12 and *ITA* VIII.2.2.

[232] See al-Qabīsī IV.8, and *ITA* VIII.2.1.

days], every degree has 12 of the days, 4 hours of the hours,[233] 12 minutes of an hour.

24 The lord[234] of the ninth-part is found thusly: they take the degrees which have ascended (of a house) or those which a planet has completed (of a sign), and they are distributed by ninths, by giving 3 1/3 degrees to each one, starting the distribution from the beginning of the movable sign of that triplicity: and where the number is ended, the lord of that sign is the lord of the ninth-part. **25** For example, the Moon was in 23° Leo: I divided those by 3 1/3, and it came to the seventh when starting from Aries, and it reached Libra: the lord of this is the lord of the ninth.[235]

	0°00'- 3°20'	3°20'- 6°40'	6°40'- 10°00'	10°00'- 13°20'	13°20'- 16°40'	16°40'- 20°00'	20°00'- 23°20'	23°20'- 26°40'	26°40'- 30°00'
♈	♂	♀	☿	☽	☉	☿	♀	♂	♃
♉	♄	♄	♃	♂	♀	☿	☽	☉	☿
♊	♀	♂	♃	♄	♄	♃	♂	♀	☿
♋	☽	☉	☿	♀	♂	♃	♄	♄	♃
♌	♂	♀	☿	☽	☉	☿	♀	♂	♃
♍	♄	♄	♃	♂	♀	☿	☽	☉	☿
♎	♀	♂	♃	♄	♄	♃	♂	♀	☿
♏	☽	☉	☿	♀	♂	♃	♄	♄	♃
♐	♂	♀	☿	☽	☉	☿	♀	♂	♃
♑	♄	♄	♃	♂	♀	☿	☽	☉	☿
♒	♀	♂	♃	♄	♄	♃	♂	♀	☿
♓	☽	☉	☿	♀	♂	♃	♄	♄	♃

Figure 60: Table of ninth-parts (Dykes)

---

[233] Omitting a puzzling *6*. The calculation in **22** assumes a year of 360 days, but in **23** Leopold (following al-Qabīsī) points out that in a year of 365.25 days, 1° is equivalent to 12 days, 4 hours, and 12 minutes (12.175 days). Leopold's use of *6* could refer to the fact that 12.175 days is very close to 12 1/6 days (12.166), which al-Qabīsī explicitly mentions.

[234] See al-Qabīsī IV.16-17, and *ITA* VII.5. Ninth-parts are discussed in a predictive context by Abū Ma'shar in *PN3*.

[235] In this method, fractions are included. So, 23° Leo is in the fiery triplicity, whose movable sign is Aries (ruled by Mars). Divide 23° / 3.333 = 6.9. Starting the count with Aries, Aries gets 1, Taurus 2, Gemini 3, Cancer 4, Leo 5, Virgo 6, and the remainder (.9) falls in Libra, which is ruled by Venus.

26 The lord[236] of the decan is found thusly: if the place of a house [cusp] or planet is in the first face of a sign, then the lord of the decan is the lord of the movable sign of that triplicity; if in the second face, then the lord is the one which is the lord of the fixed sign of that triplicity; if in the third face, then it is the lord of the common sign of that triplicity. **27** For example, Jupiter was in the second face of Leo: the lord of second sign of that triplicity is the Sun, and he was the lord of the decan of Jupiter; and [that is] because Mars was [the lord of] the first one, namely Aries, and Jupiter [the lord] of the third one, namely Sagittarius.

28 The lord[237] of the twelfth-part is found thusly: multiply the degrees which have crossed over [a cusp] (of a house), or which a planet has made in [its] sign, by 12,[238] and distribute this total from your place by 30, and where the number is finished, there is the lord, which is the lord of that sign.

	0°-2.5°	2.5°-5°	5°-7.5°	7.5°-10°	10°-12.5°	12.5°-15°	15°-17.5°	17.5°-20°	20°-22.5°	22.5°-25°	25°-27.5°	27.5°-30°
♈	♈	♉	♊	♋	♌	♍	♎	♏	♐	♑	♒	♓
♉	♉	♊	♋	♌	♍	♎	♏	♐	♑	♒	♓	♈
♊	♊	♋	♌	♍	♎	♏	♐	♑	♒	♓	♈	♉
♋	♋	♌	♍	♎	♏	♐	♑	♒	♓	♈	♉	♊
♌	♌	♍	♎	♏	♐	♑	♒	♓	♈	♉	♊	♋
♍	♍	♎	♏	♐	♑	♒	♓	♈	♉	♊	♋	♌
♎	♎	♏	♐	♑	♒	♓	♈	♉	♊	♋	♌	♍
♏	♏	♐	♑	♒	♓	♈	♉	♊	♋	♌	♍	♎
♐	♐	♑	♒	♓	♈	♉	♊	♋	♌	♍	♎	♏
♑	♑	♒	♓	♈	♉	♊	♋	♌	♍	♎	♏	♐
♒	♒	♓	♈	♉	♊	♋	♌	♍	♎	♏	♐	♑
♓	♓	♈	♉	♊	♋	♌	♍	♎	♏	♐	♑	♒

Figure 61: Table of twelfth-parts (Dykes)

---

[236] See al-Qabīsī IV.18, and *ITA* VII.6. This is an Indian version of the decans, which usually follow the "Chaldean" order: see table in Ch. IV.1, **112**.

[237] See al-Qabīsī IV.15, and *ITA* IV.6.

[238] Omitting "and add to the sum what you have multiplied," which is a relic of John's labored explanation. The method is simply to multiply the exact position of something (in minutes, degrees, and seconds) by 12, and project this number from the beginning of the sign. Where the numbering ends, is the sign indicated by the twelfth-part.

29 The lord[239] of the orb[240] is the planet which is the lord of the hour when a matter begins, or the native is a child: and this, along with the ascending lord, signifies the good health or illness of a native in the first year. **30** In the second year, the lord of the hour is the one which follows[241] the lord of the first hour; and it, along with the lord of the lord of the house of assets in the root, signifies assets, and thus through the 12 houses. **31** And in the thirteenth year, it returns to the first one.

32 The lord[242] of the circle is the lord of the sign of the profection, by giving one sign to every year; and the [lord] of that sign which the extension reaches, is the lord of the circle.

33 The *firdaria*[243] or powers of the planets in the years, were placed above by us;[244] but to which planet [certain] years belong [in mundane astrology] is known thusly. **34** The years of the *geharit* are taken and completed with the quarters which they do not have in themselves, and 18 years are subtracted from them, and what remains is divided by 75, and there is a distribution of the remainder, starting from Saturn: and where the distribution was, there is had the lord of the *firdaria*. **35** 639 years and 27 days of the year of the *geharit* are completed at noon in the year of Christ 1271, on the 13th day of March. **36** However, in nativities this distribution begins from the Sun with the participation of the *firdaria* which is according to the distribution begun from Saturn, and the native's status is according to his *firdaria*.

---

[239] See al-Qabīsī IV.19, and *ITA* VIII.2.3.
[240] Reading *orbis* with John's Latin, for "hour." In Arabic this is "period."
[241] Omitting *et*.
[242] Or, "lord of the year." See al-Qabīsī IV.8, and *ITA* VIII.2.1.
[243] In this paragraph, Leopold is describing mundane *firdaria*, of which there were several types. The one described here is the "small" version, which lasts 75 years just as the natal one does, but as Pingree describes it, it does not begin with Saturn (see Pingree 1968, pp. 62-63). Leopold wants to explain how to know what the mundane *firdaria* is for any particular year, but his discussion is opaque because of the puzzling number 18 and reference to "quarters" (**34**), not to mention using the transliteration *geharit*. But if we subtract 639 years from 1271 AD, we get 632 AD, which was the year of Muhammad's death. My sense is that *geharit* is really a transposition for *hegarit*, the Hijrah or Muhammad's flight to Medina in 622 AD (a standard reference point in Islamic calendrics). In other words, Leopold is copying a method for determining the mundane *firdaria* based on a cycle beginning with the start of the Islamic calendar. Needless to say, if one does not follow such a calendar or culture, Leopold's calculation (however he is actually doing it) is not pertinent in any case.
[244] In IV.2, under each planet.

37 A transit,[245] which is the elevation of a planet over a planet, is known thusly: take the equated place of a planet, and the mean [position] of its course; if its equated place is less than its mean course, then it is ascending from the [lower] middle of its circle towards the summit of the [epicyclic] circle; and if its equated place was greater than its mean course, it is descending from the [upper] middle of its circle towards the lower part of it. **38** And if the equated place and its mean course are equal, it will be in the middle of its circle. **39** Then [if they are unequal], subtract the lesser from the greater, and multiply what remains by 7 and divide by 22, and what comes out is the amount of the ascent or descent of any planet. **40** If however either of the two inferiors (namely, Venus or Mercury) was eastern—that is, appearing before the Sun in the morning—and its equated place is less than the equated place of the Sun, then they are ascending from the middle of their circle towards the farther longitude of each.[246] **41** And the one of them which was eastern and its equated place is greater than the equated place of the Sun, is descending toward the lower longitude of its orb from the middle of its circle. **42** And concerning the quantity of the ascent or descent, operate just as with the superiors. **43** And that one which is upper in a conjunction, that one is stronger in the impression. **44** And the impression is stronger in conjunctions than in oppositions and in squares. **45** And a northern one [in latitude]

---

[245] Lat. *almurat* (John: *almamar*). See al-Qabīsī IV.21, and Kennedy 1958. The doctrine of "transit" in Arabic astronomy and astrology is a bit more complicated than one might think, and I will just give a sketch here, especially since actually using their techniques would be impossible without special tables. Now, astrologers wanted to know which planet was dominant in any combination: that planet was said to be elevated over, or above, the other (**37, 43**). Since Venus cannot astronomically be above, say, Saturn, they needed a way of determining superiority: the answer was that the planet whose position was in some sense higher or more increased in its own circle, was the superior one (here, al-Qabīsī is only concerned with the epicycle). These terms were used in several ways and it can be rather confusing to understand. But many astrologers took the short cut that al-Qabīsī uses here. Basically, they compared the mean position of the planet to its equated or true position (see my *Comment* to Chs. II.2 and II.4 above): the mean position is the expected position of the planet based on constant motion, while the true position is its position as seen by us. For al-Qabīsī, if the true position is greater than the mean, then the planet is moving downwards from its epicyclic apogee (called the "middle," **37**); but if it is less than the mean, the planet is rising up from the perigee towards the apogee. If they are equal, then the planet is exactly on its apsidal line (**38**). Then we must compare the two planets. For each planet, multiply the difference between the two positions by *pi* (expressed in **39** as 7/22), and the result allows one to put the two planets on a circle that will show which one is higher. Then, because the cycles of Mercury and Venus follow the mean Sun, their positions are compared with his (**40-42**). Finally, al-Qabīsī points out which types of aspects are stronger (**44**), and which aspects by latitude are stronger (**45**).
[246] Reading *utriusque* for *uterque*.

rises over a southern one, and one which is more northern is above one which is less so, and one which is less southern [is] above one which is more southern.

46 The *bust*,[247] which many Indians observe, is a consideration at the hour of the conjunction of the Sun and Moon. **47** Then, 12 hours from the conjunction are given to the Sun, from there 12 to Venus, and thus according to the order of the planets (and after all of them, it returns to the Sun). **48** And the time of those hours is judged by their lords and by the lords of their triplicity. **49** And [according to some people],[248] all hours which are granted to the Sun are called "burned," and they are bad; and they[249] understand the nature of the lords which were the lords of the triplicities of the planets at the hour of the conjunction, by giving four hours to each lord.

50 "Facing" was defined above.[250]

Chapter IV.5: On Lots

1 Hermes and all of the sages of the Persians, Indians, [and] Greeks, judge through these eight things:[251] through [1] the house of the matter and [2] its lord, through [3] the planet which naturally signifies the matter, through [4] the Lot of the matter and [5] its lord, through [6] the conjunction and aspect of the planets to the house of the matter and to [7] its lord, and through [8] the changing of the planets[252] through the signs. **2** Therefore, the extraction of the Lots was necessary for making judgments.

3 A Lot[253] is the longitude between two significators over one matter by natural signification,[254] and its falling into a particular place of the circle. **4** And there must be three significators: namely, the one from which it is projected, and the one to whom it is projected (and these two are immovable); the third one is the place from which it is projected, and to which [the count-

---

[247] *Alburat.* See al-Qabīsī IV.23, and *ITA* VIII.4. For a lengthier explanation and a table, see al-Kindī's *Forty Chapters* Ch. 11.7.
[248] Adding with al-Qabīsī.
[249] *Quilibet.*
[250] See IV.3, **24**.
[251] See Leopold's other version of this list in Ch. VIII.1, **20**.
[252] Reading *planetarum* with Ch. VIII.1, **20**, for *rerum* ("matters").
[253] See *Gr. Intr.* VIII.3, lines 222-57.
[254] For example, both the Moon and Venus signify women and female figures, so they are used as the two planets for calculating the Lot of the mother.

ing ultimately comes] ([and] this one is movable). **5** And in this, equal degrees are taken—which are the degrees of the orb of the signs, not degrees of ascensions (which are the degrees of the circle surrounding the orb of the signs and all of the other [orbs] between the tips of its axis). **6** (The [obliquity of the] axis of the orb of the signs is 23° 33'.)

7 The Lots of the seven planets are just like the 80 [Lots] of the houses; and [there are] 10 others in revolutions, in nativities, and in other necessary things.[255]

[Lots of the planets]

8 The Lot of Fortune[256] is the Lot of the Moon, and it is taken in the day from the Sun to the Moon (in the night, the reverse), and on top of that are added the equal degrees of the ascending sign which have ascended, and it is projected from the beginning of the ascending sign: and where it reaches, there is this Lot. **9** And it signifies the same things as the luminaries do. **10** And [some believe][257] if you multiply the completed hours of the day by the parts of the hours of the day and project from the place of the Moon, this projection falls into the place of the Lot of Fortune (or near it).

11 The Lot of the Sun[258] is the Lot of future things,[259] and it is taken in the day from the Moon to the Sun (and in the night the reverse), and the degrees of the ascending sign which have ascended are added, and it is projected from the beginning of the ascending sign: and where it reaches, there is the Lot of future things. **12** And this a Lot which signifies the soul and body, and faith, and religion, and hidden things.[260]

---

[255] See the numerous Lots listed in **251ff**.
[256] See *Gr. Intr.* VIII.3, lines 279-87 and 310-16.
[257] Adding based on *Gr. Intr.* I am not exactly sure what this means, but it is part of the notion that the Lot is the "Ascendant of the Moon."
[258] See *Gr. Intr.* VIII.3, lines 323-34.
[259] That is, the Lot of Spirit (Gr. *Daimōn*). In Arabic this is called the "Lot of the hidden." Both "future things" and "hidden" suggest spiritual matters and intangible values, particularly since the spiritual world is taken to be our destination after death.
[260] See also **261**, which says that the Lot of Spirit signifies "the being/condition of the soul."

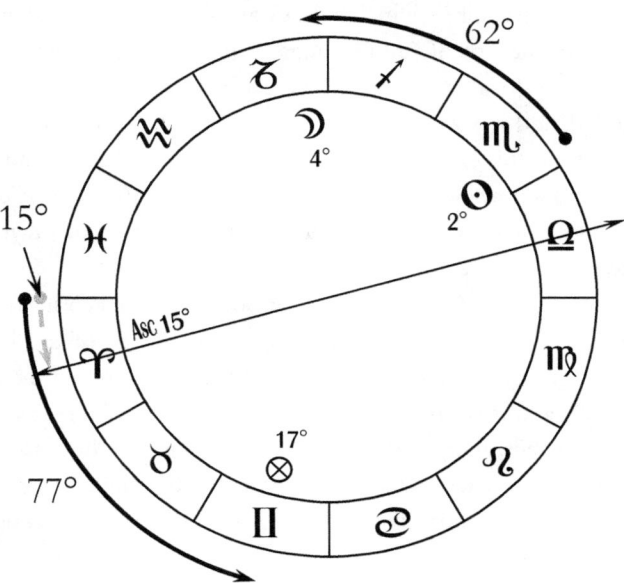

Figure 62: Medieval way of projecting Lots (Dykes)[261]

13 The Lot of Saturn,[262] or "heavy" [Lot], is taken in the day from the place of Saturn to the Lot of Fortune (in the night, the reverse), and the degrees of the sign of the Ascendant which have ascended are added [to it], and they are projected from the beginning of the ascending sign: and where it reaches, there is the Lot. **14** And it signifies things taken furtively, or which flee away, or have fallen into a well, and prison, and liberation from prison or fetters, and praise and blame.

---

[261] Leopold describes a medieval (and perhaps unnecessarily complicated) way of projecting Lots. Here, we are calculating the Lot of Fortune. It is a diurnal chart, so first we count forward from the Sun to the Moon: in this case, the distance is 62°. From here we might jump directly to projecting this from the degree of the Ascendant at 15° Aries, yielding 17° Gemini. But some medievals thought it would be easier if one counted in increments of 30°, which is more intuitively done from the beginning of the sign. So, on top of the 62° between the Sun and Moon, they added the degrees which had actually arisen, of the rising sign (8): in this case, since 15° of Aries have arisen, we add 62° + 15° = 77°. Now we can begin projecting from the beginning of the sign Aries, casting off increments of 30°: we cast off 30° for Aries, with 47° remaining; we cast off 30° for Taurus, with 17° remaining. Therefore, the Lot must be at 17° Gemini, which it is.
[262] See *Gr. Intr.* VIII.3, lines 371-83.

15 The Lot of Jupiter,[263] which is the Lot of blessedness and aid, is taken in the day from the Lot of future things to Jupiter (and in the night the reverse), and on top [of that] are added the degrees of the ascending sign which have ascended, and it is projected from the beginning of the sign: and where it reaches, there is this Lot. **16** And it signifies honor and faith, and effort in a good work, and a praiseworthy end, and victory, and the love of God, and a just judgment among brothers, and the building of places of prayer, wisdom and loftiness, trust in the good, and kindness.

17 The Lot of Mars,[264] which is that of boldness, is taken in the day from Mars (who is the significator of boldness) to the degree of the Lot of Fortune (in the night the reverse), and on top [of that] are joined the degrees of the Ascendant, and it is projected from the beginning of the ascending sign: and where it reaches, there is this Lot. **18** And it signifies honesty and sharpness and boldness, and greatness of heart with vehemence, killing and robbing, and foul and horrid words, lascivious things, and seductions and craftiness.

19 The Lot of Venus,[265] which is that of love and concord, is taken in the day from the Lot of Fortune (because it is a significator of love and [good] fortune) to the Lot of future things (in the night, the reverse), and the degrees of the ascending sign which have ascended are added on top, and it is projected from the beginning of the sign: and where it reaches, there is this Lot. **20** And it signifies pleasure and passionate desire for sexual intercourse, and the desires of the mind, and marriage-unions, and happiness and praises and delight.

21 The Lot of Mercury,[266] which is that of cleverness,[267] is the Lot of poverty and moderate cleverness: it is taken in the day from the Lot of future things to the Lot of Fortune (in the night, the reverse), and what ascends of the sign of the Ascendant is increased on top [of that], and it is projected from the beginning of the ascending sign: and where the counting reaches, there is this Lot. **22** And it signifies poverty, hatred, contention, doing business, writings and numbers, the seeking of diverse sciences, and cleverness in astronomy.

---

[263] See *Gr. Intr.* VIII.3, lines 390-404.
[264] See *Gr. Intr.* VIII.3, lines 410-19.
[265] See *Gr. Intr.* VIII.3, lines 428-37.
[266] See *Gr. Intr.* VIII.3, lines 438-49.
[267] *Ingenii*, which is a difficult term to translate from Latin: it ranges from character and temperament, to cleverness and skill.

[Lots of the 1st house]

23 There[268] follows the Lots of the 12 houses, which are of diverse significations because [the houses] necessarily have diverse [significations]: for example, in the eighth house, which signifies death, some die from a long illness, others a short one, others by the sword, others by shipwreck—the diversity of which matter happens on account of diverse significators. **24** The first Lot[269] is that of the Ascendant, and it is that of life, whose significators are Saturn and Jupiter because [these] planets are higher and slower than the others, and therefore they signify the length and duration of life; and the Ascendant participates with them, because it signifies life itself. **25** And this Lot is taken in the day from Jupiter to Saturn (in the night, the reverse), and what is ascending of the Ascendant is added, and it is projected from the beginning of the ascending sign: and where it reaches, there is this Lot. **26** And it signifies natural life and the condition of the body and the means of subsistence: and if it was of a good condition, it signifies the extensiveness of life and good health of the body, and the joys of the soul (and contrariwise).

27 The second Lot[270] of the Ascendant is that of duration and stability. **28** The Sun and Moon are the stronger significators in the world and in strength, and they signify the soul and body—through a good mixture of which there is the durability of life (and contrariwise)—and their Lots signify [good] fortune. **29** So, this Lot is taken in the day from the Lot of Fortune to the Lot of future things (and in the night the reverse), and on top is joined the degrees of the ascending sign which are ascending, and it is projected from the beginning of the ascending sign: and where it reaches, there is this Lot. **30** And it signifies the face of the native, and of his father and mother (whether he is like the father or mother), and the fitness of the native's body, and [its] soundness[271] at the hour of his nativity, and foreign travel. **31** And if this Lot and its lord were of a good condition, the native will be handsome in the face and other limbs, and healthy for his whole life, he will be successful at foreign travel; if the reverse, say the reverse. **32** And if it deviates towards the significator of the father, the native will be like the father, and likewise

---

[268] See *Gr. Intr.* VIII.4, lines 489-503.
[269] See *Gr. Intr.* VIII.4, lines 536-50.
[270] See *Gr. Intr.* VIII.4, lines 551-91.
[271] Reading *sanitatem* with John's Latin for *suavitatem* ("sweetness").

with respect to the mother. **33** And if you want to know whether a matter or man would endure, once you knew the nativity or revolution of the year or he asked about this, look at this Lot: which if it is in an aspect [with its lord][272] or with the lords of the angles, or with the lord of the Ascendant in an angle, it signifies its duration; if remote from an angle, destruction and impediments. **34** [If it was impeded][273] in an angle it will last with sorrow, in a succeedent in a middling way, in a remote [place] more so.

35 The third Lot[274] is that of reason and sense, and it is taken from Mercury in the day (because he is a significator of reason) to Mars (who is a significator of heat and motion), in the night the reverse, and it is projected from the Ascendant.[275] **36** And this Lot signifies reason and sense. **37** And if this Lot was with the lord of the Ascendant or its lord, or in a sign in which the lord of the Ascendant had testimony, and Mercury looked at them from a strong aspect, he will be reasonable and knowledgeable. **38** And if Mars looked at the lord of the Lot and [the lord of] the Ascendant, he will have the most tenacious memory and sense and sharpness.

[Lots of the 2nd house]

39 The second house[276] has three Lots. **40** The first is the Lot of assets: it is taken in the day and night from the lord of the house of assets to the degree of the house of assets, by equal degrees,[277] and on top are added the degrees of the sign of the Ascendant which have ascended. **41** And this Lot signifies success and livelihood and food by which he is sustained for his whole life. **42** And if it was in a good place, it signifies a good condition in assets and the means of livelihood and food (and the reverse). **43** But the rest of the significators of assets and fortune signify the other goods of fortune which are acquired, hoarded, and kept safe.

---

[272] Adding based on John's Latin.
[273] Adding based on John's Latin. Leopold's reading of this sentence is a bit free, but the point is that angular planets tend to show something lasting, and cadent or falling planets show it receding and disappearing.
[274] See *Gr. Intr.* VIII.4, lines 592-603.
[275] This Lot is also known as the Lot of action or work (Gr. *praxis*), a tenth-house Lot which seems to deal with the use of technical skills; one can see the similarity in the meanings here.
[276] See *Gr. Intr.* VIII.4, lines 604-17.
[277] That is, by zodiacal degrees.

44 The second Lot[278] of the house of assets, which is that of money-lenders,[279] is taken in the day and night from Saturn to Mercury, and is projected from the Ascendant. **45** And if this Lot was impeded, and it and its lord had a signification for assets,[280] the majority of assets will be had because of money-lenders and debts; but if made fortunate, it will be the reverse.

46 The third Lot[281] of the second house is that of collection, which is taken in the day from Mercury to Venus[282] (in the night, the reverse), and is projected from the Ascendant. **47** And it signifies that the native will discover a thing which has fallen to the native or been offered [to him], while on the road or elsewhere. **48** And if any of the lords of the triplicity of that same Lot, or the Sun or Moon, is with that same Lot or in a good aspect, and this Lot was in an angle, what has departed will return [to him]. **49** And likewise, if the significators of the Lot were of a good condition in their own places in nativities, he will have success which he will find on the road, and he will be made fortunate in them (and *vice versa*).

[Lots of the 3rd house]

50 The third house[283] has three Lots. **51** The first is that of brothers,[284] and it is taken in the day and night from Saturn to Jupiter, and is projected from the Ascendant. **52** And the lord of the house of this Lot signifies the matter of brothers and their concord. **53** And if this Lot falls into a sign of many children, there will be many brothers; and the number of brothers is known by the number which is between this Lot and its lord (in terms of signs), by giving one brother to each sign.

54 The second Lot,[285] concerning the number of brothers, is taken [by day and night][286] from Mercury to Saturn, and [to it] is joined, etc., and it is projected from the Ascendant. **55** And if it falls into a sign of many children,

---

[278] See *Gr. Intr.* VIII.4, lines 618-23.
[279] *Feneratorum.* Or perhaps, money-*lending*; also, "interest."
[280] Reading *fueritque ei et domino eius significatio in substantia* with John, for *fuerit levis dominatio eius significator in substantia.*
[281] See *Gr. Intr.* VIII.4, lines 624-39.
[282] Reading with *Gr. Intr.* for "Mars."
[283] See *Gr. Intr.* VIII.4, lines 646-49, and 658-68.
[284] This should be read as including sisters.
[285] See *Gr. Intr.* VIII.4, lines 672-82.
[286] Adding with John's Latin.

there will be many brothers and sisters according to the number of the signs and planets—and perhaps the counting will reach the amount of the [lesser] years of the planets (or the middle or greater ones)—and planets looking [at it] will increase [according to] their years. **56** And if this Lot falls into a sign of few children, there will be few.

57 The third Lot[287] is of the death of brothers and sisters: this is taken in the day from the Sun to the degree of the Midheaven,[288] and they are increased [by adding the degrees of the Ascendant], and it is projected from the Ascendant. **58** And it signifies the reason for the death of brothers and sisters. **59** And if this Lot reached the significators of the brothers and sisters (or conversely) by profection by sign or according to direction by degree, the brothers and sisters will have evil.

[Lots of the 4th house]

60 The fourth house[289] has eight Lots. **61** The first is that of fathers, and it is taken in the day from the Sun to Saturn (in the night, the reverse), and it is projected from the Ascendant. **62** And [this is] because the Sun is a significator of life, and Saturn that of antiquity. **63** And if the signification of Saturn is annihilated under the rays,[290] the signification is taken in the day from the Sun to Jupiter (in the night the reverse), and projected from the Ascendant. **64** And this Lot signifies the matter of the father and his nobility, and the lord of the house of the father [signifies] his assets and labors, and the fortune of the father. **65** And if this Lot was in a good condition of the circle, the father is noble; and if its lord is of a good condition, he will be made fortunate (and *vice versa*). **66** And this Lot signifies the native's rule and honor, according to [its] strength.

67 The second Lot[291] is that of the death of fathers, and it is taken in the day from Saturn to Jupiter (in the night the reverse), and is projected from the Ascendant. **68** And this Lot signifies the reason for the death of fathers: and whenever the profection reaches this Lot and its lord, it signifies evil for

---

[287] See *Gr. Intr.* VIII.4, lines 684-95.
[288] In a quadrant-based house system, the Midheaven would mark the 8th house from the 3rd: the death of siblings.
[289] See *Gr. Intr.* VIII.4, lines 696-
[290] Or rather, if *Saturn himself* is under the rays.
[291] See *Gr. Intr.* VIII.4, lines 727-33.

the father; and [also] when any of them reaches the significators of the father.

69 The third Lot[292] is that of grandfathers,[293] and is taken in the day from the lord of the place of the Sun to Saturn (in the night the reverse), and is projected from the Ascendant; and if the Sun is in the Ascendant [or][294] his own house, it is taken from the first degree of Leo in the day to Saturn (in the night the reverse), and is projected from the Ascendant—and one does not care whether Saturn is under the rays or not. **70** This Lot and its lord signifies the condition of grandfathers, and whenever it was with the bad ones it signifies the dangers of the grandfathers, and if with good ones they will find [good] fortune.

71 The fourth Lot[295] is that of parentage and origin, and it is taken in the day from Saturn to Mars (in the night the reverse), and on top are increased the degrees which Mercury has made in the sign in which he is, and it is projected from the beginning of that same sign: and where it reaches, there is this Lot. **72** And if this Lot was in an angle, and any lord of [its] dignity (or the Sun or the lord of the Midheaven) is looking at it with a good aspect, the native will be noble and of a respectable parentage. **73** And if this Lot falls from an angle and is joined to bad ones, or no lord of its dignity or the lords of the angles is looking at it, he will be disparaged in his parentage.

74 The fifth Lot[296] is that of real estate:[297] this, according to Hermes, is taken in the day and night from Saturn to the Moon, and it is projected from the Ascendant—and this Lot matches the Lot of the king or kingdom, and equally the work a native does.[298] **75** If this Lot and its lord were of a good condition and place, the native will have real estate and will be made fortunate with the cultivation of the earth, and he will acquire assets from thence; if of a bad condition, speak to the contrary.

76 The sixth Lot[299] is that of real estate according to the Persians: it is taken in the day from Mercury to Jupiter (in the night the reverse), and is

---

[292] See *Gr. Intr.* VIII.4, lines 734-45.
[293] Or, "forefathers" (*avorum*).
[294] John's Latin only has the Sun in his own house (domicile), so this is an error or amplification by Leopold.
[295] See *Gr. Intr.* VIII.4, lines 746-59.
[296] See *Gr. Intr.* VIII.4, lines 760-71.
[297] Lat. *haereditatum*. In Latin (and English) this word also has connotations of "inheritance," because inheritance was often a matter of rights to land or property.
[298] See **206** below, but also **174** and **257**.
[299] See *Gr. Intr.* VIII.4, lines 772-76.

projected from the Ascendant. **77** And through this one looks in matters of real estate just as with the preceding Lot.

78 The seventh Lot[300] is that of the cultivation of the earth and crops, and it is taken in the day and night from Venus to Saturn, and is projected from the Ascendant: and where it reaches, this is the Lot. **79** And if its lords were made fortunate, then he will have success in the cultivation of the earth; and if they are impeded, he will suffer harm and [it will be] horrible in this.

80 The eighth Lot[301] is that of the ends of things, and it is taken in the day and night from Saturn to the lord of the house of the conjunction or prevention which preceded the nativity, and is projected from the Ascendant. **81** And if this Lot and its lord were in signs rising directly or made fortunate, the ends of his matters will be good and praiseworthy; but if in signs rising crookedly or impeded, the ends of his matters will be bad. **82** And if one of them was in a straight sign and the other in a crooked sign, there will be diversity and mixture in the ends of his matters; after this, the matter will revert to what the sign in which the lord of the Lot is, signifies.[302]

[Lots of the 5th house]

83 The fifth house[303] has five Lots. **84** The first one is that of a child, and it is taken in the day from Jupiter to Saturn (in the night the reverse), and it is projected from the Ascendant. **85** And it matches the Lot of life in a nativity, and [in the night][304] the Lot of a child and that of brothers agree (that is, they meet in one place). **86** And Theophilus[305] takes it in the day *and* night from Jupiter and Saturn, while [the one stated first][306] is more true. **87** And it signifies whether a man will have a child or not; and if this Lot and its lord were in a sign of many children, he will have many children, and in sterile ones none, if one of few, few. **88** And if this Lot signifies that there will be a child and it was made fortunate, the child will live (and *vice versa*). **89** And it signifies the general condition of the child, and how he will relate with his father.

---

[300] See *Gr. Intr.* VIII.4, lines 777-83.
[301] See *Gr. Intr.* VIII.4, lines 784-95.
[302] This is a common doctrine since antiquity: a given position signifies the beginning of a matter, while its lord signifies what happens later.
[303] See *Gr. Intr.* VIII.4, lines 796-817.
[304] That is, if the Lot of brothers should be reversed; in **51** above it is not, but I believe it should be.
[305] Reading with John's Latin; Leopold has mistaken *putavit Theophilus* for *Ptolomeus plus*.
[306] Adding with John's Latin.

90 And it is taken in terms of every sign which is between the Lot and its lord: and one child is given to each [sign].

91 The second Lot[307] of the fifth house signifies the hour in which there would be a child, and the number of them, and it is taken in the day and night from Mars to Jupiter (because Mars is a significator of heat, and Jupiter moisture, which are necessary for sexual intercourse), and it is projected from the Ascendant. **92** And if this Lot and the rest of the significators of a child signified that the native will have a child, it even signifies the number of their children. **93** And if Jupiter reached this Lot bodily in the sign, or he looked by a strong aspect, it removes the child [from the womb] in that same hour—if his age was appropriate [for having a child]. **94** And if it is in a feminine sign, there will be more females, and if in a masculine one it signifies many sons. **95** Then, if this Lot and its lord are in a sign of whatever kind, this signifies the number according to the number of the lesser or middle or greater years, and perhaps those which are looking will increase according to the number of their own years.

96 The third Lot,[308] of masculine children, is taken in the day and night from the Moon to Jupiter, and is projected from the Ascendant: because the Moon signifies a young age, and Jupiter creation and increase, and Jupiter signifies masculine [children] more so than Saturn, whence he is rather taken for this Lot.

97 The fourth Lot[309] is that of daughters and females, and is taken in the day and night from the Moon to Venus, and is projected from the Ascendant (because the Moon signifies adolescence and feminine persons, Venus generation and moisture). **98** And the Moon is always put first because her signification over women is stronger than that of Venus. **99** And this Lot signifies daughters,[310] [and] the marriage-union of, and dwelling with, women. **100** And if this Lot and its lord are of a good condition (or bad), [it shows their condition to be good or bad; while if you wanted to know whether the

---

[307] See *Gr. Intr.* VIII.4, lines 821-47.
[308] See *Gr. Intr.* VIII.4, lines 848-65.
[309] See *Gr. Intr.* VIII.4, lines 868-
[310] Reading the feminine (*filiarum*), especially so as to distinguish this from the rest of the sentence (which would otherwise read, "feminine children, marriage-unions, and dwelling").

condition of][311] the male children or female children will be better, [favor the one] whose Lot and lord were better.

101 The fifth Lot[312] teaches whether [a child] would be male or female, and is taken from the lord of the house of the Moon to the Moon by day (in the night, the reverse), and is projected from the Ascendant. **102** And if it fell into a masculine sign it will be male (and *vice versa*).

[Lots of the 6th house]

103 There are[313] four Lots of the sixth house. **104** The first one is of infirmity and an inseparable accident,[314] and is taken in the day from Saturn to Mars (in the night the reverse), and is projected from the Ascendant.

105 The second one,[315] of infirmities, according to certain people is taken in the day and night from Mercury to Mars and is projected from the Ascendant.

106 The third:[316] the Lot of slaves, because male and female slaves and legates are quick things, therefore they are attributed to the quicker [planets] (namely Mercury and the Moon): and it is taken in the day and night from Mercury to the Moon and projected from the Ascendant. **107** And if this Lot and its lord are made fortunate, usefulness is had from slaves (and *vice versa*). **108** And if they fall into signs of many [children] there will be many male and female slaves, etc.

109 The fourth Lot[317] is that of captives and the conquered, and is taken in the day from the lord of the house of the Sun to the Sun, in the night from the lord of the house of the Moon to the Moon, and is projected from the Ascendant. **110** And if this Lot falls in optimal places with the fortunes, he will be liberated from captivity and from prison; if in bad [places] and with the bad ones, there will be loss. **111** And if the Sun by day is in his own house (or the Moon in the night in her own house), [that] one of them will be the significator: and see where it falls in the circle, and from whom it is

---

[311] Adding and reading with John's Latin. Leopold seems to have broken off in the middle of one sentence, and resumed several lines later.
[312] See *Gr. Intr.* VIII.4, lines 896-902.
[313] See *Gr. Intr.* VIII.4, lines 903-08.
[314] That is, of chronic or long-term illnesses.
[315] See *Gr. Intr.* VIII.4, lines 909-11.
[316] See *Gr. Intr.* VIII.4, lines 912-27.
[317] See *Gr. Intr.* VIII.4, lines 933-43.

being separated and to whom it is being conjoined, and judge according to that.

[Lots of the 7th house]

112 The seventh house[318] has sixteen Lots. **113** The first, of the marriage-union of men according to Hermes: since Saturn is a significator of antiquity and masculinity, and Venus [has signification] over femininity, and the male precedes the female, for that reason according to Hermes the Lot of marriage-union is taken in the day and night from Saturn to Venus, and is projected from the Ascendant. **114** And judge the marriage-union and its usefulness in accordance with how this Lot and its lord are situated.

115 The second Lot[319] of marriage-union [is] according to Valens, which is taken in the day and night from the Sun to Venus, and is projected from the Ascendant.

116 The third Lot,[320] of the cleverness of men towards women, is like the Lot of marriage-union [of men] according to Valens.

117 The fourth Lot[321] is of the sexual intercourse of men with women: it is like the Lot of marriage-union [of men] according to Valens.

118 The fifth Lot,[322] of sexual lewdness and sexual intercourse of men with women, is like the aforesaid Lot [of the marriage-union of men according to Valens].[323] **119** And if this Lot is in a good place, the marriage-union will be praiseworthy (and *vice versa*); and in the signification of the Lot of cleverness, [it signifies that if the place of that very Lot were good, or it was in a sign of ingenuity and cleverness],[324] he will get what he wants from women by seduction.[325] **120** And if the lord of this Lot looks at the Lot of the nuptials[326] of men [according to Hermes],[327] he will be a fornicator.[328]

---

[318] See *Gr. Intr.* VIII.4, lines 944-60.
[319] See *Gr. Intr.* VIII.4, lines 966-69.
[320] See *Gr. Intr.* VIII.4, lines 971-73.
[321] See *Gr. Intr.* VIII.4, lines 974-75.
[322] See *Gr. Intr.* VIII.4, lines 976-93.
[323] Adding with John's Latin for clarity.
[324] Adding with John's Latin.
[325] Lit., "he will seduce."
[326] Reading *nuptiarum* with John for *imperitorum*.
[327] Adding with John: this is the first, Saturn-Venus Lot mentioned above.
[328] Reading *fornicator* with John for *fortunatio*.

121 The sixth Lot,³²⁹ of the marriage-union of women according to Hermes, is similar to the reasoning for the marriage-union of men, and is taken in the day and night from Venus to Saturn, and is projected from the Ascendant—and agrees with the Lot of the cultivation of the earth. **122** And if this Lot and its lord are of a good condition, a woman is made fortunate in her marriage-union (and *vice versa*).

123 The seventh Lot,³³⁰ of the marriage-union of women according to Valens, is taken in the day and night from the Moon to Mars, and is projected from the Ascendant (and certain people took it contrariwise in the night, but the first one is better).

124 The eighth Lot,³³¹ of the cleverness of women towards men, is like the Lot of the marriage-union of men according to Hermes.³³²

125 The ninth Lot,³³³ of [the conjoining with] women, is like the Lot of the marriage-union of women³³⁴ according to Valens.

126 The tenth Lot,³³⁵ of the sexual lewdness of women and their filthiness, is like the Lot of the marriage-union of women according to Valens. **127** And if this Lot and its lord were of a good condition, a marriage-union will please a women—and vice-versa, because through a marriage-union she will be sad. **128** And pronounce this confidently³³⁶ according to the status of the Lots and their lords.

129 The eleventh Lot³³⁷ is that of the respectability of women, and is taken in the day and night from the Moon to Venus, and projected from the Ascendant. **130** Which, if it falls into a fixed sign, it signifies respectability; if in a movable one, [she is] false; if in a common one, in the middle—and [she is] more [respectable]³³⁸ if a fortune is there or is looking at that place.

131 The twelfth Lot,³³⁹ of the marriage-union of men and women, is taken in the day and night (according to Hermes) from Venus to the nuptial degree³⁴⁰ (that is, the seventh house), and is projected from the Ascendant. **132**

---

³²⁹ See *Gr. Intr.* VIII.4, lines 994-1003.
³³⁰ See *Gr. Intr.* VIII.4, lines 1004-09.
³³¹ See *Gr. Intr.* VIII.4, lines 1010-12.
³³² The sixth Lot above.
³³³ See *Gr. Intr.* VIII.4, lines 1014-15.
³³⁴ Reading with John for "men" (the seventh Lot above).
³³⁵ See *Gr. Intr.* VIII.4, lines 1016-22.
³³⁶ *Certe.*
³³⁷ See *Gr. Intr.* VIII.4, lines 1037-46.
³³⁸ Adding based on John.
³³⁹ See *Gr. Intr.* VIII.4, lines 1047-54.
³⁴⁰ Reading *gradum nuptialem* for *gradum et numerum anguli nuptiarem.*

And if this Lot is joined to the bad ones or the bad ones are looking at it, he will be blamed in his marriage-union. **133** And if the lord of the Lot is in a bad place and Venus impeded by Saturn or under the rays, he will never marry.

134 The thirteenth Lot,[341] of the hour of the marriage-union according to Hermes, is taken in the day and night from the Sun to the Moon[342] and is projected from the Ascendant. **135** And when Jupiter reaches this Lot or looks at it with a strong aspect, the man will marry a beautiful and respectable and delightful woman in that hour. **136** And this Lot is extracted from the luminaries, because one is hot and masculine and the other moist and feminine, through which universal generation happens.

137 The fourteenth Lot,[343] of the ingenuity[344] of the marriage-union, is taken in the day and night from the Sun to the Moon and is projected from Venus. **138** And if this Lot is of a good condition, fortunate in signs of cleverness,[345] the marriage-union will be good (and vice-versa).

139 The fifteenth Lot,[346] of relatives,[347] is taken in the day and night from Saturn to Venus, and is projected from the Ascendant. **140** And [if] this Lot matches the lord of the sign in which it is, [and][348] if it is of a good condition, he will meet well with relatives (and vice-versa).

141 The sixteenth Lot,[349] of those contending[350] and contentions, is taken in the day from Mars to Jupiter (and in the night the reverse), and is projected from the Ascendant. **142** Which if it falls in the Ascendant or with its lord, in any angle, the native will be contentious; and if it was impeded, he will have evil from this; and if made fortunate, it will be good. **143** And if this Lot

---

[341] See *Gr. Intr.* VIII.4, lines 1055-66.
[342] Reading with John, as Leopold has reversed them.
[343] See *Gr. Intr.* VIII.4, lines 1067-75.
[344] *Ingenii*. Or, "stratagem, ruse" (Ar.).
[345] Omitting *aut termini coniugii* ("or the bound of marriage-union"), which seems to be a puzzling misread of some aspect of John's Latin.
[346] See *Gr. Intr.* VIII.4, lines 1076-83.
[347] *Cognatorum*. I take these to be the relatives (particularly male relatives) of the spouse, both from context and by reading John's *sororii* as *soceri* ("father-in-law").
[348] Again, Leopold has left off one sentence to resume another; Abū Ma'shar was pointing out that this calculation matches a previous Lot, but also trying to talk about this Lot being in some appropriate conformity with its lord.
[349] See *Gr. Intr.* VIII.4, lines 1084-92.
[350] Reading *contendentium* with John for *concordantium*.

fell in the Ascendant along with the lord of the seventh, he will contend[351] in the presence of kings and judges.

[Lots of the 8th house]

144 The[352] eighth house has five Lots. **145** The first is that of death. **146** The Moon is the significator of bodies, and the eighth house the significator of death and loss, and Saturn signifies an ending, desolation, and destruction—just as Hermes takes this in the day and night from the degree of the Moon to the degree of the eighth house (by equal degrees), and from above are increased the degrees which Saturn has made in the sign in which he is, and it is projected from the beginning of the sign in which he is: and where it reaches, there is this Lot. **147** And if this Lot and its lord were impeded and the fortunate ones did not look at them, the native will be killed through the most foul death. **148** And if the fortunes [were looking],[353] say the contrary.

149 The second Lot[354] is said to be that of the "killing planet." **150** Because the lord of the Ascendant signifies the soul, and the Moon the body, [and] when the soul [is mixed with] the body[355] [the result] becomes well-tempered and very durable (and the contrary), therefore this Lot is taken in the day from the degree of the lord of the Ascendant to the degree of the Moon (and by night the reverse), and it is projected from the Ascendant. **151** And if the Moon alone[356] looks at this Lot, and the Moon is in a sign of severed limbs, impeded, some limb will be cut off. **152** And if this Lot and its lord, and the lords of the signs in which they are, impeded each other, he will be killed by suffering [that].

153 The third Lot,[357] of the year in which the native's death and affliction or weakening is feared, is taken in the day and night from Saturn to the degree of the lord of the house of the conjunction or prevention which was before the nativity, and it is projected from the Ascendant—because Saturn is a significator of chills, death, an end, and affliction, and likewise the degree of the conjunction or prevention. **154** And this Lot agrees with the Lot of the

---

[351] Reading *contendet* for *cadit* ("he falls").
[352] See *Gr. Intr.* VIII.4, lines 1093-1106.
[353] Adding with Abū Ma'shar.
[354] See *Gr. Intr.* VIII.4, lines 1112-25.
[355] Reading *corpori* with John for *corporis*.
[356] Reading *sola* with John for *solem et* ("the Sun and").
[357] See *Gr. Intr.* VIII.4, lines 1126-46.

end of things.[358] **155** And this Lot and its lord, if they were with the lord of the Ascendant, [impeded],[359] the native will be very much infirm and afflicted in his body and assets, and often he will approach the loss of his body. **156** And this [will be] when the Ascendant reaches this Lot, or this Lot [reaches the Ascendant by] circles (that is, profections, to which a year is given to every sign), or by direction to the Ascendant or to its lord: dangers will come to the native in his body from diseases and difficulties, and [something] horrible in [his] assets, and he will fear death from diverse directions.

157 The fourth Lot,[360] of the "heavy place," is taken in the day from Saturn to Mars (in the night the reverse), and from above are increased the degrees which Mercury has walked through in the sign in which he is, and it is projected from the beginning of that same sign: [and] where it reaches, there is this Lot (and it is like the Lot of parentage).[361] **158** And if this Lot and its lord were impeded,[362] the native will have an inseparable infirmity in the limb which the sign in which the Lot is, signifies, and his good will be delayed. **159** And if the year from the Ascendant reached this Lot, or the Lot [reached] the Ascendant or to its lord by circles (that is, profection) or by direction as was said, he will have many sorrows, and he will not complete what he began in that year; and if the bad ones are looking, it will be worse.

160 The fifth Lot,[363] of destruction, is taken in the day from Saturn to Mercury (in the night the reverse), and is projected from the Ascendant. **161** And if this Lot and its lord were impeded, and the year reached them (or any one of them) by profection or direction, the native will have evil from which he will not be liberated—and if he is liberated from one [evil], he will fall into another. **162** If the fortunate ones looked at it from strong place, they will take away a portion of that evil. **163** And if the lord of the Ascendant in the root of the nativity [was with this Lot],[364] [both] impeded, the native will be in evil for his whole life, and he will find evil in everything which he undertakes.

---

[358] In **80-82** above.
[359] Adding with John.
[360] See *Gr. Intr.* VIII.4, lines 1147-66.
[361] See **71-73** above.
[362] John has, "if this Lot were with the lord of the Ascendant, impeded."
[363] See *Gr. Intr.* VIII.4, lines 1167-81. The name for this Lot in Leopold's edition (*destructionis*) is a misread for *districtionis*, which has to do with hardships and predicaments.
[364] Adding with John.

[Lots of the 9th house]

164 The ninth house[365] has seven Lots. **165** The first is of the foreign travel of the native [by land]: it is taken from the lord of the [ninth] sign to the degree of the ninth house by equal degrees, and it is projected from the Ascendant. **166** And this Lot and its lord signify the native's foreign travel.

167 The second Lot[366] is of foreign travel by water: it is taken in the day from Saturn to 15° Cancer (in the night the reverse), and is projected from the Ascendant. **168** And if this Lot fell, along with the fortunes, in a watery sign, he will see good and prosperity in foreign travel by sea and proficiency[367] at it (and *vice versa*). **169** And if Saturn was in 15° Cancer, that very degree and the degree of the Ascendant will be significators: and judge according to the aspects of the planets to them and to the lord, etc.

170 The third Lot,[368] of faith and religion, is taken from the Moon to Mercury in the day (in the night the reverse); it is projected from the Ascendant. **171** And if this Lot and its lord fell into the Ascendant or on the significators[369] of the Ascendant (that is, with the lord of the Ascendant or with the victor over the Ascendant), the native will be religious. **172** And [it is] likewise if the significators of the Lot[370] looked at it or at the lord of the Ascendant. **173** If [it is] to the contrary, say the contrary.

174 The fourth Lot[371] is that of reason and depth of counsel and intellect: it is taken in the day from Saturn to the Moon (in the night the reverse), and is projected from the Ascendant. **175** And it signifies reason, thinking, depth of counsel [and] of intellect, and also the consideration of matters and the examination of deep matters and the discovery of forms of wisdom and praiseworthy counsels—and especially if Saturn in the day was above the earth, eastern, looking at [the Lot] and regarding it, or the Moon looked at it from an optimal place.

176 The fifth Lot,[372] of wisdom and patience. **177** Since the stability of philosophy, depth in matters and scrutiny in speaking, or the length or wide range of thought belongs to Saturn, and reason, patience, and wisdom belong

---

[365] See *Gr. Intr.* VIII.4, lines 1182-86.
[366] See *Gr. Intr.* VIII.4, lines 1187-96.
[367] *Exercitio*.
[368] See *Gr. Intr.* VIII.4, lines 1197-1204.
[369] Reading *significatores* for *significationes* ("significations").
[370] I take this to be Mercury and the Moon.
[371] See *Gr. Intr.* VIII.4, lines 1205-12.
[372] See *Gr. Intr.* VIII.4, lines 1213-27.

to Jupiter, and to Mercury [belongs] writing, wisdom, and teaching, and the testing out[373] of things, the Lot of wisdom is taken from these planets. **178** And this Lot of wisdom and patience is taken in the day from Saturn to Jupiter (in the night the reverse), and is projected from Mercury: and this signifies wisdom and patience and extensiveness.[374] **179** And if this Lot was in the aspect of Saturn and Jupiter, received [by them] or by one of them, the native will be extensive and patient and rational. **180** And if Mercury looked at it, he will be wise in connection with deep matters, and quick in the discovery of similar things.

181 The sixth Lot,[375] of histories and the rumors of men, and tales, is taken in the day from the Sun to Jupiter (and in the night the reverse), and is projected from the Ascendant; and this Lot agrees with the Lot of the father (because it is like [it] if Saturn[376] was under the rays). **182** And if this Lot falls in an angle, in the aspect of Mercury or Venus, and the lord of the Ascendant is looking at it, the native will retain ancient histories and rumors, and he will be an inventor of tales and beautiful narrations in which listeners will delight, and will laugh and have fun (and *vice versa*).

183 The seventh Lot,[377] of rumors and whether they are true or false, is taken in the day and night from Mercury to the Moon, and is projected from the Ascendant (and it is like the Lot of slaves). **184** Which, if it is in an angle or in a fixed sign or in a sign of equal (that is, "straight") ascension, the rumors will be true; if it was otherwise, it will be to the contrary.

[Lots of the 10th house]

185 The tenth house[378] has twelve Lots. **186** The first[379] is of the native's nobility and one about whom it is doubted whether he is the son of the one to whom he is imputed: it is taken in the day from the Sun to the degree of his own exaltation (namely 19° Aries), and you will take it in the night from

---

[373] *Experimenta*.
[374] Reading *spaciositas* for *speciositas* ("looking good," "being handsome"). The Arabic (*tuwadah*) means deliberateness, a calm demeanor, etc. John might have understood this to mean going on at length, being searching and extensive in one's mind.
[375] See *Gr. Intr.* VIII.4, lines 1228-37.
[376] Reading *Saturnus* with Abū Ma'shar for *haec pars* ("this Lot").
[377] See *Gr. Intr.* VIII.4, lines 1238-43.
[378] See *Gr. Intr.* VIII.4, lines 1245-68.
[379] This is the Hellenistic Lot of exaltation.

the degree of the Moon to 3° Taurus, and is projected from the Ascendant. **187** For the Sun is the luminary of the day, and in the day is the significator of the native's life and his lastingness, and it signifies life, mind, honor, loftiness, rulership, and victory, and the Moon is nocturnal and the significator by night of those things which the Sun signifies in the day. **188** And where it reaches, there is this Lot. **189** Which if it would fall into the Midheaven or with planets which were of a good condition and place, the native will reach nobility and the greatest exaltation, and the ranks of the rich; and if rulership is owed to him, he will have it. **190** And if the Sun in the day was in 19° Aries, and the Moon in the night in 3° Taurus, the signification will belong to those same degrees and to the Ascendant. **191** And if the significators of this Lot looked at it, and they were [configured] to it by any good aspects,[380] the native will be the son of the father to whom he is imputed; and if it is to the contrary, [he comes] from adultery.

192 The second Lot,[381] that of the king, is taken in the day from Mars to Moon (in the night the reverse) and is projected from the Ascendant. **193** And if this Lot and its lord were mixed with the lord of the tenth or[382] of the Ascendant, the native will be a king or general,[383] his words will be received by the wealthy, and they will be heard willingly.

194 The third Lot,[384] of managers or consuls[385] or kings, is taken in the day from Mercury to Mars (in the night the reverse), and is projected from the Ascendant. **195** For Mercury is the significator of giving and taking [and] distributing things, counseling, ruling, prohibiting, legates, letters, counting, sense and clarity, cleverness, and correction; but fear and terror and upheaval belong to Mars. **196** And if this Lot and its lord are of a good condition and place, with the lord of the Ascendant, the native will be of a subtle mind, teachable, rational, a manager with benefit,[386] or he will be a scribe of kings or a collector of the land taxes of the king, and his command and prohibition will pass to the ends of the earth.

197 The fourth Lot,[387] of the aid of the kingdom and victory, is taken in the day from the Sun to Saturn (in the night the reverse), and is projected

---

[380] Omitting a redundant *bonus*, with Abū Ma'shar.
[381] See *Gr. Intr.* VIII.4, lines 1269-73.
[382] Reading with John for "and."
[383] Or, "leader" (*dux*).
[384] See *Gr. Intr.* VIII.4, lines 1274-87.
[385] Reading with John for "the management of counsels."
[386] *Dispositor in fructum*. John has *fruetur consulatu*, "he will enjoy a consulship."
[387] See *Gr. Intr.* VIII.4, lines 1289-97.

from the Ascendant; and it matches the Lot of fathers when Saturn is not under the rays. **198** Which, if it is mixed with the lord of the Midheaven and the lord of the Ascendant, he will have rulership and honor; and if it was in a sign in which the lord of the Ascendant has dignities, he will have victory against those who contend with him.

199 The fifth Lot,[388] of those who are made lofty unexpectedly, is taken in the day from Saturn to the Lot of Fortune (in the night, the reverse), and is projected from the Ascendant; and this Lot is like the Lot of Saturn, which is the Lot of prisons.[389] **200** And if it was in an optimal place from the Ascendant and from a fortune, he will suddenly be made lofty; and if it is impeded, evil will come to him suddenly.

201 The sixth Lot,[390] of nobles or the honored, is taken in the day and night from Mercury to the Sun, and is projected from the Ascendant.[391] **202** And if this Lot and its lord are of a good condition, the native will be honored among kings and the wealthy. **203** And if it is with a planet which has strong testimony in the Midheaven, he will have the greatest dignity, [or] position of first place from which he will be famous, just as [the head] of a tribe and the citizens of cities are made famous by their own citizens.

204 The seventh Lot,[392] of soldiers and ministers, is taken in the day from Mars to Saturn (and in the night the reverse), and is projected from the Ascendant. **205** And [if] this Lot and its lord [are] commixed with the lord of the Ascendant, it signifies that the native will be of the soldiers of the king, or a minister.

206 The eighth Lot,[393] of rulership[394] and what work the native will acquire, is taken in the day and night from Saturn to the Moon, and is projected from the Ascendant. **207** For adversity and great poverty [and works] like the building of houses, and laborious and hateful works belong to Saturn, and the Moon signifies labor and quickness on account of the speediness of her motion; and the common people [belong to her], and Saturn signifies the wealthy. **208** And this Lot signifies rulership, honor, and magnificence, and the work of the native and the mastery of his hand: whence, if

---

[388] See *Gr. Intr.* VIII.4, lines 1298-1308.
[389] See **13-14** above.
[390] See *Gr. Intr.* VIII.4, lines 1309-18.
[391] Note that this Lot can only ever be in the twelfth, first, or second signs.
[392] See *Gr. Intr.* VIII.4, lines 1319-23.
[393] See *Gr. Intr.* VIII.4, lines 1324-43.
[394] Reading *regni* with John, for "king."

this Lot and its lord were of a good condition, he will acquire rulership and power. **209** And if it was in Gemini or Virgo, or in signs of arts or masteries, he will be made lofty through the works of his own hands; and if it is commixed with the significators of assets, he will acquire great assets (and vice-versa).

210 The ninth Lot[395] is of those working with their own hands: it is taken in the day from Mercury to Venus (in the night the reverse), and is projected from the Ascendant—for Mercury signifies masteries and working in gold and silver, and Venus ornaments. **211** And the native will be in the trade of [some] thing in accordance with how this Lot and its lord bear themselves.

212 The tenth Lot,[396] of the business of selling and buying according to certain people, is taken in the day from the Lot of future things[397] to the Lot of Fortune (in the night the reverse), and is projected from the Ascendant. **213** Which, if it is in the aspect of Mercury, received, the native will be experienced in business matters; and if made fortunate, he will be successful (and *vice versa*).

214 The eleventh Lot,[398] of work, is of a matter which it is necessary that it come to be: [it is taken] in the day from the Sun to Jupiter (in the night the reverse), and is projected from the Ascendant; and this Lot is like the Lot of fathers when Saturn is under the rays. **215** And if this Lot is with the lord of the Ascendant, the native will be focused[399] in every matter of his own; and if this Lot is with the fortunes, his trade work will be beneficial for him (and *vice versa*).

216 The twelfth Lot[400] is that of the mother, and is taken in the day from Venus to the Moon (in the night the reverse), and is projected from the Ascendant. **217** And this Lot signifies the condition of the mother, and it is the Lot of mothers, and is put in the tenth house for the reason that [the tenth] is opposed to the house of fathers.[401]

---

[395] See *Gr. Intr.* VIII.4, lines 1347-59.
[396] See *Gr. Intr.* VIII.4, lines 1360-69.
[397] The Lot of Spirit.
[398] See *Gr. Intr.* VIII.4, lines 1370-82.
[399] *Angustiabitur*, which has more to do with feeling cramped and hemmed in. The Arabic connotes being absorbed, preoccupied (*munkamish*), so I have opted for "focused."
[400] See *Gr. Intr.* VIII.4, lines 1383-87.
[401] That is, the tenth is the seventh from the fourth. This is a later development based on a particular reading of Ptolemy. In *Tet.* III.5 (Robbins) or III.6 (Schmidt), Ptolemy names "the culminating sign" (that is, the tenth) and "the place of the mother" (i.e., the place of the Moon by night and Venus by day) as places of the native's *siblings*; but then he proceeds to speak of these as though they were a single place, as well as the place following

[Lots of the 11th house]

218 The eleventh house[402] has eleven Lots. **219** The first is that of excellence and nobility: and because the Lot of Fortune and the Lot of future things are more excellent than the other Lots, for that reason they signify nobility and excellence—[therefore] this Lot is taken from them, in the day from the Lot of Fortune to the Lot of future things (in the night the reverse), and is projected from the Ascendant. **220** And this Lot is like the Lot of duration and the Lot of Venus.[403] **221** Which if it is with the fortunes, in an [optimal][404] place, received, and especially in the tenth and in the eleventh, falling away from[405] the bad ones, the native will be excellent and men will be in need of him, [and he will be][406] like princes in tribes, and his name will remain throughout the ages.

222 The second Lot,[407] of esteem towards men,[408] is taken in the day from the Lot of Fortune to the Lot of future things (in the night the reverse), and is projected from the Ascendant: and this Lot is like the Lot of Venus.[409] **223** Which, if it fell with the fortunes or the fortunes were the lords of the house in which it is (or of the exaltation or triplicity), he will be esteemed by men and delightful in their eyes. **224** And if [it was] with bad ones which have no dignity there, he will be hateful to men, and burdensome.[410]

225 The third Lot,[411] of one known among men and honorable among them,[412] is taken in the day from the Lot of Fortune to the Sun (in the night the reverse), and is projected from the Ascendant. **226** Which, if it is received, with Jupiter [and] the Sun and the rest of the fortunes, or they looked at it and at the lord of the Ascendant with a good aspect, the native will be

---

after it. Schmidt's translation and explanation (p. 19) convincingly translates it as the tenth sign *from* the place of the mother (i.e., the tenth *from* the Moon by night or Venus by day). But the Persians and Arabs identified the tenth *as being* the place of the mother, took it out of its context of siblings, and justified it by saying that it was the seventh from the fourth.
[402] See *Gr. Intr.* VIII.4, lines 1388-1404.
[403] See **27-29** and **19**, respectively.
[404] Adding with John.
[405] That is, "in aversion to."
[406] Adding with John.
[407] See *Gr. Intr.* VIII.4, lines 1405-14.
[408] Omitting *est*.
[409] Again, see **19**. It is also like the preceding Lot in **219**.
[410] *Ponderosus* (lit., "heavy"), but following the Arabic connotation of the word.
[411] See *Gr. Intr.* VIII.4, lines 1415-25.
[412] Reading with John for *nati...honorabiles*.

honored by the wealthy and the common people, and he will well complete many business affairs.

227 The fourth Lot,[413] of luckiness (that is, success), is taken in the day from the Lot of Fortune to Jupiter (in the night the reverse), and is projected from the Ascendant. **228** Which, if it is with the lord of the Ascendant or [the lord of the Ascendant] is looking at it, the native will be lucky in all matters; and if the fortunes are looking, he will do what he wants, and will have more of the good than he wished for.

229 The fifth Lot,[414] of cravings and enthusiasm and appetite in the love of the world, is taken in the day from the Lot of Fortune to the Lot of future things (in the night the reverse), and is projected from the Ascendant. **230** If this Lot is in an optimal place, the native will conquer his own cravings (and vice-versa).

231 The sixth Lot[415] is that of hope and trust, and is taken in the day from Saturn to Venus (in the night the reverse), and is projected from the Ascendant. **232** But certain people extract this Lot like the Lot of the marriage-union of men according to Hermes—and this is an error.[416] **233** And if this Lot is in an optimal place, made fortunate, he will have what he hoped for (and vice-versa).

234 The seventh Lot,[417] of friendships, is taken in the day and night from Moon to Mercury, and is projected from the Ascendant: because the signification of Mercury is diverse (now masculine, now female, now bad, now good), and is always inclined towards the stronger [nature],[418] and because the Moon is similar through the quickness of her motion, and likewise [the condition of men][419] is diverse with friends. **235** And if this Lot and its lord were of a good condition, in movable signs, he will have many friends; and if they were made fortunate, they will be useful to him and he to them; and if they are received, he will be loved by them. **236** And certain people think that the[420] Lot of Mercury signifies the entirety[421] of the condition of friend-

---

[413] See *Gr. Intr.* VIII.4, lines 1426-38.
[414] See *Gr. Intr.* VIII.4, lines 1439-47.
[415] See *Gr. Intr.* VIII.4, lines 1448-56.
[416] That is, according to **113** above, the marriage Lot according to Hermes should *not* be reversed at night, whereas this Lot should be.
[417] See *Gr. Intr.* VIII.4, lines 1457-72.
[418] Adding with John. That is the stronger nature among the planets to which he is connected.
[419] Adding with John.
[420] Omitting "this" (*haec*), with John.

ships, but this is inappropriate because the signification of the Lot of Mercury over friends is partial.

237 The eighth Lot,[422] of concord or discord, is taken in the day and night from the Lot of future things to Mercury, and is projected from the Ascendant. **238** And it signifies the esteem of friends [and] of a husband and wife: which, if in the nativity of men it is in the Ascendant or exaltation[423] of the other or in concordant[424] signs, they will esteem each other (and vice-versa).

239 The ninth Lot,[425] of fertility and abundance, is taken in the day and night from the Moon to Mercury and is projected from the Ascendant. **240** And if this Lot and its lord is mixed favorably with the Lot of Fortune and the lord of the Ascendant, the native will be plentiful in his own home, having resources (and if it was to the contrary, say the contrary).

241 The tenth Lot,[426] of honesty,[427] is taken in the day from Mercury to the Sun (in the night the reverse), and is projected from the Ascendant. **242** And if it falls with the fortunes (and especially with Jupiter), or Jupiter or the Sun looked at it favorably, he will be honest, sweet, and patient; and likewise if this Lot and its lord fell in signs of honesty.[428]

243 The eleventh Lot,[429] of praiseworthiness and gratefulness, is taken in the day from Jupiter to Venus (in the night the reverse), and is projected from the Ascendant. **244** And if the fortunes looked at this Lot and its lord (and especially Jupiter), or [a fortune] was with them, the native will be praiseworthy, thankful (and *vice versa*:[430] and perhaps he will do good and from thence he will be blamed).

---

[421] Reading with John and the Arabic for "diversity."
[422] See *Gr. Intr.* VIII.4, lines 1473-83.
[423] Perhaps Abū Ma'shar means "the tenth."
[424] I am not exactly sure which signs Abū Ma'shar means, as there are many ways for signs to "agree" or be in concord.
[425] See *Gr. Intr.* VIII.4, lines 1484-90.
[426] See *Gr. Intr.* VIII.4, lines 1491-98.
[427] In Arabic this is the "freedom" or "independence" of the soul (*hurriyyah*).
[428] Again, "freedom" or "independence." In Arabic, this verb has to do with heat, so perhaps Abū Ma'shar is thinking of the hot signs (both fiery and airy), or perhaps even just the fiery signs.
[429] See *Gr. Intr.* VIII.4, lines 1499-1508.
[430] That is, if infortunes are looking at it.

[Lots of the 12th house]

245 The twelfth house[431] has three Lots. **246** The first is that of enemies, which according to certain people is taken in the day and night from Saturn to Mars, and is projected from the Ascendant.

247 The second Lot[432] of enemies, according to Hermes, is taken in the day and night from the lord of the house of enemies to the degree of the house of enemies, and is projected from the Ascendant. **248** And each of these Lots ought to be used: which if they were in the opposition of their own lords or of the lord of the Ascendant, the native will have many enemies (and *vice versa*).

249 The third Lot,[433] of labor and affliction, is taken in the day and night from the Lot of future things to the Lot of Fortune, and is projected from the Ascendant. **250** And it signifies the native's labor and fortune: and if it is with the lord of the Ascendant or it was commixed[434] by any bad aspects, the native will be full of labor in his life, and his assets will not be profitable for him.

[Additional natal Lots]

251 Apart from the aforesaid Lots,[435] there are ten [other] Lots. **252** The first is that of the releaser, which is taken in nativities at the hour of the nativity, from the degree of the conjunction or opposition to the Moon, and it is projected from the Ascendant.[436] **253** And it is directed by degree just like the releaser, and a profection by signs is led forth as with the releaser: and whenever it reaches the bad ones it signifies evil. **254** And those who do not direct it do not know the causes of events, even though they observe the releaser well and they direct the other significators.

---

[431] See *Gr. Intr.* VIII.4, lines 1509-12.
[432] See *Gr. Intr.* VIII.4, lines 1513-19.
[433] See *Gr. Intr.* VIII.4, lines 1520-27.
[434] Reading *fuerit com-* to be more in line with John, for *eius*.
[435] See *Gr. Intr.* VIII.5, lines 1528-47.
[436] This Lot is based on Valens, *Anth.* III.7. For Valens, if the nativity was conjunctional (after a New Moon), the Lot is calculated from the conjunction to the natal Moon, and projected from the Ascendant. But if preventional (after a Full Moon), count from the natal Moon to the *next* conjunction after birth, and subtract this from the natal Ascendant.

255 The second Lot,[437] of thin bodies, is taken in the day from the Lot of Fortune to Mars (in the night the reverse), and is projected from the Ascendant. **256** And if it was in a moist sign, the native will be thick, with large limbs; and if it were otherwise and it was with Mercury or Mars, he will be thin in body.

257 The third Lot,[438] of the military and boldness, is taken in the day from Saturn to the Moon (in the night the reverse), and is projected from the Ascendant. **258** And if this Lot or its lord will be in a sextile aspect with Mars or Jupiter in signs of animals, he will be bold, eager, a swordsman, playing with spears and swords.

259 The fourth Lot,[439] of boldness and strength in wars, is taken in the day from the lord of the Ascendant to the Moon (in the night the reverse), and is projected from the Ascendant. **260** And if it falls in the sextile aspect of Mars or Jupiter or [in] the houses of the bad ones, received, in strong signs, it signifies that the owner of [the chart] is spirited, bold, and strong in his body, and a killer.

261 The fifth Lot,[440] of cunning, is taken in the day and night from Mercury to the Lot of future things,[441] and is projected from the Ascendant—because the significator of character and cleverness and memory is Mercury, and all of these are referred to the soul, and the Lot of future things signifies the being of the soul. **262** And if this Lot was with Mercury, the native will be clever, with many arts and a sharp mind. **263** And if it was made fortunate, these matters will be beneficial for him, and if the contrary it will happen contrariwise. **263** And if Mercury is with Mars and in his mixture, and he had some signification in the Lot, the owner of [the chart] will be of those who open doors and bolts through ingenuity and cleverness and robbery.

264 The sixth Lot,[442] on the place of a thing and searching for it. **265** Since the destruction and scattering of all things is from the two bad ones, and Mercury [has] partnership in things, and the bad ones [destroy and delay matters] (unless they were fit and of a good condition, [for then] they differ

---

[437] See *Gr. Intr.* VIII.5, lines 1553-61.
[438] See *Gr. Intr.* VIII.5, lines 1562-69.
[439] See *Gr. Intr.* VIII.5, lines 1570-76.
[440] See *Gr. Intr.* VIII.5, lines 1577-90.
[441] Leopold is in error: according to *Gr. Intr.*, this is reversed at night.
[442] See *Gr. Intr.* VIII.5, lines 1591-1604.

and to the contrary become good), this Lot is taken in the day and night from Saturn to Mars, and from above are increased the degrees of Mercury, and it is projected from him. **266** Which, if it is free of Mars in the day (and from Saturn in the night), it signifies the effecting of matters (and vice-versa). **267** And this Lot is used for unknown things.

268 The seventh Lot,[443] of necessity[444] and the postponement [of needs] according to the Egyptians, is taken in the day and night from Mars to the degree of brothers, and is projected from the Ascendant.

269 The eighth Lot,[445] of necessity and the postponement [of needs] according to the Persians, is taken in the day and night from the Lot of esteem[446] to Mercury, [and] is projected from the Ascendant. **270** And both Lots[447] will be used: which if they were with the bad ones (and especially with Saturn), and [the Lot] and its lord were with the lord of the Ascendant, the native will be slow and will hardly be moved towards [obtaining] his needs, unless necessity forces him or another stirs him up. **271** And if the lord of this bad one impedes the significators of assets, they will destroy his assets.

272 The ninth Lot,[448] of retribution, is taken in the day from Mars to the Sun (in the night the reverse), and is projected from the Ascendant. **273** Which, if it is in the angles or in any dignity, or with the lord of the Ascendant, the native will be engaged in retribution (and vice-versa).

274 The tenth Lot,[449] of good work and truth, is taken in the day from Mercury to Mars (in the night the reverse), and is projected from the Ascendant. **275** Which, if it is in a strong angle, he will be truthful and wielding truth, and will have benefit from that; and if it is in a bad angle, he will wield truth and will have evil from that; and if it is remote from [its own] dignities, in a movable sign, he will know the good but will not do it.

276 And[450] these ten Lots are used in nativities and revolutions.

---

[443] See *Gr. Intr.* VIII.5, lines 1608-11.
[444] Reading *necessitatis* with John, for *nativitatis* ("nativity").
[445] See *Gr. Intr.* VIII.5, lines 1612-22.
[446] *Dilectionis*. Perhaps the second Lot of the eleventh house, above.
[447] I.e., this and the previous one.
[448] See *Gr. Intr.* VIII.5, lines 1623-28.
[449] See *Gr. Intr.* VIII.5, lines 1629-38.
[450] See *Gr. Intr.* VIII.5, lines 1639-42.

[The relation between a Lot and its significators and lords]

277 Once[451] the aforesaid about the individual Lots is known, one must know that sometimes a Lot has one [planetary] significator [in its calculation]—like the Lot of foreign travel, and that of assets, [if they fell into the houses of travel or assets, respectively.][452]

278 [But[453] a Lot which had two significators is] like if [the Lot of foreign travel] falls into the house of assets: it has two significators,[454] since one is that from which it begins and the other the one in whose house it falls: and the more worthy one is the one in whose house it falls.[455]

279 And[456] the Lot which has one significator is strengthened when its significator is looking at it. **280** And [a Lot which has] two [is strengthened] when those two are looking at it—and the lord of the house of the Lot is the stronger one between them. **281** And one which has three significators is stronger if all the significators are looking at it: because then it will have perfect strength, [since] all are signifying it equally—and if some are looking and others not, the Lot will be less perfect. **282** And those of the [significators] which are retrograde, burned, or in their own descension, make the signification of the Lot weak. **283** And if none of the significators looks at the Lot, the Lot will be weak and its signification will not appear.

284 And[457] if the significators of the Lot are looking at the Lot from a good aspect, he will see what he desires because of that matter which the Lot signifies; if from a bad one, he will have evil. **285** And if a planet similar to its nature looks at the Lot and the significators of the Lot are not looking at it, there will be an impediment of that same Lot, and it will be modest or will

---

[451] See *Gr. Intr.* VIII.8, lines 2054-60.
[452] Leopold has blended two paragraphs together, so I have supplied the missing parts of this paragraph in my own words, and the beginning of the next paragraph based on his example.
[453] See *Gr. Intr.* VIII.8, lines 2061-71, and 2076-77.
[454] Omitting "since one is the lord of the house in which it fell," as Leopold has mixed two sentences together.
[455] What Abū Ma'shar means is this. The Lot of foreign travel is taken from the lord of the ninth to the ninth. Obviously, if the Lot ends up being in the ninth itself, then it will have only one associated planetary significator: the lord of the ninth itself. But if it fell into the second, then it would have two associated planets: the lord of the ninth (which was used for the calculation), and the lord of the second (the house in which it falls).
[456] See *Gr. Intr.* VIII.8, lines 2081-98.
[457] For the rest of this section, see *Gr. Intr.* VIII.8, lines 2099-2102.

not be [at all]: whence it is thought that the planet should have testimony in the Lot.

286 For example, [if] you want to know the assets, and you take the signification from the Lot of assets, and its significators are not looking at it, but if Jupiter (who is the natural significator of assets) is looking at it. **287** Or,[458] if you want to know about the marriage-union and you take the signification from the Lot of marriage-union, and the significators of the Lot are not looking at the Lot, but Venus (who is the significator of a marriage-union by nature) is. **288** Or, if you want to know about slaves and you take the signification from the Lot of slaves, and the significators of the Lot are not looking at it but Mercury (who is the significator of slaves by nature) is. **289** If it is so, then see if a fortune through its own nature is looking at such a Lot, and the planet is received in an angle: it signifies the effecting of that same matter, but it will be moderate or less than what one thought, and it will be through the help of one man. **290** And if the one looking at the Lot is in its own house or one in which it has dignity, [the effecting of] this will be from the direction in which he seeks it, and through the assistance of those known to him; and if it is in a foreign[459] sign, it will be from the direction of one unknown and through the aid of one unknown. **291** And if the planet looking at the Lot is made unfortunate, not receiving the Lot, or remote and impeded, there will be changes and fears in it, and nothing will move forward with what the Lot signified. **292** And if that same unfortunate one is in an angle or following an angle, and it is direct, the impediment or destruction of it will be after it was thought to be completed. **293** If it is Saturn and he is retrograde, the impediment will be because of some accident; and if it is Mars, it will be because of some contention; if Mercury was impeded, the impediment will be because of business or letters or writing; and if the Moon ([and she is] waxing), it will be because of rumors or the increase of a thing (and if [she is] diminished, because of a diminution); if Venus, because of women; if the Sun, because of kings and the wealthy and greater [people]; if Jupiter, because of faith and religion, the religious, judge, and men entering in between them; and if the Tail was joined to the Lot, it will be because of distinguished people[460] and princes.

---

[458] Reading "or" for *et* ("and") here and in the sentences below, to make the sentence divisions natural.
[459] *Peregrino*. That is, from a peregrine sign or one in which it had no dignity.
[460] Reading *capitaneorum* with John for *captivorum* ("captives").

[When the place of one of the significators is unknown][461]

294 Know that every Lot is extracted from a number of significators. **295** And the first is the one from which it begins, the second the one to which it proceeds, and the third the one from which it is projected, and the fourth the place of the Lot:[462] if at any rate three of them are known and one unknown, you are able to know the unknown place. **296** If therefore the places of the Lot and the two significators are known and you want to know the degree of the Ascendant, take from the first significator to the degree of the second significator by equal degrees, and project what was collected from the degree of the Lot in reverse order (that is, from the end towards the beginning): and where the numbering is ended, there is the degree of the Ascendant. **297** And if the places of [the last] three significators are known and the place of the first significator unknown, take from the third significator to the Lot by succession [of degrees], and project what was collected from the degree of the second significator, as above ([backwards], from the end of the [sign of the] second[463] significator towards the beginning: and where it reaches, there will be the degree of the [first] significator. **298** And if the places of three[464] significators were known and the degree of the second[465] significator unknown, take from the degree of the third significator to the degree of the fourth significator, and add from above what the first significator has gone through [in its own sign], and project this from the degrees of the first significator in forward order (namely from the beginning of the sign to its end), giving 30° to each one: and where the numbering is ended, there is the degree of the [second] significator.

---

[461] For this whole section, see *Gr. Intr.* VIII.9, lines 2149-93.
[462] Reading the singular for clarity.
[463] Reading for "first."
[464] Reading for "two." Leopold has mixed up the significators here, but so has John.
[465] Reading for "third."

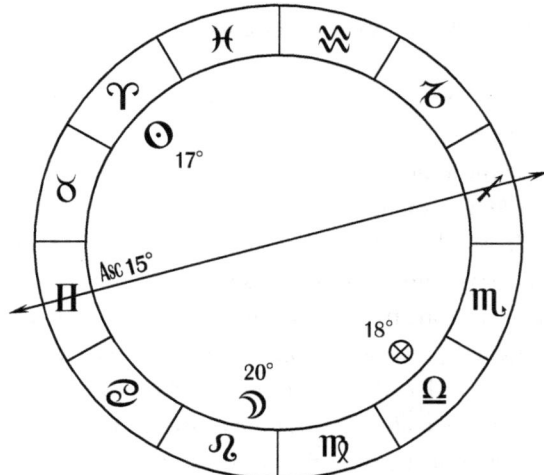

Figure 63: Abū Ma'shar's example chart (Dykes)

299 For example, the Sun in 17° Aries was the first significator, and the Moon in 20° Leo (which is the second significator), and the Lot of Fortune in 18° Libra (which is the fourth significator): and thus we know the places of three significators, and we do not know the degree of the Ascendant. **300** Which, if we wanted to know it, we take from the Sun to the Moon by equal degrees, and there come to be 4 signs [and] 3° (namely 123°), which we project backwards from 18° Libra by equal degrees, and the numbering runs out in 15° Gemini: and thus we know that the Ascendant is 15° Gemini according to the numbering of those degrees. **301** And if the degree of the Sun was unknown we take from the degree of the Ascendant to the Lot, which is four signs and 3°: afterwards we project this backwards from the place of the Moon (from the end of the sign towards the beginning), and it will be at an end at 17° Aries—[and] we said that the Sun was in that same place. **302** And if the degree of the Moon was unknown, we take from the Ascendant to the Lot (and there was four signs and 3°): we added from above what the Sun had gone through in his own sign, and we project it from the beginning of the sign of the Sun in forward order, and the numbering is ended in 20° Leo, and we know that the Moon is there.

[Three political Lots][466]

303 We have found three Lots which are employed in revolutions and conjunctions signifying the basis for a kingdom and its durability. **304** And the first Lot is called the Lot of rulership or authority, and it is employed in the revolution of years of the world, and is taken from Mars to the Moon, and is projected from the Ascendant of the conjunction which signifies the changing of the rulership. **305** And it [also] comes to be otherwise: namely from the degree of the Ascendant of the conjunction to the degree of the conjunction, and it is projected from the degree of the Ascendant of the revolution. **306** Moreover, it is otherwise taken from the degree of the Midheaven of the revolution to the Sun, and is projected from the degree of Jupiter.[467]

307 The Lot of the duration of the rulership (that is, how long the rulership ought to last) is taken at the hour of the election[468] of the king from the Sun to 15° Leo, and is projected from the Moon (in the night, from the Moon to 15° Cancer and projected from the Sun). **308** (Others have it from 3°.)[469]

309 Another Lot of the time of the election[470] is taken at the hour of the election of the king, in the day from Jupiter to Saturn (in the night the reverse), and is projected from the Ascendant of the revolution of the year in which the king accedes. **310** And if Jupiter was in a common sign and the revolution [was] diurnal, and Jupiter falling from an angle, it is taken from Saturn to Jupiter, and from above are added 30°, and it is projected from the Ascendant. **311** And if Jupiter and Saturn were opposed, and[471] both falling from the Ascendant, what comes out should be halved—that is, one-half of the degrees which are between them is taken, and is projected from the Ascendant. **312** And if Jupiter [was] in his own exaltation and the revolution was nocturnal, it should be counted from him to Saturn, and projected from the Ascendant.

---

[466] For this section, see al-Qabīsī V.17, and discussions and examples in *AW2*.
[467] This is backwards, as it should be from the Sun to the Midheaven, not the Midheaven to the Sun.
[468] Or rather, "accession" (Ar.), which is different.
[469] Leopold might be thinking of the natal Lot of exaltation, from the tenth house above.
[470] Or rather, "accession" (Ar.), here and in the rest of the sentence.
[471] This should be read as "or."

[The two "greatest" Lots][472]

313 These are two Lots from which especially the time of the election[473] of the king and his duration is extracted. **314** The first is that you should look at the hour of the king's election, in which the profection then arrived from the conjunction of the triplicity which signifies the sect, by giving one year to every 30°, and one month to every two-and-a-half degrees. **315** And when you know in which sign and degree it comes to be, preserve this, because this is the place from which you will equate[474] the first Lot. **316** And when you know it, calculate the Ascendant of the revolution of the year in which the elected one acceded. **317** After this, take from the planet eastern from the Sun in that year (namely, either Saturn or Jupiter) and project up to the degree of the equation[475] of the first Lot which you preserved, and project from the Ascendant of the revolution: and where it reaches, that is the place of the first Lot.

318 The second Lot is that you should look from the conjunction in which the king acceded, [at which sign or degree the profection of the year has reached, from the amount of which one year is given to every 30°, to the month and day in which the king acceded],[476] and it is the place of the equation of the second Lot: preserve it. **319** After this however, [take] from the planet western from the Sun (namely Saturn or Jupiter) up to the place of the equation of the second Lot which you preserved, and project from the Ascendant of the revolution: and where it reached, there is the place of the second Lot. **320** And these are the Lots which signify the strength of the king and his duration.

---

[472] For this section, see al-Qabīsī V.18, and my discussion and examples in *AW2*, Section I.2.

[473] Again, this should be the "duration of the accession."

[474] In ancient Ptolemaic and medieval astronomy, an "equation" is a number used to correct or fine-tune some other, provisional amount. Thus with these Lots Abū Ma'shar (in the words of al-Qabīsī) takes the positions of Saturn, Jupiter, and the Ascendant at the revolution of the year in which a king accedes, and then adds a second amount which he calls its "equation," to get a final position for the Lot. Then he does the same for the second Lot.

[475] Reading *aequationis* as above, for *aptationis*.

[476] Adding on the basis of John's Latin, as Leopold has skipped several lines.

[*Lots for commodities*][477]

321 Thus far I have found Lots which we use in the revolutions of the years of the world, and through them is known what will be of an expensive or cheap price, and much or little [in amount]. **322** Therefore we should look, at the revolution, to see in which planet's house or exaltation or bound or triplicity a Lot [is]—namely of the [commodity] about which we are asking whether it will be expensive or cheap—like the Lot of wheat, or the Lot of whatever sort it is. **323** Which if [its lord] was retrograde, burned, or in a malign place, the thing of that Lot will be cheap and of a small price; but if it was in a place of strength or in an angle, and especially in the Midheaven, that thing will become burdensome and will be of an expensive price. **324** And if the lord of that house reached the place of its own exaltation, it will again be of an expensive price; and if it reached the place of its fall (that is, descension), its thing will be cheap and will be of a small price. **325** Consider the aspects of the planets (the good [planets] and the bad ones) both to the Lot and to the lord of its Lot: and if a fortune (and the Moon) is looking at the Lot, that thing will be multiplied, and if bad ones [look], it will suffer detriment.

326 The Lot of wheat[478] is taken from the Sun to Mars.
327 The Lot of water, from the Moon to Venus.
328 The Lot of barley, from the Moon to Jupiter.
329 The Lot of chickpeas,[479] from Venus to the Sun.
330 The Lot of lentils, from Mars to Saturn.
331 The Lot of beans, from Saturn to Mars.
332 The Lot of millet,[480] from Saturn to Mars.
333 The Lot of dates, from the Sun to Venus.
334 The Lot of honey, from the Moon to the Sun.[481]
335 The Lot of rice,[482] which is a kind of grain, from Jupiter to Saturn.
336 The Lot of olives, from Mercury to the Moon.

---

[477] For this section, see al-Qabīsī V.19, and my discussion in *AW1* Section II.13.
[478] Or in some manuscripts, "food." We should consider wheat as the staple food, since it is the basis of most bread.
[479] Reading with the Ar. for "air."
[480] Or, "Indian peas" (Ar.).
[481] Reading with the Ar. for "the Sun to Venus."
[482] Reading with the Ar. for *alsationis*.

337 The Lot of silk,[483] from Mercury to Venus.

338 The Lot of sesame,[484] which is a kind of white seed in the likeness of flax, and doctors use it, and a useful ointment comes from it, from Saturn to Jupiter or Venus.

339 The Lot of grapes, from Saturn to Venus.

340 The Lot of *al-baṭṭīkh* (that is, melons),[485] from Mercury to Saturn.

341 The Lot of acidic herb-foods,[486] from Saturn to Mars.

342 The Lot of sweet foods, from the Sun to Venus.

343 The Lot of foods with the taste of celery,[487] from Mars to Saturn.

344 The Lot of bitter foods, from Mercury to Saturn.

345 The Lot of sour medicines, from the Sun (or from Saturn) to Jupiter, or from Mars to the Moon.[488]

346 The Lot of salty medicines, from Mars to the Moon.

347 The Lot of poisoned things, from the Head of the Dragon to Saturn.

348 And all of these are projected from the Ascendant.

---

[483] Or rather, "cotton" (Ar.).
[484] Reading with the Ar. for *aleoten*, and reading Saturn for "Mercury" in the formula.
[485] Reading the proper Arabic transliteration for *almatig*, and "melons" for the incorrect "saffron."
[486] Or, "sour foods" (Ar.).
[487] Or, "pungent foods" (Ar.).
[488] Or rather, "purgative and sour medicines" (Ar.). Leopold's entry here might be due to different manuscript readings, or confusion on his part.

Treatise V: On the Revolutions of Years

[Chapter V.1: Introduction]

1 As the four Treatises on the spheres, on the planets, on the proving of [astrological] knowledge, and on the introductory [matters] of judgments have been set forth, in this fifth Treatise is collected [information] on the revolutions of years.

2 The revolution of the year of the world is the entrance of the Sun into the beginning of Aries—at which entrance, the philosophers judge what things are going to be for peoples, kings, cities, the changing of the atmosphere, famine, mortality, earthquake, concerning floods, wars, and comets in that year; and all of these things just stated fall under[1] the first part of judgments (and it is said to be general).[2] **3** The second part of astronomy, which is called particular, is that concerning nativities, questions, elections, and intentions.[3] **4** (The revolution of the year of a native or another personal root, is when the Sun returns to the same point in which he was when someone was born or when that matter began.)

5 Therefore, in the revolution of the year which you wanted, proceed thusly: arrange the figure of heaven for that hour, and equate the planets,[4] and put the individual [planets] in the places given to them.[5] **6** See if the Ascendant at the revolution is fixed: the figure which you made suffices for the whole year. **7** If it is a common sign, make another one when the Sun enters Libra. **8** If it is movable, make four: at every entrance of the Sun into the tropical signs in the revolution of the year of the world, or in the quarters of the root (whatever it was).[6]

---

[1] Lit., "brought back to" (*reducuntur*).
[2] That is, mundane astrology is general in its application, to large groups of people and lands.
[3] These are encompassed by Treatises VII-X, respectively.
[4] In geocentric astronomy, to "equate" means to convert positions from their provisional, mean positions to their exact ones. So, Leopold is telling us to calculate the exact positions of the planets (which we find nowadays in the ephemeris).
[5] Reading *deditis* for *debitis* ("required, obligated").
[6] Leopold seems to mean that we could apply the same principle to any solar revolution, whether natal, electional, an event chart, or whatever. At any rate, we are now focusing on mundane ingresses.

9 You should say that the planet which has many dignities in the figure of the circle is the "lord of the year," and judge the state of the world or the native or other matter principally through it.

10 Five things should be considered in the revolution: [1] the distributor, that is, the lord of the bound which the distribution or direction has reached; [2] the lord of the rays of the distribution; [3] the partner or receiver; [4] the lord of the year; [5] and the lord of the profection.[7]

[Chapter V.2: General evaluation of an ingress][8]

1 Judge the state of the common people through the Ascendant of the revolution of the year of the world, and its lord. **2** If the lord of the Ascendant falls away from the Ascendant into the eighth house, it signifies the mortality of the common people; in the sixth, diseases; in the twelfth, enemies.

3 Judge the state of the king through the Sun, the Midheaven, and its lord. **4** That [land] is stronger than [other] kings, whose lord is the lord of the year,[9] and more so if it was in the degree of its own exaltation. **5** The lord of the Midheaven entering under the rays of the Sun in the revolution, signifies the death of the king. **6** The significator of the king[10] being conjoined to a bad one in the revolution (or in its square or opposite aspect), in the eighth, signifies the death of the king; in the sixth, diseases. **7** Mars under the rays of the Sun at the revolution, signifies the killing of the king.

---

[7] These five planets seem to be the following. First is [1] the distributor of the directed *mundane* Ascendant, which moves around the zodiac every 360 years; then [2] perhaps a planet casting rays into the bound; then [3] the partnering planet of that mundane distribution; then [4] the lord of the year from the ingress chart, as mentioned above; finally [5] the lord of the *mundane* profection, probably the profected Ascendant from the most recent triplicity shift (see *AW2* for a description of these).

[8] Virtually every sentence in this section can be traced back to Māshā'allāh's *RYW* (see *AW2*, Section II.2).

[9] This probably derives from *RYW* Ch. 16, **7**. For Māshā'allāh, this means that the rulers of lands attributed to the lord of the year, will be more powerful than those of other regions. So, if Venus is the lord of the year at some ingress, then the kings of Venusian lands or peoples will be more powerful (such as Arabs or Muslims, *etc.*). For an entire treatment of chorography, see *AW1* Part IV.

[10] This planet is often the lord of the Midheaven, but there are numerous rules for finding it: see *AW2*.

8 How[ever] the significator of any [person] is at the revolution, such will be his state.[11]

9 A bad one in the Ascendant at the revolution, impedes the body; in the second, assets; and so on. **10** The bad ones being direct and receiving, do not impede. **11** The bad ones in their own house or exaltation [still signify evil], but slowly; however, they signify a good end.

12 The good ones repel evil by aspect, unless they are retrograde or burned up. **13** The signification of a good one is diminished if [it is] retrograde, if burned up, if descending,[12] [or] if in the opposite of its own house.[13]

14 That year will be worse, in which Saturn and Jupiter are conjoined. **15** The year will be severe if the bad ones were in the upper half of the circle of their apogee, and if they were northern. **16** The worst that it could be will be for a land in whose sign there is a retrograde bad one at the revolution. **17** [But] a good one in the sign of a clime, signifies good for that clime. **18** A retrograde planet signifies nothing of the good until it goes direct.

19 Mars in the Midheaven at the revolution signifies that the king will hang many in that year; in the Ascendant and the west he will cut off hands, and in the angle of the earth the feet.

20 Among combatants, the one whose clime Mars is more associated with, will win.

21 If Mars is in the Ascendant at the revolution, and the Moon in his square or opposite aspect, this is a deadly impediment. **22** Mars destroys Jupiter through the conjunction and through the opposition, and the square aspect. **23** They are bad when they impede the lords of the fourth, seventh, and twelfth.

24 A slow planet at the revolution, signifies war; retrograde, flight; direct, peace (and especially if a good one is looking at it from the Midheaven).

25 An infortune signifies according to the sign and house in which it is: and in the sixth, disease, in the eighth, death.

26 The Head with Saturn signifies evil: in Aries, in beasts and wolves. **27** The aspect of a bad one[14] to the Tail signifies[15] famine, cold, and pestilence.

---

[11] For example, Mercury for scholars and teachers.
[12] This probably means being in its own fall.
[13] That is, in its detriment.
[14] Or more likely, "Mars" (see *RYW*, Ch. 24, 8).
[15] Reading the singular, with *RYW*.

28 If an eclipse occurred, and the lord of the house of the eclipse is the significator of the king, the king should have fear when the Sun reaches the Midheaven of the eclipse; if [it is the significator] of the common people, the common people should have fear when the Sun reaches the Ascendant of the eclipse.

29 The significator of the king in the Midheaven at the revolution, gives war to him; in the Ascendant, rest; in the west and the angle of the earth, [it gives] the destruction of the common people by means of the king.

30 Saturn along with the Moon is in charge of the upper part of the world (this is the northern [part]); Jupiter along with Mercury, the middle part of the world; Mars along with Venus, the lower part of the world (namely, the southern).[16]

31 Jupiter direct at the revolution, without the aspect of an infortune, gives strength and rulership in which there will not be injustice.

32 The east and south are hot, the west and north cold. **33** The winds from the east are hot and dry, from the west cold and moist, from the south hot and moist, from the north cold and dry.

34 The signs signify parts of the world not through their own places, but by nature.[17]

35 Many planets conjoined in watery [signs] at the revolution, signify rains; in fiery ones, dryness and sterility; in airy ones, winds; in earthy ones, cold and snows.

36 The aspect of Mars to the lord of the year at the revolution, in the earthy triplicity, overwhelms that whole people.

37 Give solid things[18] to Saturn, city councilors and magnates to Jupiter, soldiers to Mars, Arabs and women to Venus, scribes, to Mercury, [and] merchants and travelers to the Moon.

38 The[19] cities of the world are 12, and every planet has two (except for the Sun and Moon, of which each has only one): judge concerning them according to the state of their lords at the revolution. **39** Cities which were founded with Mars appearing in the Midheaven, [will have] many princes die by the sword.

---

[16] This refers to the northern hemisphere, divided into three broad regions.

[17] That is to say, Virgo signifies certain lands because of its and their Virgoan nature, not by Virgo occupying some place in the ingress chart.

[18] *Solidas res.* It would be better to read this as austere religious people, farmers, estate managers, and other kinds of Saturnian people.

[19] For this unusual sentence, see *RYW* Ch. 34 and *Skilled* VIII.34, **13-15** (in *AW2*).

40 Avert your eyes from a figure in which Mars is in an angle, and more so if the angles are slanted—that is, signs of slanted ascensions[20]—and if Scorpio is ascending (because Scorpio is a sign of falsity).

41 Saturn and Mars in fixed signs signify fixed impediments, and *vice versa*; in dry ones, a fall from a height; in moist ones, a fall on level ground; in airy ones, evil by means of powerful winds.

42 Mercury with Mars at the beginning of the year, or in any quarter of the year, signifies mortality and powerful winds, or fires, and more so in a fiery sign at the conjunction of the bad ones.

43 If the Moon is joined to Saturn in latitude, there will be famine and mortality; if to Mars, the shedding of blood.

44 Saturn[21] configured to Mercury in an earthy [sign] makes an earthquake; Mercury configured to Mars from an earthy one, makes an earthquake.

[Abū Ma'shar: BRD VIII.1]

45 Earthquakes and floods are known beforehand in the revolution through Saturn: for if then his rays are in earthy or watery signs, and the revolution belongs to him, [or his] ray [is] in earthy signs and the Moon made unfortunate, there will be submersions;[22] and in watery ones, moistures; in airy ones, snows and deadly hail destroying [things], and cold, and the darkness of the air, and powerful winds.

46 In[23] a revolution of the year of the world, if the revolution and the conjunction or prevention which preceded the revolution, and their Ascendants, were safe from the infortunes, they signify good health; and if to the contrary, mortality. **47** If the lords of the lords of the aforesaid Ascendants (or either one) or the Moon is then with an infortune, and on top of that they are being connected with the lord of the eighth, this signifies excessive death by reason of pests. **48** If the said significators (or many [of them]) were

---

[20] *Obliquae.* Leopold means the "crooked" signs. Of course, there will always be crooked signs on two of the angles, so it is hard to know what Leopold means here. Probably the Ascendant and Midheaven are meant.

[21] This sentence is based on 'Umar al-Tabarī: see *Skilled* VIII.27 (in both *AW1* and *AW2*).

[22] Or rather, earthy signs indicate sinkholes, while watery ones indicate flooding (Abū Ma'shar).

[23] This paragraph is based on *BRD*, but Abū Ma'shar has taken it from al-Kindī, *Forty Chapters* Ch. 39 (included in *AW1*, Section I.4).

connected with the lord of the eighth, there will be much sudden death. **49** And if Mars was the one making [them] unfortunate, and in hot signs, and especially if he is quick and strong, it signifies hot illnesses. **50** If Saturn was the one making [them] unfortunate, there will be long-lasting illnesses, and more so if he is in cold and dry signs.

51 If the Moon (being separated from the conjunction or prevention which more closely preceded the Sun's entrance into Aries) is being joined to a good one, the year will be good; and contrariwise [if] to a bad one.

[Other views]

52 At a revolution of the year of the world, if the lord of the *firdārīyyah* is good and in a good condition, the year will be good (and contrariwise).

53 At a revolution of the year, there will be many difficulties and battles if Saturn and Jupiter were in their own exaltations. **54** Mars stirs up wars if he was in any angle of the figure of heaven at the revolution. **55** The time of the war is when Mars is in the opposite or square aspect of Jupiter or Saturn. **56** The winner will be the one who invades, if the lord of the fourth or seventh was in the first or in the tenth. **57** The winner will be the one who invades if the lord of the Ascendant is made fortunate and strong; if [it is] the lord of the seventh, say the contrary.

58 The king should not go out to do battle if Cancer is ascending. **59** The king should fear to go out to battle if the Moon is with the bad ones or under the rays of the Sun, or with the Tail: otherwise he will be killed or conquered.

60 The winner in the war will be the one whose mansion Mars is more associated with.

[Abū Ma'shar: BRD VIII.1][24]

61 The conjunction of Saturn and Jupiter, and the square aspect or opposite, signals wars. **62** The time of the war is when the Sun is equidistant from[25] Saturn, or looks [at him]. **63** Moreover, when the Ascendant of the year reaches the place of an infortune by direction, giving a month to a sign. **64** Moreover, when the year reaches the conjunction of the bad ones by body

---

[24] Not every sentence below can be traced to *BRD* VIII.1, but most can.
[25] *Equidistat*, translating the Ar. for "parallel," a term sometimes used by Abū Ma'shar in *BRD* to refer to conjunctions.

or by a bad aspect, one month [per sign]. **65** Moreover, when the year reaches the opposite of the Ascendant of the year of the world. **66** Moreover, by means of the distance between the two bad ones,[26] by giving one month to every two-and-a-half degrees [between them].

67 You would know the place of the war thusly: divide the sign of every clime by 7, and to each seventh they give 4° 17' 08" 35'".[27] **68** And give the first division of the sign [to that] clime, [and the next one to the next clime] according to what follows it in [geographical] position, and thus up to the seventh from that clime: and where there are fortunes, say good (and contrariwise).

69 The infortunes in the eighth signify much evil at the revolution.

70 The Lot of victory at the revolution signifies victory in the war—which is taken from Mars to the Moon, and is projected from the place of the Sun: and where it leaves off, there is the Lot of combat. **71** Which, if it is strong, it signals that in that place they who have a just cause for war will conquer; and if it is weak, the side of falsity will conquer.

72 If the Moon applies to Mars at the revolution, this signals killing among kings, and the decline of nobles from their positions, and the elevation of one over another because of that.

73 A revolution of peace is one in which Saturn does not look at Jupiter. **74** Moreover, if Saturn does not look at Mars, this signals the negation of wars. **75** If Mars, being received, looks at Saturn, the wars will be weak. **76** If Saturn receives Mars, [they will be] weaker; and if they look at each other without reception, there will be many wars.

77 Moreover, whatever is signified in a movable sign at the revolution of the year, will be at the beginning of the year; what will be in a common one,

---

[26] In *BRD*, this is the distance between *either* of the malefics and an axial degree, not between the malefics themselves.

[27] Reading with *BRD* for *34*. Abū Ma'shar's instructions are unclear to me here, but he is evidently dividing the signs much in the way that the twelfth-parts do (see Glossary). First, a zodiacal sign of 30° is attributed to some clime (perhaps through its lord, so that Scorpio indicates the clime of Mars)—but whether this sign is the Ascendant, or Midheaven, or something else, we do not know. Then, this sign is divided by seven to yield 4° 17' 08" 35'" for each clime. If the sign is (say) Scorpio, then the first 4° 17' 08" 35'" belongs to the clime of Mars, the next to the clime of Jupiter, then Saturn, then the Moon, and so on in order. But again, we do not know whether we are supposed to go in the ascending or descending order of the planets. Anyhow, whichever portion has the rays or bodies of benefics, will indicate good for the clime attributed to it; malefics show the opposite. For more on climes, see *AW1*.

will be in the middle of the year; what [is] in a fixed sign, will be at the end of the year.

[Chapter V.3: "Al-Qabīsī" on planetary conjunctions in the signs][28]

1 With the Sun entering Aries, [consider the following]:[29]

2 If Saturn and Jupiter were in Aries or near [it], they indicate a new future sect. **3** If Jupiter, Venus, and Mercury, the Sun, and the Moon were there (or at least three of them), there will be fertility and good men, much rain and hail, writers will profit, beasts will be had for a cheap price, [and] fresh waters will be increased. **4** If Jupiter and the Moon were in one degree of that same sign, in the east[30] the king will make a judgment and justice, and [do] many good things. **5** If Saturn and Mars, or Mars and Jupiter, or Mars and Mercury, or Mars and Venus are in that same place, there will be war in the east, much blood will be shed in the temples of the Arabs, and [they] will be overthrown, their women will be captured and dragged away.

6 If Venus and Mars were in Taurus in one degree, women will initiate seditions against men, demanding illicit sex from them, and animals will die. **7** If Mars [was] in Taurus, war will come to be toward the south, and wind so that the fruits of trees will fall, and many of them will perish and dry out. **8** If Mars, Jupiter, Venus, and the Moon (or three of these) were [in Taurus], men will be extreme liars, and [there will be] much hatred between them, [and] earthquake, and beautiful people will die in that year (for Jupiter and Venus signify beautiful people; Mars kills them [by being] with them in the same degree or sign); there will be much steady rain, and the water of the sea and

---

[28] This section is Leopold's rendition of a short Latin text attributed to al-Qabīsī (in *AW2*, Section I.6); but the essentials are already found in Arabic and attributed to Hermes, in al-Rijāl's *Skilled* VIII.5 (in *AW2*, Section IV.2).

[29] I have omitted the rest of this sentence, which is not found in either the Latin translation by John of Spain or in the Arabic. Each part of the sentence means something on its own, but all of the pieces together do not make much sense: *venturo signo fortunatus dicitur gradus Arietis 19 quod tunc oritur facta figura iuxta hoc signorum omnium et planetarum*. It evidently wants to connect the Sun's ingress with the degree of his exaltation at 19° Aries, but the phrases say (in one way of stitching them together): "it being the sign to come, the nineteenth degree of Aries is said to be fortunate, which then arises, with the figure being made according to this, of all the signs and planets."

[30] This could indicate the east because Aries is an eastern sign, or else the author means that they are conjoined *in the east of the chart*. But it is probably the former: compare **5** and **17** below.

springs will be abundant. **9** Men will go out from the southern side, desiring to kill their own lord (which they will not be able [to do]). **10** If Saturn, Jupiter, and Mars were in the same degree of Taurus, emperors and kings will abandon what belongs to them, thoroughly terrified from excessive fear or they will die; monks will become apostates or die. **11** If Saturn and Mars are there together, women will become infirm in their breasts and throat, and men in their testicles and bladder.

12 If Mercury, Venus, and the Moon are together in Gemini, writers will profit little, the dull man will disdain to obey [his] master, [and it signifies] much grain, troublesome robbers on the road. **13** If Mars and Saturn or Mars and Jupiter were there, there will be war in Armenia, the Moabites will rush in upon them, and will kill their elders and go to mountainous areas, trusting in the divinations of seers. **14** Wind will rush in from the east.

15 If Saturn, Jupiter, Mars, the Sun, and the Moon were together in Cancer, panic will surround the people who incite God through [their] offenses; some men will harass others, and then signs will be seen in the sky, and torches flying [in the sky] in the morning, there will be earthquake, not many waters, produce will perish, and soldiers and seafarers will be disturbed by horrible fear, [and] the north wind will be very harmful in that year.

16 If Saturn, Mars, the Moon, and Jupiter were in Leo, the eastern people will make war amongst themselves, and men will be vexed with pains of the belly, stomach, and other things. **17** If Jupiter, Mars, and the Sun were there, merchants will fear their own masters and the Arabs;[31] a vehement wind will rush in from the east.

18 If Saturn, Mars, and Mercury stood still in Virgo, every fruit will perish by means of locusts or animals. **19** If Saturn and the Sun were obscured there,[32] and the Tail and Mars were there, in the land of the Nubians[33] and in the south war and sedition will arise between the wealthy and the poor. **20** If Saturn and Jupiter were in that place, there will be much rain, wind from the south, virtually all things (and especially grain and wine) will be expensive.

21 If Mars and Jupiter [were] in Libra, it will redden the sky, which is a sign of the infirmity of men or the shedding of blood. **22** If the Sun, Jupiter, and the Moon were there, women will die and there will be much rain. **23** If

---

[31] Or, merchants *and* the Arabs will fear their own masters.
[32] Or rather (following the Arabic), if the Sun was eclipsed there—the Arabic does not include Saturn, which would make the statement confusing.
[33] Reading with "al-Qabīsī" for *nubilorum*.

Mars and Saturn [were] there together, there will be war, [and] robbers will have hold of the roads.

24 If Saturn, Mars, and Venus were in Scorpio, the king will be killed by poison, then [people] will slander and hate each other. **25** And if the Moon was with one of these, there will be rain so that the world will be nearly swamped by the rains. **26** But if Jupiter and Saturn [were] there, you may be certain that false prophets are going to come, sowing a new sect.

27 If Mars and the Moon [were] in Sagittarius, war will come to be next to the sea. **28** If Saturn, Jupiter, Mercury, and the Moon are there together, the world will virtually perish from flooding, rivers and seas will be greatly increased, [and] scribes, medical doctors, astrologers, [and] priests will be venerated by the people. **29** If Mars and Saturn [were there] together, robbers will plunder the rustics, and estates, and ships on the sea. **30** If Mars and Venus, prostitutes will snatch away boys and girls, leading them into captivity.

31 If the Sun, Mars, and Mercury were together in Capricorn, many lords will die, and there will be much infirmity, and men will burn the harvests and homes, and the wind will be excessive, little grain will be harvested, [and] thieves will get hold of the sea and lands. **32** If Saturn and Mars are together [there], there will not be so much war [among] men; the class of men will fear God.

33 If Saturn, Mars, and the Moon were together in Aquarius, the rain will be little, [but] springs will have water enough, robbers will get hold of the roads, the sky will be disturbed by clouds but will not give rain; concerning a man born then, the joy is great [and] many peoples will be subject to him, every mastery will be abundant, there will be many monks and those fearing God.

34 If Jupiter [is] in Pisces, there will be much religion.

35 He who desires to judge concerning future things in the year, should examine much the mixtures of the planets, the conjunctions, [and] significations from [these] statements and others, and [the natures][34] of the signs in which they are: and so he will judge securely.

36 In[35] all things, detest Mars when the Moon is separated from him or is in his square or opposite aspect. **37** And you should know that the aspect of the good ones breaks the malice of the bad ones.

---

[34] Adding with "al-Qabīsī."
[35] These sentences are not from the Latin work attributed to al-Qabīsī.

[Chapter V.4: Prices]

1 At[36] the revolution of the year, if the Ascendant is Aries, fish become cheap and meat becomes expensive. **2** If Taurus, wheat will be expensive, and meat cheap. **3** If Gemini, all things will be expensive, except that wheat will be cheap. **4** If Cancer, waters and dews will be diminished, and there will be many conflagrations. **5** If[37] Leo, fruit will be multiplied, likewise produce of the fields and all provisions. **6** If Virgo, it makes olive oil very expensive. **7** In Libra, few coins will be had, whence silver will be expensive but gold becomes cheap; finally, all provisions will be expensive. **8** If Scorpio, it draws away waters and makes rivers[38] moderate, [but] fertilizes trees. **9** If Sagittarius, it makes wars and seditions, and there will be many provisions. **10** Capricorn makes meats cheap, but the fruit of palms [and] dates [and] black mulberries [become expensive], and vegetables cheap. **11** Aquarius diminishes waters and makes provisions expensive. **12** Pisces makes for mediocrity in all things.

13 For[39] the price of things for sale,[40] consider the Ascendant of the conjunction or prevention preceding the revolution, and see by how much Saturn is distant from the beginning of Aries. **14** Discard 30 from the total, divide the remainder by 13 1/3 (beginning from the Pleiades),[41] and see what is there where the number has terminated. **15** If that place is in one knot[42] with Saturn or the Moon,[43] and they are between the Ascendant and the fourth, it signals the expensiveness of provisions. **16** Between the fourth and the seventh, mediocrity. **17** Between the seventh and tenth, things for sale

---

[36] For this paragraph, see Jirjis in *Judges* §7.70, itself based ultimately on Māshā'allāh's *On Prices* (see *AW1* Section II.3, **A99-111**).

[37] For Leo through Libra, Leopold has mixed up the significations, putting Virgo's in Libra, and some of Libra in Leo; I have put them in their proper places, according to *Judges*.

[38] The Ar. reads, "prices."

[39] For this paragraph, see Jafar in *AW1*, Section II.2. This technique is based on the 27-mansion system of the Indians (360° / 27 mansions = 13° 20' apiece, as in **14**). The idea is really to measure the distance between the Pleiades and Saturn, and project this from the Ascendant of the New or Full Moon preceding the ingress; then, see what planets are in or aspecting the mansion where the counting ends.

[40] *Pro venalitate.*

[41] *Aloraye (al-Thurayyā).*

[42] In *AW1* I suggest that a "knot" here means a mansion, or perhaps an aspect considered as falling into a mansion.

[43] Omitting *si supra* ("if above"), which might be a mistake for *sic supra* ("just as above"), referring to an earlier sentence in Jafar.

will be much sought. **18** Likewise, [between] the tenth and the first, they will be reputed cheap. **19** But the presence of the fortunes and [their] aspect, confine the evil of Saturn.

[Chapter V.5: General conjunctional theory][44]

1 General and greater alterations of the world are known through these:

2 Through the conjunction of Saturn and Jupiter at the beginning of Aries, in 960 years.

3 Through the conjunction of the same according to the changing from one triplicity to another, in 240 years.

4 Through the conjunction of Saturn and Mars [in Cancer], in every 30 years.[45]

5 Through the places of the planets in the conjunctions or preventions preceding the Sun's entrance into the tropical signs.

6 Through the places of the planets at the very hour[46] of the [Sun's] entrance [into Aries].

7 Through the lords of the orb containing 360 years,[47] and through the signs ruling from the conjunction signifying the Flood.[48]

8 Through the lords of the Quarters, each one of which has 90 years.

9 Through the lords of the Ascendants in the Quarters and in the orb.

10 Through the profection from the root, by giving one year to each sign.[49]

11 Through the direction from the root, a year per degree.[50]

---

[44] For this section, see generally *AW2* Part I, and *Skilled* VIII.39 (in *AW2*, Section IV.2).
[45] Note that Leopold omits the 20-year period of the lesser Saturn-Jupiter conjunctions.
[46] Reading in the singular.
[47] This is the mundane "mighty" *fardār*, here called an "orb" but more accurately the "Turn" (see my introduction to *AW2*, and its Appendix containing a table of the Turns).
[48] These are the signs which successively partner with the planets in the list of Turns. At the Flood posited by Abū Ma'shar in 3102 BC, the time lords were Cancer-Saturn, then Leo-Jupiter, and so on. According to this system, we are currently in Virgo-Saturn, and will change to Libra-Jupiter in 2020 AD.
[49] This is either the profection from the sign of the triplicity shift, or from its Ascendant at the Aries ingress in that year.
[50] This must be the direction of the Ascendant at the Aries ingress at the triplicity shift.

12 Through the lord of the bound which the distribution has reached.⁵¹

13 Through the rays of the planets, which, when they return after the conjunctional years to the roots, signal as they did before.⁵²

14 In the stated places, the good and fortunate [planets] signal good, eastern ones [do so] quickly, angular ones [signify] strength.

15 Through Jupiter, a distinction of sects; according to others, a connection with him.⁵³

16 Through the lords of the Ascendant which signals a sect.

17 Through the place of the Lot of rulership.

18 Through the houses of the planets, the changing of sects.

19 Through the changing of conjunctions in the triplicities.

20 Through the revolutions of Saturn and Jupiter in 360 years.⁵⁴

21 Through the greater years of the planets.

22 Through the advancing and retreating of the orb by 8° in 640 years.⁵⁵

---

⁵¹ That is, the lord of the bound in which **11** falls at any given time.

⁵² I am not exactly sure what this means, but it undoubtedly is a reference to *BRD*.

⁵³ I am not sure what this last clause means. Indeed, throughout the following sentences it is unclear to me what Leopold is doing. To be sure, he is listing things we should look at, but how does he mean us to use these?

⁵⁴ I am not sure what this refers to.

⁵⁵ This refers to an early theory of trepidation reported by Theon of Alexandria (see my *Comment* to Ch. I.1). Not only is the theory incorrect and so inapplicable, but even by Leopold's time a new trepidation theory attributed to Thābit b. Qurra had arisen.

Chapter V.6: Comets[56]

1 A comet is an earthy vapor having thick parts powerfully hurling [and] ascending to the upper part of the [region] of heat, signifying the alterations of kingdoms and other great things in this world—which some say happens from the conjunction of two planets, [and] others from the adherence of vapor to the light of a planet or star. **2** John of Damascus says a comet comes from God in order to signal the deaths of kings, and is dissolved by God.[57]

[Types of comets]

3 There are 9 comets:[58]

4 The first belongs to Saturn, and is black or blue, and when it appears it signifies mortality and famine.

5 The two following ones belong to Jupiter: silver and rose. **6** The silver one has a very beautiful ray in the manner of purest silver, which cannot be looked at, and when it appears it signifies fertile years, and more so if Jupiter was then in a watery sign. **7** The rose one is great and round[59] and has a face in the manner of a man, and its color is like that of silver mixed together with gold; and appearing, it signifies the death of kings and the wealthy, and things of the world are changed, and better ones will come.

8 Four belong to Mars: the javelin,[60] measuring rod,[61] the tray,[62] and red dawn,[63] and all signify battles and terrors in the world, and [from] their color is known the evil which they signify, and from the nature of the sign in which they first appear. **9** And if they appear in the east, then what they signify will come about quickly; in the west, it will be slowed.

---

[56] Reading in the plural, for *cometa*. For more on comets, see *AW1*, Part III.

[57] John of Damascus (fl. 8th Century AD) was a Syrian monk who wrote among other things on comets (see Hellman p. 45). According to John, comets not only foreshadow or foretell events (as astrologers claimed), but they were created and abolished directly by God for that purpose, as opposed to being only natural phenomena.

[58] Compare the following with Bonatti's descriptions (in his Tr. 8 Part 1 Ch. 104, or *AW1* Section III.11). In *AW1* I give extensive notes on some of my translation choices.

[59] Reading *rotunda* with Bonatti, for *munda* ("clean, elegant").

[60] Reading *veru* with Bonatti for *feru*.

[61] Reading *pertica* for *partica*.

[62] *Tenacula*.

[63] Reading *matutina* with Bonatti for *matura rubea*.

10 One belongs to Venus, and it is called the soldier, and it is large in the manner of the Moon, and it showers hairs and rays behind [itself], and travels through the twelve signs. **11** And it is harmful to kings and powerful people, and men will rise up in the world who want to change the ancient laws and introduce new ones; and the worse signification is from the direction of [its] tail.

12 One belongs to Mercury, and it is called the lord of *astoriae*,[64] and it is blue and small, and a tail which is long, and when it appears it signifies death and fights.

13 The javelin is horrible to look at, and goes near the Sun.

14 The measuring rod has a thick body and signifies in particular a scarcity of waters, and more so [if] conjoined to Venus. **15** If to Mercury, youths and sages will die. **16** If to the Moon, the people will die. **17** If to Saturn, the mortality will be severe. **18** If to Mars, there will be fights and mortality by the sword. **19** If to Jupiter, whatever it signifies will appear in kings and the wealthy.

[Abū Ma'shar: comets in the angles and signs]

20 If[65] a comet appeared in the Ascendant of a nativity or the foundation of some place, or other root, or in the sign of the profection or in the Ascendant of the revolution, or in the degree of the direction, it signifies the death of the native or the destruction of that matter whose Ascendant that sign was. **21** And if it appeared in the sign of the Midheaven when someone was elevated to a dignity, the elevation of the dignity will threaten danger (understand by "the sign which was in the Midheaven" as being at the time of his elevation).

22 If[66] a comet appeared in the equinox of Aries, it signifies the detriment of the kingdom of Babylon, and wars between the Greeks and barbarians, and between the Italians and Alexandrians, the misfortune of the Romans, great dryness and pains of the eyes, and the death of cows, and the descending of the nobles and elevation of the lowest people, and many minerals of gold and silver, with great heat in the summer, and that the religious ought to

---

[64] See my discussion of this uncertain word in *AW1*, in the section on Bonatti.
[65] This paragraph (like **58** below) seems to be based on Abū Ma'shar's *BRD* V.7, **15**, but sentence **21** is from somewhere else.
[66] The following descriptions of comets in the signs are based on Abū Ma'shar's *BRD* V.7.

get themselves involved in[67] many deeds forbidden to them. **23** And if it appears in the east, hatred will fall between the Persians and others, and many regions will obey the king of Babylon. **24** If in the west, magnates will have evil from kings, and slaughter in the west, and many rains, the flooding of rivers, and snows.

25 If a comet appeared in Taurus, there will be fights and terrible rumors in the lands of the Romans and Babylon, powerful illnesses with a small agricultural yield, the misfortune of Italy with captivity and oppression and mortality, many dry pains (like eczema and itching), and the death of cows, the cutting of roads, and a certain part of the year will be left desolate through earthquake, and there will be intense cold and the corruption of the harvests, and the falling of the fruits of the trees, and a scarcity of cultivation and planting. **26** And if in the east, the king will fear his enemies, and buboes[68] will fall in men, and this will endure in the following years, and many illnesses in the summer quarter. **27** And if in the west, it signifies many rains.

28 If a comet appeared in Gemini, the king of the Romans will have difficulties and misfortunes, the king of Egypt [will have difficulties][69] which will introduce death to him, and a thief who is not of the Egyptians will reign after him, and there will be illnesses and deaths, and famine, and the death of children, and the miscarriage of pregnant women, and the death of birds, and great thundering and flashes of light, [and hot dust storms][70] burning the fruits. **29** And if this [were] in the east, many magnates will fall from their own ranks. **30** If in the west, it signifies much captivity and many rains and inundations.

31 If a comet appeared in Cancer, it signifies wars and much death and many evils, and submersion, and the sudden death of certain people, many rains, few fish. **32** And if it appears in the east, there will be difficulties and the cheapness of the annual yield at the end of the year. **33** If in the west, it signifies a quarrel between kings, and peace after this.

34 A comet in Leo signifies a fight between kings at the end of the year, and much shedding of blood in the east, and the death of certain nobles, and

---

[67] Or perhaps, "would be responsible for getting involved in" (*debeant se intromittere*). This is not in the Arabic version.
[68] A bubo is the painful, dark swelling of the lymph nodes in victims of bubonic plague (hence the name of the plague).
[69] Adding with the sense of *BRD*, to make it more grammatical.
[70] Adding with *BRD* (which specifically lists "simooms" or desert storms), replacing *venenosa* ("poisonous").

difficulty urinating, and pains of the eyes, the illness of wolves, rabies in dogs. **35** And if [it is] in the east, many contentions and dryness. **36** If it appears in the west, it signifies many illnesses and the strength of wolves, and rabies in dogs.

37 If a comet appeared in Virgo, it signifies the despising of goods,[71] with injury, and many pains of fevers and trembling, and the windiness of women, and ulcers and blisters, [and] the miscarriage of pregnant women. **38** And if it was appearing in the east and the Sun in Virgo, the Persians will conquer al-Ahwāz.[72] **39** And in the west, the fighting of Babylon.

40 A comet in Libra signifies the harshness of the king of Babylon, and the intensity of his injustice, and the death of kings of the west, and much death of princes and nobles, and the shedding of blood, and mortality, and the cutting off of merchandise, a scarcity of rains and much clear [weather], the forcefulness of the winds, the dryness of rivers, the scarcity of plants, the destruction of foliage. **41** And if it appears in the east, there will be many misfortunes of the king of Babylon, and horses and mules will be expensive, and battles in the lands of the Romans, and they will kill each other. **42** In the east, [it signifies that] slaves will not obey their masters, and mediocre produce.

43 A comet in Scorpio signifies pain of the testicles, bladder, ribs, and the quarreling of kings, and evil for those in labor, and many harmful rains, and the destruction of fruits through ice, and the darkness of the atmosphere, and moisture, and the scarcity of waters, and the drying out of rivers, and the horrible state of fish. **44** And if it is in the east, there will be good health for the Babylonians, and little death, and that will last for 6 years, and rabies in wolves and dogs. **45** And if in the west, there will be locusts, and they will harm little.

46 If a comet [appeared] in Sagittarius, it signifies the kings imperiousness over the common people, and the desire to gather money, and the death of certain nobles, and the intensity of the heat, and a scarcity of the fruits of palms. **47** And in the east [it signifies] the death of kings, and fighting, and robberies, and few returns on real estate and produce. **48** In the west, much imaginativeness in dreams, with the miscarriage of women.

---

[71] In the Arabic, this has to do with enemies capturing people.
[72] Lat. *Alanem*. This is a city in Persia.

49 A comet in Capricorn signifies war between kings, and many misfortunes in the west and for the king in that place, and quarreling and terrible rumors in Persia, and towards the south a multitude of robbers, the plundering of the religious and [their] goods, and death, and excessive hail and snows, and planets will be destroyed (and especially gardens). **50** And [if it is] in the east [it signifies] the impediments of kings from their enemies, and they will be the cause of their death and the renewal of rulership by magnates, and there will be many snows and rains, and the salvation of vineyards and produce. **51** In the west, the grassiness[73] of the year and abundance of the waters.

52 A comet in Aquarius signifies the death of the king in the direction of the east, and of men who seek rulership, and much death, slaughter, and fighting in the direction of the west, and this will last a long time; and leprosy and the darkness of the atmosphere, and many thunders and flashings of light and lightning strikes, and the death of many on account of this, a scarcity of birds and fish, and the cheapness of the annual yield. **53** And if it is in the direction of the east, with the Sun in Aquarius, there will be much grassiness. **54** If it is in the west, there will be many terrible rumors in Persia, and plundering.

55 A comet in Pisces signifies the death of some of the common people, and much slaughter among the kings of the blacks and the Egyptians, and this because of reasons of faith; and there will be portents, and the king will go out and burn cities, and he will have evil and will be abused among men, and the religious will kill each other, and poverty will appear, and fish will die, and there will not be profit in waters. **56** And if it appears in the east and the Sun is in Pisces, there will be violence in leaders and princes, and they will be disobedient to the king, and will destroy the treasury of the king, and there will be fear in many climes, and misfortune in Persia with many rains. **57** And if in the west, there will be many distresses of men, and death in many climes, and especially in the direction of the west, and it will last for 3 years, and there will be many birds and fish, and the flooding of rivers.

58 And if it was with [Ascendant of] any of these,[74] it signifies their distresses, and wars coming to them, and there will be envy and injury among

---

[73] That is, fertility which leads to much grass and other vegetation.

[74] Adding with Abū Ma'shar, and omitting *dominis* ("masters, lords"). What Abū Ma'shar means is that if the comet appears on the Ascendant of the *nativities* of powerful people or of other charts, it will cause problems.

men, and especially in high men, and in middling men it even signifies enemies and misfortunes on account of this.

[Chapter V.7: Planets' rulerships over places and regions]

1 As regards knowing the sign or planets of any particular place, or the lord of an estate, I believe there is a fourfold path:

2 One, through the founding of the estate or place, because the sign ascending then is the sign of the estate or place, and the more powerful planet in that hour is the planet of that estate or place, and is called the "victor": and this the more certain path which could be had.

3 Another path is through the great events (whether good or bad) which happen to the estate or place:[75] because if the event is good, it is right that the planetary significator of the estate or place be powerful in the figure, and its sign be in one of the angles, and the good planets in it or looking at it. **4** But if the event was bad, it is right that the planet of the estate or place be weak and conjoined with the bad one, or looking at them with a malevolent aspect, and its sign be falling, and the bad ones in it or looking at it malevolently.

5 The third path is through the consideration of the tenth house of the nativity of the lord who founded the estate: and this third path is put in the *Tetrabiblos* of the glossator, in Part II, Chapter 3, at the end.

6 The fourth path is posed by some as being by the day of the market day of that estate: wherefore if it is on the day of Venus, Venus is the planet of that estate.

---

[75] I.e., important event charts, or perhaps the ingress charts in years of great events.

TREATISE VI: ON THE CHANGING OF THE ATMOSPHERE

[Introduction]

1 Intending to have foreknowledge about the changing of the atmosphere, I examined many volumes of the philosophers carefully—from which I have judged that every change of the atmosphere happens either from the nature of the signs (or of the [fixed] stars which are in them), or from the nature of the planets in themselves and in the signs (and their conjunctions and applications). **2** And therefore I have first gathered the nature of the signs and [the fixed] stars which are in them; secondly, the nature of the planets in themselves and in signs, and their conjunctions and applications; thirdly, the rules of foreknowledge,[1] which the philosophers put down concerning the changing of the atmosphere.[2]

[Chapter VI.1: The signs and fixed stars][3]

1 Aries generally[4] thunders and flashes. **2** And its beginning makes rains and winds, the middle is temperate, the ends [of it] burn up and generate mortality. **3** And the northern [portions] heat and destroy, the southern ones freeze and chill.
4 Taurus generally bears each complexion, but inclines more towards heat. **5** And the stars around its beginning (and especially those which are around the Pleiades) make earthquakes and winds and mists, in the middle they moisten and chill, at the end then, around Aldebaran, they make fires, flashings, and thunders. **6** The northern ones are temperate, the southern ones unstable: they make disorderly motions.
7 Gemini generally makes a temperate balance. **8** At the beginning they moisten and destroy, in the middle they temper, at the end they commingle.

---

[1] This could also be read as, "rules which must be known beforehand" (*regulas...praesciendas*).
[2] This seems to refer to the rules about winds (among some other things) in Ch. VI.3 below.
[3] The following division of the signs is based on Ptolemy, *Tet.* II.11 (Robbins). See also *AW1*, Section I.2.
[4] Or, "universally" (*universaliter*).

9 The northern ones make winds and earthquake, the southern ones are fiery and burn up.

10 Cancer generally makes fair weather and heat. **11** And at the beginning around Praesepe it makes the air hot and turbid,[5] and earthquakes; those which are in the middle temper, at the end they make winds. **12** The northern and southern ones are burned up.

13 Leo generally makes the air hot and turbid,[6] and likewise its beginning, as well as mortality; the middle tempers, the end moistens and destroys. **14** The northern ones are fiery and burn up, the southern ones moisten.

15 Virgo generally moistens and thunders. **16** The beginning heats and destroys, the middle tempers, and the end [moistens].[7]

17 Libra generally varies. **18** The first [part] and middle temper, the end is watery. **19** And the northern [parts] make winds, the southern ones what is moist, and mortality.

20 Scorpio generally thunders and is fiery. **21** And at the beginning it makes winds excessively,[8] and in the middle it tempers, and its stars at the end make earthquake. **22** The northern ones burn up, the southern ones moisten.

23 Sagittarius generally makes winds. **24** The beginning moistens, in the middle it tempers, at the end it is fiery. **25** And the northern ones add winds, the southern ones moisten powerfully and vary.

26 Capricorn generally moistens very much. **27** The beginning burns up and destroys, the middle tempers, at the end it makes rains. **28** The northern and southern ones moisten powerfully and destroy.

29 Aquarius generally chills and is watery. **30** At the beginning it is moist, in the middle temperate, at the end windy. **31** The northern ones burn up, the southern ones make winds excessively.

32 Pisces generally chills and makes winds. **33** The beginning tempers, in the middle it moistens powerfully, the last stars burn up. **34** The northern ones make winds, the southern ones are watery.

35 These, therefore, are the natures of the twelve signs and of the stars which are in them: and these are the twelve statements of my compilation.

---

[5] Or more simply, "stormy" (*turbidus*).
[6] See above.
[7] Adding with Ptolemy.
[8] In Ptolemy, this part makes snow.

36 Also,[9] the moist signs are Cancer, Leo, Scorpio, and Aquarius; Sagittarius is added on account of the seas which occur at its end,[10] and Pisces on account of the streams which it is in charge of. **37** The moist parts of the signs are the end of Aries and the beginning of Taurus, Cancer, the end of Capricorn and the beginning of Aquarius, and the beginning of Leo.

[Moisture in the lunar mansions][11]

38 However, not yet has it come to be noted that certain ones of the mansions of the Moon (about which we spoke before)[12] are moist, certain ones dry, certain ones bearing a mean between moisture and dryness. **39** [Table follows:]

1.	The horns of Aries	have a mean
2.	The belly of Aries	dries up
3.	The head of Taurus	moistens[13]
4.	The eye[14] of Taurus	moistens
5.	The head of the strong Dog	dries up
6.	The Small Star (with great light)	has a mean
7.	The Arm [of Leo]	moistens
8.	Two cloudy stars with a middle cloud	has a mean
9.	The Eye [of Leo]	dries up
10.	The Brow [of Leo]	moistens
11.	The Fur [of Leo]	has a mean
12.	The Tail of Leo	moistens
13.	The Dog	has a mean
14.	Spica	has a mean
15.	The Covered	moistens
16.	The Horns[15]	moisten

---

[9] This seems to be a mixture of opinions based on Hermann of Carinthia and John of Spain: see *AW1*, especially the section on rainy signs in the Introduction.

[10] This may refer to the numerous constellations of sea animals in the later part of the zodiac.

[11] The following is based on John of Spain, in his *Treatise on Rains* (see *AW1*, Section I.16). See also the table in Ch. I.2, **50**.

[12] See Ch. I.2, **48**.

[13] Leopold is following John's comment that the *Arabs* call this moist; John himself says it is temperate.

[14] Reading *oculus* with John for *cornu* ("horn").

17.	The crown above the head of Scorpio	moistens
18.	The Heart of Scorpio	dries up
19.	The Tail of Scorpio	moistens
20.	The Beam	moistens
21.	The Desert	has a mean
22.	The Shepherd	moistens
23.	The Gulping	has a mean
24.	The Star of Fortune	has a mean
25.	The Butterfly	dries up
26.	The first Pourer	dries up
27.	The second Pourer	moistens
28.	The Fish	has a mean

40 I see therefore that there are 12 moist mansions, 6 dry; the rest are temperate. **41** Certain people[16] put the mansions of the Moon as being only 27, and thus they grant to each one precisely 13° 20': and they do not posit 28 because the Moon is under the rulership of the Sun.[17]

[Chapter VI.2: Planets and their combinations in the signs]

1 Concerning the natures or proper qualities of the planets, the philosophers say that the rainy planets are Venus, Mercury, and the Moon: and understand thusly the works of these and of the others.[18]

[Superior planets as lords of the year]

2 If Saturn were in charge of the year[19] without the aspect of Mars or another planet, it will bring forth cold in the north, animals, and seeds; and more so if he is ascending from the middle of the circle of his apogee. **3** And then, on account of Saturn's rulership, lands will be tempered extremely

---

[15] That is, the pans of Libra.
[16] Namely, the Indians.
[17] See *AW1*, Ch. I.1.
[18] Venus, Mercury, and Moon form one group of rainy planets, the malefics the other. See *AW1* Ch. I.1.
[19] For rules on this, see *AW2*, my *Introduction* §12.

quickly,[20] and animals there and seeds will be strengthened: and their atmosphere will be good. **4** If Saturn were descending, likewise in the north there will be vermin in animals, and deadly expensiveness. **5** Saturn in a fiery sign signals the greatest heat. **6** Saturn in signs of the portion of the Sun (which is from Leo to Aquarius) signals submersion in waters; in the portion of the Moon (which is from Aquarius to Leo), it signals thirst.

7 If Mars were in charge of the year, the cold of winter will be tempered in the north, and because of this animals and seeds will be strengthened if this is without the aspect of Saturn or another planet. **8** And in hot signs[21] there comes to be the destruction of animals and seeds, and more so than this if he would be ascending from the middle circle of the apogee: and then there will be battle, quick death, and collusion. **9** Mars in a hot sign makes great heat. **10** In a human sign, it stirs up war, and more so if he is being concealed by the Sun or if he is in the sign of his own disgrace (which is Cancer).

11 The Sun varies the quarters of years according to the conjunction and aspect of the hot or cold planets to him. **12** For, Saturn with the Sun in the winter without the aspect of Mars or another, increases the cold; in the summer with the Sun it diminishes heat. **13** And Saturn operates more strongly in the cold signs and quarters, and Mars in the hot ones. **14** Jupiter with the Sun without the aspect of another, tempers the atmosphere and makes northern, temperate winds from which animals and seeds are strengthened; likewise if he is charge of the year, and he is the occasion of [good] fortune. **15** Whenever Venus is either with the Sun or in charge of the year, it increases moisture in the winter and spring, and it diminishes dryness in the summer and autumn: so that if another would not look at her, she gives good marriage-unions and sexual intercourse, and many feasts and loves. **16** Mercury conjoined the Sun, or when he is in charge of the year, varies the weather and corrupts with wind and dryness; and he gives a subtle character, and his signification is diverse. **17** The Moon at the first quarter of the month is hot and moist, in the second hot and dry, in the third she is cold and dry, in the fourth cold and moist. **18** And in any month she visits all the signs, and commixes and tempers and strengthens [their] natures so that animals and seeds are able to endure. **19** And if she is in charge of the year or

---

[20] Reading tentatively for *ultra modum calide*, though it does not make sense to me.
[21] Reading *signis* for *terris* ("lands").

is mixed with the Sun, she operates through the quarters of the year as I said;[22] and so the Moon operates in the month as the Sun does in the year.

[Ptolemy on weather][23]

20 Since these general things have been noted beforehand, for the quarters of the year observe the entrance of the [Sun into] the equinoxes and solstices, the conjunctions or preventions of the Sun and Moon preceding [them], and the angles of heaven in those hours—and this [is] in every clime—and the lords of the places of the conjunctions or preventions and angles, and judge the quality of the atmosphere according to the powers of the stars ruling in them. **21** Alterations of the atmosphere come to be more frequently three days before the conjunction of the Moon with the Sun, or three after.

22 If planets appear in the morning or at a late hour, more clearly than usual, in the east or west according to the affinity of the Sun,[24] then they alter the weather according to their own natures. **23** Moreover, the luminaries in the angles of heaven alter the weather. **24** Likewise, winds do not arise except through the course of the two luminaries to those pivots,[25] and they come to be towards the direction to which the Moon inclines.

25 If the Moon were black or green or condensed, it denotes wintry and rainy air. **26** Moreover if a clear circle surrounds her and it is gradually abbreviated[26] it signals fair weather. **27** Likewise if two or three circles surround her, they signal wintry air. **28** Again, if they incline to a clear redness and are as though cut off, they signal wintry air and extremely powerful winds. **29** Moreover, if they are turbid and thick, they signify wintry air which comes to be through winds and snows. **30** Again, if they incline towards the black and green [and appear] cut off, they signify wintry air through winds. **31** Likewise,

---

[22] This probably refers to the use of New and Full Moons before each quarterly ingress. Ptolemy recommends we cast the lunation chart just before the ingress, and use the charts of that same type of Moon (Full or New) for the rest of the season. Just before the next season, we cast the chart for *that* type of lunation. See *AW1*.

[23] See *Tet.* II.12-13 (Robbins).

[24] This must refer to their sect, so that diurnal planets rise before the Sun in the morning, and nocturnal ones after the Sun in the evening. Or, it may mean the superior planets rising before the Sun in the morning, and inferior ones after him in the evening.

[25] Following Ptolemy's meaning by reading *cardines* for *ordines* ("ranks").

[26] *Breviabitur*, which has no basis in Ptolemy. Perhaps Leopold means that it will dissipate quickly.

clear circles around the other planets and stars signify in a similar way. **32** Moreover, if the Pleiades and Alphecca (and others which many stars approach [in a group])[27] are clearer than usual and appear larger, they signify winds from the direction in which they are. **33** Again, if Alphecca and Praesepe and those like them virtually do not appear in clear weather, or they are thickened, they signify a multitude of rains and wintry air. **34** Likewise, clear and shining stars signify powerful winds.

35 Comets and *assub*[28] always signify dryness, and this according to their multitude and the extent of their size.

36 Moreover, the shooting[29] of the stars from one of the angles signifies winds from that direction, disorderly winds from different[30] angles, [and] if it comes from the four angles, wintry air from many different [directions], along with thunders and flashings of light, and the like.

37 Also, clouds like tufts of wool denote wintry air.

38 Moreover, a rainbow in clear weather signifies wintry air, and clear skies in rainy [weather]; and colors always signify what is like themselves.

39 Observe,[31] in a rainbow, that its altitude and the Sun does not exceed an altitude of 42°: and it has redness from fire, and is purple from water, crimson[32] from the air, green from the earth, and it is called a rainbow from the air.

[Some reports by John of Spain and Hermann][33]

40 With the Sun entering Aries, if Saturn is in a moist [sign], judge moisture; likewise with the other watery [planets], but Saturn more signifies cloudiness and cold. **41** If then Saturn, Venus, Mercury, and the Moon are ruling, it will rain much, especially if they are in rainy signs (namely at the end of Capricorn and at the beginning of Aquarius, at the end of Aries and in the beginning of Cancer, or Leo).

---

[27] In other words, clusters.
[28] This seems to be a misread for *Aladcha*, which appears here in Plato of Tivoli; but this word itself is taken from an Arabic word currently unknown to me, and at any rate does not seem to correspond to any word in Ptolemy.
[29] Reading *iaculatio* with Plato for *occultatio* ("concealment").
[30] That is, "opposite" (Ptolemy).
[31] The source of this sentence unknown.
[32] Reading *hyacinthinus* for *iactinctinus*, though crimson does not seem right for air.
[33] Much of this material can be traced back to Hermann's *Book of Heavy Rains* (see *AW1* Section I.12), or John of Spain (see *AW1* Sections I.15-16).

42 Jupiter makes a good mixture and winds from the left, Mars heat and winds from the right, Venus rains, Mercury winds, the Moon rains (and this, according to the nature of the one to which she is being joined or the one whom she looks at). **43** The Sun in the upper half of [his] eccentric makes clear weather, in the other [half] rains.[34]

44 In a revolution of the year, if Mars is in his own proper sign,[35] it will rain much; in a house of Saturn, little; in the others, in a middling way.[36] **45** At the conjunction or opposition which precedes a revolution of the year, if Mars looks at that place there will be lightning, thunderings, and meteors.

46 According to the Indians, annual rains are foreknown thus, at the conjunction of the Sun and Moon (or the opposition) before the Sun's entrance into Aries, if the Moon first looks at Saturn, and both she and he are in a moist [sign] and the aspect of Jupiter does not interrupt [their aspect], there will be black clouds and sluggish and lasting rains. **47** And if the planets below the Sun then look at Saturn, the rain will be greater and lasting more.

48 In a revolution of the year, if Venus, Mercury, and the Moon were in moist places, rains will abound. **49** In a revolution of the year, if the Lots of the planets of rain (namely Venus, Mercury, and the Moon)[37] fall into moist places, there will be rains so that they are harmful.

50 In a revolution, the Lot of Mercury is taken thusly, at the conjunction or prevention which precedes the revolution of the year: the degrees which are from Mercury to the lord of the sign in which Mercury is, are taken, and the degrees of the ascending sign which ascended are added, and the projection is from the beginning of the ascending sign. **51** And the atmosphere is judged according to the lord [of the sign] in which the numbering is ended. **52** If then[38] Mars is in the angle of the earth and in an earthy [sign], invested

---

[34] The "upper half" of his eccentric is the half towards his apogee, so roughly a little after the beginning of spring, to a little after the beginning of fall. See Ch. II.2.

[35] That is, in Aries or Scorpio.

[36] This is a view of Abū Ma'shar (see his *Flowers* Ch. III.2, in *AW2*), which ibn Ezra scorns as inaccurate (ibn Ezra 2010, p. 93).

[37] Leopold is referring to two Lots of rains and wind described below; he associates them with these three rainy planets because these planets are used in the calculations of the Lots.

[38] This information about Mars in the angles is not directly related to the question of the Lot of air and winds (or rather, Mercury) just mentioned. But by saying "then" (*tunc*), Leopold seems to think it is.

with Mercury,[39] it makes earthquake and the corruption of minerals; in a fiery one, the burning of the land and seeds; likewise in the others.

53 In a revolution, the Lot of rain is taken in the day from Venus and the Moon (in the night the reverse), and is projected from the Ascendant. **54** Which if it falls into a moist [sign], there will be many rains, and *vice versa*; and when the Moon will have reached that place, it will rain; likewise with Venus.

55 When the Sun enters a tropical sign, if then Venus looks at the Moon in a moist [sign], *from* a moist [sign], there will be many rains; if then the Moon is not in a moist one but Venus is, it will be middling.

56 In a revolution, if the Moon looks at the Moon or Mercury, and both are eastern, there will be many rains at the beginning of the year; if western, the contrary.

57 In a revolution, if the Moon then falls away from[40] Mars, it will rain on that day. **58** In a revolution, if Mars looks at Venus from Scorpio, rains will be abundant.

59 If the Sun is in Aries or Taurus, and Venus [is] then retrograde, spring will be very rainy.

60 If you made the beginning of the month in the quarters the minute of [each] successive conjunction,[41] you would know beforehand the moistures of the air.

61 And the rising of the sea is greatest at the conjunction and opposition of the luminaries, the least in the quarters; toward the quarters it decreases, from the quarters it increases.

62 The Lot of the day is to take, at the rising Sun every day, how much there is from the Sun to Saturn, and then project this from the place of the Moon. **63** If it falls into a moist [sign], it signifies moisture, and contrariwise; into a house of Venus and the Moon, rain; into the house of the Sun and Mars, fair weather; Jupiter and Mercury, winds; Saturn, clouds.[42]

64 If the Moon is with Venus or Mercury in a moist [sign], and more so with each [of them], rains will be abundant.

65 If the Moon is in Scorpio and Mars in the opposite, rains are abundant. **66** If the Moon and Mars are together in a moist [sign], and either of the inferiors from the Sun is looking at Mars, there will be terrible clouds, meteors,

---

[39] That is, a conjunction in particular but also by aspect.
[40] *Decidit.* I am not sure if this means something like "separating," or is a translation of the Arabic phrase which means "in aversion to."
[41] That is, the New and Full Moons.
[42] Or perhaps, "fog" or "mist" (*nubula* [*sic*]).

and thunders, and hail, but it will not rain unless Mars would be looking at Saturn or Jupiter or the Sun—if the arranger of the seasons, Glorious and Sublime God, wishes!

67 The Moon[43] entering Cancer at the hour of the Sun, Virgo at the hour of Venus, Libra at the hour of Jupiter, Sagittarius in her own [hour], Taurus at the hour of Mars, Gemini at the hour of Mercury—it signifies according to the nature of the lord of the hour and sign in which it is.

68 If the Moon enters Aquarius or Pisces, it changes[44] and disturbs the atmosphere. **69** If the Moon applies to a scorched Mercury, or is opposed to him from Scorpio, it makes rains. **70** If Venus applies to Mars in Scorpio, it will rain immediately. **71** If the Sun, Venus, Mercury, and the Moon are together, they make continual heavy rains on that day, even if the Moon looks at them from elsewhere.

72 If the Moon was in Scorpio and Mars in [her] opposite, and the Sun in Aquarius or Pisces, rains are abundant.

73 If the Sun is in Aquarius and the Moon in Leo, it will rain on that day.

74 When the Sun enters Libra, if Venus is with him within one sign, there will be many rains—and if she was western and under the rays, it will be more at the beginning of the year; if eastern and not under the rays, it will be at the end of the year.

75 Venus in an angle at the conjunction and opposition of the luminaries, is a certain judgment of rains. **76** Likewise the lord of the Ascendant in an angle and in a watery [sign].

77 If the Moon is in the southern hemisphere (namely from Libra to Aries), and Venus under the rays of the Sun, and the Moon applies to her, it will rain immediately on that day and hour.

78 It will rain when the Moon, in a pivot and in a watery [sign], applies to Venus or Mercury; and it lasts for as long as the application lasts.

79 If the Sun is in Pisces or Aries, and the Moon in [his] opposite or in Sagittarius, in vaporous places, there will be an abundance of heavy rains on that day.

80 If the Moon is in the opposite of the Sun or with Venus in Pisces or[45] Aries, Libra, or Scorpio, there will be meteors, thunders, and lightnings.

---

[43] For these planetary hours, see my discussion in the Introduction to *AW1*.
[44] Lit., "turns" (*vertit*).
[45] Reading *aut* for *in*.

81 Venus entering Cancer makes rains. **82** Saturn, Jupiter, and Mars being conjoined make rains and burning.[46]

83 If Saturn is at the apogee of this circle and the Moon conjoined to him at the end of the month, it signifies the increase of the thing which the sign in which she is, signifies.

84 If[47] the Moon applies to the Sun, there will be clouds and heavy rains from which rivers will be overflowing. **85** With Venus, bright white clouds, middling heavy rains, light winds. **86** With Mercury, varied clouds (saffron, reddish, black, grey, and pale); if[48] she is alone [with him], the site of the clouds will come to be a diversity of the coursing of colors, and the interruption of heavy rains. **87** With Saturn, black clouds, the severity of lightning flashes, [and] winds and rain in turn. **88** With Jupiter, bright white and black clouds (as though put next to each other),[49] meteors, thunderings, and heavy rain, and sometimes the good balance of the atmosphere. **89** With Mars, reddish clouds and a pale rainbow and heavy rain, a good heating air in the beginning (and sometimes cold). **90** And these seven judgments belong to the Indians.

91 A retrograde planet up to the opposition of the Sun, signifies rains more so than the reverse.[50]

92 With the Moon in a feminine sign, if she regards a retrograde planet in a feminine sign, it will rain immediately. **93** The Moon joined to a retrograde planet, with her being increased in light, is a sign of rain.

---

[46] *Torrentes.* But perhaps this could be read simply as "torrents" (of rain).
[47] This paragraph is very similar to some in *AW1*, and might be based on al-Kindī (*AW1*, Section I.3), but there are too many differences to be certain.
[48] From here to the end of the paragraph, reading somewhat uncertainly for *cum sola est situs nubium fit discursus colorum diversitas, et interruptio imbrium.*
[49] *Quasi invicem suppositae.*
[50] The reverse probably means being retrograde *after* the opposition up to the second station.

[The centers of the Moon][51]

94 There are twelve centers of the Moon. **95** The first is the place of the conjunction of the Sun and Moon. **96** The second is from the conjunction by 12°. **97** The third is from the conjunction by 45°. **98** The fourth, by 90° from the conjunction. **99** The fifth, from there by 45°.[52] **100** The sixth, at 12° from the opposition. **101** The seventh, the place of the opposition. **102** And the other five [are] from the opposition to the conjunction, just as from the conjunction. **103** Observe the Moon in such places: of what kind are they, whether moist or dry or middling, and to which [planets] is she being joined by body or aspect? **104** Judge according to that.

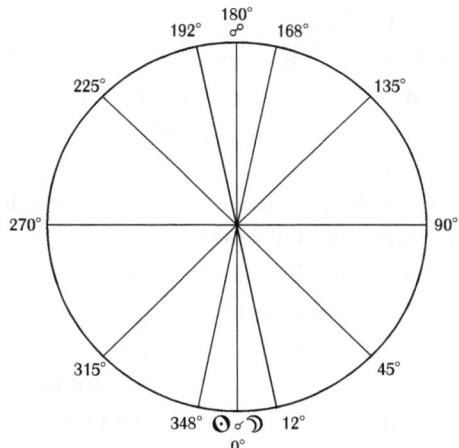

Figure 64: Centers of the Moon (Dykes, from 'Umar and al-Kindī)

[The opening of the doors][53]

105 There are ten openings of the doors, and they are between those whose houses are contrary between themselves: such as Saturn and the Sun, Saturn and the Moon, Jupiter and Mercury, Mars and Venus. **106** Whence, if the Moon is transferred from the Sun to Saturn (or conversely), from Jupiter

---

[51] This section could have been taken from al-Kindī (*Forty Chapters* Ch. 38.3) or 'Umar al-Tabarī (see *AW1*, Section I.5).
[52] That is, at 135°.
[53] For more on this, see *AW1* Ch. I.1.

to Mercury (or conversely), from Mars to Venus (or conversely), it is always an opening of the doors. **107** And thus there are ten doors of opening in which changes of the atmosphere come to be, according to the natures of those between which the transfer is; and the one which receives the conjunction or aspect is the lord of the matter.

[Other views][54]

108 The Indians know the day of rain by the distance of the conjunction or opposition of the luminaries (or square) to the degree of a rainy planet: so that if the Moon is in a movable sign they give one hour to every degree, in a fixed one a day, in a common one they give a day in her first half but they give an hour in the second half; and then it will rain. **109** And if Mars is then looking at Saturn, rain is deferred up to where the Moon looks at Saturn by the opposite or square aspect in a dry [sign], or she gives power to Jupiter; with each one appearing in a moist [sign], and either of the inferiors looks at Jupiter, then it will be cloudy. **110** With the Moon and Jupiter bearing themselves thusly [to one another], if neither of the inferiors looks at Jupiter, if Jupiter himself looks at Saturn, it will rain.

111 There is no diversity in the heaven nor in the planets, except according to their situation in longitude, latitude, [going] upwards and downwards. **112** And the diversity of the atmosphere comes to be through the eccentric of the Sun and [the bearing] of the planets in relation to the Sun, and among themselves through their diversity [of relationship] to the earth. **113** And the greatness of the body of the Sun and his heat conquers over planets which are under his rays.

114 And if the planets descend to the base of [their] epicycle they are hot, but if in addition they are at the summit of [their] eccentric, their heat does not appear, but cold.[55] **115** And it must be known that if the center of the planet is less than six signs [from its apogee], it is descending in the eccentric; if more [than six], it is ascending. **116** And if the argument of the planet is less than six signs, it is descending in the epicycle; if more, it is ascending.

117 And if in the summer quarter five [planets] are direct, the summer will be suitable on account of their cooling; if at that time [they are] retrograde, it

---

[54] Some of the following can be traced to al-Kindī's letter on rain (see *AW1*, Section I.3).
[55] *Non apparet eorum calidum sed frigidum*, which I read as *calor sed frigus*.

will be hot, and a hot wind will exhaust the northern areas: for retrograde, they heat up, direct they cool down.

118 If the Sun is between Capricorn and Aries (this is in the winter), and one retrograde [planet] is with him, there will be dryness; if two, a corresponding moisture; if three, adding moisture; if four there will be a flood ([and] for the superiors, this cannot be except by aspect). **119** If all are retrograde when the Sun is in the autumnal quarter, and they to direct in the winter, it will be the height of dryness in every clime.

120 The light ones being burned up in the quarter of autumn make cold and moisture; in the wintry quarter, gloominess and southern winds; in the spring one, gloominess; in the summer one, hotness and thunders. **121** And likewise the heavy ones. **122** And from a latitude of 9° from the equator up to 60°, rains come to be.

123 If Saturn, Jupiter, the Sun, and the Tail of the Dragon or Venus are conjoined, they make torrents destroying cities (and more so in the winter). **124** If a retrograde Mars looks at the Sun, burning lightning-flashes will fall; with Mars regarding Venus and the Moon, if Mercury accompanies him or her, there will be heavy rains with thick drops.

125 When[56] the Sun enters 18° Scorpio, if Venus is then in a watery [sign], there will be rains [leaning towards] submersion. **126** If the Sun is in Aquarius, and Venus, and the Moon applies to Venus or is opposed to her, it will rain immediately. **127** If Venus is retrograde and eastern, and the Sun in Capricorn, Aquarius, or Pisces, it gives few heavy rains in the spring, [but] abundant ones at the beginning of winter. **128** Moreover, Venus being direct [and] eastern in the winter, it gives few rains at the beginning, but at the end of winter many (unless any star should traverse more closely to the Sun).

129 The Sun in the bounds of Mars in the summer, increases heat; in the winter and spring it makes dryness and a scarcity of rains. **130** Saturn and Mars are dry: which [if they are] conjoined in Cancer with the testimony of Jupiter, the Sun, and the Moon, they signify dryness at all horizons.

---

[56] This paragraph is based on Hermann's *Book of Heavy Rains* (see *AW1*, Section I.12).

[Chapter VI.3: Rules about winds]

1 Wind is an earthy vapor climbing across[57] the atmosphere and impelling it powerfully. **2** Moreover, another person says: wind is dense atmosphere stirred up to the point of a stormy shock.[58] **3** When the Sun is between Aries and Cancer, the winds will be eastern; to Libra, northern; to Capricorn, western; to Aries, southern.

4 The configuration of Mercury with the Moon makes winds. **5** With Saturn (if he is not retrograde), winds with black clouds; the retrogradation of Saturn speaks against winds, and more so in an earthy sign. **6** Likewise, Mars in an earthy sign speaks against [them]. **7** With Jupiter, health-giving [winds], with Mars hot and fiery ones, with the Sun (in a windy [sign]) it makes hot or bad winds. **8** Moreover, if the Sun were in Capricorn and the Moon was in Scorpio or Capricorn or Taurus or Virgo, the coldest winds will blow.

9 The principal winds are four, and each one has two contributing ones.[59] **10** From the east, Subsolanus; it has Vulturnus from the left, Eurus from the right. **11** From the south, Auster; from the left [it has] Nothus, from the right Africus. **12** From the west, Zephyrus; from the left it has Circius, from the right Favonius (even though Favonius is put as the principal one by certain people). **13** From the north, Aquilo; from the left it has Boreas, from the right Chorus.

14 There are twelve winds on account of the twelve portals of the Sun through which they go out, and he makes them. **15** And a dry and subtle and cold vapor elevated into the atmosphere, makes wind; and a dry and thick one shut up in the earth, makes earthquake; and a dry vapor enveloped by a moist one makes flashings of light and thunders; however, a moist vapor is the matter of rains and what is of this kind.

16 The Sun raises up the eastern winds, Mars the southern ones, the Moon the western ones, Jupiter the northern ones. **17** The matter of the wind goes out or is drawn forth from down below to up above, but the return down below is crooked, whence in this it imitates the motion of the stars above the arc of the horizon. **18** While however it presses down the

---

[57] Or, "climbing over" (*transcendens*).
[58] *Offensionem*.
[59] According to one online source (en.wikipedia.org/wiki/Classical_compass_winds), Latin sources on winds tend to mix up the winds, so this description may be at odds with others.

wind from above to below, it is cold because of[60] the upper part of the air; and its motion is not continuous, because once pressed down it is strengthened by the heat of the lower place, and is raised up again.

19 The eastern winds are hot and dry, because that is the path of the Sun from which he [makes the atmosphere] subtle and heats up. **20** The western ones [are] the reverse for the contrary reason: namely [they are] cold and moist, because when they go out from the hot region, the northern winds find them from the coldest places which they open up, constricted by cold, and they bear moisture. **21** The northern ones are cold and dry on account of the cold which condenses the vapors there. **22** And in every vapor is something of the three elements, air, water, and earth: whence what steams cannot be wholly simple, and on account of the earthy [element] which is in the vapor of the wind.

23 The wind darkens[61] like smoke, which is even black on account of earthy burning.

24 The winds which are in the mountains are joined to the air which strikes every vapor and impels the atmosphere.

25 And the wind is not able to go up above on account of the cold encountering it, nor down below on account of the heat encountering it, nor backwards on account of the impelling coldness: whence it is forced to go into the opposite. **26** And the wind does not leave its own natural place, because, taking on the nature of the atmosphere, it is moved in its [own] region.

27 And Auster is winding, because Aquilo, encountering it, reflects and curls it [back]: it is reflected in its own place. **28** But Aquilo blows in a straight line, because the bluntness[62] of Auster cannot reflect it.

[Thunder and other portents]

29 If it thundered[63] in the second sign from the first, the signification of the first [sign] will perish. **30** If it thundered in Aries, herbs will abound, there will be difficulty for the children of men, [and] hangings will be multi-

---

[60] Adding *causa*.
[61] Reading tentatively for *denigrat* (*de* + *niger*); Leopold's source might be thinking of how the atmosphere's ability to bear moisture darkens it.
[62] *Obtusum*, though this is not really a noun.
[63] The topic has now changed, but I am not sure to what: surely this cannot mean any kind of thunder, but thunder at a specific time.

plied. **31** In Taurus, a good annual yield in the mountains, little in the valleys, wine and beasts of the field will be multiplied. **32** In Gemini, there will be many rains and hail, much grain and beans, few birds, many creeping things. **33** In Cancer, famine and upheaval,[64] locusts will lay waste[65] to the fruits of the earth. **34** In Leo, there will be sedition between kingdoms, the means of subsistence expensive at the beginning, the sedition of the people at the end, and a great man will die. **35** In Virgo, virtually all men will plot,[66] and four-footed things will die. **36** In Libra, dryness at the beginning, rains at the end of the year, and the means of subsistence expensive at the end. **37** In Scorpio, few raisins, fish and cattle will die, women will miscarry, the winds will be great; the Moon in the east will be obscured. **38** In Sagittarius, the winds will be appropriate, the fruits of trees will fall, the slaves of the king will do battle. **39** In Capricorn, many peoples will be dispersed, and there will be a great pestilence, [and] mortality in the children of men from every direction. **40** In Aquarius, great winds, terror for men, the wind will bring in coughing and itching, and there will be great upheaval in the world. **41** In Pisces, frost and dryness in the earth, the fruits of the earth will be deficient, much wine will abound, men of riches will become ill (but not many will die).

42 The thunders of January signify powerful winds and an abundance of the produce [of the field]. **43** Those of February pronounces the death of many men, and especially the rich. **44** Of March, powerful winds and an abundance of produce, and lawsuits in the people. **45** April, good and a pleasant year. **46** May signals famine. **47** June, the abundance of the produce and especially the means of subsistence, and bad infirmities. **48** July [indicates] the good means of subsistence in that year, but the produce of fruit trees will perish. **49** August, the prosperity of the matter of the public, but men will become very ill. **50** September, an abundance of produce and the killings of the powerful. **51** October brings powerful wind and the scarcity of the means of subsistence and the fruits of trees. **52** November, an abundance of grain and having fun in that year. **53** December, the abundance of the means of subsistence, peace and concord in the people.

54 If the kalends of January[67] were on Sunday, the winter will be good but windy, the spring moist, summer and autumn windy, and the means of sub-

---

[64] *Commotio.*
[65] Reading *vastabunt* for *fastabunt*.
[66] Reading *homines* for *hominibus*. If the text were correct, it would mean that some other plural subject would plot *against* men—but no such subject is evident.
[67] That is, January 1.

sistence and cattle and honey [will be] enough; the vintage, beans, the fruits of gardens, and youths will perish; discord among kings, many robberies. **55** If on Monday, the winter middling, the spring temperate, the summer hot, floods, fears and infirmities, low-class people will die, war between women, the moving [away] of princes,[68] matrons will mourn, much ice, kings will die, great devastation by the sword, a bad vintage, bees will die. **56** If on Tuesday, a great winter, and snow and flooding, the spring and summer moist, autumn dry, grain expensive, the sudden death of cattle, resident aliens will rule, much honey, expensive wood, many burnings, excessive pestilence, good beans, the fruits of trees will perish, oil will abound, the Romans will be improved in something, women will die, and kings, and a bad vintage. **57** If on Wednesday, a cheap means of subsistence, a good vintage, hot and prosperous winter, a bad and moist spring, temperate autumn, the dangers of the sword, an abundance of oil, the loosening of the belly and insides,[69] women will die, there will be famine in diverse places, and something new will be heard, youths will die. **58** If on Thursday, a storm winter, good spring, bad summer, dry autumn, little grain, a good vintage, the inflammation of the eyes, infants will perish, wars and the sedition of soldiers, earthquake, the dangers of kings, much oil, great rumors among princes. **59** If on Friday, a troubled[70] and dry winter, an abundance of produce, pains in the eyes, infants will die, much hail. **60** If on Saturday, a windy winter, long[71] spring, summer varied with constant storms, a dry autumn, an agreeable means of subsistence, the death of pigs, expensive wood, many tertian [fevers], men will be vexed by varied weaknesses, old men will die, many burnings, much hay, few fruits, and men will die.

61 If the night of the kalends of January has fair weather (this is without wind and rain), the coming year will be good; if with an eastern wind, cattle will die; with a western one, kings; with a southern one there will be mortality; with a northern one there will be sterility.

62 At[72] the first Moon of January, if the Moon is at the beginning of Aries (which is called *almarach*), rains will be overpowering and grain fields will be

---

[68] Reading *principum mutationes* for *principium mutationis* ("the beginning of change/moving").
[69] *Ventris et praecordiorum solutio*, which may mean diarrhea.
[70] *Importuna*, which can also mean "stormy."
[71] *Magnum*, which normally means "big."
[72] This paragraph does not make much sense to me. First, I am not sure whether Leopold's source is speaking of separate New Moons, or *days of* a particular Moon cycle.

eradicated. **63** If the first Moon sends horns upwards, it will be dry; if turning [the other way] she has a dusky appearance, it will be rainy; if one is above, the other below, it will be semi-moist. **64** And if in the third Moon it thundered twice, there will be a storm in that month; if in the fourth, lightning and hail.

65 Farmers say that no bread-grains having hollow[73] chaff can be retained for a long time, but they will putrefy and be gnawed by worms after their harvesting, if they are sown with the Moon being much diminished.

66 A rainbow in diverse places signifies diverse things; arising from the south,[74] the great power of waters will come, for it signals the great power of waters will be in the atmosphere, which in the south can dominate or be dissolved. **67** If around setting, it will flash,[75] thunder, and lightly rain. **68** If it sprang up from the rising [of the Sun], it promises fair weather.

69 The circle around the Moon which is called a halo, if it flowed down evenly and evaporated on its own, it signifies the tranquility of the atmosphere; if it was broken on one side, the wind is cut off from there; if it was broken in many places, sailors expect a storm on the sea.

Second, in this sentence a New Moon in January can only happen when the Sun is in Aquarius, and so the Moon could not be at the beginning of Aries anyway. I would point out that the unknown word *almarach* is close to the Arabic word for Mars, *al-Mirraych*.

[73] *Concavas*, which can also mean "curved."

[74] Or perhaps, "at midday."

[75] Reading *refulgerit* for *refulserit*.

TREATISE VII: ON NATIVITIES

[Introduction]

1 In this, the seventh Treatise, I intend to gather [teachings] on nativities. **2** And first, on those about to die suddenly or who will survive a short time. **3** Second, on monsters. **4** Third, on completed births and their life, assets, and brothers, and thusly in order according to the twelve houses.[1]

5 To these [ends], I humbly invoke the aid of God, because this passage is difficult and almost not able to be [fully] comprehended by the intellect of men. **6** Having trust therefore in Him who gives abundantly to all and insults none of the philosophers, but concerning this I approach the opinions in His name, organizing [them] in such a way.

[Chapter VII.1: Early deaths]

1 The nativity is the exit of the native from the womb of his mother. **2** If the luminary whose authority it is (such as the Sun in the day, the Moon in the night) was impeded, and [also] the degree of the Ascendant, and the lords of the luminaries receded from the angles, the one who is born then will not taste food. **3** And the hour of his death is when the luminaries reach a bad one.[2]

4 If the three lords of the triplicity of the Ascendant receded from the angles, and likewise the luminaries and their lords, and the conjunction or prevention which preceded the nativity, the native will never taste [food] or will be a monster.

5 If Mars and the Moon were together in the Ascendant in the nativity, and Saturn in the eighth, the native will not go out of the mother's womb alive.

6 If Saturn, Mars, and the Moon were together, the one who is born then will not live for two hours. **7** If the lord of the Ascendant is corrupt, and Mars is in the eighth, the one who is born then will not live a month. **8** If the conjunction of the Sun and Moon was in the sixth house or the twelfth, the

---

[1] In order to organize the sections conveniently and number the sentences appropriately, I assign Ch. VII.3 to the first house only, and add extra chapters for the rest of the houses.
[2] This is probably by transit.

one who is born then will not live a year, unless Jupiter or Venus was in the eleventh. **9** But if either one was there, the native will enter [his] fourth year, but will not complete [it]. **10** If the Moon was impeded in the nativity, with the lords of the triplicity of the Ascendant falling, [and] even in addition to this a bad one is in an angle, the native will live [only] a short time.

11 If Mars and the Moon were together in the Midheaven, and the lord of the Midheaven was burned up or in its descension,[3] the mother and native will die from that birth; if [it was] only Mars, only the mother [will die].

12 By how many degrees the Tail of the Dragon was in the Ascendant, for that many years the one who is born will be blind.

13 If the lord of the fourth was in the eighth, it means the death of the woman giving birth.

[Chapter VII.2: Monsters][4]

1 He will have a monstrous shape, who is born if the luminaries were then falling from the Ascendant, and the bad ones are in the angles of this nativity: and if he is born then [he is] monstrous.

2 See the conjunction or prevention which preceded [the birth], and the places of the luminaries at the hour of the nativity, and the managing planets: because if the planets of them, and the place of the Moon or the Ascendant of them were all (or mostly) just as was stated, [his] shape will be monstrous.

3 And if in addition the luminaries were in the four-footed or feral signs, and the infortunes were in the angles, the native will not be of men. **4** And if the fortunes, along with the luminaries, did not have testimony but the infortunes testified to them, the native will be of animals which men use for work, like chickens, pigs, cows, goats, and the like which dwell with men; however, his shape will be monstrous.

---

[3] Reading *descensione* for *decursione*.
[4] This chapter is based on *Tet.* III.8 (Robbins) or III.9 (Schmidt).

TREATISE VII: ON NATIVITIES 219

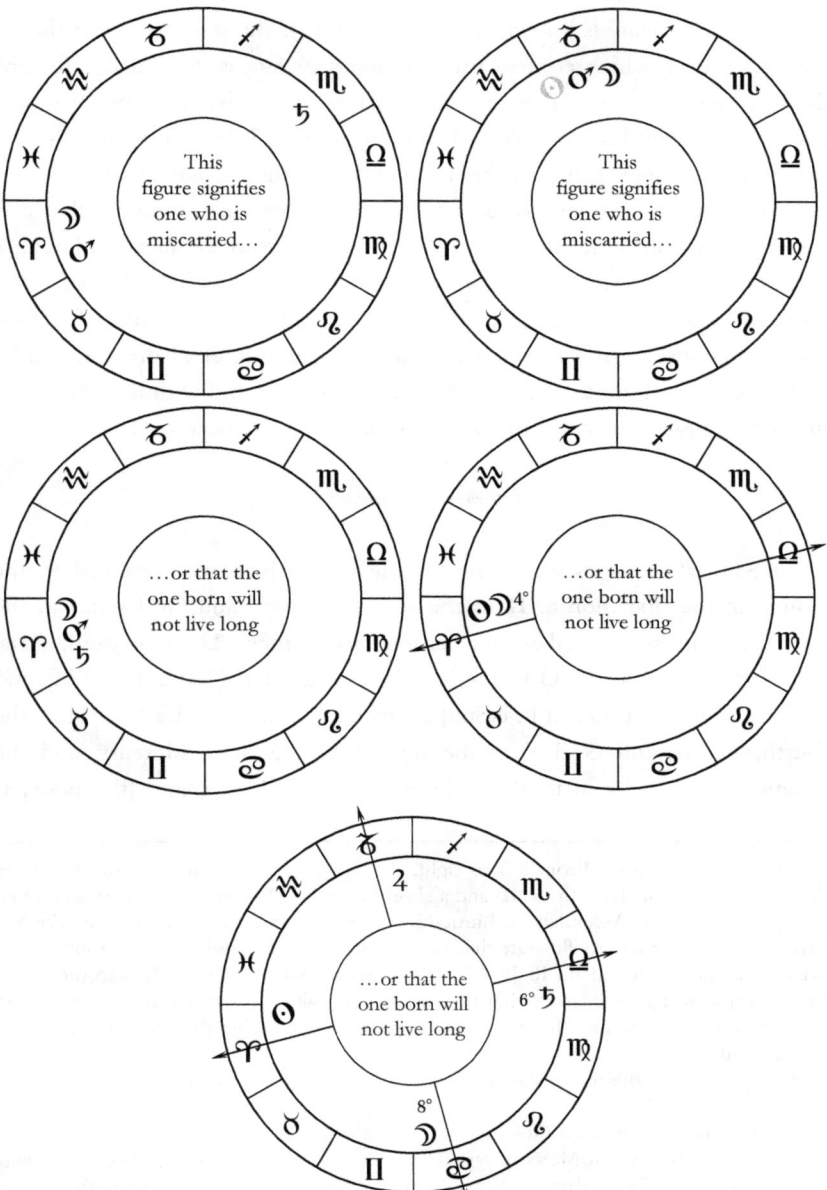

Figure 65: Examples of miscarriage and early death (Leopold)[5]

---

[5] These five diagrams were originally part of a single figure in Leopold, with the addition of the Tail (from **12**, but omitted here). I have separated them according to the sentences above, and added hypothetical axial degrees to the last two examples since that seems to

5 And his quality is known from the figures of the signs in which the infortunes stood, which contain the luminaries or angles. **6** And if a fortune does not testify to any of the aforesaid places, the native will not speak and his form will truthfully be changed and completed.[6] **7** But if Jupiter or Venus testifies, the proper quality of the native in which the change was, will be that he would be honored and lifted up, because it is from this figure that it is called a hermaphrodite[7] (and it is a figure named from Venus and Mercury). **8** And it is a property in the soul through which the soul lives, before it becomes so that someone might think he is dead, and it may be true.[8] **9** And if Mercury [alone] testifies, the native will be an interpreter of dreams, and he will have his livelihood from this, but he will be deaf and without teeth [and] in other things of the appropriate nature, and sly and a deceiver.

[The months of conception]

10 Saturn[9] manages and congeals the seed which was received in the womb, in the first month. **11** In the second, Jupiter; and God sends in the spirit and [the embryo] takes on a certain temperament. **12** In the third, Mars; and blood comes to be. **13** In the fourth, the Sun; and God imposes life and soul,[10] and for that reason [the Sun] is given a role in the releaser.[11] **14** In the fourth, Venus; and God gives the sex. **15** In the sixth, Mercury, and the tongue comes to be in it. **16** In the seventh, the Moon; and [the body] is

---

be what Leopold wants. From left to right, the figures illustrate most of the sentences about miscarriage or stillbirth (**5, 11**) and a short life (**6, 8, 10**). For **11**, I have assumed that Mars (the lord of the Ascendant) is burned by the Sun by inserting a Sun in gray. For **8**, I have added the horizon to illustrate that Leopold's Sun-Moon conjunction is above it and dynamically falling or cadent. In **10**, Leopold seems to assign degree values to the Moon and Saturn in order to illustrate that they are dynamically cadent, in earlier degrees than the axes. I am treating the Moon as being impeded by her being dynamically cadent and squaring Saturn.
[6] Ptolemy says that the native's shape will be nondescript, which must mean it has little defining character.
[7] *Armarsarip*, but reading with Ptolemy.
[8] Ptolemy says that when Mercury aspects along with Jupiter or Venus, the native may become something like a prophet. Leopold's description here is bizarre, but perhaps he is thinking of something like desert prophets and column-sitters and those who mortify the flesh, who might appear dead or in a trance.
[9] See 'Umar's *TBN* I.1.
[10] Reading *animam* for *animatam*, which (though not quite grammatical) suggests being "ensouled" or "animate."
[11] That is, the longevity releaser (also known as the *hyleg* or *hīlāj* in Arabic, or the Greek *apheta*): see below.

completed, and then the native is able to live. **17** In the eighth, Saturn returns and he will not live. **18** In the ninth, [it] returns to Jupiter, and he will live.

[Chapter VII.3: On completed births, conception, and character]

1 Concerning completed natives and those who will survive, proceed thusly:

[The Trutine of Hermes][12]

2 Once the figure is made for the hour of the nativity, and the planets are equated and arranged as they ought to be, the place of the Moon in the nativity was the ascending degree at the conception; and the place of the Moon in the conception, was the ascending degree in the nativity.

3 For an understanding of this, note that the staying of the seed in the womb is threefold: the first is said to be "lesser," and has 258 days; the second is the "middle," and has 273 days; the third is the "greater," and has 288 days. **4** Once these are known beforehand, consider the Moon: for if she is at the beginning of the seventh house, the stay of the seed will be the lesser

---

[12] For another version of this, see Abū Bakr I.4, in *PN2*. The Trutine is meant to help rectify full-term pregnancies between 8.5 and 9.5 solar months (between 258 and 288 days long). The theory is that the Moon at birth was the Ascendant at conception, and the Ascendant at birth was the Moon at conception (**2**). Since most people know their birth time close enough to find their birth Moon, the method claims that we can derive the rest of the positions almost exactly from that. First, cast the chart of the assumed (but unrectified) birth. Then, see where the rough birth Moon falls, relative to the assumed horizon: if she is on but above the Descendant, the conception was 258 days before (**4**); from there, the gestation increases to be 9 months or 273 days directly on the Ascendant (**5**), and so on up to the west again, just under the Descendant, or 288 days (**6**). By finding where the assumed natal Moon falls and converting that to days, we subtract those from the known birth date (**10-12**) and look in the ephemeris (or our computer program) to begin determining the closest Moon-Ascendant combination on that day that will rectify the chart. In the diagram, the assumed birth has an Ascendant of 15° Aries, and the Moon is at 15° Capricorn. In zodiacal degrees, she is above the earth and exactly between the Ascendant and Descendant, which comes to 265.5 days, exactly between the least days (258) and the average days (273). So, we must assume that the birth was 265.5 days before birth, and that the Ascendant at that time was roughly the Moon's current degree, 15° Capricorn. Now we must find that day in the ephemeris or electional locator, and find the time when 15° Capricorn was rising; corresponding to this will be the Moon at that time, which will be approximately the Ascendant at birth. One might then repeat the procedure with the more exact birth Ascendant, in order to refine it further.

one. **5** If the Moon is in the east, the stay of the seed in the womb will be the middle one. **6** If at the end of the sixth house, it was the greater one. **7** If between the west and the east, the stay was greater than the lesser one, and less than the middle one. **8** If between the east and west [in the lower hemisphere], the stay was greater than the middle one and less than the greater one.

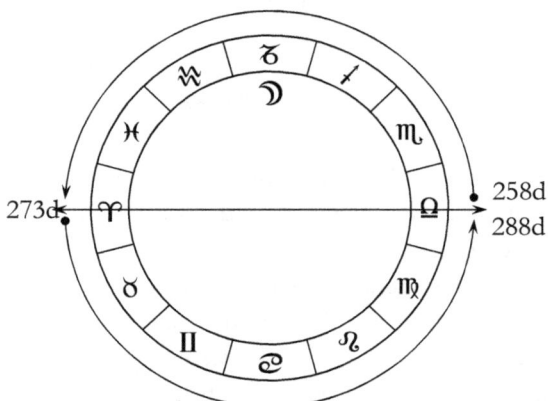

Figure 66: Trutine of Hermes (Dykes)

9 And so that you may know the divergence of the diminishment or decrease, proceed thusly. **10** If the Moon is in the upper half above the earth, take the equal degrees[13] which are from the west to the Moon, and double them, and divide by 24: and how much comes out, denotes the days, and how much remains is the hours. **11** And add how much you have to the lesser stay, and subtract this total [number of days] from the root of the Moon with which you equated the Moon for the hour of the nativity, and with the root (that is, with the time) that you have then, equate the Moon, and you will see that the place of the Moon in the nativity was the Ascendant at the conception, and that the place of the Moon at the conception was the Ascendant at the nativity.

12 And if the place of the Moon in the nativity is between the east and the west (that is, under the earth), take the degrees which are from the east to the Moon, and do as above, and add to the middle stay, and operate again as before. **13** If however the Moon is precisely in the place of one of the stays, you subtract the stay which it was, from the root with which you equated the

---

[13] That is, the zodiacal degrees.

Moon at the nativity, and with the root which remains (which is the conception) you equate the Moon: you will find that the place of the Moon in the nativity was the Ascendant at the conception, and that the place of the Moon in the conception is the degree which ascends in the nativity.

[Various judgments about birth]

14 By the amount of degrees that the conjunction or prevention of the Sun and Moon preceded the nativity, so many degrees of a sign will be the angle of the nativity of a human, and never of another animal.

15 Examine the nature of the [native's] background before you judge! **16** For you will judge one way concerning a noble person, and another for an ignoble one: and remove in every judgment what cannot receive the impression of the virtue of the heavens.

17 From the lords of the triplicity of the Ascendant is known whether the native would be nourished. **18** And from the lords (that is, of the ninth-part)[14] we know the native's life.

19 Whatever forms ascend at the hour of the nativity, such will be he who is born. **20** If Mars was in the Ascendant at the hour of the nativity, the native will have an ugly mark on his face; it is likewise with Saturn. **21** The 5° above the earth and 25° below the earth make the Ascendant, according to Ptolemy.[15]

[Rectification through Ptolemy's indicator][16]

22 Since the degree of the Ascendant in the conception is had through the place of the Moon in the nativity, to me it seems vain to seek the ascending degree in another way. **23** But 'Umar and al-Qabīsī, imitators of Ptolemy, seek it thusly. **24** With the figure of the nativity being established, they see whether the nativity is conjunctional or preventional (this is, whether the conjunction of the luminaries or their opposition was more nearly before the nativity). **25** And concerning the degree of the conjunction, there is no doubt; but for the degree of the prevention, the sages opined in diverse ways.

---

[14] *Novenae.* I am not sure where Leopold is getting this. But for the ninth-parts, see Ch. IV.4, **24-25**.
[15] Or at least, this is what Ptolemy uses for his longevity technique.
[16] See 'Umar Ch. I.2 (in *PN2*), and *Tet.* III.2 (Robbins) or III.3 (Schmidt).

26 Dorotheus says the degree of the prevention is that degree in which the Moon is, at the prevention. **27** Ptolemy says the degree of the prevention is the degree of that luminary which is above the earth at the hour of the prevention—and if one [luminary] is then in the east, and the other in the west, he gives the degree of the prevention to the one which is in the east.

28 Then, they consider which planet at the hour of the nativity has more dignity in that place: they equate this for the hour of the nativity and see to which of the angles (namely the Midheaven or Ascendant) that planet is closer in the number of its degrees and to which it is closer: they equate the houses according to that angle. **29** Now, it is true that I said it is vain to seek the Ascendant in a certain nativity other than through the place of the Moon in the conception. **30** But what Ptolemy says is true and necessary in a nativity which is not certain but taken by estimate: because the nativity teaches the conception, and the conception teaches the nativity, according to the method which was stated.

[Indications in pregnancy]

31 Noted signs of a conception. **32** The first is that the peaks of the breasts are extended, changed from their proper color. **33** The second is that the eyes are hollowed. **34** The third, that the vision of the woman is sharp. **35** The fourth, that the pupil is clear. **36** The fifth, that the white of the eye is filled and solid. **37** The sixth, that the body is extended.[17]

38 The signs of a masculine conception are these. **39** The first is a full and round belly, beautiful, hardened. **40** Second, the color of the breasts [is] red (but this sometimes fails). **41** Third, the color of the woman is gleaming. **42** Fourth, thick and coagulated milk between the fingers. **43** Fifth, milk dripped over an iron mirror placed in the Sun is compressed like a pearl in the space of one hour.

44 Concerning other children that will be, know it beforehand thusly. **45** If, on the head of one born already born you see a crown of hairs, it signals that another is going to be born; and if two, say two are going to be born at the same time. **46** Moreover, if there are knots in the length of the umbilical cord in the direction of the womb, and a spike after she gives birth, how many there are is how many she will give birth to; and if [there is] not one, she will not give birth to more.

---

[17] Or perhaps, "filled out" (*laxatum*).

47 The signs of a feminine conception are a broad, long belly, a foul color, and black marks on the breasts (but this is in error), milk without coagulation and flowing upon an iron mirror.

[Qualities of the native, from the nativity]

48 If Mars was in charge, the native will be stinking; if Saturn, he will be dirty. **49** Every native whose Ascendant was not a human sign, nor the lord of the Ascendant in a human one, will not associate with men.

50 Judge the morals of the native through Venus and her sign in the nativity. **51** Judge the sociability of the native through Mars: because his is an irascible power.

52 The Sun is the origin of living virtue. **53** The Moon, natural [virtue]. **54** Saturn, retentive [virtue]. **55** Jupiter, growing [virtue]. **56** Mars, irascible and attracting[18] [virtue]. **57** Venus, [the virtue] of longing. **58** Mercury, rational [virtue]. **59** Whence judge concerning these virtues according to the proper significators.

60 A male native will be masculine if the lord of the eastern face was masculine and in a masculine sign. **61** A female one will be feminine if the lord of the eastern face was feminine and in a feminine sign. **62** A [male] native will be effeminate if the lord of the eastern face is feminine, in a masculine [sign]. **63** A female [native] will be mannish if the lord of the eastern face is masculine, in a feminine sign.

64 In the nativities of men, if the luminaries are in masculine signs, their actions will be that of a masculine person; thus in the nativities of women, if the luminaries are in feminine signs, their actions will be those of a feminine person. **65** And if [it was] to the contrary, the actions will be immoderate and unnatural. **66** And Mars and Venus likewise. **67** And if these two [were] eastern, they make for masculinity; Saturn adds impurity, and Mercury [adds] impetuosity, delight, and the contrary.

68 He will be tall, whose significators are in the height of the heavens, ascending in the beginnings of signs, and eastern in the second station, and in signs of long ascensions; and [if] to the contrary, he will be short.

---

[18] *Attractive*, meaning unclear here.

69 He will be thin, whose significators of the Ascendant do not have latitude in the zodiac. **70** And if they have southern latitude from the zodiac, the native will be stout and nimble. **71** If northern, he will be fat and slow.

72 He who does any work by natural instinct can be known by which planet has rulership in his nativity.

73 The configuration of the Moon with the planets (this is [her] aspect or application or conjunction) makes the native be moved to what it signifies: with Jupiter, to justice; with Mars, to wickedness; with Saturn, to endurance; with Venus, to love; with Mercury, the wisdom and discernment. **74** And this, according to the strength or weakness of the planets.

75 If the bad ones were in charge over the Ascendant, the native will be delighted in unseasoned and bitter things,[19] and sometimes in stinking ones.

76 If Mercury was in either of the houses of Saturn, one who is born then will understand matters inwardly, provided that he is strong. **77** If in a house of Mars, he will be treacherous, clever—and Aries is the stronger house of Mars. **78** And if Mercury is in charge, he will be sharp and more [inclined] to understanding by hearing rather than discovery. **79** And if the nativity is diurnal and Mercury is in either house of Saturn, the native will exercise himself in the sciences.

80 Judge the status of anyone on any day through the one which was the victor in Aries.[20]

81 He will never lose his sense in whose nativity the Moon goes toward Mercury.

82 He will be famed like a king, and none will surpass his command, in whose nativity Jupiter and the Moon are in the same degree, [each] ascending toward its own apogee.

83 He will be most powerful, in whose nativity the Sun is in the Midheaven and Saturn eastern from him in a masculine sign.

84 One in whose nativity Jupiter and Venus were united with the Sun, his words will be received as though by a prophet. **85** Mars and Venus united with the Sun, in a dignity of Venus, make the words of the native be received as though by a prophet, and so on.

---

[19] That is, foods.
[20] *Almuz* [*almubtazz?*] *in Ariete.* Meaning unclear. But perhaps this is the victor over the *nativity* (reading *nativitate* for *ariete*).

[Chapter VII.4: Longevity and natal predictions]

1 Whatever is said concerning life is justly appropriate to the first house, for life itself is brought back to the first house. **2** Therefore the releaser, which is the lord of life and [its] status, is sought thusly:

[The longevity releaser and house-master][21]

3 Look at the Sun, the Moon, the Ascendant, the Lot of Fortune, [and] the degree of the conjunction or prevention which more closely preceded the nativity. **4** And first, [look at] the Sun if the nativity is diurnal: see therefore if at the hour of the nativity the Sun is in the first house, or the tenth or eleventh, whether he is in a masculine or feminine sign: he himself is the releaser. **5** In the seventh, eighth, and ninth, the Sun is not the releaser unless he was in a masculine sign. **6** And understand this in a diurnal nativity, so that, however, the lord of the house, bound, or exaltation, or triplicity of the place of the Sun would be looking at him: otherwise, he will not be the releaser.

7 Then, look at the Moon:[22] which if she is in an angle or a succeedent, she will be the releaser if any of the four aforesaid [lords] looked at her. **8** And if the Moon is not the releaser, regard the Ascendant: which if it is regarded by the lord of any of the four dignities, the Ascendant will be the releaser. **9** And if not, look at the Lot of Fortune if it is looked at as before. **10** And if it is not, take the degree of the conjunction which more closely preceded the nativity (and this is in the day, and in a conjunctional nativity).[23]

11 In the night, the Moon is put ahead of the Sun. **12** Look then at the Moon: which if she were in the Ascendant or in the second or third, or in the seventh or eighth, she will be fit to be the releaser, whether the sign was masculine or feminine. **13** And if she was before the degree of the Ascendant by 5° or less, or she was in the fourth or fifth sign, a feminine one, she is

---

[21] This seems to be a version of al-Qabīsī IV.4-5 (see *ITA* VIII.1.3). The releaser (often called the *hyleg* or *hīlāj*, after the Persian) is the planet or position which signifies the life force of the native, and is an example of a victor "among" places, as explained in *Search* and my workshop on victors (www.bendykes.com). The house-master (often called the *alchocoden* or *kadukhudāh*, again from the Persian) is one of the lords of the releaser (see below).

[22] That is, if the Sun does not qualify.

[23] For preventional and nocturnal nativities, see **15** below.

made fit for being the releaser. **14** If however she was in any of these places in a masculine sign, she will not be fit to be the releaser.

15 In a preventional [nativity], the degree of the prevention is taken instead of the degree of the conjunction. **16** And prefer the degree of the Lot of Fortune to the degree of the Ascendant in a nocturnal nativity, and consider as before.

17 And the releaser is interpreted as the wife, and signifies the native's life; the house-master is interpreted as the man, and is the giver of years and the significator of the limit of life, and is the one which projects the rays to the releaser—provided that it is the lord of the place (or the bound, or exaltation, or triplicity) to which it projects [the rays]. **18** And if many are looking, choose that one for the house-master which holds onto more dignities—and if in addition it looks at the place, its power will be stronger for being the house-master.[24] **19** And if the Sun is in Leo or Aries, he himself is the releaser *and* the house-master in the day; in the night, it is the Moon [if] in Cancer or Taurus.[25]

[Directions and distributions][26]

20 And if you want to know the status of the native, for his life take it from the degree of the Ascendant, for the state of his assets from the Lot of Fortune, for his influence and honor from the Sun, for the habit of the soul along with the body from the Moon, [and] for mastery and work from the Midheaven.

21 However, you will direct from the Ascendant thusly:[27] take the ascensions of the degree of the Ascendant in the native's clime, and add one degree for every year, and look at the lord of the place which the extension [of the degrees] reaches, and more so the lord of the bound. **22** And then judge according to that concerning the state of the native's life, and observe what is there by body or aspect.

---

[24] This is ambiguous, as the only candidates allowed for the house-master are precisely those which *do* look at the releaser.
[25] The material on longevity continues below with a misplaced account of Ptolemy's *horimaia* (**49-52**), and the years given by the house-master (**56ff.**).
[26] Much of this section seems to be based on al-Qabīsī VI.11 (see *ITA* VIII.2.2).
[27] This is distributions through the bounds, which I have created an audio workshop for (see www.bendykes.com). But for any direction where the Ascendant is the significator, it is measured strictly in oblique ascensions.

23 For example, in a nativity the 10th complete degree of Libra was arising, in the seventh clime. **24** The ascensions of this place are 193° 40' [as measured from Aries]. **25** I wanted to know where the direction reached after 50 years. **26** I add 50° on top of the stated ascensions, and they come to be 243° 40', which respond in equal degrees to the sign of Scorpio, 16° 20': and these degrees are the bound of Mercury. **27** Whence, I said that Mercury is the distributor, and manages the 51st year of the native's life.[28]

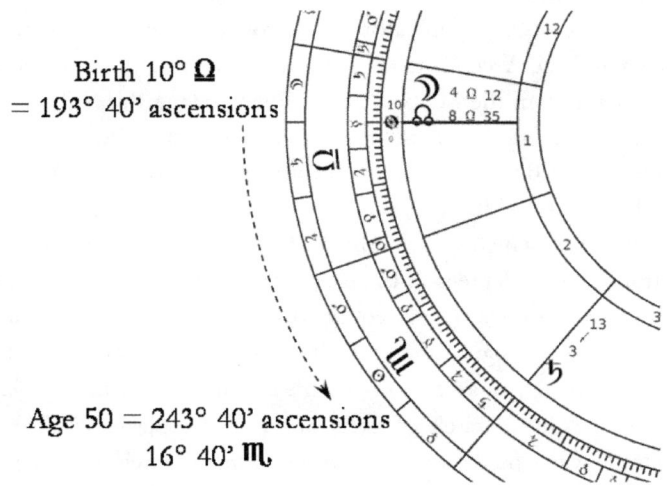

Figure 67: Distribution of the Ascendant to age 50 (Dykes)

---

[28] The number of ascensions between 0° Aries and 0° Libra are 180, for any latitude. So if the 10° Libra Ascendant is worth an extra 13° 40' in ascensions (for a total of 193° 40' as measured from Aries), then each degree of Libra at the birth latitude is worth 1° 22' or 1.366 ascensions (13° 40' / 10° = 1° 22' or 1.366). In the table of ascensional times this corresponds to latitude 48° N. So Leopold has a birth at latitude 48° N, and wants to direct or distribute the Ascendant through the bounds until age 50 (**25**). Since each equatorial degree is worth 1 year, we must add 50° of ascensions to the oblique ascension of the Ascendant, to get 243° 40' (**26**). At a rate of 1.36 ascensions per degree, the rest of Libra will take up 27.33 ascensions, for a total of 221 ascensions at the beginning of Scorpio. Since we need to get to 243° 40' in ascensions, we still have 22° 40' in ascensions to go. At that latitude each degree of Scorpio gets 1.36 ascensions per zodiacal degree, age 50 or the 22° 40' we still need will correspond to 16° 40' Scorpio (22° 40' / 1.36 = 16° 40'), which is in the bounds of Mercury (**26-27**). Therefore at age 50, the native's life in general will be governed by Mercury (**20, 27**).

28 Moreover, if any significator is in the Midheaven, direct it thusly: by how many years are completed, add that many degrees of the right circle,[29] and where this is terminated, there is the direction from the Midheaven.[30]

29 If the significator is in the west, direct the degree of the nadir of the west, and where the extension [of degrees] reaches, the direction will be in the opposite of that.[31]

30 And if the significator is in the angle of the earth, operate through the right circle as with the Midheaven above the earth.[32]

31 If however[33] the significator which you want to direct is between the Midheaven and the Ascendant, see by how many hours the one you want to direct is distant from the Midheaven. **32** For knowing this, subtract the right circle (that is, the ascensions of the right circle of the Midheaven) from the right circle of the degree of the significator, and divide what remains by the parts of the hours of the degree of the significator, and [what] comes out [will be] the hours which you sought.[34] **33** Then, add to the right circle of the significator as many degrees as there are years which have transpired (that is, how many years you want to direct [it for]), and see where that sum reaches in the circle of the signs, and note its place. **34** Likewise, add that same amount on top of the ascensions of the significator in the clime, and see where it reaches in the circle of signs, and note the place. **35** Then, take the difference between the places of extensions in the circle of signs, and take out one-sixth of the difference, and multiply it by the hours which you found earlier, and add the product to the place to which the extension in the right circle reached (if it is greater), or subtract (if it is less). **36** And where this reaches, there is the direction of the significator.

---

[29] That is, in right ascensions.

[30] That is, when the MC is the significator, measure directly in right ascension.

[31] What Leopold really means is this. *Because* degrees of oblique descension (near the Descendant) are always opposite those of oblique *ascension* (near the Ascendant), we should first direct the Ascendant by oblique ascensions, convert it to a zodiacal degree, and then find the degree opposite to it in the zodiac in order to find the directed Descendant (or rather, the significator which is on it).

[32] That is, when the MC is the significator, measure directly in right ascensions.

[33] From **31-39**, the instructions are for Ptolemy's proportional semi-arcs, or directions between any points that are neither the ASC/DESC nor MC/IC. For explicit instructions on this topic (which are easier than what you find here), see my audio lecture "Primary Directions Without Tears" (www.bendykes.com), Appendix E to *ITA*, and Gansten (2009).

[34] In other words, divide (a) the meridian *distance* in RA by (b) the amount of *time* it takes for the planet to move by diurnal motion *to* the Midheaven. This tells us how far the planet moves in any given time.

37 Do³⁵ likewise if the significator is between the Ascendant and the angle of the earth, by taking the difference between the right circle of the significator, and that of the angle of the earth. **38** Divide the difference by the parts of the hour of the degree of the nadir and above the earth, by the proper parts of the hour of the degree in the middle of the descending circle. **39** Take the ascensions of the degree of the nadir in the ascending half as proper and ascribed ascensions.³⁶

40 And if³⁷ one significator is in one quarter, and the other in another, first direct to the angle which is before the significator as I taught [you] by the right circle or by the ascensions in the clime. **41** From there, [calculate in the same way] to the place of the one to which you want to direct, whether by the right circle or by ascensions in the clime, as I said. **42** Join both directions together, and you will know the time in which the direction reaches the one to which you directed, always by giving one year to one degree.

43 And according to this, 5' [of ascensions] are granted to one month, and 1' to 6 days. **44** And to the 5 days and 6 hours which are in the year beyond [these] 360 days, there fall 12 minutes of an hour to one minute.³⁸

*[Zodiacal directing by handing over daily management]*³⁹

45 There is also another direction by equal degrees⁴⁰ for the status of the native in individual days, so that from the significator to a place of the circle in front of it (whatever that is) they take 59' 08".⁴¹ **46** And for this to come⁴²

---

³⁵ This paragraph is a version of al-Qabīsī (as mentioned before), but highly truncated and incomplete.
³⁶ *Proprias et ascriptas*. Meaning unclear.
³⁷ This is for directions across quadrants. The point is that one must perform two different directions: (a) a direction to the angle, and (b) a proportional semi-arc to the promittor. The sum of the two results gives the total arc, which is then converted into time.
³⁸ Leopold is referring to the extra 5 and almost ¼ days beyond the 360-day year implied in **43**, but I do not understand his phrasing here or how he intends these to be fit in.
³⁹ This method is very simple. Start with some significator, count the zodiacal degrees between it and the next one, and divide by 59' 08": the result is the number of days of the year which the first significator manages. Then measure from the second one to the next one, and do the same: this is the number of days of the year which the second planet will manage; and so on.
⁴⁰ That is, zodiacal degrees.
⁴¹ This is probably meant to be used in a solar revolution, and it is very similar to al-Qabīsī IV.13 (*ITA* IV.2.2*f*). However, al-Qabīsī clearly intends only to direct the Ascendant, and explicitly uses oblique ascensions, not zodiacal degrees.

to any other known significator, it is necessary that it have more degrees in the sign in which it is. **47** And the equal degrees of the first [significator] are subtracted from the equal degrees of the second one, and the difference is divided by 59' 08": and however much comes out from the difference, so many days are had in which that first significator manages the native's life.[43] **48** And from that, the second significator likewise is directed to a third one which is in more degrees, and it is judged as before.

[Ptolemy's horimaia][44]

49 And pay attention that in the ascending half (which is from the angle of the earth up to the Midheaven above the earth),[45] the direction is forward (that is, according to the succession of signs); and what is in the other half (from the Midheaven to the angle of the earth)[46] it is backwards, because it does not have degrees of descensions, but [they] take the degrees of the ascensions of the opposite degrees: for thus these descend just as those ascend. **50** Whence, the direction in the descending half is against the succession of signs.

51 And you should know that the degrees[47] are always directed, and when the direction comes to be according to the succession of signs, then the killer goes towards the releaser; when the direction happens against the succession of the signs, then the releaser goes toward the killer (namely, to the degree of

---

[42] Reading for "if this would come to…" (*si hoc fiat ad…*).

[43] This is a fancy way of saying that the degrees between them (moving forward in the zodiac) are divided by 59' 08", and the result is the number of days which the first significator will manage the life. For example, let the Moon be in 15° Gemini, and Mars in 12° Leo. There are 57° between them: 57° / 59' 08" = 57.8 days.

[44] This short section is Leopold's version of Ptolemy's *horimaia* (*Tet.* III.10 in Robbins, III.11 in Schmidt), part of his longevity calculation. Once Ptolemy has found his longevity releaser (let it be the Sun), he wants to see on what half of the chart it falls. If it is on the eastern or rising side of the chart (see diagram), then it acts as a significator to which malefic planets and other things are directed as promittors by primary motion towards him (**49-51**). For example, if the Sun were in the 11th, then some malefic later in the zodiac or "in the succession of signs" would be moved as a promittor towards him, making a direction that threatens life. However, if he were on the western or setting side (say, in the 9th), then *he* would be directed as promittor towards the *Descendant* (which symbolically indicates death and the underworld), again making a direction that threatens life (**51-52**). Ptolemy's method is actually a bit more complicated than it appears here.

[45] Reading the converse of Leopold, who has it from the Midheaven down to the IC.

[46] Again, reading the converse for Leopold's "from the angle of the earth to the Midheaven."

[47] *Partes* ("parts, Lots, degrees, portions").

the west). **52** And because of this, the planets which are between the releaser and the west do not kill (namely, towards the degree of the west); but the degree of the west does kill.

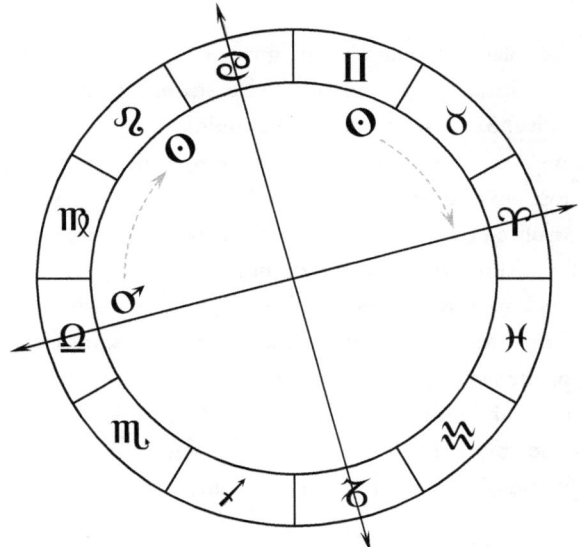

Figure 68: Ptolemy's releaser by primary direction and *horimaia* (Dykes)

[Continuous annual profections][48]

53 For the profection from the Ascendant of the root, give one sign to every year, and to every degree they grant 12 days, 4 hours, 12 minutes. **54** And just as you make directions and profections from the Ascendant for life, do likewise for assets from the Lot of Fortune, for influence and honor from the Sun, and for the habit of the soul along with the body from the Moon, for mastery and work from the Midheaven. **55** And see which planets or stars

---

[48] See al-Qabīsī IV.8 (*ITA* VIII.2.1). Although al-Qabīsī speaks here of profecting at a rate of one sign per year, these are really continuous increments of 30°, starting from the degree of the Ascendant. For example, if the Ascendant were at 15° Gemini, a whole-sign profection would jump: Gemini-Cancer-Leo, *et cetera*. But continuous profections would go: 15° Gemini - 15° Cancer, 15° Cancer - 15° Leo, *et cetera*.

are in the place which the profection reaches, and which arrive there in that year by body or aspect, and judge according to that.

[*Longevity through the house-master*][49]

56 And the planet which is the giver of years (namely, the house-master),[50] if it is in an angle and otherwise strong, it gives its own greater years to the native. **57** In succeedents, the middle ones; in declining ones, the least [years]. **58** And if it is burned up or retrograde, or peregrine or in its own descension, instead of years it signals [that many] months or days. **59** And if it is corrupted by all of these defects, it signals hours.[51]

60 And if a fortune (not retrograde nor burned up) regards the giver of years, it adds its own lesser years; and if retrograde or burned up, it adds that many months instead of years. **61** And if the bad ones are looking at it by a square or opposite aspect, or they are with it in the same sign, they subtract years according to the number of lesser years. **62** And if Mercury is with adding fortunes, he gives the lesser years, and with the bad ones and with subtracting [fortunes] he subtracts that same amount.

---

[49] This short section seems to be a combination of several sources, such as 'Umar's I.4.3 (in *PN2*) and Abū 'Alī's Chs 3-4 (in *PN3*).

[50] Otherwise known as the *alcochoden* or *kadukhudah* (Pers.).

[51] Below is my corrected table of Leopold's periods for longevity (the printed edition had some errors of calculation, some rounding up and down, and a couple of transcription errors, such as reading *6* as a *0*). Column [2] assigns years to the planets, based on the number of their lesser years (see the table Ch. IV.2). Column [3] assigns the name number, but as months (I have inserted in brackets the number of days this yields, based on 30-day months). The exception is Capricorn, which, as in the Hellenistic method of "zodiacal releasing," only gets 27 instead of Saturn's usual 30. Column [4] is nothing more than the total number of days in [3] divided by 12. Columns [5]-[6] go together, and are column [4] divided by 12. So for example, the signs of Mars (Aries, Scorpio) get 15 years [2] or 15 months of 30 days apiece [3], which is the same as 450 days. These 15 months (or 450 days) divided by 12 yields 37.5 days [4]. Finally, these 37.5 days divided by 12 equal 3.125, or 3 days and 3 hours [5]-[6].

[1] Signs	[2] Years	[3] Months	[4] Days	[5] Days	[6] Hours
♈	15	15 [450d]	37.5	3	3
♉	8	8 [240d]	20	1	16
♊	20	20 [600d]	50	4	4
♋	25	25 [750d]	62.5	5	5
♌	19	19 [570d]	47.5	3	23
♍	20	20 [600d]	50	4	4
♎	8	8 [240d]	20	1	16
♏	15	15 [450]	37.5	3	3
♐	12	12 [360d]	30	2	12
♑	27	27 [810d]	67.5	5	15
♒	30	30 [900d]	75	6	6
♓	12	12 [360d]	30	2	12

Figure 69: Table of planetary periods for longevity (Leopold)

[Personality traits through the Ascendant]

64 One who is born at the beginning of Aries will be bad to brothers [and] full of adversities, clever, liable to anger, and before the anger will have clouded eyes; a woman [is] likewise at the beginning. **65** And at the end of Aries, he will be good in everything, a strong man, praiseworthy, friendly, without anger, of a black color; and likewise a woman.

66 At the end of Taurus, [he is] low-class, poor.

67 In Gemini (through all [of it]): good, but sterile and angry, even of a bloody[52] color.

68 In all of Cancer: good, a women pure, his throat has a knot from an abundance of moisture.[53]

69 All of Leo: good, strong, wise, liable to anger at those doing him dishonor; a manly woman.

70 Virgo: in all things [a woman is] good, a pure, friendly man, a woman pure [and] good; humble, wealthy, of good morals because of all of the aforesaid.

---

[52] Or, "sanguine" (*sanguineus*).
[53] This probably indicates hacking and coughing up phlegm.

71 The beginning of Libra: bad in all things, a false man, a traitor, bad for everything, a woman extravagant[54] and the worst in all things; the end of Libra [is] good.

72 The beginning of Scorpio good, in the middle bad, distressed; at the end, extravagant, a murderer; a woman will be bad and a prostitute.

73 The beginning of Sagittarius good, a women will die from childbirth or blood or in the water; likewise at the end.

74 All of Capricorn: good; a woman [will be] a prostitute.

75 The beginning of Aquarius [*missing*], in the middle good, at the end a low man; a woman [is] a prostitute.

76 Pisces: mediocre, a poor man with many children, a small voice, an estate manager,[55] or a paralytic.

[*More on longevity: killing places*][56]

77 Once the years of the native are known (which he had through the house-master and by addition), see the direction of the releaser: when it reaches the places of the bad ones in the nativity or to their bad aspects, and the fortunes were not there, nor did they look benignly, the native will die. **78** And pay attention to the same thing if, at the beginnings of the subsequent years the places which were encountered were made unfortunate, and the places of the stars impede the ruling places: because death is what follows from this. **79** If it was either[57] of these, the native will have a danger like death.

80 And the ruling places are: the Sun and Moon, the Ascendant, the Lot of Fortune, and the Midheaven. **81** And a difference in the aspects in the latitude of those which are looking, reduces what it signifies.

82 The killers are 18:[58] Saturn, Mars, the Sun by square and the opposite [and conjunction];[59] the Moon by square and the opposite aspect; the Moon in the degree of the Ascendant, when she is the releaser;[60] nebulous places[61]

---

[54] Or, "voluptuous" (*luxuriosa*).
[55] *Vilicus*.
[56] See 'Umar I.4.8 (in *PN2*).
[57] This could probably read "neither," so that it is a danger like death but not death itself.
[58] The following list seems to be more than 18; nor does it quite duplicate 'Umar's list.
[59] Adding with 'Umar.
[60] Or more likely, when the *Ascendant* is the releaser.
[61] That is, nebulous fixed star clusters.

[and] dark places; the hearts of the signs;[62] the Head and Tail; Mercury by square and the opposite aspect; the degree of the seventh house; the degree of the conjunction or prevention; a comet.

83 And there comes to be a diversity of conjunctions, on account of the diversity of the significators.

84 And the astrologer cannot turn away from a death known beforehand.

[Bodily form][63]

85 The form and shape of the body is known through the Ascendant and the planets which are ruling there, and stronger, and of greater testimony, and through the condition of the Moon: because that is known from the nature of these lords, and the planets ruling there, and their commixture, and the fixed stars which ascend with them, and those [planets which are] more strong (since they rule over the arrangement of the body); and the proper quality of their place aids them. 86 But the arrangement of the native's body is known specifically, thus:

87 If Saturn were eastern and the sole manager, the native will have a honey color, middling in thickness, black curly hair on the head [and] thick on the chest, average eyes, a body temperately large, and moisture conquers in the complexion of the body. 88 If western, he will be blackish, thin, with a small body, straight and sparse hair on the head, of fit assembly [of limbs], and dryness will conquer in him.

89 If Jupiter were the manager of the stated places, and eastern, the native will be white, with average hair and likewise the eyes, of a fit stature of moderate size, heat and moisture will prevail. 90 If western, he will be white, not so fitting as before, straight hair on the head, bald in front, average eyes, and an average body, moisture will conquer in the complexion.

91 If Mars [were] eastern, the native will be white and red, of good size, suitable fleshiness, varying eyes, average [and] thick hair on the head, heat and dryness will conquer in him. 92 If western, he will be only red, with a moderate body, small eyes, sparse straight and blond hair on the head, dryness will conquer in the complexion.

---

[62] That is, Antares (*Cor Scorpionis*) and Regulus (*Cor Leonis*).
[63] See *Tet.* III.11 (Robbins) or III.12 (Schmidt).

93 The activity of Venus is likened to the activities of Jupiter, but she makes [bodies] more beautiful and as though with the beauty of a woman, of better figure, and a more appropriate quality of soul, and a softer body, and she gives reddish and suitable eyes.

94 Mercury gives the color of honey,[64] a moderate body, fitting assemblage [of limbs], small eyes, average hair on the head, heat prevails—and [it is] thus if he is eastern. **95** If western, he will be blackish, of a saffron color, commonly thin, small voice, polite, hollow eyes,[65] and the pupil is like a goat's, leaning towards redness; dryness prevails.

96 The Sun and Moon, too, aid any one of these if they are associated with them in the figure: the Sun [aids] in shape and beauty and plumpness, the Moon in proportion and thinness or moisture, and especially when she is separated from him (however, in particular [her aid will be][66] according to the property of her light.[67] **97** And the Sun and Moon, when they manage, give what is more well-balanced in that region.

98 The eastern stars and those appearing, generally give large bodies, and in the first station they give vigor and make good mixtures. **99** In the second [station], weaker ones, [and] when they sink [below the rays], misery and impediments.

100 And the places themselves in which they are, denote the form and figure and complexion of the native. **101** In a general way, one born between[68] the spring equinox and the summer solstice is of good color, fitting stature, good eyes, heat and moisture will conquer in him. **102** One [born] between the summer solstice and the autumnal equinox will have a well-balanced and middling size of the body and fleshiness, large eyes, thick and curly hair on the head, and heat and dryness will conquer in him. **103** In the third quarter is given a honey color, thin, a weak voice, wide shoulders,[69] average hair on the head, appropriate eyes, coldness and dryness will conquer. **104** In the last quarter, a black color, well-balanced size, straight hair on the head, and sparse, a fit assemblage [of limbs], coldness will conquer, and dryness.

---

[64] Reading *mellis* with Plato of Tivoli for *metallivum*.
[65] Reading *cavos orbes* with Plato of Tivoli for *orbatus*.
[66] Reading *erit eius auxilium* with Plato for a redundant *separatur*.
[67] That is, in her first quarter she will be more warming and moistening, in the second more warming and drying, *et cetera*.
[68] But I believe this refers rather to the zodiacal quarter in which the key planets are, not the time of year.
[69] Reading *scapulae* for *spatulae* ("shoulder blades").

105 Moreover, in a particular way the signs of human figures and the figures within the circle of signs and outside [of that] make well-balanced bodies; those which are not of [a human] kind make limbs in a harmonious way [but] likened to themselves, or they make [bodies tending] toward largeness [and] smallness, strength and weakness, a fitting or unfitting coordination [of limbs]. **106** Large ones [are]: Leo, Virgo, Sagittarius; small ones [are]: Pisces, Cancer,[70] Capricorn. **107** And the beginnings of Aries, Taurus, and Leo make for fatness, the ends thinness. **108** In Sagittarius and Gemini and Scorpio, the beginning [tends] toward thinness, their ends towards fatness. **109** Likewise, Virgo, Libra, Sagittarius [tend] toward a coordination, [but] Scorpio, Pisces, and Taurus the contrary. **110** And if in addition the other figures are observed, and compared amongst themselves, the properties and complexions of bodies will be known from them.

[Another review of the planets][71]

111 If Saturn was the lord of the native, it makes him black, marked by infirmity, dressed and going along repulsively, marked temples,[72] easily getting angry, foul, with a sparse beard, serious, lazy, rarely and hardly laughing, of a greyish color, with much rough hair on the body, with a bad face, he always gives a burdensome art like laboring in gardens, vineyards, lands, and other things with labor.

112 Jupiter [indicates] a beautiful look with a thick face, friendly, with straight hair on the head, respectable, with beautiful eyes, two larger upper teeth, religious, walking in a mellow way, speaking briefly, does not want to bear heavy burdens, he loves merry things like the table, he exchanges [money] or sells [things], works at beautiful fabrics with a needle, writes well and studies; and if the whole[73] is above the earth in the nativity, it makes an orator.

---

[70] Reading with Plato and Ptolemy for *Scorpio*.
[71] These descriptions are somewhat similar to al-Qabīsī's version of Māshā'allāh, but seem to be drawn more likely (though only in part) from the source Bonatti identifies as "Sacerdos" and "al-Dawla" (*BOA* Tr. III, Part 1, Chs. 1-7).
[72] *Timpora (tempora)*.
[73] *Totus*. But perhaps this should be read as *orbus*, his orb or body.

113 Mars makes a man curved, brown, red dots on the face, thin hair in the beard like eunuchs, a schismatic, blacksmith, baker, small eyes, crooked teeth, suspicious, red, always joking.

114 The Sun [indicates] full flesh with a beautiful face, eyes sometimes large, a face of a white color mixed with citrine, a full beard, in the service of great men, a counselor, originator of cities and principal man of provinces, a thick and unsuitable voice, sharp eyes, suspicious, a mark on the face, a burn on the body, faithful in the service of a lord, seeking rulership.[74] **115** If the Sun ascends [only] a little, [it makes] a gold worker, while[75] if he is eastern in his exaltation[76] he will work gold; if he is in fall, copper.

116 Venus [indicates someone] bright white in the face, studious, with beautiful hair on the head, playing instruments, teaching singing, delighting in good-smelling things, a curved nose, marked on the face, with thicker lips below the mouth, extensive hair [on the body], loving song, a master of women's ornaments (such as are rings and the like).

117 Mercury is of average standing, with small eyes, a large nose, acquiring and losing friends easily, of a light soul, with sparse hair in the beard, thin lips, long hair on the head, thin, crooked teeth, wounded by a blow or iron in the mouth,[77] hurried, scuffing the earth with his feet, a writer, studious, easily having knowledge of number, and he will be a chancery-clerk or something of this kind.

118 The Moon [indicates] a man of no service,[78] traveling, with a round face, large stature, thick skin, bulging eyes, not lacking a defect in the eyes, flowing beard, marks on the face, fat from the first Moon to the fifteenth [day], white and thin from the fifteenth to the thirtieth, and she makes those leasing [land] to others who bear[79] [produce], like honey, olive oil, figs, and what is of this kind.

---

[74] Reading *dominationem* for *durationem* ("lastingness").
[75] *Ita*.
[76] Reading *exaltatione* for *erectione*.
[77] This seems odd and unlikely.
[78] That is, not formally attached to a certain career or person.
[79] Reading uncertainly for *locantes aliis ferentes*, which could refer to al-Qabīsī's "supplying foods" (II.37).

[Chapter VII.5: Prosperity and wealth]

1 Concerning[80] the second house, see in the nativity if the lord of the Ascendant and the Moon are in angles, and either one is joined to planets in angles or the lords of the angles, or[81] if the luminaries are joined to the lord of the Ascendant and to the lords of the angles, and if the lord of the Ascendant is received in an angle: the one who is born will be high [in wealth] and will stay that way. **2** If it was to the contrary,[82] the one who is born is wretched and will stay that way.

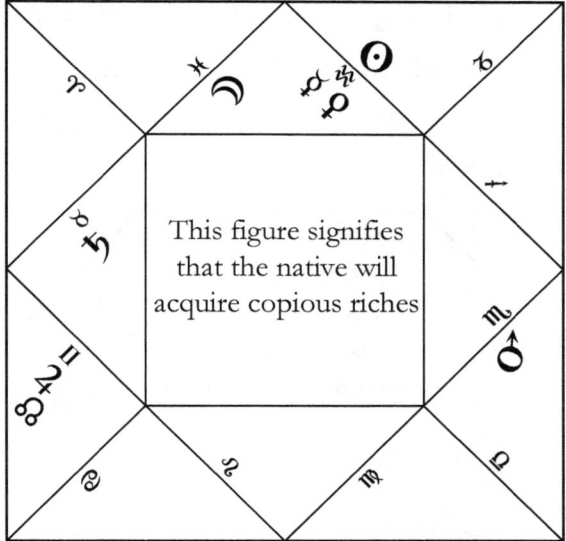

Figure 70: A nativity showing copious riches (Leopold)

3 If[83] the lord of the Ascendant, and the Moon and Sun, and the lords of the angles are in the angles, and they are joined to declining planets and bad planets, and the bad ones are the lords of the declining lords, the native will be born high and be brought [down] to misery and sometimes to servitude.

---

[80] See 'Umar's Ch. III.1.1, item [3.1-2].
[81] Reading *aut* with 'Umar, for *ut* ("so that").
[82] That is, if the significators are in bad and cadent places, and are being joined to cadent planets and the lords of cadent places.
[83] See 'Umar's Ch. III.1.1, item [3.4].

4 If[84] the lord of the Ascendant [and] the Moon and Sun are declining or in their own descensions, and they were joined to fortunes in the angles, or bad ones which receive them in angles, and they themselves are the lords of the angles, he is born miserable and will be high.

5 And[85] if the Moon would be setting out from [her] lesser motion to the greater one (or from the average [motion]), the native will be raised up (and *vice versa*).

6 The[86] one to which the Moon proceeds first in the birth of the native, signals the dignity.

7 [But] if[87] the Moon is being joined to none, and is separated from none, then the native will be [a man][88] of the wilderness, and in no place is it worse.

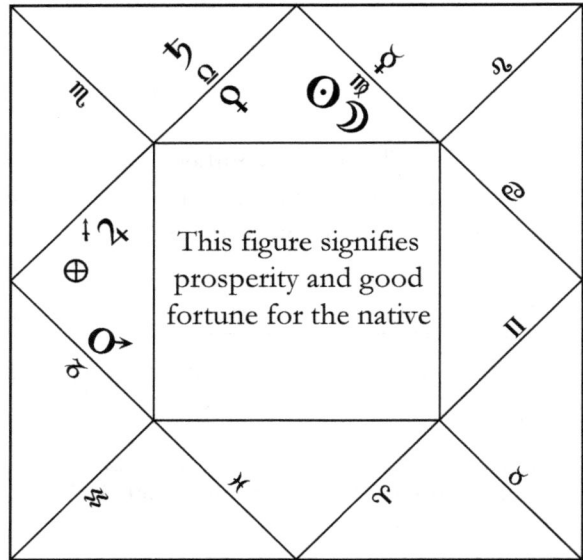

Figure 71: **A nativity showing prosperity and good fortune (Leopold)**

8 Understand[89] the prosperity or adversity of the native according to Ptolemy, thus. **9** Consider the [following] four: the Sun, Ascendant, Moon, and

---

[84] See 'Umar's Ch. III.1.1, item [3.3].
[85] See 'Umar's Ch. III.1.1, item [6].
[86] See 'Umar's Ch. III.1.1, item [4].
[87] See 'Umar's Ch. III.1.1, item [7].
[88] Reading simply *homo* and following the meaning of 'Umar, for the puzzling *excitatio*.
[89] The next two paragraphs represent a version of *Tet.* IV.2 (Robbins and Schmidt).

Lot of Fortune. **10** And as the Sun is related to the Ascendant, so the Moon is to the Lot of Fortune; and as the body belongs to the Ascendant (because through it I know the condition of the body), so assets belong to the Lot of Fortune, which is the Ascendant of the Moon, and through it I know the native's assets: namely, through its place, and [its] lord and its condition, and the bearing of the other planets towards these, and through the stars, the sign in which the Lot of Fortune falls, and the testifying and partnership of them amongst themselves in any power and association in the figure by conjunction or aspect. **11** For Saturn being the lord of the Lot of Fortune, in himself signifies attaining riches through buildings, agriculture, or navigation. **12** Jupiter, from commendations or estate management[90] or honesty. **13** Mars, through rulership, the army, and a kingdom. **14** Venus, by means of women. **15** Mercury, through the industry of commerce.

16 And if Jupiter would associate with Saturn (with him being the lord of the Lot of Fortune), or[91] should there be reception, he will be enriched from real estate: for[92] just as a bad one or good one would be joined, so in the succession of an inheritance evil would happen to the dead person and good to the successor. **17** If Mars was thus with Saturn, it would be of the native's will that he would be a robber, and in profession that he would be a leader of soldiers, and the native will be a cutter of roads, and would plunder foreign places by force; and if he wants to be just and by profession a medical person, [then] he will be a surgeon. **18** And that Saturn, if he makes a commixture with Jupiter, it will be good[93] if Jupiter was in the high angles (that is, the Ascendant, Midheaven, and the seventh). **19** Or if the Moon had a connection: this signifies that he will inherit the goods[94] of foreigners. **20** And if the stars which are of the sect[95] of the stars having the management, would testify, the native's possession will remain safe with him; and if of the contrary sect would be elevated above the places of the authorities [over assets] or would go following after them,[96] they will designate the loss of assets.

---

[90] That is, taking care of or managing someone else's affairs or estate.
[91] This should probably be read as "and."
[92] Again, this should probably be read as "and."
[93] Reading with Ptolemy for "bad."
[94] Reading the plural.
[95] *Hayz*, here and later in the sentence.
[96] The "elevation" here suggests overcoming, and particularly decimation (being in the tenth sign from the Lot or its lord, so as to be in a superior square from it), and "following after" refers to coming after them in the zodiac.

21 But the time of the events is discovered from the aspects of the stars to the angles or to the arising places.

22 Pay[97] attention to the spear-bearing of the planets, which is that the planets superior to the Sun are eastern from the Sun in the day, and the inferior ones are western from the Moon in the night—and in addition they are in their own houses or exaltations, likewise the Sun and the Moon, and they were in the angles and looked at each other: the king will be like a king or prince. **23** And if not all were in the angles but it was otherwise as before, he will be great. **24** If declining and peregrine, he will be mediocre. **25** And if wholly to the contrary, he will be low.

26 The[98] lords of the triplicity of the Sun in the day should be considered, and the one which is the first lord of the triplicity of the Sun: if this one is in an angle within 15°, the native will be a king or like a king. **27** If beyond [that] and within 30°, he will still be a prince of [great][99] memory. **28** If up to 45°, he will be mediocre, [and] if beyond [that], one who is miserable. **29** Do likewise with the Moon [in a nocturnal chart].

30 The[100] Head of the Dragon with the fortunes signifies great eminence beyond all others.

31 The[101] native will have profit if the lord of the Ascendant is in the second, but [it will be] with labor. **32** And if the lord of the second [is] in the first, he will have profit without labor.

33 As[102] the first lord of the triplicity of the Sun is, so will be the first status of the native; as the second one is, such will be his status in the middle of life, and so on: and this is more so if it is the Sun in the day or the Moon in the night (or whichever one was the releaser).[103]

34 He[104] will never be poor whose lord of the nativity was Jupiter. **35** The Sun in Leo in the Ascendant of the nativity, and the Moon in Taurus, makes it very fortunate.

---

[97] See 'Umar's version of Ptolemy IV.3, in his own Ch. III.1.1, item [1]. There is some confusion here between diurnal planets and superior ones on the one hand, and nocturnal planets and inferior ones on the other.
[98] See 'Umar's Ch. III.1.1, item [2].
[99] Adding based on 'Umar. This means that he will be remembered well by *others*.
[100] Source uncertain.
[101] See Abū 'Alī Ch. 11.
[102] See 'Umar's Ch. III.1.2.
[103] This parenthetical remark seems to be Leopold's own.
[104] Source uncertain.

36 Judge[105] the status of life according to the status of the Moon and her lord, and according to those to whom the Moon is being joined.

37 Consider[106] the Lot of Fortune and its lord, [and] the Lot of assets[107] and its lord, the second and its lord, and the one who is there, the lords of the triplicity of the luminary whose authority it is, the tenth and its lord and one who is there, and judge the fortune of the native according to this—and Jupiter, because he naturally signifies assets.

38 The[108] lord of the second being eastern, signifies [assets] in youth; western, it signifies [it] in old age. **39** And before all things, [look at] the victor in those places.

40 The[109] lords of the triplicity of the Sun being eastern, and those of the Moon western, and increased in light, greatly strengthens [assets].

41 Jupiter,[110] the Sun, and Mercury, give riches.

42 The[111] lord of the Ascendant, the lord of the eleventh, the Moon, the Lot of Fortune, [all] being surrounded by fortunes,[112] is very fortunate.

43 The[113] Sun in the Midheaven in a fiery [sign] and the Moon in his trine aspect, is very fortunate.

44 The[114] Ascendant in the beginning,[115] [and] the Midheaven, [being] fiery or airy, is very fortunate.

45 A[116] revolution like the root, is very fortunate.

46 He[117] will gain treasure in whose nativity the same planet is the lord of the first and the fourth. **47** He will live splendidly, in whose nativity the same planet is the lord of the tenth and first.

48 If[118] the lord of the Ascendant and the Moon (or either of them, and the stronger one) is joined to the lord of the house of assets, and it receives

---

[105] This is probably based on the longer paragraph in 'Umar's Ch. III.1.2.
[106] See Abū 'Alī Ch. 11.
[107] Reading with the similar paragraph in Abū 'Alī, for Leopold's "diminution." For this Lot, see Ch. IV.5, **40-43**.
[108] Source uncertain, but possibly Abū 'Alī's Ch. 8.
[109] Source uncertain.
[110] Source uncertain.
[111] Source uncertain.
[112] This probably means being besieged by benefics: see *ITA* IV.4.2.
[113] Source uncertain.
[114] Source uncertain.
[115] This probably means "at the nativity."
[116] Source uncertain.
[117] Source uncertain.
[118] This is very similar to Abū 'Alī Ch. 11.

[the lord] or her, whether it is a good or bad one (or even if it is a good one and does not receive [the lord] or her), the native will be rich through his own labor. **49** If the lord of assets is joined to the lord of life and to the Moon (or the stronger one), he will be rich without labor. **50** If the lord of life, and the Moon (or the stronger one between them) hands over its management to a bad one, and it does not receive it, it will not be perfected. **51** For reception cannot be annulled, and a planet is not said to be received unless the one receiving it would look at it.

52 If[119] the luminaries were in the same minute, and a fortune in the degree of the Ascendant, the one who is born then will be fortunate in the acquisition of assets, because his Lot of Fortune is in the Ascendant. **53** If however the luminaries are opposite each other and a fortune is in the seventh, the one born then will likewise be fortunate, because the Lot of For-Fortune for him is in the seventh.

54 The[120] greater fortune is from the fixed stars and from the spear-bearing of the planets, and that the angles of the conjunction or prevention which more closely preceded the nativity are the angles of the Ascendant. **55** The fixed stars give exceeding gifts, but often they are ended in evil.

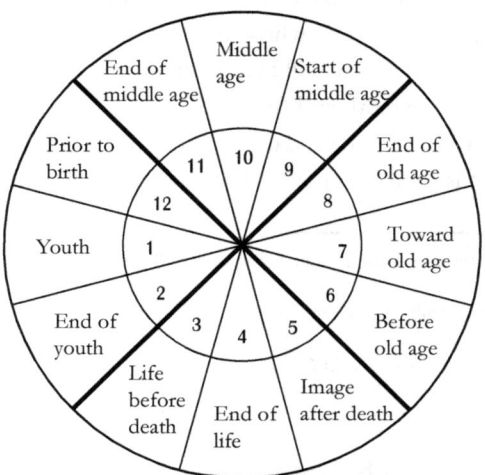

Figure 72: Angular triads for ages of life (Dykes)

---

[119] Source uncertain.
[120] Source uncertain.

56 Divide[121] the life into four: into the beginning, middle, end, and death, and each part into three: beginning, middle, and end. **57** And distribute [the parts] thusly: give the twelfth and first and second to the first part of life, the ninth, tenth, [and] eleventh to the second part, and so on.

58 The[122] status of all men is changed when the likeness of the signs is changed, and the figures of the planets which indicate good and evil for them.

59 If[123] the degree of the Midheaven in the revolution of the year was the native's Ascendant, and the luminaries were in the heart of their exaltation, one who was born then will be free of misfortunes like a king, and his seed will inherit the earth.

60 If[124] a retrograde, declining, burned up infortune contrary to its nature is looking at the significator, it signals the contrary, or an evil which none would be able to turn away from, unless God [wills].

61 And[125] the direction to a good one (such as to Jupiter) signifies profit, and when the direction reaches a bad one (such as to Mars), [it indicates] the loss of assets.

---

[121] See 'Umar's Ch. III.1.2.
[122] Source uncertain.
[123] Source uncertain.
[124] Source uncertain.
[125] This may be based on Abū 'Alī Ch. 8. Abū 'Alī does mention directing all of the planets, but the Lot of Fortune in particular.

[Chapter VII.6: Siblings]

1 For brothers,[126] consider the third house and its lord, and the lords of its triplicity, and the victor over these, moreover the Lot of brothers (from Saturn to Jupiter in the day, contrarily by night). **2** And [see] if any [planet] is in the third or is looking there, and Mars and the lords of the triplicity [of Mars], and the lord of the Ascendant, and if there is any concord between these.[127]

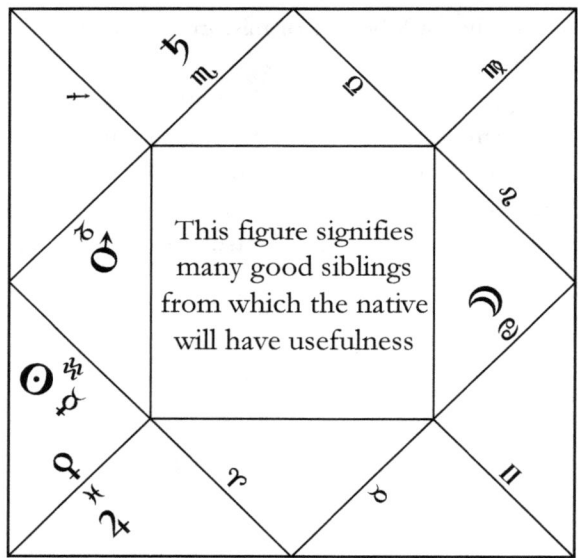

Figure 73: A nativity showing many good siblings (Leopold)[128]

3 Moreover, if the sign of brothers is one of many children, he will have many brothers and sisters. **4** And if the significators are in masculine signs, they will be brothers; in feminine ones, they will be sisters.

5 And [if] the significators[129] of the first [house] and the third look at each other benignly, they will be in concord; and *vice versa*.

6 Likewise, see which of the significators is stronger, and that [sibling] will be more powerful. **7** Moreover, which of the lords of the triplicity of Mars is

---

[126] This whole chapter is based on 'Umar's Ch. III.3.
[127] Leopold has mixed up the instructions: we are to look at the configuration between the victor over the places indicating brothers (above), and the lord of the Ascendant.
[128] This figure is unlikely to be a real chart, as it is a bit too good.
[129] Or rather, "victors" ('Umar).

stronger: [as the first one is], so [are] the older brothers, as the second one so the middle, and the third so the last.

8 Likewise, if there are fortunes between the Midheaven and the Ascendant, there are surviving [brothers] before him; if bad ones, then they are deceased; if mixed, and in common signs, some will live and some will not. **9** If there are planets between the Ascendant and the angle of the earth, [there are] male children and sisters after him, according to the number of planets which are there. **10** And if they are bad, they signify their death; and good ones, their lastingness.

11 Moreover, the Sun and Saturn signify the father, Venus and the Moon the mother.[130]

12 Likewise, the separation of the Moon from the planets signifies those born before; a conjunction with [other] planets signifies future ones.

[Chapter VII.7: Parents]

1 For[131] the father, look at the fourth sign and its lord, and the Lot of the father and its lord, the Sun and Saturn, and the victor over these places, and the planets which are in the fourth, and make these the significators of the father. **2** And direct from the one which is more worthy, to the good ones and to the bad ones, and it will be the number of his years according to what the victor signified. **3** And if this one were impeded in the day by Mars, and in the night from Saturn, from a square aspect or the opposite, without the aspect of the fortunes and without reception, this signifies the severity of his death. **4** And if the impeding bad one was the lord of the Ascendant or the victor over the Ascendant, perhaps the native will kill his own father.

---

[130] This sentence from the Latin version of 'Umar should be replaced with the following from Māshā'allāh and Dorotheus (*Carmen* I.21.10): "Also, the Sun and Saturn indicate older brothers, but Jupiter and Mars the middle ones, and Mercury the younger ones; Venus indicates younger sisters and the Moon older ones."

[131] Except for **8** and **14** below, this chapter is based on 'Umar's Ch. III.4.

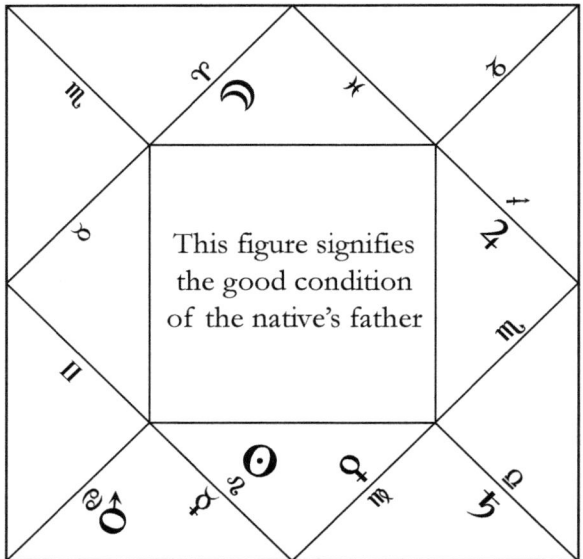

Figure 74: A nativity showing the good condition of the father (Leopold)

5 And the native will have concord with the father if the victor of the child and that of the father are concordant, or the victor of the house of the father is so with the victor of the Ascendant; and *vice versa* [if they are not concordant].

6 And the native is not legitimate, nor the father the one he supposes, if the Sun in the day is impeded by Mars (and in the night by Saturn) by a square aspect or the opposite. **7** The same, if the lord of the house of the father does not look at the house of children, nor the Sun the lord of his own house, nor the lord of the Lot of the father the Lot of the father: the native will not be the son of the one he supposes.

8 Judge[132] the end [of the father] through the one to which the Moon applies, and through the fourth and its lord.

ಐ ಐ ೧

---

[132] Source uncertain; this sentence should probably involve the Sun (not the Moon), and track him by directions—as mentioned in Abū 'Alī Ch. 17. Abū 'Alī also points out that in the night we should use Saturn.

9 For the mother, consider the tenth and its lord, and the Moon, Venus, and the Lot of the mother and its lord, and the victor over these places: and it will be the significator of the mother. **10** Then see what it signals in terms of years, and what increases and decreases [those years], and judge the status of the mother according to the aforesaid. **11** And [do the same] from the spear-bearing of the said [planets], and from the Moon and Venus by night and day [respectively]; and look at the Lot of the mother. **12** And direct from [her] releaser to the good ones and bad ones, and judge according from that, and likewise from the Moon.

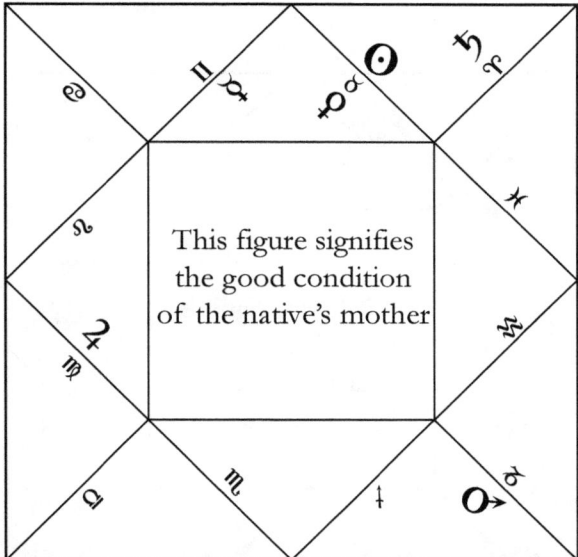

Figure 75: A nativity showing the good condition of the mother (Leopold)

13 And consider the victor of the mother and child, and just as they bear themselves toward each other, so [it will be between] mother and child.

14 And[133] which of the parents will die first, is known through the victor of each one (namely that of the father and the mother).

---

[133] Source unknown, but again this echoes statements in Abū 'Alī's Ch. 19.

[Chapter VII.8: Marriage]

1 For[134] a marriage-union which is a legitimate conjoining of husband[135] and woman, consider the seventh and its lord, and the one which is in the seventh, and its lord, the Moon and Venus, and the Lot of marriage-union and its lord, and the victor over these places (whether it was one or two), and look at the concord between the victor of the Ascendant[136] and its victor. **2** And if there is concord, the native will marry. **3** And if the seventh is one of many children, or there was a commixture (that is, an aspect) of the sign[ificator]s and the signs of many children,[137] the native will have many women.

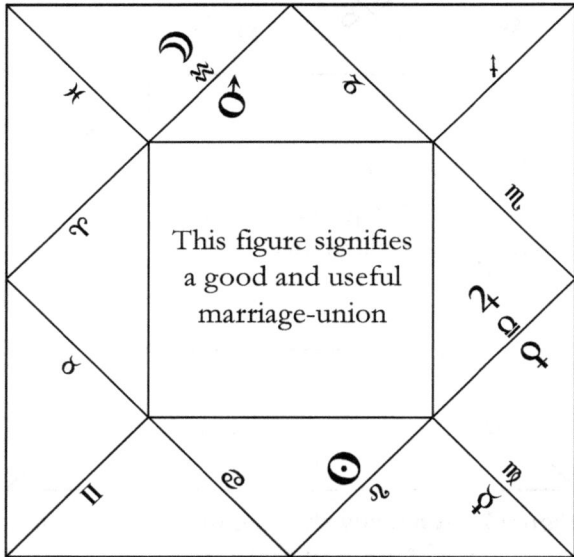

Figure 76: A nativity showing a good and useful marriage union (Leopold)[138]

---

[134] Except for **19-20**, this chapter is based on 'Umar's III.5.
[135] Reading *mariti* or *viris* for *maris*.
[136] Reading *ascendentis* for *ascendens*.
[137] Or rather, aspects *from out of* such signs ('Umar).
[138] Note that Saturn is missing.

4 And if the Moon was between the Midheaven and the Ascendant, the native will marry in youth; likewise if it was between the angle of the earth and the seventh. **5** In other quarters, [he will marry] in old age.

6 Moreover, look at the lords of the triplicity of Venus: if they are all (or many) eastern and of a good place and without impediment, nor under the rays nor otherwise impeded, the native will be fortunate in women and will marry in youth; and *vice versa* (and especially through the rays of the Sun). **7** And if they were western, he will not marry except at the greatest age.

8 And if Saturn is exalted over[139] Venus or in her square or opposite aspect, the native will be cold. **9** If Venus [is exalted over] Saturn, he will have a marriage-union in middle age (that is, at an appropriate time).

10 If Venus were eastern, in any of her own dignities, women will be elevated over him.

11 And if Venus and the Sun and the Lot of marriage-union, and many significators of the native, and the lord of the house of marriage-union, were in foul signs or those of foul conjoining, the native will be overflowing in an abundance of the most filthy things. **12** The foul signs are: Aries, Leo, Libra, Capricorn.

13 If Venus[140] was in the square or opposite aspect of Mars, or with him in one sign, and in addition Mars would be in his own house or exaltation, the native will then be most filthy in sexual intercourse. **14** And if Mars was in a feminine sign, the native will be deluded; and if he is in a masculine sign, he will be a sodomite. **15** And if a woman is born, and Mars is thus (as was stated) in a feminine sign, she who is born will be a prostitute; and if he is in masculine signs, they will abuse women. **16** And in the nativities of women, if many significators were feminine and in feminine signs, the female native will be soft and effeminate; and [if] the reverse, women will be mannish: and such will live [only] a short time and will not be nourished due to the multitude of moisture in men, and dryness in women. **17** And eastern [planets] make for masculinity, western ones femininity. **18** And Mercury adds the impulse of delights.[141]

---

[139] This means "overcoming" her from the tenth sign from her (see Glossary).
[140] Reading with 'Umar for "the Sun."
[141] For 'Umar, Mercury being the victor over the significators of marriage indicates an interest in younger males.

19 If[142] a bad one in the nativity of one, fell in the place of a fortune in the nativity of the other, the second [native] will sustain something horrible from the first, and the kind of evil will be according to the nature of the planet; but [the area of life] in which it is, will be from the nature of its place. **20** And this applies in all things.

[Chapter VII.9: Children]

1 Concerning[143] children, as to whether the native is going to have one or more, consider the fifth sign and its lord, Venus, Jupiter, and the Lot of children and its lord, and the victor over these places (whether it was one or two). **2** Then see whether there is any mixture or concord between it and the victor over the Ascendant [or the victor][144] over the Moon. **3** And if it is so, the native will have a child. **4** And apply the fifth and its lord: and if the sign of children, and the sign of the victor over the native, and the Ascendant, are those of many children, the native will abound in children.[145] **5** And if in addition Jupiter is burned up and the Moon impeded, the native will be sterile; and if the Ascendant is a sterile sign and many significators are in sterile signs, the native will be sterile for his whole life. **6** And the sterile signs are Taurus, Leo, Libra, Capricorn, [and] Aquarius—and this is according to 'Umar. **7** According to Abū Ma'shar, [they are]: the beginning of Taurus, Gemini, Leo, Virgo.[146]

8 And if the victor, or Jupiter, or the lord of the house of the victor over the house of children,[147] and the Lot of children, is in the Ascendant, he will have children in youth; if in the Midheaven, in middle age; if in the seventh or the fourth, at the end of life. **9** If it is eastern, in youth; if western, in old age.

10 If Jupiter and Venus were the victors [over] children, he will have many; if Saturn and Mars, few; if the Sun and Moon, in the middle (and Mercury with them [signifies] few).

---

[142] Source uncertain.
[143] Except for **7-8**, this chapter is based on 'Umar's III.6.
[144] Reading with 'Umar for "and either one."
[145] Omitting "and on this side of him" (*et citra eum*), which might be an odd misread for 'Umar's "if God wills."
[146] See Ch. IV.1, **23**.
[147] Or perhaps simply, the victor over the house of children.

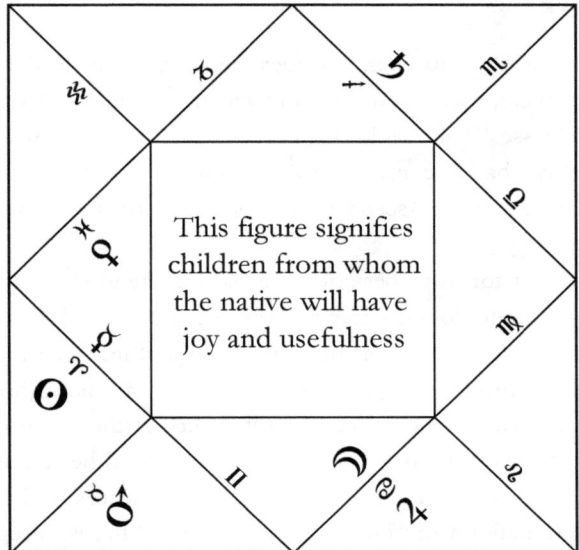

Figure 77: A nativity showing many good children (Leopold)

11 For children consider even the eleventh and its lord, and the planets which are there, [and] from the Midheaven in the day and from the angle of the earth in the night; also in the day from the Sun and Saturn and the Midheaven.[148]

12 And the victor over the house of children (whether it was one or two), [if] one or many agrees with the lord of the Ascendant and the victor over the Ascendant, the children will be just and loving their father. **13** And if [the significator over children is a bad one and][149] impedes the Moon, the native will impede the mother. **14** And if the indicators of children are safe, the children will be safe and rejoicing; and contrariwise [they will be] rarely rejoicing.

---

[148] Reading with 'Umar for "Jupiter." At night 'Umar recommends Saturn and Jupiter and the angle of the earth, whence Leopold's error.
[149] Adding with 'Umar.

[Chapter VII.10: Infirmities][150]

1 For the native's infirmities, consider the sixth and its lord, and the planets which are there, [also] from Mercury and from the Lot of infirmities and inseparable illnesses[151] and its lord, and the victor over these places. **2** Which if [the victor] is a bad one and commixed with the lord of the Ascendant, or it was in an angle and the Ascendant impeded by it, the native will have many infirmities.

3 And if the victor over these places is Saturn, the infirmities will be from cold and dryness, and long-lasting: like cancer, gout,[152] and dropsy.[153] **4** And if it was Mars, and he looked at the Ascendant and impeded [it] and was in the angles, the infirmities will be from red choler and blood flow. **5** And if there was a fortune in these places, and it looked at the victor over the Ascendant, this signifies the native's prosperity and good health, and salvation from infirmities, and he will be fortunate in animals, slaves, and domestics.

6 And if in addition the Lot of chronic illness (that is, inseparable accident) is with the Moon in the ninth, and Mars in the eighth, and in signs of severed limbs, in the nativity, some limb of the native's will be cut off by iron. **7** And the Lot [is] likewise if the Moon were in another quarter and the Ascendant was impeded by a bad one: the native will suffer in the limb of the sign in which the Moon was. **8** [And it will be] in the left eye in a diurnal nativity, in a nocturnal one in the right one.

9 If the luminaries were in the conjunction or prevention, and the bad ones in the square aspect of the conjunction or prevention, and a bad one ascended afterwards,[154] the native will lose the right eye (from the Sun), and the left one (from the Moon). **10** Moreover, the luminaries being impeded by the square or opposite aspect of the bad ones, or if [it was] with them in one sign, or it even ascendant and the fortunes would not be looking, he will lose his eyes.

---

[150] For **1-17**, see 'Umar's III.7.
[151] That is, "chronic illness." This is calculated by day from Saturn to Mars (reversed by night), and projected from the Ascendant: see Ch. IV.5, **103**.
[152] *Podagra*, which can also mean arthritis of the foot.
[153] In modern terms, edema. Note that all of the Saturnian illnesses involve an accumulation of tissue and/or fluid.
[154] That is, ascending in the sign after the luminaries.

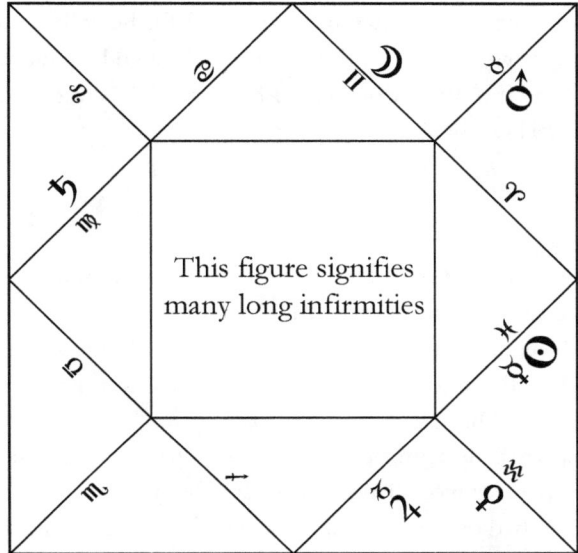

Figure 78: A nativity showing many long infirmities (Leopold)

11 The Moon impeded by the bad ones (that is, in one sign) without the projection of the rays of the fortunes to that bound, [means] the native's limb which pertains to the sign in which the Moon is, will be destroyed.

12 If the Moon were in signs impeding the eyes (such as Cancer, Leo, Scorpio, Sagittarius, Capricorn, Aquarius), they signify the impediments of the eyes.

13 Moreover if the Moon decreases [in light] in[155] Sagittarius, whether she is impeded or not, it impedes the native's eyes and it is feared that he will be blind.

14 And[156] she being impeded in Gemini and its triplicity by Mars, signifies white leprosy, gout, cancer, and an evil of the throat.

15 If the Moon was in any sign with the Sun or Mars in a square or opposite aspect, the native will be burned.

16 The Moon[157] impeded by Saturn, by Mars, and by Mercury, without the aspect of the fortunes, signifies that the native's testicles will be cut off; and

---

[155] Reading for "ascends with" with *Carmen* IV.1, **110**.
[156] Leopold has combined two sentences in 'Umar. First, if he Moon is impeded by Mars in Gemini and its triplicity, it indicates leprosy if a fortune did not look at her; second, if the Moon is impeded by Saturn in Cancer and its triplicity, it indicates white leprosy and cancer and throat problems if a fortune did not look at her.

if then the lords of the triplicity are strong and fit, he will acquire a dignity from that; and if weak, labor and affliction will be added, and he will be in servitude. **17** And if it was a woman, her breasts will be cut off, and the comfort of Venus will not be in her.

[Decumbitures][158]

18 If at the beginning of an illness the Moon is in a sign in which there is a bad one in the root, one must have fear.

19 If the Ascendant of the infirmity was contrary to the sign of the nativity (as is the seventh, fourth, eighth), one must have fear; and if the direction reached there, it will be easier.[159]

20 An eastern Saturn impedes exceedingly, [and] a western Mars. **21** A northern Jupiter saves more, [and] a southern Venus.

22 Eastern[160] bad ones make impediments, western ones make diseases.

23 The most detestable things in the signification of the one getting sick, is if the significator is going under the rays of the Sun. **24** And [likewise] if the Lot of Fortune were unfortunate.

[Significations and indications continued: Various authors]

25 Epileptics[161] are those in whose nativities the Moon is [not] mixed with Mercury, and [not] going to unite with the Ascendant.[162] **26** And if in addition Mars is in an angle in a diurnal nativity and Saturn in the night, one who was born then will be insane.

27 For the sick person, Hermes considers only the one of whose nature it is,[163] and which planet is there by body or aspect. **28** Hippocrates judges the passions[164] by the signs, insofar as the limbs are deputed to them, through the Moon in them, and through the good and bad planets in that same place by body or aspect.

---

[157] 'Umar has Venus here.
[158] The source of most of the following is unknown to me at this time.
[159] Mean unclear to me.
[160] This sentence is based on *Tet.* III.12 (Robbins) or III.13 (Schmidt).
[161] For this paragraph, see *Tet.* III.14 (Robbins) or III.15 (Schmidt).
[162] Adding "not," based on Ptolemy. In other words, the Moon and Mercury would be in aversion to each other and to the Ascendant.
[163] "It" here might refer to the sign on the Ascendant, or on the sixth.
[164] But this could also mean, "sufferings" (*passiones*).

[Some medical elections]¹⁶⁵

29 If someone took a purgation with the Moon appearing with Jupiter, its work will be shortened and the effect diminished. **30** It is praiseworthy to take a purgation with the Moon appearing in Scorpio, and the lord of the Ascendant going towards a planet which was under the earth; but if it went toward a planet which was above the earth, he will vomit up the medicine.

31 One must fear touching a limb with iron, with the Moon appearing in the sign of that limb (such as Gemini [for] the arms), nor should you induce vomiting when the Moon is in Leo, nor should you circumcise a boy when the Moon is in Scorpio.

32 If the seventh and its lord were impeded, remove the medical doctor from the sick person.

33 To be trusted¹⁶⁶ are the hours in which changes of diseases for the good or bad are declared: and they are the places of the Moon in the squares. **34** Alterations which come to be are in the octagons,¹⁶⁷ and they come to be through the middle, through the quarters and through the middles of the quarters, and through the middles of the middles:¹⁶⁸ and the days of these alterations are called "critical days."

[Ptolemy on infirmities]¹⁶⁹

35 For infirmities which do not last forever and induce pain, and concerning impediments which last forever and do not induce pain, Ptolemy considers five things: the east, west (the angles of the hemisphere), and especially the setting [angle and the sixth], and the two infortunes and how they bear themselves towards these places.¹⁷⁰ **36** For if both or either [infortune] were in that same place or in the square or opposite aspect with respect to

---

¹⁶⁵ See also Tr. IX for other medical elections.
¹⁶⁶ *Certae*.
¹⁶⁷ These are either the quarters and cross-quarters of the Moon in her actual movement, or in relation to her original position at the time of the decumbiture.
¹⁶⁸ Either Leopold has made this sentence hopelessly redundant, or he now advocates sixteen critical days: the eight mentioned earlier, and the middle points of *those*. I suspect that only eight are meant.
¹⁶⁹ For this chapter, see *Tet.* III.12 (Robbins) or III.13 (Schmidt).
¹⁷⁰ In other words, the Ascendant, Descendant, sixth, and both malefics.

the ascending degrees to those places and the sixth,[171] they signify infirmities and impediments in the native's body.

37 And see if each of the luminaries (or either one) was in the angles, so that they are in one angle or the opposites, and then will be strengthened the infirmities which the places of the hemisphere (and the places of the fortunate stars and infortunes, and the stars associated with them in the figure) signify; and this [is] whether [the infortunes] ascend after the luminaries or before [them].[172]

38 Because the parts of any sign surrounding the [injured] portion receiving the light (of the parts of the hemisphere, namely the impeded, receiving part),[173] signify that very part of the body in which it is going to occur; and this will be in the limb which is attributed to the planet. **39** In[174] one whose [injured part][175] is the east and west, and which proceed before them or after, and these signal that the infirmity or impediment ought to come, and this is especially of the nature of the stars.

40 Of the principal parts of a man, Saturn has the right ear, the spleen, bladder. **41** Jupiter, touch, the lung, ribs, and spine of the back. **42** Mars, however, [has] the kidneys, veins, and testicles. **43** The Sun: vision, brain, nerves, and all limbs on the right. **44** Venus: smell, the liver, flesh. **45** Mercury: the tongue, speech, deliberation, memory. **46** The Sun: the nose.[176] **47** The Moon: the throat and taste, stomach, belly, the private parts of women and all limbs on the left.

48 For the most part, impediments[177] come to be through eastern infortunes, infirmities through western ones: and this happens according to the corresponding[178] positions of the stars.[179] **49** For vision will be lost in either

---

[171] This is badly stated, but Ptolemy is not very helpful either: he wants to know if either or both of the malefics are on, squaring, or opposing "the pre-ascensional degrees of these places."

[172] This seems to mean that the luminaries are angular as well as the malefics, and the malefics are in earlier degrees—normally Ptolemy is interested if the malefics ascend *after* other planets.

[173] This seems to mean: look at the parts of the constellations around where the malefic planets are indicating harm (i.e., along the Ascendant or Descendant), and this will give indications about the illness.

[174] This sentence seems to be a redundant combination of **37** and **38**, and should be ignored.

[175] Adding speculatively to make the sentence make sense.

[176] Source of this sentence unknown.

[177] Or rather, injuries.

[178] *Consimiles.*

of the eyes when the Moon is alone in the aforesaid angles[180] at the hour of the conjunction or prevention, or when she is in the seventh sign with the Sun[181] and has a commixture with any star which is likened to clouds: and they are in the circle of signs and are the nebulous ones which are in Cancer, and *al-Thurayyā* in Taurus (that is, the Pleiades), and the tip of the arrow [in Sagittarius, and] the tail of Scorpio, and what is around *Al-Dahifaron*[182] of the parts of Leo, and the Pitcher of Aquarius. **50** [It is also when[183] the Moon is any of the angles of the west and Mars (alone or with him Saturn), eastern, and the Moon goes toward their conjunction; and [also] if the Sun were in any angle and these two stars ascend before him. **51** Or, if [the infortunes] would associate with the two lights in the figure, and each of the luminaries is in one and the same sign or in the opposite, and morning stars are in the regard of the Sun and evening ones in the regard of the Moon, he will be impeded in each eye: by Mars, through iron or striking; and Mercury being joined will make these things happen through wrestling or a game or from bad people; Saturn, from a cataract of the eyes, or coldness, or hurling,[184] or the like.

52 Venus in an angle (especially the western one), being with Saturn or associated [with him] in the figure, and Mars elevated above her,[185] or if he is opposed to her, the native then will not generate [children], a woman will miscarry, and sometimes the mutilation[186] of boys will happen: particularly in Cancer, in Virgo, and Capricorn. **53** And if the Moon has a connection with Mars from the east, and Venus[187] is associated with Mercury and Saturn, and Mars is elevated above her or opposed to her, the native will be without tes-

---

[179] Following Schmidt's footnote (p. 52 n. 1), this seems to mean that planets arisen out of the rays (or eastern) signify one-time injuries because the planets stand so to speak individually on their own; but planets under the rays (or western) continue to be oppressed by the Sun, like ongoing illnesses.
[180] That is, the Ascendant or Descendant.
[181] Ptolemy has the Moon being in any other of her phases with the Sun.
[182] This could be a misread for several stars or lunar mansions, but Ptolemy means the mane of Leo, *Coma Berenices*.
[183] This sentence is not quite as how Ptolemy has it. Rather, Ptolemy seems to mean that the Moon is waning and angular, while Mars/Saturn, being eastern, are directed to the Moon by primary directions. Likewise, if the infortunes are in an earlier degree than the Sun while they are angular.
[184] *Iaculatione*. This should read "glaucoma," with Ptolemy.
[185] That is, "overcoming" (see Glossary).
[186] *Detruncatione*. In Ptolemy this is "abortions."
[187] In Ptolemy, this seems to be the Moon, not Venus.

ticles, or a hermaphrodite, or lame. **54** And if in addition she would be associated with the Sun in the figure, and the Sun and Moon and Venus are in masculine signs and quarters, and the Moon western[188] and the infortunes[189] in the following degrees, the native will be emasculated[190] or impeded in the testicles, and especially if this was in Leo, Aries, Scorpio, or Capricorn or Aquarius. **55** If a women, she will be sterile. And perhaps one of these will not escape an impediment of the eyes.

56 Mercury with Saturn in the said angles, with the Sun, makes the tongue be impeded, and especially if the Moon would be associated with them[191] in the signs—namely Aries, Leo, Scorpio, Capricorn, or Aquarius. **57** And if Mars is there, it will denote for the most part the holding back[192] of tongue.

58 Moreover, if the Moon went toward the unfortunate stars in the angles,[193] or they were in the opposition of the luminaries, and especially if the Moon was in either of the two Nodes (which is the Head and Tail of any planet) or in a bending[194] or in the infirmity-producing signs (which are Aries, Taurus, Cancer, Scorpio, Capricorn), he will be hunchbacked, or some limb will be destroyed or lame or dislocated. **59** And if the luminaries are thus at the hour of birth, it will be likewise. **60** And if in the Midheaven the infortunes would be elevated above the luminaries in longitude (namely by a square or opposite aspect), this however [will happen] by falling or robbers or through four-footed [animals], and always according to the nature of the sign. **61** If Mars would be the elevated one and would dominate, it will be from the burning of fire or from the greatest plagues; if Saturn would be elevated and dominate them, it will be from falling or submersion or paralysis.

62 The Moon in the point of the vernal equinox, makes morphew (that is, white marks);[195] in the summer solstice, impetigoes and *alboras*[196] (that is, marks sprinkled around[197] the mouth); [near the autumn equinox, leprosy];[198]

---

[188] Or rather, "waning."
[189] Reading *infortunae* for *in fortitudine* ("in strength").
[190] Reading *emasculabitur* for *emulabitur*.
[191] Reading *eis* with Ptolemy's sense, for *ei* ("him").
[192] *Tenacitatem*. But actually, Ptolemy says that Mars will loosen up the impediment.
[193] Omitting *Fortunae* ("of Fortune").
[194] *Casmon* (unknown), so reading with Ptolemy. That is, the points 90° between the Nodes of each planet, when it is at its greatest northern or southern zodiacal latitude.
[195] That is, white leprosy.
[196] Word unknown; Ptolemy seems to have fungal infections.
[197] *Perfundatas ad*.
[198] Adding with Ptolemy.

in the winter solstice, lentigo.[199] **63** And the infortunes being associated with the Sun in the aforesaid way, and the aforesaid [planets] western of the Moon, make marks.[200] **64** Saturn makes wind, very cold phlegm or moistures descending to the limbs, they will become thin through an illness, a plague of the intestines, leprosy, [and] pain of the womb in women. **65** Mars signifies the spitting of blood, ulcers in the lung, and melancholy, burning, and cutting in hidden members, such as[201] hemorrhoids, fistulas, [and] abortion for women. **66** Mercury aids Saturn in the flowing down of moistures to the palate, chest, and stomach, and [he aids] Mars in drying out in these things which come to be with dryness: like ulcers, sacred fire,[202] impetigo, maniacal behavior, epilepsy.

67 With these in the forested signs and Pisces, they make ulcers,[203] flayings,[204] scrofulas, fistulas, and leprosies; Gemini and Sagittarius [make] epilepsy; and[205] in the first part of the body, and the last one in the lower [part], whence they make arthritis and gout.

68 And if the fortunes then [did not][206] associate with the infortunes, these things will be incurable; [and] likewise if the infortunes are elevated above[207] the fortunes associated[208] [with them]. **69** But if the fortunes are strong,[209] the foul things and infirmities will be light, and if in addition the fortunes are eastern.[210] **70** And Jupiter conceals [the illness] through money or honesty, and Mercury with him will give the work of medicines. **71** Venus [helps] on the occasions of the Divine or prophecies, and Saturn with her makes it public; [but] Mercury with her makes this [better] with the profit of the one suffering.

---

[199] Dark spots on the skin, including liver spots.
[200] *Maculas.* Or rather, illnesses. Also, Ptolemy has the malefics western of the Sun, and eastern of the Moon.
[201] Reading *sicuti* for *uti.*
[202] This is probably either shingles or erysipelas.
[203] Reading with Ptolemy, for *corrosivas* ("gnawings"); but ulcers do produce this painful, gnawing feeling.
[204] Or perhaps, the sloughing off of skin (*excoriationes*).
[205] The rest of this sentence is very confused: Ptolemy says that if these starts are in the *last* degrees of the *signs*, they will make these diseases in the *extremities* of the *body.*
[206] Adding with Ptolemy.
[207] That is, overcoming them.
[208] Reading *associatas* with the sense of Ptolemy, for *inassociatas.*
[209] That is, overcoming the infortunes.
[210] Reading with the sense of Ptolemy, for "western."

[Chapter VII.11: Qualities of the soul][211]

1 However, we recognize qualities of the soul through Mercury, the Moon, and their signs. **2** The movable signs make one love universality,[212] union, praise, riches, but a liberal character towards others of good opinion, and experienced in the stars. **3** The common [signs indicate] what is multiform, unstable, cunning, easily changeable, difficult to understand, nimble, a lover of music, but clarity of the intellect. **4** The fixed ones [indicate] one of good character, immovable, suffering, a bearer of labors, rigid, restraining pleasures, an unchangeable lover of honor. **5** And the eastern stars make souls good, firm, open, and prosperous; but the contrary ones [make them] hidden and imperfect. **6** And those above the Sun, being eastern of the Sun in the Ascendant or Midheaven, are good in the day, the lower ones [being] western are good in them; and in the night the reverse.

7 But understand the qualities of the soul in a particular way, thusly. **8** When Saturn alone is in charge of the management of ensouled things, and he was the lord of the Moon or Mercury, and [dignified] with respect to the world and the angles, the native will love the just, be rigid, he will be of deep counsel, and fixed in this, full of labor, a disputer (but sometimes he will veer from the truth), he desires riches, black, hairy, a hoarder of treasure, envious, hidden; and if Saturn bore himself to the contrary, say the contrary. **9** But if Saturn is assimilated to[213] Jupiter, and commendable [in his condition], the native will be just, he will honor his associates, and will be of sound counsel, an aide to the king, a giver, of good memory, a lover of friends, quiet, intelligent, patient, a philosopher; and if to the contrary, say the contrary. **10** If Saturn is assimilated to Mars, and he himself is of a good condition, the native will be understanding, intelligent, very full of labor, miserable, unsound, doing great harm, he will tempt with fear, greedy, he will hold all things in contempt, be bad in everything; [but] if Mars is to the contrary, say the contrary. **11** If Saturn is assimilated to Venus and he is of a good condition, the native will abhor beautiful women, be badly envious, solitary in association, and in will have confidence in his own counsel, he will revere God through divination; [but] if Venus was to the contrary, the native will be a fornicator and envious, venereal in all ways, speaking evil, proud, and will do it with

---

[211] See *Tet.* III.13-14 (Robbins) or III.14-15 (Schmidt).
[212] That is, things pertaining to the public and politics.
[213] Or, "has familiar ties with" (*Ptolemy*).

beasts contrary to law, he will not revere God, he will have contempt for the just, [and] will be a black magician. **12** If Saturn is assimilated to Mercury, and he is of a good condition, the native will be an investigator of laws and matters, he will love medicine, will do wondrous things, will be a sophist [and] of a sharp mind; if Mercury is to the contrary, he will be nervous, full of labor, he will be disturbed at night, [and be] a black magician [and] enchanter.

13 If Jupiter alone manages [the soul] and he is of a good condition, the native will be great-souled, generous, just, modest, cheerful, he will do well to men; if weak, it will be similar to the aforesaid, [but] if more weak in these, [he will be] more wasteful in great things, instead of just he will serve the Devil, and instead of modest he will be inhibited, instead of gentle he will be proud. **14** If Jupiter is assimilated to Jupiter and he was of good condition, the native will be cunning, tripping others up, bellicose, humble to none, and he will make himself God; he will be a discoverer of things and will know the truth, great-souled, liable to anger; [but] if he bears himself to the contrary, the native will be a blasphemer, impudent, a concealer of nothing, false piety, proud, he will be easily stirred up, and will be a scoffer. **15** If Jupiter is similar to Venus and is of a good condition, the native is simple and will love truth, jokes, eating, and he will have a good quality of soul, he will love God and serve Him; and if it is to the contrary, say the contrary. **16** If to Mercury, and he was of a good condition, the native will be persistent in reading, he will love calculation, and he will be a geometer and versifier, humble, of good counsel, of good morals, costly, he will suddenly complete things begun, he will be a doctor of the king, he will love God and his blood-relatives; [but] if he bears himself to the contrary, the native will be stupid, saying stupid things, frequently making mistakes, [and] will lose his sense.

17 Speak about Mars in himself and according to his commixture with Venus and Mercury, and likewise about the others, according to their natures and properties, in accordance with the aforesaid.

18 And the Sun and Moon are not able to rule the stated qualities, but they are in charge of live-giving[214] ones; yet they help and impede according to their condition in nativities. **19** And the Moon in the Nodes gives sharpness, but [when at the bendings], the northern and southern [limits],[215] it

---

[214] *Vegetabilibus.*
[215] Reading and adding with Ptolemy, for Leopold's tortured: "in the Nodes gives sharpness, but southern, that is, northern and southern…". The "bendings" are the places where she has greatest northern and southern ecliptical latitude.

makes one easily alterable; and the Moon arising and increased in light makes the significations open, and more true, [but] diminished in light or under the rays she conceals [the qualities]. **20** And the Sun[216] [with] the planets makes the qualities of the soul more straightforward, and the native is more powerful, more generous, and civil; and in a contrary [condition] it makes [him] worse and stupid.

[Ailments of the soul]

21 The spirit-possessed[217] are those in whose nativities Mars is in an angle by day (Saturn by night), and the Moon is not complected with Mercury, and neither [of them] with the Ascendant.[218] **22** And if an infortune rules over the Moon, and she rises under the rays of the Sun, and especially with Mars in Aries or Sagittarius and Pisces, and if both infortunes conquer, these passions will be incurable. **23** If however Jupiter or Venus are like them, and if the infortunes are in the angle of the west and the fortunes in the angle of the east, even if these are lasting, they will still be curable. **24** Jupiter makes this [happen through a doctor, Venus through Divine aid. **25** And if the fortunes and infortunes are to the contrary, the passions will be incurable, and manifest, and [it will be] epilepsy with wailing and the fear of death, it will last, and the insane will not be able to be held back, and they will say foul things, the spirit-possessed will jump upon men and beat them. **26** And the places of the Sun and Mars contribute to insanity, Venus and Mercury to epilepsy; however, [with] Venus prophecies will be spoken, Saturn hidden places, and the Moon the spirit-possessed.

27 If the luminaries alone are in the male signs, men will practice what is natural for themselves [but] in excess, [but] women [will practice] what is unnatural[219] for themselves and what is natural for men.

28 Moreover, if Mars or Venus (or either of them) was masculine, a man will excessively unnatural and contrary to law, and women will be unnatural amongst themselves. **29** And [with] a masculine Venus the deeds will be hid-

---

[216] Omitting "and Mars."
[217] Ptolemy: epileptics.
[218] That is, the Moon and Mercury are in aversion both to each other and to the Ascendant. However, this condition is not possible: all places in aversion to the Ascendant are configured with each other. But Ptolemy has them being unconnected to the "rising horizon," which may mean simply that while they are in aversion to each other they lack a degree-based aspect to the degree of the Ascendant.
[219] Reading with Ptolemy for "natural."

den, [but with] a masculine Mars they will be manifest, and they will have other women as quasi-wives. **30** Likewise, if the luminaries are in feminine [signs] women will be carrying out natural[220] things excessively, [but] men [will be] unnatural and soft. **31** Again, if Venus alone is feminine, women will pursue Venus excessively, and natural things more frequently, and they will deny no one; men [will be] effeminate and more unnatural, but in a hidden way. **32** Moreover, if Mars is feminine, they will commit fornication and foul deeds and without shame, and for that reason they will be blamed. **33** The eastern and morning qualities of Venus and Mars [pertain to] masculinity and they uncover; evening and western, and [pertaining to] women, they conceal. **34** Saturn with them [makes] what is horrid, and foulness, and incurs great shame, for he is cooperation with them. **35** And if Jupiter was with them he will increase the propriety and modesty. **36** Mercury with them aids in detection and the hastening of future [acts], and the multitude of their types, and [their] increase.

[Chapter VII.12: Travel and faith]

1 For[221] foreign travel and journeying, consider the ninth and its lord, and the planet which is there, and Mars,[222] and the Lot of foreign travel and its lord, and the victor over these places (whether it is one or two). **2** If there is any combination or commixture between one of these and the one over the Ascendant according to the fourteen[223] ways, the native will travel abroad and[224] he will not have a livelihood in his own home.

---

[220] Reading with Ptolemy for "unnatural."
[221] From **1-6**, see 'Umar's Ch. III.8.
[222] Reading *Martem* with 'Umar for *circum* ("around").
[223] Reading with 'Umar for "four."
[224] Reading "and" for "if." But 'Umar's fuller version says that if no combination is found, then he *will* seek his livelihood at home: so Leopold has attached two unconnected sentences together, and this is the easiest way to correct him.

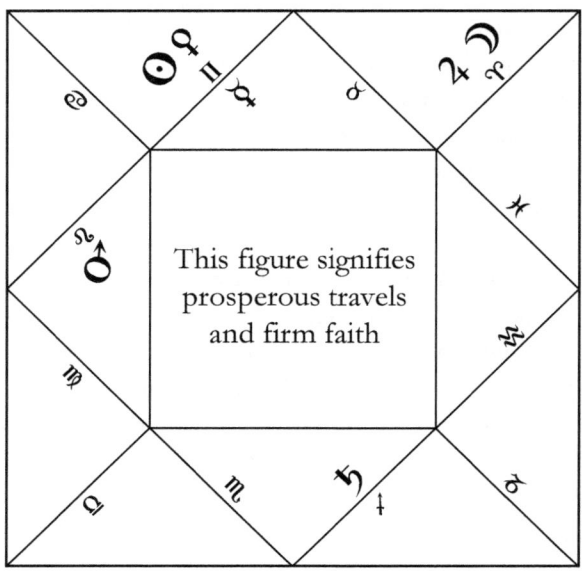

Figure 79: A nativity showing prosperous travels, firm faith (Leopold)

3 Likewise, if Mars is an angle, and if the Moon [did not]²²⁵ look at the lord of her own house, he will live in other regions. **4** The lord of the triplicity of Mars, if it was in better places and quarters, it makes it so that the native's exile is better, *etc.*²²⁶

5 If the lord of the ninth was impeded, the native will be of bad faith, of much pretending, and seeing a commixed matter in faith, and traveling abroad will not be useful for him, and he will lose his assets. **6** And likewise if the bad ones were in the ninth house.

7 Or,²²⁷ [if] the victor over it was Mercury, and it matched²²⁸ the lord of the Ascendant, the native will be contending in faith, and a disputer, having teaching in his words. **8** And if Mercury is then made fortunate and eastern, his end will be great and praiseworthy from this; if impeded and western, evil will befall him from this.

8 The²²⁹ Lot of Fortune in places signifying travels (as are the declining houses and the point of the west), signifies a long exile; and if the good ones

---

²²⁵ Adding "not" with 'Umar.
²²⁶ That is, travel will be better for him than staying in one place.
²²⁷ For this paragraph, see 'Umar's Ch. III.12.
²²⁸ *Congrueret.*
²²⁹ Source uncertain.

are looking into the places of foreign travel, the native's exile will be good (and *vice versa*).

9 If[230] the significators of foreign travel were in the ascending half [of the chart],[231] the native will be an exile towards the east; in the descending half, towards the west.

10 For faith,[232] consider the ninth and its lord, the victor in that same place, the Lot of faith and its lord, and the third[233] and its lord: which if Saturn is in them,[234] and he was free of impediments, or Jupiter or Mars [were in them] and these [were] without impediment, the native will be a worshipper of one faith, without diversity.

11 Moreover,[235] look at the lord of the triplicity of the Lot of faith, and which one of these is more fortunate: in that same age [of his life], the native will have a better faith.

12 He[236] will be turned away from his faith, in whose nativity Mercury is in the eighth, and whose Lot of faith[237] was impeded.

13 [For travel],[238] beware of infortunes in the seventh and eighth [when] going out (and the lord of each); in returning, the first and second (and the lord of each): because the seventh signifies the place to which one goes, and the eighth the profit there; but the first [signifies] his person and the second the profit.[239]

---

[230] Source uncertain.
[231] That is, on the eastern half from the IC up to the degree of the Midheaven; the descending half is the western half, from the MC down to the IC.
[232] See 'Umar's Ch. III.12.
[233] Reading with 'Umar for "fourth."
[234] In 'Umar, Saturn is understood here to be the victor over the places of faith, not in them.
[235] See 'Umar's Ch. III.12.
[236] Source uncertain.
[237] Reading *fidelitas* (sc. *fidei*), for *felicitatis* ("happiness").
[238] Compare with Ch. IX.4, 22. I have moved the position of "returning," so as to make the sentence read better.
[239] Omitting *doni* ("of the gift").

[Chapter VII.13: Rulership and mastery]

1 For[240] rulership and work and mastery, consider the Midheaven and its lord, the Sun, and the Lot of the native's work,[241] and its lord, [and] the victor over these places, whether it was one or two. **2** And if there is a mixture [of the victor] with the victor over the Ascendant, the native will have many works and be a king or prince, and he will be rational.

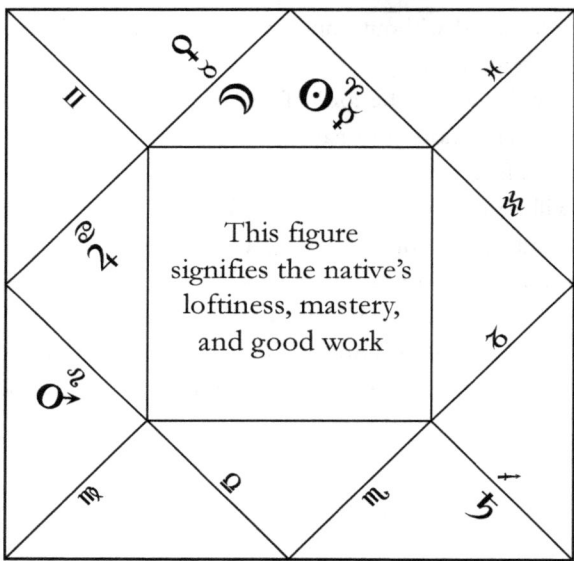

Figure 80: A nativity showing loftiness, mastery, and good work (Leopold)

3 If the Sun was in the eastern quarters, the native will be raised up[242] in youth (and contrariwise)—and more so if the victor is eastern from the Sun or Ascendant, and more so [if] from each.

4 If all the lords of the triplicity of the Sun are strong, the native will be high for the whole time of his life; if weak, contrariwise, and [if] in a mixed way, [mixed].

---

[240] This section is based on 'Umar Ch. III.9.
[241] This is the Lot of action or work, taken in the day from Mercury to Mars (by night the reverse), and projected from the Ascendant.
[242] That is, elevated or recognized.

5 Saturn in an angle in the night, and Mars in the day (and especially in the Ascendant or in the Midheaven) do not allow for rulership nor a good work within their own lesser years—beyond that, it will be according to the ascensions of the sign in which the planet is.

6 Mars in the Ascendant or Midheaven (not in the other angles, however) in the day makes danger for the native because of his work, and his body will be whipped and bound. **7** Saturn in the angles in the night makes him be chained and crucified, and he will die thusly.

8 Saturn in the Ascendant in the day makes the native be solitary, and if he had brothers and sisters he will send them before [him] in death[243] and he will be fond of fine foods.[244] **9** If the Sun were in the opposition of the Moon, the native will have hatred for his own parents and will not be guided into work or rulership, and the wealthy will despise him, and he will precede the father and mother in death.[245]

10 If the victor over the Midheaven and the Sun and the Lot of work is Mercury, the native will be an astrologer [or] mathematician. **11** If it is the Sun, he will be a prince and will be wise in the management of a kingdom, and of good discretion. **12** You should speak likewise based on the nature of this victor and the nature of those looking at it, whether it was two or three. **13** Moreover, see which planet is looking at the victor, and mix their work[246] with the work of the victor, and speak according to them.

14 The essence of the mastery is known from Mars, Venus, and Mercury, and the commixture and aspect among them.

15 And the angle of the Midheaven falling into the eleventh, increases honor; if in the ninth, it diminishes dignity; and in the withdrawing[247] places [likewise].[248]

---

[243] *Praemittet.* This does not mean he will kill them, simply that they will predecease him.
[244] *Gulosus.*
[245] In 'Umar, this means the father will precede the mother, it is not a statement about the native's death.
[246] Or, "its." That is, there might be more than one aspecting planet.
[247] *Recedentia.*
[248] Since the ninth is already a cadent or falling or withdrawing place, perhaps Leopold's source is referring to planets as well: such as if the lord of the Midheaven were also cadent.

[Other views][249]

16 If the Ascendant of a minister was the Ascendant of the king, they will be in concord with one another. **17** Likewise if the Ascendant of a captive was the sixth of the master, and the Ascendant of a wife [was] the seventh of the husband. **18** If the Ascendant of a minister was the tenth of [his] master, the minister will dominate his own master. **19** And if the lord of the sixth of the nativity is in the Midheaven, receiving management there from the lord of the Ascendant, he will have good rulership with respect to his servants; and similar [situations] convey [benefit] according to this.

[Length of rule: Sahl][250]

20 Observe the time of enthronement into a dignity or office, and see the star which is in the tenth or first, with testimony: if it will be burned up in a pivot, [the office] will be ended.[251]

21 If those two places are empty, [then] if the Sun applies to Saturn or Mars in a pivot, one should have fear [when he arrives at their degree]. **22** If the Sun applies to Jupiter or Venus, and Saturn arrives there by opposition or square, [he will be removed from office]. **23** If the Moon [in a nocturnal chart] neither applies to the Sun nor is separating from him, it supports rulership in [only] that year.[252]

24 Moreover, if the lord of the house[253] of the Sun was unlucky in that revolution, it deprives [him] of rulership in that year. **25** Likewise, if the Moon applies to unfortunate [planets] in the revolution or is corrupted by burning, the degrees of the application [show when his time] is finished.

26 Likewise if the Moon is not received, [or] the lord of her house or sovereignty[254] will be corrupted, it comes to an end within a year, unless the lord

---

[249] Source currently unknown.

[250] This section is based on Sahl's *On Times* §12, which itself is taken from Māshā'allāh; in the future I will have translations of both from Arabic. Leopold has highly abbreviated this long section, in some cases almost unintelligibly, so I have supplied brief statements in brackets to clarify.

[251] Omitting the apparent sentence fragment, which also does not correspond to Sahl: *Si in oriente plus de vita imetur* ("If in the east, more concerning life [*unclear*]").

[252] Sahl seems to say that if she *is* applying to or separating from the Sun, then we may still use the timing mechanism of the Sun as just described.

[253] In John's Sahl, this is the *exalted* lord of the Sun's place.

[254] That is, exaltation.

is strong. **27** And if she is received, it will last until an infortune reaches the degree of the Ascendant of the rulership.

[Other views]

28 If the direction of the significator of the rulership reached the star which cuts off [the light], perhaps the king or another powerful man of the kingdom will die: which if it is Saturn, he will be a hidden man; if Jupiter, a judge or counselor; if Mars, a courageous[255] man; if the Sun, the king or other noble man; if Venus, a wanton woman; if Mercury, a sage or scribe; if the Moon, a great minister of the king.

29 The native will have honor if the lord of the east or the lord of the tenth or Jupiter was in its own house, or the Head [was] with any of these. **30** If the lord of the first regards the lord of the tenth or fourth or seventh, this will be in his own land; in the following [places], near that land; in the remote [places], remote [from it].

31 If Mars was the lord of the Ascendant of the enthronement, in the second and mixed with his own lord, it will destroy the assets of the enthronement;[256] and more so if the lord of assets was Jupiter. **32** It hardly or never is but that he whose Ascendant is Virgo or Pisces will be the cause of his own rulership; and he whose Ascendant is Scorpio or Taurus will be the cause of his own death. **33** And he whose Ascendant is Aries or Libra, is the cause of his own death. **34** Because always in these [matters], those signs which belong to one planet, work together for the matter indicated by its houses.[257]

35 If Mars was in the eleventh and he had a strong indication[258] in the Ascendant, the native will be unfaithful to his own prince. **36** Those relatives[259] of the king will succeed [him] in rulership whose nativity agrees with the hour in which the king was enthroned. **37** The Ascendants of the enemies of the king [are those] which are falling from his Ascendant, [those which are

---

[255] Or, "violent" (*animosus*).
[256] Or better, "accession."
[257] *Unum cooperantur ad rem signatam per domos illius.*
[258] *Signator.*
[259] *Propinqui.*

the] angles[260] belong to those ruling with him; the succeedent ones are those of the ministers of the king.

38 The Ascendants of cities at their building, judge all things which happen to them. **39** But those which ascend at the ordaining of the kings of those same cities, pronounce all things which happen under their rule. **40** And the Ascendant of appearances in them,[261] warns of whatever is going to happen in those cities.

[Chapter VII.14: Friendship]

1 For friends,[262] you should regard the eleventh and its lord, Venus, and the Lot of friends, and the planet which is in the eleventh, and the victor over these places (whether it is one or two). **2** And if one of these has one combination of the four[teen] [combinations] with the victor of the Ascendant,[263] he will have many friends. **3** And if [the victor over the eleventh] is Venus, there will be many friends from among women; if the Sun, they will be men.

4 And if many significators [are] in movable signs, friendship will not last. **5** And if many were bad,[264] he will have evil from them (and *vice versa*).

6 Friendship exists between those [whose] Ascendants are interchanged or matching, and an obeying sign is of greater friendship. **7** Likewise, for those in whose nativities the luminaries look at each other benignly, there will be friendship between them (and likewise to the contrary with other [configurations]).

8 The bad condition of the eleventh house and its lord, signals that there will be evil for the counselors of the king and his assets; and a bad condition of the second signifies that the people will get little [of value] under that king.[265]

---

[260] Reading for *are the remaining angles*.
[261] Such as the time of strange omens.
[262] Except for **8-9**, this chapter is based on 'Umar's Ch. III.10 (in *PN2*).
[263] In 'Umar this is only a configuration between the victor of the eleventh and the victor of the Ascendant, *not* all of the others.
[264] In 'Umar, this is only the victor over the Ascendant, not the others; but Leopold's interpretation makes more sense.
[265] This sentence must refer to mundane charts and question charts.

9 If in the night the lord of the eleventh and the first bear [themselves well] toward one another,²⁶⁶ the native will have what he hopes for.

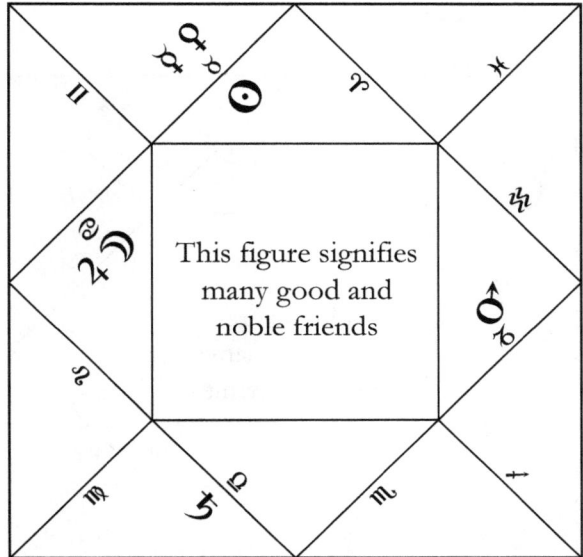

Figure 81: A nativity showing many good and noble friends (Leopold)

[Chapter VII.15: Enmity]

1 For enemies,²⁶⁷ consider the twelfth and its lord, and the Lot of enemies,²⁶⁸ and Saturn, and the planets which are in the twelfth, and the victor over these places (whether it is one or many).

2 And if the victor over the Ascendant and the twelfth meet according to any configuration,²⁶⁹ the native will have many enemies. **3** If the victor of the twelfth looks at the victor of the Ascendant and impedes [it], the native will be destroyed by his enemies. **4** If the lord of the Ascendant has any power in the eighth and the lord of the twelfth impedes it, the native will die at the hands of his enemies; and if it is Mars, it will be in a war. **5** And if the victor

---

²⁶⁶ Adding *bene*. That is, if they have a good bearing or configuration or relationships.
²⁶⁷ For this chapter, see 'Umar's Ch. III.11.
²⁶⁸ We should also consider its lord.
²⁶⁹ Following 'Umar instead of reading the puzzling *partem*.

of the twelfth did not look at the victor[270] of the Ascendant, the native will have few enemies. **6** And if the victor of the Ascendant is bad and corrupts the victor of the twelfth, the native will conquer his enemies and they will perish at his hand.

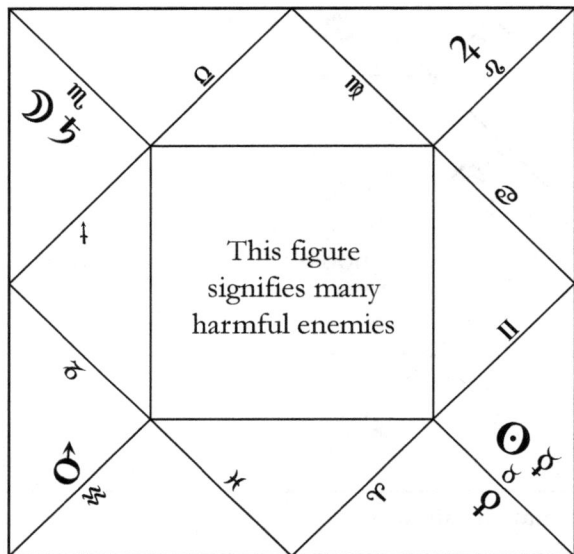

Figure 82: A nativity showing many harmful enemies (Leopold)

7 And the native always hates the twelfth sign and its images.[271]

8 And if Saturn [is in the house of enemies, he will destroy the house of [his] enemies; and if he impeded the victor over][272] the house of enemies, the native will rejoice in his enemies and will send them to death before himself; speak likewise about Mars [in the twelfth].

---

[270] Omitting *in secundo* ("in the second").
[271] In 'Umar, this is the location of the Lot of enemies, not the twelfth itself; but Leopold's version makes astrological sense.
[272] Leopold or the typesetter has missed an entire line: reading with 'Umar for "destroys."

[Chapter VII.16: Death]

1 For[273] the "end," [which] I have put down for "death," which is the end: look at the eighth and its lord, and the Lot of death and its lord, and the victor over these places, and the planet which is there.

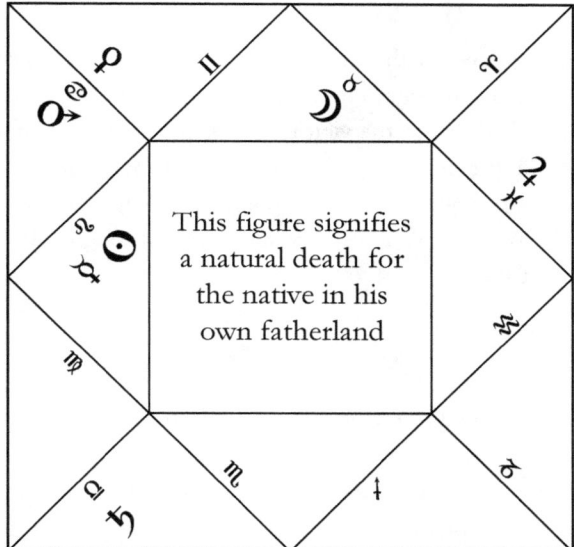

Figure 83: A nativity showing a natural death in the fatherland (Leopold)

2 If[274] especially the Moon or the victor was impeded in Ophiuchus[275] or Serpentarius or in the place of the serpent which is called "Bold," or the serpent which is at the place of the Head of the Dragon in Scorpio, the native will die through the bite of a serpent or from something venomous or otherwise through poison. **3** If she was impeded in the place of the Vulture, at death he will not be buried but birds will eat him. **4** If she was impeded in the place of Aries or Taurus or Capricorn, or in Leo, he will be killed by an animal. **5** Moreover, if she is impeded in the place of *Caput Algol* (because there Perseus holds the Head of the Gorgon, and there is [her] head without

---

[273] This paragraph seems to be Leopold's own, using the previous chapters as a model.
[274] Sentences **2-9** represents 'Umar's interpretation of Ptolemy, in 'Umar's Ch. III.13.
[275] Lat. *Offulto*.

a body), it signifies that the native's head will be cut off. **6** Likewise if in the place of the native's death the partners were the Sun or Moon or Jupiter, and after this they are impeded by the bad ones, they signify the worst death; and if they were opposite there, the death will be at the hand of a rich person. **7** Moreover, impeded significators of death being above the earth signify being hung or crucified; if they are under the earth, being buried or dying from shipwreck.

8 The Moon joined to the Sun in one sign, or by the square aspect of Mars or with him in one sign, makes the native be burned up in fire. **9** And the significator of death and the victor over it, if it is impeded in earthy signs, he will die from the falling of something on top of him; in fiery ones, through fire; in airy ones through the pillory or being hung at the hands of men [or] on the backs of animals; in watery ones, through submersion or he will be food for fishes.

[Other views]

10 If Mars was joined to *Caput Algol* and a fortune is not looking at the ascending degree, nor was there a fortune in the eighth, and the lord of the shift of the luminaries[276] was opposite Mars or in his square aspect, the native will then be decapitated; if then the Sun [is] then in the Midheaven, he will be hung, and if the bad ones are looking from Gemini and Pisces his hands and feet will be cut off. **11** If Mars was joined bodily to the lord of the Ascendant in Leo, and Mars does not have any dignity in the Ascendant, and in addition there is not a fortune in the eighth, the native will be burned by fire. **12** If Mars was the victor of the Ascendant and he was not with the benevolent ones, then the native will be burned. **13** If Saturn was in the Midheaven, and the one whose shift it is[277] was in his opposite, and the fourth sign is dry, then the native will die from falling ruins; if it is moist, he will be submerged; and if in the form of a man, he will be strangled or die [by] being beaten by rods unless it was a fortune; then [for] him whose [chart] it was, the aforesaid will come to be but he will not die from thence.

---

[276] That is, the sect light; the word for "shift" (*nauba*) is from the Ar. *nawbah*, referring both to the regular shifting between night and day, and the shift or role the planets play in a diurnal or nocturnal chart.
[277] That is, the sect light (see above).

14 If at the beginnings of subsequent years[278] the places of hostile encounters were made unfortunate and the places of the stars impede the ruling places, the native will die; if [something else],[279] he will have a danger like death.

15 Another person says that when the releaser arrives to the rays of the bad ones (according to the years established as a year for a degree by degrees of ascensions), or the Tail or to the square or opposite aspect of the Moon, once the years of the house-master are completed the native will die or will have a danger like death.

[Chapter VII.17: Planets in their own and others' houses][280]

1 Abū 'Alī, a chapter on nativities: how the individual planets signal [things] in their own houses and in others.

2 Saturn in a diurnal nativity in his own house, signals the friendship of nobles and the greatest assets if he was in the Ascendant with the Lot of Fortune; in a nocturnal one, labor and a multitude of diseases. **3** In a house of Jupiter, beauty; in the day an abundance of assets, and truth; in the night the contention of nobles and death of the father. **4** In a house of Mars, a stony heart without sympathy, an abundance of anger. **5** In the house of the Sun in the day, the native's good fortune and that of his father; in the night, the contempt of each. **6** In a house of Venus, the destruction of the native's faith, the esteem of women, the poor, and infirmity and impediment from them. **7** In a house of Mercury, the investigation of forms of knowledge, and hidden things [become] manifest (whence he will suffer evil from thence) and his tongue is heavy, bad in spirit, he will suffer envy concerning something he did not do.[281] **8** In the house of the Moon, [it signifies] the infirmity of the native and the mother, and it will destroy the mother's assets.

9 Jupiter in a house of Saturn, the anguish of the heart, a multitude of profit but he will present himself as being a pauper; weak in heart, and he will think about evil (whence he will support[282] evil). **10** In his own house in the

---

[278] That is, at annual solar revolutions.
[279] *Alterum*, lit. "another, the other."
[280] This chapter is based on Abū 'Alī's *JN*, Chs. 39-45.
[281] Reading *fecit* for *facit* ("does"), with Abū 'Alī.
[282] Or perhaps merely "endure" (*sustinebit*).

day, the native will be fortunate, wealthy, esteemed, and be influential among kings; in the night it will be less than this. **11** In a house of Mars, unfortunate, [he will be] an associate of kings, and if he was then in angles or succeedents and in masculine signs, he will be the leader of an army. **12** In the house of the Sun he will be wise, of good character,[283] esteemed by kings and all the people; and if in addition he is in the angles or succeedents he will be a king or like a king, especially in a diurnal nativity. **13** In a house of Venus in a masculine nativity, mixing with the nobles, joy and advancement in the overseeing of noble women; in a female nativity, advancement because of faith and religion. **14** In a house of Mercury, a faithful businessman, having many assets beyond [what] others [have]. **15** In the house of the Moon in the day, in angles or succeedents, he will be fortunate, mixing with kings; in the night, notable in the [surrounding] regions.

16 If Mars is in a house of Saturn, the native will be a king, bold, and completing whatever he begins, but he will squander the assets of his own parents, and his older brothers will die. **17** In a house of Jupiter [he will be] noble, esteemed by kings, the general of an army (especially if Jupiter is then made fortunate in a house of Mars). **18** In his own house, great, clever, a geometer (especially in a nocturnal nativity); in a diurnal one in Aries, and a fortune is not looking at him, [the native] will be malignant, bringing injuries[284] to others, and he will have hidden pains and he will fall from a height (in Scorpio, less than that). **19** In the house of the Sun, the destruction of the native, an infirmity in the eyes and stomach, and he will be a master in the work of iron, his death will be sudden or he will be killed or die a foreigner. **20** In a house of Venus, he will be lascivious (and with his own blood relatives), or he will be betrothed to a woman with whom he'd earlier had an affair, and he will have evil from thence. **21** In Libra, from fire or iron in a hidden [place] of the body, in Taurus it gives falseness and betrayal. **22** In a house of Mercury, negligent but clever, he will profit in a bad way, he describes false things, and he will conquer [his] associates through his cleverness and knowledge. **23** In the house of the Moon, an agile person, inquiring into deep things, bold in bad things, he will have evil in hidden things, [and] his mother [will have] a long infirmity; his death is sudden, and he will squander the assets of his mother.

---

[283] *Ingenii.* This word can also speak of someone's cleverness, ingenuity, etc.
[284] Reading with John's Abū 'Alī for *vim* ("power, force").

24 The Sun in a house of Saturn in a diurnal nativity signifies that the native will be complete in all of his own works; in the night, unstable. **25** In a house of Jupiter [it signifies] matters of faith and he will be great in his own clan; in the night,[285] a fornicator and unjust with the wife of his own father. **26** In a house of Mars, liver pain, his father will die the worst death (and this is in Scorpio); in the day in Aries,[286] the exaltation of his life, in the night it will be less than this. **27** In his own house in the day, in an angle or succeedent, he will be a king, wealthy, great, strong, and riches will come to him from foreigners; in the night the sorrow of the father and he will die quickly, and he himself will have good on foreign journeys. **28** In a house of Venus, an explainer of dreams and investigator of concealed things, and truthful, and he will love travels. **29** In a house of Mercury, [he will have] many forms of knowledge and good works, be an astronomer, esteemed by nobles if the nativity is diurnal; in a nocturnal [nativity], a poor man doing evil things, poor in his youth [but] he will abound in riches in middle age, he will hurt in his stomach and his eyes, and partner with men practicing the works of demons.

30 If Venus is in a house of Saturn, he will be a fornicator of betrothed women; his wife will die. **31** In a house of Jupiter, [it signifies] good through noble women, and he will be hated by his own parents; in a diurnal [nativity] it will be less than this. **32** In a house of Mars, contentions and mixing with bad women, and perhaps he will kill his own wife. **33** In a house of the Sun, a lover of young women, abounding in horrible excess. **34** In her own house, a multitude of joy, esteem with stupid[287] women (whence evil will be said [about him]); he himself is fortunate, [and] will get good in all of his works. **35** In a house of Mercury, he will be with the religious and will do the works of women and love extravagance. **36** In the house of the Moon, impetuous extravagance, and always in the movable signs she signals instability in a single thing.

37 Mercury in a house of Saturn [indicates] the heaviness of the tongue, he is joined to religious people and sages. **38** In a house of Jupiter, mixing with kings and he will be a sage in the law of judges. **39** In a house of Mars, false and a malicious liar: on account of this [he will get] evil for himself (nor

---

[285] Reading with Abū 'Alī for "day."
[286] John's Abū 'Alī only mentions Scorpio in diurnal nativities.
[287] This does not appear in Abū 'Alī.

however will many evils follow him from that).[288] **40** In the house of the Sun, [he has] a good memory, deep in forms of knowledge. **41** In a house of Venus, a multitude of noble friends and works of knowledge pertaining to joy. **42** In his own house, all sciences of the trivium and quadrivium and philosophy and medicine, and [especially][289] in Virgo. **43** In the house of the Moon, it signifies a good and pure will, and [he is] faithful.

44 The Moon in a house of Saturn [signifies] laziness and a poor reputation, pain from coughing, and punishment, especially in the night—in the day, [it is] less than this. **45** In a house of Jupiter he will be as though a king among notables and of good reputation, extravagant with women with whom it is not permitted to be so. **46** In a house of Mars, mixing with bad men and robbers. **47** In the house of the Sun, joy with kings, an infirmity of the head, and especially at the beginning or end of the sign. **48** In a house of Venus, a lover of women, rejoicing with them, and he will have benefit from thence. **49** In a house of Mercury [he will be] of a good life, great understanding, he will esteem small girls. **50** In her own house, royal interactions and advancement from them; conjoined or applying to bad ones, [it indicates] diverse illnesses, if to fortunes the good health of the body.

[Chapter VII.18: Planets in the twelve places][290]

1 The Sun in the Ascendant signifies sovereignty and loftiness. **2** The Sun in the second, beauty and the happiness of the eyes. **3** In the third, an office of the king and changing[291] through [various] regions. **4** In the fourth, treasure and the revelation of the future, praise, loftiness. **5** In the fifth, reverence from the common people. **6** In the sixth, infirmity, tribulation through slaves and the ignoble. **7** In the seventh, contrariety from the powerful and wealthy. **8** In the eighth, loss, death, and the plundering[292] of princes. **9** In the ninth, divine culture, faith, and fear of God Most High. **10** In the tenth, rulership, great honor, and advancement. **11** In the eleventh, joy through friends, the wealthy, and ministers, and cleverness in men. **12** In the twelfth, the killing of

---

[288] This last clause is not in Abū ʿAlī.
[289] Adding with Abū ʿAlī.
[290] This chapter is based on *Twelve Domiciles*, attributed to Māshāʾallāh or Jirjis (see *WSM*); it is very similar to Abū ʿAlī, Chs. 47-48.
[291] That is, traveling.
[292] Lit., "taking away" (*ablationem*).

the wealthy,[293] the taking away of honor, tribulation from slaves and enemies and from ignobles.

13 Venus in the Ascendant, joy and happiness and the appearance of desire,[294] eating, drinking, clothing, golden ornaments and good-smelling things, respectability of morals and greatness of blessing and the enjoyment of the body. **14** In the second, assets and success from women. **15** In the third, a lack of self-control[295] and evil from bad works, and a multitude of friends against God.[296] **16** In the fourth, sorrow at the beginning in connection with the mother, but the end is praiseworthy. **17** In the fifth, tribulation because of a child, afterwards joy. **18** In the sixth, tribulation through male and female slaves and the mother;[297] however, he will have what he wants. **19** And if it was an interrogation about an infirm person, he will be freed: for if a fortune was in the house of infirmity, the infirmity of the one suffering will be alleviated (and *vice versa*). **20** In the seventh, a marriage-union and joy in women, and in every thing sought which he will have easily. **21** In the eighth, the death of the mother and nurse and their older relatives. **22** In the ninth, [pleasure and fortune from][298] foreign travel[299] and changing,[300] from the houses of religion, divine worship and religion and true dreams. **23** In the tenth, joy by means of the king. **24** In the eleventh, friendship, joy, the occurrence of goods and trust in friends, and good fortune with them. **25** In the twelfth, tribulation, the greatest enmity from women (and especially from ignobles).

26 Mercury in the Ascendant signifies wisdom, trust, disputations, geometrical and mathematical things. **27** In the second, the profit of assets [and] honor with the king. **28** In the third, the strength of brothers and sisters and friends. **29** In the fourth, grief and contention.[301] **30** In the fifth, letters and rumors, and joy from a preceding grief, and good fortune by means of a child. **31** In the sixth, robbing, deception by means of women and extrava-

---

[293] John's Abū 'Alī more appropriately has, "the enmities of kings."
[294] *Velle*.
[295] *In continentiam*.
[296] This does not make sense, nor does it match Abū 'Alī, who more sensibly speaks of joy from friends and the charm of the brothers and sisters.
[297] Or rather, the wife (Abū 'Alī).
[298] Adding with Abū 'Alī.
[299] *Peregrinationem*. In medieval Latin in particular, this can mean "pilgrimage."
[300] That is, moving house.
[301] *Twelve Dom.* reads, "and deliberation." John's Abū 'Alī reads, "a good memory, and precision in [one's] crafts."

gance. **32** In the seventh, contention from women, and extravagance. **33** In the eighth, the greatest enmities from neighbors, and lying because of the dead. **34** In the ninth, teaching, wisdom, astronomy, praise from noted people. **35** In the tenth, a sense of devotion from mathematical and geometrical writing. **36** In the eleventh, many friends, joy, the association of wise people. **37** In the twelfth, stupidity, shallowness, and asking about those things which lack a foundation, and perhaps he will knowledge about four-footed things.

38 The Moon[302] in the Ascendant signifies sovereignty and changing from place to place, and joy from mothers and great women. **39** In the second, loss and grief. **40** In the third, joy because of the wealthy, loftiness from kings, foreign travel,[303] friends, and being with noble people. **41** In the fourth, sorrow at the beginning if it was in the day, and the end will be praiseworthy; in the night, ruin at the beginning and the end, unless it was an interrogation about hidden treasure or a buried thing: for in this it is best and the thing will appear and be uncovered—and God knows more. **42** In the fifth, many sons if the interrogation is nocturnal (in a diurnal one, many daughters), and rumors from far away, good ones about a child and in accordance with the quality of the planet from which the Moon is being separated. **43** In the sixth, a quarrel from parents, profit from four-footed things, and the soundness of the body. **44** In the seventh, good from women. **45** In the eighth, ruin and deposing [because] of the king, false testimony, a quarrel and flight, anxiety such as lunatics suffer. **46** In the ninth, evil thoughts, changing throughout the regions, and the management of the kingdom. **47** And if this was a house of Mercury, [it indicates] astronomy; if one of Venus, singing and happiness; if of Mars, the work of arms and instruments; if Jupiter, divine worship and knowledge in the law; if Saturn, the knowledge of alchemy; if of the Sun, knowledge and foresight in four-footed things; if in Cancer, the knowledge of all things which go out of the water (and this is a peculiar property of the Moon among the planets). **48** In the tenth, the effecting of things and [of an] interrogation.[304] **49** In the eleventh, joy from friends and the attainment of every thing hoped for. **50** In the twelfth, [the matter asked about will be][305] at the hour of the Moon's exit

---

[302] In this paragraph, Leopold's (or rather, *Twelve Dom.'s*) text departs more radically from Abū 'Alī.
[303] Again, this can mean "pilgrimage" (see above).
[304] John's Abū 'Alī has: "A great love for beautiful things, riches, offices, honors among kings and princes."
[305] Adding with *Twelve Domiciles*.

from this place, and especially if it was at the end of the lunar month, and the Moon was impeded by Saturn: for then the judgments are horrible.

51 Saturn in the Ascendant: death because of debt and lands. **52** In the second, the taking away of assets and the confusion of friends. **53** In the third, the destruction of brothers. **54** In the fourth, the destruction of a building and lands and seeds and treasures, and danger from them. **55** In the fifth, the destruction of children and a contention with a legate. **56** In the sixth, the disobedience of slaves. **57** In the seventh, the destruction of the wife and the effecting of evil at the end. **58** In the eighth, grief and sorrow because of death and long lamentation. **59** In the ninth, the destruction of faith and going out to [do] evil. **60** In the tenth, sorrow and danger from the king, and long imprisonment. **61** And if the Sun was the lord of the house, the king will kill him in his prison; and the Moon in the same place[306] signifies what the Sun does, unless she is joined to Saturn. **62** And if Jupiter was the lord of the tenth, the king will kill him without fault; if Mars, he will perish of his own fault; if Venus, he will have benefit [after the][307] tribulation; if Mercury, he will be killed with injury and lying. **63** And if Mercury is looking at Mars, he will be struck with whips; if Mercury is with the Sun, the king will do injury to him,[308] and this is the property of Saturn in the tenth house among the other planets. **64** In the eleventh, much grief in friends and little in things despaired of. **65** In the twelfth, impediments from the king, and he will be captured by enemies, and will be panicky in all of his matters.

66 Jupiter in the Ascendant [indicates] reverence, respectability. **67** In the second, much assets, a good character, and management. **68** In the third, good fortune in brothers and sisters, joy in relatives.[309] **69** In the fourth, joy from what is left behind by the dead [and] inherited lands, treasure, security from horrible things. **70** In the fifth, many good and useful children, praise, it confers the accompaniment of wealthy people in matters of success.[310] **71** In the sixth, a scarcity of infirmities, loftiness through slaves, benefit from four-footed things. **72** In the seventh, joy from women and victory over all enemies. **73** In the eighth, [it means] that he would fall into the hands of his enemies, and from this he will have a praiseworthy end. **74** In the ninth, joy

---

[306] Or rather, *ruling* the same place.
[307] Reading with *Twelve Dom.* for "from."
[308] Reading *iniuria* for *sibi cara*, with the sense of *Twelve Dom.*
[309] Or, "neighbors" (*propinquis*, lit. "those who are close").
[310] *Prosperatis.*

from foreign travel, respectable faith and the explanation of dreams, and truth; for the explanation of [the content of the][311] dreams, see the planet from which Jupiter is separating or which one [separates] from him, and speak according to the nature of that same one (make an interpretation of a dream in a similar way). **75** In the tenth, enrichment, praise,[312] and loftiness. **76** In the eleventh, praise from friends, benefit through things hoped for. **77** In the twelfth, servitude, poverty, need, sorrow from four-footed things and slaves.

78 Mars in the Ascendant [signifies] sorrow, contention, and a horrible matter, the taking away of assets and without praise, and getting into a matter which does not pertain to him. **79** In the second, the taking away of assets, need, the confusion of ministers. **80** In the third, the enmity of brothers and their killing of each other. **81** And if [it is a house] of Venus, there will be joy from brothers and sisters; if Jupiter, there will be a multitude of assets and business; if Saturn, the digging up of tombs and walls; if Mercury, the subtlety of divinations and false testimony, and he will have dangers; if [it is] the house of the Moon, the breaking of walls and the impediment of stolen goods in the public market; if the Sun, the cutting of roads and plundering of roads (and this is a particular property of Mars with the planets). **82** In the fourth, killing, the shedding of blood, and the end [of life] is a long tribulation. **83** In the fifth, many fornicating children.[313] **84** In the sixth, a multitude of infirmities, hot and dry fevers from the blood, and grief from slaves. **85** In the seventh, doing business and contention, sexual intercourse, loss, tribulation in every matter. **86** In the eighth, killing, the cutting off of hands and feet, the most foul blaming, he will have the greatest assets, and he will suffer violence on account of that, and he will fall into the greatest poverty. **87** In the ninth, the seeking out of wars and horses, the drinking of wine and lack of self-control, unfaithfulness, many false dreams. **88** In the tenth, tribulation, beating by whips, prison, need in the means of subsistence, much war, contention in things not pertaining to him. **89** In the eleventh, a scarcity of benefit, the enmity of friends, loss of assets, the taking away of faith.[314] **90** In the twelfth, the cleverness of a robber in every way, delay in all things which he can do, the taking away of assets, a multitude of enemies, grief because of beasts.

---

[311] Adding with *Twelve Dom*.
[312] Reading with John for "the enrichment of praise."
[313] Or rather, children *from* fornication.
[314] Or more likely, "hope."

91 The Head in the Ascendant signifies loftiness and good fortune according to its conjunction with the planets. **92** In the second, the increase of assets and the greatest good fortune. **93** In the third, the acquisition of profit,[315] the appearance of faith and the truth of dreams. **94** In the fourth, benefit if it is in fiery signs or airy ones; in the earthy and watery ones turn the opinion around and speak to the contrary. **95** In the fifth, an increase of children and liberation from all things. **96** In the sixth, the strength of infirmities,[316] the increase of slaves, and the selling of beasts [for profit].[317] **97** In the seventh, the association of women. **98** In the eighth, the strength of life, a scarcity of grief. **99** In the ninth, faith according to the planets which are with it (good or bad). **100** In the tenth, asking about God Most High and about a good, invisible matter, and it signifies loftiness, reverence, and good fortune in masteries. **101** In the eleventh there is no work in it, and likewise the Tail. **102** In the twelfth, an increase of evils [and] a scarcity of good fortunes.

103 The Tail in the Ascendant, the uprooting, tribulation, [and] diminution of matters. **104** In the second, poverty and falling from places which one does not believe [could happen]. **105** In the third, the destruction of brothers. **106** In the fourth, need and inquiring into things without benefit. **107** In the fifth, the expulsion of children[318] and the descent of horrible things upon them, the old age of clothing, the lack of children. **108** In the sixth, infirmity and the laziness of male and female slaves, and the weakness of beasts. **109** In the seventh, destruction for the wife,[319] the strength of enemies. **110** In the eighth, [a bad] death and what is left behind by the dead, and loss. **111** In the ninth,[320] moving,[321] and a scarcity of faith. **112** In the tenth, being put down, dangers, traveling abroad without a reason. **113** In the eleventh, nothing. **114** In the twelfth, a scarcity of evils.

115 Speak according to this, and do not doubt!

---

[315] Or rather, the good status of siblings (John's Abū 'Alī).
[316] John's Abū 'Alī has strength *against* infirmities.
[317] Reading *mutuationem* (lit. "exchanging") for *mutationem* ("changing").
[318] This may refer to miscarriage and abortion, not (or not only) sending children away.
[319] Reading *uxori* for *thori* (a misprint).
[320] Omitting *fortitudinem* ("strength") which may have been carried down from **109**.
[321] Lit., "changing" (*mutationem*).

TREATISE VIII: ON INTERROGATIONS

[Chapter VIII.1: Introduction]

1 The[1] human condition, out of an inspiration[2] of eternal love, does not cease to imitate the nature and order of the heavenly bodies: and because of this, how it is in the [celestial] circle, so also is it in the soul. **2** For the features of this world are subject to the features of the heavens: and so the response to questions is certified.

3 However, questions arise concerning six things: concerning nations, families, kings and their actions, concerning the nativities of men, concerning inceptions, [and] concerning the intentions of minds.[3] **4** In addition to these however, things are asked about in a seventh way:[4] whether it would be in part or in full, how many parts, and how, from what, when, and what the end [will be]—all of which Apollonius[5] reduced down to four. **5** He[6] attributes the one asking[7] to the Ascendant, the thing asked about[8] to the west, the reason for the thing asked about to the Midheaven, the end to the angle of the earth.

6 Therefore, the querent will make a simple and absolute question. **7** The judge should take care that his instrument is true, and that the Sun is not at the angle of the Midheaven. **8** And if the testimonies of the good ones and bad ones came out to be equal, so that one could not avoid error, he defers the question to another time, and then it should be done again.

9 The[9] Arabs call the leader[10] of the question the "victor": take the one which has many dignities in the figure of the circle, according to house, exal-

---

[1] Sentences **1-4** and **6-8** are based on Māshā'allāh (*Judges* §A.127), and 'Umar al-Tabarī (*Judges* §A.128).
[2] Or, "instinct" (*instinctu*).
[3] That is, thought-interpretation (see Tr. X).
[4] That is, through a horary question.
[5] That is, the medieval Bālīnūs, probably from his *On the Secrets of Nature*, translated by Hugo of Santalla.
[6] I take this to be Apollonius, but this is a general enough scheme found from the earliest treatments by Dorotheus.
[7] That is, the "querent" (*quaerentem*), which I will use from now on.
[8] Often known as the "quaesited" (*quaesitum*).
[9] Sentences **9-18** are based on 'Umar (*Judges* §A.129-31).
[10] *Ducem*. This should be "indicator" or "significator," but the Arabic verb at the root of this word can also mean to point to, direct attention to, etc., so some Latin translators (most notably Hugo of Santalla, who compiled *Judges*) called it a "leader."

tation, bound, triplicity and face.[11] **10** And if two are equal in this, prefer the one which the Moon favors more,[12] and the one which looks at the east: it is the leader. **11** Which if it is falling,[13] the one which the Moon is looking at will be the leader. **12** And the victor of the business is the star which is more powerful in the place of the thing asked about; and always bring the Moon to bear.

13 And see to whom the leader applies, or which one to him: for good ones hasten, the bad ones change it. **14** Now if the leader of the east, being in a pivot or succeedent, applies to the lord of the thing asked about, it promises the effect; in a falling one[14] it removes [it] unless the question is about travel or some change. **15** Speak likewise about the transfer or collection of light.

16 Difficulty and delay comes from Saturn; from Mars, lying and frauds (however, it promotes venereal things if he is benignly configured[15] to Venus), the Sun has kingdoms,[16] Jupiter rulership and the business of kingdoms, Venus women. **17** The Tail of the Dragon stains both fortunes with its own perversity, and it will be worse if Mercury is present—likewise [it stains] Mercury and even the Sun and others: for the Moon and the four others[17] are corrupted [when] less than 12° from the Head or Tail.[18]

18 The[19] acceptor of counsel[20] is principally the central[21] [planet to watch]: for this one signifies what is going to be concerning the matter.

19 And[22] the degrees of the application designate days (if the application is in the tropical signs, and their arising is in less than two hours); in common

---

[11] This is somewhat misleading. In *Judges*, ʿUmar is looking for the victor of both the Ascendant (for the querent) and the quaesited or the object of the question (such as the fifth for children, *etc.*), not the victor over the chart as a whole. The victor of the quaesited is mentioned in **12**. For some pointing systems, see Ch. IV.1, **120**.
[12] That is, the one to which she applies.
[13] This must mean that it is "falling away" from view of the Ascendant, namely in aversion to it: "falling away" is an idiom in Arabic astrology that refers to being in aversion.
[14] That is, a cadent place.
[15] *Conformetur*.
[16] Or, "rulership" (*regnum*).
[17] The Sun, Mercury, and both benefics.
[18] Lit., "within the Head or Tail by 12°."
[19] See Māshāʾallāh (*Judges* §A.132).
[20] That is, the one to which other planets apply: it accepts or takes on the "counsel" or "management" (the latter term is more faithful to the Arabic).
[21] *Medius*.
[22] See al-Kindī, *Forty Chapters* Ch. 2, and *Judges* §A.133.

ones months (provided that their rising is in less than two hours); and in fixed ones, years (provided that they are raised up in more than two hours).

༄ ༄ ༄

20 And generally, in every judgment observe these eight things so that you may judge concerning the matter proposed:[23]

21 First, through the house of the matter.
22 Second, through the lord of that house.
23 Third, through the planet which signifies that matter naturally.
24 Fourth, through the Lot of that matter.
25 Fifth, through the Lot of the house.[24]
26 Sixth, through the lord of the Lot.
27 Seventh, through the conjunction and aspect of the planets to the house of the matter and its lord.
28 Eighth, through the changing of the planets through the houses.

29 Love[25] and hatred remove a man from the rightness of judging: love subverts reasoning by means of longing, hatred through a liability to anger.

30 If the strength of the significator of the interrogation was fixed,[26] look at its strength in the Ascendant of the revolution of that same year, and in the Ascendant of the lesser conjunction, and in the sign of the profection; and once it is known, judge the strength and weakness in all of these.[27]

31 The[28] first and its lord (which are significators of the querent) and the seventh and its lord (which are the significator of the thing asked about),[29] if

---

[23] See Ch. IV.5, **1**, where Leopold attributes these to Hermes and others. But here Leopold has listed the same thing twice (the Lot of the matter, here the fourth and fifth), and combined two others as one (the aspects to the house and to its lord, the seventh).

[24] Again, **24** and **25** are the same thing, and Leopold should have distinguished the aspects to the house and aspects to its lord in **27**. See previous footnote.

[25] This is a version of pseudo-Ptolemy's *Centiloqium*, Aphorism 12 (with thanks to Wade Caves for identifying it). This is an extremely important principle, and is one of the reasons that one must be careful about judging one's own question, or a question in which one has an emotional stake.

[26] This probably means "angular."

[27] This is quite a lot of trouble to go through for any question, and should probably be ignored.

[28] Omitting *quantus error erit astronomicum*, an ungrammatical phrase that suggests "how much astronomical error there will be"—but I have not located the source, and it does not make sense here.

they were impeded, then the response and questions should be deferred to another time. **32** If the significators were equal in anything (and in the contrary of that), look at the Ascendant of the conjunction and prevention which more closely preceded [the question]: and if those which are there are equal, you should not hasten to give a judgment. **33** The lord of the angle of the conjunction and prevention, and the quarters, if it was strong, will [act] strongly in all those things which they signify; and if weak, it will be low. **34** Likewise if it was fast or slow. **35** And if the significator is in the middle of the Ascendant[30] and quick, and applies to a quick one, it signifies the occurrence of the thing in that same hour; being removed by one [degree], within the day; by two, within a month.

[Chapter VIII.2: Questions of the 1st house]

[A general appraisal of the chart][31]

1 Since there is a distribution of all matters throughout the twelve houses, judgments are arranged according to the order of their questions.
2 If a question about life is proposed, then once the east is discovered (which is the root of the question), if the lord of the east and the Moon look at it benignly they signify a lucky querent or native; and if you found the lucky [planets] safe and cleansed, say [he is] lucky. **3** Concerning corrupted ones, less lucky; with the unlucky [planets being corrupted], unlucky.
4 Once[32] that has been accomplished, consider the Ascendant and the lord of the Ascendant, and the lord of the conjunction or prevention which preceded the interrogation, and speak according to them. **5** And direct to the good ones and bad ones.[33]

---

[29] Leopold is now reverting to the model in **5** above.
[30] Reading *ascendentis* for *ascendente*.
[31] This entire section (except for a few sentences) comes from Sahl's *On Questions* §1 (*Judges* §1.1).
[32] This paragraph does not seem to be from Sahl.
[33] This probably means to direct the Ascendant to them, to find the length of life.

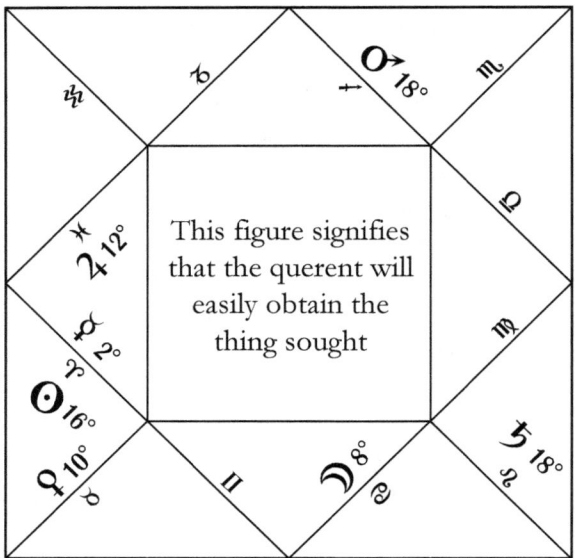

Figure 84: A figure showing that the querent will obtain it easily (Leopold)

6 Concerning those things which are going to come in life, once a question has been proposed, see the agreement between the lords of the east and the question: if there is an application and reception, and each are free of the bad ones, or [they are] corrupted.

7 If the lord of the east and the Moon apply to the lord of the question (that is, to the one in whose house the question falls), the querent will have what is sought, with labor; [if] conversely, without labor. **8** Or, if the lord of the east[34] is in the house of the question, or the leader of the question is in the east, there is no doubt [of his getting it] unless it would be burned there or have [its] fall. **9** It is the same if the lord of the east or the Moon applies to a planet in the place of the question,[35] [it] having dignity in that same place, or [if] the lord of the question [applies to a planet][36] in the east.

10 Say the same about the transfer and collection of light, [but] so that there is no corruption by retrogradation or burning or fall: for if [it was] thus, it will be acquired and afterwards lost. **11** However, the thing will be had easi-

---

[34] Reading *orientis* with *Judges* for *eorum* ("their, of them").
[35] I have reversed the clauses, with *Judges*. Leopold has the lord of the Ascendant or the Moon applying *in* the place of the question, *to* a planet having dignities there.
[36] Reading with *Judges* for Leopold's puzzling *aliorum* ("of the others").

ly if the application or transfer or collection of light comes to be through a good aspect (and *vice versa*).

12 And if this [application] was to a planet in the place of its own fall (such as to Mars in Cancer [or] to Jupiter in Capricorn),[37] the business will be corrupted; likewise concerning the Moon if she is in 3° Scorpio, or if Mars (he being the lord of the east) would regard her by a bad aspect or the Moon would apply to him, or, if the one to which the application came did not receive her, it is the worst sign. **13** But concerning a favorable figure,[38] it does not threaten so dangerously.

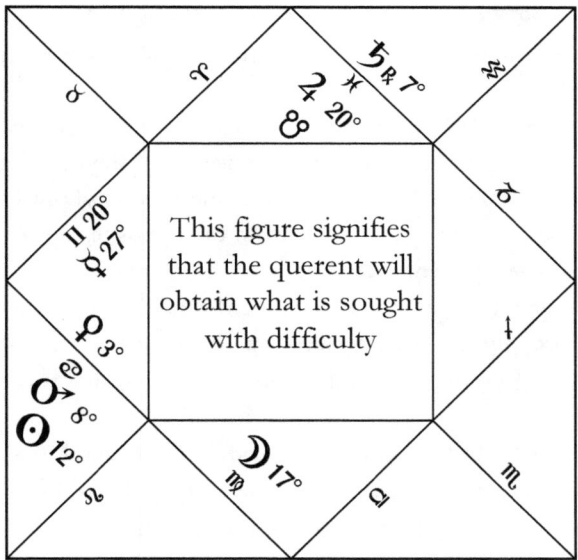

Figure 85: A figure showing that the querent will obtain it with difficulty (Leopold, after Sahl)[39]

14 And if the same planet is the lord of the east and of the question, safe from the infortunes and received, it shows a firm and stable business. **15** And

---

[37] This may be so, but what Sahl actually means is that one applies to a planet *from* that planet's fall: such as applying to Mars *from* Cancer, or to Jupiter *from* Capricorn. The idea is that Mars or Jupiter would be given light from a place they detest, which is not good for the outcome of the question. The rest of the sentence is likewise garbled, and one should consult Sahl.
[38] That is, a sextile or trine.
[39] This example is Sahl's own (see below), and can be dated to 824 AD.

[it is the same] if the Moon, being free and safe, would apply herself to [such a planet, even if she should apply to][40] no [other].

16 Note that three things establish a judgment: the lord of the east, the Moon, and the lord of the question.

[Sahl's example]

17 And in order that it might be judged more easily, let this example about rulership be posed.

18 The east was 20° Gemini, the Sun was in 12° Cancer, the Moon in 17° Virgo, Mercury 27° Gemini, Mars 8° Cancer, Venus in 3° of the same, Jupiter in 20° Pisces (in his first station), Saturn in 7° of the same, retrograde, the Tail with Jupiter.

19 Mercury has the leadership of the east, at the end of the sign, already separated from Jupiter. **20** Jupiter was the leader of the question and in the house of the question. **21** I crossed over to the Moon, whom I found in the pivot of the earth, applying to Jupiter from the opposite, and having the signification of the querent. **22** Because the application was from the opposition, it denoted that the matter sought would come to be with difficulty; but because Jupiter [was] picking up the counsel[41] and standing still, getting ready to go retrograde, it denoted that the gift that was obtained will be quickly lost.

23 And if the lord of the east had picked up the counsel [from the lord of the tenth], and was weak as the lord of the tenth is [here], [we would assign] blame to the one taking [the political dignity, and] the dignity would have been lost.[42]

24 And the lord of the east wanting to enter into the second sign, signifies him hastening to the thing sought, but he does not get it there because, being in Cancer [and] applying to Mars, [Mars] does not accept [the application].[43]

25 And because Mars is the lord of the sixth (which is [the house] of slaves), it was signaling loss on the occasion of slaves.

---

[40] Adding and reading with *Judges* for Leopold's *domino*.
[41] *Consilium legens*. That is, accepting her application.
[42] Leopold's and Hugo's Latin is extremely compressed here, so I have filled it out a bit based on John's Sahl.
[43] That is, Mercury moving into the second house shows the querent trying to make a livelihood (second house). However, when in Cancer his next application would be to Mars, from the sign of Mars's fall (Cancer): thus Mars will not accept what is given to him. This is an example of what Leopold was trying to explain in **12** above.

26 And the Tail with Jupiter, in his rulership, signifies that he would be not a little disturbed. **27** Also, the separation of Mercury from Jupiter [shows] that he had formerly fallen into the hope of [obtaining] this, and portends that he is already pretty forsaken; but the Moon seemed to draw [us] back [to this conclusion].[44] **28** Operate according to this example in the others.

[A question about longevity: al-Khayyāt][45]

29 The east truly signifies life: whence, concerning the quantity of life [that is left] consider principally the lord of the east and the Moon. **30** Now, a separation of the Moon (namely from Saturn)[46] denotes the finished part of life, an application what is left.

31 Therefore the lord of the east already entering into burning, if the malicious [planets] are in the east or in the seventh, really suggests death. **32** Take the hour of death by means of the lord of the east: for by how many degrees it is distant from burning, it testifies that he will survive that many years in firm signs, months in common ones, days in convertible[47] ones—but it is more so if a malicious one is in the east (or regards it) [and it] rules the fourth or eighth lodging-place.[48] **33** But if benevolent testimonies are in the east, and the lord of the east and the Moon are cleansed of infortunes, it signifies a long-lasting state of life.

34 And the number of degrees [from] the Moon to the malevolent which corrupts her, denotes damages to life, and [its] impediments; from the lord of the east to [its] burning, signifies the quantity of life.

[A question about life: "Dorotheus"][49]

35 And say that that quarter of life is better, in which you found the Lot of Fortune and the better stars—namely, the eastern, southern, western, [or]

---

[44] That is, that there would be problems (see **22**).
[45] See *Judges* §1.2.
[46] This mention of Saturn is not in *Judges*, and I do not know where Leopold is getting it.
[47] That is, "movable" or "cardinal" ones (Aries, Cancer, Libra, Capricorn).
[48] This is the word sometimes used by Hugo of Santalla for "house."
[49] See *Judges* §1.3.

northern [quarters].⁵⁰ **36** Judge likewise if it is asked in which direction it is better to go, and likewise concerning the day and doing business (and thus the day is divided artificially into four [parts]).⁵¹ **37** But Hermes takes the natural day,⁵² and orders that one very much avoid the quarter which the infortunes occupy.

[A question about life: Jirjis]⁵³

38 Concerning life that has passed and is yet to be, see how many degrees in its own sign the lord of the eastern face has gone through, and how many [degrees of the Ascendant have arisen]:⁵⁴ multiply the first by the second, and if the total goes beyond 100, cast away 100 and what remains signifies the years already transpired. **39** Then multiply the degrees remaining to the star which are left over in the sign, by the remaining degrees of the east: and if they cross [beyond] 100, cast away 100 and the remainder undoubtedly signifies the future years of life.

40 Likewise, multiply⁵⁵ the degrees which the lord of the eastern triplicity has crossed over in the face of its own sign, by the crossed-over degrees of the eastern bound, and if [they are more than] 100, *etc.*, as before. **41** Multiply⁵⁶ the remaining degrees of the eastern bound by those which are left to its lord in its own face: and if [they are more than] 100, *etc.*, as before, above.

[A question on life: "Aristotle"]⁵⁷

42 And you should know that the eastern lord in a pivot signals long life; after the pivots, a lesser one; in the remote ones, shorter.

---

⁵⁰ Moving clockwise, between the Ascendant and Midheaven is the first, eastern quarter (and first part of life); then the second, southern quarter; then the third, western quarter; then the fourth, northern quarter.
⁵¹ That is, if one asks a question about the best time of day to do business.
⁵² This means that if benefics are (say) between the Ascendant and Midheaven, then the time from sunrise to local noon is best (and so on with the rest).
⁵³ See *Judges* §§1.4-5.
⁵⁴ Reading with *Judges* for "lord of the lord of the east."
⁵⁵ Reading *multiplica* for *deduc* (which would imply subtraction).
⁵⁶ See footnote above.
⁵⁷ See *Judges* §1.6.

[Chapter VIII.3: Questions of the 2nd house]

[On acquiring wealth: Sahl][58]

1 Concerning the second house, it is asked about profit and about assets. **2** About this, before everything you should consider the leaders of the question (which are the lord of the east and the Moon), from thence the second and its lord, and Jupiter (because he naturally signals resources). **3** If in particular the Moon or the lord of the east applies to the leader of the question (or conversely [it applies to the] eastern [lord]), or if there is a transfer of light between them, it is a certain judgment of profit. **4** Venus and Jupiter, being found in the lodging-place of resources, do the same.

5 And if you did not find the aforesaid, profit is denied. **6** And the malevolents in the second do not only deny profit, but they even bring in loss. **7** And the Moon being solitary[59] makes a long-lasting and stable misfortune.

[On acquiring wealth: ʿUmar][60]

8 If however it is asked in an indeterminate way, if the lord of the east and the Moon (or either one) regards the east, or any star collects the light of each and reflects the light of each or one of them to the east, that [planet] will obtain the duty of being the leader. **9** Therefore, this [significator] applying to the fortunate ones and being received, greatly bestows money from that party which it regards:[61] with difficulty from the square or opposite aspect, [but] easily from the trine and sextile.

10 He will get [it] easily from the king while [the significator] is joined to the lord of the Midheaven—[but not] without its reception—and by an aspect to the lord [of the eleventh].[62]

---

[58] See *Judges* §2.1.
[59] That is, being void in course (see Ch. IV.3, **62**). The word I have translated as "being" (*incidens*, "to fall, happen") translates an Arabic word that means "to fall," but more colloquially, "be, happen."
[60] See *Judges* §2.2.
[61] I believe this refers to the nature, rulerships, and location of the fortunate planets which it applies to.
[62] Adding with *Judges*.

[On acquiring wealth: al-Kindī][63]

11 Moreover, if the lord of the Ascendant applies to the lord of money, being received by it, with the regard of the Sun and Moon (if [the lord of] the house of money regards the lord of the Ascendant), it gives the hope of profit.

12 The application of the lord of the Ascendant[64] with the lord of the Lot of Fortune does the same, and [an application of the lord of the Lot] with the Sun and Moon; and the same thing if the Moon regards the Lot of Fortune.

13 In the signification of money, Jupiter is stronger if he is in the second with the lord of the Ascendant and the leader of money, or in the Ascendant or the eleventh or tenth, or the remaining pivots, or even if he appears after the pivots.

14 Moreover, the lord of the Ascendant and of the second, and Jupiter, being together in the pivots, show great and lasting riches—in which the Ascendant is the best, then the tenth, then the seventh, lastly the fourth. **15** In the succeedents, first we take the eleventh, then the second, third, fifth, fourth, [and] sixth.

16 Moreover the lord of money applying to the lord of the Ascendant signifies it will be easily acquired; contrariwise [it is acquired but] not without labor: and with good aspects, it comes to be unexpectedly; with bad ones, with difficulty; retrogradation makes for the impediments of the leaders.

17 Moreover, if someone wants to get something from a specific person, the Ascendant belongs to the one seeking, the seventh belongs to the one from whom it is sought. **18** Then judge concerning getting it just as they bear themselves amongst themselves: the lord of the Ascendant, and the lord of the seventh, and the lord of the second, and the Lot of Fortune and its lord.

---

[63] See *Forty Chapters* Ch. 13.1, and *Judges* §2.3.
[64] The version of al-Kindī in al-Rijāl has the lord of the second.

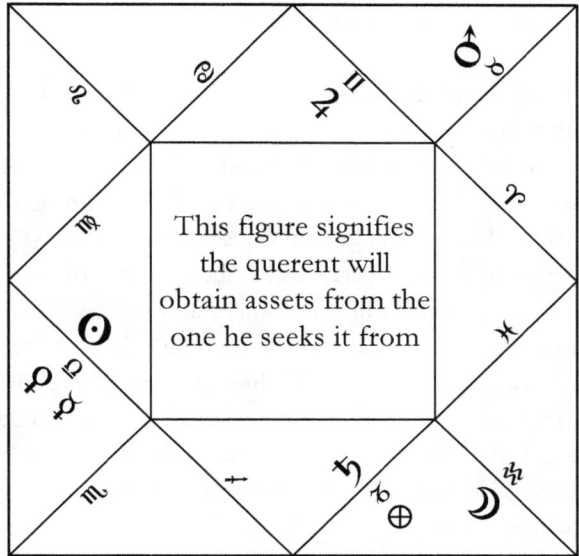

Figure 86: A figure showing that the querent will obtain assets (Leopold)

[On acquiring wealth: al-Khayyāt][65]

19 Likewise if the lord of the Ascendant and the Moon apply to the lord of the second, or the Moon applies to the lord of the second [from] the eastern lord, it gives the hope of acquiring money. **20** It is the same if a lucky [planet] is in the house of resources, or at least the Moon or the lord of the east applies to a benevolent. **21** Moreover, a lucky one [applying] to the lord of the Ascendant, provided that it looks at the east, promises honor [and] dignity with great convenience; speak to the contrary with malevolents.

22 Likewise, the Lot of Fortune [being] lucky, along with the lord of the east and the Moon, strengthen the hope of profit and bless many times over. **23** And if the lord of the east is corrupted, it takes away much; and if in addition the Lot of Fortune is corrupted and an unlucky Moon regards [the Lot], it speaks completely against the things asked about.

---

[65] See *Judges* §2.4.

[The source of wealth: Sahl][66]

24 But whence the profit will come forth, you will know thusly: for if the leaders gather counsel amongst each other in the east or in the second, he acquires the riches through his own business and labor; in the third, through the assistance of brothers and sisters; in the fourth, through parents and fields; in the fifth, through children; in the sixth, the infirmity of bodies and the common people was the occasion; in the seventh, from women and a controversy; in the eighth, from inheritances and old matters; in the ninth, through journeys, teachings, and laws; in the tenth through kings and magnates; in the eleventh he will have aid through friends, and many wares; in the twelfth, from enemies. **25** And if [the twelfth] is four-footed, with four-footed animals; if of a human form, prison and captives.

26 And judge good or bad thusly through the houses, just as you find the lucky or unlucky [planets].

[The source of wealth: ʿUmar][67]

27 And [if he seeks wealth from someone other than the king, and] the leader itself applies to the lord of that same house, or if there is a transfer between them, or one who transfers the light to the lord of the east, resources will come [to him] from that class [of things]; lacking that, however, not. **28** Judge likewise about the square and opposite aspect and assembly.

[The source of wealth: al-Khayyāt][68]

29 And if something is hoped for from the king, certain people observe the place of the Sun and Jupiter, and they do not care about the east and its lord. **30** For both the Sun and Jupiter holding onto a pivot along with the Lot of money or its lord, or if they are in the house of money with Mars falling [away] from them and averse, he will easily have what is sought. **31** But if Mars is stronger than Jupiter and running along in [Jupiter's] pivot, [and] he regards the lord of the second or the lord of the Lot of Fortune, there will be

---

[66] See Sahl's *On Questions* §2.2, and *Judges* §2.6.
[67] See *Judges* §2.7.
[68] See *Judges* §2.9.

labor and difficulty[69] from the owner of the resources, and [there will be] much dissipation of things. **32** And if it is Saturn instead of Mars, there will be a delay through the king or powerful people. **33** Saturn in the place of Jupiter,[70] even though it takes away little, still over individual days it restores a modicum of it.

[The amount of wealth: al-Khayyāt][71]

34 The quantity and number of money acquired[72] is known through the [lord of the second and the][73] Lot of resources[74] and through Mercury: for the one among these which is stronger in place and aided by more testimonies, is the leader.

35 If Mercury is falling and placed awry,[75] it confers 20 *denarii* or *solidi*;[76] in his own triplicity, 200; in his own house 2,000 and in [his] kingdom [20,000][77]—and likewise the others acquit what is promised according to their lesser years[78] and their number, unless they were falling or would be going towards falling. **36** In their own bounds, they change [the amount] by the number of [their] lesser [years], in tens; in [their own] houses, by hundreds; in [their] kingdoms they give thousands.

37 And if a star is retrograde, one-half is subtracted. **38** If burned, [subtract] according to the manner of burning and its distance from the Sun ([which] is ended at 12°): for by 6° it gives half, by 4° one-third, and so on; and with the Sun, nothing.

---

[69] Reading *difficultas* for *dissipat*. Leopold has greatly mixed up this sentence and the next, and I have moved some clauses to their proper place.
[70] *Judges* reads "the traversal of Saturn *from* the place of Jupiter," which I take to mean that he is in one of Jupiter's whole-sign angles.
[71] See *Judges* §2.11.
[72] Reading *acquisitae pecuniae* for *acquirendae pecuniae*, as being more natural.
[73] Adding with *Judges*.
[74] That is, the Lot of money (see Ch. IV.5, 40).
[75] This suggests a cadent place or one in aversion to the Ascendant, especially the sixth and twelfth. But in context it could also mean, "peregrine."
[76] Both of these are types of ancient coinage.
[77] Adding based on *Judges*. See the footnote there for further information and citations that led to these corrections.
[78] See the table in Ch. IV.2.

[*The time of acquisition*: 'Umar]⁷⁹

39 For then the thing will be had when the leaders apply with the lord of the one seeking, in some dignity [or] pivot of the signs or planets—if, however, there is reception between them.

[*On debts*: al-Khayyāt]⁸⁰

40 The east is given to the querent (whether he is the debtor or creditor), the seventh to the one about whom it is asked, the money is deputed to Mercury and the Moon. **41** For if each [regards] from a trigon or hexagon, [the debt will be settled with peace and concord; but with a regard being denied],⁸¹ the money of each is denied. **42** And should the Moon or any other transfer the light, it restores [the money] unexpected through a mediator. **43** The luckiness of the Moon [means] it is received well and respectably.

44 And if Mercury is corrupted by the malice of Saturn, the creditor will seek again the money that was accepted, and in addition it introduces false witnesses; being corrupted by Mars, it will mix in discord and quarrels. **45** Concerning a burned Moon, speak as above.

[*Good fortune based on angularity*: al-Kindī]⁸²

46 The fortune of worldly things, and their worthiness, is known through the pivots and the stars which are in them, for these designate the most renowned things; however, those which are remote from the pivots and falling, are said to be the contrary. **47** The ninth and third⁸³ [are] obscure and unknown; the twelfth and sixth belong to what is abject and suchlike, and every misfortune.

48 If the lords of the pivots are in the pivots, they make fortunate and take away ruin; contrariwise in the remote [places]. **49** In those which [are] after the pivots: after the tenth⁸⁴ they give hope, fulfill, and apply friends;⁸⁵

---

⁷⁹ See *Judges* §2.13.
⁸⁰ See *Judges* §2.14.
⁸¹ Adding with *Judges*.
⁸² See *Forty Chapters* Ch. 2.3, and *Judges* §2.15.
⁸³ Reading *tertium* with *Judges*, for "second."
⁸⁴ That is, in the eleventh house.
⁸⁵ Reading *amicos* with *Judges* for *annos* ("years").

those after the fourth[86] introduce middling fortune and favors with every exultation, because of children; those after the Ascendant,[87] through money and family; after the seventh,[88] they give inheritance and because of ancient things.

50 However, the summit is the prosperity which the lord of the Ascendant signals: which if it is in the Ascendant, it will come to be through his own personal labor and power; in the Midheaven, through the king or grand duties; in the seventh, because of borrowing[89] and adversaries and betrothals; in the fourth, through lands, fathers, and the channeling of waters.

51 They likewise signal their effects according to the houses in which the good and bad ones are.

[On things lent or deposited for safekeeping: "Aristotle"][90]

52 For things deposited for safekeeping and lent out, if the lord of the second is falling or burned up or retrograde, part is restored and part lost. **53** And if the bad ones are in the second or with its lord, the one to whom they have been committed will return [them] negligently.[91] **54** And if Mars is the lord of the second, holding onto either one of his own houses, he would [not] be able to recover [them] unless by war or force.

55 The benevolents in the second make [the goods] be restored in a benign way. **56** Mercury in the second, he being the lord of the second, the whole is restored because he persuades [the other person] to it.[92]

57 Moreover, with the lord of the second bearing itself well with respect to it, with the bad ones being averse and from the second, the whole is restored; if you saw the contrary, say the contrary.

☼ ☾ ☊

---

[86] That is, the fifth house.
[87] That is, in the second house.
[88] That is, the eighth house.
[89] Reading *mutuationis* with *Judges*, for *mutationis* ("moving"). But it is true that the seventh signifies the destination of travels, so perhaps Leopold's misreading is correct after all.
[90] See *Judges* §2.16.
[91] *Judges* says that he will neglect to return them, but I suppose both interpretations make astrological sense.
[92] Reading with the better spelling and more complete phrasing sentence in *Judges*.

58 If[93] the fortunes were in charge of the fearful places, they import harm in these places; the fearful [places] are the places of the bodies or rays of the infortunes, which the indicators of nativities reach by direction or profection. **59** But if the fortunes looked at [a fearful place] or were there, the fear will be annulled. **60** And convey it according to this with the four commixtures: if good, good; if bad, bad.[94]

[Chapter VIII.4: Questions of the 3rd house]

1 Concerning[95] the third house and brothers, consider the third and its lord, and the regard of the good ones and bad ones to them. **2** If therefore the lord of the third applies to the lord of the sixth or traverses in the sixth, or the lord of the sixth [was] in the third, the brother will grow ill. **3** If the lord of the third is in the fifth or eleventh, he has moved [from] his place.

4 And any corruption of the leader denotes the adversity of the brothers. **5** The leader being burned and unlucky, never puts an end to infirmities and miseries.

6 Judge likewise about the fourth for parents, about the fifth for children, about the sixth for slaves, about the seventh for marriage-unions and controversies, and likewise about the others.

---

[93] I am not sure of the source of this paragraph, but it seems to be taken from another context.

[94] Leopold might mean something like combinations of benefics and malefics ruling and aspecting houses: such as a benefic ruling the twelfth, but a malefic in it, versus a malefic ruling it and a benefit in it.

[95] For this section, see Sahl's *On Questions* §3, and *Judges* §3.1.

[Chapter VIII.5: Questions of the 4th house]

[Questions of the 4th: Sahl][96]

1 Concerning the fourth house (such as for lands and the status of fields, and other things which pertain to the fourth house). **2** If it is asked about the status of these, give the leadership of the querent to the lord of the east and to the Moon; the status of the land or field to the fourth and its lord. **3** If these apply to each other, or at least they are in the fourth, they signal good.

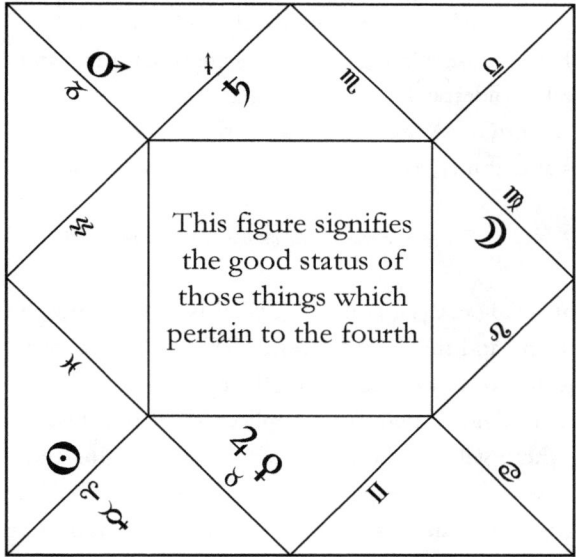

Figure 87: A figure showing the good status of fourth-house matters (Leopold)

[On purchasing fields: Sahl][97]

4 And the east signals the inhabitants, the fourth the status of the fields, the seventh the produce, the tenth denotes the trees which are there. **5** Therefore, that matter whose angle has a good significator, and conforming

---

[96] See Sahl's *On Questions* §4.1, and *Judges* §4.1.
[97] See Sahl's *On Questions* §4.2, and *Judges* §4.5.

to it, its matter is good (and vice-versa) **6** And if the leader of the inhabitants is retrograde, they themselves will destroy the field.

7 And a lucky one in the tenth, direct, signifies many and fertile trees; retrograde, cutting them down. **8** And if none is there, and the lord of the tenth regards it, it testifies that trees are present; if [it is] in aversion,[98] to the contrary. **9** And the lord of the tenth being eastern denotes new [trees], western old ones, direct lasting ones, retrograde ones about to perish.

10 Speak about the fruits through the seventh and its lord, the nature and quality [of the land] through the fourth. **11** For, this being fiery signals hard and mountainous land, earthy [means] plains, airy partly mountains [and] partly plains, watery infused or watery [land], and near waters.

11 But[99] that same sign being common signals that that same land is partly cultivated, partly wilderness.

12 And[100] Saturn in a watery sign wastes the harvests through rot, deprives and dissolves at maturity; Mars burns the fruits with heat and dryness.

[On selling real estate or houses: 'Umar][101]

13 And for selling estates, houses, or what is of this kind, the east belongs to the one buying and the seventh to the seller.[102] **14** Whence, if lord of the east applies to the lord of the seventh, the buyer asks for it; if the reverse, the seller does so. **15** And if there is no application or transfer or collection between them, there will not be a sale between them. **16** And if there is an application between them from the square or opposition or assembly, it will be difficult; from the trine or sextile, easy; and reception makes it easier.

17 And the infortunes in the fourth corrupt reclaimed land, if in that same place [they are] made firm[103] and peregrine; the fortunes in that same place, save.

18 And the lord of the Midheaven indicates[104] the amount of the price: in its own house, thousands or hundreds; in [its own] trigon, hundreds.[105] **19**

---

[98] *Adversus.*
[99] This sentence is from al-Khayyāt, *Judges* §4.8.
[100] This sentence is from al-Kindī, *Forty Chapters* Ch. 14.1, and *Judges* §4.2.
[101] See 'Umar, *Judges* §§4.6-7.
[102] Or rather, the east is the client.
[103] I am unclear what this means.
[104] Reading *indicat* for *mutat* ("changes").
[105] That is (according to *Judges*), one multiplies the planets lesser years by this amount.

And if it is retrograde or burned or descending,[106] it takes away from the price.

20 Also, of the Lots, note the Lot of real estate, which you have in the fourth house, and speak according to it and its lord.[107]

21 But the usefulness of the purchase is known through the lord of the seventh and the Moon, and the Lot of Fortune[108] and its lord (this is, through their application with the lord of the east): and whatever kind of application it is, such is the advantage of the one obtaining [it] with [good] fortunes.

[Building houses and cities: al-Kindī][109]

22 In the building of cities or houses, the Moon should be made fortunate by lucky [planets] and eastern ones; and let there be reception in a place of her own power. **23** It is the same if the Moon is ascending in a pivot in the north, quick in course, in a fixed and straight sign, and the Lot of Fortune is in a fortunate pivot, the pivots firm and immovable (nor let them be drawn back),[110] the lord of the fourth and the Ascendant in its own power, eastern, and let all the pivots be free of the bad ones.

24 Let the lord of death fall away from[111] the lord of the Ascendant, and from the Moon, nor let it be in the pivots. **25** The[112] Tail [should be in] the twelfth, [and] let the lord of the sixth or eighth [be in aversion to the Ascendant and Moon, and] the [lord of the] degree of the conjunction or prevention [be in a place of its own power], and[113] the eastern lord in a place of its own power, [and] let them be free of the infortunes and let them be in

---

[106] This probably means being in its own fall.
[107] According to *Judges*, this is taken from the lord of the fourth to Saturn, and projected from the degree of the IC. But according to al-Rijāl (and Ch. IV.5, **74** above), this is by day or night from Saturn to the Moon, and projected from the Ascendant.
[108] *Judges* simply has "the Lot," which would imply the Lot of real estate mentioned above.
[109] See *Forty Chapters* Ch. 15, and *Judges* §§4.13-14.
[110] That is, the MC-IC axis should not be in the ninth sign.
[111] That is, "be in aversion to."
[112] Leopold's sentence is horribly mangled here, so I have added much material in brackets from *Judges*.
[113] This following bit about the lord of the Ascendant is good advice, but results from Leopold's mangled reading of *Judges*.

a pivot or after the pivots, and let Venus or Jupiter be in the fourth[114] or tenth: for this introduces much money or the greatest joy.

26 Venus gives the greatest joy in the fourth: let Mercury,[115] being with her, make the lord of the second and the Lot of Fortune and the Lot of money fortunate. **27** And Saturn and Mars should in no way be in a pivot, because Saturn lays waste, constrains the inhabitants, slows success, blocks joy, tries to snatch away the good. **28** Mars professes rapine, burning, the constant attacks of enemies, and as though disposed to swallowing [them up], the detriment of the citizens, and inappropriate wars.

29 Therefore, in building cities it is important that Mars be restrained from the corruption of those who are aiding the lord of the Ascendant and the fourth[116] and the Moon (and Saturn forces them to suffer). **30** In order that [they] may favor with health, let them or a portion of them be mixed by some kind of reception; **31** Therefore, Venus being established in a trigon or hexagon introduces no little triumph from the subjects.[117]

32 For digging out[118] riverbeds, let the Moon be in the first tetragon of the Sun,[119] fortunate, received in a pivot, let the pivots be firm and upright, the lord of the Ascendant eastern, in any dignity of its own, let it be in a pivot or after the pivots, and let the Ascendant be watery and made fruitful by Jupiter or another fortunate [planet], and the fourth made fortunate or not deprived of the blessing of the lucky [planets], and let the lord of the Moon be in a place of its own dignity, received and blessed, and let the Lot of Fortune be supported in the regard of the Sun and Moon, [let] the degree [of the assembly] be made fruitful by the regard of the fortunes, and the application of the Moon from the conjunction or opposition of the Sun should be with a strong fortune in a pivot or after the pivots, and [the infortunes should be falling away] from the Moon and from the Lot of Fortune and from the lord of the Moon. **33** For if these things were observed, the impediments are repelled, waters multiplied, and there will be much usefulness, [and] it preserves ships unharmed.

---

[114] Reading with *Judges* for "eighth."
[115] This mention of Mercury is Leopold's own.
[116] Reading with *Judges* for "eighth."
[117] *De subiectis*. *Judges* reads, "from plowing."
[118] Reading *effodiendis* with Hugo (*Judges* §4.14), for *excidendis* ("cutting off").
[119] That is, at her first quarter.

[*Buried treasure:* '*Umar*][120]

34 With a question being proposed indeterminately[121] about treasures, first see whether there is anything in the place or not: if therefore the fortunes occupy the seventh, something is there; if the infortunes are there, it has been taken out. **35** And if it *is* there, the quality is sometimes known thusly: for the one which is in the seventh, and its partner[122] (if it is a fortune), show that the thing dug [out] is the same as the seventh house and their nature;[123] which if [the planet] in the seventh is without all dignity in that same place, [the nature of the object] agrees with the lord of the seventh. **36** If therefore the Sun is there in Aries or Leo, it indicates gold or a precious substance, but of a red color. **37** If [it is] Saturn, in either of his own houses, lead. **38** If Mars, iron or stones (such as a magnet), and what is of this kind. **39** If Jupiter in his own house, pearls, coral, and such things as the sea brings forth. **40** If Mercury in his own house, liquid quicksilver, leather books, little pots, and what is like these are indicated. **41** And if the said stars, being outside of their own proper houses, are with those who do not give up their own lodging-places, or those which apply to them, it is necessary to [make them] comply [with each other] or be united in some way.[124]

42 If,[125] I say, the star designating the thing is found in the seventh (possessing something [of dignity] there), [it] or the lord of the seventh itself should principally be noted. **43** Which if it would apply to the lord of the east, or [the latter] to it, or if there is a transfer between them or one who collects their light, it testifies that it [can be] obtained; and if this is by the square or opposite or assembly, it will come to be after labor. **44** And know the extent of the place within which the thing is contained: see what sign and what part of the circle the leader is holding onto: for if [it is in the] eastern

---

[120] See 'Umar, *Judges* §4.15.

[121] *Indeterminate.* That is, if the querent wants to know *if* a treasure is buried in a place—a determinate or specific question would be about a specific, known treasure.

[122] This is the lord of the seventh; see my rendition of al-Rijāl's version in *Judges,* which is fuller and makes more sense than Hugo's compressed version.

[123] Reading somewhat loosely for *sit idem quod septima domus eiusdemque naturae suffossum ostendunt.*

[124] That is (in the version in al-Rijāl), if the preferred significator is peregrine, its meaning should be combined with another planet to which it is joined. (In this version by Hugo, he prefers that the other planet be in *its* own house, too.)

[125] The question now turns to whether or not the object can be recovered: see 'Umar, *Judges* §4.16.

[direction], they show the direction of the place to be towards the east; in the western, towards the west; and the leader being in a firm sign [shows] the thing is under the earth, in a double-bodied one in the wall,[126] in a convertible one in the [ceiling][127] of that whole quarter. **45** Then, see how many degrees of its own sign the leader of the hidden thing has crossed, and whether it is in the first face of the sign or [not], and so on. **46** For if it is in the first [face], then the things are in the first third of the place—and likewise with the others (namely, eastern or southern, [or] western). **47** But [after this], take [that] lesser portion of the space by means of the degrees of the transit in the decans, and thus you will find the smallest portion of the place.[128]

[Buried treasure: al-Kindī][129]

48 Likewise, a lucky [planet] in the Ascendant signifies that the thing is in the place: the concealed thing [will be] according to its manner and nature, strength or weakness, and [one will know its] proper quality and price according to its nature. **49** For a lucky one being corrupted by a strong infortune disperses the whole, or portends that the majority [of it] has been taken away. **50** Which if it would be blessed by any luckiness of the others, the thing sought is in that same place. **51** And a common application of the lord of the Ascendant and the Moon with the leader of the concealed thing, confirms the finding of the thing; and if it is otherwise, let [your judgment] be changed.

52 And once the discovery of the thing is known, the certain place is had thusly. **53** From the center of the discovered place, draw 12 lines towards the circumference, making right angles. **54** And from the sign in which the leader is, in the triangular space let a line be drawn outside from the center. **55** And by the amount of the portion which the leader has crossed, the line makes or enclose that large a portion of the triangle: for the line drawn forth from the center separates out the whole portion of the space which we established at the outermost [limits] of the sign. **56** By how many [degrees] the leader has

---

[126] Reading *in pariete* with Hugo for *impartite*.
[127] Adding with Hugo.
[128] This seems to mean the following: once we know what quarter the object is in, we subdivide it further based on the portion of the decan actually traveled.
[129] See al-Kindī, *Forty Chapters* Ch. 35.1, and *Judges* §4.17.

already gone through in the sign,[130] you should draw out that much of the sign on the line; and by how much the leader is northern or southern [in latitude] from the zodiac, take that much in distance from the line, toward that direction. **57** And the leader being with the apogee of its own circle, denotes that the hidden thing is up high; at the opposite of the apogee, in the lowest parts; in the middle of the circle, in the middle.[131]

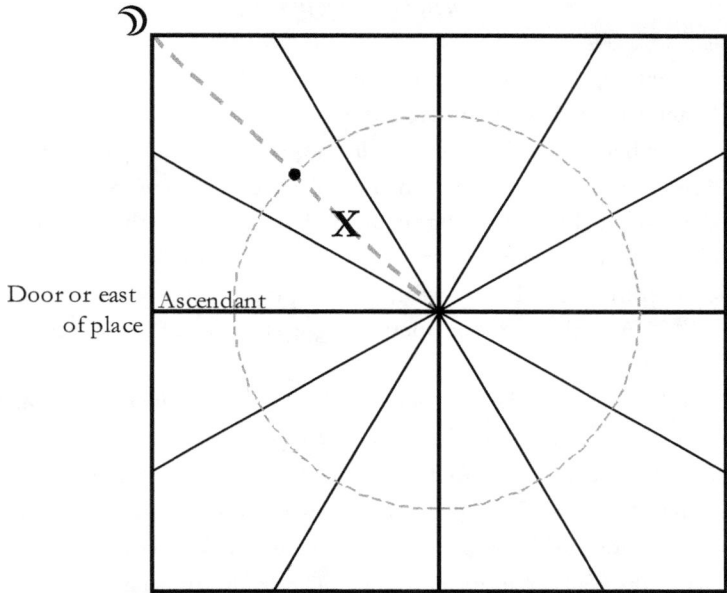

Figure 88: Al-Kindī's example of finding treasure[132]

---

[130] Reading more with Hugo here (for *in zodiaco*) and in the following clause, as Leopold seems to be confused about the procedure.
[131] For the apogees, see the table at Ch. II.4, **37**.
[132] In this example from al-Kindī's *Letter* (Burnett 1997, pp. 70-71), the treasure is in a house, and the Ascendant represents the door. The square house is divided into twelve equal parts representing the signs. The Moon happens to be the significator of the treasure, and is 45° to the south of the Ascendant, with 2° northern latitude. Hugo's version has us estimate which third of the sign the planet is in, but al-Kindī's *Letter* recommends using the exact degree. We draw a dotted gray line from the center of the house towards the southeast, at an angle of 45° from the Ascendant. Then, divide this line in half with a mark, and use a compass to draw a circle representing the ecliptic (the circle is actually unnecessary, what matters is dividing the line). Then, determine what the maximum latitude of the planet is, and what its latitude actually is at the time: in this case, the Moon's maximum latitude is 5°, but she is actually at 2° N. Northern latitudes will be between the mark and the center of the house, southern latitudes between it and the circumference of the figure. Since she is 2/5 of the way towards her northernmost latitude, the treasure will be at a distance 2/5 of the way from the mark to the center of the house, marked by the

58 And if you want to dig [it] up, choose so that the Moon is with the leader (it being fortunate) or applies to it, and let there be an application of the lord of the Ascendant of that hour with it.[133] **59** And the stronger thing for each is the assembly in this [situation]. **60** [And] do not let the infortunes be in the pivots.

[Buried treasure: Jirjis][134]

61 Moreover, once the seventh from the east has been noted, if any fortunate [planet] is in that same place, there is a treasure or something hidden there (and a benevolent in a pivot [indicates] the same). **62** Whenever the Sun and Moon support the east with their own aspect, the thing is in the place. **63** And the lord of the hour being in the east signifies that the hidden thing is then at the door of the house; in the Midheaven, in the middle of the house; in the seventh, towards the west; in the pivot of the earth, towards the north.[135] **64** And that same [planet] being eastern signifies the thing is new; western, old.

65 And Mercury in the east [indicates] it is buried under the earth; Venus in the same place, towards the couch;[136] Jupiter, in the wall; Saturn, in an obscure place or in a collapsed building; the Sun, in [a middle place of the house; the Moon, in][137] the place of a woman or a storage space; Mars, in a pathway or kitchen or where fire tends to be lit; the Head of the Dragon, in a high place; the Tail, in an obscure one. **66** And the traversing[138] of the [Sun and] Moon in the east, or if they are received, denote that it can be found quickly. **67** And the star which is in the seventh teaches what is hidden; and if none is there, the lord of the seventh is the leader of that same thing.

68 And the place must be divided into four parts: eastern, western, southern, and northern. **69** Then, see how many degrees the lord of the hour has made in the sign in which it is, and multiply these by 12, and distribute the sum [in increments of] 30, beginning from the eastern degree. **70** And if the distribution is ended in an eastern sign, the thing is in the eastern quarter

---

X. Her distance towards or away from her apogee (or perhaps, her elevation in the sky) will determine how high up or low the treasure is.

[133] I take this to be the significator or leader.
[134] See Jirjis, *Judges* §4.18.
[135] Reading *septentrionem* for *austrum* ("south").
[136] Or, "bed" (*lectum*).
[137] Adding with *Search*.
[138] Lit., "traveling down" (*decursus*).

(likewise with the other [quarters]). **71** Then, divide the discovered quarter by four as before, and see how many degrees the lord of the sign (in which the counting was ended) has made in the sign in which it is, and give 7.5 [degrees of it] to [each] sign in which it[139] is: and the kind [of sign] in which this distribution ends (namely, eastern, and so on), it is hidden in this quarter—and do likewise until you come to the smallest portion of the place.

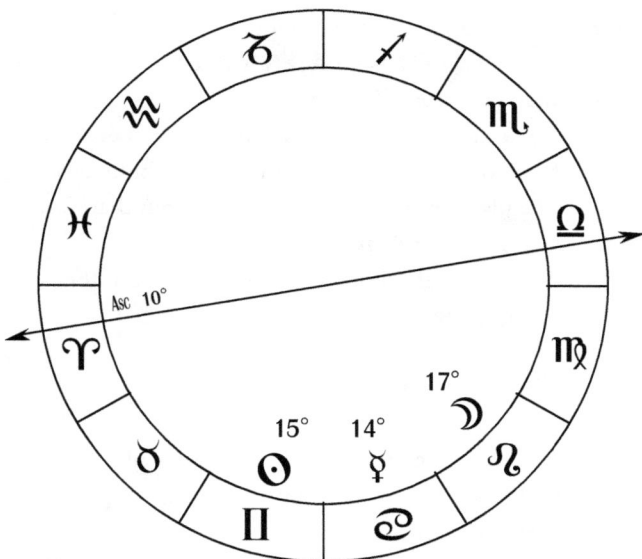

Figure 89: Finding a hidden object (Dykes, from Jirjis)

72 For example, the east was 10° of Aries, Mercury (the lord of the hour) had made 14° in Cancer. Multiply [the degrees of Mercury] by 12: they make 168.[140] **73** These, being drawn out from the degree of the east, are ended in Virgo, which is a southern sign: therefore, the thing is in this quarter of the place (namely, the southern).

---

[139] Leopold has "the lord of the hour," which may be correct. Unfortunately, the example below is a bit ambiguous, because Mercury is both the lord of the hour and the lord of the sign in which the counting has ended—and Leopold then remarks that we project from Mercury *because* he is the lord of that sign (not stated in Hugo). Because the example then goes on to use the successive domicile lords of the planets, I believe that Jirjis does mean to project now from the domicile lord of the sign where the counting has ended.
[140] Leopold erroneously has "144."

74 Therefore, after dismissing the other [quarters], divide this quarter into four. **75** And the degrees of Mercury are 14° (because he is the lord of Virgo): distribute [them in 30° increments] by 7.5, beginning from Cancer and from the place of Mercury, and even this is ended in Virgo: therefore in this division it is in the southern quarter.

76 Divide that quarter likewise into four, and because Mercury is in the lodging-place of the Moon, and the Moon in the house of the Sun (namely 17° Leo), once 7.5 of these have been granted (beginning from the place of the Moon), the distribution reaches Libra, a western sign: whence, the thing is in the western quarter of that division.

77 Moreover, once the division of that quarter has been done, since the Sun (the lord of the Moon) was in 15° Gemini, after these have been distributed from that same place by 7.5, it is ended in Cancer: therefore the thing is in the northern quarter of that division.[141]

78 And[142] if the lord of the hour is in the sign of another planet, begin from the place and sign in which *it* is.

[Hidden objects: Māshā'allāh][143]

79 Likewise, if someone conceals something in a place and says to you that you should find it, divide the place into four parts, and establish the Ascendant **80** And if the lord of the Ascendant is in the eastern quarter, [then] according to the figure it was hidden in the eastern quarter. **81** Divide [this area of the house] into four, the other [quarters] being discarded. **82** Then, see the lord of the aforesaid eastern sign (from which sign you found the lord of the Ascendant): which if it is in an eastern sign by nature, or a southern one, then take[144] that quarter (after the others are discarded), and see where is the lord of *that* sign, and divide [that quarter] by four, and do thusly until you come to the place of the hidden thing.

---

[141] To review: the object is in the northern (**77**) part of the western (**76**) part of the southern (**75**) part of the southern (**73**) quarter of the house.
[142] This sentence is not in Hugo.
[143] See *On Hidden Things* §3, in *WSM*.
[144] Omitting *occultum*.

[More on hidden objects: Māshā'allāh][145]

83 Moreover, the one which is stronger (between the lord of the Ascendant and the lord of the hour) is the significator. 84 Which [if] it is in the degree of the east, the hidden thing will be in the middle of the east; in [the degree of] the tenth, towards the south; of the seventh, in the west. 85 And [if] in the second, [it is] nearer the east than the north, in the sixth nearer the west than the north.[146] 86 And if the Moon looks at the significator and the Ascendant, it will be found quickly (and vice-versa).

87 And in a house, the signs which are airy signal the ceiling, the fiery ones the walls, the watery ones the foundations, the earthy ones the floors—according to al-Kindī and according to the positing of geomancy.[147]

88 Moreover, for the finding of a hidden or lost thing, if the lord of the Ascendant or the lord of the hour is in the angles, the thing will be found; if in houses which do not look at the Ascendant, it will not be found. 89 And if the lord of the Ascendant or lord of the hour is in the Ascendant, the thing is with the one seeking [it], where it is lost;[148] and if one or both of them are in the seventh, he will find [it] after some days. 90 Likewise, if the lord of the Ascendant or the lord of the hour is looking at the Sun, he will find it. 91 And if the Moon looks at the lord of the Ascendant,[149] it will be better. 92 And wherever the lord of the hour was, the thing is in that same place.

[Hidden objects: miscellaneous sources]

93 In order to know this, make the twelve houses: if you found a fortune in any of the four angles, without the aspect of the bad ones, a thing is in the place. 94 And[150] whether [it is] much or little, you will know thusly, by the strength which the fortune has in the place where you found [it]. 95 And if

---

[145] See *On Hidden Things* §4, in *WSM*.
[146] Reading *septentrioni* for *meridiei*.
[147] This last statement about al-Kindī and geomancy seems to be an addition by Leopold, as the Māshā'allāh text attributes the triplicities in this way but does not (and could not) have referred to al-Kindī.
[148] This is ambiguous; the Māshā'allāh text says that it is not really lost, *because* it is with (*apud*) him. But it is unclear to me how close to the querent it must be for this to be true.
[149] In the Māshā'allāh text, this seems to be the Sun.
[150] The rest of this paragraph is not in the "Dorotheus" text, but is in harmony with al-Kindī above (**48-57**).

the bad ones look at that fortune with a bad aspect, there is not anything there; and if there is not an impediment there, something is there.

96 And so that you might know whether the one who sought [it] would find [it], look at the lord of the Ascendant and the Moon: which if they were joined to the aforesaid fortune, or they looked with a good aspect, or they even received [it], he will find [it]; and if it was the contrary, he will not find [it].

97 Judge[151] the color by means of the sign of the leader: in Aries, white mixed with red; in Taurus, white mixed with citrine; in Gemini, white with red; in Cancer, green; In Leo, red; in Virgo, gray; in Libra, black; in Scorpio, black with citrine; in Sagittarius, red-yellow; in Capricorn, black;[152] in Aquarius, sky-colored; in Pisces, white.

[Whether something would happen or not: ʿUmar][153]

98 For an uncertain matter, as to whether it would happen or not, consider the tenth and its lord: for [the lord] being in a pivot, not scorched, means the effecting [of the matter]. **99** In the east or tenth, the effect follows clearly on that day or hour. **100** And if the lord of the tenth falls away from the Midheaven, it is a sign of what has already passed; in the third or sixth or twelfth, it removes the effect altogether.

101 And the Lot to apply is the one taken from the lord of the hour to the lord of the east, and it is projected from the Midheaven. **102** See, then, what sign and bound it arrives in: if the lord of that same bound is looking at the east, there is no ambiguity in the effect; and if it happens otherwise [it is] to the contrary.

103 And so that you may know the particular hour of the outcome, take from the lord of the east to the rising degree itself, and give one month to [every] 2.5°.

---

[151] For this sentence, see *Search* Ch. II.1.3.
[152] In *Search*, Capricorn is citrine and Scorpio is simply black—if Hermann is correct, then Leopold has accidentally added citrine to Scorpio and perhaps come up with his own attribution for Capricorn.
[153] See ʿUmar, *Judges* §§4.19-20.

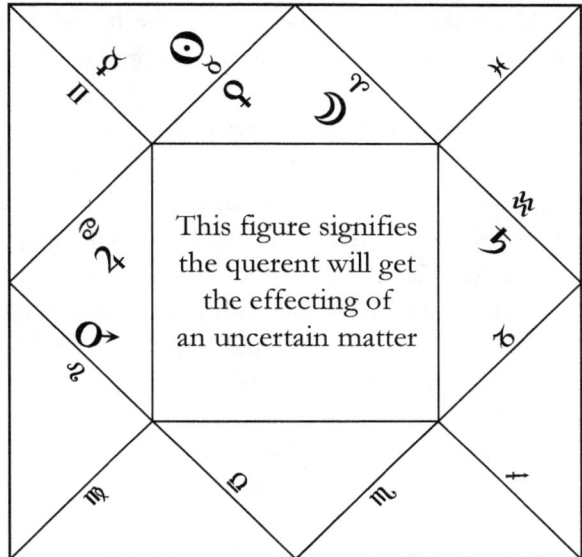

Figure 90: A figure showing the effecting of an uncertain matter (Leopold)

104 Take even from the lord of the hour to the Midheaven: and with the lord of the Midheaven falling away from [the Midheaven], take the degrees placed in between [it] to the lord of the hour, and grant individual days or months or years to the individual degrees.

105 The knowledge of this matter depends greatly on each light, and the east, and the Lot of Fortune, and their lords. **106** Because [the lords'] regards to them[154] shows the effecting [of the matter]; and if two are regarding and two not, [then] once the stronger regard is noted, the end and integrity or corruption is known from it. **107** And with all of these being deprived of an aspect, consider the luminaries and the lord of the Ascendant, for these ones in pivots or after the pivots show the effecting [of it]; falling ones wholly pervert the effect.

108 Moreover, the Moon being found in the second, holding to the tetragon of the fortunes and a double-bodied sign, really signifies the business is done or going to be; and in the east, it will be. **109** In the second [it is] the same, with delay. **110** And the lord of the east regarding [the east], and the lords of the luminaries [regarding] them, and the regard of one to the other,

---

[154] Reading more closely with Hugo, for *quare eorum in eodem respectu*.

[and] with the Moon regarding[155] [the lord] of the bound of the twelfth-part,[156] and the [lord of the] Lot of Fortune the Lot, give a certain testimony.

[Hidden objects: "Ptolemy"][157]

111 If the significator looked at the Ascendant, the kind the hidden thing will be of the substance of the Ascendant; but if it does not look, it will be of the substance of the significator. **112** The lord of the hour signifies the color of the thing. **113** The Moon above the earth [indicates] a new thing, under the earth an old one. **114** The lord of the Lot of Fortune [indicates] the length or shortness. **115** The lord of the bound of the degree of the fourth house, and the lord of the bound of the degree of the Midheaven (namely the one which is in an angle), and the lord of the bound of the degree of the Moon, [indicate] the nature of the thing.

[Chapter VIII.6: Questions of the 5th house]

[Having children with a specific person: Sahl][158]

1 Concerning the fifth house, such as on having children, consider thusly: if the lord of the east or the Moon applies to the lord of the fifth, or they are in the fifth, or the lord of the fifth [applies] to the lord of the east or more preferably is in the east, it generates the sweetest production of offspring. **2** A transfer [indicates] the same but more slowly, and [any planet] gathering counsel[159] [should be] cleansed of the infortunes. **3** And if any of these is retrograde or scorched, it conveys offspring that are going to last [only] a short time.

4 And a well-placed Jupiter, if he would regard the east, being free of corruption, [it is] well for him. **5** [But] Venus conjoined to the bad ones and the Moon applying to the bad ones deny the hope of offspring. **6** And a benevo-

---

[155] Reading with Hugo for *rōne* (*ratione?*).
[156] Hugo has the Moon regarding the bound of the twelfth-part, which is equally puzzling to me.
[157] See *On Hidden Things* §6, in *WSM*.
[158] See Sahl in *Judges* §5.1, or *On Questions* §5.1 (in *WSM*).
[159] That is, a planet accepting or receiving the application.

lent in the fifth denotes she is already[160] pregnant. **7** An infortune there, or[161] regarding it, speaks against [children].

[Having children generally in the future: Sahl][162]

8 And a fortune in the east, or with the lord of the east being in the east or tenth or fifth or seventh, with Jupiter being well placed, hastens [it]. **9** A malevolent in the east or regarding it perversely, or with the lord of the east being in a perverse place, and with Jupiter being averse, retrograde, or scorched, and in the eighth, it is a sign of broken[163] offspring, nor those who will remain long.

10 And a benevolent in the fifth hastens conception, a bad one delays and removes it.

11 And an eastern Jupiter [in a pivot] hastens, [but] western and in a pivot (even should the lord of the east be well placed), the conception will be with a delay.

[Will a pregnant woman miscarry: 'Umar][164]

12 And if the lord of the fifth is not retrograde nor scorched, nor descending nor unlucky from the tetragon or opposition or assembly, being received from a trigon or hexagon, the birth will be unharmed.

[Will a pregnant woman have twins: Sahl][165]

13 And [if] the east and fifth are double-bodied, and the Sun and Moon are in common [signs], she will give birth to twins; otherwise, only one.

---

[160] Reading *iam* with Hugo for *tam*.
[161] Reading *aut* with Hugo for *autem*.
[162] See Sahl in *Judges* §5.1, or *On Questions* §5.2 (in *WSM*).
[163] *Ruptae*; John's and Hugo's Sahl simply has "few" or a "scarcity" of them.
[164] See 'Umar in *Judges* §5.16.
[165] See Sahl in *Judges* §5.27, or *On Questions* §5.5 (in *WSM*).

[Will the child be male or female: Sahl][166]

14 Moreover, if the east and fifth are masculine, a male will be born, and vice-versa; and if one is masculine and the other feminine, the judgment should be directed according to the sign in which the Moon is. **15** And an eastern Mercury signifies a masculine [birth], western the contrary.

[Is he the child of his father: "Aristotle"][167]

16 Moreover, the one who is thought to be his father: [see] if Mars or Saturn or the Tail of the Dragon are not in the east or in the fifth, for if they *are* there, he is not the father.

[Will a woman have a child: "Aristotle"][168]

17 Whether a woman is going to have a child, is known thusly: if the ascending sign is Gemini, Leo, or Virgo, and the lord of the fifth is in any of these, she will have nothing[169] from the impregnation [unless][170] the lord of the fifth is with the lord of the first (and if not, not).

[Is a rumor true: 'Umar][171]

18 Rumors are true concerning what is sought, if the east and luminaries are free from the bad ones, and their lords in pivots or in those following [the pivots], invested with the fortunes.[172] **19** Which if they were less than [this], you will judge [them] more loosely; and if contrariwise, it will decline towards the contrary direction.[173]

---

[166] See Sahl in *Judges* §5.32, or *On Questions* §5.6 (in *WSM*).
[167] See "Aristotle" in *Judges* §5.39. It seems to me that this question might also be, "Am *I* the father of the unborn child?"
[168] See "Aristotle" in *Judges* §§5.5 and 5.13.
[169] Reading *nihil* for *numquam* ("never").
[170] Tentatively adding, replacing *si* ("if").
[171] See 'Umar in *Judges* §5.40.
[172] That is, "with" or "aspecting/looking at." In Arabic texts, mixtures between planets are sometimes thought of as one being dressed in the clothing of another.
[173] Namely, they will be false.

[Will a messenger reach his destination: al-Kindī][174]

20 The lord of the Ascendant and the Moon respond concerning a messenger, whether he would reach the desired place. **21** For if both or either is in the seventh, or they apply to the lord of the seventh, he has reached the intended place. **22** Also, being withdrawn from fortunes has conferred health[175] and opportunity on the journey; withdrawn from the infortunes, the contrary. **23** And this judgment is according to the strength and weakness of the fortunes and infortunes.

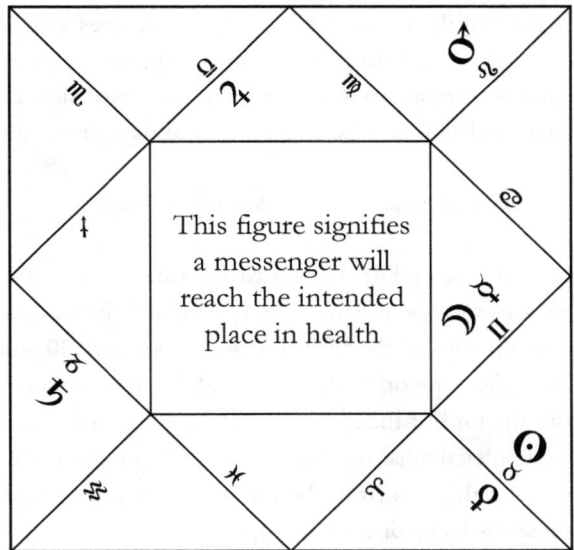

Figure 91: A figure showing that a messenger will arrive safely (Leopold)

[Whether someone is absent: Jirjis][176]

24 And if the lord of the east is in the east, one who is thought to be absent is in his own home; outside[177] the pivots, it means he is absent.

---

[174] See al-Kindī in *Judges* §5.48, or *Forty Chapters* §604.
[175] Reading *salutem* for *salutis*.
[176] See Jirjis in *Judges* §5.49.

[Will a messenger return: al-Kindī][178]

25 Also, he returns [from his journey] if each leader (or either one) is drawn back from[179] either the seventh or the pivots or withdraws from the lord of the seventh. **26** And if it applies with its own lord [while] it is drawn back from the pivots, [the same]. **27** Should it be mixed with[180] the infortunes, it speaks against the messenger [and his return].

[When will a messenger return: al-Kindī][181]

28 And the hour of the return is known by the degrees which are between the one who is applying and the one to whom it applies, according to whether the application is from a movable or common or fixed sign, and according to their quickness and slowness (whether hours or days or months or years).

[Will a legate return with money: ʿUmar][182]

29 And the east and its lord belong to the one sending [the legate], the seventh and its lord the one to whom he is sent, and likewise the Moon [for the legation] and the lord of the fifth [for the messenger]. **30** And the one of these which occupies a pivot, is the leader. **31** If therefore [the significator] withdraws from the lord of the seventh and[183] applies to the lord of the east, the legate has completed what has been imposed [upon him]. **32** And if, with this withdrawal, it withdraws from the lord of the house of money (whether the lord of the east is lucky or corrupted), he brings money with him. **33** Another judgment should not be given in the rest of the signs.

---

[177] Reading the rest of this sentence with Hugo, as Leopold seems to have jumbled the rest of the passage, partially omitting statements about the Midheaven and Ascendant (*et in eadem absens in succedente in medio*).
[178] See al-Kindī in *Judges* §5.51, or *Forty Chapters* §606.
[179] This probably means, "cadent from," i.e. in the cadent houses.
[180] Reading the subjunctive for *commiscetur*.
[181] See al-Kindī in *Judges* §5.52, or *Forty Chapters* §607.
[182] See ʿUmar in *Judges* §5.55.
[183] Reading with Hugo for "or."

[When will a legate return: Sahl/Māshā'allāh][184]

34 If the lord of the hour is stronger than the Moon, and is in the ascending half of the circle, the traveler will return in fewer hours than there are degrees between it and the Ascendant. **35** If the Moon is stronger than the lord of the hour, [then] if there are 13° between the Moon and the Ascendant, he will return within that many days. **36** If both are in the descending half, [give] a day for an hour, a month for a day.[185]

[When the rumored event will happen—Jirjis][186]

37 That which the rumor announces, will be within three days or elapsed hours of the day, if the lord of the east is in the east; in the Midheaven it portends hours; in the west, months; in the pivot of the earth, years.

[More on rumors and reports: Jirjis][187]

38 The quality of the rumors is known through the one from whom the Moon is being separated.
39 And the Moon regarding Mercury and applying to him (so that she is withdrawing from the lord of the seventh), signifies that the news is conveyed[188] in writing; if otherwise, the messenger will speak without writing.
40 And the one from whom Mercury is being separated, signifies the rumors as being good or bad.
41 And the number of lines of script is known by the number of the ascensions of the sign in which Mercury is.

---

[184] See Sahl's *On Times* §10 (in *WSM*).
[185] That is, while the units of time on the eastern side of the chart are measured in hours and days, those on the western side are measured in days and months.
[186] See Jirjis in *Judges* §5.45.
[187] See Jirjis in *Judges* §5.46.
[188] *Inferri*.

[More on rumors and reports: "Aristotle"][189]

42 And Saturn, Mars, or the Tail of the Dragon in the east signify lies; Jupiter, Venus, [or] the Head of the Dragon, truth.

[More on an absent person: pseudo-Ptolemy]

43 If[190] you were asked about an absent person, you should not judge death for him until you remove [the possibility] of drunkenness from him, nor should you say he was wounded until you remove [the possibility] of bloodletting, nor that money was acquired until you remove [the possibility] of money stolen.[191]

[Chapter VIII.7: Questions of the 6th house]

[On illness: Sahl][192]

1 Concerning the sixth house, such as on the status of one who is sick, consider thusly whether he would be freed: give the doctor to the east, the one who is sick to the tenth, the disease to the seventh, the medicine to the fourth. **2** And if an infortune is in the east, the doctor is not useful (and contrariwise). **3** If an infortune is in the tenth, the occasion of the disease is due to the sick person; if a fortune, good health [comes] from him. **4** If a bad one [is] in the seventh, he is changed from disease to disease, if a good one is in the seventh, he will be cured without any medicine. **5** If a bad one [is] in the fourth, once the medicine is introduced it will increase the pain; a lucky one in the same place, cures.

---

[189] See "Aristotle" in *Judges* §5.47.
[190] See the *Centiloquy*, Aph. 59.
[191] *Commissam.*
[192] See Sahl in *Judges* §6.1, and *On Questions* §6.1 (in *WSM*).

TREATISE VIII: ON INTERROGATIONS

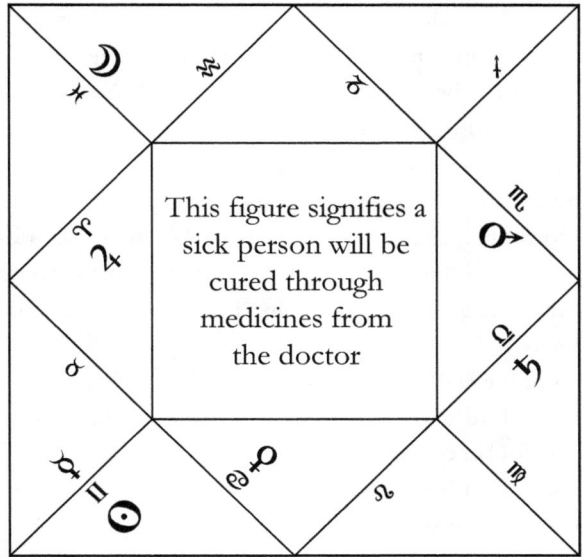

Figure 92: A figure showing that a sick person will be cured (Leopold)

6 And if the lord of the east and the Moon, or either of the planets, is in a pivot or regards the east, being safe, not scorched, certainly with the lord of the eighth being averse from the east, he will escape. **7** An application of either one with the benevolents does the same; this same benevolent being retrograde prolongs the illness but does not cancel the hope of good health. **8** And the Moon under the earth (from the second to the sixth), applying to a planet going out into the upper hemisphere, announces good health unless the star which gathers the counsel of the Moon[193] is scorched. **9** And if she applies [to one going] from the upper [hemisphere] to the lower one, it is fatal.

10 And if the Moon is waxing both in light and computation, and applies to the eastern lord (though it may even be staying under the earth), good health is near.

11 And an application of the Moon with a star in the eighth is fatal. **12** And the lord of the east applying to the lord of the eighth, if in addition the Moon is corrupted, signals death. **13** With the Moon even transferring the light from the lord of the east to the lord of the eighth, it is to be feared; and

---

[193] That is, the one to which she applies. Leopold has mixed up the roles of both planets in the sentence: reading *stella quae lunae legit consilium* for *stella cui luna legit consilium*.

the reception[194] of the Moon prolongs the disease. **14** And the eastern lord appearing in a pivot, applying to the lord of the eighth, does not kill until the lord of the eighth reaches the degree of the east. **15** And should the Moon transfer from the lord of the east to the lord of the eighth, and the eastern [lord] is falling or scorched, and the adverse [lord][195] occupies a pivot, it is deadly. **16** The lord of the eighth in the east, with the lord of the east and the Moon being corrupted, signals the same thing. **17** The same is if,[196] with the Moon being corrupted, the lord of the east would regard a malevolent in the eighth. **18** If the one gathering the counsel of the Moon is a malevolent, it repeats the disease.

19 The lord of the eighth staying in a pivot is to be feared.

20 The eastern lord under the earth, if it applies to the lord of the eighth appearing in the fourth or eighth, is a judgment of death.

21 The eastern lord being scorched within 12°, but not received, is fatal. **22** And if the lord of the east is of the heavier stars, not scorched, [and] does not apply [to any other star], and in addition the Moon is safe, it saves.

23 And if the sixth sign is of the convertible ones, it alternates the disease; a two-parted one changes it; a firm one preserves [him] in the same status.

24 And the Moon separated from a western star is a sign of having had the disease for a long time; from an eastern one, a recent disease.

---

[194] Reading *receptio* with Hugo and John, for *corruptio* ("corruption").
[195] Reading *adversus* for *aversus*. Leopold's Sahl is referring to the lord of the eighth.
[196] Omitting *aliqua malivola*. This sentence reads differently in Hugo. Hugo has a malefic regarding the lord of the east, *while* the lord of the east is in the eighth (and with the Moon being corrupted). Nevertheless the Arabic reads differently.

[The relation of the lunar mansions to disease: Unknown]

25 These are the lucky and unlucky mansions designating the limbs of the body:[197]

		Alburator, lucky. The head.	
Unlucky: *Azima*. The eye.		Lucky: *Azarpha*. [Al-Ṣarfah] The eye.
Unlucky: *Alhau*. The ear.		Unlucky: *Alanato*. [Al-Nathra?] The ear.
Unlucky: *Alothem*. The arm.[198]	Lucky: *Algebera*. [Al-Jabha?] The neck.	Lucky: *Azimeth*. [Al-Simāk] The arm.
Unlucky: *Aldebari*. [Al-Dabarān] The hand.		Lucky: *Algofra*. [Al-Ghafr] The hand.
Unlucky: *Alchoraie*. [Al-Thurayyā] The side.	Unlucky: *Altarff*. [Al-Ṭarf] The heart.	Unlucky: *Alichil*. [Al-Iklīl] The side.
Lucky: *Albuthan*. [Al-Buṭayn] The belly.		Unlucky: *Alkalb*. [Al-Qalb] The belly.
Unlucky: *Anathehel*. The kidneys.		Lucky: *Alfenila*. The kidneys.

---

[197] Compare with the list in Ch. I.2, **50**. Normally in medieval literature, there are 28 mansions, but this table lists only 27 (unless the double name for the hip in the left column is two mansions). I have included the correct names for the mansions I can identify, and suggested some others. The procedure here seems to be that the mansions were divided around #10, with the mansions from #10 onwards flowing down the right side of the body (or the right column), until about #23. Then, from #23 and circling back to the beginning, the mansions flow up the left side of the body (or the left column).
[198] *Humerus*, actually the shoulder. But this word can sometimes refer to the arm (Lat. *brachium*) as well.

Lucky: *Alhehit/ aldurach.* The hip.		Lucky: *Alnabaa.* [Al-Na'ā'im?] The hip.
Unlucky: *Albumabher.* [No limb given] [Al-Fargh al-Mu'akhkhar?]		
Unlucky: *Almudede.* [Al-Fargh al-Muqaddam?] The shin.		Lucky: *Albelda.* [al-Balda] The shin.
Lucky: *Alhabia.* [Sa'd al-Akhbiyah?] The foot.	Lucky: *Alvazre.* The house of life.	Unlucky: *Maldaboha.* [Sa'd al-Bula'?] The foot.
Lucky: *Azood.* [Sa'd al-Su'ūd?] The testicle.		Lucky: *Zadazeben.* The testicle.

Figure 93: Lunar mansions applied to the body (Leopold)

27 With[199] a question being proposed about an infirm person, see into which mansion the east of the preceding conjunction or prevention[200] falls. **28** Begin therefore from *Alvazre*, and see if the mansion which the Moon hold onto is more associated with the eastern [*degree?*]. **29** Count therefore from the house of life (which is *Alvazre*),[201] and consider if it is terminated in a lucky or unlucky mansion: for it denotes the cause of the disease which the limb deputed to it is suffering.[202] **30** Moreover, [see] whether the Moon is there or what mansion she holds onto, namely a lucky or unlucky one. **31** Likewise, note how the infortunes look at that mansion or the Moon: for if the malevolents happen to be found with [the mansion] or with the Moon, it is fatal; however, with the fortunate ones being interposed in a straight line (that is, with a sextile aspect),[203] the infirm person will return to his former

---

[199] The instructions from **27-36** are unfortunately very confusing, and seem typical of a Hugo of Santalla or Hermann of Carinthia (more interested in the fanciness of his style than in communicating information), as filtered through the wretched and compressed style of Leopold.
[200] That is, the most recent New or Full Moon.
[201] Note that Leopold has not told us exactly what we are counting.
[202] This does not quite seem right—perhaps Leopold's source means, "the mansion will show the part of the body in which the disease is."
[203] This seems to mean, "if benefics also aspect closely," so that they mitigate the malice of the malefics.

health. **32** However, if the Moon and that mansion do not travel together in the line of an equal bond, provided that any malevolent would be staying in that same bond with the Moon or mansion, it prolongs the evil; with the fortunate ones mediating in that same place, the pushing away of the illness will take place. **33** Again, an application of a malevolent made with the Moon and not with the mansion, denotes the illness as long-lasting; an application made with that mansion and not the Moon (provided that a fortunate Moon happens to be the mediator)[204] denotes that death is to be feared.

34 The advancement of the benevolents or Moon or a mansion[205] through a Node hastens good health, unless (as was stated above about the benevolents), any of the malevolents occupies the middle line between each: and thus in accordance with its nature and the quantity of its power and the proper quality of the mansion (to which limb it is ascribed), it worsens the limb and wounds the body.

35 In addition, there are certain mansions[206] which, if the malevolent stars are in them, they do not harm; benevolents in that same place do not help. **36** Therefore, observe these diligently [to see] of what kind they are: *Alhalva*,[207] *Achoiaie*,[208] and those configured with these, because the lines do not even touch each other.

[In what part of the body the patient suffers: al-Kindī and Jirjis][209]

37 The leader being corrupted above the earth signals that he suffers on the right side of the body; under the earth, on the left.

38 And, [a malevolent] traversing with the Sun weakens the right side, with the Moon the left. **39** At the beginning of a sign, the upper parts of the body; in the middle, the middle ones; at the end, it infects the lower parts. **40** And the [malevolent] leader in a diurnal sign [indicates it is in] the front parts;

---

[204] *Dummodo Luna fortunata mediatrix incidat*, meaning unclear.
[205] Reading *mansionis* for *mansioni*.
[206] I have greatly abbreviated this phrase (*quasdam subiectae formae esse mansiones*) and changed the case to the nominative, as I can think of no other way to make sense of what Leopold means.
[207] Possibly *Alhabia* (the foot in the left column of the table above).
[208] Or *Alchoraie* in the table above (the Pleiades).
[209] For **37** and **42** see al-Kindī in *Judges* §6.13 and 6.14, and *Forty Chapters* §618 and 620. For **38-40**, see Jirjis in *Judges* §6.14.

in a nocturnal one, in the rear ones. **41** He[210] suffers in that limb which is referred to the sixth sign.

42 Moreover, if the lord of the seventh makes the lord of the Ascendant fortunate, the doctor who is introduced is useful to the infirm person (and contrariwise).

[*Bloodletting, cupping, and surgery: al-Kindī*][211]

43 Bloodletting and cupping have this in common: that in both cases blood is drawn out. **44** For which, let the lord of the east and the Moon be put in airy or fiery signs, fortunate, in a pivot or after [one], in their own light, and let their lords be fortunate.

45 And in each [operation] let it be observed with the greatest diligence that the limb of the sign in which the lord of the Ascendant or the Moon is, never be wounded by iron: such that Aries has the head, Taurus the neck, Gemini the arms[212] and hands, Cancer the chest, Leo the stomach and vital organs and what is adjacent to them, Virgo the loins and ribs and sides, Libra the hips[213] and what is adjacent to these, Scorpio the rod,[214] bladder, and [those] regions, Sagittarius the testicles [and] colon, Capricorn the thighs and knees, Aquarius the shins, Pisces the feet.

46 And in the purging of blood the earthy[215] [signs] should be preferred, so that the lord of the Ascendant and the Moon should be put in them. **46** In the purging of choler,[216] prefer the watery to the airy and fiery. **47** If melancholy,[217] [prefer] the airy to the fiery. **48** If you want to purge phlegm, choose the fiery.

49 And let the lord of the Ascendant and the Moon be deprived of the companionship of the lord of the eighth, and [let the lord of the eighth be] estranged[218] from a pivot. **50** And it is best if the lord of the Midheaven is

---

[210] This sentence does not appear in Jirjis.
[211] See al-Kindī in *Judges* §§6.29-30, and *Forty Chapters* §§626-34.
[212] Again, this particularly denotes the shoulders (*humeros*).
[213] Reading *coxas* for *suras* ("calves").
[214] *Virga*, Latin slang for "penis." This should be understood as the genitals of either sex.
[215] Reading with al-Rijāl for Hugo's (and Leopold's) "airy." In this paragraph, the humor to be purged is contrasted with an element of a contrasting type: choler and fire are contrasted with phlegm and water, and blood and air are contrasted with black bile and earth.
[216] That is, yellow bile.
[217] That is, black bile.
[218] Reading *alienus* for *alieno*. Reading from Hugo, this means that it should not be in a pivot; Leopold has omitted the part of the sentence that makes the lord of the eighth also

lucky [and] regards the Moon or the lord of the Ascendant. **51** And the Moon or lord of the Ascendant should in no way be in the fourth.

52 And in bloodletting, choose the prior half of the month; in cupping the end of the month [after] the opposition of the Sun and Moon.

53 For surgery, observe [the procedure] as above with respect to the limb and sign. **54** And the lord of the Ascendant or the Moon should not fall from the pivots, nor should they be scorched nor retrograde, [but] they should be in a pivot: the lord of the Ascendant in the Ascendant or Midheaven, the Moon in the tenth or seventh, and both (namely the lord of the Ascendant and the Moon) should be strong and without the infortunes. **55** And let the lord of the sixth be weak.

[Critical days: Sahl][219]

56 "Critical" or declarative days are those in which a determination of diseases to the good or bad comes to be, and they are computed from the hour of taking to bed[220] or from the hour of the question: and they are [days] 7, 14, 21, and 28. **57** For in each of these, if the Moon applies to fortunate ones or is looked at by them, it will be a sign of good health (and contrariwise).

58 However,[221] the medicinal month according to Galen has 26 days, 22 hours: whence they grant 6 days and 17.5 hours to individual quarters for the crisis. **59** Because the third crisis comes to be after 20 days and 4 hours and 30 minutes of an hour (which is a half-hour).[222]

[Laxatives and purgatives: al-Kindī][223]

60 Take a [laxative] potion when the Moon is in the last[224] half of Libra or first one of Scorpio. **61** And her lord should be fortunate and strong, eastern,

---

be estranged from (in aversion to) the lords of both the lord of the Ascendant and of the Moon.
[219] See Sahl in *Judges* §6.19 and *On Questions* §6.2.
[220] Also known as a "decumbiture" chart, from the Lat. *decumbo*, "to take to bed."
[221] This paragraph seems to be Leopold's own.
[222] I do not know why Galen's month is only 26.916 days, but it may have to do with the visibility of the Moon. Regardless, this number divided by four quarters yields 6.729 days per quarter, which means the third crisis will happen after 20.1875 days, as Leopold says.
[223] See al-Kindī in *Judges* §6.29, and *Forty Chapters* §§635-38.
[224] Reading with Hugo for "figure" (*figura*). This region is one version of the so-called *via combusta* or "burned path."

and in a pivot, and the one by which it is made fortunate eastern and in a pivot. **62** And likewise the lord of the Ascendant. **63** And the infortunes should be remote or falling from the pivots. **64** And if the [lord of] the Moon is unlucky, let it regard her from a trigon [or hexagon].[225]

65 And in addition, let any fortune be put in the sign whose limb is to be cured,[226] and let the lord of the Ascendant[227] be situated as the lord of the Moon is.

66 And beware lest any leader be put in the sign of [an animal] chewing the cud, because the potion would be vomited up—but this *is* valuable in purgation through the upper parts, provided that the signs and leaders are made fortunate as before (that is, the leaders should not be falling nor should they be unfortunate).

67 And the lord of the house of death should not be in a pivot, nor should the leaders participate with him.

[The hour of health and death: ʿUmar][228]

68 The hour of health is when the lord of the east reaches its own house or sovereignty, or when it goes more quickly in a direct course, with the lord of the house of death falling away from it: for that hour introduces health. **69** The hour of death is certain when the lord of the east and the lord of the eighth are conjoined by body or the square aspect or opposite: for then he would in no way be able to avoid death.

[On urine: Unknown]

70 The sage likewise judges concerning urine not seen, and by the nature of the cause and the departure of the disease. **71** For it is known that the urine is cooked and colored[229] in the liver, and the fifth house signals the liver.

---

[225] Adding bracketed material with Hugo and al-Rijāl.
[226] That is, a particular limb or organ supposed to be purged by a potion.
[227] Reading with Hugo, but al-Rijāl only has the fourth.
[228] See ʿUmar in *Judges* §6.3.
[229] Reading *coloratur* for *colatur*.

72 Therefore, once the urine is presented by its owner or by another who brings it out of a sense of responsibility,[230] the east is taken as the Ascendant of the infirm person, and the liver is judged by means of the fifth house from the Ascendant. **73** But if the brother brought it, the third house from the Ascendant is the Ascendant of the owner of the urine, and the victor of the fifth house [from that], which is the seventh from the Ascendant, signifies the liver. **74** And if a slave brought it, the tenth[231] will be the Ascendant, and the second from the Ascendant the place of the liver, and so on.

75 With[232] the figure organized thusly, take the victor (the recognition of which is had as in the introductory parts):[233] it is disclosed by the dignities of the house or exaltation or bound or triplicity or face, moreover by the strength or regard of the houses. **76** For the first house has 12 dignities, the tenth 11, the seventh 10, the eleventh 9, from thence the fifth, fourth, ninth, third,[234] eighth, twelfth, sixth, always by subtracting [one point] up to 1. **77** This therefore is the victor or leader which obtains more dignities in these: consider it through the whole circle. **78** For the one which is more worthy in dignities, more powerful in strength, [and] more blessed by regard, [is the victor]: and in this, more worthiness or strength wins out over the advantageousness of the places.[235]

79 Once [the victor] is known, see who is being separated from it, or from which one it itself [is separating]: for the soundness or illness of the owner of the urine will be had according to its status, and according to the sixth: the one which has victory in this, corrupting this victor, makes clear the nature

---

[230] Or perhaps, "piety" or "devotion" (*ex pietate*). This seems to mean, "by the patient himself" or someone specifically sent by him, so that the patient it initiating the consultation.
[231] The idea here is that the tenth means "the master," even though slavery is normally a sixth-house relationship.
[232] The victor in this paragraph seems to be taken by adding up the dignities of all planets in their places, and then seeing which of the highest-scoring planets is in a house with the most points. For more on this type of procedure, see *Search* and my audio workshop on victors, at www.bendykes.com.
[233] See for example Ch. IV.1, **120**.
[234] I believe the second should come after this.
[235] That is, being dignified and otherwise strengthened by planetary condition (such as being aspected by benefics, eastern, etc.) is more important than house points. For more on the advantageous or busy places, see *ITA* III.3-4.

of the disease; and its domicile looked at by it [makes clear] the cause.[236] **80** And the place of the victor of the disease reveals the foundation [of it].[237]

81 For with [the victor] ascending, the head suffers, and thus with respect to the other houses.[238] **82** Which if it is solitary, [that planet alone indicates] the nature of the disease, and that house of it which is more strongly looked at denotes the occasion [for the disease], and its place [denotes] the place of the suffering. **83** But the one to which the victor applies, or that one to it, announces hope or fear according to [it being] a fortune or infortune.

84 Then, see the leader of the liver (namely, which lord of the fifth, the place of the liver, is more worthy and stronger, and better in place in the circle), and [the significator] over the place of Jupiter and Mars and Venus, and over the Lot of the liver (which is taken in the day and night from Jupiter to Mars and is projected from Venus).[239] **85** Once it is had, one must see who is being separated from it, or from whom it [is being separated]: because the status and tenor of the liver's virtues are according it (and likewise the stomach). **86** Which if it is solitary, [judge] according to the nature of it and the portion[240] of its place.

87 Judge according to the condition[241] of the whole body, which the victor over the Ascendant shows. **88** And judge according to the condition[242] of the liver, from what is contained in the urine: namely,[243] if the retentive virtue was weak (the expulsive [virtue] expelling it), a retention of the humors will occur in the urine, and it will appear to be excessively cooked. **89** How-

---

[236] That is, see which of its own domiciles the planet indicating the disease, aspects: that sign will indicate something about the cause. Leopold offers an example in **115** below.

[237] By the "cause" of the disease, the author may mean the physical cause, such as the imbalance of a particular humor, while the "foundation" (*fundamentum*) may reveal something like the external source of the disease—a brother, or animals, etc. But this is only my conjecture.

[238] That is, the victor in the second means the neck, the third the shoulders and arms, and so on.

[239] It is unclear to me exactly how this victor is supposed to be calculated, with all of these places.

[240] This probably means "degree."

[241] *Consistentiam*.

[242] *Consistentiam*.

[243] From here through the end of the paragraph, my translation is somewhat speculative. In a technical situation like this (which requires real precision in expression), Leopold's habit of condensing and abbreviating his source texts really does us a disservice. The text reads: **88** ...*scilicet si virtus contenta claudicans fuerit expulsiva ipsam expellens accidit in urina contentum de humoribus et ipsam nimis coctam apparere.* **89** *Econtra autem in his virtutibus facta : tenuior est urina et contentis carens.* **90** *Si autem digestiva estu excessit in naturali et separata claudicat erit urina livida et turbata : econtra vero temperata erit in colore substantia limpida.*

ever, it being made to the contrary in these virtues, the urine is thin and free of contents. **90** If however the digestive [virtue] was excessive in natural heat and deficient in the separative [virtue], the urine will be livid[244] and muddy; but contrariwise, if temperate it will be clear in color [and] substance.

Virtue	Humor	Planet	Function
Digestion	Blood/Air	♃	Digests & processes nourishment.
Attraction	Choler/Fire	♀	Heats, enables distribution of nourishment.
Retention	Black bile/Earth	♄	Retains nourishment; density & tissue strength.
Expulsion	Phlegm/Water	☽	Expels excrement & toxins.

Figure 94: Humoral virtues, planets, & functions (Dykes, after Saunders 1677)

91 And you know how the virtues are attributed to the planets, such as the appetitive to Venus, and so on, and the expulsive to the Moon. **92** Whence, whichever one of these is mixing itself more strongly with the place of the liver, the virtue of this one prevails. **93** If a lucky one, it will work naturally in nature, unnaturally if corrupted; [and] with none of these looking [at it], the virtue of the lord of the bound will prevail.

94 Thus comes to be the consideration that there should be a comparison[245] between the victor of the Ascendant and that of the fifth, and between [their] virtues, so that a discerning judgment may proceed by means of all things. **95** And understand this to be more for the healthy than for the sick: for the sick, the place of the liver along with the admixture of the victor (or the place alone, if it does not have a victor), or the planet which is in the place of the liver, or the nature of the place [itself], plainly shows the color and substance.

96 The four humors correspond to the triplicities (which are four): choler to the fiery, blood to the airy, phlegm to the watery, melancholy to the earthy. **97** And the essence of the humors remains natural and unchanged, following this essence of the signs. **98** For their commixture or staining of

---

[244] *Livida*, a dark greyish.
[245] *Collatio*.

one another, or the tension of qualities, is from the planet which is in the place of the liver or looks at it. **99** And a natural commixture comes to be if it is a partner[246] of the place, tension if it lacks testimony. **100** Saturn is implied in melancholy, Jupiter blood, Mars and the Sun choler,[247] the Moon and Venus phlegm; Mercury is commixed according to application or according to separation with another bearing upon him.

101 Also, if Aries is the place of the liver, and Mars is there or looks at it, the disposition of the body is that of fever, and the substance of the urine mediocre on account of the weakness of the separating virtue in the liver, in a livid color or somewhat tending to blackness from the choleric burning. **102** But if the disposition of the body were sound, the urine will be thin throughout and reddish, or an intense[248] urine on the verge of[249] fever.

103 Moreover, if the place of the liver is Capricorn, and Saturn is there or looks at it, the body is feverish and the urine is livid, with blackness from mortification, with mediocre substance from the admixture of the thicker humors on account of the weakness of the separating virtue in the liver. **104** And if the body is sound, the color or urine will be thinner, with a citrine-lead [color].

105 Likewise, if the place of the liver is Pisces, and Jupiter looks at it from Capricorn, the disposition of the body is one of fever: this is a commixture of cold blood on account of Capricorn, and of phlegm on account of Pisces (and Cancer is a sweet phlegm): and then the urine is a little dense with a red color. **106** But if the body is sound, the urine is like citrine or golden in color, with a mediocre substance. **107** If Mars is there, the phlegm will become salty by mixture; if the Sun, the color of the urine is red on account of [his] staining, with a mediocre substance.

108 If the disposition is fit, [the color is] yellowish bordering on pale: therefore, if it is sound, which humor abounds is according to the present disposition of the body, and the natures of the signs and stars, and the tension or relaxation of the disposition is found; and let the judgment be according to every comparison of them.[250]

---

[246] Here one should understand, "lord," i.e., having some dignity there.
[247] Reading *colerae* for *calore* ("heat"). Note the tension between Mars and the Sun for choler, and Venus as the indicator for the choleric, attractive faculty above.
[248] I take this to be a more concentrated color.
[249] *Cum apparatu ad.*
[250] Or rather, "a comparison of all of them."

TREATISE VIII: ON INTERROGATIONS

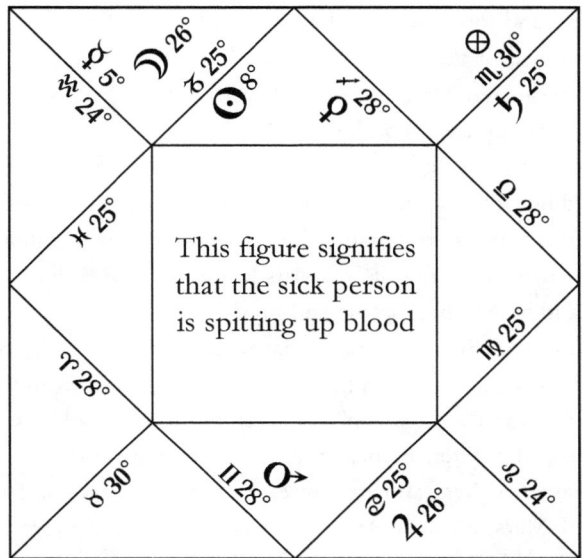

Figure 95: A figure showing that a sick person is spitting up blood (Leopold)[251]

109 This is an example of all of the aforesaid. **110** The Ascendant was 25° Pisces, Venus 28° Sagittarius, the Sun 8° Capricorn, the Moon 26°, Mercury 5° Aquarius, Mars 28° Gemini, Saturn 25° Scorpio, Jupiter 26° Cancer, the Lot of the liver 30° in Scorpio.[252] **111** Therefore, Venus was the victor over the Ascendant, Jupiter the victor over the place of the liver. **112** Therefore the leader of the liver signifies that bloody phlegm abounds, for Jupiter denotes blood, Cancer phlegm. **113** And on account of Mars corrupting the Ascendant, [it means] the present disposition is sick. **114** In substance the urine was somewhat condensed, on account of the commixture of Mars in the Ascendant and the Moon in the place of the liver.[253] **115** And because

---

[251] This chart can tentatively be dated to about January 7, 1220 AD, JC (or January 14, 1220 AD, GC). But apart from the usual small errors in planetary positions, the Sun would have been at about 23° Capricorn, not 8°. Also, there seems to be some confusion between the values of some planets like Mars and Venus, and the degrees of some cusps (such as the MC-IC, or the second and eighth).

[252] Recall (**84**) that this Lot is calculated (by day at least, if not by night) from Jupiter to Mars and projected from Venus. It is designated here by the symbol for the Lot of Fortune.

[253] Leopold may mean that Mars is closely aspecting the degree of the Ascendant, and the Moon closely aspects both the cusp of the fifth and Jupiter in it.

Mars corrupts, and looks at Aries better than he does Scorpio,[254] it was certain that the cause of the illness was from hotness and dryness in the head: for Aries likewise signifies the head. **116** And because Mars is in the fourth house, which has the chest and lungs and whatever wounds the chest inside, it was certain that he suffered around the lungs. **117** And because Mars signifies the shedding of blood, it was certain that the sufferer was spitting blood. **118** Also, Venus was entering under the rays towards the burning of the Sun: it was certain that he would die towards 2 months and 8 days—and it happened thus, and he was hemoptoic and ptysic.[255]

119 The house of Saturn signifies that what is feared will be by reason of coldness and moisture, such as a flowing of expectoration from the belly, and particularly if it was Capricorn; if Aquarius, because of coldness and winds. **120** The house of Jupiter, namely Sagittarius, by reason of heat and winds; Pisces, by reason of heat and moisture, such as abscesses and the like. **121** The house of Mars, such as Aries, [means] this will be more in the head; Scorpio is heat with moisture, and there will be suffering in the lower parts. **122** The house of the Sun, by reason of heat and dryness, and more so if the Sun was made unfortunate by Mars. **123** The house of Venus, by means of medicines and poisons, and what happens will be festive: and if it is Taurus, it will be because of coldness and dryness, and because of beasts; and if it is Libra, through heat and moisture, and in connection with pains of the throat, especially if Venus is in Aries. **124** The house of Mercury, such as Gemini, by reason of heat and moisture and pain in the liver, and madness, and the loss of one's senses; if Virgo, by reason of the destruction of the liver, gallbladder, and viscera. **125** The house of the Moon, by reason of coldness and moisture—and commingle the planets joining in with her, and judge according to that: for if the planets joining in with her match the aforesaid, the judgement will be more certain (and with these, the aspects are even observed).

126 Regard the sixth of the ill person by means of the victor: from whom is it being separated, or which is separating from it.

---

[254] Mars looks at his own house, Aries, from a sextile; but he is in aversion to Scorpio.

[255] That is, "coughing up blood" and "expectorating," respectively (*emoptoicus et ptisicus*). The time frame here may be when Venus actually reached the 7° or 7.5° limit of being burned by the Sun's rays (and not just merely being under them): this did indeed happen about 2 months and 8 days later.

[On slaves and captives: Sahl][256]

127 Concerning a slave or captive, if the lord of the Ascendant or the Moon (and this [means] the stronger one) is being separated from the lord of the Midheaven or from the Sun or from the infortunes, and it applies to none of these, the slave or captive will be freed.

[On slaves and captives: 'Umar][257]

128 And the lord of the east or the Moon (or the majority of them) being in a firm sign, detains [the slave from leaving], and more so in a pivot of the house of the east. **129** And the [lord of the east and the][258] Moon being in the east, and the lord[259] of the Moon and the Moon in a convertible [sign], being drawn back or falling, hasten his departure. **130** The stated leaders (or many) in common [signs] do the same thing;[260] [if] otherwise, speak otherwise.

[On captives: al-Kindī][261]

131 And observe the hour in which someone captured, is led [into captivity]: if then the lord of the Ascendant or the Moon (the stronger one in the Ascendant, I say, or the question) withdraws from an infortune or the lord of the twelfth or sixth or eighth and applies to fortunes, it signals freedom and good health. **132** The leaders being withdrawn from the pivots do the same thing.

---

[256] See Sahl in *Judges* §6.30, and *On Questions* §6.4.
[257] See 'Umar in *Judges* §6.31.
[258] Adding with Hugo.
[259] Reading *dominus* for *domus*, with Hugo.
[260] But Hugo's text points out that common signs can also indicate a change of affairs, or going from one type of captivity to another, or simply a middling time-period for the captivity.
[261] See *Forty Chapters* Ch. 23.1, and *Judges* §6.34.

[Whether a captive would be killed: 'Umar][262]

133 And observe if the leader applies to Mars from the square or opposite or assembly, or to the Lot of the crucified (which is called the Lot of death)[263] or its lord. **134** And if Mars or the Lot of the crucified or its lord is in the Midheaven, and the leader (being in Gemini or its triplicity) applies [to them], he will be hanged; and otherwise it is not to be feared.

[Buying a slave: Sahl][264]

135 And buy a slave when the lord of the east and the Moon applies to the lord of the sixth, [with them being] in the sixth, or [if] the lord of the sixth is in the east, or if there is a transfer of light between them.

[Whether the querent will be captured: "Aristotle"][265]

136 And the lord of the east being in the twelfth (or vice-versa) signals that the one seeking is going to be captured without a doubt. **137** For the lord of a falling [place] and [its] point are places of foreign travel and misery.[266]

---

[262] See 'Umar in *Judges* §6.48.

[263] In *Judges* §6.47, 'Umar defines this as being from the Moon to Saturn, and projected from the degree of the sixth (i.e., in quadrant houses). If this were a Lot of death, it should probably use the eighth house; but there we are discussing torture and imprisonment, which belongs to the sixth.

[264] See Sahl in *Judges* §6.59, and *On Questions* §6.8.

[265] See "Aristotle" in *Judges* §6.67.

[266] This sentence is not in "Aristotle." By "point" (*punctum*) I take Leopold to mean a house cusp. While all four of the falling or cadent places are sometimes said to pertain to travel, it is also true that the ninth and the third do so specifically, while the sixth and twelfth have to do with kinds of misery.

[Chapter VIII.8: Questions of the 7th house]

[Whether one would be married: Sahl and 'Umar][267]

1 On the seventh house, such as concerning a marriage union, whether it would come to be. **2** It is known thusly: if the lord of the east and the Moon (which belong to the one seeking) apply to the lord of the seventh, or either one is in the seventh, it will come to be with the effort of the one seeking; if conversely, it will be with the effort of the other party. **3** And if there is a transfer between them, it will be arranged by messengers. **4** And an application by good aspects signal that it will come to be without difficulty, by bad ones with difficulty.

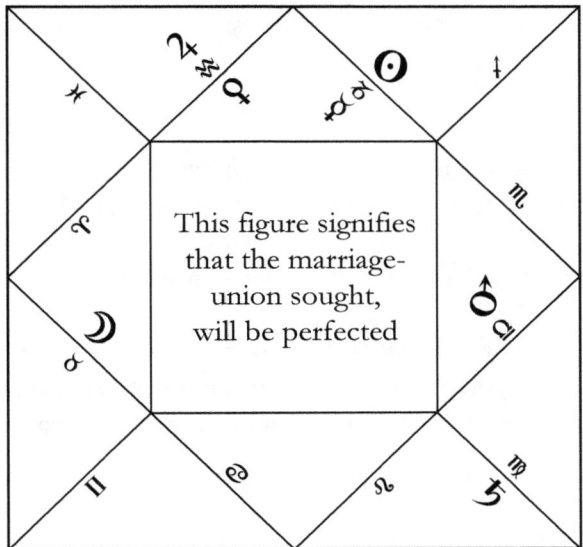

Figure 96: A figure showing that a marriage-union will be perfected (Leopold)[268]

---

[267] See Sahl in *Judges* §7.1 (or *On Questions* §7.1, in *WSM*), and 'Umar in *Judges* §7.2.
[268] This can tentatively be dated, in the Fagan-Bradley sidereal zodiac, to about January 8, 1275 AD JC (or January 15, GC). My Sun symbol replaces Leopold's upside-down Venus symbol in the same place.

[Whether one would be married: 'Umar][269]

5 Moreover, the Lot of marriage-union is taken from the degree of the seventh to the degree of its lord, and once the degrees of the east have been added on, it is projected from the beginning of the rising sign. **6** And [if] the degree of the Lot and its lord is in the east or seventh, or at least with the Sun and Venus, or if the lord of the Lot regards the eastern or seventh house, and if there is a collection or translation, they will be furnished with the womanly endowment of the marriage-bed.[270] **7** And if there is nothing of the aforesaid, either it will not come to be or will be quickly broken up. **8** And an application of the lord of the Ascendant and of the lord of the seventh in the pivots or after the pivots, consecrates a marriage-union. **9** An application of the Moon with Venus, and she being received by Venus, [indicates] the same; the Sun being received, regarded by his own lord, the same.

[Whether the fiancée is beautiful: al-Kindī][271]

10 And [as for] whether the fiancée is beautiful, look through the signs just as the limbs [of the body] are deputed to them (the head through the Ascendant, and so on), and with what sign the Moon is, not corrupted: it signifies beauty in its limb. **11** And the one in which she is corrupted, spoils it.

12 And the increase of the Moon signifies something in the body that is beyond proper proportion,[272] decreasing that it is less [than that].

13 And the signs in which fortunate [planets] are, commend [those] limbs (and conversely).

---

[269] See 'Umar in *Judges* §7.2.
[270] In other words, the querent will be married; whether he does this out of over-excitement or literary boredom, these typical phrasings by Hugo of Santalla on the topic of marriage are rather obnoxious. See also **16** below.
[271] See al-Kindī in *Judges* §7.15, or *Forty Chapters* §526-28, and 532.
[272] Or, "measure" (*modum*).

*[Who will die first: Jirjis]*²⁷³

14 And if the lord of the east enters into burning first, the man will die first; if that of the seventh, speak to the contrary.

15 And²⁷⁴ the one whose significator has an application with the lord of the eighth, will die first.

*[The woman's sexual experience: "Aristotle"]*²⁷⁵

16 And the one with whom the woman has committed adultery, is known thusly: if the Ascendant belongs to Mars or Saturn, and the Moon is acknowledged there (and [therefore] the light of the candle²⁷⁶ was there), if [it is] in the hour of Venus, [she is] plump and young. **17** And if Venus and the Moon are in the house of Mars and in the diameter of the Midheaven, she is menstruous.²⁷⁷ **18** If Venus was in her own house, he has [already] known his own wife. **19** If Gemini is rising and the Moon is there, she is pregnant. **20** If Venus is in the east and Saturn in the seventh, she has had one dependent on her.

---

²⁷³ See Jirjis in *Judges* §7.28.
²⁷⁴ Source unknown at this time.
²⁷⁵ See "Aristotle" in *Judges* §7.21. This question is a confused mixture of information about sexual experience and overall age and condition. Nevertheless, Leopold's wording departs from it in so many ways it is worth repeating Hugo's Aristotle here: "In order that this may be discovered, the east should be noticed. For, Aries or Scorpio being in the east, or Aquarius or Capricorn, while Venus should happen to be staying in one of these, reveals a young girl. Moreover, with Mercury occupying one of these, while the Moon would go through any of them (it being the east), it testifies that the light of the candle was not absent. This being done at the seventh hour (which belongs to Venus), it is clear that she was chubby and fair and a young girl. But if Venus were together with the Moon, and she is oppressed by [some] power. Moreover, Venus with the Moon in a domicile of Mars: she had really reached menstruation. Should Taurus or Libra be setting, with Venus lingering there, [it means] he has been acquainted with his wife. With the sign of Gemini arising, he knew her once; with the Moon lingering in her own proper house, she has become pregnant. If Venus would possess the east with the [Head of the] Dragon, it testifies she is noble and of good stock. But if she would be staying with Saturn in the west, it testifies she was someone dependent on him and of a lower rank."
²⁷⁶ The "candle" probably refers to the Moon, especially since the Moon herself naturally signifies marriage and the wife.
²⁷⁷ That is, she is already menstruating.

[Lawsuits: Sahl][278]

21 Concerning a legal case or controversy, judge thusly: give the east and its lord to the one seeking, the seventh and its lord to the adversary. **22** If they each apply to each other benignly, they will make peace; if malignly, not. **23** And if they were together in the same sign, they will make peace by themselves. **24** And if there is a transfer between those leaders, there will be peace between them by means of intermediaries.

[Significators in lawsuits: 'Umar][279]

24 The Midheaven and its lord determine what will happen between them. **25** The fourth and its lord [indicate] the end of the matter. **26** And the star from which the Moon is being separated signifies the one accusing, and the one to whom she applies, the one defending. **27** And the lord of the Moon is the leader of the end. **28** And the second and its lord aid the one accusing, [the eighth and its lord] the one defending. **29** And the tenth holds onto the judge.

[Who will win: "Dorotheus"/others][280]

30 And the judge is contrary to that party whose significator the lord of the Midheaven corrupts; and the one whose significators are stronger, will win.

[Who will win: "Aristotle"][281]

31 For a hostile negotiation,[282] if the lord of the east is in an angle (wherever [it is]), and the lord of the seventh is in the seventh or fourth or tenth from the seventh, both are strong, and neither will win. **32** If the lord of the first is in a falling [place], the one seeking will lose, and thus if the lord of the seventh is in the said place; if the contrary, say the contrary. **33** And if the

---

[278] See Sahl in *Judges* §7.37, or *On Questions* §7.8 (in *WSM*).
[279] See 'Umar in *Judges* §7.38.
[280] See "Dorotheus" in *Judges* §7.41, and others from §7.40-46.
[281] See *Judges* §7.47.
[282] *Pro placito*.

lord of the first is in a falling [place], that one will win who has more fear; speak thusly about the seventh.

[On business deals: 'Umar]²⁸³

34 Concerning business deals and trade, you should know that the Moon is in charge of them, whence she should be chosen and she should then be waxing and ascend to the north (namely from the east to the tenth).²⁸⁴ **35** From thence to the seventh, every business deal will be useful and advantageous (and understand [her to be] increasing in number and light). **36** And if the aforesaid were to the contrary, speak to the contrary. **37** And let Mercury likewise be made fortunate, and let the application of the Moon be good, and the aspect good.

[On business deals: al-Khayyāt]²⁸⁵

38 And the buyer has the east, the seller the seventh: whence, [if] its lord applies to the lord of the other, he will pursue the business deal more.

39 A benevolent in the east signifies a good buyer, likewise in the seventh; an infortune, the contrary.

40 The profit depends on the Midheaven.

41 (Certain people even give the seller to the east, the buyer to the seventh, and this is a difference according to whether one seeks the other.)²⁸⁶

42 And the star from which the Moon is being separated entering into burning, signifies death for the buyer before the price is accepted.

[On prices: 'Umar]²⁸⁷

43 Concerning things for sale, judge by means of the luminaries: therefore, in individual months know their conjunction beforehand, and the

---

²⁸³ See 'Umar in *Judges* §7.57.
²⁸⁴ I believe this means she should be rising in northern ecliptical latitude as well as being in this quadrant.
²⁸⁵ See al-Khayyāt in *Judges* §7.58.
²⁸⁶ This is a nice reminder by Leopold that the Ascendant denotes the person who is initiating and seeking the matter—we should not always give the Ascendant to the buyer.
²⁸⁷ See 'Umar in *Judges* §7.65.

Ascendant of the conjunction and its lord. **44** For these, being strong and fortunate, make the things deputed to them expensive.

45 On this question, Thābit the Egyptian resembled the philosophers of Egypt in his time, and agreed with them thusly, that they put the conjunction of the Sun and Moon as generating the renewal of all worldly thing, but their opposition as the cause of the alteration and variation of all things. **46** They said the Moon was the beginning of all transitory things (planets and animals and metals), [and of their] increase and diminishment. **47** From that, they applied the Sun as what gives the assembly[288] and opposition of the Moon.

48 And they judged with respect to things for sale according to the bearing of these [two luminaries] and the other planets, considering through the years and months that if the planets were fortunate, the things deputed to them are made expensive (and conversely).

[On prices: al-Kindī][289]

49 And they used to observe the conjunction or prevention which preceded the Sun's entrance into Aries, and the victor at that hour. **50** For if [the victor] was adding or applying to an adding [planet], the price of things for sale became expensive according to the nature of the sign in which it was. **51** And the good ones in the pivots [also increase the price], likewise the bad ones the contrary.

52 The Sun and Moon in a pivot [make] coin expensive, the Sun gold, the Moon silver; attributed Venus to the Moon in this, Mercury to the Sun. **53** Whence, these falling from the pivots make gold and silver cheap. **54** Moreover, the lord of the Ascendant and the lord of the assembly being in the pivots make things expensive, and conversely.

[Fugitives: Sahl][290]

55 Concerning a lost or runaway thing, as to whether it would be recovered, it is valuable to know the Ascendant and its lord, along with the Sun—give [them] to the one seeking; give the seventh and its lord, and the Moon, to what is lost. **56** If in particular the lord of the east applies to the lord of

---

[288] Reading *conventum* for *ortum* ("arising," which I suppose could refer to the New Moon as it comes out of the Sun's rays).
[289] See al-Kindī in *Judges* §7.66, and *Forty Chapters* §662-67.
[290] See Sahl in *Judges* §7.72, and *On Questions* §7.10.

the seventh, the one seeking will recover [it] through his own effort; it is the same if the lord of the east is in the seventh. **57** Moreover, if the Moon, being separated from the lord of the east, applies to the leader (that is, the lord) of the seventh, it announces the rumors about the lost thing are true;[291] if to the contrary, it is restored to his possession. **58** Moreover, if the lord of the seventh applies to the eastern lord, or if it is in the east, he will recover it without labor, and [a fugitive] will return on his own.

59 Likewise, if the leader applies to a malevolent appearing in a pivot, the one fleeing will fall into foreign fetters.[292] **60** Moreover, if either of the luminaries applies to the leader, the fugitive will not be able to be hidden. **61** Likewise, if the leader is scorched, the fugitive will be caught, especially if the lord of the east regards it. **62** Moreover, the Moon applying to a malevolent prepares a cell for the fugitive, and if she applies to a benevolent it promises escape—unless it[293] is perhaps entering into scorching or if it is retrograde or corrupt; and being scorched signifies death. **63** And if in addition it was corrupted otherwise [in addition to scorching], even after his death revenge will be taken on his corpse.

64 Moreover, an application of the Moon to the Sun denies escape. **65** Again, the Moon applying to a retrograde [planet] brings the fugitive back on his own. **66** Likewise, the Moon applying to a star in a pivot or after one, signifies that the path of the fugitive is impeded.[294] **67** If it is in the first station, the fleeing one is led back, severely ruined; if in the second station, he is caught as was already set forth, but cannot be held for long. **68** And if it is a malevolent with whom the Moon applies, and it is direct, he is led back without severe ruin. **69** Again, a scorched Moon applying to Mars gives burning [to the fugitive], if Saturn the dangers of waters. **70** A benevolent wholly frees [him].

---

[291] Namely, that the thing or person *is* lost and gone away, because the Moon is transferring the light from the owner (who signifies possession and ownership) to the thing (fleeing, missing).
[292] Or, the ownership of someone else (*aliena*).
[293] Leopold reads this as the feminine, as though it is the Moon; but I take it to be the significator of the fugitive.
[294] Reading *quod via fugientis impeditur*, more logically and with Hugo for *quod fugiens viam impedit* ("that the one fleeing will impede the path/way").

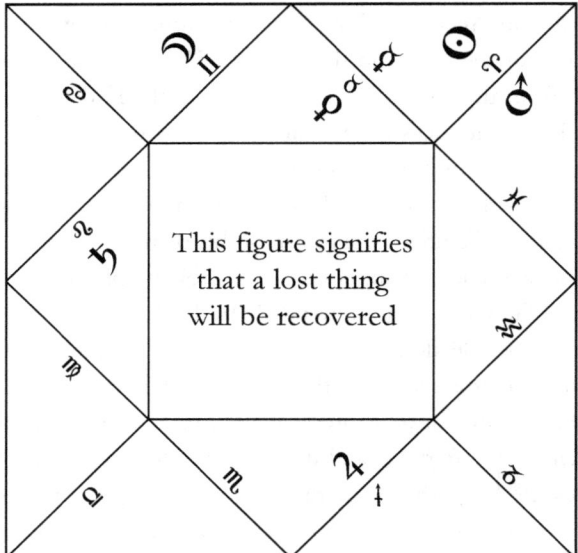

Figure 97: A figure showing that a lost object will be recovered (Leopold)[295]

71 With the Moon waxing and adding, whoever has fled will be aided; with her waning and subtracting, it is the contrary.

[Lost objects: Sahl][296]

72 The Moon lays open the place of the lost thing or fugitive: for if she is in the east, [it is] toward the east; if in the Midheaven, towards the south; if in the seventh, towards the west; in the fourth, towards the north. **73** And if the Moon is outside the pivots, judge according to the nature and signification of the places.

74 And the return is good for the fugitive if the Moon is separated from a benevolent; from a malevolent, say the contrary.[297]

---

[295] This chart could tentatively be dated, in the Fagan-Bradley sidereal zodiac, to April 3, 1272 AD JC (or April 10-11, GC). But Venus should be back in Pisces, and the positions of the Sun and Mars are switched.

[296] See Sahl in *Judges* §7.79, and *On Questions* §7.11.

[297] The reasoning here is that if the Moon (the fugitive) separates from a benefic, it shows that he is leaving a good master and so is more likely to return; but if from a malefic, he has left a bad master and is unlikely to.

[The location of lost objects: al-Kindī][298]

75 Moreover, the lunar lord[299] in a human sign signifies the lost thing will be in a place frequented by men. **76** If it is in Aries or Capricorn, in a sheep-related [place]. **77** In Taurus, one given to cows or oxen or camels. **78** In a four-footed sign (such as Sagittarius), it signifies a place of quadrupeds. **79** In Leo, a place of wild beasts, forests, or the desert. **80** In Scorpio, one of creeping things. **81** In Cancer, cisterns [and] springs. **82** In Pisces, sweet waters and a place full of fish. **83** In Aquarius—even though it is reputed a human sign—mountainous places, rivers, and larger streams. **84** From the middle of Pisces [and] beyond, the habitations of birds. **85** And the Moon in a fiery signs [indicates] places of fire, and likewise with the rest.

[The location of the thief: al-Khayyāt][300]

86 And if an infortune gathered the counsel of the Moon in a pivot, he has not withdrawn far.

[Whether he has gotten rid of the goods: ʿUmar][301]

87 And, any star being established between the east and the fourth, or better being between the leader of the thief and 90°,[302] signifies that the thief had handed the stolen goods over to someone; and if it bears itself otherwise, he has handed it over to no one.

[The religion of the thief: ʿUmar][303]

88 So that you may know the law of the thief,[304] take the lord of the hour. **89** Which if it is the Sun and in a convertible [sign], it testifies [that he goes] from law to law; if Venus, it signifies the Arab law; if Mercury, the law of the

---

[298] See al-Kindī in *Judges* §7.81, and *Forty Chapters* §255-57.
[299] That is, the lord of the Moon: reading with Hugo and al-Rijāl 1485, for *dominus luminaris* ("lord of the luminary").
[300] See al-Khayyāt in *Judges* §7.84.
[301] See ʿUmar in *Judges* §7.130.
[302] Reading *nonaginta* with Hugo for *coniunctio* ("conjunction").
[303] See ʿUmar in *Judges* §7.143.
[304] That is, his culture or religion.

Indians; the Moon, that of the Persians; if Saturn, the Jews; if Mars, the Romans (and 'Umar says these things); if Jupiter, the pagans.

[The name of the thief: 'Umar][305]

90 For the name of the thief, note which letters or which signs or houses are denoted: for if 1° or 11° has arisen in the east, it signifies the first letter (namely, *a*); which if it is otherwise, see the house of the seventh. **91** Which [if] it has 2° or 12° at its beginning, take the second letter (namely, *b*). **92** And if it bears itself otherwise, see the tenth: it being 3° or 13°:[306] they denote the third letter. **93** Which if it was not so, take the fourth sign: it being 4° or 9°,[307] they denote the fourth later. **94** Beyond that, turn back to the east and see the second: take the sixth [letter] from the second, the seventh [letter] from the one following the Midheaven, the eighth from the one following the fourth, the ninth from the third from the Midheaven, the tenth from the third from the pivot of the earth. **95** Proceed uniformly, always by adding one, up to the twentieth inclusively: the sixth from the east judges the twenty-first [letter], the seventh sign designates the twenty-second, that of the Midheaven gives the twenty-third, the pivot of the earth indicates[308] the twenty-fourth.[309]

[Partnerships: Sahl][310]

96 Concerning an association and partnership, give the one seeking to the east and its lord, give the associate to the seventh and its lord, the association to the tenth and its lord, the end to the fourth and its lord. **96** And just as these bear themselves to each other, so judge concerning their love and profit and loss.

---

[305] See 'Umar in *Judges* §7.145. This chapter by 'Umar is extremely difficult in the Latin, and will have to remain obscure until I translate it from Arabic for my forthcoming 'Umar volume.

[306] Reading with Hugo for *cuius est aut undecimum* ("whose it is, or the eleventh").

[307] Hugo reads 15°. Nevertheless all of 'Umar's procedures are so vexed and difficult to understand in Hugo's Latin, that it would be best to wait for my translation of 'Umar's book on questions before trying to figure it out oneself.

[308] Reading *indicat* for a redundant *quartam* ("fourth").

[309] 'Umar's method seems to use only 24 letters.

[310] See Sahl in *Judges* §7.147, and *On Questions* §7.23 (in *WSM*).

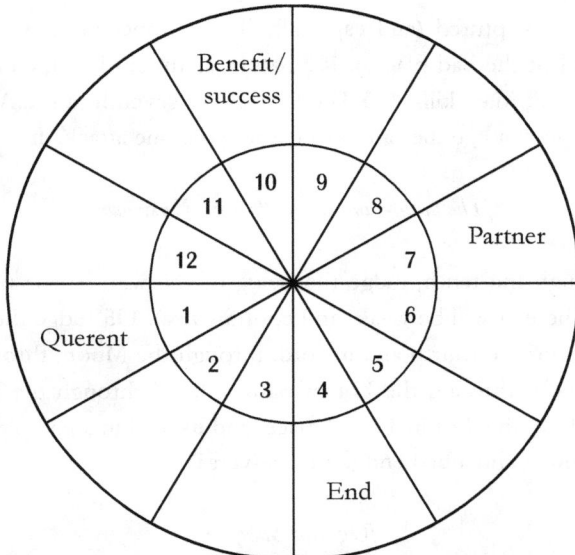

Figure 98: Sahl's angular significations for partnerships (Dykes)

*[War: Various]*³¹¹

97 Being asked about war, give the Ascendant and its lord to the one attacking, the second and its lord to his allies, the seventh and its lord to the one attacked, the eighth and its lord to his allies. **98** Through the tenth you may know the essence of the war, through the fourth the outcome.

99 And judge thusly according to their lords: if the significators of the first and seventh regard each other malignly, without reception, and more so from fixed signs, the war will be strong and the one whose significator is stronger will win. **100** Moreover, the one whose significator is peregrine, will have a failure of counsel.

*[On capture and death: al-Kindī]*³¹²

101 Likewise, the lord of the Ascendant in the seventh, impeded or under the rays or retrograde, if the one impeding is Mars or the Sun,³¹³ the attack-

---

³¹¹ These significations and descriptions match many authors (see *Judges* §§7.160-7.198).
³¹² See al-Kindī in *Judges* §7.172, and *Forty Chapters* §389-90a.

ing one will be captured (and especially if it is impeded from an angle, or he[314] is a lord of the bad places). **102** Saturn as the lord of the eighth makes him be captured, Mars kills. **103** The lord of the seventh in the Ascendant, if it were corrupted: judge the same concerning the one attacked.

[The nature and end of the war: Unknown]

104 Through the tenth, judge the being of the war: if it is movable and Mars is not there, it will be weak (and contrariwise). **105** Judge the end of the war by means of the fourth and its lord, through the Moon, through the Lot of the planets,[315] through the Lot of battles, [and] through the Lot of Fortune and its lord: this Lot in a good place, and its lord in a bad place, signifies a good beginning and a bad end (and vice-versa).

[On war: Sahl][316]

106 Moreover, the star from which the Moon is being separated should be given to the one seeking [the war], and the one to which she applies to the one defending: and if the Moon applies to none and is being separated from none, the Moon should be left behind in this business. **107** And in this business, the power of the superior planets is greater than that of the inferiors.

108 In particular, if the leaders regard each other benignly, with reception, this is a sign of peace; if malignly, there will be peace after discord.

109 Moreover, the Moon being with Mars (the fortunate [stars] being turned away), threatens death or captivity to the one seeking. **110** The Sun with the Head or Tail allows few or none on either side to escape.

---

[313] Al-Kindī does not mention the Sun here, but Leopold might be thinking of being under the rays.
[314] I take this to be Mars (or Saturn, whichever is making the lord of the Ascendant unfortunate).
[315] There is no Lot of the planets, so this must be Leopold's or a scribe's mistake.
[316] See Sahl in *Judges* §7.160, and *On Questions* 7.25 (in *WSM*).

[Who will win: al-Kindī][317]

111 If the lord of the seventh is falling or under the rays or in the conjunction of Mars without reception, the one invaded will be killed.

112 If the significators of both parties are equal, seek Mars and Mercury: for the one which they favor more, will win. **113** Say the same about Jupiter and Venus, with them not being impeded by the bad ones.

114 If[318] the lord of the first is impeded by the lord of the second, the attacking supporters will kill him.

[Quality of the parties and the war: Unknown][319]

115 And the lord of the fourth being impeded by the lord of the seventh or eighth, in the seventh or eighth, if it has any dignity in the Ascendant, the end of the one attacking will be wrong; speak conversely with respect to the one attacked.

116 Moreover, consider the Lot of Fortune according to its place and lord and bearing. **117** If the Lot of Fortune and its lord are in good places and [are] good, the one attacking will have a good beginning and good end. **118** If the Lot is [placed] well and its lord badly, the beginning is good and the end of the one attacking bad (and conversely).

[The quality and manner of the war: Sahl][320]

119 The quality or manner of the war is had through Mars and his place from the east, and from the star regarding [him], and the quantity of the slaughter from the Moon and her place. **120** And the army of each follows the proper quality of its leader.

121 And the star from which Mars is being separated belongs to the one seeking or attacking, and the one to which he applies belongs to the other party.

---

[317] See al-Kindī in *Judges* §7.162, and *Forty Chapters* §§396 and 398.
[318] This seems to be from *Forty Chapters* Ch. 12.1, §424 (*Judges* §7.185).
[319] I do not seem to be able to find these sentences in *Judges*.
[320] See Sahl in *Judges* §7.167, and *On Questions* §7.25 (in *WSM*).

122 And the Moon regulates all of our actions.[321] **123** If Mars is being separated from the good ones in a question or at the inception of a war, the invasion is just (and conversely).

124 Moreover, Mars in his own exaltation makes great war; but in [his] descending,[322] a small one.

125 Likewise, Mars in movable signs or in the angles [indicates] a glorious war;[323] in fixed ones and not in the angles, not glorious.

[The reason for the war: Julianus of Laodikaia][324]

126 If Mars (or the one with whom he is joined) is stationary, the war will have many pauses; if direct, few.

127 Mars in the Midheaven says the war comes to be because of rulership, in the Ascendant because of life, in the west because of a loss, in the fourth because of land or burials. **128** In the ninth, because of neglected gods or laws, in the third because of a clan or human gods,[325] in the sixth because of someone's mutilation or a malicious charge, in the twelfth because of subordinates. **129** In the eleventh because of friends or children, in the fifth because of a wife or city, in the second because of money, in the eighth because of ancient things or the dead.

130 And if Mars is western,[326] it makes the war hidden, but eastern[327] out in the open.

131 If Mercury looks at those to which Mars is joined, with a good arrangement and with the testimony of the good ones, it will hand over the attacking one to the one attacked. **132** But if [he looks at] those from whom Mars is being separated, the contrary. **133** And if Mercury is under the rays, the traitor will escape, and if eastern not.

---

[321] This sentence is not precisely in *Judges*, but Leopold seems to be taking these two sentences from Sahl in §7.177; the next paragraph resumes §7.167.

[322] That is, his fall.

[323] In Hugo's Sahl, this refers to how fervently the people fight.

[324] I do not know where or how Leopold got this passage from Julianus, but it will be published in full in 2016 in the extant astrological works of Theophilus of Edessa (translated by Eduardo Gramaglia). Some of these sentences are also reflected in Sahl.

[325] This might be a deliberate paganizing of this phrase, so that it does not refer to "God." At any rate, Julianus has "female gods."

[326] That is, under the Sun's rays.

[327] That is, having arising out of the rays.

[The beginnings of wars: Various]

132 At the beginnings of wars, if the Moon is conjunctional, give the Moon to the one undertaking [it], the Sun to the enemy; if preventional, the contrary, and judge who would win according to their bearing and the attacking places.[328]

133 Moreover,[329] in entering into war, let the Ascendant be one of the houses of Mars, and Mars or Jupiter in the tenth (or their places interchanged and configured to one another),[330] and with the Lot of Fortune, with them appearing well [in their condition], as well as the signs in which they are, and those which are the causes of the army and war [should be] effective for victory.[331]

134 In this chapter (namely on war), judge according to Petosiris (whom Julius Caesar held as most famous): by the Ascendant and its lord for the querent or the one beginning the war, and through the second and its lord for his supporters, through the seventh and its lord for the adversary, through the eighth and its lord for his supporters, through the tenth and its lord [for] the cause and essence of the war, through the fourth and its lord [for] the outcome and end of the war. **135** Fifthly, through the Lot of Fortune, as to whether it falls in the half of the one beginning or attacking, or the one defending. **136** Sixthly, through the planets, beginning from the Moon, then the Sun, from there through Saturn and the rest according to the order of planets.

137 And Hermes gives war to Mars, the one from whom he is separating to the one attacking, the one to whom he is joined to the one defending---and he judges the war and triumph according to this.

---

[328] *Impugna*. I take this to be the first and seventh houses.
[329] This sentence is ultimately based on Theophilus of Edessa's *On Military Labors* Ch. 24, to be published by me in full in 2016 (translated by Eduardo Gramaglia).
[330] This would be a case of classical mutual reception: in each other's domiciles, and looking at each other at least by sign, if not by a degree-based aspect.
[331] Reading *victoriae* for *victoria*. I am uncertain about this last clause concerning the army and war, because it does not quite make grammatical or astrological sense, and I do not know the source.

[Hunting: Sahl][332]

138 For hunting, consider the east and the lord of the hour [for the hunter], the seventh and its lord for the thing which you want to hunt, so that the significators of the first are stronger than the latter significators. **139** And if they apply to each other benignly, what is sought will be caught easily (and vice-versa). **140** And if four-footed things are sought after, a four-footed seventh should be chosen. **141** And the prosperity or corruption of Mars should be maintained, because he is the leader of the hunt.

[Fishing: Sahl][333]

142 For fishing, consult the lord of the east and the Moon, and the lord of the seventh. **143** So[334] with the east being watery, if the Moon or lord of the hour applies to Mars, and Venus is averse to the aspect of the Moon, and falling, one should absolutely desist [from fishing], because you will have nothing without the greatest labor and impediment. **144** Likewise, if the Moon applies to Saturn, and Venus looks at her, the fishing will be great, for in this kind [of thing] Saturn does not impede the Moon unless Mars looks at her.[335] **145** And then Venus is weakened, because in [his] aspect Mars is adverse to Venus and threatens shipwreck.

[Chapter VIII.9: Questions of the 8th house]

[Whether someone is alive or dead: Sahl][336]

1 Concerning the eighth house, as to whether someone is living or dead, judge thusly: if the lord of the east and the Moon are in the fourth or eighth, or if they are being scorched or are falling, or preferably conjoined to the lord of the eighth, it is certain that he is dead. **2** If either one of them bears itself thusly, from there judge how each leader bears itself in status and posi-

---

[332] See *On Questions* §§13.15-16, and *Judges* §§7.199-200.
[333] See Sahl in *Judges* §7.202, and *On Questions* §13.16.
[334] Reading *quidem* for *quidam* ("certain people").
[335] Reading *eam* with Hugo and John's Sahl, for *eum* ("him").
[336] See Sahl in *Judges* §8.1, and *On Questions* §8 (*in WSM*).

tion, and how it looks at the good or bad ones, and according to the testimonies of these.

3 Moreover, if the lord of the east is in the twelfth[337] or falling or in the eighth or if it withdraws from a retrograde lord of the eighth, it will be feared for [his] death. **4** But if it is adjoined to a retrograde [planet], death is near.[338]

5 The application of the Moon to any [planet] staying under the earth, is fatal; above the earth, the contrary.

6 Moreover, the lord of the east being conjoined to malevolents ([and] not without the lord of the twelfth), or being regarded by them, if along with this either of the luminaries is corrupted, it is deadly.

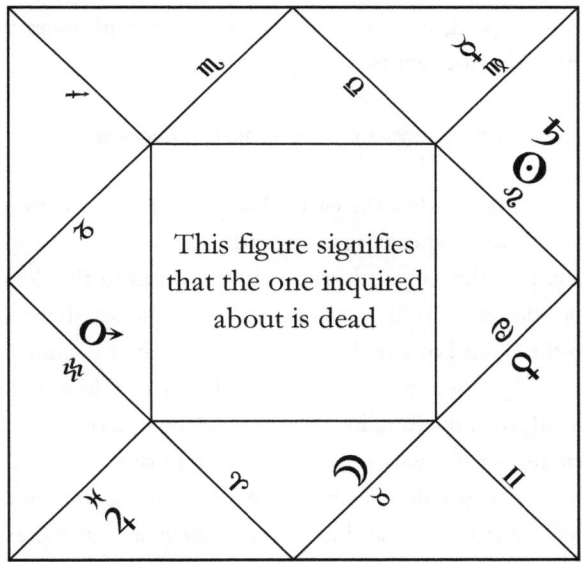

Figure 99: A figure showing that someone inquired about is dead (Leopold)

7 Likewise, the Moon along with Mars in the fourth (with the benevolents being wholly turned away), [indicates the same].

---

[337] John's and Hugo's Sahl understand this to be its fall or descension, not the twelfth.
[338] John's and Hugo's Sahl seems to understand that it is retrograding *into combustion*, not that it is joined to a retrograde planet.

8 And in addition the Lot of fortune with the wicked [planets and possessing] the fourth or sixth or twelfth, without aid of the fortunes, has testimony [for death].

9 Moreover, a star in the upper hemisphere generally has a judgment of life; in the lower one, the contrary.

10 Again, with the lord of the east being scorched and the benevolents turned away, or[339] if the Moon is below the earth in the remote [places], it signifies death.[340] **11** And this is without any doubt if the Moon is staying within the third degree of Scorpio[341] and is corrupted by Saturn (whose nature is death-bringing).

12 And[342] never should a judgment of death come to be unless either of the leaders is corrupted, or one weakens the other, with even the fortunate [planets] falling from the pivots.

[Whether someone is living or dead: "Dorotheus"][343]

13 Moreover, if the lord of the east is lucky or withdraws from the degrees of the house of death, it speaks against death.

14 Likewise, take the Lot of death from the Moon to the degree of death, and draw [that] down from the east, and where it reaches, there is this Lot. **15** If it falls into the bound of a malevolent or the receiver is unlucky, it is deadly[344] for the one about whom it is asked. **16** Moreover if Mercury is the leader and far removed from the Sun, in the aspect of the bad ones, it is deadly; and Venus and the rest of the stars signify according to this.

17 Moreover, if you knew death by means of the scorching of the leader of death, it will be from heat and a hidden disease; and at the extreme point of a pivot,[345] it signifies the worst kind of death.

18 Again, Saturn corrupting the leader in Aries or in its triplicity, signifies death from a fall from a height or by means of a beast. **19** Or (particularly in

---

[339] Both John's and Hugo's Sahl reads "and."
[340] Omitting *signis*.
[341] This is the degree of her fall.
[342] This sentence is taken from the end of al-Khayyāt's version of the same material, in *Judges* §8.2.
[343] See "Dorotheus" in *Judges* §8.3-4.
[344] Reading *fatale* with Hugo for *facile* ("easy").
[345] Reading *in cardinis extremo* with Hugo for *in cardine extremo*. I take this to mean that it is burned on or near the very degree of the axis, but I am not sure: *extremus* normally means "last, end," but can also mean the "point, tip."

Taurus or its triplicity), from cold and dryness. **20** In Gemini and its triplicity, if it is in the tenth, he will tumble from a height or, in the pivot of the earth, he will either die by slipping or something will fall upon him. **21** In Cancer and its triplicity, he will die from submersion or dysentery, unless perhaps Saturn is ascending,[346] for then [it will be] by apoplexy and what is of this kind.

22 Mars being the one corrupting, if he is in Aries or its triplicity, threatens a fall or impels a heavy thing upon him, or he will die by the sword. **23** Likewise, Mars in the tenth prepares the cross or hanging. **24** In Cancer and its triplicity he gives death through water.

[The kind of death: "Aristotle"][347]

25 Leo in the eighth signifies death from a beast. **26** Scorpio in the eighth, by poisonous things. **27** Saturn in Scorpio, Pisces, or Cancer, and with the lord of the eighth, [indicates] death by waters. **28** Mars in the eighth or with its lord [means it is] by means of a feverish heat and often the sword.[348] **29** The Tail in the eighth or with its lord, prepares the sword. **30** Likewise, if the lord of the eighth is traversing alone, it signifies its own proper [kind of] death.[349]

[Chapter VIII.10: Questions of the 9th house]

[On travel: Sahl][350]

1 Concerning the ninth house, such as on travel, whether it would come to be or not: give the one seeking to the lord of the east and the Moon, the road to the ninth and its lord. **2** If in particular the lord of the east or the Moon is in the ninth or applies to the lord of the ninth, the one who has asked will go of his own will. **3** Contrariwise, if the lord of the ninth is in the

---

[346] I am not sure whether this means rising in latitude, or arising in the east, or even rising toward his apogee.
[347] See "Aristotle" in *Judges* §8.5.
[348] Or, "iron" (*ferro*).
[349] That is, apart from any significations of Saturn or Mars.
[350] See *On Questions* §9.1, and *Judges* §9.1.

east or applies to the lord of the east, he will proceed because of a reason forcing [him to it]. **4** A transfer between them procures travel, [and so does collection of light, if the collecting planet aspects the ninth];[351] contrariwise,[352] travel is denied.

5 And the east belongs to the one going, the tenth to the business [he is traveling for], the seventh the place to which he heads, the fourth sums up[353] the end: whence, judge regarding this according to the status of the signs and their lords.

[On travel: Jirjis][354]

6 And if the lord of the east is in the east, in a firm sign, the one seeking it will not go; but if it is a convertible one, [he will go]. **7** [If it is in the east, he goes] towards the east; if after the east, in the Midheaven,[355] to the south or to foreign nations; if it is in the seventh or eighth, it signifies death or prison; in the pivot of the earth to the north.

[Whom he will meet: Sahl][356]

8 And through the Moon is known to which men he heads. **9** For if she applies to the Sun, [it is] to kings or princes; if to Saturn, to common people; if to Jupiter, to magnates; if to Mars, to soldiers; if to Venus, to women; if to Mercury, to wise people. **10** And if she goes in a solitary way, because of doing business. **11** If she withdraws from Saturn, it frees him from a debt, if from Mars it protects him from tight spots and captivity. **12** And if the one to whom she applies is in its own house, he heads to those who are native [to the area], in the triplicity to strangers but inhabitants of his own land.

13 And if the lord of the east or the Moon applies to a malevolent in a human sign, robbers should be feared on the road. **14** In Aquarius, he should not sail. **15** In a four-footed [sign] he should fear the attack of wild animals; if this is in Leo, cruel wild animals, and [in Scorpio] he should fear poisonous

---

[351] Adding based on Hugo; Leopold has omitted virtually an entire sentence.
[352] That is, if the collecting planet does *not* aspect the ninth.
[353] *Absolvo*, borrowing from a Latin idiom instead of the usual "absolves, acquits," *etc.*
[354] See Jirjis in *Judges* §9.7.
[355] Leopold seems to understand "after the east" to mean "diurnal motion from the Ascendant towards the Midheaven"; but Hugo's Jirjis is referring to the second sign, indicating east-northeast.
[356] See Sahl in *Judges* §9.11 and *On Questions* §9.1 (in *WSM*).

vermin. **16** In Pisces, sea monsters and the dangers of the waters. **17** And Saturn is more serious for waters than for lands; on the other hand, the wickedness [is worse] on lands than in waters.

[Whether it is better to go or stay: Sahl][357]

18 And it is better to move than to remain still if the lord of the Ascendant and the Moon are being separated from the infortunes and apply to the fortunes, and vice-versa.

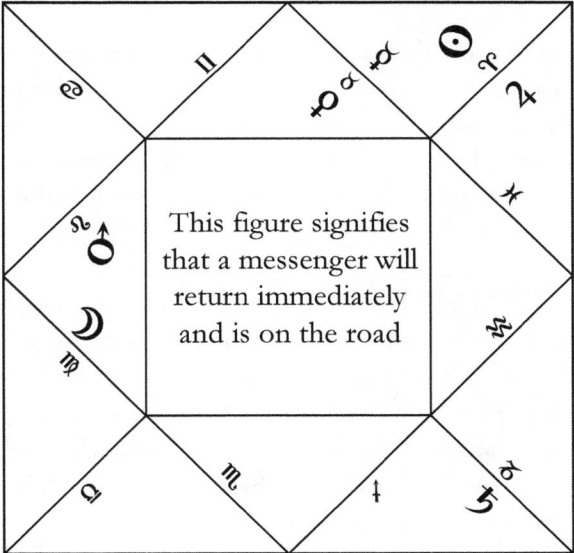

Figure 100: A figure showing that a messenger is returning immediately (Leopold)

---

[357] See Sahl in *Judges* §9.13 and *On Questions* §9.4 (in *WSM*).

[What will happen to him: Sahl][358]

19 Moreover, if [the lord of the second upon his arrival] is in the first station, he will stay but it will profit nothing; in the second station he will have a profit not expected. **20** And if the lord [of the second] is in the east or tenth or eleventh, the journey is useful; in the seventh, the contrary; if in the ninth or third he will not stay there. **21** If the Moon meanwhile is in the fourth, [it is] fatal.[359]

[What will happen to him: Sahl][360]

22 If it is asked about the return of an absent person, see if the lord of the east is in the east or in the Midheaven, or at least should it apply to one appearing in them: he will return quickly. **23** In the seventh[361] or fourth, slowly, for on the contrary he is yet staying there. **24** If in the ninth or third, and applying to one in the east, he has undertaken to return and is on the road; likewise if it would apply from the eighth or second[362] to a star placed in the tenth.

25 And if the lord of the east applies to a retrograde [planet], nor does it in any way look at the east, it signals an impediment. **26** If however it[363] would regard the east, he will return quickly unless it is otherwise[364] corrupted. **27** If these things do not pertain to the lord of the east, [then] have recourse to the Moon: for if she renders counsel to the lord of the east while [it] is placed in the east or near the east, he will return quickly; in the seventh or after the Midheaven, he will slow down.

---

[358] See Sahl in *Judges* §9.12, and *On Questions* §9.2 (in *WSM*). Leopold or the medieval typesetter has mutilated the following sentences. Here, Sahl (following Māshā'allāh's version of Dorotheus's *Carmen* V.22, **7-13**) instructs us to look at the lord of the second sign when the traveler arrives at his destination. Nevertheless it seems to me that one ought to do this in the inception chart of the journey itself, or in the question chart.

[359] This is particularly if she were with the lord of the second, or Mercury, or Mars (Sahl).

[360] See Sahl in *Judges* §9.20, and *On Questions* §9.6 (in *WSM*).

[361] Reading with John's Sahl and *Carmen* for "eighth."

[362] Reading with Hugo and John for "third."

[363] Hugo's and John's Sahl seem to take this to be the retrograde planet.

[364] Reading *alias* for *alius* ("another").

[The hour of the return: 'Umar][365]

28 The hour of the return is when the lord of the house of the thing sought, or the lord of the Moon, applies to the pivot[366] of the east, or at least to the pivot of the lord of the east. **29** For a pivot of the signs is one thing, and the pivot of stars another.[367] **30** If therefore any star occupies the pivot of another star, the effecting [of the matter] is fulfilled.

[Whether the traveler is safe: 'Umar][368]

31 And the [person] about which it is asked, is safe if its lord is direct, in its own house or kingdom,[369] lucky, and the Moon waxing, not in fall, they being cleansed of the infortunes (and vice-versa).

32 However, he is dead if the lord of the question[370] and the Moon (being under the earth) are looked at by the lord of the eighth, or if [the lord of the eighth] itself is the leader of the question. **32** And if it does not regard them, it is not yet deadly. **33** And if they are above the earth, and the lord of the eighth falls away from them, it is life-giving.

[On dreams: 'Umar][371]

34 Concerning dreams, principally see their truth by means of the east.[372]

35 Indeed, Saturn placed with the Tail in the ninth makes fearful things be seen, as serpents, monsters, stinking things. **36** And the house of Saturn[373] should be noted, for it also signals horrendous things. **37** Jupiter in the same place [indicates] what belongs to magnates; Mars what [pertain] to hunting or

---

[365] See 'Umar in *Judges* §9.30.
[366] Reading *cardini* for *domino*, with Hugo.
[367] By "pivot of the stars," 'Umar means the whole-sign angles from the position or sign of a particular star. So, if the lord of the Ascendant is in Gemini, then its pivots or whole-sign angles are all of the common signs: Gemini itself, Virgo, Sagittarius, and Pisces.
[368] See 'Umar in *Judges* §9.31-32.
[369] That is, exaltation.
[370] That is, the significator of the absent person—probably, the lord of the Ascendant.
[371] See 'Umar in *Judges* §9.36.
[372] 'Umar is vague on exactly how to determine whether a dream is true or not, but Sahl (in his *On Questions* §9.7) suggests that if there is no planet in the ninth, nor the angles, nor the third, then the dream does not represent something true or that will manifest.
[373] Hugo's 'Umar makes it seem that the lord of the ninth (in such a situation) should be noted, not the house of Saturn.

to killing; Venus to good-smelling things, pearls, nuptials, sexual intercourse; Mercury books, temples, and the rest of what is his; the Sun whatever flies between the heaven and earth, or kings; the Moon, what is aquatic, and so on.

38 An[374] infortune in the east or house of law,[375] [indicates] evil and difficulty; a fortune, advantage and joy.

[On alchemy: Sahl][376]

39 You will know whether someone knows alchemy by means of the lord of the east and the Moon. **40** For if they are cleansed of the infortunes, he does know; the corruption of these signals a liar. **41** And for gold, the Sun should be made fortunate, for silver the Moon.

[On the knowledge of anything: 'Umar][377]

42 Also, the quality of the knowledge of anything, [is known] by means of the east (which belongs to the one knowing), and by the ninth (which belongs to the knowledge), through their lords, and those which are there or with their lords, by body or aspect. **43** And Saturn there speaks against knowledge, unless perhaps his own lord receives him and regards him benignly.

[Choosing between ships: Unknown]

44 For choosing [between] four ships, the one which occurs more to the mind of the one asking should be given to the east; the one [which does so] less, to the tenth; the third, to the seventh; the fourth, to the fourth: the one which the fortunes favor more, should be chosen. **45** Likewise when it is asked and judged about other multiple things.

---

[374] This sentence comes from "Dorotheus", in *Judges* §9.37.
[375] That is, the ninth.
[376] See Sahl in *Judges* §9.38; **41** can be traced to his *On Elections* §41 (in *WSM*).
[377] See 'Umar in *Judges* §9.40.

[Danger and safety when sailing: al-Kindī][378]

46 And Mars corrupting the lord of the Ascendant and the Moon (or either one) will burn the boat, Saturn breaks or submerges [it]. **47** Jupiter making [the Midheaven][379] fortunate preserves the good health of the ship and those sailing, in one piece; Venus fertilizes and makes [them] rejoice; Mercury [signifies] the ship's impediment.[380]

[More on danger and winds: Various]

48 If[381] Mars was not in the tenth or eleventh [it will be better]:[382] for if he were there, what is in the ship will be lost through pirates. **49** And if in addition there is then ascending one star from the hearts[383] of the signs, the ship and whatever is in it will be burned.

50 For raising the sail, if Aquarius is rising the wind will be great (and if Saturn is of a good condition); if Libra the wind will be middling; if Gemini, the wind will be variable (and let Mercury be of a good condition).

[Chapter VIII.11: Questions of the 10th house]

[On attaining a dignity: Sahl][384]

1 Concerning the tenth house, whether someone ought to attain a dignity is known thusly: if the lord of the Ascendant and the Moon apply to the lord of the tenth, so that it [also] regards the Midheaven,[385] he will have the dignity through his own effort. **2** It will be the same if both are in the tenth, so that however they are cleansed of the bad ones. **3** The same if the lord of the Midheaven is in the east or applies to the lord of the east, [but] he will have

---

[378] See al-Kindī in *Judges* §9.42 (*Forty Chapters* Ch. 17, §§491-93).
[379] Reading with al-Kindī, for *illa* ("them").
[380] This phrase about Mercury does not appear in the Latin al-Kindī.
[381] See pseudo-Ptolemy's *Centiloquy*, Aph. 55.
[382] Tentatively adding, else the sentence could not make sense.
[383] *Cordibus*. Ptolemy reads this as being one of the fixed stars of the nature of Mars; I do note that three of the traditional royal stars in the fixed signs (Aldebaran, Regulus, Antares) were held by Ptolemy to be wholly or partly of the nature of Mars.
[384] See Sahl in *Judges* §§10.1-2, and *On Questions* §§10.1-2 (in *WSM*).
[385] Adding *caeli* ("heaven").

the dignity without labor. **4** The same if the lord of the tenth applies to a fortune appearing in the east.

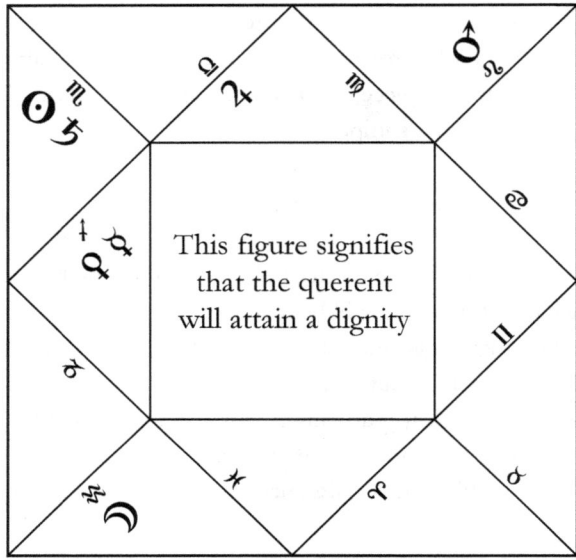

Figure 101: A figure showing that the querent will attain a dignity (Leopold)

5 It will be the same if there is a transfer between both leaders. **6** The same if the one who receives [the light] is cleansed [of the infortunes] and free, and regards the tenth: he will have the dignity. **7** And its corruption will cut off the effecting [of it] after certain hope. **8** And if the bad ones corrupt by means of a square or the opposite, it will cease with a severe rebuff; but if they corrupt by a sextile or trine, the dignity will be denied in a nice way.

9 Moreover, if there comes to be a collection of light, and if the one which collects is in the east or tenth: if then the Moon applies to either of these leaders, he will have the honor; and if an application does not take place, provided that she is cleansed [of the infortunes], he will obtain [it] by means of many helping. **10** And if the Moon bears herself otherwise than was stated, if the star which collects the light is in the tenth or regards it, even so that it is neither remote from[386] the east and cleansed of the infortunes, nor

---

[386] This seems to mean, "in aversion to."

does it go out of[387] the sign before both leaders (or either one) apply to it or conjoin to it, it does not stand in the way of having the dignity.

11 Then however, the honor will be had when the application between the leaders is completed, and more quickly so if the Moon confers [her management] to one.

12 And[388] the eleventh and its lord signifies the rendering[389] of the dignity.

[On attaining a dignity: 'Umar][390]

13 Moreover, if at the hour of the nativity the Sun is in the tenth or in his own house or in the degree of exaltation,[391] provided that Jupiter is not scorched [and] appeared as an associate with him, or Venus [is] in a pivot and the infortunes do not regard him from a square or opposite aspect, it is necessary that the one seeking[392] (or the native) rule the world. **14** The Sun not being in his own house nor in his own sovereignty,[393] takes [it] away, unless he arises from a royal family or one of magnates. **15** For, if placed [thusly], it subjects the ends of the kingdom to him.

16 Likewise, with Mercury in the east, if it is his sovereignty, it signifies the secretary or scribe of the king.

[On attaining a dignity: Jirjis][394]

17 Jirjis plainly says that an aspect discovered between the eastern and Midheaven lords [means] no ambiguity arises with respect to acquiring an honor; but not so without one.

18 When however it would happen, is known thusly: for how many degrees of application there are between the leaders, take that many days or months or years, according to the signs being tropical or double-bodied or firm.

---

[387] Reading *ab signo* for *ad signum*.
[388] Source unknown at this time.
[389] *Reditus*.
[390] See 'Umar in *Judges* §10.4.
[391] The "or...or" here could also mean "either...or."
[392] Omitting *si*.
[393] *Regnum*. That is, his exaltation.
[394] See Jirjis in *Judges* §10.9.

[How the reign will be: Sahl][395]

19 If some prince enters the rulership, or, sitting on the imperial seat he first administers the affairs, note: for if the entrance is diurnal and the Sun is with Saturn, he will quickly step down. **20** Moreover, the Sun being regarded by the benevolents while he and the lord of the east are in a good place from the east and in a firm sign,[396] he will have the principal place according to his wishes. **21** Again, with the Sun in the east, if he is in a tropical sign and Mars holds onto the tenth and regards him, one of the citizen subjects will turn against him or it threatens death at the end. **22** If Jupiter is in the Midheaven, made fortunate while the Sun holds onto a good place and firm sign, the kingdom will increase, it multiplies [his] name and reputation and resources. **23** Likewise, if the Sun is in the eighth or sixth, if the lord of the east is good and in the east or in the Midheaven, even though it supports the prince in all things, still [it indicates] the death of him[397] from whom he had received the rulership.

24 Moreover, if the dignity is had by night, speak about the Moon in the night just as about the Sun in the day. **25** For if she is cleansed of the infortunes and in a safe place, it preserves [his] body unharmed. **26** If [she is] with the bad ones or applies to them, he will be deposed. **27** Again, the Moon being distant from the Head or Tail by 4° or less signifies an unprofitable rulership; beyond 4° it harms less, beyond 12° he will escape the dangers, free.

[The interpretation of the timing of the chart: Various][398]

28 In one place, the hour of the receiving of the honor signifies what there is between men and their prince (that is, at the hour of the enthronement of its prince). **29** In another place, the hour in which an honor is given to a vassal[399] by [his] lord signifies what will be between the lord and him. **30**

---

[395] See Sahl *Judges* §10.11, and *On Questions* §10.6 (in *WSM*).
[396] Omitting "or they are diurnal," which does not appear in Hugo.
[397] Reading with Hugo and John, for "death *from him*" (which would imply his being killed by his own predecessor).
[398] Sources uncertain at this time, but these passages bear a resemblance to Abū Ma'shar's *BRD* and some of 'Umar's questions.
[399] *Fasaleo*.

And the hour at which he enters the dignity signifies what there will be between him and the subject people.

31 You[400] should not presume to liken the figures and compare the significators of kingdoms between them prior to the knowledge of the comparison of what they intend,[401] because kings are changed in every[402] conjunction. **32** And once you have certified the rankings, you will give to the king and those over whom he is in charge, what is owed to them because of the rank, and you will be safe from error. **33** In another passage: you should not judge that the matters of the world will change from [just] one planet, before you understand the whole figure: for kingdoms are [normally] changed in the great conjunctions. **34** And once you have looked at all things well, you should know of what nature their lords were, and their vassals[403] in anything, and you will not go astray.

35 ...argument that the dignity of a leading person in society is reduced to [being signified by] the tenth.[404]

[How long the reign will be: 'Umar][405]

36 Also, Valens determines the duration of the king in the rulership thusly: by how many degrees the Sun is distant from the degree of the east, he will reign for that many years or months or days.

37 The same is through the Lot of the king and office, which is taken from the Sun to the degree of the Midheaven and projected from the degree of Jupiter; and where the projection is ended, there is this Lot. **38** If the lord of the place of the bound is in its own house or sovereignty, it completely attributes the lesser years [of the planet]; and if the [the lord of the] bound is under the rays or rather[406] unlucky, or in a sign or bound of the bad ones, or scorched, take months or days for how many [its] lesser years are.

---

[400] The rest of this paragraph is pretty opaque, due no doubt to a combination of the lofty vagueness of the original translator (probably Hugo of Santalla) and Leopold's frustrating tendency to compress and abridge.
[401] *Assimilationis propositorum.*
[402] This should probably read either *magno* ("great") as below, or should read "kings are *not* changed...".
[403] *Fasalli.*
[404] This is evidently a sentence fragment which may not be connected to the preceding material.
[405] See 'Umar in *Judges* §10.13.
[406] Reading *potius* for *post* ("after").

[When he would be expelled: ʿUmar][407]

39 Concerning the expulsion of someone in power, proceed thusly according to Valens.[408] **40** If the lord of the Midheaven is corrupted, or the Midheaven itself, when the Moon reaches [by aspect] the degree of the infortune which is corrupting the Midheaven or its lord, or is assembled in the same degree, he will leave the dignity [he had] collected, unless that infortune, having left it, would cross over to the next one[409]—[or], unless Jupiter or Venus would reach that same degree: for if it is so, they preserve [him] in that same status, but they cannot cancel [his] cares, stings, and groaning. **41** Moreover, he says if an infortune is in the Midheaven or looks at it, the king will have trouble[410] in that hour.

42 Likewise, compute the degrees from the degree of the Midheaven up to the infortune, and give years, months, or days to individual degrees. **43** The same: give two days or months or years to individual degrees.[411]

44 Moreover, according to the Lot which is taken from the lord of the twelfth to the degree of the twelfth: however much the number of degrees [is], it preserves the dignity through that many [years].

[Knowing his predecessor and successor: al-Kindī][412]

45 You should know [his] predecessor by means of the star which is in the ninth; lacking that, through the lord of the ninth. **46** His successor is by means of a star in the eleventh; lacking that, through the lord of the eleventh. **47** And for each, judge concerning their good or bad according to that.

48 You would know the stock and fatherland of the predecessor and successor through the planets ruling those places. **49** Saturn signifies an Indian or Arab, Jupiter from Babylonia or Persia, Mars a Roman, Venus an Arab, Mercury from the places of the west, the Moon a Thracian,[413] the Sun from the east or the family and house of a king.

---

[407] See ʿUmar in *Judges* §10.14.
[408] Again, this attribution to Valens comes from ʿUmar.
[409] This probably means either the next bound or sign.
[410] Reading *incommodum* for *in como*.
[411] Reading loosely (and with Hugo) for *Idem da signulis horis rectis dies aut menses aut annos duabus semper duos dies*. Hugo's Latin already needed a little massaging, and Leopold's Latin condensing of it is almost incomprehensible.
[412] See al-Kindī in *Judges* §10.18-19, and *Forty Chapters* §§341-47b.
[413] Reading with Hugo for *in terra*, but Robert's version of al-Kindī has "Parthian."

50 And whichever it was, if it is in a house of Saturn it signifies an ignoble person or old man. **51** In a house or bound of Jupiter of the wise and merchants or the ranks of the law. **52** In a house or bound of Mars, the leader of an army or prince of wars, and a victor and shedder of blood, who frequently encourages fire. **53** Those of the house of the Sun, from a royal family or an augur or astrologer or hunter or some excellent profession. **54** In a house or bound of Venus, a singer, lover of women, or one delighting in jokes. **55** In a house or bound of Mercury, a scribe or consul. **56** [In the house of the Moon, a courier or messenger or legate or of the common people.]^414 **57** And in an eastern quarter it signifies an adolescent, in a western one a man of full age.

58 And the hour when he supplies^415 [his] precepts [and] begins to reign,^416 undoubtedly lays bare his vigor and how long he is going to reign.

[How long he would reign: "Dorotheus"]^417

59 When someone is promoted to an honor or will first sit down as a tribune, in the hour of the question that is made [see] if there is a star which is the lord of the sovereignty^418 of the sign in which the Moon is. **60** [If] it is cleansed of the infortunes, he will reign for a full year and beyond. **61** And if the Moon is not appropriate for that,^419 [look at] the next one to which the Moon applies: it being unlucky or close to scorching, however many degrees it is distant from scorching, give that many months. **62** The Moon being [well] placed, when a malevolent^420 reaches the degree of the star which receives the Moon's [light], and it is scorched [as was stated above], it is a sign of deposing.

63 Moreover, if the luminaries are in the east or Midheaven, and either of the infortunes meets with their places, it deprives [him of] the dignity.

64 Saturn in the east or in the Midheaven, under the aspect of the fortunes, preserves the honor according to his own lesser years (namely, 30); in a wicked place or in his own fall, for 30 months. **65** Jupiter in the east or

---

414 Adding based on Hugo.
415 Reading *suggerit* with Hugo for *fugerit* ("he will flee").
416 Omitting *praecepta fugerit* as incomprehensible or a bad misspelling, and following Hugo.
417 See "Dorotheus" in *Judges* §10.22.
418 That is, "exaltation."
419 That is, if her sign has no exaltation.
420 Reading *malivola* with Hugo for *benivola*.

Midheaven, for 12 years; being corrupted, for that many months. **66** Mars in the same place, for 15 years; being corrupted, for that many months. **67** The Sun, for 8 years; being corrupted, for that many months. **68** Venus in either of the places and eastern, in [her own] house or sovereignty, 10 years; falling or applying to bad ones, for that many months. **69** Mercury for 10 years;[421] being corrupted, [that many] months. **70** The Moon, for 25 years; being corrupted, for that many months. **71** And all of them thusly.

[Whether someone would return to a dignity: Sahl][422]

72 Moreover, one who has lost an honor will recover [it] if, at the hour of the question, the lord of the east applies to the lord of the tenth: and this comes to be with labor. **73** If conversely the lord of the tenth applies to the lord of the east, [it will be] without labor. **74** The Moon applying to a star in the tenth or east means the same thing. **75** The lord of the east [means] the same thing if it is retrograde, and if the Moon is in a tropical [sign] he will return quickly.

[Whether a ruler will please his subjects: ʿUmar][423]

76 And someone in power will please [his] subjects according to the way that the lord of the seventh and lord of the first bear themselves towards each other.

ଔ ଔ ଔ

77 In these things you should convey what I have noted with respect to nativities (in the tenth house), and thus you could be able to judge securely with respect to dignities.

---

[421] Omitting *dux* ("leader").
[422] See Sahl in *Judges* §10.23, and *On Questions* §10.8.
[423] See *Judges* §10.35.

[Chapter VIII.12: Questions of the 11th house]

[Things hoped for: Sahl][424]

1 Concerning the eleventh house, such as on something hoped for: it is known through the lord of the eleventh. **2** For if the lord of the east applies to it, or the other way around, what is hoped for will be had; and if by a good aspect, easily, and if by a bad one with difficulty. **3** The same if the lord of the eleventh[425] is received in a pivot.

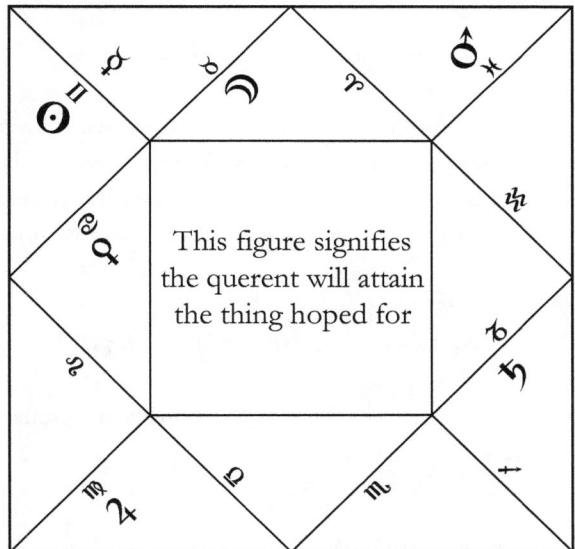

Figure 102: A figure showing that the querent will attain the thing hoped for (Leopold)

4 Moreover the one which receives[426] the Moon being in a double-bodied [sign] conveys a moderate portion of the thing hoped for; in a tropical one, difficulty occurs; in a firm one, it perfects it fully. **5** Likewise if the receiver of the Moon is corrupted, it will destroy what was gained. **6** And if the one

---

[424] See Sahl in *Judges* §11.1, and *On Questions* §11.1.
[425] Reading with Hugo for "east."
[426] That is, the one to which she applies, reading *recipit* with Hugo for *respicit* ("regards").

which gathers the Moon's counsel is received, it conveys everything according to his wish.

[On things unstated by the querent: Sahl][427]

7 And if you want to know about this thing which the one seeking does not want to express, see the lord of the east and the Moon. **8** For if there is an application from the pivots or after the pivots, he will get what he hopes for; but lacking this, not at all.

9 But if he, being worried about the attainment of something, would express it, look into the signification of the twelve houses, and judge.

[On love and hate: 'Umar and others][428]

10 Concerning love and hate between two people, see it by means of the Ascendant and the seventh and their lords; likewise through the Ascendant and eleventh and their lords. **11** Moreover, the lord of the eleventh in a good aspect with the lord of the first signifies concord, and it is more so with reception.

[Whether someone is a friend or flatterer: Jirjis][429]

12 Moreover, a benevolent in the east or Midheaven signifies a true love; if conversely a bad one, a bad one.

---

[427] See Sahl in *Judges* §11.2, and *On Questions* §11.3.
[428] See 'Umar in *Judges* §11.7, and various statements about the eleventh house throughout §§11.6-11.
[429] See Jirjis in *Judges* §11.12.

[Chapter VIII.13: Questions of the 12th house]

13 Concerning the twelfth house, such as on enemies, judge thusly: the star from which [the lord of the twelfth] is separated signifies the one attacked, the one to which it is joined the attacked one. **14** Therefore, that one of them which is stronger, will win. **15** Do likewise with the lord of the Ascendant and the seventh.

16 Concerning horse racing, I will put everything which I have noted here in the ninth Treatise (on elections).

17 Concerning questions through the individual houses, bring together [along with this Treatise] those things which I have collected in the order of houses from nativities, and judge securely through these and those. **18** For if you will have considered both sciences well, you will readily understand what you doubt, even though [natal questions] are natural ones; these however are *like* natural ones.[430]

ʘ ʘ ʘ

[How questions are corrupted: Sahl][431]

19 And concerning similar [matters] the sages give a similar judgment, [so that] with respect to the Ascendant you produce what corrupts questions as well as the life of a native.[432] **20** And do thusly: look at the star which acts as the leader[433] in nativities and questions, the star to which the lord of the Ascendant or lord of the matter is joined, and the one to which the Moon is conjoined (because the Moon is the partner of the lord of the Ascendant), or

---

[430] See al-ʿImrānī Ch. I.4 for this. Al-ʿImrānī means that nativities are "natural," because births are natural and the natal chart shows the natural influences of the planets upon the native at that time; but although horary questions do not arise by nature, they can be answered in ways very similar to natal topics. Thus, questions are not natural things but they are *like* them.

[431] The following material is from the rest of the introductory portions of Sahl's *On Questions* in Hugo's translation (omitted in *Judges*): see *On Questions* I.9 in *WSM* (mistakenly labeled I.8 in the first edition).

[432] Omitting *nato non est* (approximately, "it is not for one born"). What Sahl means is that certain configurations in the chart will show similar problems for different types of charts—if a question chart, they harm the question; if a nativity, the native.

[433] Reading *ducentem* for *lucentem* ("shining"). This refers to the victor of the chart.

the one acting as leader[434] over the Ascendant and its lord, and the lord of the matter.

21 Consider therefore the conjoined star, and the one with whom it is being conjoined. **22** For if it is being conjoined with a fortune which does not receive [it], or with a retrograde star or a falling one or a burned one, or with an unfortunate one with cut-off light,[435] the matter is corrupted. **23** And if it is being conjoined with a star and [the star] is safe, and that star has the connection of some star with which it will be conjoined, then until the conjunctions are ended we look from those [which are] conjoined with it: then if it has a cutting [planet] (as was stated at the beginning), the matter will be corrupted after it is put right. **24** And if it does not have a cutting [planet], then the question is received.[436] **25** And if it is being conjoined with an unfortunate one at the beginning of the matter, it is cut off with corruption. **26** Which if the unfortunate one [has] reception without a square and without an opposition and without [a conjunction] to the degree,[437] the matter will be established. **27** And if it is without transposition[438] and without a square, and if it is being conjoined at the beginning of a matter with a fortune and there is not a conjunction with an infortune, the matter is completed. **28** Which if a star transfers between each, [if the star] to which it is transferred [is] falling, unfortunate, not received, the matter is corrupted. **29** And if it groups together[439] the light of two stars, and the one grouping it between each is unfortunate, the matter is corrupted. **30** And if it is receiving one of them and is not receiving the other, it is corrupted.

31 And Sahl says[440] that Māshā'allāh concealed this chapter, the knowledge of which is very necessary in nativities and questions—but I do not believe he did this intentionally.

---

[434] See footnote above.
[435] *Abscisi luminis*. Perhaps this could be read as "made unfortunate *because of* a cut-off light."
[436] John's Sahl has "complete" or "completed," which makes more sense.
[437] Reading as *partilitate*.
[438] *Transpositione*. That is, a transfer of light.
[439] That is, "collects."
[440] This is so in the Latin versions, but the Arabic manuscripts I have used for the Arabic edition of Sahl omit the whole discussion of cutting off the light, as well as the reference to Māshā'allāh.

Treatise IX: On Elections & Images

[Chapter IX.1: Principles of elections]

1 An election is the fitness of the signs and planets in strength and fortune, for the hour of beginning some matter. **2** However, it happens according to the differences of men: of age, honor, duty, and sect. **3** Man was made so that he might think and choose, beasts so that they may be tamed[1] and hasten.

[General features of elections]

4 Therefore[2] let the Moon be made fit, because she has a signification over all things. **5** Make the Sun fit (he being like a king), likewise the planets which naturally signify the proposed matter, such as Venus [signifies] nuptials, Jupiter assets, and likewise with the others, just as they signify. **6** The Ascendant and its lord should be made fit, the Moon and her lord, the fourth and its lord, the tenth and its lord, the Lot of Fortune and its lord. **7** Also, the sign of the proposed matter: a watery sign for navigation, an earthy one for going by land (so that these are free from the bad ones and their aspects), masculine for masculine [people], feminine ones for feminine [people].[3] **8** Moreover, the sign of the thing sought.[4]

9 And[5] the good ones should be in the angles, cleansed of the bad ones, not in falling or impeded signs, and it is better if a good one is with a good one.[6]

10 There[7] should not be a contrariety between a planet and its own place. **11** One which looks at the significator from its own dignity, is good.[8] **12** It is

---

[1] Reading *perdomentur* for the abbreviated *perdent* ("they may lose").
[2] See al-'Imrānī Ch. I.1.2.
[3] Reading *masculina* and *feminina* (neuter plural, indicating the signs) for *masculini, feminini* (masculine/feminine plural).
[4] What Leopold seems to mean is that one should adapt both the sign *naturally* signifying the matter, as well as the sign which falls on the house topic that is desired (such as the 5th for children, and so on).
[5] See al-'Imrānī, Ch. I.2.5.
[6] That is, without the aspect of a malefic.
[7] See al-'Imrānī, Ch. I.2.7.
[8] This is backwards, as compared with the Latin al-'Imrānī. Rather, planets aspecting a significator should have dignity in the place where the significator itself is: so if a key significator is in Virgo, Mercury should look at it, and so on.

good if the lord of [the significator's bound] looks at the Sun.[9] **13** If the lords of the angles look at each other benignly by degrees and by ascensions, and especially [if they look at] the Ascendant (and this is from an angle), it signifies exaltation and a great name. **14** Let there be fixed stars of the nature of the good ones, in the Ascendant or in the tenth or in the [house signifying the matter].[10]

15 The[11] house of the significator should not be a sign besieged between the two bad ones; if a fortune is there it will not harm if it is besieged or falling from an angle. **16** Moreover, the lord of the sign should be made fit, because it has its own signification as well as that of the place in which it is: [so][12] in hastened matters, [the signs should be] the fast ones, and vice-versa.

17 For[13] kings, the eastern [signs] should be made fit, and especially Leo. **18** For investigating the truth, the signs ascending straight.

19 All[14] things cannot be made fit, because the bad ones cannot be removed from the heavens.

20 According[15] to Ptolemy and according to Abū Ma'shar, the Moon in the Ascendant is good [particularly for travels]; according to Māshā'allāh, the contrary.

21 A fortune[16] in the Ascendant [is good], and better in the ascending degree or a little lower [than it].

22 The[17] place of the conjunction or prevention [most] nearly preceding [the election] should be made fortunate and cleansed of the bad ones. **23** And the prevention is [the degree] of the light which is then above the earth or in the east, according to Ptolemy. **24** Whence, one must observe what is then in that degree by body or by aspect, to the degree or equation.[18] **25** Thus [also] with respect to the lord of the degree of the conjunction or pre-

---

[9] This is a bit odd in the Latin al-'Imrānī too, and will have to be corrected based on the Arabic in a future edition.
[10] Reading with al-'Imrānī for "the ninth."
[11] See al-'Imrānī Ch. I.2.5.
[12] The rest of this sentence does not seem to be in al-'Imrānī, and seems misplaced.
[13] See al-'Imrānī Ch. I.2.7.
[14] See al-'Imrānī Ch. I.2.4.
[15] See al-'Imrānī Ch. I.2.8.
[16] See al-'Imrānī Ch. I.2.9.
[17] See al-'Imrānī Ch. I.2.10.
[18] This word does not appear in al-'Imrānī. In traditional astronomy, an "equation" is a correction applied to a planet so as to get its precise location *as viewed by us*, as opposed to its mean position (based on the center of its epicycle). So, Leopold seems to be saying that it is not enough for a planet's epicycle to be on or near the degree of the prevention, but rather its true or equated ("correct," "corrected") position or aspect must be there.

vention. **26** [Note] how the Moon bears herself from the conjunction or prevention: if she goes to a good one, it signifies a good end; from a good one to good one, the beginning is good and the end good (and vice-versa). **27** The lord of the conjunction or prevention being eastern in that hour, and in its own house or exaltation, or in a good aspect of it,[19] or [its own] triplicity, signifies good, and that the native will escape evils by means of prudence. **28** And if the place of the conjunction or prevention falls from an angle, it will be less than this.

29 Let[20] the lord of the conjunction or prevention preceding the election, and the quarter of the year, and the lord of the year, be made fit. **30** And [if the lord of the election was][21] the lord of the sign of the Moon in the revolution of the year or the lord of the year, [and it] is fortunate at the hour of the election,[22] it signifies the increase of honor of the one beginning [the action], and the praiseworthy end of the matter. **31** And the degree of the conjunction or prevention being in a good place signifies a firm matter, and then the native or person elevated.

32 The[23] lords of the triplicity of the Moon at the conjunction or prevention should even be made fit, because they are the guardians of the native and the undertaking.

33 And[24] the Moon in an angle, increased in light, is good in things to be increased,[25] and vice-versa.

34 The[26] Moon and the other significators being above the earth signal a matter is going to be revealed; quick significators signal a matter is going to happen quickly (and vice-versa). **35** The luminaries looking at each other benignly signals the strength of the thing undertaken, and of the native, and especially if the Moon is in the sign of her own joy, which is where the Head is.[27]

---

[19] This phrase is not in al-'Imrānī.
[20] See al-'Imrānī Ch. I.2.10.
[21] Adding with al-'Imrānī.
[22] Reading with al-'Imrānī, for *elevatione* ("elevation," suggesting an accession to the throne or elevation to a dignity).
[23] See al-'Imrānī Ch. I.2.11.
[24] See al-'Imrānī Ch. I.2.11.
[25] Reading the verb *augere* with al-'Imrānī for *angulis* ("angles").
[26] See al-'Imrānī Ch. I.2.11.
[27] The Head or North Node is where the Moon crosses into northern latitude, so is not to be equated with the third house, the *house* of the Moon's joy.

36 A planet[28] eastern from the Sun is strong, [or] western from the Moon: choose according to this. **37** The Moon is strong in the night, as the Sun is in the day.

38 Above[29] all else, the Ascendant and the Moon and their lords should be made fit, because it is better to guard the body and soul than to perfect any matter.

39 The[30] [motion of the] stated Moon being similar to the motion of Saturn,[31] signals slowness and difficulty.

40 If[32] it is necessary to undertake something and the Moon is made unfortunate, let the one making her unfortunate[33] be the lord of the Ascendant, [if it is] free and a [good] condition, and it is better if it receives the Moon.

[Things to beware of][34]

41 One must beware of a conjunction of the bad ones, lest it be with any significator in that same sign (nor in the opposite nor in the square); from the trine and sextile they do not impede. **42** And according to Māshā'allāh, they become fortunes if there is any reception between them.

43 The bad ones should not be with the places[35] from which we take the significators or significations, nor, in the square nor opposite, nor in their pivot.[36] **44** The significators should not be falling, nor should they be weak.

45 Beware much of an eclipse at the hour of the undertaking,[37] and [especially] if it was in the sign in which the luminaries were in the nativity of the one for whom we are electing.

46 The Moon should not be under the rays nor otherwise impeded.

47 There should not be a [fixed] star of the nature of the bad ones in the ascending degree or Midheaven, or the lord of the matter to be chosen.

48 The significator should not be joined to the Sun, nor should [the Sun] be united with it. **49** The significator should not be in the square or opposite

---

[28] See al-'Imrānī Ch. I.2.11.
[29] See al-'Imrānī Ch. I.2.11.
[30] See al-'Imrānī Ch. I.2.11.
[31] That is, if she goes less than 12° per day.
[32] See al-'Imrānī Ch. I.2.11.
[33] Reading *infortunans* with al-'Imrānī, for *fortunans*.
[34] For this whole section, see al-'Imrānī Ch. I.2.12.
[35] Reading *locis* with al-'Imrānī for *carcere* ("prison").
[36] In other words, the malefics should not be in the whole-sign angles from these places.
[37] Reading *inceptionis* for *coniunctionis*.

aspect of the Sun. **50** However, if there is reception between them, it will be easier, but [only] a little bit. **51** The opposite [aspect] always gives quarrels and contrarieties.

52 The bad ones should not be in an angle, especially in the Ascendant or in the tenth, and especially if the bad ones were the lords of a sign signifying evil (as is the sixth, eighth): for then this signals what their houses[38] do.

53 The ascending sign should not be one which was impeded at the revolution of that same year.

54 The Moon should not be slower in what we want to happen quickly, for then it delays it and makes the matter difficult, unless there are many quick significators.

55 And remove the movable signs in durable [matters].

56 [For durable matters] the angles should not be remote, falling: which is when the ninth according to number becomes the tenth according to equation, but [rather] according to accident when the eleventh [by number] becomes the tenth [by calculation]—and this is valuable in matters which we want to last forever.[39]

57 Neither the lord of the Ascendant, nor the lord of the matter, nor the planet signifying the matter [naturally], nor the lord of the house of the Moon, nor the planet to which the Moon is being joined, should be in its "senility," which is when it is close to the Sun, setting in the evening. **58** But being away from the Sun will not harm, except that it signifies slowness.[40]

---

[38] Reading *domus* for *domi*.
[39] This is an important principle. By "number," al-'Imrānī means "whole signs"; by "calculation" or "equation," he means "by quadrant divisions." (These are standard phrases in Arabic, showing the overlap between whole sign and quadrant houses.) That is to say, we do not want the ninth *sign* to be the location of the Midheaven or tenth *quadrant house*, because then the Midheaven will be on a sign that is falling by whole signs. Rather, we want the Midheaven to be either on the tenth sign, or on the eleventh sign: in the latter case, the Midheaven will fall on a succedent sign that is moving into the tenth position by whole signs.
[40] Omitting *sed prope in munditiam* ("but close in cleanliness").

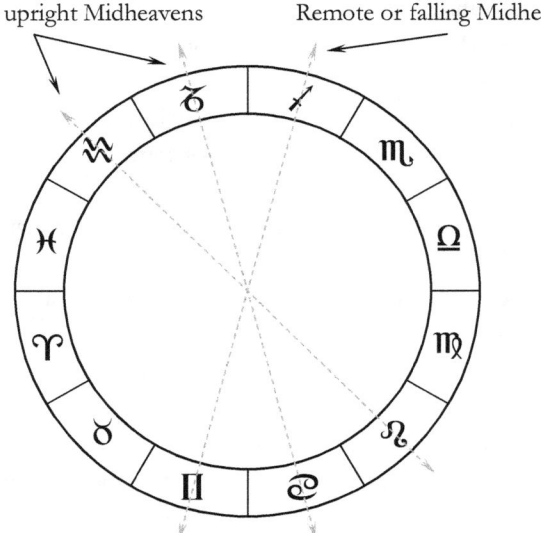

Figure 103: Advancing/upright and remote/falling Midheavens (Dykes)

59 Moreover, if it were necessary to undertake something in praiseworthy hours and the Moon is being joined to Mars and Saturn, and if the matter is signified[41] by the fortunes, begin with these, and commix something of the nature of the bad one. **60** Received bad ones are better than they can [otherwise] be, and worse if they were horrible [in condition].

---

[41] Reading *significatur* for *significant*.

[Chapter IX.2: A few specific elections][42]

1 For[43] doing something publicly, make it so that the Ascendant is in the aspect of the Sun, and the Sun is looking at the good ones, the Ascendant, and the Moon in a good aspect, and the luminaries should look at each other with a good aspect. **2** And if the matter could not be hidden, then one fleeing will be captured. **3** But if the aspect was a bad one, it will even be uncovered—but not as it ought to be. **4** The significators even being above the earth uncover [the matter].

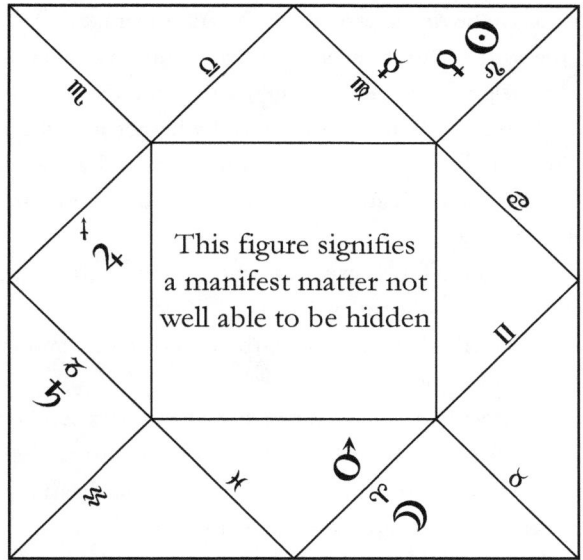

Figure 104: A figure showing that something cannot be well hidden (Leopold)

5 For[44] concealing, let the lord of the Ascendant and the Moon be under the earth, and one under the rays, or the luminaries falling from[45] the Ascendant, not looking at each other. **6** When the Moon is in the same degree with the Sun, and Venus in the Ascendant, a journey that is undertaken and

---

[42] This material is still part of al-ʿImrānī's long introductory book, but Leopold presents it as a combination of specific elections and general rules.
[43] See al-ʿImrānī Ch. I.2.12.
[44] See al-ʿImrānī Ch. I.2.12.
[45] That is, "in aversion to."

concealed will be known by none. **7** In concealing [something], if the lord of the Ascendant is a bad one, much evil will follow from that, and especially if the luminaries were impeded.

8 A stronger concealment is when the significators are embodied with the Sun.[46] **9** In clandestine things, the Moon should be under the rays, not entering [them], but going out. **10** If the lord of the conjunction or prevention was in an angle of [the thing] sought, the matter is perfected; and with the Sun it conceals something. **11** When the lord of the conjunction or prevention is in an angle, it would not be able to be hidden. **12** When the significator looks at the Ascendant, the hidden thing will be of the essence of the significator; if it does not look, it will be of the essence of the Ascendant.

13 And[47] the lord of the hour signifies the color. **14** Likewise the Moon [above] the earth [signifies something] newly dug up, under the earth not yet. **15** The Lot of Fortune and its lord [indicate] whether it is short or long. **16** The lord of the bound of the fourth or tenth (namely, the one which is in an angle), and the lord of the degree of the bound of the Moon, [show] the nature of the hidden thing.

17 No building[48] should be raised up, whose significators were joined to a planet appearing under the earth.

18 Regard the [fixed] stars in the construction of cities, and the planets in the putting-together of houses.

19 The[49] impediment of Mars is taken away in ships when he is not in the tenth or eleventh, for if he were there whatever was in the ship will be lost through pirates. **20** And if in addition one star of the hearts[50] of the signs were in the Ascendant, the ship and whatever is in it will be burned up.

21 A house[51] will fall down quickly, at whose beginning [the Moon] is southern in latitude, in Scorpio or in Pisces.

22 When[52] the fortunes rule in the roots, the evils which follow[53] should not be worried about; if however the following [charts] are praiseworthy, the good fortune[54] is doubled.

---

[46] This at least means being in a bodily conjunction, but might even refer to being in the heart with him ("cazimi"), being in the same degree as he is.
[47] See *On Hidden Things* §6 (in *WSM*).
[48] See pseudo-Ptolemy's *Centiloquy*, Aph. 54.
[49] See pseudo-Ptolemy's *Centiloquy*, Aph. 55.
[50] *Cordibus*. Ptolemy reads this as being one of the fixed stars of the nature of Mars; I do note that three of the traditional royal stars in the fixed signs (Aldebaran, Regulus, Antares) were held by Ptolemy to be wholly or partly of the nature of Mars.
[51] Source unknown at this time.

23 Moreover,[55] undertake [a matter not disclosed to the astrologer] in the hours of the rulership of Jupiter, Venus, and the Sun.)

24 The[56] lord of the seventh should be weakened when we want to go on a hunt or to battle.

25 [A strong natal planet][57] should never be weakened.[58]

26 In electing[59] for kings, make the Sun fit, and the tenth and its lord; Mercury for scribes, Mars for boxers and blacksmiths and butchers, Jupiter for judges and merchants, Venus for women and Arabs, Saturn for old men and farmers and Jews. **27** And usually, [do the same for his] class and land and sect and work, a masculine sign and diurnal hours for masculine [people], for women the contrary.

28 For[60] buying slaves and animals (which belong to [one's] assets), make the second sign fit, and its lord.

29 For[61] dyeing red, Mars, for green, Jupiter; for leaden-blue, Saturn; for citrine, the Sun; for white, Venus; for a varied [color], Mercury; for the color of silver, the Moon.

30 All[62] hours which belong to the Sun, burn (which we have explained in the fourth Treatise,[63] on introductory things), because they are bad for life.[64]

---

[52] See al-'Imrānī Ch. I.2.13.
[53] In this context, al-'Imrānī means "subsequent charts," such as looking at someone's solar revolution. Thus, if the fortunes are powerful and ruling in someone's nativity, then one does not need to review the recent solar return to see if an election is possible this year.
[54] Reading *fortuna* with al-'Imrānī for *persona*.
[55] See al-'Imrānī Ch. I.2.13.
[56] See al-'Imrānī Ch. I.2.13.
[57] See al-'Imrānī Ch. I.2.13.
[58] Omitting *a lumine in nativitate vel in revolutione* ("by a light in the nativity or in the revolution").
[59] See al-'Imrānī Ch. I.2.13.
[60] See al-'Imrānī Ch. I.2.13.
[61] See al-'Imrānī Ch. I.2.13.
[62] See al-'Imrānī Ch. I.2.13.
[63] In Ch. IV.4, **46-49**.
[64] Omitting *earum* ("of them").

[Adapting the nativity and revolution to the election]

31 If[65] the nativity is known, put the victor of the nativity in an angle or succeedent of the election, and it is better above the earth, and let it be free from the bad ones and joined to strong fortunate [planets]. **32** Which if it were a bad one, let it be put in a succeedent, lest (being placed in an angle) it destroy the matter. **33** And it is better if the lord of the revolution and the lord of the Lot of fortune [are made fit, and some astrologers] observe the lord of the profection and the lord of the orb[66] or victor of the nativity.[67]

34 Moreover,[68] the Ascendant of the root (or the Midheaven) should be the Ascendant of the election, free from the bad ones, and it is better if a fortune is there or looks at the Ascendant benignly. **35** If that could not happen, let it be the fifth sign [or] eleventh of his revolution or profection, or the sign of the Lot of Fortune in the root or revolution, so that however it is free from the bad ones. **36** Moreover, make the house of the matter in the nativity or revolution, be the Ascendant in the election. **37** And the Moon should look at the Ascendant and a bad one should not be looking—and if a bad one *does* look and it is the lord of the nativity, it does not impede, and such a perfection of the matter will be very good.

38 In[69] no way should the Ascendant of the election be the house of infirmities in the root, nor that of death or enemies.[70] **39** Let the lord of the Ascendant of the election be in a good place from the Ascendant of the root, [and] do the same thing with the Ascendant of the revolution (if it could happen) and the sign of the profection, and the place of the Lot of Fortune (and more so the Lot of Fortune in the root of the nativity). **40** The strength of the significators[71] and the aspects of the fortunes annul every evil.

41 If[72] the lord of the Ascendant of the nativity or revolution or election is in the house of the matter in the nativity or revolution or election, the matter is perfected with the labor of the one choosing; and if is the other way

---

[65] See al-ʿImrānī Ch. I.3.
[66] This might refer to the "lord of the turn," a predictive technique that became rare in the Latin West: see *ITA* VIII.2.3.
[67] Modifying the case endings a bit to match the meaning of al-ʿImrānī.
[68] See al-ʿImrānī Ch. I.3.
[69] See al-ʿImrānī Ch. I.3.
[70] That is, the sixth, eighth, and twelfth, respectively.
[71] Reading *significatorum et aspectus fortunarum* with al-ʿImrānī for *significatur et aspectus significatorum fortunatorum*.
[72] See al-ʿImrānī Ch. I.3.

around,[73] [it will be perfected] without labor—if however it is strong and free from the bad ones. **42** If the lords of the two places look at each other benignly, it is good, and more so if they are conjoined, and especially if there is reception between them.

43 Moreover,[74] if in the nativity evil is signified for the native in such a year, he should not undertake a grand work in that year, especially one which pertains to that evil that is signified. **44** But if it is necessary to undertake it, let the significator of evil be made to be falling, and let us make the Ascendant as fit as we can, and the lord of the end of the matter, and their lords. **45** And let a fortune be put in a place in which that bad one was in the root, or the rays of a fortune, or at least let the bad ones be removed from the angles, and particularly the significator of the evil.

46 If[75] the nativity signifies the fitness[76] of the matter, the matter will be perfected in that hour, even if the election is not perfectly good.

47 The[77] evils that are signified in nativities are sometimes diminished, sometimes even wholly cancelled (according to all the astrologers), and because of this it was necessary to know the nativities. **48** Moreover, if you do not know the Ascendant of the nativity, use the Ascendant of the revolution of the year of the world. **49** Even when something of great good[78] happens to someone, the Ascendant should then be made the Ascendant [of the election]. **50** Moreover, if a planet is strong when a good thing happens to someone, that planet should be put as belonging to him.[79] **51** Likewise with respect to regions and cities.

52 And[80] if the evil is weak, it[81] is necessary to use the infortunes in elections just as expert doctors use poisons in a suitable amount.

---

[73] That is, if the lord of the topic we are electing for, is in the Ascendant. The symbolism here is as follows: if the lord of the Ascendant is in another house, it means the client needs to go to the topic (i.e., with labor); but if the lord of the topic is in the Ascendant, the topic comes to him (i.e., without labor). This is discussed again in Ch. VIII.2, **7** above.
[74] See al-'Imrānī Ch. I.3.
[75] See al-'Imrānī Ch. I.3.
[76] Reading *aptationem* for *optationem* ("wishing").
[77] See al-'Imrānī Ch. I.4.
[78] Reading somewhat loosely for *aliquod magni in bonis*.
[79] That is (following al-'Imrānī), we can suppose that that planet plays a good role in his nativity, and so should be strengthened in the election.
[80] See pseudo-Ptolemy's *Centiloquy*, Aph. 10.
[81] Omitting "whence."

53 You[82] should not elect except for one who has revealed his intention to you, as to the nature of the matter for which you are electing, and unless you knew the end of [his] intention in it.

54 And[83] prepare what there is between the spherical virtue and your own experience, and do likewise in all things.

[Going to races or games]

55 In[84] the racing of horses, the one who goes out of his own home with the lord of the hour in the Ascendant, will be first; if the lord of the hour is in the tenth, [his horse] will be second; if in the seventh, it will come in between the first and last; in the fourth, it will be last. **56** And if lord of the hour is in the place of [its own] fall, the one whom it signifies will suffer a fall. **57** And the Moon should be in Sagittarius[85] or in the middle of Libra—and thus counsels al-Kindī.[86] **58** The[87] age of [the horse] is known through the lord of the twelfth: if eastern, he has changed two teeth; if western, all.

59 For[88] a game, leave your house under a movable sign, and in no way under a fixed one; and let the Moon be joined to Mars from a trine, and not Saturn. **60** And your face and chest [should be] against the Moon,[89] and let the Moon be above the earth.

---

[82] Source unknown at this time.
[83] Source unknown at this time, nor does it make sense to me.
[84] See al-'Imrānī Ch. II.1.12.
[85] Reading with al-'Imrānī, for *in signo*.
[86] Actually, al-'Imrānī attributes only the first part of **55** to al-Kindī (and he seems to be wrong about that anyway); the rest follows Sahl, except for the rule about the Moon in **57**.
[87] For this sentence, see Sahl's *On Questions* §12.3.
[88] See al-'Imrānī Ch. II.1.12.
[89] That is, "facing" the Moon.

[Chapter IX.3: Making magical images]

1 If you want to make an image for someone, for good health or illness,[90] let these things be made fortunate or unfortunate: the Ascendant and its lord, and the lord of the house of the lord of the Ascendant, the Moon and her lord, the tenth and its lord, the lord of the eighth, the lord of the hour.

2 These things are inscribed: the name of the matter, the name of the Ascendant, the name of the lord of the Ascendant, the name of the lord of the day, the name of the lord of the hour, the Lot of good or bad things (that is, the lord of the Lot).[91]

3 And it is said [that][92] the image is set aside or buried, the Midheaven [being] as above.[93] **4** If it is for benefiting a man, he should carry it with him or leave it in the house under a fortunate Ascendant for strong good fortune.[94] **5** Do likewise in making a place fortunate or the destruction of a region.

6 For acquiring assets easily, let the Ascendant and its lord be made fortunate, the second and its lord, the lord of the second should be in reception[95] with the lord of the first (the lord of the second should be in an obeying [sign], the lord of the first in a commanding [sign]), [and] the tenth and its lord, the eighth and its lord, the eleventh and its lord, the Moon and her lord. **7** The Lot of Fortune should be in the first or eleventh.

7 For having a desired thing, or recovering a lost thing, there come to be two images. **8** The first comes to be under the Ascendant of the one who seeks the thing or demands it back, according to the nativity or interrogation. **9** And let the Ascendant and its lord be fortunate, let the Ascendant and its lord be made fit in strength and fortune, so that it is even put in a commanding sign. **10** And let it be put in the conjunction or good aspect (with reception) of the significator of the one who then holds or is detaining the

---

[90] Normally, astrological authors do not provide elections for hurting people, but the author of this magical material does.
[91] This is probably simply the lord of the Lot of Fortune.
[92] Omitting *intendit* ("he intends").
[93] Reading somewhat uncertainly for *ut supra medium coeli*. I believe Leopold's source means this: *make* the image with the Ascendant according to the conditions stated above, but *bury/leave* it when that ascending sign is on the Midheaven. Then in the next sentence, he states what one should do for carrying it around.
[94] Or perhaps, "with a strong fortune" (*fortunio forti*).
[95] Reading *receptione* with the sense of Thābit, for "retrogradation" (*retrogradatione*).

thing. **11** And let it be stated what is intended.⁹⁶ **12** So that if [the one possessing the thing] is the king [it is the lord] of the tenth, if the father the fourth, if a brother the third, and thus with the others. **13** And the image should be named with a famous name of the one for whom it is made.⁹⁷ **14** And when it is done, let the name of the Ascendant be inscribed, [and] the name of the lord of the Ascendant, the name of the lord of the day, the name of the lord of the matter, and the name of the lord of the hour.

15 The second [image] will come to be under the Ascendant of the one who holds or detains the thing. **16** And let the Ascendant be made fortunate, and let its lord be made fit in strength and fortune, except that it should be put in an obeying sign and put in the conjunction or good aspect (with reception) of the significator of the first image. **17** Let it be stated what is intended. **18** And let the image be named with a famous name of the one for whom it is made. **19** And when it is done, let the name of the matter be inscribed, the name of the Ascendant, the name of the lord of the Ascendant, the name of the lord of the day, and the name of the lord of the hour. **20** And when both are finished, let them be placed with the owner of the first image.

21 For making a place fortunate (and its destruction), proceed just as you did above with respect to health and infirmity, [but] with this added: that in good things you should make the lord of the hour a good planet, and it should be in a good bearing; but in bad things, a bad planet (and particularly Saturn), so that you make him unfortunate.

22 For having an honor, let the Ascendant and its lord be made fortunate, let the lord of the tenth be in reception with the lord of the first, [and] let the Lot of Fortune be in the tenth or eleventh.

23 For the support of a greater [person], let there be a conjunction or reception by a good aspect between the lord of the first and the tenth, or both should be free from the bad ones. **24** And the lord of the Ascendant [should be] in the Ascendant or should look at it benignly.⁹⁸ **25** And the lord of the tenth should not impede the lord of the Ascendant. **26** Make a second [image] under the Ascendant of the tenth,⁹⁹ along with the stated conditions,

---

⁹⁶ At this point the prayer or invocation should be made, as well as in **17** below.
⁹⁷ The "famous name" (here and below) is probably a magical name or statement.
⁹⁸ Omitting a redundant "or both should be free from the bad ones."
⁹⁹ I believe this means "when the tenth house of the first image comes to be on the Ascendant." So if the tenth of the first image was Libra, then make the second image when Libra is arising.

and put the hand of the second [person] toward the neck of the first [person].

24 For the hatred of a greater [person], do the contrary: the lord of the tenth should be in the opposite of [the lord of] the first, with separation.

25 For[100] having the love of someone, make an image for the one whose love you want to acquire on the day and hour of Jupiter, under the Ascendant of the nativity or interrogation. **26** Make the Ascendant and its lord forfortunate, and remove the bad ones from them. **27** Let the lord of the tenth be a fortune and joined to the lord of the Ascendant with bodily reception or by a good aspect. **28** Name the image with a famous name of the one for whom you are making it. **29** Make a second image under the Ascendant of the eleventh[101] for a friend, under the Ascendant of the seventh for a wife, [and] even name this image with the famous name of the one for whom you are making it. **30** Put the second [image] with the first one so that they embrace each other, put in a clean cloth, and [put] both images with the owner of the first image. **31** The power [of the image] is not in the metal or wax or clay from which it comes to be, because an observation of the Ascendant with the memorized conditions is enough.

32 For repulsing some animal (for example, a scorpion), make the image of a scorpion with Scorpio ascending, [and] let the Moon be in that same place, made unfortunate. **33** Let the lord of the Ascendant be unfortunate in the eighth, [and] let the lord of the fourth be made unfortunate by the seventh[102] or square aspect of a malevolent. **34** Let these things be inscribed: the name of the Ascendant, the name of the lord of the Ascendant, the name of the lord of the day, the name of the lord of the hour, the name of the Moon. **35** And for good things which you inscribe, put them on the front; for bad things, on the back. **36** Bury the reversed[103] image in the middle of the place (it will be better if you make four and you buried all reversed [images] in the four directions of the place). **37** Once the right place has been divided into four, and while you bury, say: "this is the burial of the scorpion, so that it might withdraw from this place and not return, forever."

---

[100] This is similar to *Picatrix* I.5, pp. 40-41 and 43.
[101] That is, let the eleventh of the nativity (or whatever chart has confirmed that friendship is possible).
[102] That is, the opposition.
[103] *Versam.* I should think that the scorpion side would face down, as though held down by the power of the good names on the front of the talisman. This word does not appear in Thābit.

38 [For someone who wants to be in charge of a city or region or other work, or a place of first importance],[104] sculpt the head of a shape (you create[105] the image, I say) under the Ascendant in which the Head of the Dragon is, and let the lord of the Ascendant be of good condition. **39** [Sculpt] the body under the Ascendant in which the Moon is increased in light, joined to a fortune. **40** The shoulder-blades and chest under the Ascendant in which Jupiter is, the belly under the Ascendant in which Venus is, the hips under the Ascendant in which the Sun is (in any dignity of his), the thighs under the Ascendant in which Mercury is (neither retrograde nor burned up, but in any dignity of his), the feet under the Ascendant in which the Moon is associated with Venus.

41 The book of images is completed; an addition to it follows:

42 On top [of what was said], note that the angular hours are moderate, the eleventh the best, likewise the Lot of Fortune: observe each if it is possible. **43** But you should retain the chapters of the said book by means of these verses: a body which holds firm, having a thing, honor and favor (love participates in this), and devastating or repelling [something] harmful.

44 Moreover, those things which are made fortunate for making images, [are done so] by carefully considering nativities (good or bad) and revolutions and questions and inceptions, for bodies, assets, honor, support, love, repelling, and [their] contraries, through the Moon in the good or bad mansions I know a good day or bad one. **45** Always observe the Ascendant and its lord for the status of the body, how they bear themselves in their own right and with the Ascendant, and who is there by body or aspect. **46** The Lot of Fortune and its lord for the status of assets, the Sun for success[106] and honor, the Moon for the condition of the soul along with the body, the Midheaven for mastery and work.

---

[104] Adding with Thābit, else these instructions would make little sense.
[105] Reading *fundas* for *fundis*.
[106] *Valentia*.

[Chapter IX.4: Individual elections]

1 For contracting an association [with someone], let the Moon be in a movable[107] sign. **2** In Scorpio and Aquarius, it is ended badly, in Taurus it is good with an equal, in Leo it is absolutely good.

3 If[108] you are going where you want to be in charge, put Jupiter in the Ascendant or in the ninth, and you will have good there; in the fourth it is terrible. **4** Moreover, let the Moon and Venus testify to Jupiter, do not let there be a bad one in an angle, [and] the Moon should not be under the rays of the Sun or with the Tail, nor with the bad ones (because then the traveler will not return, [and] an infirm one will then die).

5 If[109] you are going to war, the lord of the Ascendant should not be in the seventh or eighth or in the ninth, nor should the lord of the first be going towards the lord of the seventh (because then the one going to war will be killed or overwhelmed).

6 For[110] a quick and prosperous return, Jupiter and Venus should be in the square of the Sun and Moon, and the Moon should be between the two fortunes, separated from one and joined to the other—and the Moon should be increased in light and number. **7** The infortunes slow down and impede with the greatest impediment, and if a fortune is with them, prosperity will follow. **8** And the Moon in the eighth house signifies a long stay [abroad].

9 In[111] changing one's lodging-place, let the fourth house be Taurus or Leo, and the house will be clean; for if it is Scorpio, poisonous animals will be had [there], and especially in the aspect of Saturn. **10** And there should not be an infortune in the fourth, nor should it look at it in an unfriendly way. **11** Venus should be in the fourth, Jupiter in the second, the Moon in a good place appropriate for her. **12** But what makes the one who enters another house become rich, is [that] when you change house Jupiter should be in the second, and the Moon in a good place, and you will be enriched.

---

[107] This does not make astrological sense, and contradicts passages such as al-'Imrānī Ch. II.8.2. Rather, we should prefer a common (mutable) sign, because we want a profitable relationship or association to be repeated, with a back-and-forth movement.
[108] See Sahl's *On Elections* §123 (in *Choices*).
[109] This bears a resemblance to Sahl's *On Elections* §§86a-86b.
[110] See al-'Imrānī II.1.8.
[111] See al-'Imrānī II.3.6, which only covers **15-17**.

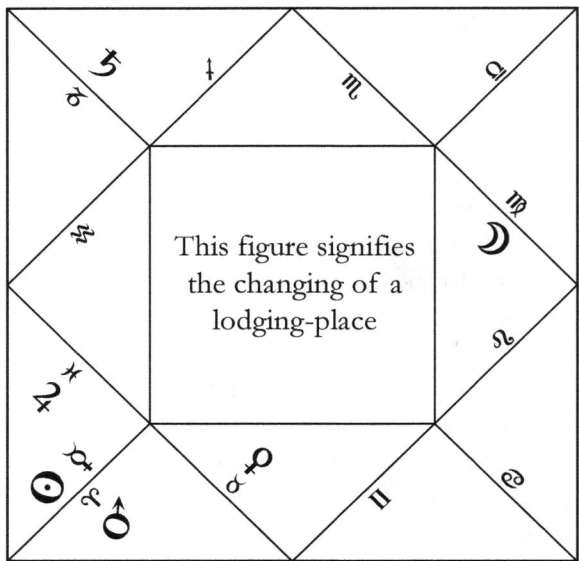

Figure 105: A figure showing the changing of a lodging-place (Leopold)

13 With a planet whose business is in the Midheaven,[112] it is good to undertake a work [of its kind].

14 A fit Sun makes a good and quick return, and let the Moon be between the two good ones.

15 Undertake no journey when the Moon is increased[113] with light; for the road, the Moon should not be in the square or opposite aspect of the Sun. **16** Moreover, in leaving and returning the Moon should not be in the eighth or seventh. **17** For returning, the Moon should not be in the first, second, or fourth: the Moon should be in the Midheaven, looking at Mercury benignly.

18 Moreover, make the lord of the hour and the Moon fit for [having] a fortunate road,[114] and make the lord of the Ascendant fortunate.

19 For[115] the road, let Mercury have gone out from burning, joined to a fortune (and especially for merchants).

---

[112] This probably means that it rules the Midheaven, or closely aspects it, or is in it.
[113] This probably only means when she is full, i.e., totally filled with light—for after that, her light wanes.
[114] Tentatively reading *pro via fortunata*, for *pro via infortunae* ("for the path of an infortune"). But perhaps this means that *if* one knows the road is likely to be difficult or unfortunate already, one should at least do these things.
[115] See al-ʿImrānī II.1.8.

20 If no planet is in the ninth, go confidently provided that the lord of the ninth is of a good condition.

21 When[116] you go to ecclesiastical people, make Jupiter and the Moon fit; if to writers, Mercury, to women Venus and the Moon, to old men let the Moon be in the trine or sextile aspect of Saturn.

22 For leaving, make the seventh and the eighth and their lords fit; for returning, the first and second and their lords. **23** Join the Moon to the planet whose matter you want to seek or have.

24 If[117] you want to seek something, let the Moon be increased in light and number.

25 If[118] someone demanded something from another with the Head appearing with Jupiter in the Midheaven, and in addition the Moon goes towards him, or if the Moon goes towards the lord of the Ascendant, withdrawing from Jupiter, or if the lord of the Ascendant goes to him, he will obtain [what he wants] quickly.

26 If you want to buy something, let the Moon be in her half [of the zodiac], from Aquarius to Leo.[119]

27 If[120] you want to buy arms or instruments of war, let the Moon be with Mars at the end of the [lunar] month.[121]

28 For beginning teachings, choose above all the day of the Sun and Mercury, and never Saturn;[122] and Mercury and the Moon should be well placed.

29 Also, the day of Venus is useful for letting [blood]; the Moon should not be in Gemini nor in Pisces, because Jupiter and Mercury deny the increase of cut-off things.[123] **30** And let the Moon be increasing in number and light.

31 Cure the eyes when the Moon is increased in light, without the aspect of the bad ones.

---

[116] See Sahl's *On Elections* §108a*ff.*
[117] See Sahl's *On Elections* §132c.
[118] See Vescovini, *Albumasar in Sadan* §6.
[119] Or rather, from the beginning of Aquarius to the end of Cancer.
[120] See Sahl's *On Elections* §91.
[121] Or rather, between the Full Moon and the New Moon, while she is waning. This rule is a sect consideration: when the Moon is increasing or waxing in light (which is akin to the day and heat), it is all right for her to be joined to Saturn (a cold, diurnal planet) but not Mars (a nocturnal, hot planet, which would exacerbate the heat). Conversely, it is all right for her to be waning or decreasing in light while joining with Mars, but not Saturn.
[122] These are Sunday, Wednesday, and Saturday, respectively.
[123] This must mean that new blood will not be produced quickly.

32 And always, in all things, beware lest the lord of the Ascendant be[124] in the eighth, for in questions this is found to be deadly.

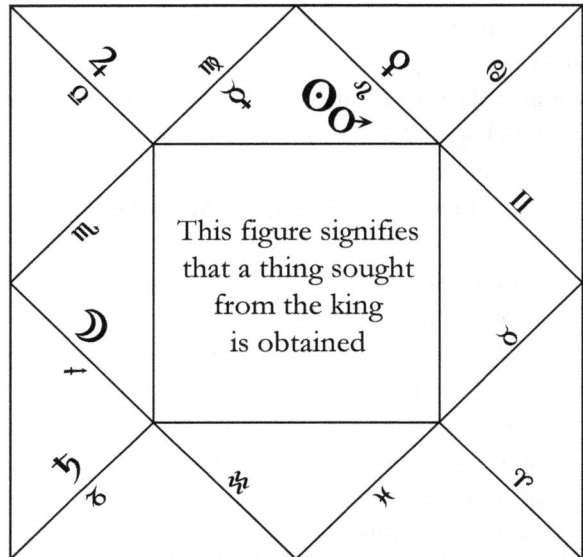

Figure 106: A figure showing that something sought from the king will be obtained (Leopold)

33 When each of the luminaries applies to the lord of the east (it appearing in a pivot), from a pivot, you will have or obtain whatever you sought from the king. **34** And either of the luminaries holding onto the rulership of the Midheaven, gives the greatest increase. **35** One who approached the king with the Moon appearing in Aquarius, will not receive it from him, nor will the king care about him.

36 In[125] every undertaking of a matter, make the circle fit for the nature of what you are going to undertake: because [there is a relationship] between the circle of heaven and the nature of lower things, such as between a magnet and iron, and between a father and son, and one eating and food.

37 Choose[126] movable signs for changes, fixed ones in lasting things (and Scorpio is the easier one among the fixed ones, Aquarius slower and worse).

---

[124] Omitting *non* ("not"), which would have led to a double negation.
[125] See Sahl's *On Elections* §10 (in *WSM* and *Choices*).
[126] See Sahl's *On Elections* §§12a-14a (in *WSM* and *Choices*).

38 You[127] should not make the Moon be waxing in the Ascendant, or the one for whom you choose will become ill—unless the lord of the Ascendant looks at the degree of the Ascendant—or [the lord] will be as though absent from its own house, not able to defend its own matter. **39** [But] if the lord of the Ascendant [were an infortune], it should look at it with a good aspect, and the Moon not be impeded in the angles, and there [should] be a fortune in the angle of the Ascendant.

40 In beginnings,[128] the Lot of Fortune should not be falling from[129] the aspect or conjunction of the Moon, unless it would look at the Ascendant or the Moon, or at least the lord of the Ascendant. **41** The lord of the Ascendant should be put with the Lot of Fortune or its aspect (which is better).

42 The Moon[130] should not be put in the falling signs.

43 If[131] the Moon is impeded and the matter can in no way be deferred, you should not give her a dignity in the Ascendant, and put a fortune in the Ascendant; and make the lord [of the Ascendant] lord fortunate by means of the presence or aspect of the fortunes.

44 They are called "chosen hours," in which the Lot of Fortune falls in an angle, and it is best if in the eleventh house. **45** Bad hours [are] if [it is] in falling houses; in succeedents, middling.

46 And I have carefully inserted the book of images along with the rules of elections, for the [book] on elections is also made [to be] about obtaining [things].

47 If you want to obtain something, choose so that the Ascendant is empty, and the lord of the Ascendant should be in the seventh, or the lord of the ninth in its conjunction, or the lord of the bound or the lord of the hour, or at least it should be eastern from the Sun or should look at the Moon, or

---

[127] See Sahl's *On Elections* §§23a-24 (in *WSM* and *Choices*).
[128] See Sahl's *On Elections* §§25a-25b (in *WSM* and *Choices*). Leopold has misunderstood part of this sentence. Sahl's points are that (a) the lord of the Lot is not that important, (b) the Lot should always be with or aspecting the Moon, and (c) that even if the Lot is in aversion to the Ascendant, it should still be with or looking at the lord of the Ascendant and the Moon.
[129] Reading *ab* for *ad* ("toward"). In other words, the Lot should not be in aversion to them.
[130] See Sahl's *On Elections* §25b (in *WSM* and *Choices*). Leopold has misunderstood this sentence: Sahl does not want the Moon to be in the signs that are in aversion to ("falling away from") *the Lot*.
[131] See Sahl's *On Elections* §28 (in *WSM* and *Choices*).

Mars should be in either of his own houses, or Jupiter with the Head of the Dragon, or the lord of the matter with the lord of the Ascendant.

48 In an election, the Moon should not be with a retrograde planet, likewise the lord of the Ascendant should not be retrograde, [and] the Moon should not be in the burnt path.

49 When the king is moved to war, the Moon should not be with a bad one by body or a bad aspect, nor under the rays, nor with the Tail: otherwise he will be killed or conquered.

50 Every undertaking is to be abhorred when the conjunction or prevention which more nearly preceded it is impeded.

51 When the lord of the Ascendant goes towards the lord of the seventh, you should not begin war. **52** One in whose nativity the lord of the fourth is in the tenth, or the lord of the seventh in the first, will be the victor in wars: speak likewise for a question, and elect according to this.

53 For[132] making concord [between people], let the lord of the seventh be weak and a fortune, and it should look at the lord of the Ascendant by a trine or sextile aspect, and it should be looking at the Ascendant with a good aspect. **54** And the lord of the twelfth [should be] weak and falling, and it is good that the lord of the twelfth be impeded. **55** And the eleventh and its lord should be made fit, and let the lord of the Ascendant be in the Midheaven or going towards it. **56** Likewise the Ascendant and its lord, so that they can be stronger in strength and fortune. **57** And if the degree of the twelfth and the lord of the Ascendant were of one [and the same] strength, this is better for all in the fitness of the houses; and if both are present, Jupiter should be made fit and the lord of the Ascendant should be in an ordering sign,[133] and the lord of the seventh in an obeying one (and if it is being transacted through a legate or letters, Mercury should be made fit).

58 When[134] we want to lead enemies out from their places by trickery, let the Moon and the lord of the Ascendant be in Aries or Taurus, Gemini, Virgo, Sagittarius, Capricorn, or Pisces, and the Moon joined to one of the fortunes (or let one of them be in the Ascendant). **59** And the lord of the Ascendant should not be falling from an angle, and it should look at the Ascendant benignly, and should be in the aspect of a fortune, and the lord of the twelfth should be weak.

---

[132] See al-'Imrānī II.1.9.
[133] That is, a commanding sign.
[134] See al-'Imrānī II.1.9.

[Chapter IX.5: Elections of the first house]

1 The[135] feeding of boys with a wet-nurse should begin[136] [when] the Moon is joined to Venus by body, and both are safe, and it is better if Venus is in the Ascendant.

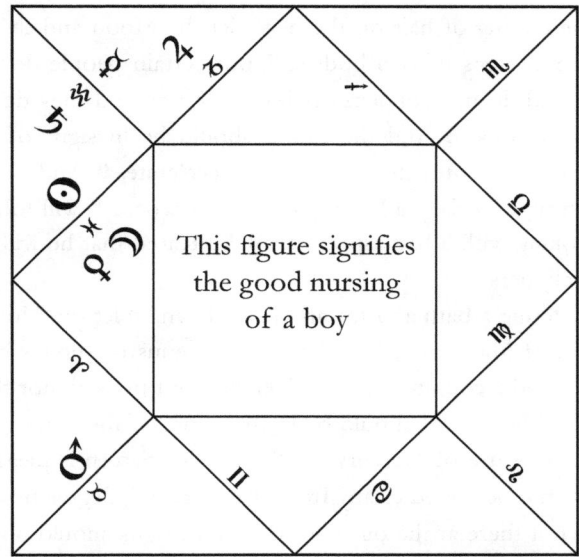

Figure 107: A figure showing the good nursing of a boy (Leopold)

2 In[137] weaning, let the Moon be away from the Sun, joined to the lord of her own house, and let [the Ascendant be in] one of the houses of the fortunes[138] (in which, the house of Venus displeases certain people, fearing that the mother of another would not take the boy[139] away from the breasts). **3** And they say when we separate infants from wet-nurses, if the Moon was in the empty course the boys will not care to nurse beyond [that].[140] **4** And oth-

---

[135] Cf. al-'Imrānī II.2.1, who however says (in the Latin) that Venus should be in the *Descendant*.
[136] Reading *incipiat* for *aspicit*.
[137] See al-'Imrānī II.2.2.
[138] Reading with al-'Imrānī for "fortunate houses."
[139] Reading *puerum* with al-'Imrānī for *cibum* ("food"). The idea behind this awkward sentence (which is also awkward in al-'Imrānī) seems to be that the mother or nurse would not want to nurse any other child in the future.
[140] Reading *alterius* with al-'Imrānī for *ulterius* ("the last one").

ers say the Moon and the lord of the Ascendant should be in the houses of crops (as is Taurus, Virgo, Capricorn), and the boy will hunger for crops.

5 In[141] the cutting of the nails the Moon should be increased in light and number, in an angle or succeedent, not in Gemini nor in Sagittarius, nor joined to their lords (for it is feared that [the nails] will not grow back), but in a house of Mars or Mercury[142] or in Cancer or Leo.

6 In[143] the cutting of hair on the head, let the Moon and the lord of the Ascendant be in signs of two bodies. **7** But certain people do not[144] commend Virgo and do not condemn Aries nor Libra, and they do not esteem Capricorn or Taurus. **8** And the Moon should be in signs of seeds (elsewhere, "burning"),[145] and the growth will accelerate. **9** And beware of the aspect of Saturn, especially a hostile one, or ringworm[146] will follow. **10** And if Mars is looking with a bad aspect, it will be feared that he will be cut with the razor or clippers.

11 In[147] entering a bath and for an oil rubdown,[148] let the Moon be in any of the houses of Mars, joined to the Sun or Venus or Jupiter by a trine or sextile aspect; and a conjunction with Venus is not praised, nor the aspect of Saturn. **12** Or, [the Moon] should be in the house of the Sun or in her own; and neither the house of Mercury nor Venus nor Saturn is pleasing. **13** The Moon should not be joined to any from the aforesaid, degree by degree.[149] **14** But if she is not there at the oil rubdown, other signs should not be blamed provided that they were safe.

---

[141] See al-'Imrānī II.2.3.
[142] Al-'Imrānī has, "Venus or Mars."
[143] See al-'Imrānī II.2.4.
[144] Al-'Imrānī omits the "not," but in context Leopold's reading sounds better.
[145] Leopold is pointing out that some manuscripts read "sowing" (*sementum*), others "burning" (*crementum*); to me it seems that "sowing" or "seeds" (al-Imrānī) is correct.
[146] *Tinea*.
[147] See al-'Imrānī II.2.5.
[148] *Unctione*. For al-'Imrānī, this includes hair removal using a depilatory cream; but in general a steam or hot bath is meant.
[149] That is, by exact degree.

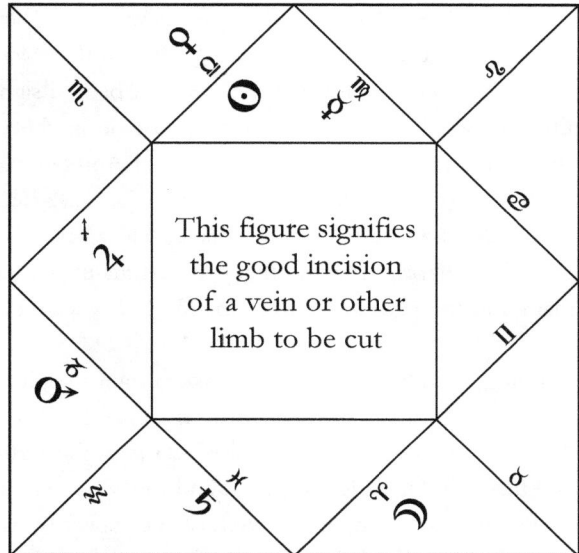

Figure 108: A figure showing the good incision of a vein or limb (Leopold)

15 For[150] bloodletting, 'Alī makes the Moon be deficient [in light], and that there should not be a conjunction of the Moon with the lord of the eighth, and the Moon should not be in the fourth house.

16 In[151] circumcising boys, let the Moon be elevated above Venus[152] and joined to Jupiter, and beware of the Ascendant and its lord, and Venus and the Moon, lest Saturn look at any [of them] by any aspect (and especially the Ascendant and the Moon): for Saturn signals the repetition of the cutting of the veins, and putrefaction. **17** The Ascendant and its lord, [and] the Moon and its lord, should be northern, going towards an angle, and Mars should not be in the Ascendant, nor the Moon in Scorpio.

18 For[153] giving purging medicines, let the Moon be in the last half of Libra or in the first [half] of Scorpio, and let her lord be fortunate and strong, and likewise the lord of the Ascendant. **19** And let the Ascendant be any of

---

[150] See al-'Imrānī II.2.8.
[151] See al-'Imrānī II.2.9.
[152] This probably means that she should "overcome" her from the superior square (see Glossary).
[153] See al-'Imrānī II.2.10.

the inferior signs,[154] and the Moon should be in them so that, being in a sign signaling that limb, she is fortunate [and] strong. **20** And if we wanted to heat or chill, dry or moisten, let the Moon and Ascendant be in a sign doing that, and any significator (or the Ascendant) should not be in the cud-chewing signs, and Capricorn is said to be more hateful.[155] **21** And Saturn should not be looking in any way (for he binds up), nor Mars (because he leads to the spilling of blood). **22** Likewise in health-inducing electuaries,[156] except that any Ascendant will not harm, provided that it is fortunate, as well as the lord of the Ascendant and the place of the Moon. **23** And beware of the lord of the eighth.

24 For[157] binding [medicines] which provoke certain people to vomiting, beware of the cud-chewing signs;[158] and if is of those, let it be weak [and] one will not have to fear them (except Taurus). **25** And the sign of the limb should be made fit so that it is clearly better, and the Moon should be in her own average course in the north, and beware of the aspect of Mars. **26** And if the Moon is in the first 3° of Taurus it is good, [because she is] going toward her own exaltation.

27 For[159] [medicines that produce] sneezing and gargling and vomiting, let the Moon and the Ascendant and the places of the significators be [in] the cud-chewing signs, with all of the other things which were stated for purges. **28** And let the Moon be diminished in light and course, rising in the circle of [her] apogee, and let the Moon and the lord of the Ascendant be in Cancer, Leo, or Virgo.

29 For[160] putting on new vestments (which pertains to the body),[161] let the Moon and the Ascendant be in movable signs, nor are the common ones bad. **93** And of the fixed signs, beware of Leo unless it is a vestment that pertains to war. **30** Let the Sun be in the Midheaven and the Moon increased

---

[154] That is, signs which indicate the lower part of the body (from Libra through Pisces).
[155] Since chewing the cud involves regurgitation, we should not have the Moon in signs such as Taurus or Capricorn when we want the medicine to be properly digested.
[156] An electuary is a medicine designed to melt in the mouth through sucking, rather than being drunk or swallowed (such as sucking on a medicinal tablet to treat thrush in the throat).
[157] See al-'Imrānī II.2.11.
[158] See footnote above.
[159] See al-'Imrānī II.2.12.
[160] See al-'Imrānī II.2.13.
[161] Omitting "hair." Leopold reads, "which is of the hairs of the body" (*quod est de capillis corporis*), but al-'Imrānī is only pointing out that this chapter belongs in this place *because* clothing pertains to the body.

in light, and make the second and its lord be fit, and especially in the purchase of vestments and their cutting.

[Chapter IX.6: Elections of the second house]

1 Concerning the second house, you have enough in nativities and questions.[162]

[Chapter IX.7: Elections of the third house]

1 Concerning[163] the third house, such as devotion to God, make the third and its lord fit, and Jupiter and the luminaries. **2** Let the Ascendant be either house of Jupiter, and make Mercury fit (and let the intention be considered subtly): and these planets [should] look at each other by a praiseworthy aspect, and each one looks at the house of the other—or we should make fit what we can of these things.
3 In[164] the issuing of commands, let the Moon be joined to that planet signaling the one to whom we are issuing [them], such as if it is the king, let her be joined to Sun (nor let them be falling); if a Jew or merchant, Jupiter. **4** And let the one to which the Moon is being joined, be free [of the infortunes].

[Chapter IX.8: Elections of the fourth house]

1 Concerning[165] the fourth house, such as building a mill, let the Moon or Ascendant be in Aries or Libra or in the last part[166] of Pisces or Virgo. **2** Do not let the Moon be in Cancer or Capricorn, because they are contrary to the quality [of the election]: for they make the days and nights unequal. **3** And if the Moon and the lord of the Ascendant are in other signs, without the aspect of an infortune, it is good.

---

[162] Nevertheless, see all of al-'Imrānī II.3.
[163] See al-'Imrānī II.4.2.
[164] Or rather, the sending of legates: al-'Imrānī II.4.3.
[165] See al-'Imrānī II.5.3.
[166] This probably means "degree."

4 In sowing,[167] let the Moon be in movable signs, or in Pisces or in Virgo. **5** In planting trees, the Moon should be in fixed [signs], and especially in Taurus or Aquarius, and Saturn direct, in what follows an angle, in a place in which he has some dignity or testimony, or in the Ascendant (and let the Ascendant be one of the aforesaid). **6** And Jupiter should be[168] looking at Saturn with a good aspect, more so [from] a place in which he has some testimony; and beware of Mars. **7** And certain people prefer the lord of the exaltation to the lord of the house when planting trees. **8** And the lord of the Moon should be looking at her[169] from a watery sign. **9** And if the Ascendant is not a fixed sign, let the Moon and her lord be eastern.

[Chapter IX.8: Elections of the fifth house]

1 Concerning[170] the fifth house, such as in the conception of a child,[171] let the Ascendant be a masculine sign of straight ascension, and the angles fixed[172] and not remote, [and] the lord of the Ascendant in the Ascendant or Midheaven or in the eleventh. **2** And let the planet which has previously reached the ascending degree through its own motion,[173] be a fortune. **3** And let the luminaries be made fit, and especially the lord of the time.[174] **4** And there should not be any infortune in an angle, but a free and strong fortune.

5 And the lord of the Ascendant should not be impeded in the ninth month, for birth often happens then; and the same is good in the seventh or tenth [month]. **6** [And] the lord of the Ascendant[175] should be strong and fortunate in this hour, and the luminaries.

7 And if the lord of the sixth or eighth is an infortune, it should not be commixed with any significator. **8** And all things unpraiseworthy in the

---

[167] See al-'Imrānī II.5.4.
[168] Omitting *non* ("not"), following al-'Imrānī.
[169] Reading *eam* for *eum* ("him, it"), following al-'Imrānī.
[170] For this whole section, see al-'Imrānī II.6.1.
[171] In this case, a male child (hence the use of masculine signs).
[172] This probably means "upright," as paired with "remote": this means that the degree of the Midheaven should be on the tenth sign (or possibly the eleventh), but not in the ninth or any other sign. See Ch. IX.1, **56**.
[173] That is, in zodiacal motion, not the diurnal rotation of the heavens.
[174] That is, the sect light (the Sun in the day, the Moon in the night).
[175] Reading with al-'Imrānī for *nam et partus tunc fit primo* ("for then the birth come to be first").

books of nativity should be made fit, and what is approved there should be taken together with the roots of elections.

9 And it is best that the Moon be in the Ascendant, in the trine aspect of the Sun, and one should beware of the burnt path. **10** And Venus should be made fit, for if Venus is impeded the woman will be corrupted (if the Moon, then the seed). **11** And make the fifth house fit, and its lord.

12 And conceptions are better in odd hours (namely, the first, third, fifth, etc.), and Libra as the Ascendant (because it is a rational sign), and Libra and its lord were free [of the infortunes]:[176] and then the Midheaven will be Cancer ([a sign] of many children). **13** And the rest of the significators should be in masculine signs, and a son will be conceived.

14 And [make sure that] there will not be a crooked limb,[177] nor the womb crooked or infirm: for the circular significations are perfected according to what the material things subject to them are able to receive.

[Chapter IX.9: Elections of the sixth house]

1 Concerning the sixth house, such as on captivity and the manumission of [captives], I have already noted [that] enough elsewhere.[178]

2 Concerning[179] the purchase of flying things which we hunt ([such as] birds), let the Moon be in Gemini or in its triplicity or in Sagittarius,[180] or in the first half of Capricorn (for the Hawk is there).[181] **3** And it is good that the Moon be in the last half of Gemini or in Leo or in Sagittarius, because the Wolf is there.[182] **4** For hunting dogs and the like, [it is the same]. **5** And it is even said [that she should be] in Cancer, because it is the house[183] of the

---

[176] Reading with al-'Imrānī for *et est bona Libra cum domino suo* ("and Libra is good with its own lord").

[177] This is Leopold's own construal of al-'Imrānī. Al-'Imrānī is here recommending that we also follow good medical practice, by not attempting such an election when other medical or physical conditions are known to interfere with conception.

[178] Perhaps referring to questions on captives in VIII.7.

[179] See al-'Imrānī II.7.4.

[180] Reading with al-'Imrānī for *in signo* ("in the sign").

[181] This is undoubtedly a reference to the constellation Aquila ("Eagle"), sometimes called *Vultur volans* ("flying vulture") in ancient literature. It sits in northern declinations just above the constellation of Capricorn.

[182] This may be Lupus (see Ch. I.3, **123**).

[183] Reading *domus* with al-'Imrānī for *dominus* ("lord").

Moon. **6** And the Moon [should be full, because then] she is quicker than at other [times].[184]

[Chapter IX.10: Elections of the seventh through tenth houses]

1 When[185] the Moon is in Cancer or Virgo, a marriage should not come to be, unless with a widow.

2 Concerning the seventh house,[186] I have noted enough elsewhere above, on questions and nativities and on those things which pertain to the other houses.

[Chapter IX.11: Elections of the eleventh house]

1 Concerning[187] the eleventh house, such as on having praise and fame,[188] the eleventh and its lord should be made fit, and let it be one of the houses of Jupiter (and if he is in the eleventh house or in the Ascendant, or if he looks at them by a good aspect, it is good). **2** And Jupiter should be free and strong, and then the lord of the eleventh in the Ascendant (or contrariwise) is good. **3** And the Sun should be in the tenth, free, and the Moon joined to him by a trine or sextile aspect; and if she is not[189] separated in this from the lord of the eleventh or from Jupiter, it will be better, for then his matter will prosper and be praiseworthy. **4** And generally, all significators should look at each other benignly, and especially the luminaries and the lords of the Ascendant and eleventh.

---

[184] Adding and reading this sentence with al-'Imrānī. The idea is that the hunting animals bought then will be very fast.
[185] See Sahl's *On Elections* §80a-b.
[186] Or rather, up through the tenth. There are other tenth-house elections below.
[187] See al-'Imrānī II.12.1.
[188] Or, "reputation" (*fama*).
[189] Al-'Imrānī omits this "not," but Leopold's reading makes more sense.

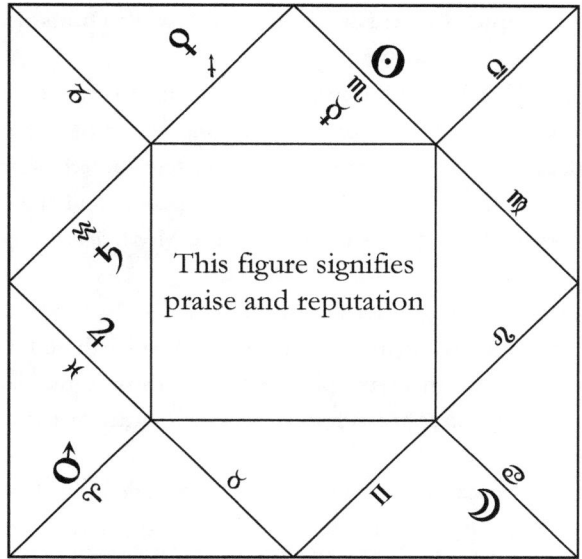

Figure 109: A figure showing praise and reputation (Leopold)

5 For having love,[190] let the Moon be made fit, along with the eleventh and its lord,[191] and let her be received by Venus in an optimal aspect;[192] and it is better if she were in [her own] house or exaltation. **6** Which if it could not happen, let [Venus] be received by the Moon[193] from a trine, and she herself should be received by Jupiter or by the lord of her own house. **7** And if is not so, let the Moon still be in some dignity of Venus, free.

8 And if the esteem of money[194] is inquired about, then let the Lot of Fortune be in the Ascendant or in its triplicity. **9** If because of real estate or land, let it be in the fourth house; and so on with the rest.

---

[190] That is, love based on friendship, not romantic love. See al-'Imrānī II.12.3.
[191] Reading with al-'Imrānī, for *cum domino undecimae et dominus eius* ("with the lord of the eleventh and its lord").
[192] That is, a sextile or trine (and perhaps the conjunction).
[193] Reading *luna* with al-'Imrānī for *bono* ("good [planet]").
[194] That is, a desire for profits. See al-'Imrānī II.12.3.

[Chapter IX.12: Elections of the twelfth house]

1 Concerning[195] the twelfth house, for impeding an enemy or another, let the Moon be impeded so that she is in the conjunction or opposition of the Sun, or by means of other impediments which I have noted elsewhere.[196] **2** And the twelfth and its lord should be impeded, and the Moon in the Ascendant: for the Ascendant is contrary to the Moon according to her own substance. **3** Or, let it be before or after an eclipse by three days or less, and let the Sun be free and cleansed [of the infortunes]. **4** And let there be a fortune in the Midheaven. **5** (And many people greatly fear those three days before an eclipse and the three after the eclipse, and they beware lest they begin anything in them.) **6** And by how much more the Moon was impeded, by that much more will those whose impediment is sought, be impeded—and especially if it is a master impeding [his] subjects, because the Moon signifies ministers and the common people.

[Chapter IX.13: Sahl on elections][197]

1 Sahl[198] says in his book of elections: if the nativity or interrogation signifies evil for a certain time, you should not elect: for it will profit you nothing [even] if you put all the fortunes in an angle and you make the bad ones fall away from the angles. **2** For you see that some people begin [some action] at the same time, and end it differently: and this is on account of the different nativities and profections and directions in their roots. **3** And[199] he says that between the circle of heaven and the natures of lower things it is just like between a magnet and iron, and between a father and child, and between the one eating and food. **4** And the fortunate stars and planets are even and temperate, and because of this [they are] good; but the bad ones on the contrary are just like thieves and [therefore] bad.

---

[195] This whole section derives from al-ʿImrānī II.13.1-2.
[196] Namely, being in the burnt path or *via combusta* (al-ʿImrānī).
[197] What follows is yet another summary of electional principles, now from Sahl's *On Elections* (see *Choices*).
[198] See Sahl's *On Elections* §5a-6b.
[199] See Sahl's *On Elections* §10a-11b.

[Quadruplicities][200]

5 For changes [of place] and roads, he chooses movable signs, and in sowing, buying, selling, [and] in getting betrothed to a woman. **6** [But] other things that are promised are not effective [in] the movable [signs]. **7** Rumors are then said to be false, nor is a planting or the placing of a foundation [good]; an infirm person will then quickly die.

8 Fixed signs are valuable in all lasting things, such as planting, building, celebrating nuptials; and then one incarcerated will be stuck for a long time, and one who becomes angry will be pleased more slowly. **9** And [legal] claims[201] will then be good. **10** And Scorpio is lighter than all the fixed ones, and Leo more [fixed], and Aquarius slower and worse.

11 He says the common signs are good in associations, and what comes to be then will be repeated; one who goes out from prison will be pushed back [inside], one convalescing will suffer a relapse, a story is not believed, advice will not stand, there will be deception in business deals.

[More general advice][202]

12 In inceptions, the Moon should not be made impeded, nor waxing[203] in the Ascendant, or the one for whom it is chosen will become infirm, unless the lord of the Ascendant would be looking at the ascending degree, else it would be as though absent from its own house, [and therefore] one which cannot defend it. **13** And if the lord of the Ascendant is a bad one, make it look there by a trine or sextile aspect, put the fortunes in the angle of the Ascendant or Midheaven.

14 And in beginnings the Lot of Fortune should not be falling away from the aspect of the Moon or her conjunction; and you should not care if it falls from the Ascendant, provided that it looks at the Moon or at least at the lord of the Ascendant. **15** And the lord of the Ascendant should be put with the Lot of Fortune or at least in its aspect (which is better). **16** And the Moon should never be put in the twelfth, sixth, or eighth, or second.

---

[200] See Sahl's *On Elections* §§12a-16a.
[201] Reading with Crofts for *mercedes* ("wages").
[202] See Sahl in §§23a-28.
[203] Reading *crescentem* with Sahl for *ascendentem*.

17 And the Ascendant and the Moon should be in straight signs. **18** And he says that the crooked signs signal slowness.

19 And[204] the good ones help little except in an angle or in the eleventh and in the fifth; in the square or opposite aspect of the good houses, they help little. **20** And the bad ones either harm little or nothing unless they are in the angles; and in the square and opposite of the lord of the Ascendant and the Moon they instill fear but cannot do [anything] else.

21 Dorotheus says, if the Moon is impeded and the matter can in no way be deferred, you should not give her dignity in the Ascendant. **22** Put a fortune in the Ascendant and strengthen the Ascendant and its lord by means of the presence or aspect of the fortunes.

[House-based elections:]

23 For[205] the second house, for alchemy the Moon should be in common signs, cleansed [of the infortunes] and let the seventh be likewise; and in a work of gold, the Sun should be made fit; silver, the Moon.

24 In[206] the fourth house, for buildings Mars should wholly be falling away from the Ascendant and from the Moon and from Mercury, and he should never be given a role there. **25** Or at least [Venus should be][207] in her own place, strong, strong over Mars, and joined to him from a trine or sextile aspect: because Mars does not impede a matter of Venus due to [her] love of him. **26** And Saturn should be falling away from Venus and from the Moon, on account of his enmity towards Venus and the Moon.

27 Against[208] the infestation of something terrible, such as a phantasm or something else, so that it would be removed from a house or man, neither the Moon nor the Ascendant should be in any[209] [of the following] signs, which are Cancer, Leo, Scorpio, Aquarius.

---

[204] For this paragraph, cf. Sahl's *On Elections* §27, which Leopold seems to have augmented with assorted phrases from Sahl's *Judgments*.
[205] See Sahl, §41.
[206] See Sahl, §§43-44.
[207] Adding based on Sahl.
[208] See Sahl, §60. Sahl is here speaking of demonic possession and electing for an exorcism; he conceives of this as a sixth-house election, perhaps because it involves the possession of the physical body or a place, and the sixth is under the earth (which typically indicates physical things and relationships).
[209] Reading *aliquo...signorum* with Sahl for *in signo fertili* ("in a fertile sign," which is incorrect).

28 Medicine[210] should[211] be [applied] to a limb which is from high up [on the body] to the chest, when the Moon is in Aries, Taurus, or Gemini; from the chest to the pubic region when she is in Cancer, Leo, Virgo; from the pubic region to the knees when she is in Libra, Scorpio, Sagittarius, etc.[212] **29** Or, from up high [down] to the pubic region it should take place when the Moon is from the angle of the earth up to the Midheaven, from the left, on account of this being the ascending part of the circle; from the pubic region downwards [when she is] from the Midheaven to the angle of the earth, whence this part is the descending[213] one. **30** And let the Ascendant be made fortunate.

31 For[214] shaving the hair of the body, this will happen when the Moon is deficient in light or is not in the hairy signs (which are Aries, Taurus, Leo, Capricorn).

32 Cure[215] the eyes when the Moon is increased in light, joined to a fortune.

[Chapter IX.14: Miscellaneous lore, and monitoring daily activities][216]

1 For having an honor, there is a special election, so that the lord of the Ascendant or lord of the tenth or Jupiter is in its own house or[217] in an angle, or the Head is with any of these three (and better in the angle of the Midheaven), and without the conjunction and aspect of a bad one, not in the feminine degrees, not in the dark ones, not in the empty ones, not in the pitted ones, and it is chosen so that it is in degrees increasing fortune. **2** And if it is in [its] house or the degree of its own exaltation, you will even judge this as being very commendable.

---

[210] See Sahl, §§65-66.
[211] Omitting *non* ("not"), following Sahl.
[212] To finish the sentence: or from the knees to the feet when she is in Capricorn, Aquarius, or Pisces.
[213] Reading with Sahl for *ascendens*.
[214] See Sahl, §70.
[215] See Sahl, §69a.
[216] Sources uncertain for most of this chapter.
[217] Reading *aut* for *ut* ("so that"). But it could be *et* ("and"), which would be even better.

Figure 110: A figure showing someone will have an honor (Leopold)

3 For finding what you seek, choose so that the lord of the Ascendant is in the Ascendant, and better if in addition the lord of the hour is with it. **4** Moreover, that the lord of the Ascendant or lord of the hour is looking at the Sun, and it is better if in addition the Moon is looking at the lord of the Ascendant.

ଓ ଓ ଓ

5 Recognize daily success thusly. **6** See how much has arisen, of the ascending sign: and if in the remaining part of the sign there is any star, so that the lord of the Ascendant looks at it, he will obtain it (according to the nature of that star) in the leftover part of the day. **7** But if the lord of the Ascendant does not look at it, it will be deferred to the night.

8 If the lord of the east is placed in the east, trouble will be removed, especially on that same day.

9 If the lord of the second is in the Ascendant, and is looked at by the lord of the Ascendant, it greatly bestows profit on that same day; but if the lord of the Ascendant does not look at it, he will pay money in tribute on that day.

10 If the lord of the third is in the east, regarded by the lord of the Ascendant, it gives advantage and those things which pertain to brothers.[218] **11** If the lord of the fourth is in the Ascendant, looked at by the lord of the first, he will acquire useful real estate,[219] or what is of this kind. **12** The lord of the fifth in the east, if it is looked at by that same lord, [means] a useful child or friend for him is acquired, or things which are pleasing to him; and if it is not looked at, [he will have] harm in similar things. **13** Now, if a malevolent looks at it, in this area alone it neither goes forward nor obstructs.

14 The lord of the sixth in the same place, being looked at by the eastern lord, threatens a disease on that same day; with a regard being denied, it neither helps nor will obstruct (however, the aspect of a malevolent introduces detriment from the king).

15 The lord of the seventh in the east, being regarded by the lord of it, he will subdue a woman to [his] rule, or will rejoice in the success of women; but if there is not an aspect, it is neither good nor bad. **16** If a malevolent is looking, he will get tears and loss because of women.

17 The lord of the eighth being regarded as was said, rouses moderate trouble on that day; without an aspect, it neither helps nor harms. **18** If a malevolent regards, death must be feared.

19 The lord of the ninth in the east, regarded as was stated, establishes a journey on that day; without an aspect, he strives [for it] but does not begin it. **20** And a malevolent regarding [means that] although[220] he may begin it, he will defer it.

21 The lord of the tenth in the east as was stated, what he has on that day which is suitable for him, will introduce a dignity; with a regard being denied, he appears to attain it but it will not be successful. **22** A malevolent regarding it will heap on difficulty.

23 The lord of the eleventh in the east as was stated, gives what is prosperous every day; with a regard being denied, it profits nothing. **24** The regard of a malevolent wholly takes it away.

---

[218] Reading *fratrum* for *furtum* ("theft").
[219] Omitting *amicum quod [sc. qui?] est filius* ("friend who is a child"), as this seems to be taken from the following sentence and does not make sense here.
[220] Reading *etsi* for *aut si* ("or if").

25 The lord of the twelfth in the east, being regarded by the lord of the east, introduces the beating of the breast because it conveys distress on that day; without an aspect, it neither goes forward nor obstructs.

26 When[221] the lord of the Ascendant does not look at the Ascendant, with respect to him he is like a man absent from his own house, because then he cannot defend it.

27 And with all diligence, always observe the state of the victor (this is [the status] of the one which was most powerful in the root): for the matter of the one whose root it is, will always bear itself in a similar way.[222]

28 Judge what happens through the individual months, thusly. **29** From the degree of the Ascendant at the beginning of the month, the lord of the bounds is taken; if each lord of a bound regards its own degree, judge according to the nature of the one regarding[223] and the proper quality of the house in which it is.[224] **30** Which if it is a malevolent, it increases evil, [and] with a regard being denied, it suggests neither good nor evil. **31** You can choose[225] according to the houses and the lords of the houses and bounds, according to these things stated before.

32 Concerning the succeedents of the angles,[226] I have noted enough in the treatise on revolutions and in the summary of the book of questions.[227]

33 And in elections, consider much the Lot of luckiness, wisdom, [and] victory, which I have noted above in revolutions (and the lord of the bound of the Midheaven, and their bearings, and the Sun). **34** And it is the Lot of Jupiter, and is taken in the day from the Lot of secrets[228] to Jupiter (in the night the reverse), and from above are added the degrees which have ascended in the ascending sign, and is projected from the beginning of the ascending sign. **35** The significations of this [Lot are] praiseworthy: look in the introductions at the Lot of Jupiter.

---

[221] This is based on Sahl's *On Elect.*, §§23b-c.
[222] This seems to mean, "watch the condition of the victor of your nativity on a daily basis."
[223] Reading *respicientis* for *recipientis* ("the one receiving").
[224] Leopold's source seems to mean that each bound should be counted as being one month.
[225] That is, "make an election."
[226] Reading *angulorum* for *amorum* ("of loves").
[227] Perhaps referring to Ch. VIII.1, **14**.
[228] That is, the Lot of Spirit (see above, Ch. IV.5, **11**).

36 Moreover,[229] for the status of a native at every hour, take how much there is from the Sun to the place of the Moon in a nativity, and then project from the Ascendant: and where the projection reaches, there is the direction of the Lot of Fortune; and judge according to the situation of the place and its lord. **37** According to another, do the root this [way] (and according to Ptolemy, what is from the Sun to the Moon): in the night project backwards from the Ascendant (that is, against the succession of signs), in the day forward (that is, following the succession of signs).

---

[229] This paragraph presents somewhat confusing instructions for the Lot of Fortune, but the idea seems to be that we can monitor the natal Lot of Fortune throughout the day and see how one's daily activities will go. Now, according to Ptolemy, the Lot of Fortune is projected by both day and night from the Sun to the Moon, and projected from the Ascendant (**36**). However, while this procedure will indeed yield the Lot of Fortune in the day, in night charts it will give the Lot of Spirit instead. So, in **37** Leopold—while confusingly referring to Ptolemy—suggests that we can still measure from the Sun to the Moon in all charts, but in the night we must project that amount *backwards* from the Ascendant. This ensures that we will follow the normal sect rules, instead of mixing the two Lots together.

TREATISE X: ON INTENTIONS

[Leopold's method, from ibn Ezra][1]

1 You will know the intention[2] of someone wanting to pose a question to you, if he came to you for this [purpose] (with him being silent),[3] through:

2 [1] The lord of the Ascendant and its place, once the figure of heaven is arranged and the planets put into their places, in the hour at which he intended to ask. **3** For if the lord of the Ascendant is in the first house, he wanted to ask about himself; if in the second, about assets; and thusly through all the houses, just as they signify.

4 [2] If the lord of the Ascendant is retrograde or burned up, do not judge through it but [rather] as before by means of the Moon—unless she is burned up by the Sun or in the burnt path.

5 [3] And[4] then judge by means of the lord of the hour, thusly: multiply the degrees which he has finished in the sign in which he is, by 12, and distribute the sum from the Ascendant in [increments of] 30: and where it is ended, judge the intention according to that part of the sign,[5] since it signifies it.

6 [4] And if this one—namely the lord of the hour—is impeded, take up the degrees which have already ascended in the rising sign (those above the earth), [and] divide them by 2 ½, and distribute this from the beginning of the rising sign, giving 2 ½° to each sign: where it is ended, there is the intention.

---

[1] These first four methods are directly from ibn Ezra's *Particular Treatises* (see Appendix J of *Search*).
[2] Reading *intentionem* for *intentionum*.
[3] *Interposito sibi silentio.*
[4] That is, if the Moon is burned up or in the burnt path.
[5] See ibn Ezra's way of dividing the houses into subtopics, in Appendix J of *Search*.

	0°-2.5°	2.5°-5°	5°-7.5°	7.5°-10°	10°-12.5°	12.5°-15°	15°-17.5°	17.5°-20°	20°-22.5°	22.5°-25°	25°-27.5°	27.5°-30°
♈	♈	♉	♊	♋	♌	♍	♎	♏	♐	♑	♒	♓
♉	♉	♊	♋	♌	♍	♎	♏	♐	♑	♒	♓	♈
♊	♊	♋	♌	♍	♎	♏	♐	♑	♒	♓	♈	♉
♋	♋	♌	♍	♎	♏	♐	♑	♒	♓	♈	♉	♊
♌	♌	♍	♎	♏	♐	♑	♒	♓	♈	♉	♊	♋
♍	♍	♎	♏	♐	♑	♒	♓	♈	♉	♊	♋	♌
♎	♎	♏	♐	♑	♒	♓	♈	♉	♊	♋	♌	♍
♏	♏	♐	♑	♒	♓	♈	♉	♊	♋	♌	♍	♎
♐	♐	♑	♒	♓	♈	♉	♊	♋	♌	♍	♎	♏
♑	♑	♒	♓	♈	♉	♊	♋	♌	♍	♎	♏	♐
♒	♒	♓	♈	♉	♊	♋	♌	♍	♎	♏	♐	♑
♓	♓	♈	♉	♊	♋	♌	♍	♎	♏	♐	♑	♒

Figure 111: Table of twelfth-parts (Dykes)

7 For example,[6] the Ascendant was 12° Aries. 8 I distributed by 2 ½, beginning from Aries, and the distribution was ended in the fifth [house], which is Leo, the house of children.[7] 9 Therefore I know that he wanted to ask about a child. 10 And because the lord of that place (namely Leo), the Sun, was in the seventh, I know that he wanted to ask about the wife of [his] child. 11 Which if he had been in the sixth, he would have intended to ask about the illness of the child—and speak thusly about the others.

[According to "Ptolemy"]

12 Ptolemy[8] used to judge the intention by means of the stronger signifier in the circle: so that if it is in the tenth, [it is] about an honor; if in the first, about life, and so on.

[According to Māshā'allāh]

13 And [according to Māshā'allāh],[9] in every case, consider [1] the Ascendant and [2] its lord, [3] the Sun and [4] his lord, [5] the Lot of Fortune

---

[6] See also *Search* Ch. I.9.3, and *On Hidden Things* (*OHT*) §2 (in *Search* Appendix C).
[7] That is, he divided 12 by 2.5 (yielding 4.8), and gave the first 4 to the signs in order, starting with Aries (because it is the rising sign); the remainder (.8) fell into Leo. One can also simply use the above table of twelfth-parts.
[8] See *OHT* §6, paragraph 2 (in *WSM* or *Search* I.9.4) for a fuller statement of "Ptolemy's" significator of thought.

and [6] its lord, and [7] the lord of the degree of the twelfth-part of the Ascendant: and judge the intention according to the one among them which appeared stronger.

14 But he[10] teaches that one is the degree of the significator[11] which is taken from the lord of the hour to the lord of the Ascendant, and [on top of that] are added the degrees which the lord of the hour has made in the sign in which it is, and it is projected from the degree[12] of the lord of the hour: and the significator will be the planet in whose sign the projection was ended (but I believe that it ought to be projected from the beginning of the sign of the lord of the hour).[13] **15** And if the victor is in the first face of a sign, it signifies a matter indicated by the first lord of the triplicity of that sign; and speak likewise with respect to the second and third [faces].

16 Also,[14] a projection of the intention happens from the lord of the hour to the degree of the Sun;[15] the equal degrees are taken and extended from the Ascendant, and the intention is in that house where the extending is ended. **17** Whence if the Sun [himself] is the lord of the hour, the lord of the hour[16] is in the Ascendant.

[*An example from Hermes*][17]

18 Also, a figure which is said to belong to Hermes:[18] **19** I have calculated it fully for the latitude of the completed third clime.[19] **20** The Ascendant was

---

[9] This is perhaps a misunderstanding of *OHT* §2 (in *WSM*). This list is taken from a combination of the many views Māshā'allāh mentions.

[10] Source unknown. Nevertheless the calculation is unlike other Lot-like calculations, and seems to be wrong. Normally, the distance is projected from a third place, such as the Ascendant.

[11] *Pars ducis*, "leader." Leopold's use of *dux* in this section leads me to believe he was relying on Hermann or another colleague such as Hugo of Santalla for this material. Likewise, some of his phrases and vocabulary later on match *Search* exactly.

[12] As Leopold will note just below, this is an error in his source manuscript: the instructions should read "sign" or "beginning of the sign."

[13] Leopold is right in terms of normal Lot-like projections, but wrong in this case: if we projected from the beginning of the sign, the counting would always reach the lord of the Ascendant.

[14] This is very similar to the Lot-like projection in *Skilled* I.11, in which al-Rijāl projects the distance from Aries instead of the Ascendant.

[15] But probably the Moon in a nocturnal chart.

[16] This should probably read, "then the intention is in the Ascendant."

[17] This chart cannot be reliably dated without the rest of the planets, but it could certainly be from the late 8th Century or even in the 5th Century AD.

9° 55' Taurus.[20] **21** The Midheaven, 26° 29' Capricorn. **22** The eleventh, 29° 20' Aquarius (in the right circle, 61° 30').[21] **23** The twelfth, 4° 50' Aries (in the right circle, 94° 30'). **24** The first, 9° 55' (in the right circle, 127° 30'). **25** The second, 6° 25' Gemini (in the right circle, 154° 30'). **26** The third, 1° 34' Cancer (in the right circle, 181° 30'). **27** Venus was in 15° Cancer, in her own triplicity. **28** The Moon in the tenth degree of Libra, in no dignity of her own. **29** The Sun was in Cancer. **30** The Lot of Fortune in Sagittarius. **31** Saturn in Leo, in no dignity of his own.

32 Therefore, Venus was the significator of the question: but because the Moon was separated from Saturn (having been bound [to him from] the sixth), Hermes judged that the question was about the mother (for the Moon is in charge of mothers), and about an infirmity [because the Moon is in the sixth]. **33** And because the Moon was being separated from Saturn, he said that the infirmity was cold and dry; and because Leo is the stomach in the human body, he says the cause [of the infirmity] is in the stomach; and because Saturn was in the first degree of Leo, he says the infirmity is in the mouth of the stomach.

34 From there, since the Moon applies to Venus [who is] receiving [her], he said she would be cured. **35** And because there were 5° between the Moon and Venus, for that reason he said she would be cured within 5 days (because the sign was convertible).[22] **36** And if the Moon had been in a firm sign, she would have signified 5 years; if in a double-bodied one, 5 months. **37** And if the Moon had applied to Saturn in such a way, he would have said the sick woman was going to die within so many days.

---

[18] See Hermann's treatment in Ch. I.7 of *Search* (including my own proposed original chart), and the version in the complete *Thought* (in *WSM*).

[19] The chart is calculated for 30° N latitude, and Leopold is using Alchabitius Semi-Arc houses.

[20] Leopold's text omits the number, so I have supplied it from the diagram in his book.

[21] This is the right ascension (RA) of the cusp: in older tables, RA was measured from 0° Capricorn instead of 0° Aries.

[22] That is, a movable sign (often called "cardinal" signs).

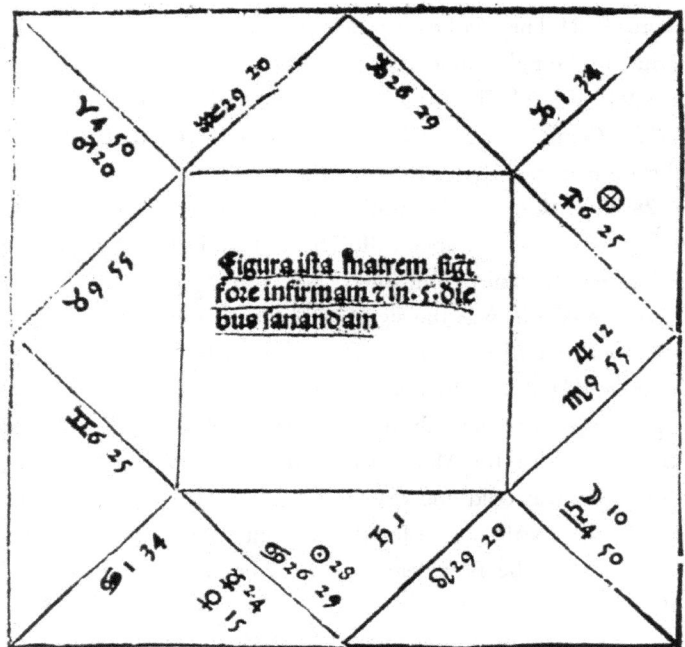

Figure 112: Hermes's thought of sick mother (Leopold)

38 Conversely, if it[23] had been Venus instead of the Moon, the question would have been about some woman of his own people; if Saturn, about his father; if Mercury, about a child; if the Sun, about the kin; if Venus [had been the significator and were] in the seventh, about betrothals. **39** The Sun is male in the day and female in the night; the contrary for the Moon. **40** Likewise, if Jupiter had been [the significator and] in the ninth, the question would have been about a dream; if Mars in the seventh, about a controversy.

41 And also al-Rāzī, looking at this figure, said: since I saw that the east was feminine and its lord feminine, and in a feminine [sign], it was plain that the question as going to be about a woman. **42** And since the lord of the lord of the east (namely, the Moon) was in the sixth, applying to Venus in the house of brothers, [and the Moon was] separated from Saturn (who was in the fourth, which belongs to parents), I know [it was] about the mother, be-

---

[23] That is, the significator. There seem to be two reasons for the Moon to be the significator. According to al-Rāzī's version in *The Interpretation of Cognition* (in *WSM*), the Moon is the lord of the lord of the Ascendant, and so shows the *cause* of the situation. But note step #2 in Leopold's own method above: if the lord of the Ascendant is burned up, we defer to the Moon.

cause mothers belong to the Moon; and because she was applying to the lord of the sixth from the sixth [itself], I knew she was infirm; and because she was being separated from Saturn (to whom the harm belongs) and is applying to Venus, it establishes that she is going to be cured. **43** And because there were five degrees within the transfer, and the transfer was happening from a movable sign, I knew that what was signaled should have happened in five days.

APPENDIX: AL-KHAYYĀT'S INTERPRETATION TEMPLATE

This short chapter from Abū 'Alī al-Khayyāt's *On the Judgments of Nativities* (in *PN1*) should be helpful as a template for interpreting houses.

Chapter 38: On the general manner or method for judging the twelve houses of heaven

1 The general manner by which you must look for the judgments of the twelve houses is in the way I will show [you] now, if God wills.

2 First, see the individual houses, and diligently observe [1] which of the fortunes or the bad ones were in them, or looked at them from the square or opposite aspect; and [2] how the lord of that house whose significations you seek is bearing itself, and what place of the circle it inhabited, and its commingling with the planets; and [3] the status of the Lot which is related to that house, and its place; moreover [4] the condition and quality of the lord [of the Lot], and its place in the circle and the commingling of the planets with it.

3 Look[1] even at [5] the condition of the significators, [and see] if they were [5.1] eastern or western, [5.2] direct or retrograde, and [5.3] with which fortunes or infortunes they would be commingled, [and] if they were [5.4] in the angles or succeedents, or in the cadents.

4 But if very many significators of some house (or the strongest of them) were made fortunate, free from the bad ones and impediments, they signify prosperity in the nature of the matter signified by that house, and especially if even a fortune, by means of commingling in good places of the circle, conferred its own testimonies [in order] to strengthen and increase [the matter].

5 But if you found the significators of some matter commingled with bad ones, or retrograde or burned up, or [5.5] in their own descension (namely, falling from their exaltation and from the angles) or in their own detriment, they signify misfortune in the matter signified, and especially if, placed (as we said) cadent and in [5.6] ill-omened places, they were even conjoined to the

---

[1] Topic [5] on planetary condition, includes [5.1] solar phase and rays, [5.2] motion and stations, [5.3] benefic/malefic configuration and natures, [5.4] angularity, [5.5] dignity or debility, [5.6] good and bad places, and [5.7] the qualities of the sign.

infortunes or in their square or oppositions. **6** And if it were one of these things in which it is necessary that [its] multitude or scarcity, increase or decrease, should be known, speak on it according to [5.7] what their position is in the signs or houses, signifying multitude or scarcity.²

---

² This must mean, for example, that in the case of children we should see whether the significators are in fruitful or barren signs.

Glossary

This glossary is an expanded version of the one in my 2010 *Introductions to Traditional Astrology* (*ITA*), with the addition of other terms from my translations since then. After most definitions is a reference to sections and Appendices of *ITA* (including my introduction to it) for further reading—for the most part, they do *not* refer to passages in this book (and if so, are labeled as such).

- **Absent from** (Ar. *ghāʾib ʿan*). Equivalent to **aversion**.
- **Accident** (Lat. *accidens*, Ar. *ḥādith*). An event which "befalls" or "happens" to someone, though not necessarily something bad.
- **Adding in course.** See **Course**.
- **Advancing, advancement** (Ar. *'iqbāl, muqbil, zāʾid*; Lat. *accedens*). When a planet is in an **angle** or **succeedent** (sometimes ambiguous as to **whole sign** or **quadrant division**), preferably moving clockwise by diurnal motion towards one of the angular axes or **stakes**. The opposite of **retreating** and **withdrawing**. See III.3 and the Introduction §6.
- **Advantageous places.** One of two schemes of **houses** which indicate affairs/planets which are more busy or good in the context of the chart (III.4). The seven-place scheme according to Timaeus and reported in *Carmen* includes only certain signs which **aspect** the **Ascendant** by **whole-sign**, and suggests that these places are advantageous for the *native* because they aspect the Ascendant. The eight-place scheme according to Nechepso (III.4) lists all of the **angular** and **succeedent** places, suggesting places which are stimulating and advantageous for a planet *in itself*.
- **Ages of man.** Ptolemy's division of a typical human life span into periods ruled by planets as **time lords**. See VII.3.
- **Agreeing signs.** Groups of signs which share some kind of harmonious quality. See I.9.5-6.
- ***Alcochoden.*** Latin transliteration for ***Kadukhudhāh***.
- **Alien** (Lat. *alienus*, Ar. *gharīb*). See **Peregrine**.
- ***Almuten.*** A Latin transliteration for ***mubtazz***: see **Victor**.
- **Angles, succeedents, cadents.** A division of houses into three groups which show how powerfully and directly a planet acts. The angles are the 1st, 10th, 7th and 4th houses; the succeedents are the 2nd, 11th, 8th and 5th; the cadents are the 12th, 9th, 6th and 3rd (but see **cadent** below). But the exact

- regions in question will depend upon whether and how one uses **whole-sign** and **quadrant houses,** especially since traditional texts refer to an angle or pivot (Gr. *kentron*, Ar. *watad*) as either (1) equivalent to the **whole-sign** angles from the **Ascendant**, or (2) the degrees of the **Ascendant-Midheaven** axes themselves, or (3) **quadrant houses** (and their associated strengths) as measured from the degrees of the axes. See I.12-13 and III.3-4, and the Introduction §6.
- **Antiscia** (sing. *antiscion*), "throwing shadows." Refers to a degree mirrored across an axis drawn from 0° Capricorn to 0° Cancer. For example, 10° Cancer has 20° Gemini as its antiscion. See I.9.2.
- **Apogee (of eccentric/deferent)**. The point on a planet's **deferent circle** that is farthest away from the earth; as seen from earth, it points to some degree of the zodiac. See II.0-1.
- **Apsides, apsidal line**. In geocentric astronomy, the line passing through the center of the earth, which points at one end to the **apogee** of a planet's **deferent**, and at the other end to its **perigee**.
- **Applying, application**. When a planet is in a state of **connection**, moving so as to make the connection exact. Planets **assembled** together or in **aspect** by sign and not yet connected by the relevant degrees, are only "wanting" to be connected.
- **Arisings.** See **Ascensions**.
- **Ascendant**. Usually the entire rising sign, but often specified as the exact rising degree. In **quadrant houses**, a space following the exact rising degree up to the cusp of the 2nd house.
- **Ascensions.** Degrees on the celestial equator, measured in terms of how many degrees pass the meridian as an entire sign or **bound** (or other spans of zodiacal degrees) passes across the horizon. They are often used in the predictive technique of ascensional times, as an approximation for **directions**. See Appendix E.
- **Aspect/regard**. One planet aspects or regards another if they are in signs which are configured to each other by a **sextile, square, trine,** or **opposition**. See III.6 and **Whole signs**. A connection by degrees or orbs is a much more intense of an aspect.
- **Assembly**. When two or more planets are in the same sign, and more intensely if within 15°. (It is occasionally used in Arabic to indicate the conjunction of the Sun and Moon at the New Moon, but the more common word for that is **meeting**). See III.5.

- **Aversion.** Being in the second, sixth, eighth, or twelfth sign from a place. For instance, a planet in Gemini is in the twelfth from, and therefore in aversion to, Cancer. Such places are in aversion because they cannot **aspect** it by the classical scheme of aspects. See III.6.1.
- *Azamene*. Equivalent to **Chronic illness.**
- **Bad ones.** See **Benefic/malefic.**
- **Barring.** See **Blocking.**
- **Bearing** (Lat. *habitude*). Hugo's term for any of the many possible planetary conditions and relationships. These may be found in III and IV.
- **Benefic/malefic.** A division of the planets into groups that cause or signify typically "good" things (Jupiter, Venus, usually the Sun and Moon) or "bad" things (Mars, Saturn). Mercury is considered variable. See V.9.
- **Benevolents.** See **Benefic/malefic.**
- **Besieging.** Equivalent to **Enclosure.**
- **Bicorporeal signs.** Equivalent to "common" signs. See **Quadruplicity.**
- **Blocking** (sometimes called "prohibition"). When a planet bars another planet from completing a **connection**, either through its own body or ray. See III.14.
- **Bodyguarding.** Planetary relationships in which some planet protects another, used in determining social eminence and prosperity. See III.28.
- **Bounds.** Unequal divisions of the zodiac in each sign, each bound being ruled by one of the five non-**luminaries.** Sometimes called "terms," they are one of the five classical **dignities.** See VII.4.
- **Bright, smoky, empty, dark degrees.** Certain degrees of the zodiac said to affect how conspicuous or obscure the significations of planets or the Ascendant are. See VII.7.
- **Burned up** (or "combust," Lat. *combustus*). Normally, when a planet is between about 1° and 7.5° away from the Sun. See II.9-10, and **In the heart.**
- **Burnt path** (Lat. *via combusta*). A span of degrees in Libra and Scorpio in which a planet (especially the Moon) is considered to be harmed or less able to effect its significations. Some astrologers identify it as between 15° Libra and 15° Scorpio; others between the exact degree of the **fall** of the Sun in 19° Libra and the exact degree of the fall of the Moon in 3° Scorpio. See IV.3.
- *Bust*. Certain hours measured from the New Moon, in which it is considered favorable or unfavorable to undertake an action or perform an **election.** See VIII.4.

- **Busy places.** Equivalent to the **Advantageous places.**
- **Cadent** (Lat. *cadens*, "falling"). This is used in two ways: a planet or place may be cadent from the **angles** (being in the 3rd, 6th, 9th, or 12th), or else cadent from the **Ascendant** (namely, in **aversion** to it, being in the 12th, 8th, 6th, or 2nd). See I.12, III.4, and III.6.1.
- **Cardinal.** Equivalent to "movable" signs. See **Quadruplicity.**
- **Cazimi:** see **In the heart.**
- **Celestial equator.** The projection of earth's equator out into the universe, forming one of the three principal celestial coordinate systems.
- **Centers of the Moon.** Also called the "posts" or "foundations" of the Moon. Angular distances between the Sun and Moon throughout the lunar month, indicating possible times of weather changes and rain. See *AW1*.
- **Choleric.** See **Humor.**
- **Chronic illness (degrees of).** Degrees which are especially said to indicate chronic illness, due to their association with certain fixed stars. See VII.10.
- **Cleansed** (Ar. *naqiyy*, Lat. *mundus*). Ideally, when a planet in **aversion** to the **malefics** (but perhaps some would consider a **sextile** or **trine** acceptable?).
- **Clothed.** Equivalent to one planet being in an **assembly** or **aspect/regard** with another, and therefore partaking in (being "clothed in") the other planet's characteristics.
- **Collection.** When two planets **aspecting** each other but not in an applying **connection**, each apply to a third planet. See III.12.
- **Combust.** See **Burned up.**
- **Commanding/obeying.** A division of the signs into those which command or obey each other (used sometimes in **synastry**). See I.9.
- **Common signs.** See **Quadruplicity.**
- **Complexion.** Primarily, a mixture of elements and their qualities so as to indicate or produce some effect. Secondarily it refers to planetary combinations, following the naturalistic theory that planets have elemental qualities with causal power, which can interact with each other.
- **Confer.** See **Pushing.**
- **Configured.** To be in a whole-sign **aspect**, though not necessarily by degree.
- **Conjunction (of planets).** See **Assembly** and **Connection.**

- **Conjunction/prevention.** The position of the New (conjunction) or Full (prevention) Moon most immediately prior to a **nativity** or other chart. For the prevention, some astrologers use the degree of the Moon, others the degree of the luminary which was above the earth at the time of the prevention. See VIII.1.2.
- **Connection.** When a planet applies to another planet (by body in the same sign, or by ray in **aspecting** signs), within a particular number of degrees up to exactness. See III.7.
- **Conquer** (Lat. *vinco*). Normally, the equivalent of being a **victor**, which comes from the same Latin verb.
- **Convertible.** Equivalent to the movable signs. See **Quadruplicity**. But sometimes planets (especially Mercury) are called convertible because their **gender** is affected by their placement in the chart.
- **Convey.** See **Pushing**.
- **Corruption.** Normally, the harming of a planet (see IV.3-4), such as being in a **square** with a **malefic** planet. But sometimes, equivalent to **Detriment**.
- **Counsel** (Lat. *consilium*). See **Management**.
- **Course, increasing/decreasing in.** For practical purposes, this means a planet is quicker than average in motion. But in geometric astronomy, it refers to what **sector** of the **deferent** the center of a planet's **epicycle** is. (The planet's position within the four sectors of the epicycle itself will also affect its apparent speed.) In the two sectors that are closest to the planet's **perigee**, the planet will apparently be moving faster; in the two sectors closest to the **apogee**, it will apparently be moving slower. See II.0-1.
- **Crooked/straight.** A division of the signs into those which rise quickly and are more parallel to the horizon (crooked), and those which arise more slowly and closer to a right angle from the horizon (straight or direct). In the northern hemisphere, the signs from Capricorn to Gemini are crooked (but in the southern one, straight); those from Cancer to Sagittarius are straight (but in the southern one, crooked).
- **Crossing over.** When a planet begins to **separate** from an exact **connection**. See III.7-8.
- **Cutting of light.** Three ways in which a **connection** is prevented: either by **obstruction** from the following sign, **escape** within the same sign, or by **barring**. See III.23.
- *Darījān.* An alternative **face** system attributed to the Indians. See VII.6.

- **Decan**. Equivalent to **face**.
- **Declination**. The equivalent on the celestial **equator**, of geographical latitude. The signs of northern declination (Aries through Virgo) stretch northward of the **ecliptic**, while those of southern declination (Libra through Pisces) stretch southward.
- **Decline, declining** (Gr. *apoklima*, Ar. *saqaṭa*). Equivalent to **cadence** by whole sign, but perhaps in some Arabic texts referring rather to cadence by **quadrant house** divisions.
- **Decreasing in number**. See **Increasing/decreasing in number**.
- **Deferent**. The large circle off-center or **eccentric** to the earth, on which a planet's system rotates, or at least its **epicycle**. See II.0-1.
- **Descension**. Equivalent to **fall**.
- **Detriment** (or Ar. "corruption," "unhealthiness," "harm."). More broadly (as "corruption"), it refers to any way in which a planet is harmed or its operation thwarted (such as by being **burned up**). But it also (as "harm") refers specifically to the sign opposite a planet's **domicile**. Libra is the detriment of Mars. See I.6 and I.8.
- **Dexter**. "Right": see **Right/left**.
- **Diameter**. Equivalent to **Opposition**.
- **Dignity** (Lat. "worthiness"; Ar. *ḥazz*, "good fortune, allotment"). Any of five ways of assigning rulership or responsibility to a planet (or sometimes, to a **Node**) over some portion of the zodiac. They are often listed in the following order: **domicile, exaltation, triplicity, bound, face/decan**. Each dignity has its own meaning and effect and use, and two of them have opposites: the opposite of domicile is **detriment**, the opposite of exaltation is **fall**. See I.3, I.4, I.6-7, VII.4 for the assignments; I.8 for some descriptive analogies; VIII.2.1 and VIII.2.2*f* for some predictive uses of domiciles and bounds.
- **Directions**. A predictive technique which is more precise than using **ascensions**, and defined by Ptolemy in terms of proportional semi-arcs. There is some confusion in how directing works, because of the difference between the astronomical method of directions and how astrologers look at charts. Astronomically, a point in the chart (the significator) is considered as stationary, and other planets and their **aspects** by degree (or even the **bounds**) are sent forth (promittors) as though the heavens keep turning by **primary motion**, until they come to the significator. The degrees between the significator and promittor are converted into years of life. But

when looking at the chart, it seems as though the significator is being **released** counterclockwise in the order of signs, so that it **distributes** through the bounds or comes to the bodies or aspects of promittors. Direction by **ascensions** takes the latter perspective, though the result is the same. Some later astrologers allow the distance between a significator/releaser and the promittor to be measured in either direction, yielding "converse" directions in addition to the classical "direct" directions. See VIII.2.2, Appendix E, and Gansten.

- **Disregard**. Equivalent to **Separation**.
- **Distribution**. The **direction** of a **releaser** (often the degree of the **Ascendant**) through the **bounds**. The bound **lord** of the distribution is the "distributor," and any body or ray which the **releaser** encounters is the "**partner**." See VIII.2.2f, and *PN3*.
- **Distributor**. The **bound lord** of a **directed releaser**. See **Distribution**.
- **Diurnal**. See **Sect**.
- **Division** (Ar. *qismah*). In the context of **house** theory, it refers to any **quadrant house** system, as these are derived by dividing each of the the **quarters** by three. Synonymous with houses by **equation**, and opposed to houses by **number**.
- **Domain**. A **sect** and **gender**-based planetary condition. See III.2.
- **Domicile**. One of the five **dignities**. A sign of the zodiac, insofar as it is owned or managed by one of the planets. For example, Aries is the domicile of Mars, and so Mars is its domicile **lord**. See I.6.
- **Doryphory** (Gr. *doruphoria*). Equivalent to **Bodyguarding**.
- **Double-bodied**. Equivalent to the common signs. See **Quadruplicity**.
- **Dragon**: see **Node**.
- **Drawn back** (Lat. *reductus*). Equivalent to being **cadent** from an **angle**.
- **Dodecametorion**. Equivalent to **Twelfth-part**.
- *Duodecima*. Equivalent to **Twelfth-part**.
- *Dustūriyyah*. Equivalent to **Bodyguarding**.
- **East** (Lat. *oriens*). The Ascendant: normally the rising sign, but sometimes the degree of the Ascendant itself.
- **Eastern/western (by quadrant)**. When a planet is in one any of the **quadrants** as defined by the axial degrees. The eastern quadrants are between the degrees of the **Ascendant** and **Midheaven**, and between those of the **Descendant** and *Imum Caeli*. The western quadrants are between

the degrees of the Midheaven and Descendant, and between those of the *Imum Caeli* and the Ascendant.
- **Eastern/western (of the Sun)**. A position relative to the Sun, often called "oriental" or "occidental," respectively. These terms are used in two major ways: (1) when a planet is in a position to rise before the Sun by being in an early degree (eastern) or is in a position to set after the Sun by being in a later degree (western). But in ancient languages, these words also refer mean "arising" or "setting/sinking," on an analogy with the Sun rising and setting: so sometimes they refer to (2) a planet arising out of, or sinking under, the **Sun's rays**, no matter what side of the Sun it is on (in some of my translations I call this "pertaining to arising" and "pertaining to sinking"). Astrological authors do not always clarify what sense is meant, and different astronomers and astrologers have different definitions for exactly what positions count as being eastern or western. See II.10.
- **Eccentric**. As an adjective, it describes circles that are "off-center" to the earth; it is also a synonym for the **deferent circle**, the larger circle in a planetary model (which is likewise eccentric or off-center).
- **Ecliptic.** The path defined by the Sun's motion through the zodiac, defined as having 0° ecliptical latitude. In tropical astrology, the ecliptic (and therefore the zodiacal signs) begins at the intersection of the ecliptic and the celestial equator.
- **Election** (lit. "choice"). The deliberate choosing of an appropriate time to undertake an action, or determining when to avoid an action; but astrologers normally refer to the chart of the time itself as an election.
- **Element**. One of the four basic qualities. fire, air, water, earth) describing how matter and energy operate, and used to describe the significations and operations of planets and signs. They are usually described by pairs of four other basic qualities (hot, cold, wet, dry). For example, Aries is a fiery sign, and hot and dry; Mercury is typically treated as cold and dry (earthy). See I.3, I.7, and Book V.
- **Emptiness of the course.** Medievally, when a planet does not complete a **connection** for as long as it is in its current sign. In Hellenistic astrology, when a planet does not complete a connection within the next 30°. See III.9.
- **Enclosure**. When a planet has the rays or bodies of the **malefics** (or alternatively, the **benefics**) on either side of it, by degree or sign. See IV.4.2.
- **Epicycle**. A circle on the **deferent**, on which a planet turns. See II.0-1.

- **Equant.** In Ptolemaic astronomy, a mathematical point in outer space from which measurements are made. At the equant, planetary motion is seen as virtually constant and unchanging in speed. See II.0-1.
- **Equation.** (1) In astronomical theory, a correction that is added to the **mean motion/position** of a planet, in order to convert its idealized position to its **true motion/position**. Equations are found in a table of equations calculated individually for each planet. (2) In **house** theory, it refers to any **quadrant house** system, where house divisions are derived by exact calculation or equation (Ar. *al-taswiyah*); synonymous with house division by **division**, and **whole-sign** houses by **number**.
- **Equation of the center (planetary theory).** The angular difference between where the center of a planet's **epicycle** is, as seen from the **equant** (also known as its **mean position**), and its **true position** as seen from earth.
- **Equation of the center (solar theory).** The angular difference between the **mean Sun** (where we expect it to be) and the **true Sun** (where we observe it to be).
- **Equator (celestial).** The projection of the earth's equator into space, forming a great circle. Its equivalent of latitude is called **declination**, while its equivalent of longitude is called **right ascension** (and is measured from the beginning of Aries, from the intersection of it and the **ecliptic**).
- **Escape.** When a planet wants to **connect** with a second one, but the second one moves into the next sign before it is completed, and the first planet makes a **connection** with a different, unrelated one instead. See III.22.
- **Essence** (Lat. *substantia*). Deriving ultimately from Aristotelian philosophy, the fundamental nature or character of a planet or sign, which allows it to indicate or cause certain phenomena (such as the essence of Mars being responsible for indicating fire, iron, war, *etc.*). This word has often been translated as "substance," which is a less accurate term.
- **Essential/accidental.** A common way of distinguishing a planet's conditions, usually according to **dignity** (essential, I.2) and some other condition such as its **aspects** (accidental). See IV.1-5 for many accidental conditions.
- **Exaltation.** One of the five **dignities**. A sign in which a planet (or sometimes, a **Node**) signifies its matter in a particularly authoritative and refined

way. The exaltation is sometimes identified with a particular degree in that sign. See I.6.
- **Excellent place** (Ar. *jayyid*). Includes several of the **advantageous places**, among which the Ascendant, Midheaven, and eleventh are consistently mentioned. (These may be the only excellent places.)
- **Face.** One of the five **dignities**. The zodiac is divided into 36 faces of 10° each, starting with the beginning of Aries. See I.5.
- **Facing.** A relationship between a planet and a **luminary**, if their respective signs are configured at the same distance as their **domiciles** are. For example, Leo (ruled by the Sun) is two signs to the **right** of Libra (ruled by Venus). When Venus is **western** and two signs away from wherever the Sun is, she will be in the facing of the Sun. See II.11.
- **Fall** (Gr. *hupsōma*, Ar. *hubūṭ*, Lat. *casus, descensio*). The sign opposite a planet's **exaltation**; sometimes called "descension." See I.6.
- **Falling** (Lat. *cadens*, Ar. *saqaṭa*). Refers to being **cadent**, but sometimes ambiguous as to whether dynamically by **quadrant division** or by **whole sign** (which is also called **declining**).
- **Falling away from** (Ar. *sāqaṭ ʿan*). Equivalent to **aversion**.
- **Familiar** (Lat. *familiaris*). A hard-to-define term which suggests a sense of belonging and close relationship. (1) Sometimes it is contrasted with being **peregrine**, suggesting that a familiar planet is one which is a **lord** over a degree or **place** (that is, it has a **dignity** in it): for a dignity suggests belonging. (2) At other times, it refers to a familiar **aspect** (and probably the **sextile** or **trine** in particular): all of the family houses in a chart have a **whole-sign** aspect to the **Ascendant**.
- *Fardār*. See *Firdārīyyah*.
- **Feminine.** See **Gender**.
- **Feral** (Ar. *waḥshiyy*, Lat. *feralis*). Equivalent to **Wildness**.
- **Figure.** One of several polygons implied by an **aspect**. For example, a planet in Aries and one in Capricorn do not actually form a **square**, but they imply one because Aries and Capricorn, together with Libra and Cancer, form a square amongst themselves. See III.8.
- *Firdārīyyah* (pl. *firdārīyyāt*). A **time lord** method in which planets rule different periods of life, with each period broken down into sub-periods (there are also mundane versions). See VII.1.
- **Firm.** In terms of signs, the **fixed** signs: see **Quadruplicity**. For houses, equivalent to the **Angles**.

- **Fixed.** See **Quadruplicity.**
- **Foreign** (Lat. *extraneus*). Usually equivalent to **Peregrine.**
- **Fortunate.** Normally, a planet whose condition is made better by one of the **bearings** described in IV.
- **Fortunes.** See **Benefic/malefic.**
- **Foundations of the Moon.** See **Centers of the Moon.**
- **Free** (Ar. *nazīah*, Lat. *liber*). Sometimes, being **cleansed** of the **malefics**; at other times, being out of the **Sun's rays**.
- **Gender.** The division of signs, degrees, planets and hours into masculine and feminine groups. See I.3, V.10, V.14, VII.8.
- **Generosity and benefits.** Favorable relationships between signs and planets, as defined in III.26.
- **Good ones.** See **Benefic/malefic.**
- **Good places.** Equivalent to **Advantageous places.**
- **Governor** (Ar. *mustawlī*). A planet which has preeminence or rulership over some topic or indication (such as the governor over an eclipse); normally, it is a kind of **victor**.
- **Greater, middle, lesser years.** See **Planetary years.**
- **Ḥalb.** Probably Pahlavi for **sect**, but normally describes a rejoicing condition: see III.2.
- **Ḥayyiz.** Arabic for **domain**, normally a gender-intensified condition of *ḥalb*; but sometimes seems to refer to **sect**. See III.2.
- **Hexagon.** Equivalent to **Sextile.**
- **Hīlāj** (From the Pahlavi for "releaser"). Equivalent to **releaser**.
- **Hold onto.** Hugo's synonym for a planet being in or **transiting** a **sign**.
- **Horary astrology.** A late historical designation for **questions**.
- **Hours (planetary).** The assigning of rulership over hours of the day and night to planets. The hours of daylight (and night, respectively) are divided by 12, and each period is ruled first by the planet ruling that day, then the rest in descending planetary order. For example, on Sunday the Sun rules the first planetary "hour" from daybreak, then Venus, then Mercury, the Moon, Saturn, and so on. See V.13.
- **House.** A twelve-fold spatial division of a chart, in which each house signifies one or more areas of life. Two basic schemes are (1) **whole-sign** houses, in which the **signs** are equivalent to the houses, and (2) **quadrant houses**. But in the context of dignities and rulerships, "house" is the equivalent of **domicile**.

- **House-master.** Often called the *alcochoden* in Latin, from **kadukhudhāh** (the Pahlavi for "house-master"). One of the lords of the longevity **releaser**, preferably the **bound lord**. See VIII.1.3. But the Greek equivalent of this word (*oikodespotēs*, "house-master") is used in various ways in Hellenistic Greek texts, sometimes indicating the **lord** of a **domicile**, at other times the same longevity planet just mentioned, and at other times a kind of **victor** over the whole **nativity**.
- **Humor.** Any one of four fluids in the body (according to traditional medicine), the balance between which determines one's health and **temperament** (outlook and energy level). Choler or yellow bile is associated with fire and the choleric temperament; blood is associated with air and the sanguine temperament; phlegm is associated with water and the phlegmatic temperament; black bile is associated with earth and the melancholic temperament. See I.3.
- **IC.** See *Imum Caeli*.
- *Imum Caeli* (Lat., "lowest part of heaven"). The degree of the zodiac on which the lower half of the meridian circle falls; in **quadrant house** systems, it marks the beginning of the fourth **house**.
- **In the heart.** Often called *cazimi* in English texts, from the Ar. *kaṣmīmī*. A planet is in the heart of the Sun when it is either in the same degree as the Sun (according to Sahl b. Bishr and Rhetorius), or within 16' of longitude from him. See II.9.
- **Increasing/decreasing in calculation.** A planet is increasing in calculation when its **equation** is added to the **mean motion/position**, because the **true motion/position** is farther ahead in the zodiac than the mean one. It is decreasing in calculation when the equation is subtracted. See *Compilation* IV.3, **6**.
- **Increasing/decreasing in number.** When the daily speed of a planet (or at least the speed of the center of its **epicycle**) is seen to speed up (or slow down). When moving from its **perigee** to its **apogee**, it slows down or decreases in number, because it is moving farther away from the earth; when moving from the apogee to the perigee, it speeds up or increases in number because it is coming closer to the earth.
- **Indicator.** A degree which is supposed to indicate the approximate position of the degree of the natal **Ascendant**, in cases where the time of birth is uncertain. See VIII.1.2.
- **Inferior.** The planets lower than the Sun: Venus, Mercury, Moon.

- **Infortunes.** See **Benefic/malefic**.
- **ʾIttiṣāl**. Equivalent to **Connection**.
- **Joys.** Places in which the planets are said to "rejoice" in acting or signifying their natures. Joys by house are found in I.16; by sign in I.10.7.
- **Jārbakhtār** (From the Pahlavi for "distributor of time"). Equivalent to **Distributor**; see **Distribution**.
- **Kadukhudhāh** (From the Pahlavi for "house-master"), often called the *alcochoden* in Latin transliteration. See **House-master**.
- **Kardaja** (Ar. *kardajah*, from Sanskrit *kramajyā*). An interval used in the rows of astronomical tables such as in the *Almagest*. Each row begins with a value (called an "argument"), and one reads across to find the corresponding value used to correct such things as planetary positions. The increment or interval between each argument is a *kardaja*. A single table may use different increments based on theoretical considerations, levels of accuracy needed, *etc*. Some books of tables defined the *kardajas* in terms of sine functions. According to al-Hāshimī (1981, p. 143), the lower **sectors** of a planet's epicycle (closer to the earth, where it is retrograde) are the "fast" *kardajas*. But this probably also refers to the lower sectors of the eccentric or deferent circle, closer to a planet's **perigee**.
- **Kaṣmīmī**: see **In the heart**.
- **Kingdom.** Equivalent to **exaltation**.
- **Largesse and recompense.** A reciprocal relation in which one planet is rescued from being in its own **fall** or a **well**, and then returns the favor when the other planet is in its fall or well. See III.24.
- **Leader** (Lat. *dux*). Equivalent to a **significator** for some topic. The Arabic word for "significator" means to indicate something by pointing the way toward something: thus the significator for a topic or matter "leads" the astrologer to some answer. Used by some less popular Latin translators (such as Hugo of Santalla and Hermann of Carinthia).
- **Linger in** (Lat. *commoror*). Hugo's synonym for a planet being in or **transiting** through a **sign**.
- **Lodging-place** (Lat. *hospitium*). Hugo's synonym for a **house**, particularly the **sign** which occupies a house.
- **Look, look at** (Lat. *aspicio*, Ar. *naẓara*). Equivalent to **aspect**.
- **Lord of the year.** The **domicile lord** of a **profection**. The Sun and Moon are not allowed to be primary lords of the year, according to Persian doctrine. See VIII.2.1 and VIII.3.2, and Appendix F.

- **Lord.** A designation for the planet which has a particular **dignity**, but when used alone it usually means the **domicile** lord. For example, Mars is the lord of Aries.
- **Lord of the question.** In questions, the lord of the **house** of the **quaesited** matter. But sometimes, it refers to the client or **querent** whose question it is.
- **Lord of the year.** In mundane ingress charts, the planet that is the **victor** over the chart, indicating the general meanings of the year.
- **Lot.** Sometimes called "Parts." A place (often treated as equivalent to an entire sign) expressing a ratio derived from the position of three other parts of a chart. Normally, the distance between two places is measured in zodiacal order from one to the other, and this distance is projected forward from some other place (usually the Ascendant): where the counting stops, is the Lot. Lots are used both interpretively and predictively. See Book VI.
- **Lucky/unlucky.** See **Benefic/malefic**.
- **Luminary.** The Sun or Moon.
- **Malefic.** See **Benefic/malefic**.
- **Malevolents.** See **Benefic/malefic**.
- **Management** (Ar. *tadbīr*). A generic term referring to how a planet "manages" a topic by signifying it. Typically, planets "push" and "accept" management to and from each other, simply by **applying** to one another. See III.18.
- **Masculine.** See **Gender**.
- **Maximum equation (solar theory).** The greatest angular amount of the **equation of the center**, which occurs when the **mean Sun** is perpendicular to the **apsidal line**.
- **Mean motion/position.** The motion or position of a planet as measured from the **equant**, namely assuming a constant rate of speed. To be contrasted with **True motion/position**.
- **Mean Sun.** A fictitious point which revolves around the earth in exactly one year, in a line parallel with the **true Sun**. The mean Sun represents where we would expect the Sun to be, if it traveled in a perfect circle around the earth. It coincides with the true Sun at the Sun's **apogee** and **perigee**.
- **Meeting** (Ar. *ijtimāʿ*). The conjunction of the Sun and Moon at the New Moon, which makes it a **connection** by body.

- **Melancholic**. See **Humor**.
- **Midheaven**. Either the tenth sign from the **Ascendant**, or the zodiacal degree on which the celestial meridian falls.
- **Minister**. A synonym for **Governor**.
- **Movable signs**. See **Quadruplicity**.
- *Mubtazz*. See **Victor**.
- **Mutable signs**. Equivalent to "common" signs. See **Quadruplicity**.
- *Namūdār*. Equivalent to **Indicator**.
- **Native**. The person whose birth chart it is.
- **Nativity**. Technically, a birth itself, but used by astrologers to describe the chart cast for the moment of a birth.
- **Ninth-parts**. Divisions of each sign into 9 equal parts of 3° 20' apiece, each ruled by a planet. Used predictively by some astrologers as part of the suite of **revolution** techniques. See VII.5.
- **Nobility**. Equivalent to **exaltation**.
- **Nocturnal**. See **Sect**.
- **Node**. The point on the ecliptic where a planet passes into northward latitude (its North Node or Head of the Dragon) or into southern latitude (its South Node or Tail of the Dragon). Normally only the Moon's Nodes are considered. See II.5 and V.8.
- **Northern/southern**. Either planets in northern or southern latitude in the zodiac (relative to the ecliptic), or in northern or southern declination relative to the celestial equator. See I.10.1.
- **Not-reception**. When an **applying** planet is in the **fall** of the planet being applied to.
- **Number** (Ar. *ᶜadad*). In the context of **house** theory, it refers to **whole-sign** houses (namely, by assigning the house numbers by counting to each sign); it is opposed to **quadrant houses** (by **division** or **equation**). For its use in calculating planetary positions, see **Increasing/decreasing in number**.
- **Oblique ascensions**. The **ascensions** used in making predictions by ascensional times or primary **directions**.
- **Obstruction**. When one planet is moving towards a second (wanting to be **connected** to it), but a third one in a later degrees goes **retrograde**, connects with the second one, and then with the first one. See III.21.
- **Occidental**. See **Eastern/western**.

- **Opening of the portals/doors.** Times of likely weather changes and rain, determined by certain **transits**. See VIII.3.4, and *AW1*.
- **Opposition.** An **aspect** either by **whole sign** or degree, in which the signs have a 180° relation to each other: for example, a planet in Aries is opposed to one in Libra.
- **Optimal place** (Lat. *optimus*). See **Excellent place**.
- **Orbs/bodies.** Called "orb" by the Latins, and "body" (*jirm*) by Arabic astrologers. A space of power or influence on each side of a planet's body or position, used to determine the intensity of interaction between different planets. See II.6.
- **Oriental.** See **Eastern/western**.
- **Overcoming.** When a planet is in the eleventh, tenth, or ninth sign from another planet (i.e., in a superior **sextile**, **square**, or **trine aspect**), though being in the tenth sign is considered a more dominant or even domineering position. See IV.4.1 and *PN3*'s Introduction, §15.
- **Own light.** This refers either to (1) a planet being a member of the **sect** of the chart (see V.9), or (2) a planet being out of the **Sun's rays** and not yet **connected** to another planet, so that it shines on its own without being **clothed** in another's influence (see II.9).
- **Part.** See **Lot**.
- **Partner.** The body or ray of any planet which a **directed releaser** encounters while being **distributed** through the **bounds**. But in some translations from Arabic, any of the **lords** of a place.
- **Peregrine** (Lat. *peregrinus*, Ar. *gharīb*), lit. "a stranger." When a planet is not in one of its five **dignities**. See I.9.
- **Perigee (of eccentric/deferent).** The point on a planet's **deferent circle** that is closest to the earth; as seen from earth, it points to some degree of the zodiac. It is opposite the **apogee**. See II.0-1.
- **Perverse** (Lat. *perversus*). Hugo's occasional term for (1) **malefic** planets, and (2) **places in aversion** to the **Ascendant** by **whole-sign**: definitely the twelfth and sixth, probably the eighth, and possibly the second.
- **Phlegmatic.** See **Humor**.
- **Pitted degrees.** Equivalent to **Welled degrees**.
- **Pivot.** Equivalent to **Angle**.
- **Place.** Equivalent to a **house**, and more often (and more anciently) a **whole-sign** house, namely a **sign**.

- **Planetary years**. Periods of years which the planets signify according to various conditions. See VII.2.
- **Portion** (Lat. *pars, portio*; Ar. *juz'*). Normally equivalent to a degree, but sometimes to the **bound** in which a degree falls.
- **Possess**. Hugo's synonym for a planet being in or **transiting** a **sign**.
- **Post** (Ar. *markaz*). A **stake** or **angle**. (The Arabic verb is virtually equivalent to Ar. *watada*, used for a stake.) Sometimes translated as **center**, as in the centers of the Moon.
- **Posts of the Moon**. See **Centers of the Moon**.
- **Prevention**. See **Conjunction/prevention**.
- **Primary directions**. See **Directions**.
- **Primary motion**. The clockwise or east-to-west motion of the heavens.
- **Profection** (Lat. *profectio*, "advancement, setting out"). A predictive technique in which some part of a chart (usually the **Ascendant**) is advanced either by an entire sign or in 30° increments for each year of life. See VIII.2.1 and VIII.3.2, and the sources in Appendix F.
- **Prohibition**. Equivalent to **Blocking**.
- **Promittor** (lit., something "sent forward"). A point which is **directed** to a **significator**, or to which a significator is **released** or directed (depending on how one views the mechanics of directions).
- **Pushing**. What a planet making an **applying connection** does to the one **receiving** it. See III.15-18.
- *Qasim/qismah*: Arabic terms for **distributor** and **distribution**.
- **Quadrant**. A division of the heavens into four parts, defined by the circles of the horizon and meridian, also known as the axes of the **Ascendant-Descendant**, and **Midheaven-IC**.
- **Quadrant houses**. A division of the heavens into twelve spaces which overlap the **whole signs**, and are assigned to topics of life and ways of measuring strength (such as Porphyry, Alchabitius Semi-Arc, or Regiomontanus houses). For example, if the Midheaven fell into the eleventh sign, the space between the Midheaven and the Ascendant would be divided into sections that overlap and are not coincident with the signs. See I.12 and the Introduction §6.
- **Quadruplicity.** A "fourfold" group of signs indicating certain shared patterns of behavior. The movable (or cardinal or convertible) signs are those through which new states of being are quickly formed (including the seasons): Aries, Cancer, Libra, Capricorn. The fixed (sometimes "firm") signs

are those through which matters are fixed and lasting in their character: Taurus, Leo, Scorpio, Aquarius. The common (or mutable or bicorporeal) signs are those which make a transition and partake both of quick change and fixed qualities: Gemini, Virgo, Sagittarius, Pisces. See I.10.5.
- **Quaesited/quesited**. In **horary** astrology, the matter asked about.
- **Querent**. In **horary** astrology, the person asking the question (or the person on behalf of whom one asks).
- **Questions**. The branch of astrology dealing with inquiries about individual matters, for which a chart is cast.
- **Reception**. What one planet does when another planet **pushes** or **applies** to it, and especially when they are related by **dignity** or by a **trine** or **sextile** from an **agreeing** sign of various types. For example, if the Moon applies to Mars, Mars will get or receive her application. See III.15-18 and III.25.
- **Reflection**. When two planets are in **aversion** to each other, but a third planet either **collects** or **transfers** their light. If it collects, it reflects the light elsewhere. See III.13.
- **Refrenation**. See **Revoking**.
- **Regard**. Equivalent to **Aspect**.
- **Releaser**. The point which is the focus of a **direction**. In determining longevity, it is the one among a standard set of possible points which has certain qualifications (see VIII.1.3). In annual predictions one either directs or **distributes** the longevity releaser, or any one of a number of points for particular topics, or else the degree of the **Ascendant** as a default releaser. Many astrologers direct the degree of the Ascendant of the **revolution** chart itself as a releaser.
- **Remote** (Lat. *remotus*, prob. a translation of Ar. *zāyīl*). Equivalent to **cadent**: see **Angle**. But see also *Judges* §7.73, where 'Umar (or Hugo) distinguishes being **cadent** from being **remote**, probably translating the Ar. *zāyīl* and *sāqiṭ* ("withdrawn/removed" and "fallen").
- **Render**. When a planet **pushes** to another planet or place.
- **Retreating** (Ar. *'idbār*). When a planet is in a **cadent** place (but it is unclear whether this is by **whole sign** or **quadrant divisions**); see also **withdrawing**. The opposite of **advancing**. See III.4 and the Introduction §6, and **Angle**.
- **Retrograde**. When a planet seems to move backwards or clockwise relative to the signs and fixed stars. See II.8 and II.10.

- **Return, Solar/Lunar.** Equivalent to **Revolution**.
- **Returning.** What a **burned up** or **retrograde** planet does when another planet **pushes** to it. See III.19.
- **Revoking.** When a planet making an applying **connection** stations and turns **retrograde**, not completing the connection. See III.20.
- **Revolution.** Sometimes called the "cycle" or "transfer" or "change-over" of a year. Technically, the **transiting** position of planets and the **Ascendant** at the moment the Sun returns to a particular place in the zodiac: in the case of nativities, when he returns to his exact natal position; in mundane astrology, usually when he makes his ingress into 0° Aries. But the revolution is also understood to involve an entire suite of predictive techniques, including **distribution, profections**, and *firdārīyyāt*. See *PN3*.
- **Right ascensions.** Degrees on the celestial **equator** (its equivalent of geographical longitude), particularly those which move across the meridian when calculating arcs for **ascensions** and **directions**.
- **Right/left.** Right (or "dexter") degrees and **aspects** are those earlier in the zodiac relative to a planet or sign, up to the **opposition**; left (or "sinister") degrees and aspects are those later in the zodiac. For example, if a planet is in Capricorn, its right aspects will be towards Scorpio, Libra, and Virgo; its left aspects will be towards Pisces, Aries, and Taurus. See III.6.
- **Root.** A chart used as a basis for another chart; a root particularly describes something considered to have concrete being of its own. For example, a **nativity** acts as a root for an **election**, so that when planning an election one must make it harmonize with the nativity.
- **Safe.** When a planet is not being harmed, particularly by an **assembly** or **square** or **opposition** with the **malefics**. See **Cleansed**.
- *Sālkhudhāy* (from Pahlavi, "lord of the year"). Equivalent to the **lord of the year**.
- **Sanguine.** See **Humor**.
- **Scorched.** See **Burned up**.
- **Secondary motion.** The counter-clockwise motion of planets forward in the zodiac.
- **Sect.** A division of charts, planets, and signs into "diurnal/day" and "nocturnal/night." Charts are diurnal if the Sun is above the horizon, else they are nocturnal. Planets are divided into sects as shown in V.11. Masculine signs (Aries, Gemini, *etc.*) are diurnal, the feminine signs (Taurus, Cancer, *etc.*) are nocturnal.

- **Sector** (Ar. *niṭāq*). A division of the **deferent** circle or **epicycle** into four parts, used to determine the position, speed, visibility, and other features of a planet. See II.0-1.
- **Seeing, hearing, listening signs**. A way of associating signs similar to **commanding/obeying**. See Paul of Alexandria's version in the two figures attached to I.9.6.
- **Separation**. When planets have completed a **connection** by **assembly** or **aspect**, and move away from one another. See III.8.
- **Sextile**. An **aspect** either by **whole sign** or degree, in which the signs have a 60° relation to each other: for example, Aries and Gemini.
- **Share** (Ar. *ḥazza*). Equivalent to **dignity**.
- **Shift**. (1) Equivalent to **sect** (Ar. *nawbah*), referring not only to the alternation between day and night, but also to the period of night or day itself. The Sun is the lord of the diurnal shift or sect, and the Moon is the lord of the nocturnal shift or sect. (2) In mundane astrology, it refers to the shift (Ar. *intiqāl*) of the Saturn-Jupiter conjunctions from one **triplicity** to another about every 200 (tropical zodiac) or 220 (sidereal zodiac) years.
- **Sign**. One of the twelve 30° divisions of the **ecliptic**, named after the constellations which they used to be roughly congruent to. In tropical astrology, the signs start from the intersection of the ecliptic with the celestial equator (the position of the Sun at the equinoxes). In sidereal astrology, the signs begin from some other point identified according to other principles.
- **Significator**. Either (1) a planet or point in a chart which indicates or signifies something for a topic (either through its own character, or house position, or rulerships, *etc.*), or (2) the point which is **released** in primary **directions**.
- **Significator of the king**. In mundane ingress charts, the **victor** planet which indicates the king or government.
- **Sinister**. "Left": see **Right/left**.
- **Slavery**. Equivalent to **fall**.
- **Sovereignty** (Lat. *regnum*). Equivalent to **Exaltation**.
- **Spearbearing**. Equivalent to **Bodyguarding.**
- **Square**. An **aspect** either by **whole sign** or degree, in which the signs have a 90° relation to each other: for example, Aries and Cancer.
- **Stake**. Equivalent to **Angle.**

- **Sublunar world.** The world of the four **elements** below the sphere of the Moon, in classical cosmology.
- **Substance** (Lat. *substantia*). Sometimes, indicating the real **essence** of a planet or sign. But often it refers to financial assets (perhaps because coins are physical objects indicating real value).
- **Succeedent.** See **Angle**.
- **Sun's rays** (or Sun's beams). In earlier astrology, equivalent to a regularized distance of 15° away from the Sun, so that a planet under the rays is not visible at dawn or dusk. But a later distinction was made between being **burned up** (about 1° - 7.5° away from the Sun) and merely being under the rays (about 7.5° - 15° away).
- **Superior.** The planets higher than the Sun: Saturn, Jupiter, Mars.
- **Supremacy** (Lat. *regnum*). Hugo's word for **Exaltation**, sometimes used in translations by Dykes instead of the slightly more accurate **Sovereignty**.
- **Synastry.** The comparison of two or more charts to determine compatibility, usually in romantic relationships or friendships. See *BA* Appendix C for a discussion and references for friendship, and *BA* III.7.11 and III.12.7.
- *Tasyīr* (Ar. "dispatching, sending out"). Equivalent to primary **directions**.
- **Temperament.** The particular mixture (sometimes, "complexion") of **elements** or **humors** which determines a person's or planet's typical behavior, outlook, and energy level.
- **Testimony.** From Arabic astrology onwards, a little-defined term which can mean (1) the planets which have **dignity** in a place or degree, or (2) the number of dignities a planet has in its own place (or as compared with other planets), or (3) a planet's **assembly** or **aspect** to a place of interest, or (4) generally *any* way in which planets may make themselves relevant to the inquiry at hand. For example, a planet which is the **exalted** lord of the **Ascendant** but also **aspects** it, maby be said to present two testimonies supporting its relevance to an inquiry about the Ascendant.
- **Tetragon.** Equivalent to **Square.**
- **Thought-interpretation.** The practice of identifying a theme or topic in a **querent's** mind, often using a **victor**, before answering the specific **question**. See *Search*.
- **Time lord.** A planet ruling over some period of time according to one of the classical predictive techniques. For example, the **lord of the year** is the time lord over a **profection**.

- **Transfer**. When one planet **separates** from one planet, and **connects** to another. See III.11. Not to be confused with a **shift** of triplicities in Saturn-Jupiter conjunctions, or the annual **revolutions**, either mundane or natal.
- **Transit**. The passing of one planet across another planet or point (by body or **aspect** by exact degree), or through a particular sign (even in a **whole-sign** relation to some point of interest). In traditional astrology, not every transit is significant; for example, transits of **time lords** or of planets in the **whole-sign angles** of a **profection** might be preferred to others. See VIII.2.4 and *PN3*.
- **Translation**. Equivalent to **Transfer**.
- **Traverse** (Lat. *discurro*). Hugo's synonym for a planet being in or **transiting** through a **sign**.
- **Trigon**. Equivalent to **Trine**.
- **Trine**. An **aspect** either by **whole sign** or degree, in which the signs have a 120° relation to each other: for example, Aries and Leo.
- **True motion/position**. The motion or position of a planet as measured from the earth, once its **mean motion/position** has been adjusted or corrected by various types of **equations**.
- **True Sun**. The zodiacal position of the Sun as seen from the earth.
- **Turn** (Ar. *dawr*). A predictive technique in which responsibilities for being a **time lord** rotates between different planets. See VIII.2.3 for one use of the turn, and *AW2* for an explanation of the mundane Turns. But it can occasionally refer more generally to how the planets may equally play a certain *role* in a chart: for example, if the lord of the Ascendant is Saturn, it means X; but if Jupiter, Y; but if Mars, Z; and so on.
- **Turned away**. Equivalent to **Aversion**.
- **Turning signs**. For Hugo of Santalla, equivalent to the movable signs: see **Quadruplicity**. But *tropicus* more specifically refers to the tropical signs Cancer and Capricorn, in which the Sun turns back from its most extreme declinations.
- **Twelfth-parts**. Signs of the zodiac defined by 2.5° divisions of other signs. For example, the twelfth-part of 4° Gemini is Cancer. See IV.6.
- **Two-parted signs**. Equivalent to the double-bodied or common signs: see **Quadruplicity**.
- **Under rays**. When a planet is between approximately 7.5° and 15° from the Sun, and not visible either when rising before the Sun or setting after

him. Some astrologers distinguish the distances for individual planets (which is more astronomically accurate). See II.10.
- **Unfortunate.** Normally, when a planet's condition is made more difficult through one of the **bearings** in IV.
- **Unlucky.** See **Benefic/malefic.**
- **Upright** (Ar. *qāʾim*). Describes the axis of the MC-IC, when it falls into the tenth and fourth signs, rather than the eleventh-fifth, or ninth-third.
- *Via combusta*. See **Burnt path.**
- **Victor** (Ar. *mubtazz*). A planet or point identified as the most authoritative over a particular topic or **house** (I.18), or for a chart as a whole (VIII.1.4). See also *Search*. Dykes distinguishes procedures that find the most authoritative and powerful planet ruling one or more places (a victor "over" places) or the member of a list of candidates which fulfills certain criteria (a victor "among" places).
- **Void in course.** Equivalent to **Emptiness of the course.**
- **Well.** A degree in which a planet is said to be more obscure in its operation. See VII.9.
- **Western.** See **Eastern/western.**
- **Whole signs.** The oldest system of assigning house topics and **aspects**. The entire sign on the horizon (the **Ascendant**) is the first house, the entire second sign is the second house, and so on. Likewise, aspects are considered first of all according to signs: planets in Aries aspect or regard Gemini as a whole, even if aspects by exact degree are more intense. See I.12, III.6, and the Introduction §6.
- **Wildness** (Ar. *waḥshiyah*, Lat. *feralitas*). When a planet is not **aspected** by any other planet, for as long as it is in its current sign. See III.10.
- **Withdrawing.** In some Latin translations (*recedens*), equivalent to one planet **separating** from another. But in Arabic (*zāʾil*), a withdrawing planet is dynamically **cadent**, moving by diurnal motion away from the degree of the axes or **stakes**—a near-synonym of **retreating**, and the opposite of **advancing**.
- *Zīj*. The Arabic for a Persian word meaning a set of astronomical tables for calculating planetary positions and other things. Ptolemy's *Almagest* can be considered a *zīj*.

BIBLIOGRAPHY

Abū Ma'shar al-Balhi (Richard Lemay ed.), *Liber Introductorii Maioris ad Scientiam Iudiciorum Astrorum* [*The Great Introduction to the Science of the Judgments of the Stars*] (Naples: Istituto Universitario Orientale, 1996)

Abū Ma'shar al-Balhi, *The Abbreviation of the Introduction to Astrology*, ed. and trans. Charles Burnett, K. Yamamoto, and Michio Yano (Leiden: E.J. Brill, 1994)

Abū Ma'shar al-Balhi, *On Historical Astrology: The Book of Religions and Dynasties (On the Great Conjunctions)*, vols. I-II, eds. and trans. Keiji Yamamoto and Charles Burnett (Leiden: Brill, 2000)

Al-'Imrānī, *The Book of Choices* [*Liber de Electionibus*], in Dykes 2008 (*WSM*).

Al-Khayyāt, Abū 'Alī, *The Judgments of Nativities*, trans. and ed. Benjamin N. Dykes, in Dykes 2009 (*Persian Nativities I*)

Al-Qabīsī, *The Introduction to Astrology*, eds. Charles Burnett, Keiji Yamamoto, Michio Yano (London and Turin: The Warburg Institute, 2004)

Al-Rijāl, 'Alī, *De Iudiciis Astrorum* [*The Book of the Skilled in the Judgments of the Stars*] (Venice: Erhard Ratdolt, 1485)

Allen, Richard Hinckley, *Star Names: Their Lore and Meaning* (New York: Dover Publications Inc., 1963)

Bonatti, Guido, *The Book of Astronomy*, trans. and ed. Benjamin N. Dykes (Golden Valley, MN: The Cazimi Press, 2007)

Burnett, Charles, "Al-Kindī on finding buried treasure," *Arabic Sciences and Philosophy* Vol. 7, 1997, pp. 57-90.

Carmody, Francis, *The Astronomical Works of Thābit b. Qurra* (Berkeley and Los Angeles: University of California Press, 1960)

Coppock, Austin, *36 Faces: The History, Astrology and Magic of the Decans* (Three Hands Press, 2014)

Dorotheus of Sidon, *Carmen Astrologicum*, trans. David Pingree (Abingdon, MD: The Astrology Center of America, 2005)

Dykes, Benjamin trans. and ed., *Works of Sahl & Māshā'allāh* (Golden Valley, MN: The Cazimi Press, 2008)

Dykes, Benjamin, trans. and ed., *Persian Nativities* Vols. I-III (Minneapolis, MN: The Cazimi Press, 2009-2010)

Dykes, Benjamin trans. and ed., *Introductions to Traditional Astrology: Abū Ma'shar & al-Qabīsī* (Minneapolis, MN: The Cazimi Press, 2010)

Dykes, Benjamin, *Traditional Astrology for Today: An Introduction* (Minneapolis, MN: The Cazimi Press, 2011)

Dykes, Benjamin trans. and ed., *The Book of the Nine Judges* (Minneapolis, MN: The Cazimi Press, 2011)

Dykes, Benjamin trans. and ed., *The Forty Chapters of al-Kindī* (Minneapolis, MN: The Cazimi Press, 2011)

Dykes, Benjamin, trans. and ed., *Choices & Inceptions: Traditional Electional Astrology* (Minneapolis, MN: The Cazimi Press, 2012)

Dykes, Benjamin, trans. and ed., *Astrology of the World I: The Ptolemaic Inheritance* (Minneapolis, MN: The Cazimi Press, 2013)

Dykes, Benjamin, trans. and ed., *Astrology of the World II: Revolutions & History* (Minneapolis, MN: The Cazimi Press, 2014)

Evans, James, *The History and Practice of Ancient Astronomy* (New York and Oxford: Oxford University Press, 1998)

Gansten, Martin, *Primary Directions: Astrology's Old Master Technique* (England: The Wessex Astrologer, 2009)

Gingerich, Owen, "Ptolemy and the Maverick Motion of Mercury," Sky & Telescope (1983), pp. 11-13.

Goldstein, Bernard R., "The Arabic Version of Ptolemy's *The Planetary Hypotheses*," *Transactions of the American Philosophical Society*, Vol. 7, Part 4 (1967), pp. 3-55.

Hellman, C. D., *The Comet of 1577* (New York: Columbia University Press, 1944)

Hermann of Carinthia, Benjamin Dykes trans. and ed., *The Search of the Heart* (Minneapolis, MN: The Cazimi Press, 2011)

Ibn Ezra, Abraham, *The Book of the World*, Shlomo Sela trans. and ed. (Leiden and Boston: Brill, 2010)

Kennedy, E. S., "The Sasanian Astronomical Handbook *Zīj al-Shāh* and the Astrological Doctrine of 'Transit' (*Mamarr*)," *Journal of the American Oriental Society* Vol. 78, No. 4 (Oct. – Dec. 1958), pp. 246-62.

Kunitzsch, Paul and Tim Smart, *A Dictionary of Modern Star Names* (Cambridge, MA: New Track Media, 2006)

Leopold of Austria, *Compilatio Leupoldi ducatus Austriae filii de astrorum scientia decem continens tractatus* (Augsburg: Erhard Ratdolt, 1489)

Māshā'allāh, *On the Revolutions of the Years of the World*, in Dykes 2013 (*Astrology of the World I: The Ptolemaic Inheritance*)

McKay, David, *Cassell's New Biographical Dictionary* (Philadelphia: David McKay, 1899)

Nevalainen, Jukka, "The Accuracy of the Ecliptic Longitude in Ptolemy's Mercury Model," *Journal of the History of Astronomy* Vol. 26 (1996), pp. 147-60.

Pedersen, Olaf, ed. Alexander Jones, *A Survey of the Almagest* (New York: Springer, 2011)

Pingree, David, *The Thousands of Abū Ma'shar* (London: The Warburg Institute, 1968)

Pseudo-Ptolemy, *Centiloquy*, in James H. Holden trans., *Five Medieval Astrologers* (Tempe, AZ: American Federation of Astrologers, Inc., 2008)

Ptolemy, Claudius, *Ptolemy's Almagest*, trans. and ed. G.J. Toomer (Princeton, NJ: Princeton University Press, 1998)

Ptolemy, Claudius, *Tetrabiblos* vols. 1, 2, 4, trans. Robert Schmidt, ed. Robert Hand (Berkeley Springs, WV: The Golden Hind Press, 1994-98)

Ptolemy, Claudius, *Tetrabiblos*, trans. F.E. Robbins (Cambridge and London: Harvard University Press, 1940)

Saunders, Richard, *The Astrological Judgement and Practice of Physick* (Abingdon, MD: Astrology Classics, 2003)

Thomas, J., *Universal Dictionary of Biography and Mythology* (New York, NY: Cosimo Inc., 2009, a reprint from 1887)

Valens, Vettius, *The Anthology*, vols. I-VII, ed. Robert Hand, trans. Robert Schmidt (Berkeley Springs, WV: The Golden Hind Press, 1993-2001)

Vescovini, Graziella Federici trans., "La versio Latina degli *Excerpta de Secretis Albumasar di Sadan*," *Archives d'histoire doctrinale et littéraire du Moyen-âge*, vol. 65, 1998, pp. 273-330.

www.ingramcontent.com/pod-product-compliance
Lightning Source LLC
Chambersburg PA
CBHW060448170426
43199CB00011B/1129